# THE ANNALS OF AMERICA

"The Residence of David Twining as It Looked in 1787" by Edward Hicks

# THE ANNALS
# OF
# AMERICA

# THE ANNALS OF AMERICA

## Volume 3

## 1784 - 1796

### Organizing the New Nation

William Benton, *Publisher*

ENCYCLOPÆDIA BRITANNICA, INC.

*Chicago London Toronto Geneva Sydney Tokyo Manila*

Printed in the U.S.A.
Library of Congress Catalog Card Number: 68-20888



The editors wish to express their gratitude for permission to reprint material from the following sources:

Morris Morgenstern and B'nai B'rith for Selection 86, from MSS in their possession.

Princeton University Press for Selection 21, from *The Papers of Thomas Jefferson,* ed. by Julian P. Boyd *et al.,* Vol. X, Copyright 1955 by Princeton University Press.

University of Pittsburgh Press for Selection 116, from *Anthony Wayne: A Name in Arms — The Wayne-Knox-Pickering-McHenry Correspondence,* ed. by Richard C. Knopf.

# CODED SOURCES IN THIS VOLUME

| | |
|---|---|
| C. F. Adams | *The Works of John Adams, Second President of the United States, with a Life of the Author.* Edited by Charles Francis Adams. In 10 vols. Boston, 1850-1856. |
| *Debates* | [Annals of Congress] *The Debates and Proceedings in the Congress of the United States with an Appendix Containing Important State Papers and Public Documents and All the Laws of a Public Nature; with a Copious Index.* In 42 vols. Washington, 1834-1856. |
| Elliot | *The Debates in the Several State Conventions on the Adoption of the Federal Constitution, etc., etc.* Edited by Jonathon Elliot. 2nd edition in 5 vols. Philadelphia, 1861. Vols. 1-3 reprinted 1866, Vol. 4 reprinted 1876. |
| Ford | *The Writings of Thomas Jefferson.* Edited by Paul L. Ford. In 10 vols. New York and London, 1892-1899. |
| H. A. Washington | *The Writings of Thomas Jefferson: Being his Autobiography, Correspondence, Reports, Messages, Addresses and Other Writings, Official and Private.* Edited by H. A. Washington. In 9 vols. Washington, 1853-1854. Vol. 8, Philadelphia, 1871. |
| Hening | *The Statutes at Large; Being a Collection of all Laws of Virginia, from the first Session of the Legislature in the year 1619.* Edited by William W. Hening. In 13 vols. covering the years 1619 to 1792. New York and Philadelphia, 1819-1823. |
| J. C. Hamilton | *The Works of Alexander Hamilton, etc., etc.* Edited by John C. Hamilton. In 7 vols. New York, 1850-1851. |
| Johnston | *The Correspondence and Public Papers of John Jay.* Edited by Henry P. Johnston. In 4 vols. New York, 1890-1893. |
| *Journals* | *Journals of the American Congress: from 1774 to 1788.* In 4 vols. Washington, 1823. |
| McMaster | *Pennsylvania and the Federal Constitution 1787-1788.* Edited by John Bach McMaster and Frederick D. Stone. The Historical Society of Pennsylvania, 1888. |
| *Madison Letters* | *Letters and Other Writings of James Madison, Fourth President of the United States.* Congress edition. In 4 vols. Philadelphia, 1865. |

| | |
|---|---|
| Malloy | [*Senate Foreign Relations Committee*] *Treaties, Conventions, International Acts, Protocols and Agreements between the United States of America and other Powers 1776-1909.* Edited by William M. Malloy. In 2 vols. Washington, 1910. |
| MHSP | *Proceedings of the Massachusetts Historical Society.* Boston, 1791 *et seq.* |
| Niles | *Principles and Acts of the Revolution in America.* Edited by Hezekiah Niles. Centennial edition, New York, 1876 (first published Baltimore, 1822). |
| *Pamphlets* | *Pamphlets on the Constitution of the United States, Published During Its Discussion by the People 1787-1788.* Edited by Paul L. Ford. Brooklyn, 1888. |
| Poore | *The Federal and State Constitutions, Colonial Charters, and Other Organic Laws of the United States.* Edited by B. P. Poore. In 2 vols. Washington, 1877. |
| Randolph | *Memoirs, Correspondence, and Private Papers of Thomas Jefferson.* Edited by Thomas Jefferson Randolph. In 4 vols. London (and Charlottesville, Va.), 1829. |
| Richardson | *A Compilation of the Messages and Papers of the Presidents 1789-1897.* Edited by James D. Richardson. In 10 vols. Washington, 1896-1899. New edition extended to 1908. Washington, 1909. |
| Scott | *The Federalist and Other Constitutional Papers by Hamilton, Jay, Madison and other Statesmen of Their Time.* Edited by E. H. Scott. In 2 vols. Chicago, 1894. |
| Sparks | *The Works of Benjamin Franklin, etc., etc.* Edited by Jared Sparks. In 10 vols. Boston, 1836-1840. |
| *Statutes* | *The Public Statutes at Large of the United States of America from the Organization of the Government in 1789, etc., etc.* In 79 vols. as of August 1966. 1845 *et seq.* Vol. 1 edited by Richard Peters. Boston, 1848 (1853). |
| WGW | *The Writings of George Washington.* Edited by Worthington C. Ford. In 14 vols. New York, 1889-1893. |

# Contents

## 1787-1788



## 1788

## 1789

## 1789 - 1790



## 1790

## 1791



## 1792



## 1792 - 1793



## 1793

# ORGANIZING THE NEW NATION
## In Pictures

---



After the war Americans moved in ever larger numbers into the newly acquired territory between the Appalachians and the Mississippi, and there came into conflict with the Indians and with the Spanish and British colonists already established there.



The government established by the Articles of Confederation in 1781 proved ineffective in handling the postwar economic crisis and the increasing unrest throughout the country. The Constitutional Convention met at Philadelphia in May 1787 to create a new form of government adequate to the task of preserving the Union.



The new Constitution produced the first clash between champions of states' rights and the advocates of a strong central government. In newspapers and pamphlets and on the floors of state legislatures and conventions the debate was often heated, and it was several months before the Federalists attained the needed support.



The federal government trod on shaky ground as its leaders tried to put into practice the system sketched out in the Constitution. Although thousands of miles from Europe, the new nation found it hard to remain aloof from the tumults brought on by the French Revolution on that continent.

American artists continued to be influenced by styles popular in European capitals. Portraits were still the dominant form, and artists, sensing the historical significance of the period, were eager to paint the leaders of the nation.



Americans sought to restore order to their farms and cities after years of war. Commerce and industry had to be reorganized to meet peacetime needs, and Americans in all walks of life were confronted with the task of producing for themselves things previously acquired from England.



A new interest in beauty could be seen in the homes of many Americans. Popular European trends were followed on the whole, but original touches were added, and a definite American design was created, particularly in artifacts.



George Washington was the first great popular hero in America. However, he did not much enjoy the limelight, and instead was anxious to retire to his Mount Vernon estate.

# Introduction

The United States in 1784 was free (the treaty with Great Britain formally ending the Revolution was ratified by Congress on January 14), but there was grave doubt in the minds of many of its ablest men about whether it had yet created a government worthy of the sacrifices of the war, and capable of withstanding the pressures to which the fledgling nation was already being exposed. The Articles of Confederation (see Selection 134 in the previous volume) had been approved by the states in 1781, and the country limped along under their mild rule for half a decade, but there were problems and difficulties almost from the first. Finally, the Articles foundered on the same rock that had wrecked Britain's whole colonial venture in the southern half of North America. The United States could not govern because it could not tax. The Revolution had been fought, to a large extent, over taxation, but now, in the opinion of men like Jay, Alexander Hamilton, and even George Washington, the immortal hero of the war, the hand that had pulled the purse strings tight must loosen them again (see, for example, Selection 18).

Noah Webster, not yet famous as a linguist and compiler of dictionaries, saw this as clearly as anyone. In his essay "Diseases of the Body Politic" (Selection 19), he pointed, in 1786, to a whole series of failures that could properly be charged to the fact that the central government of this sparsely populated, sprawling nation, strung up and down a seacoast and extending for nearly a thousand miles, was simply too weak for any kind of effective action. Many felt the same way, and a convention was called in Annapolis, Maryland, in the fall of the same year, to consider measures to improve the situation (see Selection 20). Not enough of the states sent fully accredited delegations for anything final to be done, but the convention broke up at the end of the year with a firm decision to meet again in Philadelphia the following spring.

The year 1787 opened with much agitation about the Articles of Confederation, and with widespread feeling that the government was inadequate in many ways. Shays's Rebellion in Massachusetts (see Selections 16 and 17) was only one sign that all was not well with the body politic, and although some felt, as did Thomas Jefferson (see Selections 22 and 23), that a little rebellion now and then (as he put it) was a good thing, most feared that this small, provincial uprising could be repeated on a larger scale and with more serious results.

The problem, as the Connecticut poet Joel Barlow saw it (Selection 26), was that the revolution that had seemed to end with the victory at Yorktown in 1781 was in reality unfinished. Benjamin Rush, the Philadelphia doctor, was another to point out defects in the Confederation (Selection 24), and Jefferson concurred, observing that, among other lacks, that of an executive (for which the Articles did not provide) was of gravest import (Selection 27). As a modern might say, it was government by a committee — and what is more, a committee the members of which were disaffected and without power.

It was hoped that the convention that had been called for the spring would find a way to improve the situation, and in most men's minds the way was clear: a new government would have to be created, which meant that a constitution would have to be written under which all Americans could live, as in some sense citizens — the sense not yet defined — of a single nation.

The convention opened in Philadelphia on May 25. One of its first acts was unanimously to elect as its president George Washington, the one man in the country about whom all agreed, and to whom all were equally devoted. But unanimity was not enjoyed for long. The delegates, who included many of the best theoretical and practical politicians in the land, soon found themselves at odds on almost every point. Yet they stuck to their task through the long, hot summer, hewing the lean phrases of a governing document out of the massive blocks of their individual interests, needs, and wants. The proceedings were secret, but James Madison kept a diary that was later published, and from it (parts of it appear here, as Selection 28) we can learn something of the passions, as well as the restraint, of this assembly (as Jefferson later called it) "of demi-gods."

The document that emerged from the deliberations of that famous summer was of course the U.S. Constitution (Selection 29). It was presented to the world, and (from a practical point of view this was more important) to the people of the various states, on September 17.

The battle for the Constitution was not won with its drafting. It had still to be ratified by the legislators, and accepted by the people of the country. Men like Madison, from Virginia, and John Jay and Alexander Hamilton, from New York, were fully aware of the opposition that the document was likely to meet and in fact did meet from both sources, and they went immediately to work. The three men began to publish the series of papers known as *The Federalist* — it is one of the great political books of the Western world — at the end of October (several of the papers appear here as Selection 47).

Opposition to the proposed Constitution took many forms. Some felt that the new government had an imbalance of powers rather than, as its authors claimed, a new and better balance (see, for example, Selection 33). Others feared that the Constitution was an instrument of aristocracy (see, for example, Selections 35 and 58). Still others held that the new government would infringe on commerce, both between the states and with foreign nations (see, for example, Selections 33 and 40). But probably the most widely shared feeling was that the document lacked a positive guarantee of individual rights, including those of speech and assembly, of a fair trial, and of worship according to the dictates of one's conscience (see, for example, Selections 30, 39, and 60).

The fight for the Constitution was won, of course, although not without setbacks, and not without bitterness. The document was ratified by the legally necessary two-thirds of the thirteen states when New Hampshire voted yes on June 21, 1788, but it was still practically necessary for Virginia and New York, the two most powerful and populous states, to join the fold. The three collaborators on *The Federalist* led their forces in their respective state ratifying conventions — Madison in Virginia, and Hamilton and Jay in New York. Virginia was the tenth state to ratify, on June 25; New York the eleventh, a month later. Rhode Island held out the longest; its legislature did not accept the new government until May 29, 1790.

Many votes had been won by the promise that a Bill of Rights would be added to the Constitution, and this in fact was done. A long list of amendments was proposed, a shorter list was presented to the states, and ten of these were declared ratified on December 15, 1791. They appear here as Selection 73.

The new government called for a chief executive, or President, and the obvious choice was Washington, who somewhat unwillingly — he had already spent most of his life in his country's service — accepted the post (he was elected by a unanimous vote). John Adams was named Vice-President, and Jefferson and Hamilton joined the new administration as secretary of state and secretary of the treasury, respectively.

Much of the history of the next eight years is the story of the growing animosity, or at least disagreement on political principles, of the last two men. The government was faced at the beginning by severe economic problems, and it later had to weather serious international ones. Hamilton, whose sympathies, on the whole, lay with the few as against the many, tended to support the monied interest of the large cities in fiscal matters, and to take a conservative and pro-British position in foreign policy. Jefferson, in opposition to the brilliant young New Yorker, put his faith in the farmers and small shopkeepers — the yeomanry, as they were called; and he tended to support France in the great European conflict that raged without letup after the French Revolution of 1789. Selections 104-107 and 109 throw light on their foreign policy differences; the crux of the matter was Washington's Proclamation of Neutrality of 1793 (Selection 103). Hamilton's economic ideas were expressed in such documents as his First Report on the Public Credit (Selection 82) and his Report on Manufactures (Selection 92), and Jefferson's critical view of what he called the Hamiltonian system is seen in Selections 83 and 91.

There were other political events, as well. The Northwest Ordinance of 1787 (Selection 42 — and see also Selections 1 and 9 in this volume, and Selection 147 in Volume 2), one of the triumphs of the otherwise undistinguished Congress of the Confederation, organized the territory north of the Ohio River and east of the Mississippi. The basis of the Ordinance was a report prepared in 1784 by Jefferson, who seemed to have his hand in almost everything that was going on. The Proclamation of 1763 had temporarily forbidden this area to settlement; now the fledgling nation declared to the world not only that the area would be settled but that it would eventually become a part of the United States. The Judiciary Act of 1789 (Selection 75) set up the Supreme Court, and three circuit and thirteen district courts. It was the first in a long series of such acts, and one of the most important. President Washington's Proclamation on the Whiskey Rebellion of 1794 (Selection 110) was also of great importance. A group of Pennsylvania farmers had risen in armed protest against the imposition of an excise tax on liquor. The President's call for 15,000 volunteers to suppress the uprising rather surprised the country, and put it on notice that there was now a central government that had some teeth in it, and that intended to use them. The insurgents were defeated and tried for treason in May 1795, and convicted. Washington pardoned the rebels, feeling that the principle was the thing, and not the imposition of punishments. We may grumble about federal excise taxes on things like tobacco and liquor, but we pay them. The Whiskey Rebellion is one reason why we do.

The last great political document in this volume is Washington's Farewell Address (see Selection 121), which established a tradition almost as enduring as his refusal to accept a third term in office. Most of our Presidents who have lived through two terms have offered similarly sage advice to the nation, and have put what they had to say in similarly lofty language. Washington's advice was more than merely typical. He urged the nation, among other things, to avoid alliances with other countries, and thereby helped to confirm the isolationist foreign policy that, on the whole, endured for more than a century, and that served us well during the period..

All was not exclusively political, however, even in this most political of times. Jefferson's "Virginia Statute of Religious Freedom" (see Selection 12) was, in his own opinion, one of his most important accomplishments. Benjamin Rush was worried as early as 1787 about the education of women (see Selection 46); in general, he was for it. Rufus Putnam and Philip Freneau were concerned in 1788 about our treatment of the Indians (see Selections 62 and 64). Noah Webster was calling in the next year for a national language (see Selection 77); the dictionary that he produced some years later was intended, in part at least, to promote this end. A memorable episode in the history of religious toleration in our country was the exchange of letters between Moses Seixas, a member of the Hebrew Congregation at Newport, Rhode Island, and President Washington, in 1790 (see Selection 86). The 1791 petition, by the free Negroes of Charleston, South Carolina, for equality under the law (Selection 88) is a moving document. Gustavus Vassa's account of what it meant to be a slave (see Selection 114) is not only moving, it is also almost unique, for few Negroes could write up until the Civil War. And although one selection is not political at all, it points to far-reaching political effects. This is a letter of Eli Whitney to his father, written in September 1793, telling him of his work on the cotton gin (see Selection 108). This machine, which had been invented by Whitney in April of that year, had the effect of reviving the Southern cotton industry, and thus of immensely increasing the South's dependence on slave labor. Without the cotton gin, slavery might have disappeared from the South within a generation after 1800, and the Civil War might not have occurred.

But in the end it was politics that most occupied the minds of Americans during this first decade of our national history. Above all, they were proud of their accomplishment in creating a government and making it work. They wrote about it, and they talked about it; they even sang about it. One song, "The Right of Free Elections" (Selection 120), poetically awkward as it is, will make the point.

# Chronology: 1784 - 1796

## 1784

**Feb. 22.** Captain John Greene sails the *Empress of China* from New York, reaches Canton, China, by way of Cape Horn on August 30. Cargo of tea and silks brought back in 1785 leads other U.S. merchants to send more ships to China in effort to make up for losses due to shrunken British market for U.S. goods.

**March 1.** Committee headed by Thomas Jefferson presents to Congress a plan for interim government of Western lands, proposing eventual division of territory into states to be admitted on equal terms with original 13. **April 23.** Plan is adopted and becomes basic idea in the Northwest Ordinance of 1787.

**May 28.** Superintendent of Finance Robert Morris requests that he be replaced by a board of three commissioners. **Nov. 1.** He leaves office having accumulated a precarious surplus of $21,000 (after meeting army's demobilization pay in 1783 from his own pocket). Recent foreign loans are largely responsible for the surplus, since Congress has no power of taxation under the Articles of Confederation but is dependent on requisitions from states for funds. Of an $8 million requisition voted in October 1781, only about $1,500,000 has been paid by January 1784.

**Aug. 23.** Convention of settlers west of Appalachian Mts. organizes independent state of Franklin in area ceded to U.S. by North Carolina. After four years of nominal statehood under John Sevier settlers accept renewed jurisdiction of North Carolina.

**Dec. 23.** New York City selected as temporary national capital until a federal district on the Delaware River can be set up.

Potomac Company organized with George Washington as president to build route connecting Potomac River with Ohio Valley. Canal is begun, and first water locks in U.S. built, but project proves unprofitable and is never completed.

First American theological college is established in New Brunswick, New Jersey.

John Filson publishes *The Discovery, Settlement, and Present State of Kentucke* which contains, in addition to Filson's account, an alleged autobiography of Daniel Boone.

## 1784 - 1797

**1784.** Judge Tapping Reeve establishes law school in Litchfield, Connecticut; followed by Peter Van Schaack's law school at Kinderhook, New York, in 1786; law lectures at University of Pennsylvania in 1790; and Columbia College in 1797.

## 1785

**Jan. 24.** Congress, being unable to obtain commercial concessions from foreign countries because Article IX of Articles of Confederation allows each state to set its own duties on foreign commerce, appoints committee to appeal to the states. Committee recommends amending Article IX but no action is taken by the states. Maryland, South Carolina, Pennsylvania, New York, Rhode Island, and North Carolina all have discriminatory duties on imports from Britain. **June 23.** Massachusetts and New Hampshire act to prohibit British ships from carrying their exports.

**March 28.** Commissioners from Virginia and Maryland meet at Mount Vernon, Virginia, to consider problems of navigation on Chesapeake Bay and Potomac River. Agreement recommends that Virginia and Maryland legislatures adopt uniform currency, uniform commercial regulations, and other measures of common commercial interest. **Dec. 5.** Maryland legislature endorses plan and proposes that Delaware and Pennsylvania be included.

**Aug. 24.** Beginning of a year of futile negotiations with Spain over U.S. right of navigation on the lower Mississippi River, which Spanish minister to U.S. refuses to concede, claiming title by virtue of 1763 Treaty of Paris. Issue is unresolved until Pinckney Treaty of 1795.

Automatic flour mill, invented by Oliver Evans, is put into operation in Maryland. New features, such as elevator and conveyor belt, cut labor needs in half.

Postwar dumping of British manufactures raises imports nearly to prewar level, but exports, no longer given preferential treatment in Britain, reach only 50 percent. British restrictions on trade with West Indies after 1783 further reduce American commerce which is only partly helped by opening of China trade and development of Pacific Northwest fur trade.

## 1785 - 1790

New York Society for Promoting Manumission (freeing of slaves) established with John Jay as president; similar societies established in other states, including several in the South, to 1788. Legislation to abolish slavery has been enacted in Pennsylvania in 1780, Connecticut and Rhode Island in 1784, New York in 1785, and is passed in New Jersey in 1786. Massachusetts constitution had abolished slavery in 1780. Slavery is prohibited in Northwest Territory by its ordinance. By 1790 about 93 percent of slaves in U.S. are in Southern states.

## 1786

**Jan. 16.** Virginia Assembly adopts Thomas Jefferson's Statute for Religious Freedom, model for First Amendment to the U.S. Constitution. Measure is virtually the same as one originally written and proposed in 1779 and not adopted.

**Feb. 28.** British notify U.S. that they will not evacuate Great Lakes posts, as promised by 1783 Treaty of Paris, until U.S. honors its debts to Britain.

**June 28.** Treaty with Morocco leads to suspension of Moroccan piracy on American commerce in Mediterranean Sea and off Spanish coast, but pirate raids from Algiers, Tunis, and Tripoli continue off Barbary coast until 1797.

**Sept. 11-14.** Following James Madison's suggestion of January 21, Virginia legislature invites all states to discuss interstate commercial problems at Annapolis, Maryland. Convention assembles at appointed time with only delegates from New York, New Jersey, Delaware, Pennsylvania, and Virginia present; those from New Hampshire, Massachusetts, Rhode Island, and North Carolina arrive too late to participate, and the rest of the states do not join in. Meager representation frustrates aim of convention but Alexander Hamilton, in address endorsed on September 14, calls upon the states to meet at Philadelphia in May 1787 to discuss all matters necessary "to render the constitution of the federal government adequate to the exigencies of the Union."

Imports and exports drop from 1785 levels, farm wages are down 20 percent; shortage of money, insistent creditors, and high taxes contribute to general economic depression. Pressure for paper money results in $800,000 issue from seven states, alarming creditors. They are further disturbed by the outbreak of Shays's Rebellion in Massachusetts, where debt-ridden farmers in western part of state rise in arms against constituted authorities, protesting economic injustice and legal discrimination. Rebellion led by Daniel Shays is not finally put down until February 1787, after unequal struggle with state troops.

First American steamboat, invented by John Fitch, is granted franchise for use on New Jersey waters; it is launched on Delaware River in 1787.

## 1787

**May 25.** Constitutional Convention opens at Philadelphia 11 days late, after waiting for quorum of seven states; all states except Rhode Island eventually attend. George Washington is unanimously elected to preside but takes no part in debates. William Jackson is made secretary. **May 29.** Edmund Randolph offers Virginia Plan which goes beyond revision of Articles of Confederation; Plan is debated until June 13. This proposal, in which states are represented in proportion to population, is opposed by small states, who hope to retain equality of states as under Articles of Confederation, but with enlarged powers of central government. **June 15.** Delegates of small states propose New Jersey Plan, a revision of the Articles. Plan is debated for four days. **June 19.** Virginia Plan is adopted by 7 states to 3, committing Convention to frame a new basis for central government rather than merely revise Articles.

**July 13.** During Convention debate on proposed Constitution, Congress of the Confederation passes Northwest Ordinance. Based on Jefferson's Report of 1784, Ordinance provides for government of territory east of the Mississippi River and north of the Ohio; it includes provision for division of territory into three to five states and their admission into the Union when population is large enough.

**July 16.** Convention adopts Connecticut Compromise. The work of Benjamin Franklin and others and introduced by Roger Sherman, it resolves issue of state representation by providing for equal votes for states in proposed Senate but votes according to population in House. **Aug. 6 - Sept. 10.** Draft Constitution as prepared by five-member Committee of Detail is submitted to Convention and debated on all points; the debate is led by James Madison and George Mason of Virginia, Gouverneur Morris and James Wilson of Pennsylvania, Roger Sherman of Connecticut, and Elbridge Gerry of Massachusetts. Morris is assigned to prepare final draft. **Sept. 17.** After making a few changes, state delegations approve final draft, and 39 of the 42 delegates still in attendance sign (Gerry, Mason, and Randolph refusing), transmit the Constitution to Congress of the Confederation, and adjourn.

**Sept. 20.** Congress of the Confederation receives draft Constitution and defeats motion to censure Convention for exceeding instructions merely to revise Articles of Confederation. **Sept. 28.** Congress votes to send draft Constitution to the individual states for consideration by special ratifying conventions (ratification cannot be by legislatures or popular vote). Nine ratifications are needed for adoption.

**Oct. 27.** First of 85 "Federalist" papers published. Federalists, who approve the Constitution, and anti-Federalists, who oppose it, flood the states with written arguments. Most distinguished and influential are those written by "Publius" (Alexander Hamilton, James Madison, and John Jay), which appear in New York newspapers. Two-volume collection, *The Federalist,* is published in 1788.

**Dec. 7.** Ratification begins with convention of Delaware which ratifies unanimously.

**Dec. 12.** Pennsylvania convention, which has met on November 21, ratifies by vote of 46 to 23 after much delaying debate by strong anti-Federalist factions.

**Dec. 18.** New Jersey ratifies unanimously only a week after meeting on December 11.

Royall Tyler's comedy, *The Contrast,* is performed by a professional acting group in New York City; it is first American play with an American hero.

## 1788

**Jan. 2.** Georgia convention meets, ratifies Constitution unanimously. Debates on Constitution continue in other states.

**Jan. 9.** Connecticut convention, which has met on January 4, ratifies by vote of 128 to 40.

**Feb. 6.** Massachusetts convention, having met since January 9, ratifies by vote of 187 to 168. Opponents are persuaded to vote favorably when Samuel Adams proposes as condition of ratification that nine amendments be recommended at once to Congress and the other states. One of these is the basis for present-day Article X of the Bill of Rights, which reserves to the states powers not expressly delegated to the federal government.

**March 24.** Rhode Island rejects Constitution by direct vote. Federalists have refused to take part because a state convention has been rejected; thus only about half the qualified voters cast ballots, and only 237 out of about 3,000 voters favor ratification.

**April 7.** Marietta, Ohio, founded by settlers sent West by the Ohio Company, organized in 1786 for land speculation and development of land granted by Congress in exchange for Continental securities.

**April 28.** Maryland convention, which has met on April 21, ratifies by 63 to 11.

**May 23.** South Carolina anti-Federalists in legislature almost prevent holding ratifying convention, but resolution is passed, convention meets May 12 and ratifies 149 to 73.

**June 21.** New Hampshire convention, having met on February 13 and adjourned until June to see what action other states will take, ratifies by 57 to 47 after proposing 12 amendments. This ninth ratification is last needed for acceptance of Constitution among the ratifying states.

**June 25.** Virginia convention ratifies by vote of 89 to 79 after three weeks of heated argument led by Patrick Henry (against) and James Madison (for ratification). Convention recommends a bill of rights of 20 articles.

**July 2.** Congress of the Confederation accepts the new Constitution as ratified. **Sept. 13.** Congress arranges for conduct of government under new order to begin on March 4, 1789, when first Constitutional Congress will meet in New York. **Oct. 10.** Congress transacts its last official business under the Articles.

**July 26.** New York convention, having met on June 17, ratifies by 30 to 27. Anti-Federalists are majority, but Alexander Hamilton manages to delay vote until ninth ratification and Virginia's vote are announced, feeling correctly that this will sway convention. Additional factor is threat of New York City to secede from the state and ratify separately. Convention urges amendment to secure a federal bill of rights.

**Aug. 2.** North Carolina convention, meeting on July 21, refuses to ratify without a bill of rights, although Federalist feeling is strong.

**Dec. 23.** Maryland cedes 10 square miles on the Potomac River to Congress as site for federal capital of government under the new Constitution.

## 1789

**Feb. 4.** Presidential electors, chosen in each ratifying state as provided by new Constitution, cast ballots (counted in Senate on April 6) unanimously electing George Washington first President; John Adams, with 34 votes, becomes vice-president.

**March 4.** Majority of members of Congress for new government, elected in January and February, are still en route to New York and Congress does not have quorum present on date specified by Congress of the Confederacy. **April 1-8.** House of Representatives (30 of 59 members) and Senate (9 of 22 members) organize for conduct of business.

**April 30.** President Washington inaugurated at temporary capital in New York City on balcony of Federal Hall; he delivers inaugural address in Senate Chamber of Hall. Executive departments — War, Treasury, Foreign Affairs — continue temporarily as under Articles of Confederation.

**May 5.** Beginning of the French Revolution with meeting of Estates General at Versailles and formation by the third estate (commons) of the National Assembly. **July 14.** Paris mob storms the Bastille in attempt to get arms and to free political prisoners. Spontaneous uprisings all over France follow, as peasants revolt against feudal lords. **Aug. 27.** Assembly adopts the Declaration of Rights, preamble to first Constitution, which is largely based on American Declaration of Independence. Eventually most of Europe is involved and hostilities continue for 10 years.

**July 4.** New Congress passes first tariff bill, setting duties varying from 5 to 15 percent on various specified imports, to raise revenue for government expenses. A 10 percent reduction is allowed for goods imported in U.S.-owned and U.S.-built ships.

**July 27.** Organization of new executive departments begins with creation of Department of Foreign Affairs (later changed to Department of State). Thomas Jefferson is appointed secretary of state on September 26 but John Jay manages this department until Jefferson's return in March 1790 from post as minister to France. **Aug. 7.** War Department, created in 1785, is carried over intact to new government; General Henry Knox is appointed secretary of war on September 12. **Sept. 2.** Treasury Department is organized with Alexander Hamilton appointed secretary of the treasury on September 11. **Sept. 22.** Office of Postmaster General created and Samuel Osgood appointed on September 26, but Post Office is not permanently organized until 1795.

**Sept. 9.** House of Representatives begins action to adopt a federal bill of rights. Twelve amendments of the many proposed by various state ratifying conventions are recommended by Congress for adoption and proposed to states on September 25. Ten amendments are ratified by the necessary number of states and become part of the Constitution on December 15, 1791.

**Sept. 24.** Congress passes Federal Judiciary Act, setting up Supreme Court with a chief justice and five associate justices, also 13 district courts. **Sept. 26.** John Jay appointed first Chief Justice of the United States; Edmund Randolph appointed Attorney General.

**Nov. 21.** Submission to states by Congress of 12 amendments of a bill of rights results in second North Carolina ratifying convention which approves Constitution with amendments by vote of 194 to 77.

Georgia legislature grants to group of land companies for speculative purposes over 25 million acres in the region of the Yazoo River (Alabama and Mississippi); later grant of 35 million acres in 1795 leads eventually to Yazoo land fraud case of *Fletcher* v. *Peck* (1810), in which Supreme Court invalidates a state law for the first time.

Dr. John Jeffries, loyalist surgeon, holds first public lecture on anatomy in Boston; gathering is broken up by mob of citizens already indignant about dissection practised for study and teaching.

Protestant Episcopal Church organized independently of Church of England at first triennial convention held in Philadelphia.

*Gazette of the United States,* newspaper founded in New York by John Fenno and moved to Philadelphia in 1790, becomes leading Federalist weekly.

First American novel, *The Power of Sympathy,* is published; author is William Hill Brown.

University of North Carolina founded, becoming first state university to function; instruction begins in 1795.

End of Revolution and beginning of the new nation lead to a new architecture, a revival of classic Roman styles (later Greek also). Revival is inspired in part by Thomas Jefferson whose design for Virginia Capitol in Richmond is first Roman-style American building; his University of Virginia designs follow same trend. Classical influence is shown in buildings in Washington, D.C., designed by various architects, notably Benjamin Henry Latrobe, as well as a number of state capitols and commercial buildings. In spite of new style, architects such as Charles Bulfinch continue to build Adam (English) types of houses, especially in New England, for 30 years after the Revolution. Most architects of this period are not professionals but carpenter-builders.

Beginning of early period of historical, panoramic and religious painting such as "The Declaration of Independence" by John Trumbull, John Vanderlyn's "The Panorama of Versailles," and "The Bearing of the Cross" by William Dunlap.

## 1789 - 1796

General business depression of 1784 to 1788 halted; period of prosperity begins, stimulated by Hamilton's fiscal policies, American expansion into Ohio Valley, and opportunities for neutral trade during European wars of the French Revolution.

## 1790

**Jan. 14.** At request of Congress, Alexander Hamilton submits to House of Representatives first *Report on Public Credit* recommending that the federal government be responsible for national debt (foreign and domestic) carried over from the Confederation (about $56 million), and assume most of the burden of debt (about $21 million) incurred by the states during the Revolution. Southern states, whose debt payments are already arranged for, object especially to U.S. assuming state debts, since they will be taxed for debts of Middle and New England states. Hamilton and Madison arrange compromise by which South agrees to accept share in debt of Northern states in return for location of national capital on Potomac River instead of at Philadelphia. **July 26.** Hamilton's proposal is passed over objection of those who have been forced to sell securities at depreciated rates.

**Feb. 11.** Society of Friends (Quakers) make first petition to Congress for emancipation of slaves.

**April 17.** Benjamin Franklin dies in Philadelphia at age 84. Half of Philadelphia, 20,000 people, attend his funeral.

**May 29.** Rhode Island's state convention, having first met in January, finally ratifies Constitution and becomes the thirteenth state of the United States. Decision is due in part to the passing by the Senate of a bill severing commercial relations between the United States and Rhode Island.

**Dec. 6.** Congress assembles at Philadelphia, voted temporary national capital until 1800.

**Dec. 14.** Hamilton submits report to House recommending establishment of a national bank. Bank is opposed by Jefferson but charter is signed by President Washington February 25, 1791.

Hamilton submits second *Report on Public Credit* recommending an excise tax on manufacture of liquor to increase federal revenue; tax is opposed by farmers of backwoods areas where distilling is only available means of marketing surplus grain, prohibitively expensive to transport in bulk even where roads exist. Whiskey tax bill is passed on March 3, 1791.

**Dec. 21.** Cotton spun for first time by water power by Samuel Slater in factory at Pawtucket, Rhode Island. Slater had emigrated from England in previous year when England prohibited export of textile machinery plans and constructed from memory Richard Arkwright's spinning machine, thus initiating cotton industry in U.S.

First national census sets United States population at 4 million (including 800,000 Negro slaves) distributed approximately 25 percent in New England, 25 percent in Middle States, and 50 percent in South. Largest city is Philadelphia, with 42,000 inhabitants; followed, in order, by New York, Boston, Charleston (South Carolina), and Baltimore; but total urban population (in towns of 2,500 or more) is only 5.4 percent. Life expectancy at birth is 34.5 years for males, 36.5 for females.

First American Roman Catholic bishop, John Carroll, is consecrated (in England) at a time when only four states have absolute religious tolerance and only Pennsylvania has Catholic churches.

Samuel Hopkins receives first federal patent for his process for manufacturing pot and pearl ash (crude and commercial carbonate of potassium) used in glass making.

## 1791

**March 4.** Vermont admitted to the Union as the fourteenth state. Claimed by Massachusetts, New Hampshire, and New York, it had, in 1777, declared itself an independent republic, but land disputes had not been settled until 1790.

**May-June.** Disagreement with administration's fiscal policies leads Jefferson and Madison to establish a political alliance with anti-Federalist faction in New York. Conflict results eventually in formation from already existing smaller groups of the first two national political parties: Republicans (later Democratic-Republicans) led by Jefferson, and Federalists under Hamilton.

**Oct. 31.** *National Gazette,* anti-Hamilton newspaper, is founded, edited by Philip Freneau. It is soon warring with the Federalist *Gazette of the United States.*

**Dec. 5.** Hamilton's *Report on Manufactures* is submitted to Congress. It proposes protective tariffs for industry, agricultural subsidies, and internal improvements (chiefly roads and canals) financed by the federal government.

**Dec. 12.** Bank of the United States, proposed by Alexander Hamilton, opens main office at Philadelphia; eight branches are established in leading commercial centers.

Part of Benjamin Franklin's *Autobiography,* written from 1771 to 1789 and covering years to 1759, published in Paris; full text is not published until 1868.

*Charlotte Temple,* a sentimental novel by Susanna Rowson, is published and achieves wide popularity.

## 1791 - 1792

Securities exchange organized in Philadelphia in 1791, followed by New York exchange in 1792. Both deal largely in federal stock rather than local enterprise.

## 1792

**Feb. 21.** Presidential Succession Act provides that order of succession is vice-president, president pro-tempore of the Senate, speaker of the house.

**April 2.** Mint Act provides for decimal system of coinage, sets up two-metal standard at ratio of 15 (silver) to 1 (gold), and establishes mint at Philadelphia.

**April.** General Anthony Wayne appointed commander of military forces in Ohio country following defeat of General Arthur St. Clair by Indians in November 1791. **May 8.** Growing Indian hostility in Northwest Territory leads to passage of Militia Act allowing states to raise armed forces of all able-bodied free white males of 18 to 45.

**June 1.** Kentucky, formerly part of Virginia, is admitted to the Union as fifteenth state.

**Aug. 21.** Pittsburgh convention passes resolves denouncing Hamilton's whiskey tax and proposes measures to frustrate its collection; Southern states also resist this tax. **Sept. 29.** President Washington issues a proclamation insisting on enforcement.

**Dec. 5.** Electors cast their votes for President and vice-president: President Washington is reelected with 132 votes; Adams is also reelected (77 votes). George Clinton of New York gets substantial vote (50 out of 132), indicating anti-administration feeling.

Philadelphia-Lancaster Turnpike begun (completed in 1794); its success as a business venture leads to building of many other toll roads, especially in New England and Middle States.

Twelve-hundred-mile Columbia River (in present-day Washington) discovered by Captain Robert Gray of Boston in ship *Columbia* on fur trading expedition. Discovery becomes one basis for U.S. claim to Pacific Northwest.

Return of portraitist Gilbert Stuart from study and professional success in England and Ireland inaugurates his career in New York, Philadelphia, Washington, and Boston as most famous of American portrait painters.

Completion of publication of Thomas Paine's *The Rights of Man*, written to defend measures used by French republicans during the early part of the French Revolution. *Modern Chivalry* by Hugh Henry Brackenridge describes frontier conditions satirically.

Russian Orthodox Church begins missionary work in Alaska; resident bishop arrives in 1798.

## 1793

**Jan. 21.** Execution of Louis XVI following proclamation of French Republic in September 1792 divides American opinion on French Revolution. **Feb. 1.** France's declaration of war on England and Holland (a month later on Spain) helps to establish party line between pro-British Federalists and anti-British Jeffersonians.

**Jan. 23.** Representative William Branch Giles of Virginia proposes resolutions in House for inquiry into state of Treasury; Hamilton is forced to defend himself (February 4 and 13) against charges of corruption and mismanagement. **Feb. 28.** Resolutions of censure are submitted by Giles and others, but defeated.

**April.** Citizen Genêt Affair. French Minister to United States, Edmond Charles Genêt, takes advantage of warm popular welcome to commission American privateers and send them to plunder British shipping. **May 18.** Genêt is coldly received by President Washington. **June 5.** He is ordered by Jefferson to cease organization of hostile projects on American soil. Genêt promises to comply but reneges, threatening to appeal to American people. **Aug. 2.** Cabinet decides to demand his recall but accession of Jacobins to power in France leads to his remaining in America as U.S. citizen.

**April 22.** President Washington declares American neutrality in Anglo-French war; some Americans sympathize strongly with Britain or France but Washington warns them against hostility toward either power.

**July 31.** President Washington's supposed partiality for the Federalists and for Hamilton's opinions on foreign affairs leads Jefferson to resign as secretary of state, effective December 31. He is succeeded by Edmund Randolph.

**August-October.** Yellow fever outbreak in Philadelphia becomes worst epidemic in any U.S. city; leads to improved methods of sewage disposal and more sanitary water systems.

Eli Whitney invents cotton gin for removing seed from green cotton. Mechanical process greatly increases output and revives dying slave economy of South.

## 1794

**March 5.** Congress proposes to states eleventh constitutional amendment exempting states from suits by citizens of other states and foreign countries. Amendment is declared ratified on January 8, 1798.

**June 5.** Neutrality Act prohibits enlistment of any U.S. citizen in service of foreign countries and forbids the supplying of foreign armed vessels in U.S. ports.

**July.** Whiskey Rebellion breaks out in western Pennsylvania, provoked by enforcement of excise tax. **Aug. 7.** President Washington orders rebels to return home and calls for 15,000 volunteers from four states. **Sept. 24.** Failure of negotiations with insurrection leaders brings second proclamation ordering suppression of rebellion. Insurgents are tried for treason in May 1795; two are convicted but are pardoned by President Washington.

**Aug. 20.** Indian resistance broken and Northwest frontier secured by victory of General Anthony Wayne at Battle of Fallen Timbers in northwest Ohio on the Maumee River.

**Nov. 19.** Jay's Treaty secures promise of British withdrawal from Western military posts by June 1796, and other concessions, but fails to settle various grievances, especially the question of British interference with neutral American shipping in Anglo-French war. Treaty is bitterly criticized in the U.S. where it becomes the focus of Federalist-Republican party conflict. Treaty is ratified by Congress after prolonged debate in June 1795, but funds for its enforcement are not appropriated until April 1796.

Act of 1794 provides for additional mail routes and stage transportation. Up to 1792, Vermont, Kentucky, Tennessee, and the West have had no mail routes, and there were only 5,000 miles of post roads in all. Typical postal rates, usually paid by recipient: 6 cents up to 30 miles; 15 cents up to 200 miles; and 25 cents over 400 miles. Much mail goes by ship, usually at double fee; city deliveries involve additional fee, paid to mail carrier.

Scientific study is stimulated by arrival in U.S. of Joseph Priestley, English clergyman and chemist, who had discovered oxygen in 1774. First American chair in chemistry is established at College of New Jersey (later Princeton) in 1795.

*Aurora* of Philadelphia succeeds *National Gazette* as principal Republican newspaper; *Aurora* had formerly been *General Advertiser*, founded in 1790 by Benjamin F. Bache, grandson of Benjamin Franklin. William Duane later succeeds Bache as editor.

*Tammany* by James Hewitt, said to be first American opera, performed in New York City.

## 1795

**Jan. 2.** Timothy Pickering of Massachusetts named secretary of war in reorganization of Cabinet. **Jan. 31.** Hamilton resigns from Treasury Department but continues as adviser and dominant voice in administration. **Aug. 19.** Edmund Randolph, having succeeded Jefferson as secretary of state, is forced to resign when President Washington becomes convinced of intrigue with French minister to prevent ratification of Jay's Treaty. Pickering succeeds to State Department, and James McHenry to War Department.

**Jan. 29.** Naturalization Act passed, making five-year residence a requirement for citizenship.

**Aug. 3.** Treaty of Greenville signed by 12 Indian tribes differentiates Indian lands and those open to settlers in Northwest Territory.

**Oct. 27.** Pinckney's Treaty (Treaty of San Lorenzo) with Spain gains Spanish recognition of U.S. Southern and Western boundaries (the 31st parallel and the Mississippi River) and right of navigation on Mississippi for U.S. Negotiations are by Thomas Pinckney, U.S. minister to Great Britain.

## 1796

**May 18.** Land Act passed by House providing for rectangular survey and public auction of land at minimum of $2 an acre, and for division of public domain into townships six miles square, with half the townships further divided into 36 sections of 640 acres each. Senate defeats attempt by Westerners to allow division of half the sections into quarter sections of 160 acres.

**June 1.** Tennessee admitted to the Union as the sixteenth state. Formerly part of North Carolina, and since 1790 "The Territory of the United States South of the River Ohio," it is the first state to be formed out of U.S. government territory.

**Sept. 19.** Washington's Farewell Address, dated September 17 but never delivered orally, published in Philadelphia *Daily American Advertiser.* Written with help of Madison and Hamilton, address, among other things, warns U.S. against "permanent" alliances, but advises temporary ones in emergencies.

**Dec. 7.** John Adams, Federalist candidate for President, elected by narrow margin, 71 to 68, over Thomas Jefferson, Democratic-Republican; Jefferson becomes vice-president. Federalist Thomas Pinckney receives 59 votes; Democrat-Republican Aaron Burr receives 30 votes.

U.S. Supreme Court passes on and upholds constitutionality of congressional act for first time in *Hylton* v. *United States* which involves tax on carriages act passed in 1794. In *Ware* v. *Hylton* Court invalidates Virginia statute of 1777 voiding debts owed to British subjects, contrary to U.S. treaty of 1783 which provides for payment, thus maintaining supremacy of national over state law.

Congress authorizes construction of Zane's Trace, road from Wheeling (now in West Virginia) to Limestone (now Maysville), Ky. Road becomes one of the main routes traveled by westbound settlers.

Cleveland, Ohio, laid out by Moses Cleaveland, agent for Connecticut Land Company that had purchased the Western Reserve (northeastern Ohio) in 1795.

# A PORTFOLIO OF MAPS

# Exploring the Continent

Spain's attention was first centered on North America because of the discovery of Florida, but the finding of vast wealth by Cortez and Pizarro in Central and South America diverted her activities southward for a time. The fact that great riches were to be found in the New World eventually encouraged Spain to seek similar benefits in North America, but she never was able to locate El Dorado there. However, by the middle of the 16th century, Spain did succeed in exploring the southern half of North America and in leaving many settlements — garrisons or missions — as outposts for the largest colonial empire any European nation has thus far founded (Map 1).

French exploration and settlement focused on Canada and what is today the midwestern United States. The early voyages of Jacques Cartier between 1534 and 1543 to find a northwest passage to the Orient or at least to discover sources of wealth comparable to the Spanish hauls became the basis for later French dominions. But it was Samuel de Champlain, and those who followed him into the interior of the continent along the St. Lawrence River, who established France's claim to colonial empire. Champlain's first voyage was in 1603, and other Frenchmen, lured by the fur trade into the interior of North America, left trading posts and forts along the way to protect their interests. Traders and missionaries opened up the water routes from the Great Lakes to the Gulf of Mexico. (Maps 2 and 3).

England came late to North America. Virginia was settled in 1607 and Plymouth in 1620; but in the course of time her empire became the dominant one. A century had to pass after the first settlement before her colonists ventured far into the interior of the continent. There were the natural barriers of mountains, as well as Indians and Frenchmen; and after 1763 there was the legal barrier of the Proclamation Line. But the very existence of a vast, unknown territory beyond the Appalachians invited exploration, no matter what the barriers. Beginning about 1750, individual exploring parties went west; Cumberland Gap was discovered in April of that year. In subsequent decades other hunters, traders, adventurers, and even farmers moved into the Ohio Valley. By the end of the century, with British rule overthrown, artificial hindrances to westward expansion were gone. The United States admitted three new states — Vermont, Kentucky, and Tennessee; and congressional land policy set aside the Northwest Territory from which future states would come (Map 4).

Maps prepared by Uni-Map Inc., Palatine, Ill.
for Encyclopaedia Britannica, Inc.

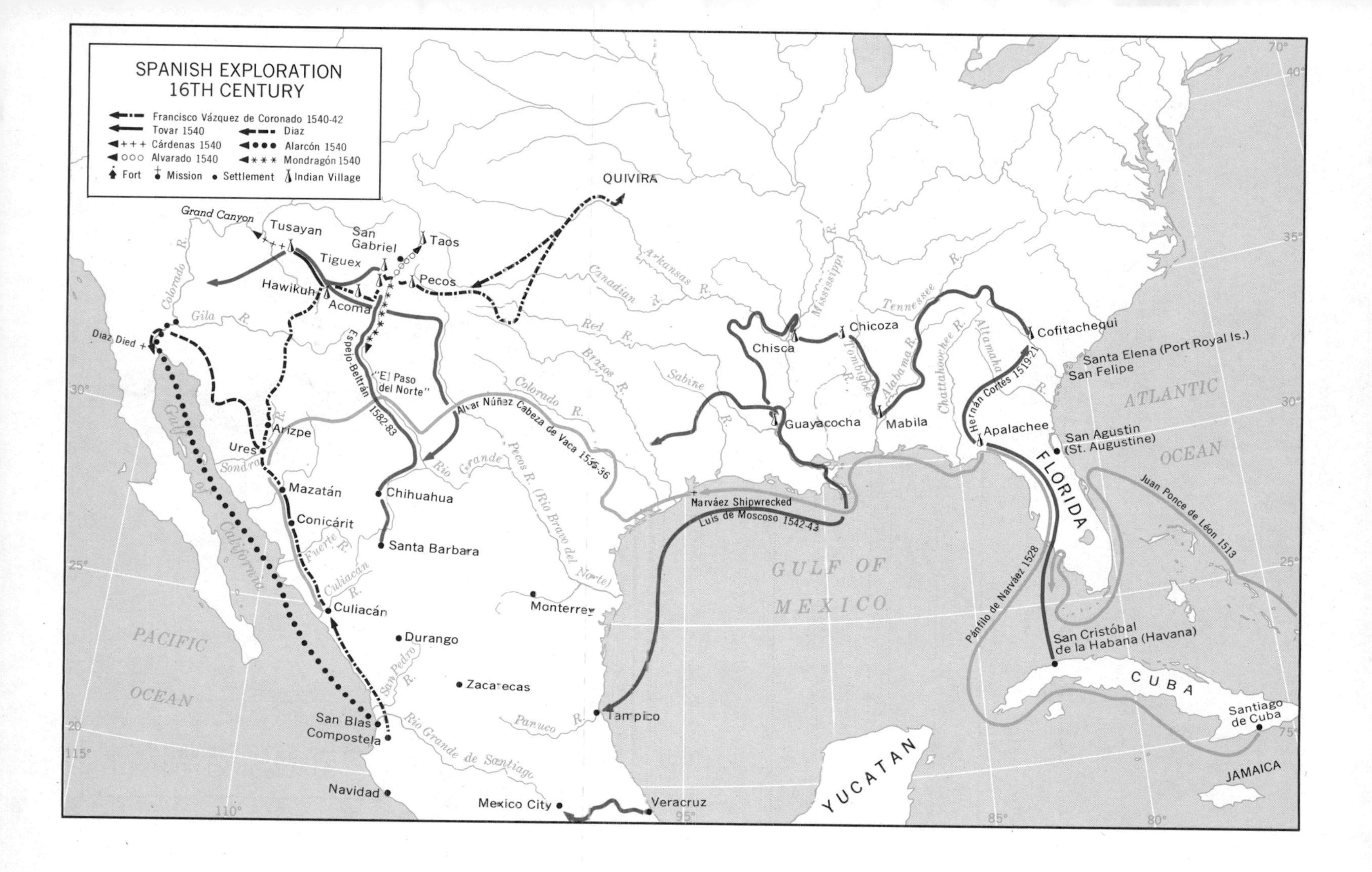

SPANISH EXPLORATION
16TH CENTURY
Francisco Vázquez de Coronado 1540-42
Tovar 1540
Diaz
Cárdenas 1540
Alarcón 1540
Alvarado 1540
Mondragón 1540
Fort
Mission
Settlement
Indian Village
QUIVIRA
Grand Canyon
Tusayan
San Gabriel
Taos
Tiguex
Pecos
Hawikuh
Acoma
Colorado R.
Gila R.
Diaz Died
Espejo-Beltrán 1582-83
"El Paso del Norte"
Alvar Núñez Cabeza de Vaca 1535-36
Arizpe
Ures
Sonora
Mazatán
Chihuahua
Conicárit
Fuerte R.
Santa Barbara
Culiacán R.
Culiacán
Durango
Zacatecas
Monterrey
San Pedro R.
San Blas
Compostela
Navidad
Rio Grande de Santiago
Mexico City
Veracruz
Tampico
Panuco R.
Gulf of California
PACIFIC OCEAN
Arkansas R.
Canadian R.
Red R.
Brazos R.
Colorado R.
Sabine R.
Rio Grande
Pecos R. (Rio Bravo del Norte)
Mississippi R.
Tennessee R.
Chisca
Chicoza
Tombigbee R.
Alabama R.
Mabila
Guayacocha
Chattahoochee R.
Altamaha R.
Cofitachequi
Hernán Cortes 1519-21
Apalachee
Santa Elena (Port Royal Is.)
San Felipe
San Agustin (St. Augustine)
ATLANTIC OCEAN
FLORIDA
Narváez Shipwrecked
Luis de Moscoso 1542-43
GULF OF MEXICO
Juan Ponce de Léon 1513
Pánfilo de Narváez 1528
San Cristóbal de la Habana (Havana)
CUBA
Santiago de Cuba
JAMAICA
YUCATAN
70°
40°
35°
30°
25°
20°
115°
110°
95°
85°
80°
75°

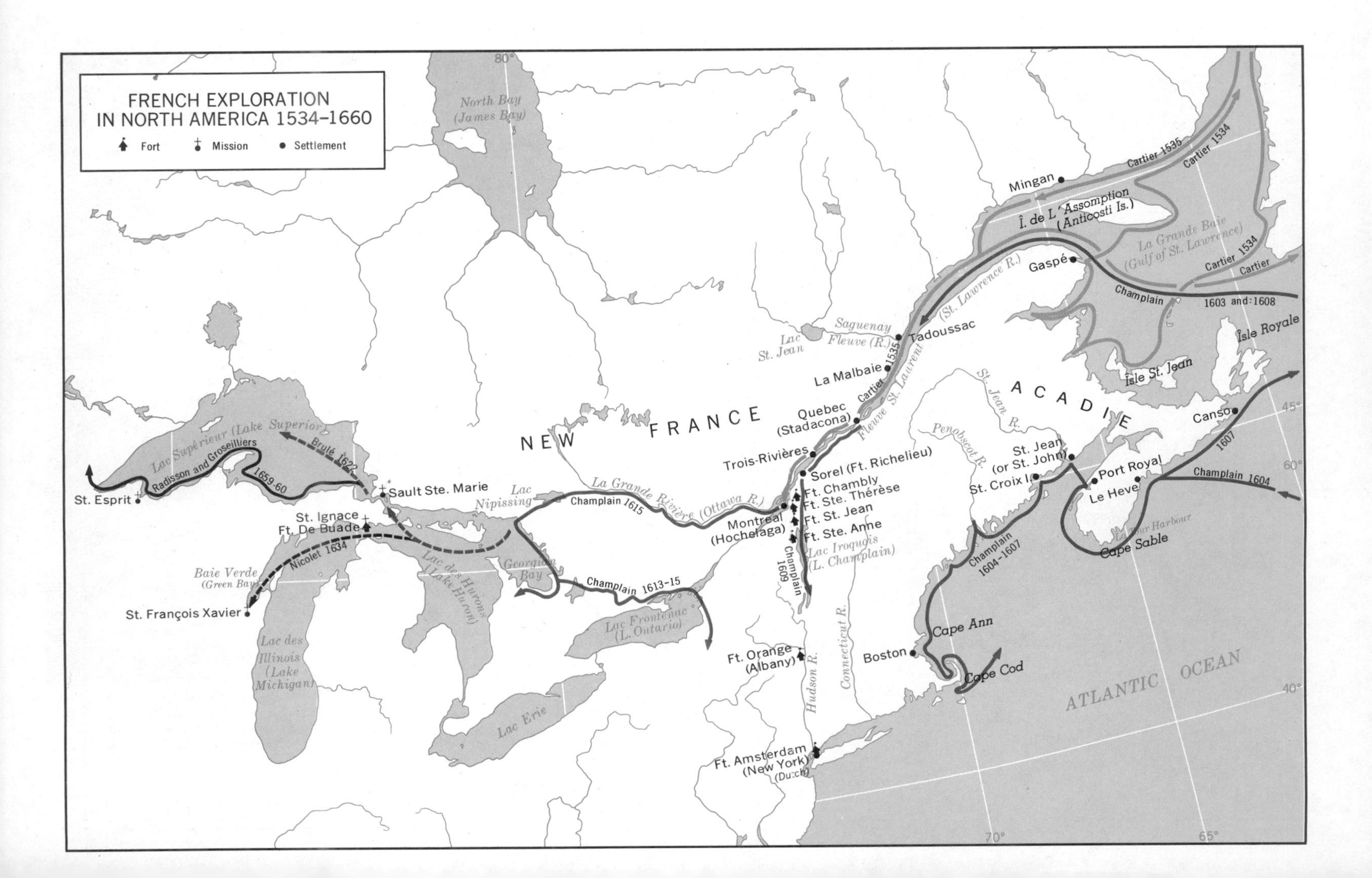

FRENCH EXPLORATION
IN NORTH AMERICA 1534–1660
Fort
Mission
Settlement
North Bay
(James Bay)
80°
Mingan
Cartier 1535
Cartier 1534
Î. de L'Assomption
(Anticosti Is.)
La Grande Baie
(Gulf of St. Lawrence)
Cartier 1534
Cartier
Gaspé
Champlain
1603 and 1608
Isle Royale
Isle St. Jean
(St. Lawrence R.)
Saguenay
Fleuve (R.)
Tadoussac
Lac
St. Jean
La Malbaie
1535
Cartier
Fleuve St. Laurent
A C A D I E
Canso
1607
Champlain 1604
Quebec
(Stadacona)
NEW FRANCE
St. Jean R.
Penobscot R.
St. Jean
(or St. John)
St. Croix I.
Port Royal
Le Heve
La Tour Harbour
Cape Sable
Trois-Rivières
Sorel (Ft. Richelieu)
Ft. Chambly
Ft. Ste. Thérèse
Ft. St. Jean
Ft. Ste. Anne
Montreal
(Hochelaga)
Lac Iroquois
(L. Champlain)
Champlain
1609
La Grande Rivière (Ottawa R.)
Champlain 1615
Lac
Nipissing
Sault Ste. Marie
Lac Supérieur (Lake Superior)
Brulé 1622
Radisson and Groseilliers
1659-60
St. Esprit
St. Ignace
Ft. De Buade
Nicolet 1634
Baie Verte
(Green Bay)
St. François Xavier
Lac des Hurons
(Lake Huron)
Georgian
Bay
Champlain 1613–15
Lac Frontenac
(L. Ontario)
Lac des
Illinois
(Lake
Michigan)
Lac Erie
Champlain
1604–1607
Cape Ann
Boston
Cape Cod
Connecticut R.
Hudson R.
Ft. Orange
(Albany)
Ft. Amsterdam
(New York)
(Dutch)
ATLANTIC OCEAN
45°
60°
40°
70°
65°

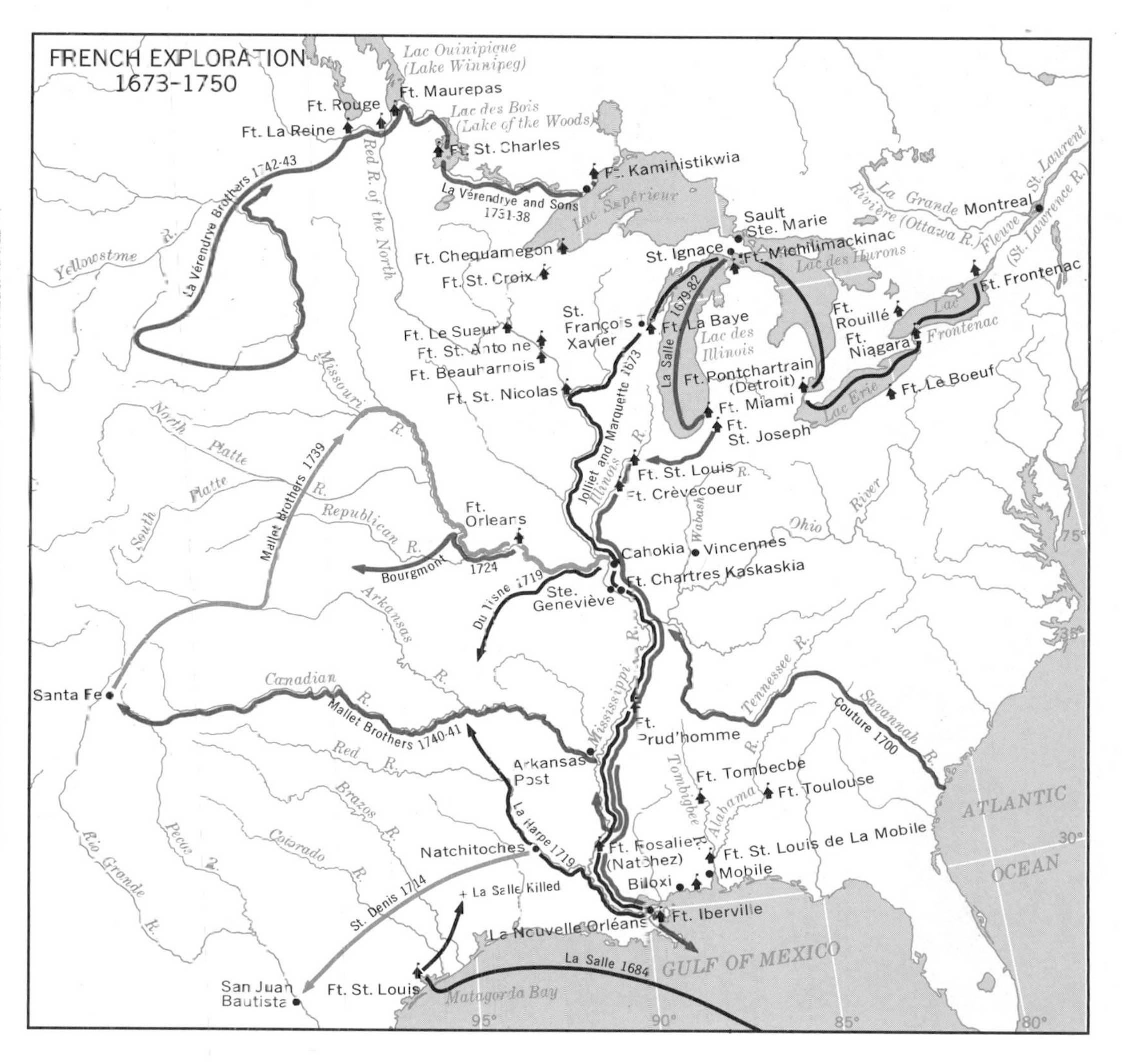

FRENCH EXPLORATION
1673-1750
Lac Ouinipique
(Lake Winnipeg)
Ft. Maurepas
Ft. Rouge
Ft. La Reine
Lac des Bois
(Lake of the Woods)
Ft. St. Charles
Ft. Kaministikwia
La Vérendrye and Sons
1731-38
Lac Supérieur
La Vérendrye Brothers 1742-43
Yellowstone R.
Red R. of the North
Ft. Chequamegon
Ft. St. Croix
Sault
Ste. Marie
St. Ignace
Ft. Michilimackinac
Lac des Hurons
La Grande Rivière (Ottawa R.)
Montreal
Fleuve St. Laurent
(St. Lawrence R.)
Ft. Frontenac
Lac Frontenac
Ft. Rouillé
Ft. Niagara
Lac Erie
Ft. Le Boeuf
St. François Xavier
Ft. La Baye
Lac des Illinois
La Salle 1679-82
Ft. Pontchartrain
(Detroit)
Ft. Miami
Ft. St. Joseph
Ft. Le Sueur
Ft. St. Antoine
Ft. Beauharnois
Ft. St. Nicolas
Jolliet and Marquette 1673
Illinois R.
Ft. St. Louis
Ft. Crèvecoeur
Missouri R.
North Platte
South Platte R.
Republican R.
Mallet Brothers 1739
Ft. Orleans
Bourgmont
1724
Cahokia
Vincennes
Wabash
Ohio River
Ft. Chartres
Kaskaskia
Ste. Geneviève
Du Tisne 1719
Arkansas R.
Mississippi R.
Tennessee R.
Savannah R.
Couture 1700
Santa Fe
Canadian R.
Mallet Brothers 1740-41
Red R.
Ft. Prud'homme
Arkansas Post
Ft. Tombecbe
Tombigbee R.
Alabama R.
Ft. Toulouse
Brazos R.
Pecos R.
Colorado R.
Rio Grande R.
Natchitoches
La Harpe 1719
Ft. Rosalie
(Natchez)
Ft. St. Louis de La Mobile
Mobile
Biloxi
St. Denis 1714
+ La Salle Killed
Ft. Iberville
La Nouvelle Orléans
La Salle 1684
GULF OF MEXICO
ATLANTIC OCEAN
San Juan Bautista
Ft. St. Louis
Matagorda Bay
95°
90°
85°
80°
75°
35°
30°

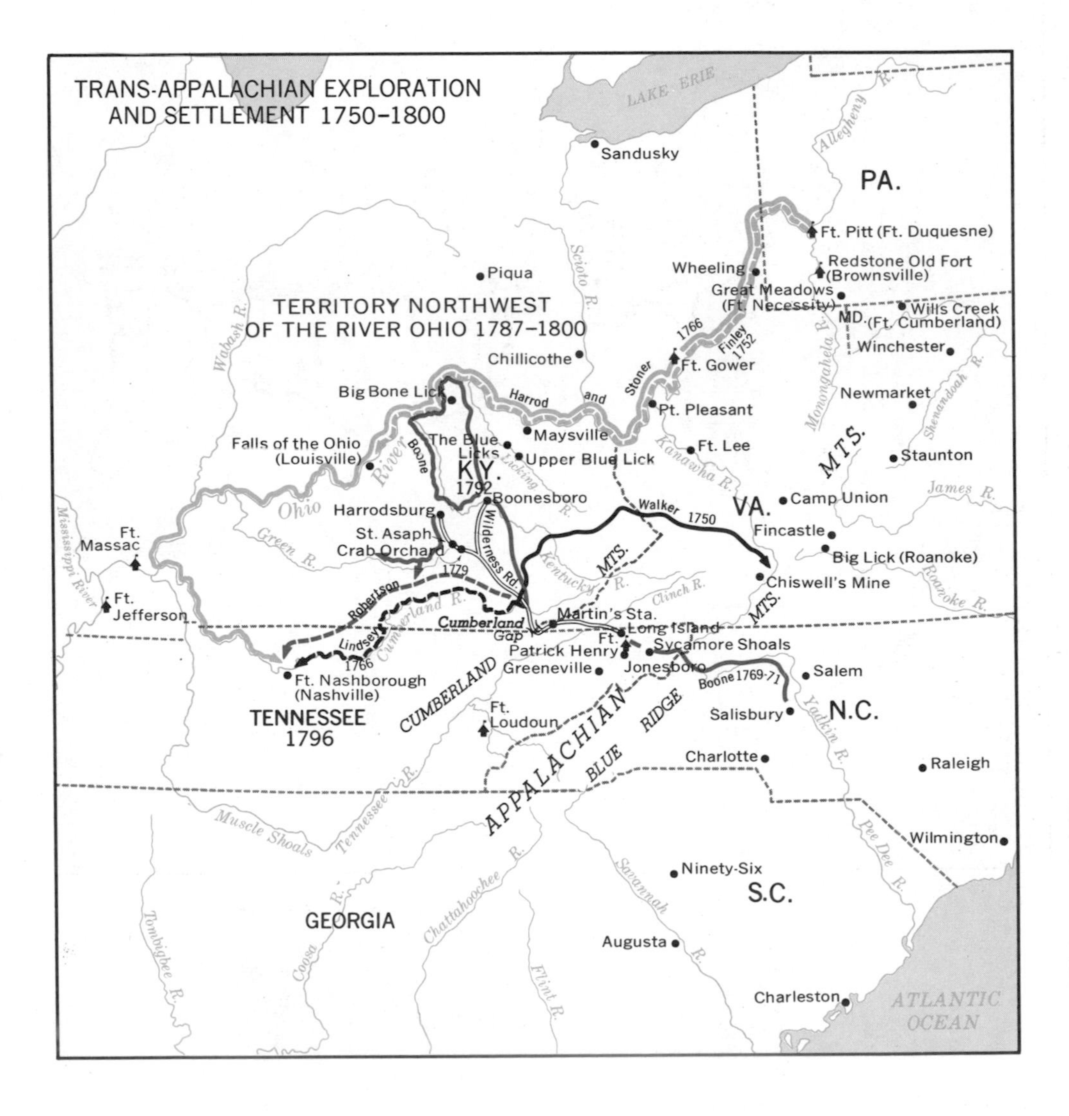
TRANS-APPALACHIAN EXPLORATION
AND SETTLEMENT 1750–1800
LAKE ERIE
Sandusky
PA.
Allegheny R.
Ft. Pitt (Ft. Duquesne)
Redstone Old Fort
(Brownsville)
Wheeling
Great Meadows
(Ft. Necessity)
MD.
Wills Creek
(Ft. Cumberland)
Winchester
Piqua
Scioto R.
TERRITORY NORTHWEST
OF THE RIVER OHIO 1787–1800
Chillicothe
Wabash R.
1766
Finley 1752
Stoner
Ft. Gower
Harrod
and
Big Bone Lick
Pt. Pleasant
Newmarket
Maysville
The Blue
Licks
Upper Blue Lick
Falls of the Ohio
(Louisville)
Boone
KY.
1792
Licking R.
Kanawha R.
Ft. Lee
Monongahela R.
MTS.
Shenandoah R.
Staunton
Ohio
River
Harrodsburg
Boonesboro
Walker 1750
VA.
Camp Union
James R.
Fincastle
Big Lick (Roanoke)
Ft.
Massac
Mississippi River
Green R.
St. Asaph
Crab Orchard
1779
Wilderness Rd.
Kentucky R.
MTS.
Chiswell's Mine
Roanoke R.
Ft.
Jefferson
Robertson
Cumberland R.
Cumberland
Gap
Martin's Sta.
Clinch R.
Long Island
MTS.
Ft.
Patrick Henry
Sycamore Shoals
Lindsey
1766
Ft. Nashborough
(Nashville)
Greeneville
Jonesboro
Boone 1769-71
Salem
CUMBERLAND
TENNESSEE
1796
Ft.
Loudoun
APPALACHIAN
BLUE
RIDGE
Salisbury
N.C.
Yadkin R.
Charlotte
Raleigh
Muscle Shoals
Tennessee R.
Pee Dee R.
Wilmington
Chattahoochee R.
Savannah R.
Ninety-Six
S.C.
GEORGIA
Coosa R.
Tombigbee R.
Flint R.
Augusta
Charleston
ATLANTIC
OCEAN

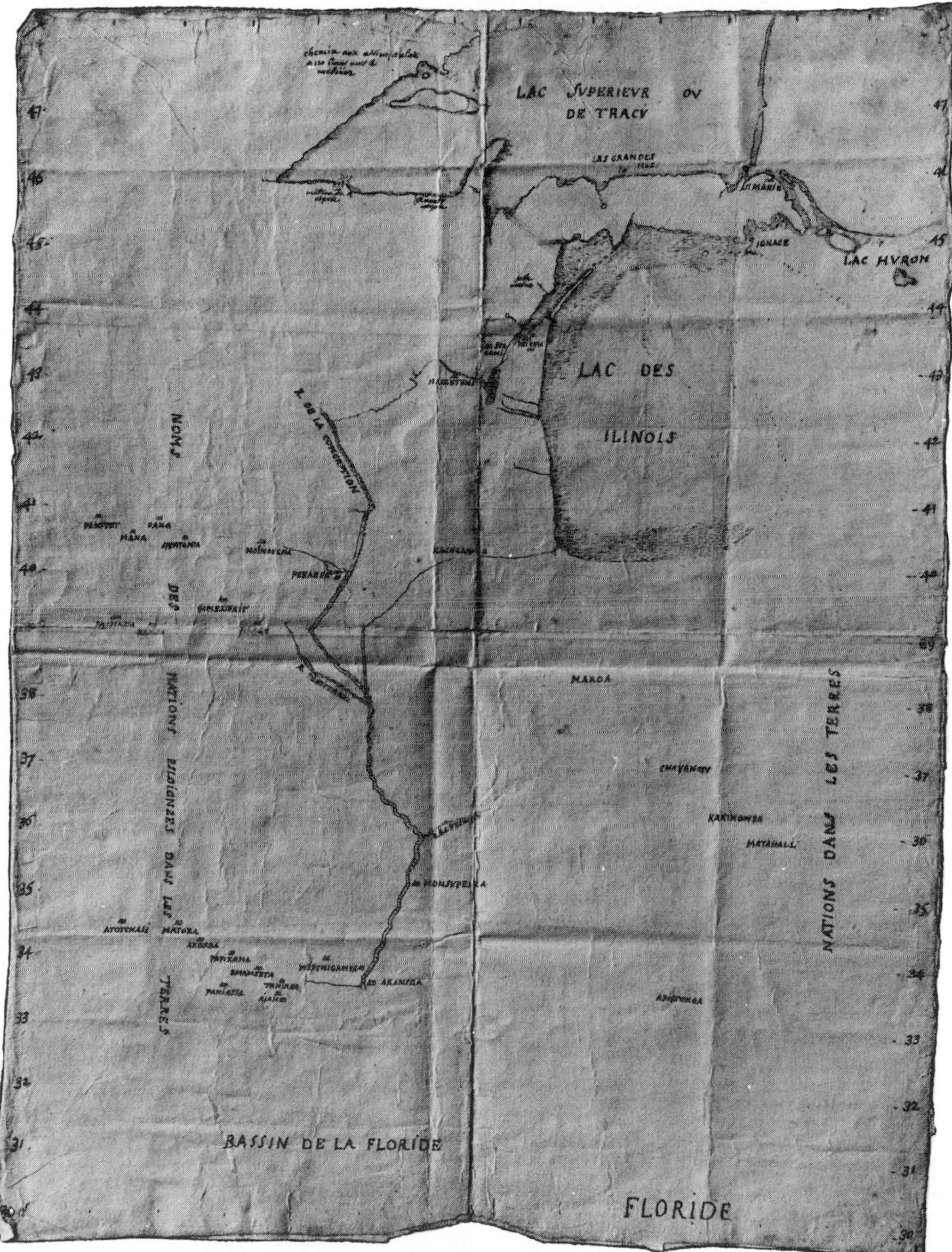


Archives of the Society of Jesus at College Saint-Marie, Montreal

**Father Jacques Marquette's map of his voyage with Louis Jolliet from Mackinac down Lake Michigan ("Lac des Ilinois"), the Illinois River and the Mississippi as far as Arkansas in 1673**

# 1784

1.

## A Plan of Government for the Western Territory

*The generally weak and ineffectual Congress under the Articles probably made its greatest contribution through its legislation on land policy. This seemed to be the one thing on which agreement was possible. So successful were its policies that they proved workable well into the nineteenth century. The territorial ordinance of April 23, 1784, reprinted here, was drafted by Thomas Jefferson. Although his clause excluding slavery from the western territory after 1800 was narrowly defeated, the ordinance did provide a plan for division of the territory and eventual admission of new states.*

Source: *Journals*, IV: "Friday, April 23, 1784."

*Resolved*, that so much of the territory ceded or to be ceded by individual states to the United States as is already purchased or shall be purchased of the Indian inhabitants and offered for sale by Congress, shall be divided into distinct states, in the following manner, as nearly as such cessions will admit; that is to say, by parallels of latitude, so that each state shall comprehend from north to south two degrees of latitude beginning to count from the completion of 45° north of the equator; and by meridians of longitude, one of which shall pass through the lowest point of the rapids of Ohio, and the other through the western cape of the mouth of the Great Kanawha. But the territory eastward of this last meridian, between the Ohio, Lake Erie, and Pennsylvania shall be one state whatsoever may be its comprehension of latitude. That which may lie beyond the completion of the 45th degree between the said meridians shall make part of the state adjoining it on the south; and that part of the Ohio which is between the same meridians coinciding nearly with the parallel of 39° shall be substituted so far in lieu of that parallel as a boundary line.

That the settlers on any territory so purchased and offered for sale shall, either on their own petition, or on the order of Congress, receive authority from them with appointments of time and place for their free males of full age within the limits of their state to meet together for the purpose of establishing a temporary government, to adopt the constitution and laws of any one of the original states, so that such laws nevertheless shall be subject to alteration by their ordinary legislature; and to erect, subject to a like alteration, counties, townships . . . for the election of members for their legislature.

That when any such state shall have acquired 20,000 free inhabitants, on giving due proof thereof to Congress, they shall receive from them authority with appointments of time and place to call a convention of representatives to establish a permanent constitution and government for themselves, provided that both the temporary and permanent governments be established on these principles as their basis:

First, that they shall forever remain a part of this confederacy of the United States of America. Second, that they shall be subject to the Articles of Confederation in all those cases in which the original states shall be so subject and to all the acts and ordinances of the United States in Congress assembled, conformable thereto. Third, that they shall in no case interfere with the primary disposal of the soil by the United States in Congress assembled, nor with the ordinances and regulations which Congress may find necessary for securing the title in such soil to the bona fide purchasers. Fourth, that they shall be subject to pay a part of the federal debts contracted or to be contracted, to be apportioned on them by Congress, according to the same common rule and measure by which apportionments thereof shall be made on the other states. Fifth, that no tax shall be imposed on lands, the property of the United States. Sixth, that their respective governments shall be republican. Seventh, that the lands of nonresident proprietors shall in no case be taxed higher than those of residents within any new state before the admission thereof to a vote by its delegates in Congress.

That whensoever any of the said states shall have, of free inhabitants, as many as shall then be in any one the least numerous of the thirteen original states, such state shall be admitted by its delegates into the Congress of the United States on an equal footing with the said original states; provided the consent of so many states in Congress is first obtained as may at the time be competent to such admission. And in order to adapt the said Articles of Confederation to the state of Congress when its numbers shall be thus increased, it shall be proposed to the legislatures of the states, originally parties thereto, to require the assent of two-thirds of the United States in Congress assembled in all those cases wherein, by the said Articles, the assent of nine states is now required; which being agreed to by them shall be binding on the new states. Until such admission by their delegates into Congress, any of the said states after the establishment of their temporary government shall have authority to keep a member in Congress, with a right of debating, but not of voting.

That measures not inconsistent with the principles of the confederation and necessary for the preservation of peace and good order among the settlers in any of the said new states until they shall assume a temporary government as aforesaid, may from time to time be taken by the United States in Congress assembled;

That the preceding articles shall be formed into a charter of compact, shall be duly executed by the President of the United States in Congress assembled, under his hand and the seal of the United States, shall be promulgated and shall stand as fundamental constitutions between the thirteen original states and each of the several states now newly described, unalterable . . . but by the joint consent of the United States in Congress assembled, and of the particular state within which such alteration is proposed to be made.

2.

# John Filson: Daniel Boone in the Wilderness

*The first descriptive history of Kentucky was written by John Filson, a pioneer of that region. His* Discovery, Settlement, and Present State of Kentucke, *published in 1784, appears to have been written to attract immigrants and thereby increase the value of the land, of which Filson owned several thousand acres. An appendix of the work contains the "Autobiography" of Daniel Boone, which fostered the Boone legend in American history.*

Source: *The Discovery, Settlement, and Present State of Kentucky, etc., etc.,* New York, 1793, Vol. II, pp. 47-78.

Curiosity is natural to the soul of man; and interesting objects have a powerful influence on our affections. . . . Thus we behold Kentucky, lately a howling wilderness, the habitation of savages and wild beasts, become a fruitful field. This region, so favorably distinguished by nature, is now become the habitation of civilization, at a period unparalleled in history, in the midst of a raging war, and under all the disadvantages of emigration to a country so remote from the inhabited parts of the continent.

Here, where the hands of violence shed the blood of the innocent; where the horrid yells of savages and the groans of the distressed sounded in our ears, we now hear the praises and adorations of our Creator; where wretched wigwams stood, the miserable abodes of savages, we behold the foundations of cities laid, that, in all probability, will equal the glory of the greatest upon earth. And we view Kentucky, situated on the fertile banks of the great Ohio, rising from obscurity to shine with splendor, equal to any other of the stars of the American hemisphere. The settling of this region well deserves a place in history. Most of the memorable events I have myself been exercised in. . . .

It was on the 1st of May, in the year 1769, that I resigned my domestic happiness for a time, and left my family and peaceable habitation on the Yadkin River in North Carolina, to wander through the wilderness of America in quest of the country of Kentucky, in company with John Finley, John Stewart, Joseph Holden, James Monay, and William Cool. We proceeded successfully, and, after a long and fatiguing journey through a mountainous wilderness, in a westward direction, on the 7th day of June following, we found ourselves on Red River, where John Finley had formerly been trading with the Indians, and, from the top of an eminence, saw with pleasure the beautiful level of Kentucky. Here let me observe that for some time we had experienced the most uncomfortable weather as a prelibation [foretaste] of our future sufferings.

At this place we encamped and made a shelter to defend us from the inclement season, and began to hunt and reconnoiter the country. We found everywhere abundance of wild beasts of all sorts, through this vast forest. The buffalo were more frequent than I have seen cattle in the settlements, browsing on the leaves of the cane or cropping the herbage on those extensive plains, fearless, because ignorant, of the violence of man. Sometimes we saw hundreds in a drove, and the numbers about the salt springs were amazing. In this forest, the habitation of beasts of every kind natural to America, we practised hunting with great success until the 22nd day of December following.

This day, John Stewart and I had a pleasing ramble, but fortune changed the scene in the close of it. We had passed through a great forest on which stood myriads of trees, some gay with blossoms, others rich with fruits. Nature was here a series of wonders and a fund of delight. Here she displayed her ingenuity and industry in a variety of flowers and fruits, beautifully colored, elegantly shaped, and charmingly flavored; and we were diverted with innumerable animals presenting themselves perpetually to our view.

Filson Club

Portrait of John Filson (1747-88) by an unknown artist

In the decline of the day, near Kentucky River, as we ascended the brow of a small hill, a number of Indians rushed out of a thick canebrake upon us and made us prisoners. The time of our sorrow was now arrived, and the scene fully opened. The Indians plundered us of what we had and kept us in confinement seven days, treating us with common savage usage. During this time we discovered no uneasiness or desire to escape, which made them less suspicious of us; but, in the dead of night, as we lay in a thick canebrake by a large fire, when sleep had locked up their senses, my situation not disposing me for rest, I touched my companion and gently awoke him. We improved this favorable opportunity and departed, leaving them to take their rest, and speedily directed our course toward our old camp, but found it plundered, and the company dispersed and gone home.

About this time, my brother Squire Boone, with another adventurer who came to explore the country shortly after us, was wandering through the forest, determined to find me, if possible, and accidentally found our camp. Notwithstanding the unfortunate circumstances of our company and our dangerous situation, as surrounded with hostile savages, our meeting so fortunately in the wilderness made us reciprocally sensible of the utmost satisfaction. So much does friendship triumph over misfortune that sorrows and sufferings vanish, not only at the meeting of real friends but of the most distant acquaintances, and substitute happiness in their room.

Soon after this, my companion in captivity, John Stewart, was killed by the savages; and the man that came with my brother returned home by himself. We were then in a dangerous, helpless situation, exposed daily to perils and death among savages and wild beasts, not a white man in the country but ourselves.

Thus situated, many hundred miles from our families in the howling wilderness, I believe few would have equally enjoyed the happiness we experienced. I often observed to my brother, "You see now how little nature requires to be satisfied." Felicity, the companion of content, is rather found in our own breasts than in the enjoyment of external things, and I firmly believe it requires but a little philosophy to make a man happy in whatsoever state he is. This consists in a full resignation to the will of Providence; and a resigned soul finds pleasure in a path strewn with briars and thorns.

We continued not in a state of indolence but hunted every day and prepared a little cottage to defend us from the winter storms. We remained there undisturbed during the winter; and on the 1st day of May, 1770, my brother returned home to the settlement by himself for a new recruit of horses and ammunition, leaving me by myself without bread, salt, or sugar, without company of my fellow creatures, or even a horse or dog. I confess I never before was under greater necessity of exercising philosophy and fortitude. A few days I passed uncomfortably. The idea of a beloved wife and family, and their anxiety upon the account of my absence and exposed situation, made sensible impressions on my heart. A thousand dreadful apprehensions presented themselves to my view and had undoubtedly disposed me to melancholy if further indulged.

One day I undertook a tour through the country, and the diversity and beauties of nature I met with in this charming season expelled every gloomy and vexatious thought. Just at the close of day, the gentle gales retired and left the place to the disposal of a profound calm. Not a breeze shook the most tremulous leaf. I had gained the summit of a commanding ridge, and, looking round with astonished delight, beheld the ample plains, the beauteous tracts below. On the other hand, I surveyed the famous River Ohio that rolled in silent dignity, marking the western boundary of Kentucky with inconceivable grandeur. At a vast distance I beheld the mountains lift their venerable brows and penetrate the clouds. All things were still. I kindled a fire near a fountain of sweet water, and feasted on the loin of a buck, which a few hours before I had killed. The sullen shades of night soon overspread the whole hemisphere, and the earth seemed to gasp after the hovering moisture. My roving excursion this day had fatigued my body and diverted my imagination. I laid me down to sleep, and I awoke not until the sun had chased away the night.

Massachusetts Historical Society

Daniel Boone, portrait from life by Chester Harding

I continued this tour, and, in a few days, explored a considerable part of the country, each day equally pleased as the first. I returned again to my old camp, which was not disturbed in my absence. I did not confine my lodging to it but often reposed in thick canebrakes to avoid the savages, who, I believe, often visited my camp, but, fortunately for me, in my absence.

In this situation I was constantly exposed to danger and death. How unhappy such a situation for a man tormented with fear, which is vain if no danger comes, and if it does, only augments the pain. It was my happiness to be destitute of this afflicting passion with which I had the greatest reason to be affected. The prowling wolves diverted my nocturnal hours with perpetual howlings; and the various species of animals in this vast forest, in the daytime, were continually in my view. Thus I was surrounded with plenty in the midst of want. I was happy in the midst of dangers and inconveniences. In such a diversity it was impossible I should be disposed to melancholy. No populous city, with all the varieties of commerce and stately structures, could afford so much pleasure to my mind as the beauties of nature I found here.

Thus, through an uninterrupted scene of sylvan pleasures, I spent the time until the 27th day of July following, when my brother, to my great felicity, met me, according to appointment, at our old camp. Shortly after, we left this place, not thinking it safe to stay there longer, and proceeded to Cumberland River, reconnoitering that part of the country until March 1771 and giving names to the different waters.

Soon after, I returned home to my family, with a determination to bring them as soon as possible to live in Kentucky, which I esteemed a second paradise, at the risk of my life and fortune.

---

3.

## "The Wayfaring Stranger"

*The freedom-loving mountaineers of the southern Appalachian Mountains expressed the hardships of their daily lives and their hopes for a beautiful hereafter in songs. "The Wayfaring Stranger" was a favorite spiritual sung at revival meetings. After the American Revolution, some of these people left the mountains and headed westward, popularizing the song among other frontier Americans.*

### THE WAYFARING STRANGER

I'm just a poor wayfaring stranger
A-trav'lin' through this world of woe,
But there's no sickness, toil or danger
In that bright world to which I go.

I'm goin' there to see my mother;
I'm goin' there, no more to roam.
I'm just a-goin' over Jordan,
I'm just a-goin' over home.

My father lived and died a farmer
A-reapin' less than he did sow.
And now I follow in his footsteps
A-knowin' less than he did know.

I'm goin' there to see my father;
I'm goin' there, no more to roam.
I'm just a-goin' over Jordan,
I'm just a-goin' over home.

I know dark clouds will gather 'round me.
My way is steep and rough, I know,
But fertile fields lie just before me
In that fair land to which I go.

I'm goin' there to see my brother;
I'm goin' there, no more to roam.
I'm just a-goin' over Jordan,
I'm just a-goin' over home.

4.

## ALEXANDER HAMILTON: The Unjust Treatment of Loyalists

*The treaty that ended the war with England provided that no revenge should be taken on those Americans who had sided with the Tories during the Revolution. Alexander Hamilton saw the dangers to which a vindictive public policy would lead in terms of creating second-class citizens without a vote or property rights. In such a society no one would know from one year to the next if he were "safe" politically. In a series of newspaper articles in 1784 under the signature, "Phocion," Hamilton undertook to defend fair treatment of Loyalists.*

Source: J. C. Hamilton, II, pp. 287-301.

WHILE NOT ONLY EVERY PERSONAL ARTIFICE is employed by a few heated and inconsiderate spirits to practise upon the passions of the people, but the public papers are made the channel of the most inflammatory and pernicious doctrines tending to the subversion of all private security and genuine liberty; it would be culpable in those who understand and value the true interests of the community to be silent spectators. It is, however, a common observation that men bent upon mischief are more active in the pursuit of their object than those who aim at doing good. Hence it is, in the present moment, we see the most industrious efforts made to violate the constitution of this state, to trample upon the rights of the subject, and to chicane or infringe the most solemn obligations of treaty; while dispassionate and upright men almost totally neglect the means of counteracting these dangerous attempts. A sense of duty alone calls forth the observations which will be submitted to the good sense of the people in this paper, from one who has more inclination than leisure to serve them; and who has had too deep a share in the common exertions in this Revolution, to be willing to see its fruits blasted by the violence of rash or unprincipled men, without, at least, protesting against their designs.

The persons alluded to pretend to appeal to the spirit of Whiggism; while they endeavor to put in motion all the furious and dark passions of the human mind. The spirit of Whiggism is generous, humane, beneficent, and just. These men inculcate revenge, cruelty, persecution, and perfidy. The spirit of Whiggism cherishes legal liberty, holds the rights of every individual sacred, condemns or punishes no man without regular trial and conviction of some crime declared by antecedent laws; reprobates equally the punishment of the citizen by arbitrary acts of legislation as by the lawless combinations of unauthorized individuals; while these men are advocates for expelling a large number of their fellow citizens unheard, untried; or, if they cannot effect this, are for disfranchising them, in the face of the constitution, without the judgment of their peers, and contrary to the law of the land.

The 13th Article of the constitution declares, "that no member of the state shall

Library of Congress

Etching showing atrocities against Loyalists

be disfranchised, or defrauded of any of the rights or privileges sacred to the subjects of this state by the constitution, unless by the law of the land or the judgment of his peers." If we inquire what is meant by the law of the land, the best commentators will tell us, that it means due process of law; that is, by indictment or presentment of good and lawful men, and trial and conviction in consequence.

It is true that in England, on extraordinary occasions, attainders for high treason, by act of Parliament, have been practised; but many of the ablest advocates for civil liberty have condemned this practice; and it has commonly been exercised with great caution upon individuals only by name, never against general descriptions of men. The sense of our constitution on this practice we may gather from the 41st Article, where all attainders, other than for crimes committed during the late war, are forbidden.

If there had been no Treaty in the way, the legislature might, by name, have attainted particular persons of high treason for crimes committed during the war; but, independent of the Treaty, it could not, and cannot, without tyranny, disfranchise or punish whole classes of citizens by general descriptions, without trial and conviction of offenses known by laws previously established, declaring the offense and prescribing the penalty.

This is a dictate of natural justice and a fundamental principle of law and liberty.

Nothing is more common than for a free people, in times of heat and violence, to gratify momentary passions by letting into the government principles and precedents which afterwards prove fatal to themselves. Of this kind is the doctrine of disqualification, disfranchisement, and banishment, by acts of legislature. The dangerous consequences of this power are manifest. If the legislature can disfranchise any number of citizens at pleasure by general descriptions, it may soon confine all the votes to a small number of partisans, and establish an aristocracy or an oligarchy. If it may banish at discretion all those whom particular circumstances render obnoxious without hearing or trial, no man can be safe nor know when he may be the innocent victim of a prevailing faction. The name of liberty applied to such a government would be a mockery of common sense.

The English Whigs, after the Revolution, from an overweening dread of popery and the Pretender, from triennial, voted the Parliament septennial. They have been trying, ever since, to undo this false step in vain, and repenting the effects of their folly in the overgrown power of the new family. Some imprudent Whigs among us, from resentment to those who have taken the opposite side (and many of them from worse motives), would corrupt the principles of our government and furnish precedents for future usurpations on the rights of the community.

Let the people beware of such counselors. However a few designing men may rise in consequence, and advance their private interests by such expedients, the people at large are sure to be the losers in the event, whenever they suffer a departure from the rules of general and equal justice, or from the true principles of universal liberty.

These men not only overleap the barriers of the constitution without remorse, but they advise us to become the scorn of nations by violating the solemn engagements of the United States.

They endeavor to mold the Treaty with Great Britain into such form as pleases them, and to make it mean anything or nothing, as suits their views. They tell us that all the stipulations with respect to the Tories are merely that Congress will recommend, and the states may comply or not, as they please.

But let any man of sense and candor read the Treaty, and it will speak for itself. The 5th Article is indeed recommendatory; but the 6th is as positive as words can make it. "*There shall be* no future confiscations made, nor prosecutions commenced against any person or persons, for or by reason of the part which he or they may have taken in the present war; and no person shall, on that account, suffer any future loss or damage, either in his person, liberty, or property."

As to the restoration of confiscated property, which is the subject of the 5th Article, the states may restore or not, as they think proper, because Congress engage only to recommend; but there is not a word about recommendation in the 6th Article.

Quotations are made from the debates in Parliament, to prove that the whole is understood as recommendatory; but the expressions in those quotations turn altogether upon those persons who have been actually proscribed, and their property confiscated; they have no relation to those who come under the 6th Article, or who might be the objects of future prosecution or punishment. And to this it may be added that it is absurd and inadmissible in fair reasoning to combat the plain, authentic language of solemn treaty by loose recitals of debates in newspapers.

The sound and ingenuous construction of the two articles, taken collectively, is this: that where the property of any persons, other than those who have been in arms against the United States, had been actually confiscated, and themselves proscribed, then Congress are to recommend a restoration of estates, rights, and properties; and, with respect to those who had been in arms, they are to recommend permission for them to remain a twelvemonth in the country, to solicit a like restoration; but with respect to all those who were not in this situation, and who had not already been the objects of confiscation and banishment, they were to be absolutely secured from all future injury to person, liberty, or property.

To say that this exemption from positive injury does not imply a right to live among us as citizens is a pitiful sophistry; it is to say that the banishment of a person from his country, connections, and resources (one of the greatest punishments that can befall a man) is no punishment at all.

The meaning of the word "liberty" has been contested. Its true sense must be the enjoyment of the common privileges of subjects under the same government. There is no middle line of just construction between this sense and a mere exemption from personal imprisonment! If the last were adopted, the stipulation would become nugatory; and, by depriving those who are the subjects of it of the protection of government, it would amount to a virtual confiscation and banishment; for they could not have the benefit of the laws against those who should be aggressors.

Should it be said that they may receive protection without being admitted to a full enjoyment of the privileges of citizens; this must be either matter of right under the Treaty, or matter of grace in the government. If the latter, the government may refuse it; and then the objection presents itself that the Treaty would, by this construction, be virtually defeated: if matter of right, then it follows that more is intended by the word liberty than a mere exemption from imprisonment; and where shall the line be drawn: not a capricious and arbitrary line, but one warranted by rational and legal construction?

To say that, by espousing the cause of Great Britain, they became aliens, and that it will satisfy the Treaty to allow them the same protection to which aliens are entitled, is to admit that subjects may, at pleasure, renounce their allegiance to the state of which they are members and devote themselves to a foreign jurisdiction; a principle contrary to law and subversive of government. But even this will not satisfy the Treaty; for aliens cannot hold real property under our government: and if they are aliens, all their real estate belongs to the public. This will be, to all intents and purposes, a confiscation of property. But this is not all. How does it appear that the persons who are thus to be stripped of their citizenship have been guilty of such an adherence to the enemy, as, in legal contemplation, amounts to a crime? Their merely remaining in their possessions, under the power of the conqueror, does not imply this, but is executed by the laws and customs of all civilized nations. To adjudge them culpable, they must be first tried and convicted; and this the Treaty forbids. These are the difficulties involved by recurring to subtle and evasive, instead of simple and candid, construction, which will teach us that the stipulations in the Treaty amount to an amnesty and act of oblivion.

There is a very simple and conclusive point of view in which this subject may be placed. No citizen can be deprived of any right which the citizens in general are entitled to, unless forfeited by some offense. It has been seen that the regular and constitutional mode of ascertaining whether this forfeiture has been incurred is by legal process, trial, and conviction. This *ex vi termini* [by the force of the term], supposes prosecution. Now, consistent with the Treaty, there can be no future prosecution for anything done on account of the war. Can we then do, by act of legislature, what the Treaty disables us from doing by due course of law? This would be to imitate the Roman general, who, having promised Antiochus to restore half his vessels, caused them to be sawed in two before their delivery; or the Plataeans, who, having promised the Thebans to restore their prisoners, had them first put to death, and returned them dead.

Such fraudulent subterfuges are justly considered more odious than an open and avowed violation of Treaty.

When these posture-masters in logic are

Public Archives of Canada

"Encampment of the Loyalists at Johnston," along the banks of the St. Lawrence River, Canada, 1784

driven from this first ground of the meaning of the Treaty, they are forced to that of attacking the right of Congress to make such a stipulation, and arraigning the impudence of Great Britain in attempting to make terms for our own subjects. But here, as everywhere else, they are only successful in betraying their narrowness and ignorance. Does not the act of confederation place the exclusive right of making war and peace in the United States in Congress? Have they not the sole power of making treaties with foreign nations? Are not these among the first rights of sovereignty? And does not the delegation of them to the general confederacy so far abridge the sovereignty of each particular state? Would not a different doctrine involve the contradiction of *imperium in imperio?* What reasonable limits can be assigned to these prerogatives of the Union, other than the general safety and the *fundamentals* of the constitution? Can it be said that a treaty for arresting the future operations of positive acts of legislature, and which has indeed no other effect than that of a pardon for past offenses committed against these acts, is an attack upon the fundamentals of the state constitutions? Can it be denied that the peace which was made, taken collectively, was manifestly for the general good — that it was even favorable to the solid interests of this country, beyond the expectation of the most sanguine? If this cannot be denied — and none can deny it who know either the value of the objects gained by the Treaty, or the necessity these states were under at the time of making peace — it follows that Congress and their ministers acted wisely in making the Treaty which has been made; and it follows from this that these states are bound by it, and ought religiously to observe it.

The *uti possidetis* — each party to hold what it possesses — is the point from which nations set out in framing a treaty of peace. If one side gives up a part of its acquisitions, the other side renders an equivalent in some other way. What is the equivalent given to Great Britain for all the important concessions she has made? She has surrendered the capital of this state and its large dependencies. She is to surrender our immensely valuable posts on the frontier; and to yield to us a vast tract of western territory, with one-half of the lakes, by which we shall command almost the whole fur trade. She renounces to us her claim to the navigation of the Mississippi, and admits us to share in the fisheries, even on better terms than we formerly enjoyed it. As she was in possession, by right of war, of all these objects, whatever may have been our original pretensions to them, they are, by the laws of nations, to be considered as so much given up on her part. And what do we give in return? We stipulate that there shall be no future injury to her adherents among us. How insignificant the equivalent in comparison with the acquisition! A man of sense would be ashamed to compare them; a man of honesty, not intoxicated with passion, would blush to lisp a question of the obligation to observe the stipulation on our part.

If it be said that Great Britain has only

restored to us what she had unjustly taken from us, and that therefore we are not bound to make compensation; this admits of several answers: First, that the fact is not true; for she has ceded to us a large tract of country to which we had even no plausible claim. Second, that however the principle of the objection might have been proper, to prevent our promising an equivalent, it comes too late after the promise has been made. Third, that as to the external effects of war, the voluntary law of nations knows no distinction between the justice or injustice of the quarrel, but in the treaty of peace puts the contracting parties upon an equal footing; which is a necessary consequence of the independence of nations: for, as they acknowledge no common judge, if, in concluding peace, both parties were not to stand upon the same ground of right, there never could be an adjustment of differences, or an end of war. This is a settled principle.

Let us examine the pretext upon which it is disputed. Congress, say our political jugglers, have no right to meddle with our internal police. They would be puzzled to tell what they mean by the expression. The truth is, it has no definite meaning; for it is impossible for Congress to do a single act which will not, directly or indirectly, affect the internal police of every state. When, in order to procure privileges of commerce to the citizens of these states in foreign countries, they stipulate a reciprocity of privileges here, does not such an admission of the subjects of foreign countries to certain rights within these states operate immediately upon their internal police? And were this not done, would not the power of making commercial treaties, vested in Congress, become a mere nullity? In short, if nothing was to be done by Congress that would affect our internal police in the large sense in which it has been taken, would not all the powers of the confederation be annihilated, and the Union dissolved? . . .

The embarrassed and exhausted state of Great Britain, and the political system of Europe, render it impossible for her ever to reacquire the dominion of this country. Her former partisans must be convinced of this and abandon her cause as desperate. They will never be mad enough to risk their fortunes a second time, in the hopeless attempt of restoring her authority; nor will they have any inclination to do it, if they are allowed to be happy under the government of the society in which they live. To make it practicable, if they should be so disposed, they must not only get the government of this state, but of the United States, into their hands. To suppose this possible is to suppose that a majority of the numbers, property, and abilities of the United States has been, and is, in opposition to the Revolution. Its success is a clear proof that this has not been the case; and every man of information among us knows the contrary. The supposition itself would show the absurdity of expelling a small number from the city, which would constitute so insignificant a proportion of the whole, as, without diminishing their influence, would only increase their disposition to do mischief. The policy, in this case, would be evident, of appealing to their interests rather than to their fears.

Nothing can be more ridiculous than the idea of expelling a few from this city and neighborhood, while there are numbers in different parts of this and other states who must necessarily partake in our governments, and who can never expect to be the objects of animadversion or exclusion. It is confirming *many* in their enmity and prejudices against the state, to indulge our enmity and prejudices against a few.

The idea of suffering the Tories to live among us under disqualifications is equally mischievous and absurd. It is necessitating a large body of citizens in the state to continue enemies to the government, ready at all times, in a moment of commotion, to throw their weight into that scale which meditates a change, whether favorable or unfavorable to public liberty.

Viewing the subject in every possible light, there is not a single interest of the community but dictates moderation rather than violence. That honesty is still the best policy; that justice and moderation are the surest supports of every government — are maxims which, however they may be called trite, are at all times true: though too seldom regarded, but rarely neglected with impunity. Were the people of America, with one voice, to ask, "What shall we do to perpetuate our liberties and secure our happiness?" the answer would be, "Govern well," and you have nothing to fear, either from internal disaffection or external hostility. Abuse not the power you possess, and you need never apprehend its diminution or loss. But if you make a wanton use of it; if you furnish another example, that despotism may debase the government of the many as well as the few; you, like all others that have acted the same part, will experience that licentiousness is the forerunner to slavery. . . .

These sentiments are delivered to you, in the frankness of conscious integrity, by one who *feels* that solicitude for the good of the community which the zealots, whose opinions he encounters, profess; by one who pursues not, as they do, the honors or emoluments of his country; by one who, though he has had, in the course of the Revolution, a very *confidential* share in the public councils, civil and military, and has as often, at least, met danger in the common cause as any of those who now assume to be the guardians of the public liberty, asks no other reward from his countrymen than to be heard without prejudice for their own interest.

*I wish the bald eagle had not been chosen as the representative of our country; he is a bird of bad moral character; like those among men who live by sharping and robbing, he is generally poor, and often very lousy.*

*The turkey is a much more respectable bird, and withal a true original native of America.*

Benjamin Franklin, letter to Sarah Bache, Jan. 26, 1784

# 1785

5.

## John Carroll: On the Selection of a Roman Catholic Bishop in America

*The Roman Catholic Church in America was under the authority of the Vicar Apostolic of London until the Revolution made a new arrangement necessary. The priests in America did not want regulation of their affairs transferred to another foreign hierarchy. Fearing such a result, John Carroll, who had been appointed by the Holy See as Superior of Catholic Missions for the United States, wrote to Rome, February 27, 1785, outlining the special problems of the church in America and giving his reasons for the selection of an American bishop. The Holy See granted permission to the American clergy to elect their own bishop. In 1789, Father Carroll was chosen to fill the post and became Bishop of Baltimore in 1791.*

Source: John G. Shea, *Life and Times of the Most Rev. John Carroll*, New York, 1888, pp. 251-256.

The Most Eminent Cardinal may rest assured that the greatest evils would be borne by us rather than renounce the divine authority of the Holy See; that not only we priests who are here, but the Catholic people, seem so firm in the faith that they will never withdraw from obedience to the sovereign pontiff. The Catholic body, however, think that some favor should be granted to them by the Holy Father, necessary for their permanent enjoyment of the civil rights which they now enjoy, and to avert the dangers which they fear. From what I have said, and from the framework of public affairs here, Your Eminence must see how objectionable all foreign jurisdiction will be to them. The Catholics therefore desire that no pretext be given to the enemies of our religion to accuse us of depending unnecessarily on a foreign authority; and that some plan may be adopted by which hereafter an ecclesiastical superior may be appointed for this country in such a way as to retain absolutely the spiritual jurisdiction of the Holy See, and at the same time remove all ground of objecting to us, as though we held anything hostile to the national independence. Many of the leading Catholics thought of laying this before His Holiness in a general memorial, especially those who have been either in the Continental Congress or the legislature of Pennsylvania and Maryland, but I induced them to refrain from any such step at least for the present. The Holy Father will perhaps see more clearly what is to be done in this matter if he considers the 6th of the Articles of Perpetual Confederation between the states, which enacts that no one who holds any office under the United States shall be allowed to receive any gift, office, or title of any kind whatsoever from any king, prince, or foreign government, and though this prohibition seems to extend only to those who are appointed to offices in the republic, it will perhaps be wrested by our opponents to apply also to ecclesiastical offices.

We desire, therefore, Most Eminent Cardinal, to provide in every way, that the faith in its integrity, due obedience toward the Apostolic See, and perfect union should flourish, and at the same time that whatever can with safety to religion be granted, shall be conceded to American Catholics in ecclesiastical government; in this way we hope that the distrust of Protestants now full of suspicion will be diminished, and that thus our affairs can be solidly established.

You have indicated, Most Eminent Cardinal, that it was the intention and design of His Holiness to appoint a Vicar Apostolic for these states, invested with the episcopal character and title. While this paternal solicitude for us has filled us with great joy, it also at first inspired some fear; for we knew that heretofore American Protestants never could be induced to allow even a bishop of their own sect, when the attempt was made during the subjection of these provinces to the king of England; hence a fear arose that we would not be permitted to have one. But some months since in a convention of Protestant ministers of the Anglican, or as it is here called, the Episcopal Church, they decreed that as by authority of law they enjoyed the full exercise of their religion, they therefore had the right of appointing for themselves such ministers of holy things as the system and discipline [of] their sect required; namely bishops, priests, and deacons. This decision on their part was not censured by the Congress appointed to frame our laws. As the same liberty in the exercise of religion is granted to us, it necessarily follows that we enjoy the same right in regard to adopting laws for our government.

Georgetown University

Portrait of Bishop John Carroll by Gilbert Stuart

While the matter stands thus, the Holy Father will decide, and you, Most Eminent Cardinal, will consider whether the time is now opportune for appointing a bishop, what his qualifications should be, and how he should be nominated. On all these points, not as if seeking to obtain my own judgment, but to make this relation more ample, I shall note a few facts.

First, as regards the seasonableness of the step, it may be noted that there will be no excitement in the public mind if a bishop be appointed, as Protestants think of appointing one for themselves. Nay, they even hope to acquire some importance for their sect among the people from the episcopal dignity. So, too, we trust that we shall not only acquire the same, but that great advantages will follow; inasmuch as this church will then be governed in that manner which Christ our Lord instituted. On the other hand, however, it occurs that as the Most Holy Father has already deigned to provide otherwise for conferring the sacrament of confirmation, there is no actual need for the appointment of a bishop until some candidates are found fitted to receive holy orders; this we hope will be the case in a few years, as you will understand, Most Eminent Cardinal, from a special relation which I purpose writing. When that time comes, we shall perhaps be better able to make a suitable provision for a bishop than from our slender resources we can now do.

In the next place, if it shall seem best to His Holiness to assign a bishop to this country, will it be best to appoint a vicar apostolic or an ordinary with a see of his own? Which will conduce more to the progress of Catholicity; which will contribute most to remove Protestant jealousy of foreign jurisdiction? I know with certainty that this fear will increase if they know that an ecclesiastical superior is so appointed as to be removable from office at the pleasure of the Sacred Congregation *de Propaganda Fide,* or any other tribunal out of the country, or that he has no power to admit any priest to exercise the sacred function, unless that congregation has approved and sent him to us.

As to the method of nominating a bishop, I will say no more at present than this, that we are imploring God in His wisdom and mercy to guide the judgment of the Holy See, that if it does not seem proper to allow the priests who have labored for so many years in this vineyard of the Lord to propose to the Holy See the one whom they deem most fit, that some method will be adopted by which a bad feeling may not be excited among the people of this country, Catholic and Protestant.

---

6.

## James Madison: Against Religious Assessments

*The occasion of Madison's "Remonstrance" was explained by him in a letter to George Mason of July 14, 1826: "During the session of the General Assembly [of Virginia], 1784-5, a bill was introduced into the House of Delegates providing for the legal support of the teachers of the Christian religion, and being patronized by the most popular talents in the House, seemed likely to obtain a majority of votes. . . . Your highly-distinguished ancestor, Col. Geo. Mason . . . and some others, thought it advisable that a remonstrance against the bill should be prepared for general circulation and signature, and imposed on me the task of drawing up such a paper. This draught having received their sanction, a large number of printed copies were distributed, and so extensively signed by the people of every religious denomination, that at the ensuing session the projected measure was entirely frustrated."*

Source: *Madison Letters,* I, pp. 162-169.

We, the subscribers, citizens of the said Commonwealth, having taken into serious consideration a bill printed by order of the last session of General Assembly, entitled "A Bill Establishing a Provision for Teachers of the Christian Religion," and conceiving that the same, if finally armed with the sanctions of a law, will be a dangerous abuse of power, are bound as faithful members of a free state to remonstrate against it, and to declare the reasons by which we are determined. We remonstrate against the said bill:

1. Because we hold it for a fundamental and undeniable truth, "that religion or the duty which we owe to our Creator and the manner of discharging it, can be directed only by reason and conviction, not by force or violence." The religion, then, of every man must be left to the conviction and conscience of every man; and it is the right of every man to exercise it as these may dictate. This right is in its nature an unalienable right. It is unalienable because the opinions of men, depending only on the evidence contemplated by their own minds, cannot follow the dictates of other men. It is unalienable, also, because what is here a right toward men is a duty toward the Creator. It is the duty of every man to render to the Creator such homage, and such only, as he believes to be acceptable to him. This duty is precedent both in order of time and degree of obligation to the claims of civil society. Before any man can be considered as a member of civil society, he must be considered as a subject of the Governor of the universe; and if a member of civil society who enters into any subordinate association must always do it with a reservation of his duty to the general authority, much more must every man who becomes a member of any particular civil society do it with a saving of his allegiance to the universal sovereign. We maintain, therefore, that in matters of religion no man's right is abridged by the institution of civil society, and that religion is wholly exempt from its cognizance. True it is that no other rule exists by which any question which may divide a society can be ultimately determined than the will of the majority; but it is also true that the majority may trespass on the rights of the minority.

2. Because if religion be exempt from the authority of the society at large, still less can it be subject to that of the legislative body. The latter are but the creatures and vicegerents of the former. Their jurisdiction is both derivative and limited: it is limited with regard to the coordinate departments; more necessarily is it limited with regard to the constituents. The preservation of a free government requires not merely that the metes and bounds which separate each department of power may be invariably maintained, but more especially that neither of them be suffered to overleap the great barrier which defends the rights of the people. The rulers who are guilty of such an encroachment exceed the commission from which they derive their authority, and are tyrants. The people who submit to it are governed by laws made neither by themselves nor by an authority derived from them, and are slaves.

3. Because it is proper to take alarm at the first experiment on our liberties. We hold this prudent jealousy to be the first duty of citizens and one of the noblest characteristics of the late Revolution. The freemen of America did not wait till usurped power had strengthened itself by exercise and entangled the question in precedents. They saw all the consequences in the principle, and they avoided the consequences by denying the principle. We revere this lesson too much soon to forget it. Who does not see that the same authority which can establish Christianity, in exclusion of all other religions, may establish with the same ease any particular sect of Christians, in exclusion of all other sects? That the same authority which can force a citizen to contribute threepence only of his property for the support of any one establishment may force him to conform to any other establishment in all cases whatsoever?

4. Because the bill violates that equality which ought to be the basis of every law, and which is more indispensable, in proportion as the validity or expediency of any law is more liable to be impeached. "If all men are by nature equally free and inde-

pendent," all men are to be considered as entering into society on equal conditions; as relinquishing no more, and therefore retaining no less, one than another, of their natural rights. Above all are they to be considered as retaining an "*equal* title to the free exercise of religion according to the dictates of conscience." While we assert for ourselves a freedom to embrace, to profess, and to observe the religion which we believe to be of divine origin, we cannot deny an equal freedom to those whose minds have not yet yielded to the evidence which has convinced us. If this freedom be abused, it is an offense against God, not against man: To God, therefore, not to man must an account of it be rendered. As the bill violates equality by subjecting some to peculiar burdens, so it violates the same principle by granting to others peculiar exemptions. Are the Quakers and Mennonites the only sects who think a compulsive support of their religions unnecessary and unwarrantable? Can their piety alone be entrusted with the care of public worship? Ought their religions to be endowed above all others with extraordinary privileges by which proselytes may be enticed from all others? We think too favorably of the justice and good sense of these denominations to believe that they either covet preeminencies over their fellow citizens or that they will be seduced by them from the common opposition to the measure.

5. Because the bill implies either that the civil magistrate is a competent judge of religious truths, or that he may employ religion as an engine of civil policy. The first is an arrogant pretension falsified by the contradictory opinions of rulers in all ages and throughout the world; the second an unhallowed perversion of the means of salvation.

6. Because the establishment proposed by the bill is not requisite for the support of the Christian religion. To say that it is, is a contradiction to the Christian religion itself; for every page of it disavows a dependence on the powers of this world. It is a contradiction to fact, for it is known that this religion both existed and flourished, not only without the support of human laws but in spite of every opposition from them; and not only during the period of miraculous aid but long after it had been left to its own evidence and the ordinary care of Providence. Nay, it is a contradiction in terms, for a religion not invented by human policy must have preexisted and been supported before it was established by human policy. It is, moreover, to weaken in those who profess this religion a pious confidence in its innate excellence and the patronage of its Author; and to foster in those who still reject it a suspicion that its friends are too conscious of its fallacies to trust it to its own merits.

7. Because experience witnesses that ecclesiastical establishments, instead of maintaining the purity and efficacy of religion, have had a contrary operation. During almost fifteen centuries has the legal establishment of Christianity been on trial. What have been its fruits? More or less in all places, pride and indolence in the clergy; ignorance and servility in the laity; in both, superstition, bigotry, and persecution. Inquire of the teachers of Christianity for the ages in which it appeared in its greatest luster; those of every sect point to the ages prior to its incorporation with civil policy. Propose a restoration of this primitive state in which its teachers depended on the voluntary rewards of their flocks; many of them predict its downfall. On which side ought their testimony to have greatest weight, when for or when against their interest?

8. Because the establishment in question is not necessary for the support of civil government. If it be urged as necessary for the support of civil government only as it is a means of supporting religion, and it be not necessary for the latter purpose, it cannot be necessary for the former. If religion be not

within the cognizance of civil government, how can its legal establishment be necessary to civil government? What influence in fact have ecclesiastical establishments had on civil society? In some instances they have been seen to erect a spiritual tyranny on the ruins of civil authority; in many instances they have been seen upholding the thrones of political tyranny; in no instance have they been seen the guardians of the liberties of the people. Rulers who wished to subvert the public liberty may have found an established clergy convenient auxiliaries. A just government, instituted to secure and perpetuate it, needs them not. Such a government will be best supported by protecting every citizen in the enjoyment of his religion with the same equal hand which protects his person and his property; by neither invading the equal rights of any sect, nor suffering any sect to invade those of another.

9. Because the proposed establishment is a departure from that generous policy, which, offering an asylum to the persecuted and oppressed of every nation and religion, promised a luster to our country and an accession to the number of its citizens. What a melancholy mark is the bill of sudden degeneracy! Instead of holding forth an asylum to the persecuted, it is itself a signal of persecution. It degrades from the equal rank of citizens all those whose opinions in religion do not bend to those of the legislative authority. Distant as it may be, in its present form, from the Inquisition, it differs from it only in degree. The one is the first step, the other is the last in the career of intolerance. The magnanimous sufferer under this cruel scourge in foreign regions must view the bill as a beacon on our coast, warning him to seek some other haven, where liberty and philanthropy in their due extent may offer a more certain repose from his troubles.

10. Because it will have a like tendency to banish our citizens. The allurements presented by other situations are every day thinning their number. To superadd a fresh motive to emigration by revoking the liberty which they now enjoy would be the same species of folly which has dishonored and depopulated flourishing kingdoms.

11. Because it will destroy that moderation and harmony which the forbearance of our laws to intermeddle with religion has produced amongst its several sects. Torrents of blood have been spilled in the Old World [by] vain attempts of the secular arm to extinguish religious discord by proscribing all differences in religious opinion. Time has at length revealed the true remedy. Every relaxation of narrow and rigorous policy, wherever it has been tried, has been found to assuage the disease. The American theater has exhibited proofs that equal and complete liberty, if it does not wholly eradicate it, sufficiently destroys its malignant influence on the health and prosperity of the state. If with the salutary effects of this system under our own eyes we begin to contract the bounds of religious freedom, we know no name that will too severely reproach our folly. At least let warning be taken at the first fruits of the threatened innovation. The very appearance of the bill has transformed "that Christian forbearance, love, and charity," which of late mutually prevailed, into animosities and jealousies, which may not soon be appeased. What mischiefs may not be dreaded should this enemy to the public quiet be armed with the force of a law?

12. Because the policy of the bill is adverse to the diffusion of the light of Christianity. The first wish of those who enjoy this precious gift ought to be that it may be imparted to the whole race of mankind. Compare the number of those who have as yet received it with the number still remaining under the dominion of false religions; and how small is the former! Does the policy of the bill tend to lessen the disproportion? No, it at once discourages those who

are strangers to the light of revelation from coming into the region of it; and countenances by example the nations who continue in darkness, in shutting out those who might convey it to them. Instead of leveling as far as possible, every obstacle to the victorious progress of truth, the bill, with an ignoble and unchristian timidity, would circumscribe it with a wall of defense against the encroachments of error.

13. Because attempts to enforce, by legal sanctions, acts obnoxious to so great a proportion of citizens tend to enervate the laws in general and to slacken the bands of society. If it be difficult to execute any law which is not generally deemed necessary or salutary, what must be the case where it is deemed invalid and dangerous? And what may be the effect of so striking an example of impotency in the government on its general authority?

14. Because a measure of such singular magnitude and delicacy ought not to be imposed without the clearest evidence that it is called for by a majority of citizens, and no satisfactory method is yet proposed by which the voice of the majority in this case may be determined or its influence secured. "The people of the respective counties are indeed requested to signify their opinion respecting the adoption of the bill to the next session of Assembly." But the representation must be made equal, before the voice either of the representatives or of the counties will be that of the people. Our hope is that neither of the former will, after due consideration, espouse the dangerous principle of the bill. Should the event disappoint us, it will still leave us in full confidence that a fair appeal to the latter will reverse the sentence against our liberties.

15. Because, finally, "the equal right of every citizen to the free exercise of his religion according to the dictates of conscience" is held by the same tenure with all our other rights. If we recur to its origin, it is equally the gift of nature; if we weigh its importance, it cannot be less dear to us; if we consult the declaration of those rights which pertain to the good people of Virginia as the "basis and foundation of government," it is enumerated with equal solemnity, or rather, studied emphasis. Either then we must say that the will of the legislature is the only measure of their authority; and that in the plenitude of that authority, they may sweep away all our fundamental rights; or that they are bound to leave this particular right untouched and sacred. Either we must say that they may control the freedom of the press, may abolish the trial by jury, may swallow up the executive and judiciary powers of the state, nay, that they may despoil us of our very right of suffrage and erect themselves into an independent and hereditary assembly; or we must say that they have no authority to enact into law the bill under consideration. We, the subscribers, say that the General Assembly of this Commonwealth have no such authority. And . . . that no effort may be omitted on our part against so dangerous an usurpation, we oppose to it this remonstrance; earnestly praying, as we are in duty bound, that the Supreme Lawgiver of the universe, by illuminating those to whom it is addressed, may on the one hand turn their councils from every act which would affront His holy prerogative, or violate the trust committed to them; and on the other, guide them into every measure which may be worthy of His blessing, may redound to their own praise, and establish more firmly the liberties, the prosperity, and the happiness of the Commonwealth.

7.

## John Adams: Foreign Commerce and Federal Union

*Under the Articles of Confederation each state regulated its own trade, making it impossible for Congress to negotiate treaties of commerce with foreign nations. Because of the intense commercial rivalry between the states Britain correctly realized that any commercial treaty would only inhibit her bargaining power. It soon became apparent to John Adams, American minister to London, that unless commercial relations were under the control of a stronger central government, the United States would continue to be victimized by unfair trade restrictions on the part of Britain. He expressed his arguments in a letter to John Jay on May 8, 1785.*

Source: C. F. Adams, VIII, pp. 242-246.

In executing the instructions of Congress of the 7th of March last, as well as all former orders which concern the court of Great Britain, the Ministry will, no doubt, find my commission and letter of credence sufficient authority. But you will see, by a letter from the Duke of Dorset, which your ministers here sometime since transmitted, that the British cabinet have conceived doubts whether Congress have power to treat of commercial matters, and whether our states should not separately grant their full powers to a minister. I think it may be taken for granted that the states will never think of sending separate ambassadors, or of authorizing directly those appointed by Congress.

The idea of thirteen plenipotentiaries meeting together in a congress at every court in Europe, each with a full power and distinct instructions from his state, presents to view such a picture of confusion, altercation, expense, and endless delay as must convince every man of its impracticability. Neither is there less absurdity in supposing that all the states should unite in the separate election of the same man, since there is not, never was, and never will be a citizen whom each state would separately prefer for conducting the negotiation. It is equally inconceivable that each state should separately send a full power and separate instructions to the ministers appointed by Congress.

What a heterogeneous mass of papers, full of different objects, various views, and inconsistent and contradictory orders must such a man pull out of his *portefeuille*, from time to time, to regulate his judgment and his conduct! He must be accountable, too, to thirteen different tribunals for his conduct; a situation in which no man would ever consent to stand, if it is possible, which I do not believe, that any state should ever wish for such a system, I suppose, too, that the Confederation has already settled all these points, and that Congress alone have authority to treat with foreign powers, and to appoint ambassadors and foreign ministers, and that the states have separately no power to do either.

Yet it is plain, from the Duke of Dorset's

letter, that the British cabinet have conceived a different opinion. This is to be accounted for only by conjecturing that they have put an erroneous construction on the *limitation, restriction,* or *exception* in the article of our Confederation which gives to Congress the power of appointing ambassadors and making treaties. This limitation is confined to treaties of commerce; all others Congress have full power to make. From this limitation, however, will probably arise a great deal of difficulty and delay to me. If the British Ministry wish and seek for delays, this will be their pretext. But even if they should wish for dispatch, which is not likely, they may have propositions to make which will fall within the limitation, and, in such case, it will not be in my power to agree with them. I can only transmit the proposition to Congress, who will perhaps transmit it to the states, and no man can foresee when the answers will be received so that the business can be brought to a conclusion.

American Philosophical Society
"The American Union" by Barleé Marbois

It is a long time that Congress have appeared to be aware of these obstructions in the way of our prosperity; but it does not yet appear that the states have been sufficiently attentive to them to remove them. It is not to be supposed that Congress will ever frame any treaty of commerce with any foreign power which shall be unequal and partial among the states, or oppressive upon any one of them; and it is very clear, from the situation and circumstances of the country, that no such treaty can ever be carried into execution or last long. If the states should be unwilling to confer upon Congress a power to make treaties of commerce unlimited in point of time, it should seem that time alone might be a sufficient restriction; or the limitation might be to a particular nation, as the English, for example, for a certain time, although it must be always remembered that we cannot favor the English with anything which will not become common to other nations — the French, the Dutch, and Swedes, at least. . . .

The last year must have been a prosperous period in the United States. The high prices of their produce, and the low prices of foreign merchandises, are a demonstration of it. Yet our shipping, our seamen, our carrying trade have been discouraged. Present ease, and even wealth, should not be our only object.

We ought to attend to considerations of strength and defense. Our situation is different from some of the powers of Europe who have neglected their own defense. Switzerland is situated so that if she should be attacked by one neighbor, she would infallibly be defended by two others. If attacked by Sardinia, she would be defended by France and the emperor; if by the emperor, France and Sardinia would support her; and if by France, the emperor and Sardinia would unite to protect her. This is so fully known to her and all her neighbors that she fears nothing and is at no expense. Holland, if attacked by France, found a friend in England; when attacked by England, France supports her; when the emperor threatened her, she found a friend in France, too, and she will forever be sure that neither of these three great powers can ever suffer her to fall a prey to any of the others. She has relied so much upon this as to neglect her defense, to her great regret at present.

But what are Switzerland and Holland — small powers limited by nature so that they never can be great — to the United States of America, destined beyond a doubt to be the greatest power on earth, and that within the life of man? This is so well known that, instead of being overlooked among the powers, like Holland and Switzerland, we shall be more an object of jealousy than any other upon earth. All the powers know that it is impossible for any, the proudest of them, to conquer us; and, therefore, if we should be attacked by any one, the others will not be fond of undertaking our defense. Knowing we can defend ourselves, they will leave us to do it; and, if they assist us at all, it will not be until we have done the work, and then it will be feebly, and only with a view of deriving more benefit and reputation from it than they do us good. They will be pleased to see us weakened and our growth a little retarded.

It behooves the United States, then, to knit themselves together in the bands of affection and mutual confidence, search their own resources to the bottom, form their foreign commerce into a system, and encourage their own navigation and seamen, and to these ends their carrying trade; and I am much afraid we shall never be able to do this unless Congress are vested with full power, under the limitations prescribed of fifteen years, and the concurrence of nine states, of forming treaties of commerce with foreign powers.

---

*Games played with the ball, and others of that nature, are too violent for the body, and stamp no character on the mind.*

THOMAS JEFFERSON, letter to Peter Carr, Aug. 19, 1785

*[Jefferson was] a gentleman of thirty-two who could calculate an eclipse, survey an estate, tie an artery, plan an edifice, try a cause, break a horse, dance a minuet, and play the violin.*

JAMES PARTON, *Life of Jefferson*

8.

## NOAH WEBSTER: The Union of the American States

*The problem of copyrighting a speller that he had compiled brought Noah Webster into politics in 1782. At that time the federal government had no authority in copyright matters, and none of the newly established states had enacted a copyright law. Webster began to promote copyright legislation in thirteen state capitals. These efforts led him to become one of the early advocates of a strong federal government. In* Sketches of American Policy, *a pamphlet printed in 1785, Webster stated his views on government.*

Source: *Sketches of American Policy,* 1785 [Harry R. Warfel, ed., New York, 1937, pp. 3-48].

NO PERSON can be said to enjoy civil liberty who has no share in legislation, and no person is secure in society unless the laws are known and respected.

In despotic governments, where the scepter is swayed by an individual, the ruler, whether denominated an emperor, a king, or a bashaw [pasha], having the sole right of making and executing laws, is the only person who enjoys any liberty. Every individual within his dominions is a slave. In this case, the interest of the individual, of the magistrate, and of the supreme power are all united, and government is of course as active as possible. Hence the vigor and decision of military operations when the power of the general is without limitation.

Despotic power is not always tyrannical; in the hands of a mild prince, it may be favorable to the rights of the subject. But such is the depravity of human nature that it is madness in a people to vest such power in an individual. Denmark furnishes the only instance of absolute power conferred on an individual by the solemn act of the people; and it furnishes perhaps the only instance of absolute power that has not been abused.

A limited monarchy, where the power of the sovereign is restrained by certain laws, is far preferable to despotism. But if a monarch has the power of making *any* laws, the people are so far slaves. However such power may be sanctified by time, custom, or hereditary succession, the exercise of it, in a single instance, is an act of tyranny. The king of Great Britain cannot make a single law binding upon his subjects, but he can defeat every bill that is proposed by Parliament. Is such a nation free? The English boast of their privileges, and with some reason, when they draw a comparison between themselves and the vassals of a Polish nobleman. But when compared with the eternal immutable rights of man, their privileges shrink into insignificance. With what face can a nation boast of their liberties, when an individual of that nation can, with a single expression, "the king will consider of it," defeat any measure that the Parliament may adopt? Neither the title nor the dignities of royalty can make a king more honest or less fallible than another man; and upon the principles of natural right, any member of Parliament might as well negative an act of that body as the king. A nation which is subject to the will of an individual is a nation of slaves, whether that nation receives its laws from the arbitrary will of its sovereign, or whether the people reserve to themselves the right of making their own laws and give their sovereign full power to annihilate them at pleasure. In either case a nation is at the mercy of an individual.

An aristocracy is a form of government of all others the most to be dreaded; I mean where the right of legislation is vested in a hereditary nobility. The idea of being born a legislator is shocking to common sense, and the fact is a reproach to human nature. In such a government, the interest of the people is out of question. The interest of the supreme power, of the magistracy, and of the individual are here blended, and they are distinct and independent of the interest of the people. The consequence is that when these interests coincide in all the members of the legislature, they are combined to oppress their subjects, and when they clash, as often happens, the state is torn with dissensions and civil war.

From the preceding consideration, I deduce this definition of the most perfect practicable system of government; "a government where the right of making laws is vested in the greatest number of individuals, and the power of executing them in the smallest number." In large communities, the individuals are too numerous to assemble for the purpose of legislation; for which reason the people appear by substitutes or agents; persons of their own choice. A representative democracy seems therefore to be the most perfect system of government that is practicable on earth. . . .

The theory of civil government exhibited in the preceding pages [is] designed as introductory to some remarks on the American states.

A tolerable acquaintance with history and a small knowledge of the English settlements on this continent teach us that the situation of these states is, in every point of view, the reverse of what has been the infant situation of all other nations.

In the first place, our constitutions of civil government have been framed in the most enlightened period of the world. All other systems of civil polity have been begun in the rude times of ignorance and savage ferocity; fabricated at the voice of necessity, without science and without experience. America, just beginning to exist in an advanced period of human improvement, has the science and the experience of all nations to direct her in forming plans of government. By this advantage she is enabled to supply the defects and avoid the errors incident to the policy of uncivilized nations, and to lay a broad basis for the perfection of human society. The legislators of the American states are neither swayed by a blind veneration for an independent clergy nor awed by the frowns of a tyrant. Their civil policy is or ought to be the result of the collected wisdom of all nations, and their religion, that of the Savior of mankind. If they do not establish and perpetuate the best systems of government on earth, it will be their own fault, for nature has given them every advantage they could desire.

In the next place, an equal distribution of landed property is a singular advantage as being the foundation of republican governments and the security of freedom. The New England states are peculiarly happy in this respect. Lands descend equally to all the heirs of the deceased possessor and perpetuities are entirely barred. In Connecticut the eldest male heir inherits two shares; this is a relic of ancient prejudices in favor of the rights of primogeniture, which the wisdom of succeeding legislatures will undoubtedly abolish. An act passed the legislature of New York a few years past, destroying and barring entailments and ordering that all intestate estates should descend to all the heirs in equal portions. No act was ever better timed or calculated to produce more salutary effects. The states of

Pennsylvania and North Carolina have made it an article in their constitutions that no estates shall be perpetual. I am not sufficiently acquainted with the constitutions of the other states to inform whether perpetuities are barred or not; but they may be avoided by a *common recovery,* a fiction often practised in the English courts of law.

But although the southern states possess too much of the aristocratic genius of European governments, yet it is probable that their future tendency will be toward republicanism. For if the African slave trade is prohibited, it must gradually diminish the large estates which are entirely cultivated by slaves, as these will probably decrease without recruits from Africa. And it is not probable that their place can be supplied by white people so long as vast tracts of valuable land are uncultivated, and poor people can purchase the fee of the soil.

But should the present possessors of lands continue to hold and cultivate them, still there is a new set of men springing up in the back parts of those states more hardy and independent than the peasants of the low countries and more averse to aristocracy. The unhealthiness of the climate in the flatlands is a circumstance that will contribute to the rapid population of the mountains where the air is more salubrious.

The idea, therefore, that the genius of the southern states is verging towards republicanism, appears to be supported by substantial reasons. It is much to be wished that such an idea might be well grounded, for nature knows no distinctions, and government ought to know none, but such as are merited by personal virtues.

The confiscation of many large estates in every part of the union is another circumstance favorable to an equal distribution of property. The local situation of all the states and the genius of the inhabitants in most of them tend to destroy all the aristocratic ideas which were introduced from our parent country.

Necessarily connected with an equal distribution of landed property is the annihilation of all hereditary distinctions of rank. Such distinctions are inconsistent with the nature of popular governments. Whatever pretensions some states have made to the name of *republics;* yet those that have permitted perpetual distinctions of property and hereditary titles of honor with a right of legislation annexed certainly never deserved the name of popular governments; and they have never been able to preserve their freedom. Wherever two or more orders of men have been established with hereditary privileges of rank, they have always quarreled till the power or intrigues of the superior orders have divested the people of all their civil liberties. In some countries they retain a show of freedom sufficient to amuse them into obedience; but in most states, they have lost even the appearance of civil rights.

Congress, aware of the tendency of an unequal division of property and the evils of an aristocracy or a mixed form of government, have inserted a clause in the Articles of Confederation forever barring all titles of nobility in the American states; a precaution evincive equally of the foresight, the integrity, and the republican principles of that august body.

Another circumstance favorable to liberty and peculiar to America is a most liberal plan of ecclesiastical policy. Dr. Price has anticipated most of my observations on this head. If sound sense is to be found on earth, it is in his reasoning on this subject. The American constitutions are the most liberal in this particular of any on earth; and yet some of them have retained some badges of bigotry. A profession of the Christian religion is necessary in the states to entitle a man to office. In some states, it is requisite to subscribe [to] certain articles of faith. These requisitions are the effect of the same abominable prejudices that have enslaved the human mind in all countries;

which alone have supported error and all absurdities in religion. If there are any human means of promoting a millennial state of society, the only means are a general diffusion of knowledge and a free unlimited indulgence given to religious persuasions, without distinction and without preference. When this event takes place, and I believe it certainly will, the best religion will have the most advocates. Nothing checks the progress of truth like human establishments. Christianity spread with rapidity before the temporal powers interfered; but when the civil magistrate undertook to guard the truth from error, its progress was obstructed, the simplicity of the gospel was corrupted with human inventions, and the efforts of Christendom have not yet been able to bring it back to its primitive purity.

The American states have gone far in assisting the progress of truth; but they have stopped short of perfection. They ought to have given every honest citizen an equal right to enjoy his religion and an equal title to all civil emoluments without obliging him to tell his religion. Every interference of the civil power in regulating opinion is an impious attempt to take the business of the Deity out of His own hands; and every preference given to any religious denomination is so far slavery and bigotry. This is a blemish in our constitutions, reproachful in proportion to the light and knowledge of our legislators.

The general education of youth is an article in which the American states are superior to all nations. In Great Britain the arts and sciences are cultivated to perfection; but the instruction of the lowest classes of people is by no means equal to the American yeomanry. The institution of schools, particularly in the New England states, where the poorest children are instructed in reading, writing, and arithmetic at the public expense, is a noble regulation, calculated to dignify the human species.

This institution is the necessary consequence of the genius of our governments; at the same time, it forms the firmest security of our liberties. It is scarcely possible to reduce an enlightened people to civil or ecclesiastical tyranny. Deprive them of knowledge, and they sink almost insensibly in vassalage. Ignorance cramps the powers of the mind at the same time that it blinds men to all their natural rights. Knowledge enlarges the understanding, and at the same time it gives a spring to all the intellectual faculties which direct the deliberations of the cabinet and the enterprises of the field. A general diffusion of science is our best guard against the approaches of corruption, the prevalence of religious error, the intrigues of ambition, and against the open assaults of external foes.

In the southern states education is not so general. Gentlemen of fortune give their children a most liberal education; and no part of America produces greater lawyers, statesmen, and divines; but the body of the people are indifferently educated. In New England it is rare to find a person who cannot read and write; but if I am rightly informed, the case is different in the southern states. The education, however, of the common people in every part of America is equal to that of any nation; and the southern states, where schools have been much neglected, are giving more encouragement to literature.

It is not my design to enumerate all the political and commercial advantages of this country; but only to mention some of the characteristic circumstances which distinguish America from all the kingdoms and states of which we have any knowledge.

One further remark, however, which I cannot omit is that the people in America are necessitated by their local situation to be more sensible and discerning than nations which are limited in territory and confined to the arts of manufacture. In a populous country where arts are carried to great perfection, the mechanics are obliged to labor constantly upon a single article. Every art has its several branches, one of which employs a man all his life. A man who makes heads of pins or springs of watches spends his days in that manufacture and never looks beyond it. This manner of fabricating things for the use and convenience of life is the means of perfecting the arts; but it cramps the human mind by confining all its faculties to a point. In countries thinly inhabited, or where people live principally by agriculture as in America, every man is in some measure an artist: he makes a variety of utensils, rough indeed, but such as will answer his purpose; he is a husbandman in summer and a mechanic in winter; he travels about the country; he converses with a variety of professions; he reads public papers; he has access to a parish library and thus becomes acquainted with history and politics, and every man in New England is a theologian. This will always be the case in America, so long as there is a vast tract of fertile land to be cultivated which will occasion emigrations from the states already settled. Knowledge is diffused and genius roused by the very situation of America.

I have already mentioned three principles which have generally operated in combining the members of society under some supreme power: a standing army, religion, and fear of an external force. A standing army is necessary in all despotic governments. Religion, by which I mean superstition, or human systems of absurdity, is an engine used in almost all governments, and has a powerful effect where people are kept in ignorance. The fear of conquest is an infallible bond of union where states are surrounded by martial enemies. After people have been long accustomed to obey, whatever be the first motive of their obedience, there is formed a habit of subordination which has an almost irresistible influence, and which will preserve the tranquillity of government, even when coercion or the first principle of obedience has ceased to operate.

None of the foregoing principles can be the bond of union among the American states. A standing army will probably never exist in America. It is the instrument of tyranny and ought to be forever banished from free governments. Religion will have little or no influence in preserving the union of the states. The Christian religion is calculated to cherish a spirit of peace and harmony in society, but will not balance the influence of jarring interests in different governments. As to neighboring foes, we have none to fear; and European nations are too wise or have too much business at home to think of conquering these states.

We must therefore search for new principles in modeling our political system. The American constitutions are founded on principles different from those of all nations, and we must find new bonds of union to perpetuate the confederation.

In the first place, there must be a supreme power at the head of the Union, vested with authority to make laws that respect the states in general and to compel obedience to those laws. Such a power must exist in every society or no man is safe.

In order to understand the nature of such a power, we must recur to the principles explained under the first head of these observations.

All power is vested in the people. That this is their natural and unalienable right is a position that will not be disputed. The only question is how this power shall be exerted to effect the ends of government. If the people retain the power of executing laws, we have seen how this division will destroy all its effect. Let us apply the definition of a perfect system of government to the American states. "The right of making laws for the United States should be vested in all their inhabitants by legal and equal representation, and the right of executing those laws committed to the smallest possible number of magistrates, chosen annually by Congress and responsible to them for their administration." Such a system of continental government is perfect — it is practicable — and may be rendered permanent. I will even venture to assert that such a system may have, in legislation, all the security of republican circumspection; and in administration, all the energy and decision of a monarchy.

But must the powers of Congress be increased? This question implies gross ignorance of the nature of government. The question ought to be, must the American states be united? And if this question is decided in the affirmative, the next question is whether the states can be said to be united without a legislative head? Or in other words, whether thirteen states can be said to be united in government when each state reserves to itself the sole powers of legislation? The answer to all such questions is extremely easy. If the states propose to form and preserve a confederacy, there must be a supreme head in which the power of all the states is united.

There must be a supreme head, clothed with the same power to make and enforce laws respecting the general policy of all the states as the legislatures of the respective states have to make laws binding on those states respecting their own internal police. The truth of this is taught by the principles of government, and confirmed by the experience of America. Without such a head, the states cannot be *united;* and all attempts to conduct the measures of the continent will prove but governmental farces. So long as any individual state has power to defeat the measures of the other twelve, our pretended union is but a name, and our confederation a cobweb.

What, it will be asked, must the states relinquish their sovereignty and independence, and give Congress their rights of legislation? I beg to know what we mean by *United States?* If, after Congress have passed a resolution of a general tenor, the states are still at liberty to comply or refuse, I must insist that they are not *united;* they are as separate as they ever were, and Congress is merely an advisory body. If people imagine that Congress ought to be merely a council of advice, they will some time or other discover their most egregious mistake. If 3,000,000 people united under thirteen different heads are to be governed or brought to act in concert by a *Resolve, that it be recommended,* I confess myself a stranger to history and to human nature. The very idea of uniting discordant interests and restraining the selfish and the wicked principles of men by advisory resolutions is too absurd to have advocates even among illiterate peasants. The resolves of Congress are always treated with respect, and during the late war they were efficacious. But their efficacy proceeded from a principle of common safety which united the interests of all the states; but peace has removed that principle, and the states comply with or refuse the requisitions of Congress just as they please.

The idea of each state preserving its sovereignty and independence in their full latitude, and yet holding up the appearance of a confederacy and a concert of measures, is a solecism in politics that will sooner or later dissolve the pretended union, or work other mischiefs sufficient to bear conviction to every mind.

But what shall be done? What system of government shall be framed to guard our rights, to cement our union, and give energy to public measures? The answers to these questions are obvious and a plan of confederacy extremely easy. Let the government of the United States be formed upon the general plan of government in each of the several states. Let us examine the constitution of Connecticut.

The inhabitants of Connecticut form one body politic, under the name of the Governor and Company of the State of Connecticut. The whole body of freemen, in their collective capacity, is the supreme power of the state. By consent and firm compact or constitution, this supreme power is delegated to representatives chosen in a legal manner and duly qualified. These representatives, properly assembled, make laws binding on the whole state; that is, the supreme power or state makes laws binding on itself. The supreme power and the subjects of that supreme power are the same body of men. As a collective body, the citizens are all an individual; as separate individuals, they are subjects as numerous as the citizens.

When laws are enacted they are of a general tenor; they respect the whole state and cannot be abrogated but by the whole state. But the whole state does not attempt to execute the laws. The state elects a governor or supreme magistrate and clothes him with the power of the whole state to enforce the laws. Under him a number of subordinate magistrates, such as judges of courts, justices of the peace, sheriffs, etc., are appointed to administer the laws in their respective departments. These are commissioned by the governor or supreme magistrate. Thus the whole power of the state is brought to a single point; it is united in one person.

If the representation of the freemen is equal and the elections frequent, if the magistrates are constitutionally chosen and responsible for their administration, such a government is of all others the most free and safe. The form is the most perfect on earth. While bills are depending before the supreme power, every citizen has a right to oppose them. A perfect freedom of debate is essential to a free government. But when a bill has been formally debated and is enacted into a law, it is the act of the whole state, and no individual has a right to resist it.

But, as it has been before observed, the acts of the supreme power must be general; it has therefore by a general law delegated full authority to certain inferior corporations to make bylaws for the convenience of small districts and not repugnant to the laws of the state. Thus every town in Connecticut is a supreme power for certain purposes and the cities are invested with extensive privileges. These corporations, for certain purposes, are independent of the legislature; they make laws, appoint officers, and exercise jurisdiction within their own limits. As bodies politic, they are sovereign and independent; as members of a large community, they are mere subjects. In the same manner, the head of a family is sovereign in his domestic economy, but as a part of the state, he is a subject.

Let a similar system of government be extended to the United States. As towns and cities are, as to their small matters, sovereign and independent, and as to their general concerns, mere subjects of the state; so let the several states, as to their own police, be sovereign and independent, but as to the common concerns of all, let them be mere subjects of the federal head. If the necessity of a union is admitted, such a system is the only means of effecting it. However independent each state may be and ought to be in things that relate to itself merely, yet as a part of a greater body it must be a subject of that body in matters that relate to the whole. A system of continental government, thus organized, may establish and perpetuate the confederation without infringing the rights of any particular state. But the power of all the states must be reduced to a narrow compass; it must center in a single body of men; and it must not be liable to be controlled or defeated by an individual state. The states assembled in Congress must have the same compulsory power in matters that concern the whole as a man has in his own family, as a city has within the limits of the corporation, and as the legislature of a state has in the limits of that state, respecting matters that fall within their several jurisdictions.

I beg to know how otherwise the states will be governed as a collective body? Every man knows by his own experience that even families are not to be kept in subordination by recommendations and advice. How much less then will such flimsy things command the obedience of a whole continent? They will not — they do not. A single state, by noncompliance with resolves of Congress, has repeatedly defeated the most salutary measures of the states proposed by Congress and acceded to by twelve out of thirteen.

I will suppose for the present that a measure recommended by Congress and adopted by a majority of the legislatures should be really repugnant to the interest of a single state, considered in its separate capacity. Would it be right for that state to oppose it? While the measure is in agitation it is the undoubted privilege of every state to oppose it by every argument. But when it is passed by the concurrence of a legal majority, it is the duty of every state to acquiesce. So far from resisting the measure, those very individuals who opposed it in debate ought to support it in execution. The reason is very plain: society and government can be supported on no other principles. The interest of individuals must always give place to the interest of the whole community. This principle of government is not perfect, but it is as perfect as any principle that can be carried into effect on this side [of] heaven.

It is for the interest of the American states either to be united or not. If their union is unnecessary, let Congress be annihilated, or let them be denominated a council of advice and considered as such. They must then be stripped of their power of making peace and war and of a variety of prerogatives given them by the Articles of Confederation. In this case we ourselves and the states of Europe should know what kind of a being Congress is; what dependence can be placed on their resolves; what is the nature of the treaties which they have made and the debts they have contracted.

But if the states are all serious in a design to establish a permanent *union,* let their sincerity be evinced by their public conduct.

Suppose the legislature of Rhode Island had no power to compel obedience to its laws, but any town in that state had power to defeat every public measure. Could any laws be rendered effectual? Could it with propriety be called a state? Could it be said that there was any supreme power, or any government? Certainly not. Suppose the smallest town in Connecticut had power to defeat the most salutary measures of the state; would not every other town rise in arms against any attempt to exert such a power? They certainly would. The truth of the case is, where the power of a people is not united in some individual or small body of individuals, but continues divided among the members of a society, that power is nothing at all. This fact is clearly proved under the first head of these observations, and more clearly felt by our fatal experience.

The American states, as to their general internal police, are *not united;* there is no supreme power at their head; they are in a perfect state of nature and independence as to each other; each is at liberty to fight its neighbor and there is no sovereign to call forth the power of the continent to quell the dispute or punish the aggressor. It is not in the power of the Congress — they have no command over the militia of the states — each state commands its own, and should any one be disposed for civil war, the sword must settle the contest and the weakest be sacrificed to the strongest.

It is now in the power of the states to form a continental government as efficacious as the interior government of any particular state.

The general concerns of the continent may be reduced to a few heads; but in all the affairs that respect the whole, Congress must have the same power to enact laws and compel obedience throughout the continent as the legislatures of the several states have in their respective jurisdictions. If Congress have any power, they must have the whole power of the continent. Such a power would not abridge the sovereignty of each state in any article relating to its own government. The internal police of each state would be still under the sole superintendence of its legislature. But in a matter that equally respects all the states, no individual state has more than a thirteenth part of the legislative authority, and consequently has no right to decide what measure shall or shall not take place on the continent. A majority of the states *must* decide; our confederation cannot be permanent unless founded on that principle; nay more, the states cannot be said to be *united* till such a principle is adopted in its utmost latitude. If a single town or precinct could counteract the will of a whole state, would there be any government in that state? It is an established principle in government that the will of the minority must submit to that of the majority; and a single state or a minority of states ought to be disabled to resist the will of the majority, as much as a town or county in any state is disabled to prevent the execution of a statute law of the legislature.

It is on this principle and *this alone* that a free state can be governed; it is on this principle alone that the American states can exist as a confederacy of republics. Either the several states must continue separate, totally independent of each other, and liable to all the evils of jealousy, dispute, and civil dissension — nay, liable to a civil war upon any clashing of interests — or they must constitute a general head, composed of representatives from all the states, and vested with the power of the whole continent to enforce their decisions. There is no other alternative. One of these events must inevitably take place, and the revolution of a few years will verify the prediction.

I know the objections that have been urged by the supporters of faction, and perhaps by some honest men, against such a power at the head of the states. But the objections all arise from false notions of government or from a willful design to embroil the states. Many people, I doubt not, really suppose that such power in Congress would be dangerous to the liberties of the states. Such ought to be enlightened.

There are two fundamental errors, very common in the reasonings which I have heard on the powers of Congress. The first arises from the idea that our American constitutions are founded on principles similar to those of the European governments which have been called *free.* Hence people are led into a second error, which is that Congress are a body independent of their constituents and under the influence of a distinct interest.

But we have seen before that our systems of civil government are different from all others, founded on different principles, more favorable to freedom, and more secure against corruption.

We have no perpetual distinctions of property which might raise one class of men above another and create powerful family connections and combinations against our liberties. We suffer no hereditary offices or titles which might breed insolence and pride and give their possessors an opportunity to oppress their fellowmen. We are not under the direction of a bigoted clergy who might rob us of the means of knowledge and then inculcate on credulous minds what sentiments they please. Not a single office or emolument in America is held by prescription or hereditary right; but all at the disposal of the people, and not a man on the continent but drones and villains who has not the privilege of frequently choosing his legislators and impeaching his magistrates for maladministration. Such principles form the basis of our American governments — the first and only governments on earth that are founded on the true principles of equal liberty and properly guarded from corruption.

The legislatures of the American states are the only legislatures on earth which are *wholly* dependent on the people at large; and Congress is as dependent on the several states as the legislatures are on their constituents. The members of Congress are chosen by the legislatures, removable by them at pleasure, dependent on them for subsistence, and responsible to their constituents for their conduct. But this is not all. After having been delegated three years, the confederation renders them ineligible for the term of three years more, when they must return, mingle with the people, and become private citizens. At the same time, their interest is the same with that of the people; for enjoying no exclusive privileges but what are temporary they cannot knowingly enact oppressive laws, because they involve themselves, their families, and estates in all the mischiefs that result from such laws.

People, therefore, who attempt to terrify us with apprehensions of losing our liberties because other states have lost theirs, betray an ignorance of history and of the principles of our confederation. I will not undertake to say that the government of the American states will not be corrupted or degenerate into tyranny. But I venture to assert that if it should, it will be the fault of the people. If the people continue to choose their representatives annually and the choice of delegates to Congress should remain upon its present footing, that body can never become tyrants. A measure partially oppressive may be resolved upon, but while the principles of representation, which are always in the power of the people, remain uncorrupted, such a measure can be of no long continuance. The best constitution of government may degenerate from its purity through a variety of causes; but the confederation of these states is better secured than any government on earth, and less liable to corruption from any quarter.

There is the same danger that the constitutions of the several states will become tyrannical as that the principles of federal government will be corrupted. The states in their collective capacity have no more reason to dread an uncontrollable power in Congress than they have, in their individual capacity, to dread the uncontrollable power of their own legislatures. Their security in both instances is an equal representation, the dependence, the responsibility, and the rotation of their representatives. These articles constitute the basis of our liberties, and will be an effectual security, so long as the people are wise enough to maintain the principles of the confederation.

I beg leave here to observe that a state was never yet destroyed by a corrupt or a wicked administration. Weakness and wickedness in the executive department may produce innumerable evils; but so long as the principles of a constitution remain uncorrupted, their vigor will always restore good order. Every stride of tyranny in the best governments in Europe has been effected by breaking over some constitutional barriers. But where a constitution is formed by the people and unchangeable but by their authority, the progress of corruption must be extremely slow, and perhaps tyranny can never be established in such government, except upon a general habit of indolence and vice.

What do the states obtain by reserving to themselves the right of deciding on the propriety of the resolutions of Congress? The great advantage of having every measure defeated, our frontiers exposed to savages, the debts of the states unpaid and accumulating, national faith violated, commerce restricted and insulted, one state filching some interest from another, and the whole body linked together by cobwebs and shadows, the jest and the ridicule of the world. This is not a chimerical description; it is a literal representation of facts as they now exist. One state found it could make some advantages by refusing the impost. Congress have reasoned with their legislature, and by incontrovertible proofs have pointed out the impropriety of the refusal, but all to no purpose. Thus one-fiftieth part of the states counteracts a measure that the other states suppose not only beneficial but necessary; a measure on which the discharge of our public debt and our national faith most obviously depend. Can a government thus feeble and disjointed answer any valuable purpose? Can commutative justice between the states ever be obtained? Can public debts be discharged and credit supported? Can America ever be respected by her enemies when one of her own states can, year after year, abuse her weakness with impunity? No, the American states, so celebrated for their wisdom and valor in the late struggle for freedom and empire, will be the contempt of nations unless they can unite their force and carry into effect all the constitutional measures of Congress, whether those measures respect themselves or foreign nations.

The Articles of Confederation ordain that the public expenses shall be defrayed out of a common treasury. But where is this treasury? Congress prescribe a measure for supplying this treasury; but the states do not approve of the measure; each state will take its own way and its own time, and perhaps not supply its contingent of money at all. Is this an adherence to the Articles of our Union? It certainly is not; and the states that refuse a compliance with the general measures of the continent would, under a good government, be considered as rebels. Such a conduct amounts to treason, for it strikes at the foundation of government.

Permit me to ask every candid American how society could exist if every man assumed the right of sacrificing his neighbor's property to his own interest? Are there no rights to be relinquished, no sacrifices to be made for the sake of enjoying the benefits of civil government? If every town in Rhode Island, even the smallest, could annihilate every act of the legislature, could that state exist? Were such a selfish system to prevail generally, there would be an end of government and civil society would become a curse. A social state would be less eligible than a savage state, in proportion as knowledge would be increased and knaves multiplied. Local inconveniences and local interests never ought to disappoint a measure of general utility. If there is not power enough in government to remedy these evils by obliging private interests to give way to public, discord will pervade the state, and terminate in a revolution. Such a power must exist somewhere, and if people will quarrel with good government, there are innumerable opportunities for some daring ambitious genius to erect a monarchy on civil dissensions. In America there is no danger of an aristocracy; but the transition from popular anarchy to monarchy is very natural and often very easy. If these states have any change of government to fear, it is a monarchy. Nothing but the creation of a sovereign power over the whole, with authority to compel obedience to legal measures, can ever prevent a revolution in favor of one monarchy or more. This event may be distant, but is not the less certain. America has it now in her power to create a supreme power over the whole continent sufficient to answer all the ends of government without abridging the rights or destroying the sovereignty of a single state. But should the extreme jealousy of the states prevent the lodgment of such a power in a body of men chosen by themselves and removable at pleasure, such a power will inevitably create itself in the course of events.

The confederation has sketched out a most excellent form of continental government. The ninth article recites the powers of Congress, which are perhaps nearly sufficient to answer the ends of our Union, were there any method of enforcing their resolutions. It is there said what powers shall be exercised by Congress; but no penalty is annexed to disobedience. What purpose would the laws of a state answer if they might be evaded with impunity? And if there were no penalty annexed to a breach of them? A law without a penalty is mere *advice;* a magistrate without the power of punishing is a *cipher*. Here is the *great defect* in the articles of our federal government. Unless Congress can be vested with the same authority to compel obedience to their resolutions that a legislature in any state has to enforce obedience to the laws of that state, the existence of such a body is entirely needless and will not be of long duration. I repeat what I have before said. The idea of governing thirteen states and uniting their interests by mere resolves and recommendations, without any penalty annexed to a noncompliance, is a ridiculous farce, a burlesque on government, and a reproach to America.

Let Congress be empowered to call forth the force of the continent, if necessary, to carry into effect those measures which they have a right to frame. Let the president be, *ex officio*, supreme magistrate, clothed with authority to execute the laws of Congress, in the same manner as the governors of the states are to execute the laws of the states. Let the superintendent of finance have the power of receiving the public monies and issuing warrants for collection in the manner the treasurer has in Connecticut. Let every executive officer have power to enforce the laws which fall within his province. At the same time, let them be accountable for their administration. Let penalties be annexed to every species of maladministration and exacted with such rigor as is due to justice and the public safety. In short, let the whole system of legislation be the peculiar right of the delegates in Congress who are always under the control of the people; and let the whole administration be vested in magistrates as few as possible in number, and subject to the control of Congress only. Let every precaution be used in *framing* laws, but let no part of the subjects be able to resist the execution. Let the people keep, and *forever keep*, the sole right of legislation in their own representatives, but divest themselves wholly of any right to the administration. Let every state reserve its sovereign right of directing its own internal affairs, but give to Congress the sole right of conducting the general affairs of the continent. Such a plan of government is practicable; and, I believe, the only plan that will preserve the faith, the dignity, and the union of these American states.

9.

## The Disposition of Lands in the Western Territory

*To encourage settlement in the territory between the Appalachians and the Mississippi, north of the Ohio River, Congress passed a Land Ordinance on May 20, 1785. The area, which had been acquired from the states upon the ratification of the Articles of Confederation, was provided by the ordinance with a system of surveying the land into townships and sections. Congress hoped to refill the treasury by land sales in this region, but the requirement of $640 in cash eliminated many potential buyers.*

Source: *Journals,* IV: "Friday, May 20, 1785."

*Be it ordained by the United States in Congress assembled* that the territory ceded by individual states to the United States, which has been purchased of the Indian inhabitants, shall be disposed of in the following manner:

A surveyor from each state shall be appointed by Congress, or a committee of the states, who shall take an oath for the faithful discharge of his duty before the geographer of the United States, who is hereby empowered and directed to administer the same; and the like oath shall be administered to each chain carrier by the surveyor under whom he acts. The geographer, under whose direction the surveyors shall act, shall occasionally form such regulations for their conduct as he shall deem necessary, and shall have authority to suspend them for misconduct in office, and shall make report of the same to Congress, or to the committee of the states. . . .

The surveyors, as they are respectively qualified, shall proceed to divide the said territory into townships of six miles square, by lines running due north and south, and others crossing these at right angles, as near as may be, unless where the boundaries of the late Indian purchases may render the same impracticable, and then they shall depart from this rule no farther than such particular circumstances may require. And each surveyor shall be allowed and paid at the rate of $2 for every mile in length he shall run, including the wages of chain carriers, markers, and every other expense attending the same.

The first line, running due north and south as aforesaid, shall begin on the River Ohio, at a point that shall be found to be due north from the western termination of a line which has been run as the southern boundary of the state of Pennsylvania; and the first line, running east and west, shall begin at the same point and shall extend throughout the whole territory, provided that nothing herein shall be construed as fixing the western boundary of the state of Pennsylvania. The geographer shall designate the townships, or fractional parts of townships, by numbers progressively from south to north, always beginning each range with No. 1; and the ranges shall be distinguished by their progressive numbers to the westward, the first range, extending from the Ohio to the Lake Erie, being marked

No. 1. The geographer shall personally attend to the running of the first east and west line, and shall take the latitude of the extremes of the first north and south line, and of the mouths of the principal rivers.

The lines shall be measured with a chain; shall be plainly marked by chaps on the trees; and exactly described on a plat, whereon shall be noted by the surveyor, at their proper distances, all mines, salt springs, salt licks, and mill seats that shall come to his knowledge and all watercourses, mountains, and other remarkable and permanent things over and near which such lines shall pass, and also the quality of the lands.

The plats of the townships, respectively, shall be marked by subdivisions into lots of one mile square, or 640 acres, in the same direction as the external lines, and numbered from 1 to 36, always beginning the succeeding range of the lots with the number next to that with which the preceding one concluded. And where, from the causes beforementioned, only a fractional part of a township shall be surveyed, the lots, protracted thereon, shall bear the same numbers as if the township had been entire. And the surveyors, in running the external lines of the townships, shall, at the interval of every mile, mark corners for the lots which are adjacent, always designating the same in different manner from those of the townships.

The geographer and surveyors shall pay the utmost attention to the variation of the magnetic needle, and shall run and note all lines by the true meridian, certifying, with every plat, what was the variation at the times of running the lines thereon noted.

As soon as seven ranges of townships, and fractional parts of townships, in the direction from south to north, shall have been surveyed, the geographer shall transmit plats thereof to the Board of Treasury, who shall record the same, with the report, in well-bound books to be kept for that purpose. And the geographer shall make similar returns, from time to time, of every seven ranges as they may be surveyed.

The secretary of war shall have recourse thereto, and shall take by lot therefrom, a number of townships, and fractional parts of townships, as well from those to be sold entire as from those to be sold in lots, as will be equal to one-seventh part of the whole of such seven ranges, as nearly as may be, for the use of the late Continental Army; and he shall make a similar draft, from time to time, until a sufficient quantity is drawn to satisfy the same, to be applied in manner hereinafter directed. The Board of Treasury shall, from time to time, cause the remaining numbers, as well those to be sold entire as those to be sold in lots, to be drawn for, in the name of the thirteen states respectively, according to the quotas in the last preceding requisition on all the states; provided, that in case more land than its proportion is allotted for sale, in any state, at any distribution, a deduction be made therefor at the next.

The Board of Treasury shall transmit a copy of the original plats, previously noting thereon the townships and fractional parts of townships which shall have fallen into the several states by the distribution aforesaid, to the commissioners of the loan office of the several states, who, after giving notice of not less than two nor more than six months, by causing advertisements to be posted up at the courthouses, or other noted places in every county, and to be inserted in one newspaper published in the states of their residence respectively, shall proceed to sell the townships, or fractional parts of townships, at public vendue in the following manner, viz.:

The township, or fractional part of a township, No. 1, in the first range, shall be sold entire; and No. 2, in the same range, by lots; and thus in alternate order through the whole of the first range. The township, or fractional part of a township, No. 1, in the second range, shall be sold by lots; and No. 2, in the same range, entire; and so in alternate order through the whole of the second range; and the third range shall be sold in the same manner as the first, and the fourth in the same manner as the second, and thus alternately throughout all the ranges; provided that none of the lands within the said territory be sold under the price of $1 the acre, to be paid in specie, or loan-office certificates reduced to specie value by the scale of depreciation, or certificates of liquidated debts of the United States, including interest, besides the expense of the survey and other charges thereon, which are hereby rated at $36 the township . . . to be paid at the time of sales; on failure of which payment the said lands shall again be offered for sale.

There shall be reserved for the United States out of every township the four lots, being numbered 8, 11, 26, 29, and out of every fractional part of a township, so many lots of the same numbers as shall be found thereon, for future sale. There shall be reserved the lot No. 16 of every township for the maintenance of public schools within the said township; also one-third part of all gold, silver, lead, and copper mines, to be sold or otherwise disposed of as Congress shall hereafter direct.

When any township, or fractional part of a township, shall have been sold as aforesaid, and the money or certificates received therefor, the loan officer shall deliver a deed . . . which deeds shall be recorded in proper books by the commissioner of the loan office. . . . The commissioners of the loan offices, respectively, shall transmit to the Board of Treasury, every three months, an account of the townships, fractional parts of townships, and lots committed to their charge specifying therein the names of the persons to whom sold and the sums of money or certificates received for the same. . . .

If any township, or fractional part of a township or lot, remains unsold for eighteen months after the plat shall have been received by the commissioners of the loan office, the same shall be returned to the Board of Treasury, and shall be sold in such manner as Congress may hereafter direct.

And whereas Congress . . . stipulated grants of land to certain officers and soldiers of the late Continental Army, and . . . to certain officers in the Hospital Department of the late Continental Army, for complying therefore with such engagements; *Be it ordained* that the secretary at war, from the returns in his office, or such other sufficient evidence as the nature of the case may admit, determine who are the objects of the above resolutions and engagements, and the quantity of land to which such persons or their representatives are respectively entitled, and cause the townships, or fractional parts of townships, hereinbefore reserved for the use of the late Continental Army, to be drawn for in such manner as he shall deem expedient, to answer the purpose of an impartial distribution. . . .

*And be it further ordained* that three townships adjacent to Lake Erie be reserved, to be hereafter disposed of by Congress, for the use of the officers, men, and others, refugees from Canada, and the refugees from Nova Scotia, who are or may be entitled to grants of land under resolutions of Congress now existing, or which may hereafter be made respecting them, and for such other purposes as Congress may hereafter direct.

*And be it further ordained* that the towns of Gnadenhutten, Schoenbrun, and Salem, on the Muskingum, and so much of the lands adjoining to the said towns, with the buildings and improvements thereon, shall be reserved for the sole use of the Christian Indians, who were formerly settled there, or the remains of that society as may, in the judgment of the geographer, be sufficient for them to cultivate.

10.

## Apprehensions About the Dangers of Aristocracy

*Many Americans who realized the weakness of their central government were still unwilling to consider replacing it. They preferred making any necessary changes purely within terms of the existing structure. Strengthening Congress to meet current needs was one thing; a new form of government which might bring with it a new form of tyranny was quite another. This thinking was reflected in the reaction of Massachusetts delegates in Congress to the instructions of the Massachusetts legislature to introduce a resolution into Congress calling for a constitutional convention. The delegates refused, replying that any commercial power granted to Congress should be temporary and restricted. The delegates replied to the legislature in the following letter of September 3, 1785, explaining their refusal.*

Source: *Letters of Members of the Continental Congress,* Edmund C. Burnett, ed., Vol. VIII, Washington, 1936, pp. 208-209.

If an alteration, either temporary or perpetual, of the commercial powers of Congress is to be considered by a convention, shall the latter be authorized to revise the Confederation *generally,* or only for express purposes? The great object of the Revolution was the establishment of good government, and each of the states, in forming their own as well as the federal constitution, have adopted republican principles. Notwithstanding this, plans have been artfully laid and vigorously pursued which, had they been successful, we think, would inevitably have changed our republican governments into baleful aristocracies. Those plans are frustrated, but the same spirit remains in their abettors. . . .

What the effect then may be of calling a convention to revise the Confederation generally, we leave with Your Excellency and the honorable legislature to determine. We are apprehensive, and it is our duty to declare it, that such a measure would produce throughout the Union an exertion of the friends of an aristocracy to send members who would promote a change of government. And we can form some judgment of the plan which such members would report to Congress.

But should the members be altogether republican, such have been the declamations of designing men against the Confederation generally, against the rotation of members, which perhaps is the best check to corruption and against the mode of altering the Confederation by the unanimous consent of the legislatures, which effectually prevents innovations in the Articles by intrigue or surprise, that we think there is great danger of a report which would invest Congress with powers that the honorable legislature have not the most distant intention to delegate. Perhaps it may be said this can produce no ill effect; because Congress may correct the report, however exceptionable, or, if passed by them, any of the states may refuse to ratify it. True it is that Congress and the states have such powers; but would not such a report affect the tranquility and weaken the government of the Union?

We have already considered the operation of the report as it would respect Congress; and if animosities and parties would naturally arise from their rejecting it, how much would these be increased if the report approved by Congress and some of the states should be rejected by other states? Would there not be danger of a party spirit's being thus more generally diffused and warmly supported?

Far distant we know it to be from the honorable legislature of Massachusetts to give up a single principle of republicanism, but when a general revision shall have proceeded from their motion, and a report which to them may be highly offensive shall have been confirmed by seven states in Congress and ratified by several legislatures, will not these be ready to charge Massachusetts with inconsistency in being the first to oppose a measure which the state will be said to have originated? Massachusetts has great weight and is considered as one of the most republican states in the Union; and when it is known that the legislature have proposed a general revision, there can be no doubt that they will be represented as being convinced of the necessity of increasing generally the powers of Congress, and the opinion of the state will be urged with such art as to convince numbers that the Articles of Confederation are altogether exceptionable.

Thus, while measures are taken to guard against the evils arising from the want in one or two particulars of power in Congress, we are in great danger of incurring the other extreme. "More power in Congress" has been the cry from all quarters, but especially of those whose views, not being confined to a government that will best promote the happiness of the people, are extended to one that will afford lucrative employments, civil and military. Such a government is an aristocracy which would require a standing army and a numerous train of pensioners and placemen to prop and support its exalted administration. To recommend oneself to such an administration would be to secure an establishment for life and at the same time to provide for his posterity. These are pleasing prospects which republican governments do not afford, and it is not to be wondered at that many persons of elevated views and idle habits in these states are desirous of the change. We are for increasing the power of Congress as far as it will promote the happiness of the people, but at the same time are clearly of opinion that every measure should be avoided which would strengthen the hands of the enemies to a free government; and that an administration of the present Confederation, with all its inconveniences, is preferable to the risk of general dissensions and animosities, which may approach to anarchy and prepare the way to a ruinous system of government.

Having thus, from a sense of duty we owe to the United States as well as to our constituents, communicated to Your Excellency our sentiments on this important subject, we request you to lay them before the honorable legislature at their next session and to inform them that their measures for a general revision of the Confederation, if confirmed, shall be immediately communicated to Congress.

*Our real disease is . . . democracy.*

Alexander Hamilton

11.

## Thomas Jefferson: An American Education for American Youth

*In the years following the Revolution, many Americans were willing to assert cultural as well as political independence from the Old World. Their notion was that since America was separated by 3,000 miles from Europe and had her own destiny, she should develop indigenous institutions in accordance with her own ideals. Higher education for an American, Jefferson felt, ought to take place in his own country, not in some foreign land whose influence might weaken his native ties. In a letter to John Banister of October 15, 1785, Jefferson made plain what to him were the differences between educating Americans at home and abroad.*

Source: Randolph, I, pp. 345-347

I should sooner have answered the paragraph in your letter of September 19, respecting the best seminary for the education of youth in Europe, but that it was necessary for me to make inquiries on the subject. The result of these has been to consider the competition as resting between Geneva and Rome.

They are equally cheap and probably are equal in the course of education pursued. The advantage of Geneva is that students acquire there the habit of speaking French. The advantages of Rome are the acquiring a local knowledge of a spot so classical and so celebrated; the acquiring the true pronunciation of the Latin language; a just taste in the fine arts, more particularly those of painting, sculpture, architecture, and music; a familiarity with those objects and processes of agriculture, which experience has shown best adapted to a climate like ours; and lastly, the advantage of a fine climate for health. It is probable, too, that by being boarded in a French family, the habit of speaking that language may be obtained.

I do not count on any advantage to be derived in Geneva, from a familiar acquaintance with the principles of that government. The late revolution has rendered it a tyrannical aristocracy, more likely to give ill than good ideas to an American. I think the balance in favor of Rome. Pisa is sometimes spoken of as a place of education. But it does not offer the first and third of the advantages of Rome.

But why send an American youth to Europe for education? What are the objects of a useful American education? Classical knowledge; modern languages, chiefly French, Spanish, and Italian; mathematics; natural philosophy; natural history; civil history; and ethics. In natural philosophy, I mean to include chemistry and agriculture, and in natural history, to include botany, as well as the other branches of those departments. It is true that the habit of speaking the modern languages cannot be so well acquired in America; but every other article can be as well acquired at William and Mary College as at any place in Europe. When college education is done with and a young man is to prepare himself for public life, he must cast his eyes (for America) either on law or physic [medicine]. For the former, where can he apply so advantageously as to Mr. Wythe? For the latter, he must come to Europe. The medical class of students, therefore, is the only one which need come to Europe.

Let us view the disadvantages of sending a youth to Europe. To enumerate them all would require a volume. I will select a few. If he goes to England, he learns drinking, horse racing, and boxing. These are the peculiarities of English education. The following circumstances are common to education in that and the other countries of Europe. He acquires a fondness for European luxury and dissipation, and a contempt for the simplicity of his own country; he is fascinated with the privileges of the European aristocrats, and sees with abhorrence the lovely equality which the poor enjoy with the rich in his own country; he contracts a partiality for aristocracy or monarchy; he forms foreign friendships which will never be useful to him, and loses the seasons of life for forming in his own country those friendships which, of all others, are the most faithful and permanent. He is led by the strongest of all the human passions into a spirit for female intrigue, destructive of his own and others' happiness, or a passion for whores, destructive of his health; and, in both cases, learns to consider fidelity to the marriage bed as an ungentlemanly practice and inconsistent with happiness. He recollects the voluptuary dress and arts of the European women, and pities and despises the chaste affections and simplicity of those of his own country; he retains through life a fond recollection and a hankering after those places which were the scenes of his first pleasures and of his first connections

He returns to his own country a foreigner, unacquainted with the practices of domestic economy necessary to preserve him from ruin, speaking and writing his native tongue as a foreigner, and therefore unqualified to obtain those distinctions which eloquence of the pen and tongue insures in a free country; for I would observe to you that what is called style in writing or speaking is formed very early in life, while the imagination is warm and impressions are permanent. I am of opinion that there never was an instance of a man's writing or speaking his native tongue with elegance who passed from fifteen to twenty years of age out of the country where it was spoken. Thus, no instance exists of a person's writing two languages perfectly. That will always appear to be his native language which was most familiar to him in his youth.

It appears to me, then, that an American coming to Europe for education loses in his knowledge, in his morals, in his health, in his habits, and in his happiness. I had entertained only doubts on this head before I came to Europe; what I see and hear since I came here proves more than I had even suspected. Cast your eye over America. Who are the men of most learning, of most eloquence, most beloved by their countrymen and most trusted and promoted by them? They are those who have been educated among them, and whose manners, morals, and habits are perfectly homogeneous with those of the country.

Did you expect by so short a question to draw such a sermon on yourself? I dare say you did not. But the consequences of foreign education are alarming to me as an American. I sin, therefore, through zeal, whenever I enter on the subject. You are sufficiently American to pardon me for it.

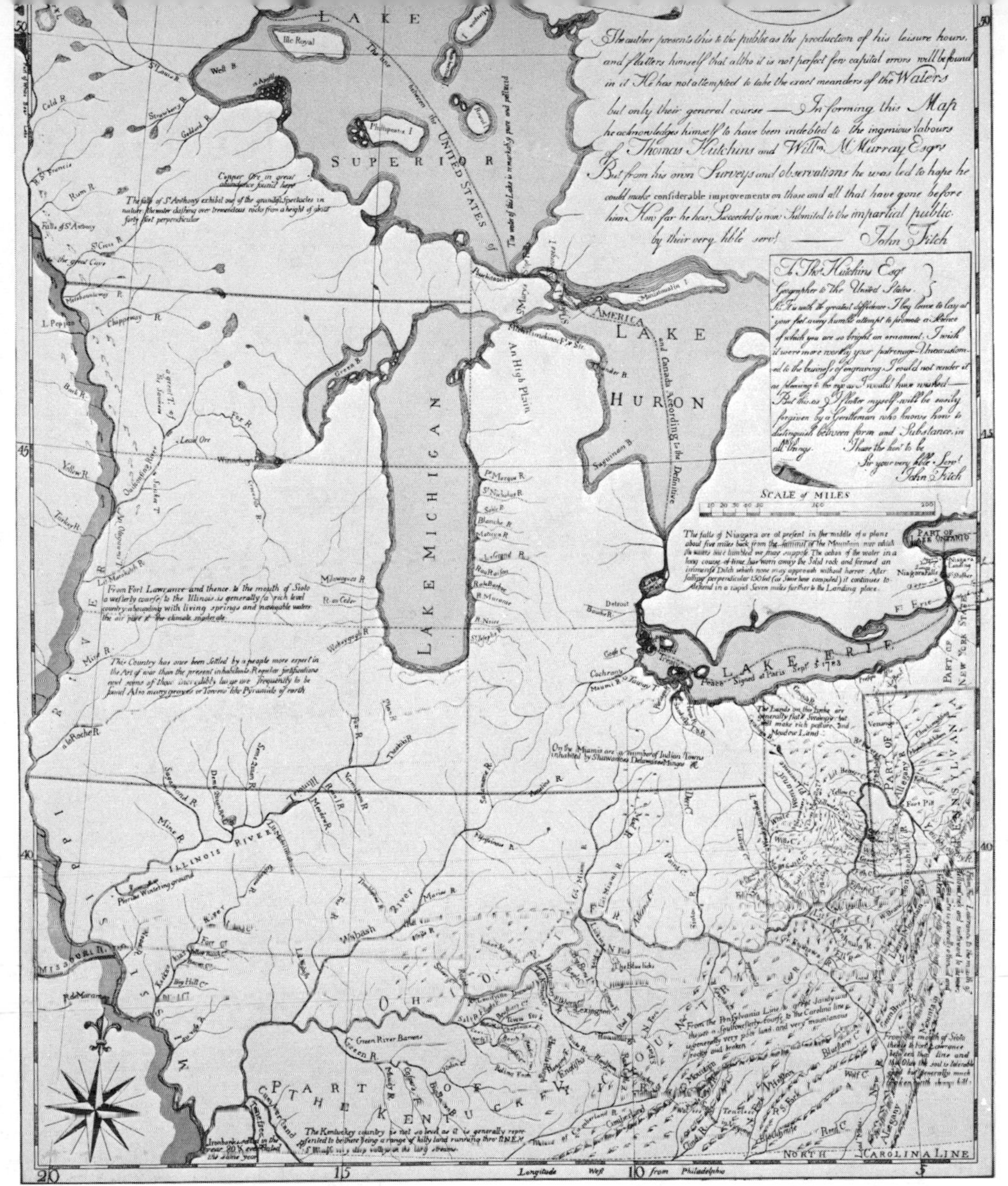

Library of Congress

# THE WESTERN FRONTIERS

Prior to the Revolutionary War the British reserved the western lands for the Indians. During the Revolution settlers began trickling westward, and with peace the trickle became a flood. After much debate the states ceded their claims to Congress, which provided a legal basis for survey and sale of land and for local governments and eventual statehood.

Inevitably the Americans collided with the interests of Spain, which had received the lands west of the Mississippi from France in 1762 and controlled shipping on the river. Tentative efforts were made to induce the settlers to secede and to join Spanish Louisiana.

In the Pacific Northwest, trading and exploration preceded settlement by many years. Captain James Cook of the British Navy skirted the Oregon coast in 1778, and Robert Gray, sailing from Boston, discovered the Columbia River in 1792.

# Settlement West of the Alleghenies

Library of Congress

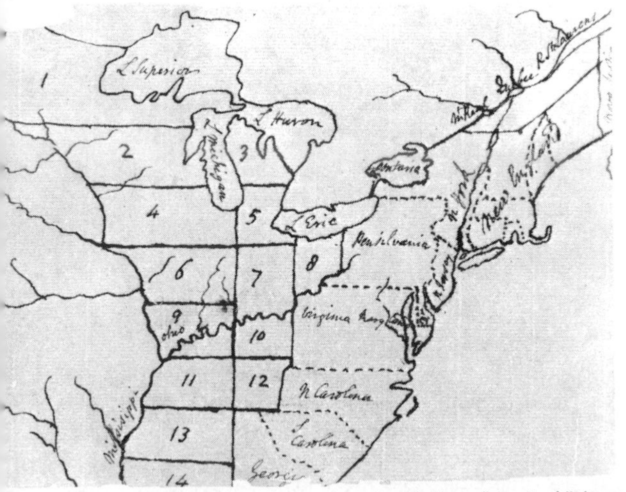

Clements Library, University of Michigan

Ever-present threats of Indian conflict tended to limit early settlements to the vicinity of the Ohio River. Moreover, flatboats were easily floated downstream; driving Conestoga wagons through the wilds was difficult, and shipment of heavy goods was practical only on the rivers. Large tracts of land in Ohio were set aside for war veterans and for development companies; elsewhere the nation still had to solidify its claims by treaty or by conquest.

**(Top) Map of Kentucky by John Filson, 1784; (left) sketch map showing Jefferson's proposal for division of the western lands ceded to America in 1784**

New York Historical Society

(Left) Fort Harmar, Ohio, built in 1784 to provide protection for the early surveyors and settlers in the territory; (center) view of Detroit in 1794; the British occupied this town until 1796 in violation of the peace treaty, using it as a base for their support of Indian raids on Americans; (bottom) the Falls of St. Anthony in the Mississippi River at the site of Minneapolis; the falls were discovered and named by Father Hennepin in 1680

Detroit Public Library, Burton Historical Coll.

Library of Congress

# Peace in Ohio

American Philosophical Society

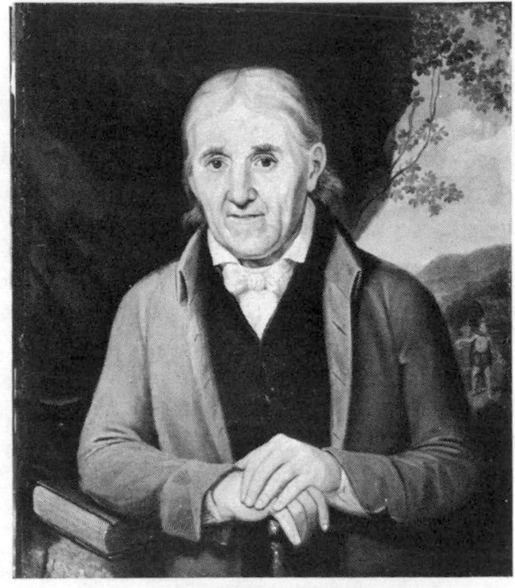

Two events in 1794 cleared the path for settlement in Ohio: Wayne's victory at Fallen Timbers and the Jay Treaty. Though the British had relinquished territorial claims, they continued to support Indian hostility to Americans. In August 1794, Revolutionary War hero Gen. Anthony Wayne defeated the Indian forces and, a year later, negotiated the Treaty of Greenville with Little Turtle and other Indian leaders. Vast territory was ceded to the Americans; they were now the undisputed proprietors of Ohio.

Library of Congress

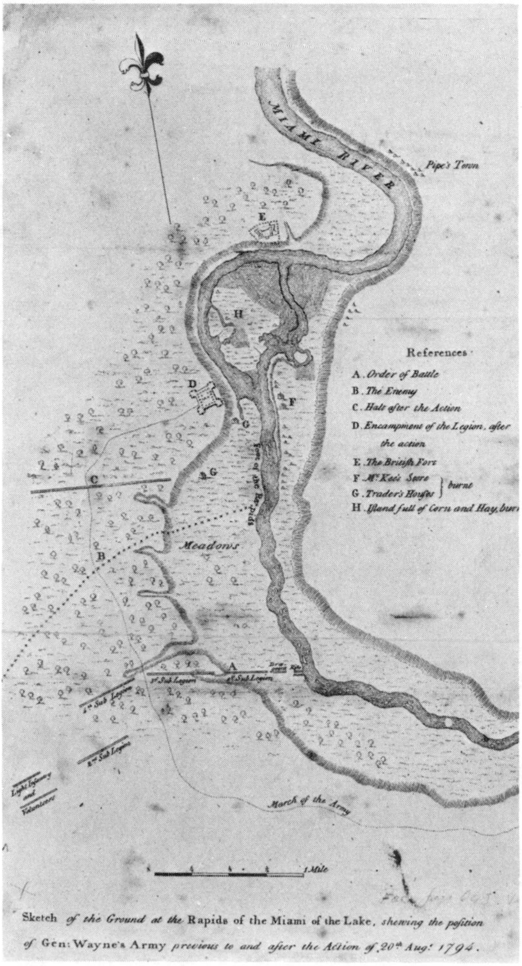
MIAMI RIVER
Pipe's Town
Meadows
References
A. Order of Battle
B. The Enemy
C. Halt after the Action
D. Encampment of the Legion, after the action
E. The British Fort
F. Mr. Kee's Store
G. Trader's Houses
burnt
H. Island full of Corn and Hay, burn
1st Sub Legion
2nd Sub Legion
March of the Army
Light Infantry and Volunteers
1 Mile
Sketch of the Ground at the Rapids of the Miami of the Lake, shewing the position of Gen: Wayne's Army previous to and after the Action of 20th Aug: 1794.

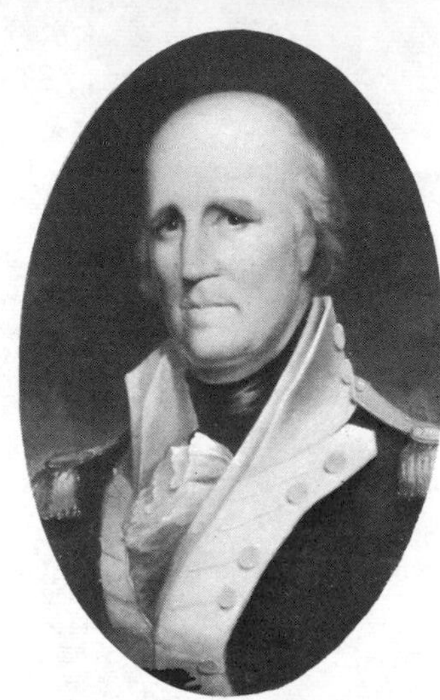

Virginia State Library

Independence National Historical Park

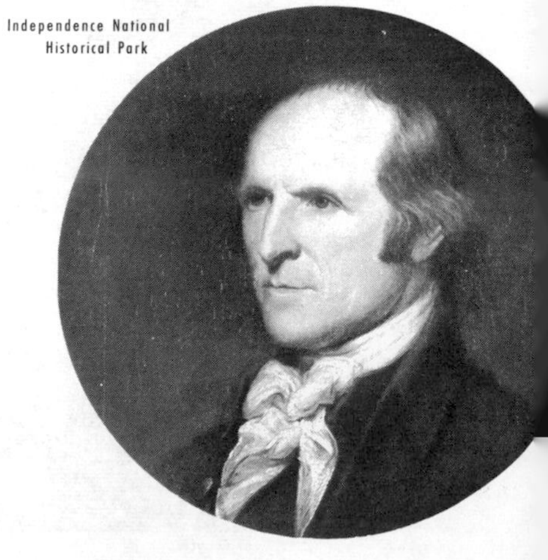

Fordham University; photo, Frick

Buffalo and Erie Co. Historical Society

Chicago Historical Society

**OPPOSITE PAGE:** (Top) John Heckewelden, missionary to the Indians, helped arrange peace at Vincennes, 1792; (center) George Rogers Clark led forces that defeated the Indians in the Revolution; (bottom) Timothy Pickering, Indian commissioner. **THIS PAGE:** (Top left) Anthony Wayne; (top right) peace medal given to Red Jacket, model for those presented at Greenville; (left) Little Turtle; (below) Treaty of Greenville, by an eyewitness

Chicago Historical Society

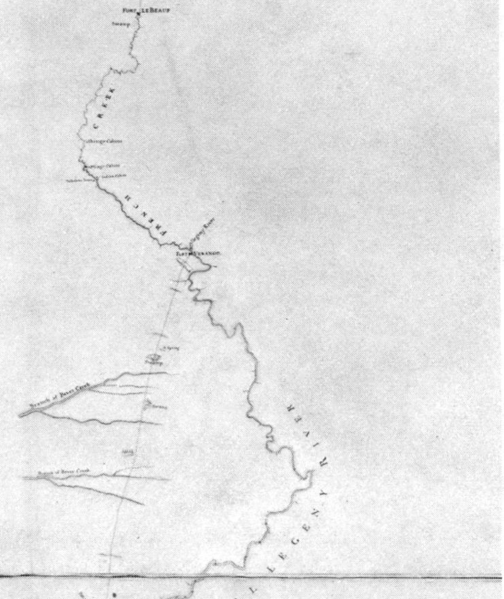


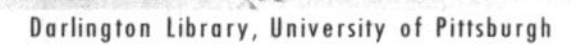

Darlington Library, University of Pittsburgh

**Early map showing the route from Fort Cumberland, Maryland, to Presqu'isle on Lake Erie**

**Payouska of the Great Osage tribe, drawing by St. Memin**

New York Historical Society

**Two young Iowas "of the Missouri," also by St. Memin**

Yale Art Gallery

**Good Peter, a chief of the Oniedas**

# Pushing Westward

As the white man moved west, so did the Indian. The Treaty of Greenville pushed the tribes in Ohio westward into the Illinois-Wisconsin region, and as the French and Spanish increased the number of towns along the Mississippi, the southern tribes moved north-westward into the Arkansas-Missouri territory to find better hunting.

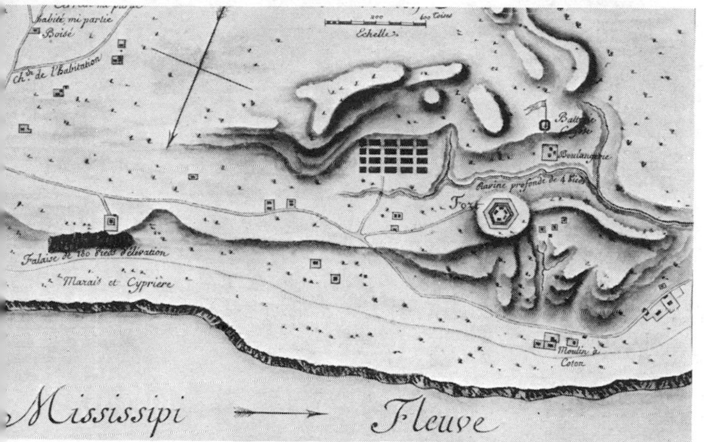

Bibliotheque Nationale

**1796 plan by Collet showing settlement at Natchez, Miss., which prospered under lenient Spanish rule from 1780 to 1798; a cotton mill is shown in the lower right**

# Spanish Empire

Spain had interests in the New World from the time of Columbus onward. By the 18th century Spain had settlements throughout South, Central, and North America. In 1762 Spain acquired Louisiana from France, giving her complete control of the Gulf Coast and the Mississippi River. To protect her holdings in North America, Spain supported the colonists against England in the Revolution. But her sparse and widely scattered settlements were unable to resist the tide of American settlers who pushed south and westward after the Revolution. Finally, unable to resist any more, Spain returned Louisiana to France in 1800, at the request of Napoleon, paving the way for the Louisiana Purchase.

Library of Congress

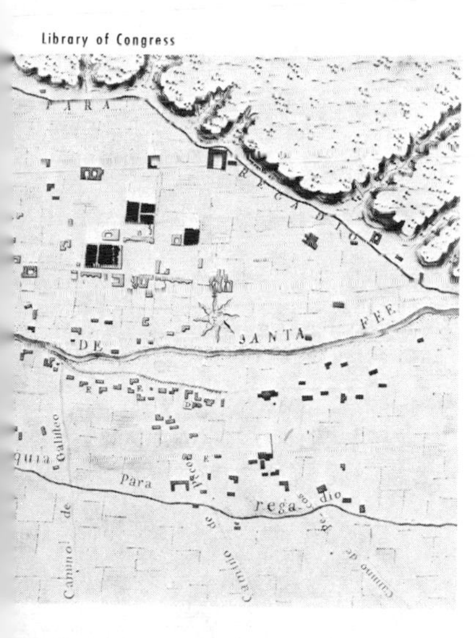


Clements Library, University of Michigan

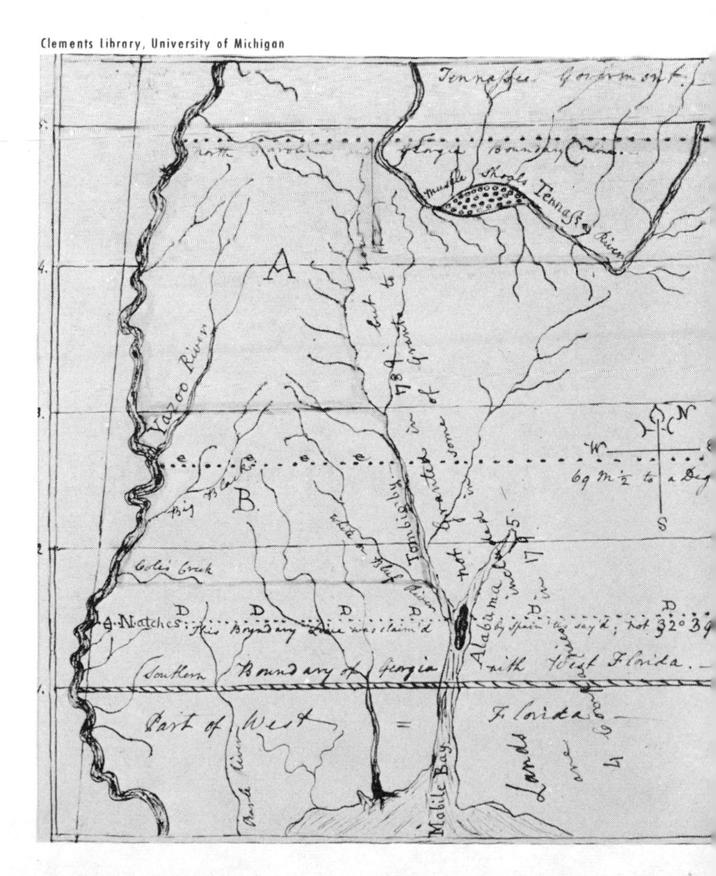


**(Above) Plan of Santa Fe, N. M., mid-18th century; (right) map of the area involved in the Yazoo Land Fraud, sold to four land companies by Georgia; when it was revealed that state legislators were shareholders in the companies, the deal was canceled**

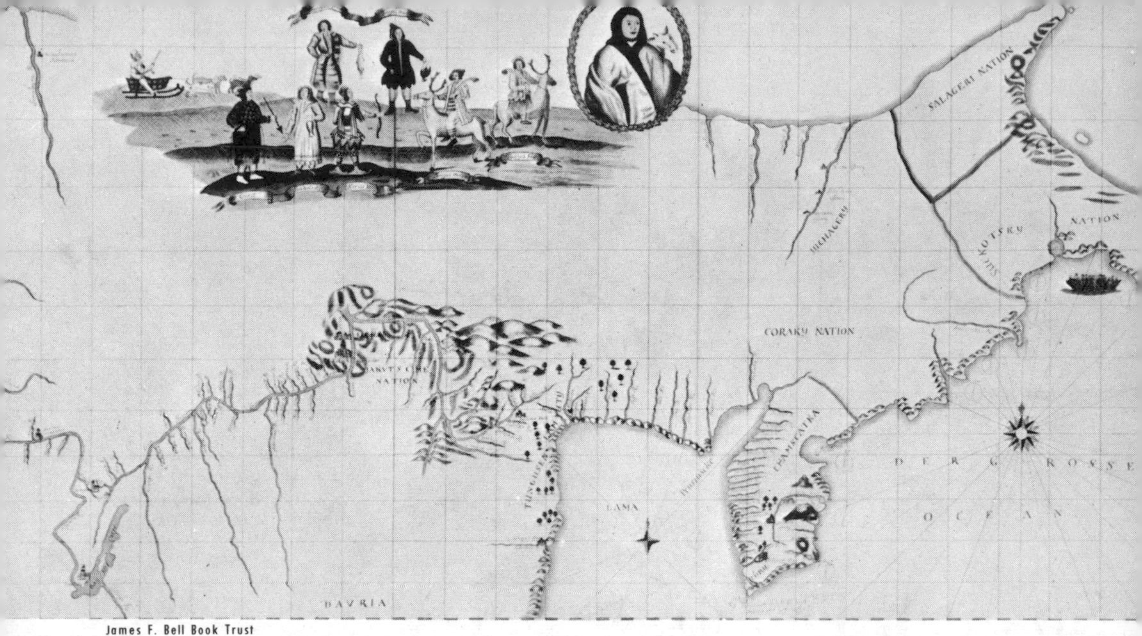


James F. Bell Book Trust

**Map of Bering's route across Siberia**

The British Museum

The British Museum

**An Indian woman; (left) a flotilla of canoes encountered by Cook in Alaska, 1778; (below) Capt. Cook by N. Dance**

National Maritime Museum, England

# The Pacific Coast

In 1728 the Danish-Russian explorer Vitus Bering crossed Siberia to the sea and strait that bear his name. In 1741, the year of his death, he made a second expedition, crossed the strait, and laid claim to Alaska for the Czar. However, knowledge of the North American coast remained hazy until an Englishman, Capt. James Cook, explored the Pacific and sailed along the American coast in 1778.

National Maritime Museum, England

**This view of the "Resolution" anchored in Hawaii gives no hint of the violence that took Cook's life**

Capt. Cook's voyages were undertaken primarily for scientific purposes. The artists and naturalists who accompanied him created a detailed account of the Pacific and its idyllic island kingdoms. After extensive exploration and charting, along the North American coast, and in the South Pacific, Cook and his party were the first Westerners to visit Hawaii. He was killed there by Hawaiians in 1779.

The British Museum

**Watercolor by John Webber of an Alaskan Indian village, 1778**

Public Record Office, London

Yale University Library

**A group of Nootka Sound Indians by John Webber**

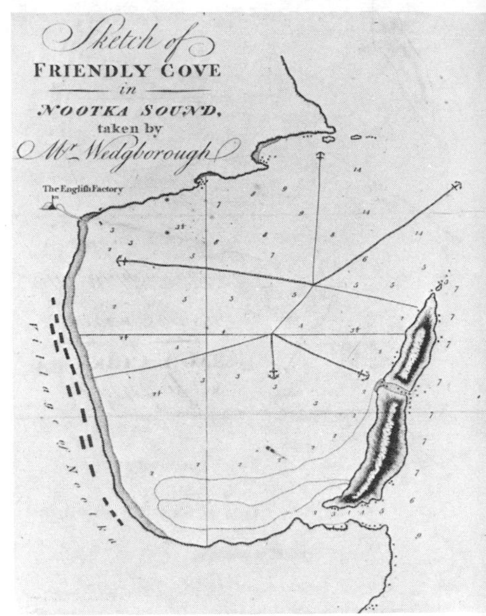


Library of Congress

**Map of Nootka Sound, Vancouver Island, from an account of the 1789 expedition and showing the British encampment**

McCord Museum, McGill University

**An Indian family in the Northwest by J. C. Young**

After Cook's expedition, several nations competed for territorial and commercial rights along the Northwest coast, from Oregon to Alaska. England, Spain, Russia, and the United States all had interests on the coast: Russia had Alaska, Spain had California, England had Vancouver Island, and the U.S. claimed the Columbia River (discovered by Captain Robert Gray in 1792). Subsequent territorial disputes would continue for over 50 years.

**Captain Robert Gray**

Oregon Historical Society

**A view of the British settlement at Fort Vancouver, a fur trading outpost**

Library of Congress

# 1786

12.

## Thomas Jefferson: Virginia Statute of Religious Freedom

*The Virginia Declaration of Rights of 1776 had asserted the principle of religious freedom, but it was not until 1779 that the Anglican Church was disestablished in the state. There were, however, many Virginians who felt that even with denominational equality all religions should be tax-supported. Public opinion was soon strongly aroused to the contrary view by Madison's "Remonstrance Against Religious Assessments" in 1785. The Statute of Religious Freedom that was drawn up by Thomas Jefferson in 1779 passed the Virginia Senate on January 16, 1786. The act made religious taxes illegal and allowed for liberty of religious opinion. This victory for the separation of church and state soon became the law for the entire Union in the First Amendment to the Constitution. Jefferson's directions for his epitaph, found after his death in his own handwriting, read: ". . . On the faces of the obelisk the following inscription, and not a word more, 'Here was buried Thomas Jefferson, author of the Declaration of American Independence, of the statute of Virginia for religious freedom, and father of the University of Virginia,' because by these, as testimonials that I have lived, I wish most to be remembered."*

Source: H. A. Washington, VIII, pp. 454-456.

I. *Whereas* Almighty God has created the mind free, so that all attempts to influence it by temporal punishments or burdens, or by civil incapacitations, tend only to beget habits of hypocrisy and meanness, and are a departure from the plan of the Holy Author of our religion, who, being Lord both of body and mind, yet chose not to propagate it by coercions on either, as was in His almighty power to do; that the impious presumption of legislators and rulers, civil as well as ecclesiastical, who, being themselves but fallible and uninspired men, have assumed dominion over the faith of others, setting up their own opinions and modes of thinking as the only true and infallible, and as such endeavoring to impose them on others, has established and maintained false religions over the greatest part of the world, and through all time; that to compel a man to furnish contributions of money for the propagation of opinions which he disbelieves is sinful and tyrannical; that even forcing him to support this or that teacher of his own religious persuasion is depriving him of the comfortable liberty of giving his contributions to the particular pastor whose morals he would make his pattern and whose powers he feels most persuasive to righteousness, and is withdrawing from the ministry those temporary rewards which, proceeding from an approbation of their personal conduct, are an additional incitement to earnest and unremitting labors for the instruction of mankind; that our civil rights have no dependence on our religious opinions, any more than our opinions in physics or geometry; that, therefore, the proscribing [of] any citizen as unworthy [of] the public confidence by laying upon him an incapacity of being called to offices of trust and emolument unless he profess or renounce this or that religious opinion is depriving him injuriously of those privileges and advantages to which in common with his fellow citizens he has a natural right; that it tends only to corrupt the principles of that . . . religion it is meant to encourage, by bribing with a monopoly of worldly honors and emoluments those who will externally profess and conform to it; that though indeed these are criminal who do not withstand such temptation, yet neither are those innocent who lay the bait in their way; that to suffer the civil magistrate to intrude his powers into the field of opinion, and to restrain the profession or propagation of principles on supposition of their ill tendency, is a dangerous fallacy which at once destroys all religious liberty, because he, being of course judge of that tendency, will make his opinions the rule of judgment, and approve or condemn the sentiments of others only as they shall square with or differ from his own; that it is time enough for the rightful purposes of civil government for its officers to interfere when principles break out into overt acts against peace and good order; and finally, that truth is great and will prevail if left to herself, that she is the proper and sufficient antagonist to error, and has nothing to fear from the conflict, unless by human interposition disarmed of her natural weapons, free argument and debate, errors ceasing to be dangerous when it is permitted freely to contradict them.

II. *Be it . . . enacted by the General Assembly* that no man shall be compelled to frequent or support any religious worship, place, or ministry whatsoever, nor shall be enforced, restrained, molested, or burdened in his body or goods, nor shall otherwise suffer on account of his religious opinions or belief; but that all men shall be free to profess, and by argument to maintain, their opinion in matters of religion, and that the same shall in no wise diminish, enlarge, or affect their civil capacities.

III. And though we well know that this Assembly, elected by the people for the ordinary purposes of legislation only, have no power to restrain the acts of succeeding assemblies, constituted with powers equal to our own, and that therefore to declare this act to be irrevocable would be of no effect in law; yet as we are free to declare, and do declare, that the rights hereby asserted are of the natural rights of mankind, and that if any act shall hereafter be passed to repeal the present, or to narrow its operation, such act will be an infringement of natural right.

13.

## BENJAMIN RUSH: On the Need for General Education

*Dr. Benjamin Rush's varied interests included enthusiastic support for all efforts to improve education in America. Rush wrote to Richard Price, a British moral philosopher, on May 25, 1786. In his letter he advanced a theory of education that involved giving greater freedom to students and encouraging their training in science and utilitarian subjects rather than in traditional disciplines.*

Source: MHSP, 2nd series, XVII, pp. 342-344.

MY LAST LETTER TO YOU by Captain Kennady contained an account of an intended convention of the states to assemble at Annapolis in Maryland, next September, for the purpose of agreeing upon certain commercial regulations and of suggesting such alterations in the Confederation as will give more extensive and coercive powers to Congress. We entertain the most flattering hopes from this convention, especially as an opinion seems to have pervaded all classes of people that an increase of power in Congress is absolutely necessary for our safety and independence.

Most of the distresses of our country, and of the mistakes which Europeans have formed of us, have arisen from a belief that the American Revolution is over. This is so far from being the case that we have only finished the first act of the great drama. We have changed our forms of government, but it remains yet to effect a revolution in our principles, opinions, and manners so as to accommodate them to the forms of government we have adopted. This is the most difficult part of the business of the patriots and legislators of our country. It requires more wisdom and fortitude than to expel or to reduce armies into captivity.

I wish to see this idea inculcated by your pen. Call upon the rulers of our country to lay the foundations of their empire in knowledge as well as virtue. Let our common people be compelled by law to give their children (what is commonly called) a good English education. Let schoolmasters of every description be supported in part by the public, and let their principles and morals be subjected to examination before we employ them. Let us have colleges in each of the states, and one federal university under the patronage of Congress, where the youth of all the states may be melted (as it were) together into one mass of citizens after they have acquired the first principles of knowledge in the colleges of their respective states. Let the law of nature and nations, the common law of our country, the different systems of government, history, and everything else connected with the advancement of republican knowledge and principles, be taught by able professors in this university.

This plan of general education alone will render the American Revolution a blessing to mankind. As you have staked your reputation upon this great event, with the world and with posterity, you must not desert us till you see the curtain drop and the last act of the drama closed. A small pamphlet addressed by you to the Congress and the legislature of each of the states, upon this subject, I am sure would have more weight with our rulers than a hundred publications thrown out by the citizens of this country. It will only be necessary in this pamphlet to be wholly silent upon those subjects in Christianity which now so much divide and agitate the Christian world. The wisest plan of education that could be offered would be unpopular among ninety-nine out of a hundred of the citizens of America if it opposed in any degree the doctrine of the Trinity.

Some of the members of the reformed Episcopal Church in the middle and southern states complained of the note you published with my letter in the English newspapers. It has injured them in the opinion of some of the English clergy. You will perceive from their prayer book that their Articles, though reduced in number, are equally Calvinistical with the Articles of the old English Church.

It is with singular pleasure that I inform you that public and private credit are reviving everywhere and that laws are gradually coming into force to compel the payment of old English debts. Whoever considers the effects of war upon morals in all countries, and then adds to these the effects of a sudden, total, and universal dissolution of all government such as took place in America during the late war will not be surprised at any of the events that have happened or at the laws that have been passed since the peace. It requires less charity than good sense to make proper allowances for all the vices of our country.

The letters written by Dr. Nisbet to his friends soon after his arrival in America, from which so many extracts have been published in the Scotch papers, were written under a deranged state of mind occasioned by a fever which fixed itself upon his brain. The doctor has since perfectly recovered his health and reason, has been reinstated in the college, and is now perfectly satisfied with our country.

Our venerable friend, Dr. Franklin, continues to enjoy as much health and spirits as are compatible with his time of life. I dined with him a few days ago in a most agreeable circle, where he appeared as cheerful and gay as a young man of five-and-twenty. But his conversation was full of the wisdom and experience of mellow old age. He has destroyed party rage in our state, or to borrow an allusion from one of his discoveries, his presence and advice, like oil upon troubled waters, have composed the contending waves of faction which for so many years agitated the state of Pennsylvania.

I beg my most respectful compliments to Mr. Adams, with whom I am happy to find you live upon the most intimate terms.

Should you conclude that the publication of any part of the intelligence contained in this letter will serve our country, you are at liberty to make that use of it, but I must request that you will not give my name to the public with it. . . .

P.S. Most of the complaints against our country which are published in your papers come from British agents, or from a set of men who have settled among us since the peace, who want either virtue or abilities to maintain themselves, and who would have been poor and unhappy in any country.

---

*What good is a newborn baby?*

Benjamin Franklin, when asked what good a balloon would be

14.

## Benjamin Rush: A Plan for the Establishment of Public Schools

*Benjamin Rush, like Thomas Jefferson, felt that education in a republic was intended to produce well-informed, useful citizens. The educational program Rush presented in 1786 called for a uniform, comprehensive system of schools for the state of Pennsylvania. His plan favored instruction for all members of society and improved education for girls.*

Source: *Essays, Literary, Moral and Philosophical,* 2nd edition, Philadelphia, 1806, pp. 1-6.

Before I proceed to the subject of this essay, I shall point out, in a few words, the influence and advantages of learning upon mankind.

1. It is friendly to religion inasmuch as it assists in removing prejudice, superstition, and enthusiasm; in promoting just notions of the Deity; in enlarging our knowledge of His works.

2. It is favorable to liberty. Freedom can exist only in the society of knowledge. Without learning, men are incapable of knowing their rights; and where learning is confined to a few people, liberty can be neither equal nor universal.

3. It promotes just ideas of laws and government. "When the clouds of ignorance are dispelled (says the Marquis of Beccaria) by the radiance of knowledge, power trembles, but the authority of laws remains immovable."

4. It is friendly to manners. Learning, in all countries, promotes civilization and the pleasures of society and conversation.

5. It promotes agriculture, the great basis of national wealth and happiness. Agriculture is as much a science as hydraulics or optics and has been equally indebted to the experiments and researches of learned men. The highly cultivated state and the immense profits of the farms in England are derived wholly from the patronage which agriculture has received in that country from learned men and learned societies.

6. Manufactures of all kinds owe their perfection chiefly to learning; hence the nations of Europe advance in manufactures, knowledge, and commerce only in proportion as they cultivate the arts and sciences.

For the purpose of diffusing knowledge through every part of the state, I beg leave to propose the following simple plan:

1. Let there be one university in the state, and let this be established in the capital. Let law, physic, divinity, the law of nature and nations, economy, etc., be taught in it by public lectures in the winter season, after the manner of the European universities. And let the professors receive such salaries from the state as will enable them to deliver their lectures at a moderate price.

2. Let there be four colleges: one in Philadelphia, one at Carlisle, a third, for the benefit of our German fellow citizens, at Lancaster, and a fourth, some years hence, at Pittsburgh. In these colleges, let young men be instructed in mathematics and in the higher branches of science in the same manner that they are now taught in our American colleges. After they have received

a testimonial from one of these colleges, let them, if they can afford it, complete their studies by spending a season or two in attending the lectures in the university. I prefer four colleges in the state to one or two, for there is a certain size of colleges, as there is of towns and armies, that is most favorable to morals and good government. Oxford and Cambridge in England are the seats of dissipation, while the more numerous and less crowded universities and colleges in Scotland are remarkable for the order, diligence, and decent behavior of their students.

3. Let there be free schools established in every township, or in districts consisting of one hundred families. In these schools let children be taught to read and write the English and German languages and the use of figures. Such of them as have parents that can afford to send them from home, and are disposed to extend their educations, may remove their children from the free school to one of the colleges.

Independence National Historical Park

Portrait of Benjamin Rush by Sharples

By this plan the whole state will be tied together by one system of education. The university will in time furnish masters for the colleges, and the colleges will furnish masters for the free schools, while the free schools, in their turns, will supply the colleges and the university with scholars, students, and pupils. The same systems of grammar, oratory, and philosophy will be taught in every part of the state; and the literary features of Pennsylvania will thus designate one great and equally enlightened family.

But, how shall we bear the expense of these literary institutions? I answer: these institutions will *lessen* our taxes. They will enlighten us in the great business of finance; they will teach us to increase the ability of the state to support government by increasing the profits of agriculture and by promoting manufactures. They will teach us all the modern improvements and advantages of inland navigation. They will defend us from hasty and expensive experiment in government by unfolding to us the experience and folly of past ages, and thus, instead of adding to our taxes and debts, they will furnish us with the true secret of lessening and discharging both of them.

But, shall the estates of orphans, bachelors, and persons who have no children be taxed to pay for the support of schools from which they can derive no benefit? I answer in the affirmative to the first part of the objection, and I deny the truth of the latter part of it. Every member of the community is interested in the propagation of virtue and knowledge in the state. But I will go further and add, it will be true economy in individuals to support public schools. The bachelor will in time save his tax for this purpose by being able to sleep with fewer bolts and locks to his doors; the estates of orphans will in time be benefited by being protected from the ravages of unprincipled and idle boys; and the children of wealthy parents will be less tempted by bad company to extravagance. Fewer pillories and whipping posts, and smaller gaols, with their usual expenses and taxes, will be necessary when our youth are properly educated than at present. I believe it could be proved that the expenses of confining, trying, and executing criminals amount every year, in most of the counties, to more money than would be sufficient to maintain all the schools that would be necessary in each county. The confessions of these criminals generally show us that their vices and punishments are the fatal consequences of the want of a proper education in early life.

I submit these detached hints to the consideration of the legislature and of the citizens of Pennsylvania. The plan for the free schools is taken chiefly from the plans which have long been used with success in Scotland and in the eastern states of America, where the influence of learning in promoting religion, morals, manners, and good government has never been exceeded in any country.

The manner in which these schools should be supported and governed — the modes of determining the characters and qualifications of schoolmasters, and the arrangement of families in each district, so that children of the same religious sect and nation may be educated as much as possible together — will form a proper part of a law for the establishment of schools, and therefore does not come within the limits of this plan.

15.

## Thomas Jefferson: On the Barbary Pirates

*The Barbary pirates of the North African states of Morocco, Algiers, Tripoli, and Tunis demanded tribute from maritime nations to ensure the safe passage of vessels through the Mediterranean. American commerce, which lacked the protection of the British Navy after the Declaration of Independence, was almost driven from the Mediterranean by the pirates in the 1780s. The removal of American competition from many of Europe's markets pleased the merchants of England. To solve the problem of the Barbary pirates, Thomas Jefferson, in a letter to John Adams of July 11, 1786, urged the use of an American naval force as the most effective means of dealing with the situation.*

Source: H. A. Washington, I, pp. 591-594.

Our instructions relative to the Barbary States having required us to proceed by way of negotiation to obtain their peace, it became our duty to do this to the best of our power. Whatever might be our private opinions, they were to be suppressed; and the line, marked out to us, was to be followed. It has been so, honestly and zealously. It was, therefore, never material for us to consult together on the best plan of conduct toward these states. I acknowledge I very early thought it would be best to effect a peace through the medium of war. Though it is a question with which we have nothing to do, yet, as you propose some discussion of it, I shall trouble you with my reasons.

Of the four positions laid down in your letter of the 3rd instant, I agree to the three first, which are, in substance, that the good offices of our friends cannot procure us a peace without paying its price; that they cannot materially lessen that price; and that paying it, we can have the peace in spite of the intrigues of our enemies. As to the fourth, that the longer the negotiation is delayed, the larger will be the demand, this will depend on the intermediate captures — if they are many and rich, the price may be raised; if few and poor, it will be lessened.

However, if it is decided that we shall buy a peace, I know no reason for delaying the operation, but should rather think it ought to be hastened; but I should prefer the obtaining it by war. (1) Justice is in favor of this opinion. (2) Honor favors it. (3) It will procure us respect in Europe, and respect is a safeguard to interest. (4) It will arm the federal head with the safest of all the instruments of coercion over its delinquent members, and prevent it from using what would be less safe.

I think that so far, you go with me. But in the next steps, we shall differ. (5) I think it least expensive. (6) Equally effectual. I ask a fleet of 150 guns, the one-half of which shall be in constant cruise. This fleet, built, manned, and victualed for six months, will cost £450,000 sterling. Its annual expense will be £300 sterling a gun, including everything; this will be £45,000 sterling a year. I take British experience for the basis of my calculation; though we know, from our own experience, that we can do in this way, for pounds lawful, what costs them pounds sterling. Were we to charge all this to the Algerine War, it would amount to little more than we must pay, if we buy peace. But as it is proper and necessary that we should establish a small marine force (even were we to buy a peace from the Algerines), and as that force, laid up in our dockyards, would cost us half as much annually as if kept in order for service, we have a right to say that only £22,500 sterling, per annum, should be charged to the Algerine War.

(7) It will be as effectual. To all the mismanagements of Spain and Portugal, urged to show that war against those people is ineffectual, I urge a single fact to prove the contrary, where there is any management. About forty years ago, the Algerines having broke their treaty with France, this court sent Monsieur de Massiac, with one large and two small frigates; he blockaded the harbor of Algiers three months, and they subscribed to the terms he proposed. If it be admitted, however, that war, on the fairest prospects, is still exposed to uncertainties, I weigh against this the greater uncertainty of the duration of a peace bought with money, from such a people, from a Dey eighty years old, and by a nation who, on the hypothesis of buying peace, is to have no power on the sea to enforce an observance of it.

So far, I have gone on the supposition that the whole weight of this war would rest on us. But (1) Naples will join us. The character of their naval minister (Acton) has known sentiments with respect to the peace Spain is officiously trying to make for them, and his dispositions against the Algerines give the best grounds to believe it. (2) Every principle of reason assures us that Portugal will join us. I state this as taking for granted what all seem to believe, that they will not be at peace with Algiers. I suppose, then, that a convention might be formed between Portugal, Naples, and the United States, by which the burden of the war might be quotaed on them, according to their respective wealth; and the term of it should be, when Algiers should subscribe to a peace with all three, on equal terms. This might be left open for other nations to accede to, and many, if not most, of the powers of Europe (except France, England, Holland, and Spain, if her peace be made) would sooner or later enter into the confederacy for the sake of having their peace with the piratical states guaranteed by the whole. I suppose that, in this case, our proportion of force would not be the half of what I first calculated on.

These are the reasons which have influenced my judgment on this question. I give them to you to show you that I am imposed on by a semblance of reason, at least, and not with an expectation of their changing your opinion. You have viewed the subject, I am sure, in all its bearings. You have weighed both questions, with all their circumstances. You make the result different from what I do. The same facts impress us differently. This is enough to make me suspect an error in my process of reasoning, though I am not able to detect it. It is of no consequence, as I have nothing to say in the decision, and am ready to proceed heartily on any other plan which may be adopted, if my agency should be thought useful. With respect to the dispositions of the state, I am utterly uninformed. I cannot help thinking, however, that on a view of all the circumstances, they might be united in either of the plans.

---

16.

# The Causes of Shays's Rebellion

*Daniel Gray, as chairman of a committee of rebels protesting the Massachusetts debtors' plight, wrote an address to the people of Hampshire County. In the address, which is reprinted here, Gray enumerated the causes for the riots that were staged under the leadership of Daniel Shays.*

Source: George R. Minot, *The History of the Insurrections in Massachusetts in the Year 1786 and the Rebellion Consequent Thereon,* 2nd edition, Boston, 1810, pp. 82-83.

WE HAVE THOUGHT PROPER TO INFORM you of some of the principal causes of the late risings of the people and also of their present movements, viz.:

1. The present expensive mode of collecting debts, which by reason of the great scarcity of cash will of necessity fill our jails with unhappy debtors, and thereby a reputable body of people rendered incapable of being serviceable either to themselves or the community.

2. The monies raised by impost and excise being appropriated to discharge the interest of governmental securities, and not the foreign debt, when these securities are not subject to taxation.

3. A suspension of the writ of habeas corpus, by which those persons who have stepped forth to assert and maintain the rights of the people are liable to be taken and conveyed even to the most distant part of the commonwealth, and thereby subjected to an unjust punishment.

4. The unlimited power granted to justices of the peace, and sheriffs, deputy sheriffs, and constables by the Riot Act, indemnifying them to the prosecution thereof; when perhaps wholly actuated from a principle of revenge, hatred, and envy.

Furthermore, be assured that this body, now at arms, depise the idea of being instigated by British emissaries, which is so strenuously propagated by the enemies of our liberties; and also wish the most proper and speedy measures may be taken to discharge both our foreign and domestic debt.

17.

## Thomas Grover: Reasons for Rebellion

*Thomas Grover, a Massachusetts citizen, listed a number of grievances of the people of Hampshire County in a letter of December 7, 1786, to the printer of the* Hampshire Herald.

Source: George R. Minot, *The History of the Insurrections in Massachusetts in the Year 1786 and the Rebellion Consequent Thereon,* 2nd edition, Boston, 1810, pp. 84-86.

It has somehow or other fallen to my lot to be employed in a more conspicuous manner than some others of my fellow citizens in stepping forth on defense of the rights and privileges of the people, more especially of the county of Hampshire.

Therefore, upon the desire of the people now at arms, I take this method to publish to the world of mankind in general, particularly the people of this Commonwealth, some of the principal grievances we complain of and of which we are now seeking redress, and mean to contend for, until a redress can be obtained, which we hope, will soon take place; and if so, our brethren in this Commonwealth that do not see with us as yet shall find we shall be as peaceable as they be.

In the first place, I must refer you to a draft of grievances drawn up by a committee of the people, now at arms, under the signature of Daniel Gray, chairman, which is heartily approved of; some others also are here added, viz.:

1. The General Court, for certain obvious reasons, must be removed out of the town of Boston.

2. A revision of the constitution is absolutely necessary.

3. All kinds of governmental securities, now on interest, that have been bought of the original owners for 2*s*. . . . and the highest for 6*s*. 8*d*. on the pound, and have received more interest than the principal cost the speculator who purchased them — that if justice was done, we verily believe, nay, positively know, it would save this Commonwealth thousands of pounds.

4. Let the lands belonging to this Commonwealth, at the eastward, be sold at the best advantage to pay the remainder of our domestic debt.

5. Let the monies arising from impost and excise be appropriated to discharge the foreign debt.

6. Let that act passed by the General Court last June by a small majority of only seven, called the Supplementary Act, for twenty-five years to come, be repealed.

7. The total abolition of the Inferior Court of Common Pleas and General Sessions of the Peace.

8. Deputy sheriffs totally set aside as a useless set of officers in the community; and constables, who are really necessary, be empowered to do the duty, by which means a large swarm of lawyers will be banished from their wonted haunts, who have been more damage to the people at large, especially the common farmers, than the savage beasts of prey.

To this I boldly sign my proper name, as a hearty wellwisher to the real rights of the people.

18.

# On the Inadequacies of the Central Government

*The men who had seen the War of Independence through to a successful conclusion were apprehensive lest their work be undone by the instability of the federal government. Thirteen separate states each going its own way would confirm what Europeans had been saying since the end of the Revolution: America was unable to govern itself and would soon fall into anarchy. The following exchange of letters between John Jay and George Washington in the summer of 1786 summed up sentiments that were becoming widespread in America. Jay's letter is dated June 27, and Washington's reply was written on August 1.*

Source: Johnston, III, pp. 203-205.
*The Writings of George Washington,* Jared Sparks, ed., Vol. IX, Boston, 1838, pp. 187-189.

I.

## John Jay to George Washington

To oppose popular prejudices, to censure the proceedings, and expose the improprieties of states is an unpleasant task, but it must be done. Our affairs seem to lead to some crisis, some revolution — something that I cannot foresee or conjecture. I am uneasy and apprehensive; more so than during the war. Then we had a fixed object, and though the means and time of obtaining it were often problematical, yet I did firmly believe we should ultimately succeed, because I was convinced that justice was with us. The case is now altered; we are going and doing wrong, and therefore I look forward to evils and calamities, but without being able to guess at the instrument, nature, or measure of them.

That we shall again recover and things again go well, I have no doubt. Such a variety of circumstances would not, almost miraculously, have combined to liberate and make us a nation for transient and unimportant purposes. I therefore believe that we are yet to become a great and respectable people; but when or how, the spirit of prophecy can only discern.

There doubtless is much reason to think and to say that we are woefully and, in many instances, wickedly misled. Private rage for property suppresses public considerations, and personal rather than national interests have become the great objects of attention. Representative bodies will ever be faithful copies of their originals, and generally exhibit a checkered assemblage of virtue and vice, of abilities and weakness.

The mass of men are neither wise nor good, and the virtue like the other resources of a country can only be drawn to a point and exerted by strong circumstances ably managed, or a strong government ably administered. New governments have not the aid of habit and hereditary respect, and being generally the result of preceding tumult and confusion, do not immediately acquire stability or strength. Besides, in times of commotion, some men will gain confidence and importance, who merit neither, and who, like political mountebanks, are less solicitous about the health of the credulous crowd than about making the most of their nostrums and prescriptions.

New York was rendered less federal by the opinions of the late president of Congress. This is a singular though not unaccountable fact — indeed, human actions are seldom inexplicable.

What I most fear is that the better kind of people, by which I mean the people who are orderly and industrious, who are content with their situations and not uneasy in their circumstances, will be led by the insecurity of property, the loss of confidence in their rulers, and the want of public faith and rectitude to consider the charms of liberty as imaginary and delusive. A state of fluctuation and uncertainty must disgust and alarm such men, and prepare their minds for almost any change that may promise them quiet and security.

## II.

### Washington to Jay

I have to thank you very sincerely for your interesting letter of the 27th of June, as well as for the other communications you had the goodness to make at the same time. I am sorry to be assured, of what indeed I had little doubt before, that we have been guilty of violating the treaty in some instances. What a misfortune it is that the British should have so well grounded a pretext for its palpable infractions! And what a disgraceful part, out of the choice of difficulties before us, are we to act!

Your sentiments, that our affairs are drawing rapidly to a crisis, accord with my own. What the event will be is also beyond the reach of my foresight. We have errors to correct. We have probably had too good an opinion of human nature in forming our confederation. Experience has taught us that men will not adopt and carry into execution measures the best calculated for their own good without the intervention of a coercive power. I do not conceive we can exist long as a nation without having lodged somewhere a power which will pervade the whole Union in as energetic a manner as the authority of the state governments extends over the several states.

To be fearful of investing Congress, constituted as that body is, with ample authorities for national purposes appears to me the very climax of popular absurdity and madness. Could Congress exert them for the detriment of the public without injuring themselves in an equal or greater proportion? Are not their interests inseparably connected with those of their constituents? By the rotation of appointment, must they not mingle frequently with the mass of citizens? Is it not rather to be apprehended, if they were possessed of the powers before described, that the individual members would be induced to use them, on many occasions, very timidly and inefficaciously for fear of losing their popularity and future election? We must take human nature as we find it. Perfection falls not to the share of mortals.

Many are of opinion that Congress have too frequently made use of the suppliant, humble tone of requisition in applications to the states, when they had a right to assert their imperial dignity and command obedience. Be that as it may, requisitions are a perfect nullity where thirteen sovereign, independent, disunited states are in the habit of discussing and refusing compliance with them at their option. Requisitions are actually little better than a jest and a byword throughout the land. If you tell the legislatures they have violated the treaty of peace and invaded the prerogatives of the confederacy, they will laugh in your face. What then is to be done? Things cannot go on in the same train forever. It is much to be feared, as you observe, that the better kind of people, being disgusted with the circumstances, will have their minds prepared for any revolution whatever. We are apt to run from one extreme into another. To anticipate and prevent disastrous contingencies would be the part of wisdom and patriotism.

What astonishing changes a few years are capable of producing. I am told that even respectable characters speak of a monarchical form of government without horror. From thinking proceeds speaking; thence to acting is often but a single step. But how irrevocable and tremendous! What a triumph for our enemies to verify their predictions! What a triumph for the advocates of despotism to find that we are incapable of governing ourselves, and that systems founded on the basis of equal liberty are merely ideal and fallacious! Would to God that wise measures may be taken in time to avert the consequences we have but too much reason to apprehend.

Retired as I am from the world, I frankly acknowledge I cannot feel myself an unconcerned spectator. Yet, having happily assisted in bringing the ship into port, and having been fairly discharged, it is not my business to embark again on a sea of troubles. Nor could it be expected that my sentiments and opinions would have much weight on the minds of my countrymen. They have been neglected, though given as a last legacy in the most solemn manner. I had then perhaps some claims to public attention. I consider myself as having none at present.

---

19.

## Noah Webster: Diseases of the Body Politic

*Noah Webster came into contact with many of the leaders of the young republic when he began agitation for an American copyright law in 1782. Promoting the legislation in thirteen state capitals, Webster became an ardent advocate of strong federal government. In 1790, he published* A Collection of Essays and Fugitiv Writings *from which the following essay of 1786 is taken. His analysis of the many problems besetting the thirteen states led him to the same conclusion that many other Americans were coming to: Only a strong federal government could save the United States from political dissolution.*

Source: *A Collection of Essays and Fugitiv Writings,* Boston, 1790: "The Devil is in You."

That the political body, like the animal, is liable to violent diseases, which, for a time, baffle the healing art, is a truth which we . . . acknowledge, and which most of us lament. But as most of the disorders incident to the human frame are the consequence of an intemperate indulgence of its appetites, or of neglecting the most obvious means of safety; so most of the popular tumults which disturb government arise from an abuse of its blessings or an inattention to its principles. A man of a robust constitution, relying on its strength, riots in gratifications which weaken the stamina vitae; the surfeiting pleasures of a few years destroy the power of enjoyment; and the full fed voluptuary feels a rapid transition to the meager valetudinarian. Thus people who enjoy an uncommon share of political privileges often carry their freedom to licentiousness, and put it out of their power to enjoy society by destroying its support.

Too much health is a disease which often requires a very strict regimen; too much liberty is the worst of tyranny; and wealth may be accumulated to such a degree as to impoverish a state. If all men attempt to become masters, the most of them would necessarily become slaves in the attempt; and could every man on earth possess millions of joes [a gold coin], every man would be poorer than any man is now, and infinitely more wretched, because they could not procure the necessaries of life.

My countrymen, it is a common saying now that the devil is in you. I question the influence of the devil, however, in these affairs. Divines and politicians agree in this, to father all evil upon the devil; but the effects ascribed to this prince of evil spirits, both in the moral and political world, I ascribe to the wickedness and ignorance of the human heart. Taking the word devil in this sense, he is in you, and among you, in a variety of shapes.

In the first place, the weakness of our federal government is the devil. It prevents the adoption of any measures that are requisite for us as a nation; it keeps us from paying our honest debts; it also throws out of our power all the profits of commerce, and this drains us of cash. Is not this the devil? Yes, my countrymen, an empty purse is the devil.

You say you are jealous of your rights, and dare not trust Congress. Well, that jealousy is an evil spirit, and all evil spirits are devils. So far the devil is in you. You act, in this particular, just like the crew of a ship who would not trust the helm with one of their number, because he might possibly run her ashore, when by leaving her without a pilot, they were certain of shipwreck. You act just like men who, in raising a building, would not have a master workman, because he might give out wrong orders. You will be masters yourselves; and as you are not all ready to lift at the same time, one labors at a stick of timber, then another, then a third; you are then vexed that it is not raised; why, let a master order thirteen of you to take hold together, and you will lift it at once. Every family has a master (or a mistress — I beg the ladies' pardon). When a ship or a house is to be built, there is a master; when highways are repairing, there is a master; every little school has a master; the continent is a great school; the boys are numerous, and full of roguish tricks, and there is no master. The boys in this great school play truant, and there is no person to chastise them. Do you think, my countrymen, that America is more easily governed than a school? You do very well in small matters; extend your reason to great ones. Would you not laugh at a farmer who would fasten a cable to a plough, and yet attempt to draw a house with a cobweb? "And Nathan said unto David, thou art the man." You think a master necessary to govern a few harmless children in a school or family; yet leave thousands of great rogues to be governed by good advice. Believe me, my friends, for I am serious; you lose rights, because you will not give your magistrates authority to protect them. Your liberty is despotism, because it has no control; your power is nothing, because it is not united.

But further, luxury rages among you, and luxury is the devil. The war has sent this evil demon to impoverish people and embarrass the public. The articles of rum and tea alone which are drunk in this country would pay all its taxes. But when we add sugar, coffee, feathers, and the whole list of baubles and trinkets, what an enormous expense! No wonder you want paper currency. My countrymen are all grown very tasty! Feathers and jordans must all be imported! Certainly, gentlemen, the devil is among you. A Hampshire man who drinks 40*s*. worth of rum in a year, and never thinks of the expense, will raise a mob to reduce the governor's salary, which does not amount to 3*d*. a man per annum. Is not this the devil?

My countrymen, a writer appeared, not long ago, informing you how to redress grievances. He gives excellent advice. Let every man make a little box, and put into it *4d.* every day. This in a year will amount to £6 1*s.* 8*d.*, a sum more than sufficient to pay any poor man's tax. Any man can pay *3d.* or *4d.* a day, though no poor man can, at the end of a year, pay £6. Take my advice, every man of you, and you will hardly feel your taxes.

But further, a tender law is the devil. When I trust a man a sum of money, I expect he will return the full value. That legislature which says my debtor may pay me with one-third of the value he received commits a deliberate act of villainy; an act for which an individual, in any government, would be honored with a whipping post, and in most governments, with a gallows. When a man makes dollars, one-third of which only is silver, and passes them for good coin, he must lose his ears, etc.

But legislatures can, with the solemn face of rulers and guardians of justice, boldly give currency to an adulterated coin, enjoin it upon debtors to cheat their creditors, and enforce their systematic knavery with legal penalties. The difference between the man who makes and passes counterfeit money, and the man who tenders his creditor one-third of the value of the debt and demands a discharge, is the same as between a thief and a robber. The first cheats his neighbor in the dark and takes his property without his knowledge: the last boldly meets him at noonday, tells him he is a rascal, and demands his purse.

My countrymen, the devil is among you. Make paper as much as you please; make it a tender in all future contracts, or let it rest on its own bottom, but remember that past contracts are sacred things; that legislatures have no right to interfere with them; they have no right to say a debt shall be paid at a discount, or in any manner which the parties never intended. It is the business of justice to fulfill the intention of parties in contracts, not to defeat them. To pay bona fide contracts for cash, in paper of little value, or in old horses, would be a dishonest attempt in an individual; but for legislatures to frame laws to support and encourage such detestable villainy is like a judge who should inscribe the arms of a rogue over the seat of justice, or clergymen who should convert into bawdy-houses the temples of Jehovah. My countrymen, the world says the devil is in you: mankind detest you as they would a nest of robbers.

Metropolitan Museum of Art, bequest of Charles Allen Munn

Pastel portrait of Noah Webster by Sharples

But lastly, mobs and conventions are devils. Good men love law and legal measures. Knaves only fear law, and try to destroy it. My countrymen, if a constitutional legislature cannot redress a grievance, a mob never can. Laws are the security of life and property; nay, what is more, of liberty. The man who encourages a mob to prevent the operation of law ceases to be free or safe; for the same principle which leads a man to put a bayonet to the breast of a judge will lead him to take property where he can find it; and when the judge dare not act, where is the loser's remedy? Alas, my friends, too much liberty is no liberty at all. Give me anything but mobs; for mobs are the devil in his worst shape. I would shoot the leader of a mob sooner than a midnight ruffian. People may have grievances, perhaps, and no man would more readily hold up his hand to redress them than myself; but mobs rebel against laws of their own, and rebellion is a crime which admits of no palliation.

My countrymen, I am a private, peaceable man. I have nothing to win or to lose by the game of paper currency; but I revere justice. I would sooner pick oakum all my life than stain my reputation, or pay my creditor one farthing less than his honest demands.

While you attempt to trade to advantage, without a head to combine all the states into systematic, uniform measures, the world will laugh at you for fools. While merchants take and give credit, the world will call them idiots, and laugh at their ruin. While farmers get credit, borrow money, and mortgage their farms, the world will call them fools and laugh at their embarrassments. While all men live beyond their income, and are harassed with duns and sheriffs, no man will pity them, or give them relief. But when mobs and conventions oppose the courts of justice, and legislatures make paper or old horses a legal tender in all cases, the world will exclaim with one voice, Ye are rogues, and the devil is in you!

---

20.

## The Annapolis Convention

*In 1785, Maryland and Virginia differed on the matter of rights of navigation on the Potomac River and Chesapeake Bay. A meeting on the question led to a general discussion of interstate commerce. As a result, the Virginia legislature called for a convention of all the states at Annapolis on September 11, 1786. But with only five states represented, the convention decided that such questions could not be effectively dealt with unless the Articles of Confederation were revised. A report, drafted by Alexander Hamilton on September 14, proposed that a convention of all the states should be held for this purpose. The recommendation was adopted by Congress, and a convention was scheduled to be held in Philadelphia eight months later.*

Source: Elliot, I, pp. 116-119.

To the Honorable, the legislatures of Virginia, Delaware, Pennsylvania, New Jersey, and New York, the commissioners from the said states, respectively assembled at Annapolis, humbly beg leave to report:

That, pursuant to their several appointments, they met at Annapolis in the state of Maryland on the 11th day of September instant, and having proceeded to a communication of their powers, they found that the states of New York, Pennsylvania, and Virginia had, in substance and nearly in the same terms, authorized their respective commissioners

> to meet such other commissioners as were, or might be, appointed by the other states in the Union, at such time and place as should be agreed upon by the said commissioners, to take into consideration the trade and commerce of the United States, to consider how far a uniform system in their commercial intercourse and regulations might be necessary to their common interest and permanent harmony, and to report to the several states such an act, relative to this great object, as when unanimously ratified by them would enable the United States in Congress assembled effectually to provide for the same.

That the state of Delaware had given similar powers to their commissioners, with this difference only, that the act to be framed in virtue of these powers is required to be reported "to the United States in Congress assembled, to be agreed to by them, and confirmed by the legislatures of every state."

That the state of New Jersey had enlarged the object of their appointment, empowering their commissioners "to consider how far a uniform system in their commercial regulations and *other important matters* might be necessary to the common interest and permanent harmony of the several states," and to report such an act on the subject, as when ratified by them, "would enable the United States in Congress assembled effectually to provide for the exigencies of the Union."

That appointments of commissioners have also been made by the states of New Hampshire, Massachusetts, Rhode Island, and North Carolina, none of whom, however, have attended; but that no information has been received by your commissioners of any appointment having been made by the states of Connecticut, Maryland, South Carolina, or Georgia.

That the express terms of the powers of your commissioners supposing a deputation from all the states, and having for object the trade and commerce of the United States, your commissioners did not conceive it advisable to proceed on the business of their mission under the circumstance of so partial and defective a representation.

Deeply impressed, however, with the magnitude and importance of the object confided to them on this occasion, your commissioners cannot forbear to indulge an expression of their earnest and unanimous wish that speedy measures be taken to effect a general meeting of the states in a future convention, for the same and such other purposes as the situation of public affairs may be found to require.

If, in expressing this wish, or in intimating any other sentiment, your commissioners should seem to exceed the strict bounds of their appointment, they entertain a full confidence that a conduct, dictated by an anxiety for the welfare of the United States, will not fail to receive an indulgent construction.

In this persuasion, your commissioners submit an opinion that the idea of extending the powers of their deputies to other objects than those of commerce, which has been adopted by the state of New Jersey, was an improvement on the original plan, and will deserve to be incorporated into that of a future convention. They are the more naturally led to this conclusion as in the course of their reflections on the subject they have been induced to think that the power of regulating trade is of such comprehensive extent, and will enter so far into the general system of the federal government, that to give it efficacy and to obviate questions and doubts concerning its precise nature and limits may require a correspondent adjustment of other parts of the federal system.

That there are important defects in the system of the federal government is acknowledged by the acts of all those states which have concurred in the present meeting; that the defects, upon a closer examination, may be found greater and more numerous than even these acts imply is at least so far probable, from the embarrassments which characterize the present state of our national affairs, foreign and domestic, as may reasonably be supposed to merit a deliberate and candid discussion, in some mode, which will unite the sentiments and councils of all the states. In the choice of the mode, your commissioners are of opinion that a convention of deputies from the different states, for the special and sole purpose of entering into this investigation and digesting a plan for supplying such defects as may be discovered to exist, will be entitled to a preference from considerations which will occur without being particularized.

Your commissioners decline an enumeration of those national circumstances on which their opinion respecting the propriety of a future convention, with more enlarged powers, is founded; as it would be a useless intrusion of facts and observations, most of which have been frequently the subject of public discussion, and none of which can have escaped the penetration of those to whom they would in this instance be addressed. They are, however, of a nature so serious as, in the view of your commissioners, to render the situation of the United States delicate and critical, calling for an exertion of the united virtue and wisdom of all the members of the Confederacy.

Under this impression, your commissioners, with the most respectful deference, beg leave to suggest their unanimous conviction that it may essentially tend to advance the interests of the Union if the states, by whom they have been respectively delegated, would themselves concur and use their endeavors to procure the concurrence of the other states in the appointment of commissioners, to meet at Philadelphia on the second Monday in May next, to take into consideration the situation of the United States, to devise such further provisions as shall appear to them necessary to render the Constitution of the federal government adequate to the exigencies of the Union; and to report such an act for that purpose to the United States in Congress assembled, as when agreed to by them, and afterward confirmed by the legislatures of every state, will effectually provide for the same.

Though your commissioners could not with propriety address these observations and sentiments to any but the states they have the honor to represent, they have nevertheless concluded from motives of respect to transmit copies of this report to the United States in Congress assembled, and to the executives of the other states.

---

*I never mean, unless some particular circumstance should compel me to it, to possess another slave by purchase, it being among my first wishes to see some plan adopted by which slavery in this country may be abolished by law.*

George Washington, letter to J. F. Mercer, Sept. 9, 1786

# CONVENTION OF 1787

By September 1786 the infant confederation was in deep trouble. "Not worth a continental" was the stock phrase for the devalued currency of the Continental Congress: it seemed to reflect the prospects of the republic, too. Only in name were the United States united; in practice each state did what it pleased — or dared. There was no separation of powers: what little federal power existed was vested in the Congress. States ignored federal calls for revenue. The depression that began in 1785 had deepened, and Daniel Shays led Massachusetts farmers in armed rebellion. The weak central government could obtain little foreign credit. States refused to comply with terms of the peace treaty, giving Britain an excuse to continue to hold the forts at Detroit and other western points. One major achievement was the passing of the land ordinances of 1785 and 1787 (Northwest Ordinance), outlawing slavery in the Northwest Territory, and providing for the sale of western lands, for public schools, and for eventual statehood. But even this forward step was undertaken under pressure from lobbying speculators who stood to gain from ownership of large tracts of land. Farsighted Americans voiced the need for a more unified government.

By the UNITED STATES in CONGRESS Aſſembled,

# A PROCLAMATION.

Thomas Mifflin

WHEREAS definitive articles of peace and friendſhip, between the United States of America and his Britannic majeſty, were concluded and ſigned at Paris, on the 3d day of September, 1783, by the plenipotentiaries of the ſaid United States, and of his ſaid Britannic Majeſty, duly and reſpectively authorized for that purpoſe; which definitive articles are in the words following.

*In the Name of the Moſt Holy and Undivided*
TRINITY.

IT having pleaſed the Divine Providence to diſpoſe the hearts of the moſt ſerene and moſt potent Prince George the Third, by the Grace of God, King of Great-Britain, France and Ireland, Defender of the Faith, Duke of Brunſwick and Lunenburg, Arch-Treaſurer and Prince Elector of the Holy Roman Empire, &c. and of the United States of America, to forget all paſt miſunderſtandings and differences, that have unhappily interrupted the good correſpondence and friendſhip which they mutually wiſh to reſtore; and to eſtabliſh ſuch a beneficial and ſatisfactory intercourſe between the two countries, upon the ground of reciprocal advantages and mutual convenience, as may promote and ſecure to both perpetual peace and harmony: And having for this deſirable end, already laid the foundation of peace and reconciliation, by the proviſional articles, ſigned at Paris, on the 30th of November, 1782, by the commiſſioners empowered on each part, which articles were agreed to be inſerted in, and to conſtitute the treaty of peace propoſed to be concluded between the crown of Great-Britain and the ſaid United States, but which treaty was not to be concluded until terms of peace ſhould be agreed upon between Great-Britain and France, and his Britannic majeſty ſhould be ready to conclude ſuch treaty accordingly; and the treaty between Great-Britain and France, having ſince been concluded, his Britannic majeſty and the United States of America, in order to carry into full effect the proviſional articles abovementioned, according to the tenor thereof, have conſtituted and appointed, that is to ſay, His Britannic majeſty on his part, David Hartley, eſquire, member of the parliament of Great-Britain, and the ſaid United States on their part, John Adams, eſquire, late a commiſſioner of the United States of America at the court

long lake and the water communication between it and the lake of the Woods, to the ſaid lake of the Woods; thence through the ſaid lake to the moſt north-weſtern point thereof, and from thence on a due weſt courſe to the river Miſſiſippi; thence by a line to be drawn along the middle of the ſaid river Miſſiſippi, until it ſhall interſect the northernmoſt part of the thirty-firſt degree of north latitude. South by a line to be drawn due eaſt from the determination of the line laſt mentioned, in the latitude of thirty-one degrees north of the equator, to the middle of the river Apalachicola or Catahouche; thence along the middle thereof to its junction with the Flint river; thence ſtraight to the head of Saint Mary's river; and thence down along the middle of Saint Mary's river to the Atlantic Ocean. Eaſt by a line to be drawn along the middle of the river Saint-Croix, from its mouth in the bay of Fundy to its ſource, and from its ſource directly north to the aforeſaid Highlands which divide the rivers that fall into the Atlantic Ocean from thoſe which fall into the river Saint Lawrence; comprehending all iſlands within twenty leagues of any part of the ſhores of the United States, and lying between lines to be drawn due eaſt from the points where the aforeſaid boundaries between Nova-Scotia on the one part, and Eaſt Florida on the other, ſhall reſpectively touch the bay of Fundy, and the Atlantic Ocean; excepting ſuch iſlands as now are or heretofore have been within the limits of the ſaid province of Nova Scotia.

ARTICLE 3d. It is agreed that the people of the United Staets ſhall continue to enjoy unmoleſted the right to take fiſh of every kind on the Grand Bank, and on all the other banks of Newfoundland; alſo in the gulph of Saint Lawrence, and at all other places in the ſea, where the inhabitants of both countries uſed at any time heretofore to fiſh; and alſo that the inhabitants of the United States ſhall have liberty to take fiſh of every kind on ſuch part of the coaſt of Newfoundland as Britiſh fiſhermen ſhall uſe, (but not to dry or cure the ſame on that Iſland) and alſo on the coaſts, bays and creeks of all other of his Britannic Majeſty's dominions in America; and that the American fiſhermen ſhall have liberty to dry and cure fiſh in any of the unſettled bays, harbours and creeks of Nova-Scotia, Magdalen iſlands, and Labradore, ſo long as the ſame ſhall remain unſettled, but ſo ſoon as the ſame or either of them ſhall be ſettled, it ſhall not be lawful for the

and between the ſubjects of the one, and the citizens of the other, wherefore all hoſtilities both by ſea and land ſhall from henceforth ceaſe: all priſoners on both ſides ſhall be ſet at liberty, and his Britannic Majeſty ſhall with all convenient ſpeed, and without cauſing any deſtruction, or carrying away any negroes or other property of the American inhabitants, withdraw all his armies, garriſons and fleets from the ſaid United States, and from every poſt place and harbour within the ſame; leaving in all fortifications the American artillery that may be therein, and ſhall alſo order and cauſe all archives, records deeds and papers, belonging to any of the ſaid ſtates, or their citizens, which in the courſe of the war may have fallen into the hands of his officers, to be forthwith reſtored and delivered to the proper ſtates and perſons to whom they belong.

ARTICLE 8th. The navigation of the river Miſſiſippi, from its ſource to the Ocean, ſhall forever remain free and open to the ſubjects of Great-Britain and the citizens of the United States.

ARTICLE 9th. In caſe it ſhould ſo happen that any place or territory belonging to Great-Britain or to the United States, ſhould have been conquered by the arms of either from the other, before the arrival of the ſaid proviſional articles in America, it is agreed, that the ſame ſhall be reſtored without difficulty, and without requiring any compenſation.

ARTICLE 10th. The ſolemn ratifications of the preſent treaty, expedited in good and due form, ſhall be exchanged between the contracting parties, in the ſpace of ſix months, or ſooner if poſſible, to be computed from the day of the ſignature of the preſent treaty. In witneſs whereof, we the underſigned, their miniſters plenipotentiary, have in their name and in virtue of our full powers, ſigned with our hands the preſent definitive treaty, and cauſed the ſeals of our arms to be affixed thereto.

DONE at Paris, this third day of September,

National Archives

**(Above) Proclamation issued by Congress telling the terms of the peace treaty signed by Britain and the United States in 1783; (below) Mr. and Mrs. Thomas Mifflin in a portrait by Copley; Mifflin was president of Congress prior to the Constitutional Convention**

Historical Society of Pennsylvania

# Congress Governs The Nation

Although named the United States, the government always acted as the "United States in Congress assembled." The chief executive was the president of Congress. For long periods no quorum could be mustered to transact business. The British spurned John Adams' efforts at a commercial treaty with the "disunited states," citing the need for thirteen treaties. The first real step toward interstate cooperation was a series of meetings in 1785 between Maryland and Virginia on navigation of the Potomac and other waterways important for opening up the West. James Madison led in calling for a meeting of all states in Annapolis.

Independence National Historical Park

Law Office of James Monroe; photo, Frick

**(Left) George Read, Delaware representative at Annapolis and Philadelphia and (right) James Monroe**

# The Annapolis Convention

From September 11 to 14, 1786, twelve men representing five states met in Maryland's Old State House to attempt to resolve interstate conflicts. Four states ignored the convention, and delegates elected by four states did not attend. But three of the four most important commercial states were represented: New York, Pennsylvania, and Virginia (the Massachusetts delegates did not appear). Connecticut and New Jersey were also represented. James Madison and Alexander Hamilton took the lead in urging another meeting in Philadelphia the following spring, to include all thirteen states and to "devise such further provisions as shall appear to them necessary to render the constitution of the Federal Government adequate." New Jersey alone had empowered its delegates to act on matters beyond those of commerce.

**State House, Annapolis, site of the brief convention, 1786**

New York Public Library

Pennsylvania Academy of Fine Arts

Historical Society of Pennsylvania

# The Philadelphia Convention

The Philadelphia Convention opened May 25, 1787, at Independence Hall (the State House), eleven days behind schedule because of the tardiness of many delegates. Rhode Island boycotted the assembly. The political leaders of twelve states were the shapers of the new Constitution, although Congress had invited them only to consider amendments to the Articles of Confederation. In the one unanimous action of the Convention (it lasted all through the summer to Sept. 17), George Washington was elected to preside. Dean of the delegates was Dr. Franklin, aged 81. After much debate, each state was given one vote, regardless of size. To ensure freedom of debate, the Convention agreed to keep proceedings confidential. The first major issue of debate was introduced by Edmund Randolph on the third day of the Convention. The Virginia plan, a "big state" plan, called for a bicameral Congress, with states electing representatives in proportion to population or to financial contribution to the federal government. Some delegates claimed the plan went far beyond the authority of Congress, but the demand for a new Constitution prevailed.

Independence National Historical Park

**(Top left) George Washington, convention chairman; (top right) Benjamin Franklin, head of the Pennsylvania delegation and oldest representative; (right) Elbridge Gerry, an early advocate of strong central government, refused to sign the final document**

WE the People of the States of New-Hampſhire, Maſſachuſetts, Rhode-Iſland and Providence Plantations, Connecticut, New-York, New-Jerſey, Pennſylvania, Delaware, Maryland, Virginia, North-Carolina, South-Carolina, and Georgia, do ordain, declare and eſtabliſh the following Conſtitution for the Government of Ourſelves and our Poſterity.

ARTICLE I.

[illegible]

II.

The Government ſhall conſiſt of ſupreme legiſlative, executive and judicial powers.

III.

The legiſlative power ſhall be veſted in a Congreſs, to conſiſt of two ſeparate and diſtinct bodies of men, a Houſe of Repreſentatives, and a Senate; ~~each of which ſhall, in all caſes, have a negative on the other. The Legiſlature ſhall meet on the firſt Monday in December in every year.~~

IV.

*Sect.* 1. The Members of the Houſe of Repreſentatives ſhall be choſen every ſecond year, by the people of the ſeveral States comprehended within this Union. The qualifications of the electors ſhall be the ſame, from time to time, as thoſe of the electors in the ſeveral States, of the moſt numerous branch of their own legiſlatures.

*Sect.* 2. [illegible]

*Sect.* 3. The Houſe of Repreſentatives ſhall, at its firſt formation, and until the number of citizens and inhabitants ſhall be taken in the manner herein after deſcribed, conſiſt of ſixty-five Members, of whom three ſhall be choſen in New-Hampſhire, eight in Maſſachuſetts, one in Rhode-Iſland and Providence Plantations, five in Connecticut, ſix in New-York, four in New-Jerſey, eight in Pennſylvania, one in Delaware, ſix in Maryland, ten in Virginia, five in North-Carolina, five in South-Carolina, and three in Georgia.

*Sect.* 4. As the proportions of numbers in the different States will alter from time to time; as ſome of the States may hereafter be divided; as others may be enlarged by addition of territory; as two or more States may be united; as new States will be erected within the limits of the United States, the Legiſlature ſhall, in each of theſe caſes, regulate the number of repreſentatives by the number of inhabitants, according to the [illegible] the rate of one for every forty thouſand.

*Sect.* 5. [illegible] drawn from the public Treaſury, but in purſuance of appropriations that ſhall originate in the Houſe of Repreſentatives.

*Sect.* 6. The Houſe of Repreſentatives ſhall have the ſole power of impeachment. It ſhall chooſe its Speaker and other officers.

*Sect.* 7. Vacancies in the Houſe of Repreſentatives ſhall be ſupplied by writs of election from the executive authority of the State, in the repreſentation from which they ſhall happen.

V.

National Archives

Museum of Fine Arts, Boston

**(Above) Nathaniel Gorham, delegate from Massachusetts who served as chairman of the committee of the whole; (left) Washington's draft copy of the Constitution; (below) William Johnson, delegate from Connecticut, who broke a major deadlock with a proposal for dividing the legislative branch**

Columbia University

Yale University Art Gallery

# Resolution . . .

The Virginia Plan was debated for two weeks, and on June 13 an amended version containing nineteen resolutions was reported out. The plan called for some separation of powers between legislative, executive, and judicial branches of government, but the executive was to be elected by the legislature, and a council consisting of the executive and several members of the judiciary would have the veto power. Madison and George Mason were the Virginia delegates who carried on the fight for Randolph's plan. On June 15 William Paterson introduced the New Jersey Plan, a "small state" plan amending the Articles of Confederation by giving the Congress some added powers.

National Archives

State of the resolutions submitted to the consideration of the House by the honorable Mr Randolph, as agreed to in a Committee of the whole House.

Resolved that it is the opinion of this Committee that a national government ought to be established, consisting of a Supreme Legislative, Judiciary, and Executive.

Resolved that the national Legislature ought to consist of two branches.

Resolved that the members of the first branch of the national Legislature ought to be elected by the people of the several States.

Resolved that the members of the second branch of the national Legislature ought to be chosen by the individual Legislatures.

Resolved that each branch ought to possess the right of originating acts.

Resolved, That the national Legislature ought to be empowered

to enjoy the legislative rights vested in Congress by the confederation; and moreover

to legislate in all cases to which the separate States are incompetent: or in which the harmony of the United States may be interrupted by the exercise of individual legislation.

to negative all laws passed by the several States contravening, in the opinion of the national Legislature, the articles of union; or any treaties subsisting under the authority of the Union

# and Compromise

After three more days of debate the delegates voted in favor of the fundamental changes envisioned by the Virginia Plan. The issues were sharply drawn: large states wanted proportional representation in the legislature; small states wanted equal representation. The Connecticut Compromise, offered by Roger Sherman and backed by William Johnson, broke the deadlock: representation would be by population in the lower house and each state would have an equal vote in the upper house. Franklin, too, called for compromise. Of fifty-five delegates, only forty-two were present Sept. 17, when the Constitution was signed. No one voted against the document, but three delegates refused to sign it.

Baltimore Courthouse Coll.; photo, Frick

National Archives

17 Resolved. that provision ought to be made for the amendment of the articles of Union, whensoever it shall seem necessary.

18 Resolved that the legislative, Executive, and Judiciary powers within the several States ought to be bound by oath to support the articles of Union

19 Resolved. that the amendments which shall be offered to the confederation by the Convention, ought at a proper time or times, after the approbation of Congress to be submitted to an assembly or assemblies of representatives, recommended by the several Legislatures, to be expressly chosen by the People to consider and decide thereon

Received this sheet from the President of the United States, with the journals of the General Convention, March 19th 1796.

Timothy Pickering
Secy of State

(Above) Luther Martin, member of the Maryland delegation; OPPOSITE PAGE: (top) Roger Sherman, delegate from Connecticut; detail of portrait by Ralph Earl; (left) Excerpts from the Virginia Plan as amended by the Philadelphia Convention; copy dated 1796; both Sherman and Martin opposed much of this plan and Martin walked out on the convention

Independence National Historical Park

# The Constitution

(Above) Charles Cotesworth Pinckney, South Carolina, proposed giving the Senate the power to ratify treaties; (below) Caleb Strong, Massachusetts, favored having money bills originate in the House

Massachusetts Historical Society

The Constitution hammered out in the hot summer of 1787 represented a long series of compromises: two legislative houses, one elected on the basis of population, the other not; a president elected for a four-year term (Gouverneur Morris had fought for a lifetime president); separation of powers among legislative, executive, and judicial instead of complete Congressional domination. Franklin told the delegates on the last day of the Convention that the government they had shaped "can only end in despotism, as other forms have done before, when the people shall become so corrupted as to need despotic government, being incapable of any other."

There were few precedents for this written frame of government: the English constitution was not a written document; the interests of the delegates were divergent. Attitudes to the Constitution familiar to the late 20th century were not yet formulated. The doctrine that the Supreme Court had power to declare an act of Congress unconstitutional (judicial review) was unknown in 1787. Not until 1803 did Chief Justice John Marshall state the idea, and then it was for the political advantage of the Federalists in their battle against Jeffersonian democracy. Charles Evans Hughes later said, while governor of New York, "the Constitution is what the judges say it is."

Library of Congress

Independence National Historical Park

**(Above) Hugh Williamson, North Carolina, active in representation compromise but frequently changed his mind during debates; (below) George Clymer, Pennsylvania, served on the financial committee**

**(Above) James McHenry, Federalist from Maryland, kept private record of debate; (below) William Richardson Davie, North Carolina, swung his delegation to support Connecticut's representation compromise**

The Pennsylvania Academy of Fine Arts

University of North Carolina; photo Frick

# 1787

21.

## Abigail Adams: On Suppressing Shays's Rebellion

*The prolific correspondence of John and Abigail Adams throws light on the political and social events of eighteenth-century America. At the time of Shays's Rebellion in 1786-1787, the Adamses were residing in London. Mrs. Adams had closely followed this event, which some Americans viewed as justification for a stronger national government. Other Americans feared a military coup d'état or even a monarchy could result from such rebellious activities. On January 2, 1787, she sent the following letter, containing her impressions of the rebellion, to Thomas Jefferson, then the American minister to France.*

Source: *Jefferson Papers,* Julian P. Boyd, ed., Vol. XI, Princeton, 1955, pp. 86-87.

With regard to the tumults in my native state which you inquire about, I wish I could say that report had exaggerated them. It is too true, sir, that they have been carried to so alarming a height as to stop the courts of justice in several counties. Ignorant, restless desperadoes, without conscience or principles, have led a deluded multitude to follow their standard, under pretense of grievances which have no existence but in their imaginations. Some of them were crying out for a paper currency, some for an equal distribution of property, some were for annihilating all debts, others complaining that the Senate was a useless branch of government, that the Court of Common Pleas was unnecessary, and that the sitting of the General Court in Boston was a grievance. By this list you will see the materials which compose this rebellion, and the necessity there is of the wisest and most vigorous measures to quell and suppress it. Instead of that laudable spirit which you approve, which makes a people watchful over their liberties and alert in the defense of them, these mobbish insurgents are for sapping the foundation, and destroying the whole fabric at once.

But as these people make only a small part of the state, when compared to the more sensible and judicious, and although they create a just alarm and give much trouble and uneasiness, I cannot help flattering myself that they will prove salutary to the state at large, by leading to an investigation of the causes which have produced these commotions. Luxury and extravagance both in furniture and dress had pervaded all orders of our countrymen and women, and was hastening fast to sap their independence by involving every class of citizens in distress, and accumulating debts upon them which they were unable to discharge. Vanity was becoming a more powerful principle than patriotism. The lower order of the community were pressed for taxes, and though possessed of landed property they were unable to answer the demand, while those who possessed money were fearful of lending, lest the mad cry of the mob should force the legislature upon a measure very different from the touch of Midas.

By the papers I send you, you will see the beneficial effects already produced: an act of the legislature laying duties of 15 percent upon many articles of British manufacture and totally prohibiting others. A number of volunteers, lawyers, physicians, and merchants from Boston made up a party of light horse commanded by Colonel Hitchbourn, Lieutenant Colonel Jackson, and Higgenson, and went out in pursuit of the insurgents and were fortunate enough to take three of their principal leaders: Shattucks, Parker, and Page. Shattucks defended himself and was wounded in his knee with a broadsword. He is in jail in Boston and will no doubt be made an example of.

New York State Historical Association

Portrait of Abigail Adams by Ralph Earl, 1785

---

*What signify a few lives lost in a century or two? The tree of liberty must be refreshed from time to time with the blood of patriots and tyrants. It is its natural manure.*

THOMAS JEFFERSON, letter to W. S. Smith, Nov. 13, 1787

22.

## Thomas Jefferson: The Good Sense of the People

*Many Americans felt Shays's Rebellion threatened their lives and property and warranted efforts for a stronger central government. Jefferson believed the real issue raised by the rebellion was not whether the people should be denied the right of independent political action but whether they needed to be better informed on public affairs. A free and vital press would enable them to form opinions and act more responsibly. The following letter was written to Edward Carrington from Paris on January 16, 1787.*

Source: Ford, IV, pp. 357-361.

The tumults in America I expected would have produced in Europe an unfavorable opinion of our political state. But it has not. On the contrary, the small effect of these tumults seems to have given more confidence in the firmness of our governments. The interposition of the people themselves on the side of government has had a great effect on the opinion here. I am persuaded myself that the good sense of the people will always be found to be the best army. They may be led astray for a moment, but will soon correct themselves.

The people are the only censors of their governors; and even their errors will tend to keep these to the true principles of their institution. To punish these errors too severely would be to suppress the only safeguard of the public liberty. The way to prevent these irregular interpositions of the people is to give them full information of their affairs through the channel of the public papers, and to contrive that those papers should penetrate the whole mass of the people. The basis of our governments being the opinion of the people, the very first object should be to keep that right; and were it left to me to decide whether we should have a government without newspapers, or newspapers without a government, I should not hesitate a moment to prefer the latter. But I should mean that every man should receive those papers, and be capable of reading them.

I am convinced that those societies (as the Indians) which live without government enjoy in their general mass an infinitely greater degree of happiness than those who live under the European governments. Among the former, public opinion is in the place of law, and restrains morals as powerfully as laws ever did anywhere. Among the latter, under pretense of governing, they have divided their nations into two classes, wolves and sheep. I do not exaggerate.

This is a true picture of Europe. Cherish, therefore, the spirit of our people, and keep alive their intention. Do not be too severe upon their errors, but reclaim them by enlightening them. If once they become inattentive to the public affairs, you and I, and Congress and assemblies, judges and governors shall all become wolves. It seems to be the law of our general nature, in spite of individual exceptions; and experience declares that man is the only animal which devours his own kind; for I can apply no milder term to the governments of Europe, and to the general prey of the rich on the poor.

The want of news has led me into disquisition instead of narration, forgetting you have every day enough of that. I shall be happy to hear from you sometimes, only observing that whatever passes through the post is read, and that when you write what should be read by myself only, you must be so good as to confide your letter to some passenger or officer of the packet. I will ask your permission to write to you sometimes, and to assure you of the esteem and respect with which I have honor to be, dear sir, your most obedient and most humble servant.

23.

# Thomas Jefferson: On the Need for a Little Rebellion Now and Then

*Shays's Rebellion prompted Thomas Jefferson to say that "a little rebellion now and then is a good thing" for a country. Rather than being alarmed by the rebellion, Jefferson saw some justification in it. He believed the people had a right to express their grievances against the government, even by such violent means. Jefferson wrote the following letter from Paris to James Madison on January 30, 1787. The letter also shows Jefferson's concern over impending negotiations with Spain, to be conducted by John Jay, the minister plenipotentiary to Spain. The proposals under consideration would give commercial privileges in Spanish ports to America, and navigation rights on the Mississippi River to Spain. Jefferson feared the agreement would be interpreted as abandoning the Mississippi River to Spanish domination and might lead to war between the Western lands and Spain. Such a war would divide the nation, an eventuality Jefferson wished above all to avoid.*

Source: H. A. Washington, II, pp. 104-111.

My last to you was of the 16th of December; since which, I have received yours of November 25 and December 4, which afforded me, as your letters always do, a treat on matters public, individual, and economical. I am impatient to learn your sentiments on the late troubles in the Eastern states. So far as I have yet seen, they do not appear to threaten serious consequences. Those states have suffered by the stoppage of the channels of their commerce, which have not yet found other issues. This must render money scarce and make the people uneasy. This uneasiness has produced acts absolutely unjustifiable; but I hope they will provoke no severities from their governments. A consciousness of those in power that their administration of the public affairs has been honest may, perhaps, produce too great a degree of indignation; and those characters, wherein fear predominates over hope, may apprehend too much from these instances of irregularity. They may conclude too hastily that nature has formed man insusceptible of any other government than that of force, a conclusion not founded in truth nor experience.

Societies exist under three forms, sufficiently distinguishable: (1) without government, as among our Indians; (2) under governments, wherein the will of everyone has a just influence, as is the case in England, in a slight degree, and in our states, in a great one; (3) under governments of force, as is the case in all other monarchies, and in most of the other republics.

To have an idea of the curse of existence under these last, they must be seen. It is a government of wolves over sheep. It is a problem, not clear in my mind, that the first condition is not the best. But I believe it to be inconsistent with any great degree of population. The second state has a great deal of good in it. The mass of mankind under that enjoys a precious degree of liberty and happiness. It has its evils, too, the principal of which is the turbulence to which it is subject. But weigh this against the oppressions of monarchy, and it becomes nothing. *Malo periculosam libertatem quam quietam servitutem.* Even this evil is productive of good. It prevents the degeneracy of government and nourishes a general attention to the public affairs.

I hold it that a little rebellion now and then is a good thing, and as necessary in the political world as storms in the physical. Unsuccessful rebellions, indeed, generally establish the encroachments on the rights of the people which have produced them. An observation of this truth should render honest republican governors so mild in their punishment of rebellions as not to discourage them too much. It is a medicine necessary for the sound health of government.

If these transactions give me no uneasiness, I feel very differently at another piece of intelligence, to wit, the possibility that the navigation of the Mississippi may be abandoned to Spain. I never had any interest westward of the Allegheny; and I never will have any. But I have had great opportunities of knowing the character of the people who inhabit that country; and I will venture to say that the act which abandons the navigation of the Mississippi is an act of separation between the Eastern and Western country. It is a relinquishment of five parts out of eight of the territory of the United States; an abandonment of the fairest subject for the payment of our public debts, and the chaining those debts on our own necks, *in perpetuum.*

I have the utmost confidence in the honest intentions of those who concur in this measure; but I lament their want of acquaintance with the character and physical advantages of the people, who, right or wrong, will suppose their interests sacrificed on this occasion to the contrary interests of that part of the confederacy in possession of present power. If they declare themselves a separate people, we are incapable of a single effort to retain them. Our citizens can never be induced, either as militia or as soldiers, to go there to cut the throats of their own brothers and sons, or rather, to be themselves the subjects instead of the perpetrators of the parricide.

Nor would that country quit the cost of being retained against the will of its inhabitants, could it be done. But it cannot be done. They are able already to rescue the navigation of the Mississippi out of the hands of Spain, and to add New Orleans to their own territory. They will be joined by the inhabitants of Louisiana. This will bring on a war between them and Spain; and that will produce the question with us, whether it will not be worth our while to become parties with them in the war in order to reunite them with us and thus correct our error. And were I to permit my forebodings to go one step further, I should predict that the inhabitants of the United States would force their rulers to take the affirmative of that question. I wish I may be mistaken in all these opinions.

24.

## Benjamin Rush: The Defects of the Confederation

*The weaknesses inherent in the Articles of Confederation evoked criticism from many commentators, among them the Philadelphia physician Benjamin Rush. He called for a continuation of the principles of the American Revolution in the forthcoming federal convention. Rush advocated not just a revision of the Confederation but an entirely new constitution and system of government. His apparently extreme position received little support at the time. Many people felt secure in the knowledge that the Revolution had successfully created an independent nation. Hoping to gain the support of the citizens of Philadelphia and generate enthusiasm for the work of the coming Constitutional Convention in May 1787, Rush gave this stirring address.*

Source: Niles: "Address to the People of the United States, by Dr. Benjamin Rush, Philadelphia, 1787."

There is nothing more common than to confound the terms of American Revolution with those of the late American war. The American war is over, but this is far from being the case with American Revolution. On the contrary, nothing but the first act of the great drama is closed. It remains yet to establish and perfect our new forms of government; and to prepare the principles, morals, and manners of our citizens for these forms of government after they are established and brought to perfection.

The confederation, together with most of our state constitutions, were formed under very unfavorable circumstances. We had just emerged from a corrupted monarchy. Although we understood perfectly the principles of liberty, yet most of us were ignorant of the forms and combinations of power in republics. Add to this, the British army was in the heart of our country spreading desolation wherever it went; our resentments, of course, were awakened. We detested the British name, and unfortunately refused to copy some things in the administration of justice and power in the British government which have made it the admiration and envy of the world. In our opposition to monarchy, we forgot that the temple of tyranny has two doors. We bolted one of them by proper restraints; but we left the other open, by neglecting to guard against the effects of our own ignorance and licentiousness.

Most of the present difficulties of this country arise from the weakness and other defects of our governments.

My business at present shall be only to suggest the defects of the confederation. These consist first, in the deficiency of coercive power; second, in a defect of exclusive power to issue paper money and regulate commerce; third, in vesting the sovereign power of the United States in a single legislature; and fourth, in the too frequent rotation of its members.

A convention is to sit soon for the purpose of devising means of obviating part of the two first defects that have been mentioned. But I wish they may add to their recommendations to each state to surrender up to Congress their power of emitting money. In this way a uniform currency will be produced that will facilitate trade and help to bind the states together. Nor will the states be deprived of large sums of money by this means, when sudden emergencies require it; for they may always borrow them, as they did during the war, out of the treasury of Congress. Even a loan office may be better instituted in this way, in each state, than in any other.

The two last defects that have been mentioned are not of less magnitude than the first. Indeed, the single legislature of Congress will become more dangerous, from an increase of power, than ever. To remedy this, let the supreme federal power be divided, like the legislatures of most of our states, into two distinct, independent branches. Let one of them be styled the council of the states and the other the assembly of the states. Let the first consist of a single delegate and the second, of two, three, or four delegates, chosen annually by each state. Let the President be chosen annually by the joint ballot of both houses; and let him possess certain powers, in conjunction with a privy council, especially the power of appointing most of the officers of the United States. The officers will not only be better, when appointed this way, but one of the principal causes of faction will be thereby removed from Congress. I apprehend this division of the power of Congress will become more necessary, as soon as they are invested with more ample powers of levying and expending public money.

The custom of turning men out of power or office as soon as they are qualified for it has been found to be absurd in practice. Is it virtuous to dismiss a general, a physician, or even a domestic as soon as they have acquired knowledge sufficient to be useful to us for the sake of increasing the number of able generals, skillful physicians, and faithful servants? We do not. Government is a science, and can never be perfect in America until we encourage men to devote not only three years but their whole lives to it. I believe the principal reason why so many men of abilities object to serving in Congress is owing to their not thinking it worth while to spend three years in acquiring a profession which their country immediately afterwards forbids them to follow.

There are two errors or prejudices on the subject of government in America which lead to the most dangerous consequences.

It is often said "that the sovereign and all other power is seated in the people." This idea is unhappily expressed. It should be, "all power is derived from the people"; they possess it only on the days of their elections. After this, it is the property of their rulers; nor can they exercise or resume it unless it be abused. It is of importance to circulate this idea, as it leads to order and good government.

The people of America have mistaken the meaning of the word sovereignty; hence each state pretends to be sovereign. In Europe, it is applied only to those states which possess the power of making war and peace, of forming treaties and the like. As this power belongs only to Congress, they are the only sovereign power in the United States.

We commit a similar mistake in our ideas of the word independent. No individual state, as such, has any claim to independence. She is independent only in a union with her sister states in congress.

To conform the principles, morals, and manners of our citizens to our republican forms of government, it is absolutely necessary that knowledge of every kind should be disseminated through every part of the United States.

For this purpose, let Congress, instead of laying out $500,000 in building a federal town, appropriate only a fourth of that sum in founding a federal university. In this university let everything connected with government, such as history, the law of nature and nations, the civil law, the municipal laws of our country, and the principles of commerce, be taught by competent professors. Let masters be employed, likewise, to teach gunnery, fortification, and everything connected with defensive and offensive war.

Above all, let a professor of what is called in the European universities economy be established in this federal seminary. His business should be to unfold the principles and practice of agriculture and manufactures of all kind; and to enable him to make his lectures more extensively useful, Congress should support a traveling correspondent for him, who should visit all the nations of Europe and transmit to him, from time to time, all the discoveries and improvements that are made in agriculture and manufactures. To this seminary young men should be encouraged to repair after completing their academical studies in the colleges of their respective states. The honors and offices of the United States should, after a while, be confined to persons who had imbibed federal and republican ideas in this university.

For the purpose of diffusing knowledge, as well as extending the living principle of government to every part of the United States, every state, city, county, village, and township in the Union should be tied together by means of the post office. This is the true nonelectric wire of government. It is the only means of conveying heat and light to every individual in the federal commonwealth. "Sweden lost her liberties," says the Abbé Raynal, "because her citizens were so scattered that they had no means of acting in concert with each other." It should be a constant injunction to the postmasters to convey newspapers free of all charge for postage. They are not only the vehicles of knowledge and intelligence but the sentinels of the liberties of our country.

The conduct of some of those strangers who have visited our country since the peace and who fill the British papers with accounts of our distresses shows as great a want of good sense as it does of good nature. They see nothing but the foundations and walls of the temple of liberty; and yet they undertake to judge of the whole fabric.

Our own citizens act a still more absurd part when they cry out, after the experience of three or four years, that we are not proper materials for republican government. Remember, we assumed these forms of government in a hurry, before we were prepared for them. Let every man exert himself in promoting virtue and knowledge in our country, and we shall soon become good republicans. Look at the steps by which governments have been changed or rendered stable in Europe. Read the history of Great Britain. Her boasted government has risen out of wars and rebellions that lasted above 600 years. The United States are traveling peaceably into order and good government. They know no strife but what arises from the collision of opinions; and in three years they have advanced further in the road to stability and happiness than most of the nations in Europe have done in as many centuries.

There is but one path that can lead the United States to destruction, and that is their extent of territory. It was probably to effect this that Great Britain ceded to us so much wasteland. But even this path may be avoided. Let but one new state be exposed to sale at a time; and let the land office be shut up till every part of this new state be settled.

I am extremely sorry to find a passion for retirement so universal among the patriots and heroes of the war. They resemble skillful mariners who, after exerting themselves to preserve a ship from sinking in a storm in the middle of the ocean, drop asleep as soon as the waves subside, and leave the care of their lives and property during the remainder of the voyage to sailors without knowledge or experience. Every man in a republic is public property. His time and talents, his youth, his manhood, his old age — nay, more, his life, his all — belong to his country.

Patriots of 1774, 1775, 1776 — heroes of 1778, 1779, 1780! Come forward! Your country demands your services! Philosophers and friends to mankind, come forward! Your country demands your studies and speculations! Lovers of peace and order who declined taking part in the late war, come forward! Your country forgives your timidity and demands your influence and advice! Hear her proclaiming, in sighs and groans, in her governments, in her finances, in her trade, in her manufactures, in her morals, and in her manners, "The Revolution is not over!"

25.

# James Madison: On the Balance of National and Local Authority

*One of the men who would be heading for Philadelphia for the Convention of 1787 was James Madison. This man, who has come to be called the Father of the Constitution, was much concerned with what the assembly would try to do. Would it attempt to revamp the Articles of Confederation to make them workable, or would an entirely new constitution be the product of debate? In the following letter to Edmund Randolph, written April 8, 1787, Madison explained his views on the problems that confronted the nation and suggested the kind of government that he felt the United States needed. Many of these ideas were eventually incorporated into the Virginia Plan, presented to the Convention in its first month.*

Source: *The Writings of James Madison,* Gaillard Hunt, ed., Vol. II, New York, 1901.

I am glad to find that you are turning your thoughts toward the business of May next. My despair of your finding the necessary leisure, as signified in one of your letters, with the probability that some leading propositions at least would be expected from Virginia, had engaged me in a closer attention to the subject than I should otherwise have given. I will just hint the ideas that have occurred, leaving explanations for our interview.

I think with you that it will be well to retain as much as possible of the old Confederation, though I doubt whether it may not be best to work the valuable Articles into the new system, instead of engrafting the latter on the former. I am also perfectly of your opinion that, in framing a system, no material sacrifices ought to be made to local or temporary prejudices. An explanatory address must of necessity accompany the result of the Convention on the main object. I am not sure that it will be practicable to present the several parts of the reform in so detached a manner to the states as that a partial adoption will be binding. Particular states may view different Articles as conditions of each other, and would only ratify them as such. Others might ratify them as independent propositions. The consequence would be that the ratifications of both would go for nothing. I have not, however, examined this point thoroughly. In truth, my ideas of a reform strike so deeply at the old Confederation, and lead to such a systematic change, that they scarcely admit of the expedient.

I hold it for a fundamental point that an individual independence of the states is utterly irreconcilable with the idea of an aggregate sovereignty. I think, at the same time, that a consolidation of the states into one simple republic is not less unattainable than it would be inexpedient. Let it be tried, then, whether any middle ground can be taken which will at once support a due supremacy of the national authority, and leave in force the local authorities so far as they can be subordinately useful.

The first step to be taken is, I think, a change in the principle of representation. According to the present form of the Union, an equality of suffrage, if not just toward the larger members of it, is at least safe to them, as the liberty they exercise of rejecting or executing the acts of Congress is uncontrollable by the nominal sovereignty of Congress. Under a system which would operate without the intervention of the states, the case would be materially altered. A vote from Delaware would have the same effect as one from Massachusetts or Virginia.

Let the national government be armed with a positive and complete authority in all cases where uniform measures are necessary, as in trade, etc. Let it also retain the powers which it now possesses.

Let it have a negative, in all cases whatsoever, on the legislative acts of the states, as the King of Great Britain heretofore had. This I conceive to be essential and the least possible abridgment of the state sovereignties. Without such a defensive power, every positive power that can be given on paper will be unavailing. It will also give internal stability to the states. There has been no moment since the peace at which the federal assent would have been given to paper money, etc.

Let this national supremacy be extended also to the judiciary department. If the judges in the last resort depend on the states, and are bound by their oaths to them and not to the Union, the intention of the law and the interests of the nation may be defeated by the obsequiousness of the tribunals to the policy or prejudices of the states. It seems at least essential that an appeal should lie to some national tribunals in all cases which concern foreigners or inhabitants of other states. The admiralty jurisdiction may be fully submitted to the national government.

A government formed of such extensive powers ought to be well organized. The legislative department may be divided into two branches — one of them to be chosen every — — years by the legislatures or the people at large; the other to consist of a more select number, holding their appointments for a longer term and going out in rotation. Perhaps the negative on the state laws may be most conveniently lodged in this branch. A council of revision may be superadded, including the great ministerial officers.

A national executive will also be necessary. I have scarcely ventured to form my own opinion yet, either of the manner in which it ought to be constituted or of the authorities with which it ought to be clothed.

An article ought to be inserted expressly guaranteeing the tranquillity of the states against internal as well as external dangers.

To give the new system its proper energy, it will be desirable to have it ratified by the authority of the people and not merely by that of the legislatures.

I am afraid you will think this project, if not extravagant, absolutely unattainable and unworthy of being attempted. Conceiving it myself to go no further than is essential, the objections drawn from this source are to be laid aside. I flatter myself, however, that they may be less formidable on trial than in contemplation. The change in the principle of representation will be relished by a majority of the states, and those too of most influence. The Northern states will be reconciled to it by the actual superiority of their populousness; the Southern by their expected superiority on this point. This principle established, the repugnance of the large states to part with power will in a great degree subside, and the smaller states must ultimately yield to the predominant will. It is also already seen by many, and must by degrees be seen by all, that unless the Union be organized efficiently on republican principles, innovations of a much more objectionable form may be obtruded, or, in the most favorable event, the partition of the empire into rival and hostile confederacies will ensue.

26.

## Joel Barlow: The Unfinished Revolution

*Despite his conservative upbringing, Joel Barlow, statesman and poet, became one of the most liberal thinkers of his time. On the eleventh anniversary of the Declaration of Independence, he addressed the Society of the Cincinnati at Hartford, Connecticut. He eulogized the goals of the Revolution but warned that "the Revolution is but half completed." With independence won, the next great challenge was to constitute an effective government.*

Source: Niles: "An Oration Delivered by Mr. Joel Barlow, at Hartford, Conn., to the Society of the Cincinnati, July 4, 1787."

On the anniversary of so great an event as the birth of the empire in which we live, none will question the propriety of passing a few moments in contemplating the various objects suggested to the mind by the important occasion. But at the present period, while the blessings claimed by the sword of victory and promised in the voice of peace remain to be confirmed by our future exertions — while the nourishment, the growth, and even the existence of our empire depend upon the united efforts of an extensive and divided people — the duties of this day ascend from amusement and congratulation to a serious patriotic employment.

We are assembled, my friends, not to boast but to realize — not to inflate our national vanity by a pompous relation of past achievements in the council or in the field but, from a modest retrospect of the truly dignified part already acted by our countrymen, from an accurate view of our present situation, and from an anticipation of the scenes that remain to be unfolded, to discern and familiarize the duties that still await us, as citizens, as soldiers, and as men. . . .

It would be wandering from the objects which ought to occupy our present attention again to recount the numerous acts of the British Parliament which composed that system of tyranny designed for the subjugation of America. Neither can we indulge in the detail of those memorable events which marked our various stages of resistance, from the glooms of unsuccessful supplication to the splendor of victory and acknowledged sovereignty. The former were the theme of senatorial eloquence, producing miracles of union and exertion in every part of the continent, till we find them preserved for everlasting remembrance in that declaratory act of independence which gave being to an empire and dignified the day we now commemorate. The latter are fresh in the memory of every person of the least information. It would be impertinence, if not a breach of delicacy, to attempt a recital of those glorious achievements, especially before an audience, part of whom have been distinguished actors in the scene, others the anxious and applauding spectators. To the faithful historian we resign the task — the historian, whom it is hoped the present age will deem it their duty as well as their interest to furnish, encourage, and support.

Whatever praise is due for the task already performed, it is certain that much remains to be done. The Revolution is but half completed. Independence and government were the two objects contended for, and but one is yet obtained. To the glory of the present age and the admiration of the future, our severance from the British Empire was conducted upon principles as noble as they were new and unprecedented in the history of human actions. Could the same generous principles, the same wisdom and unanimity be exerted in effecting the establishment of a permanent federal system, what an additional luster would it pour upon the present age! A luster hitherto unequaled; a display of magnanimity for which mankind may never behold another opportunity.

Without an efficient government, our independence will cease to be a blessing. Shall that glow of patriotism and unshaken perseverance which has been so long conspicuous in the American character desert us at our utmost need? Shall we lose sight of our own happiness because it has grown familiar by a near approach? Shall thy labors, O Washington, have been bestowed in vain? Hast thou conducted us to independence and peace, and shall we not receive the blessings at thy hands? Where are the shades of our fallen friends? and what is their language on this occasion? Warren, Montgomery, Mercer, Wooster, Scammel, and Laurens, all ye hosts of departed heroes! rich is the treasure you have lavished in the cause, and prevalent the price you have paid for our freedom. Shall the purchase be neglected? the fair inheritance lie without improvement, exposed to every daring invader? Forbid it, honor; forbid it, gratitude; and oh, may heaven avert the impending evil.

In contemplating the price of our independence, it will never be forgotten that it was not entirely the work of our own hands; nor could it probably have been established, in the same term of time, by all the blood and treasure that America, unassisted, was able to furnish for the contest. Much of the merit is due, and our warmest acknowledgments shall ever flow to that illustrious monarch, the father of nations and friend of the distressed — the monarch who, by his early assistance, taught us not to despair; and who, when we had given a sufficient proof of our military virtue and perseverance, joined us in alliance, upon terms of equality; gave us a rank and credit among the maritime nations of Europe; and furnished fleets and armies, money and military stores, to put a splendid period to the important conflict. . . .

Unite in a permanent federal government; put your commerce upon a respectable footing; your arts and manufactures, your population, your wealth and glory will increase; and when a hundred millions of people are comprised within your territory,

New York Historical Society

Engraving of Joel Barlow by A. B. Durand after portrait by Robert Fulton

and made happy by your sway, then shall it be known that the hand of that monarch assisted in planting the vine from which so great a harvest is produced. . . .

Here shall that pride of the military character, the gallant Fayette, find his compensation for a life of disinterested service; whose toils have not ceased with the termination of the war; and whose successful endeavors to promote our interest in commercial and political arrangements can only be equaled by his achievements in the field. How will the posterity of that nobleman, and that of the other brave officers of his nation who have fought by your sides, on reviewing the American history, rejoice in the fame of their fathers; nor even regret the fate of those who bled in so glorious a field! . . .

The present is justly considered an alarming crisis, perhaps the most alarming that America ever saw. We have contended with the most powerful nation, and subdued the bravest and best appointed armies; but now we have to contend with ourselves, and encounter passions and prejudices more powerful than armies, and more dangerous to our peace. It is not for glory, it is for existence that we contend.

Much is expected from the Federal Convention now sitting at Philadelphia, and it is a happy circumstance that so general a confidence from all parts of the country is centered in that respectable body. Their former services, as individuals, command it, and our situation requires it. But although much is expected from them, yet more is demanded from ourselves.

The first great object is to convince the people of the importance of their present situation; for the majority of a great people, on a subject which they understand, will never act wrong. If ever there was a time in any age or nation when the fate of millions depended on the voice of one, it is the present period in these states. Every free citizen of the American empire ought now to consider himself as the legislator of half mankind. When he views the amazing extent of territory, settled and to be settled under the operation of his laws; when, like a wise politician, he contemplates the population of future ages, the changes to be wrought by the possible progress of arts in agriculture, commerce, and manufactures, the increasing connection and intercourse of nations, and the effect of one rational political system upon the general happiness of mankind — his mind, dilated with the great idea, will realize a liberality of feeling which leads to a rectitude of conduct. He will see that the system to be established by his suffrage is calculated for the great benevolent purposes of extending peace, happiness, and progressive improvement to a large proportion of his fellow creatures. As there is a probability that the system to be proposed by the Convention may answer this description, there is some reason to hope it will be viewed by the people with that candor and dispassionate respect which is due to the importance of the subject. . . .

Those who are possessed of abilities or information in any degree above the common rank of their fellow citizens are called upon by every principle of humanity to diffuse a spirit of candor and rational inquiry upon these important subjects.

Adams, to his immortal honor and the timely assistance of his country, has set the great example. His treatise in defense of the constitutions, though confined to the state republics, is calculated to do infinite service by correcting thousands of erroneous sentiments arising from our inexperience; sentiments which, if uncorrected in this early stage of our political existence, will be the source of calamities without measure and without end. Should that venerable philosopher and statesman be induced to continue his inquiries, by tracing the history of confederacies, and, with his usual energy and perspicuity, delineate and defend a system adapted to the circumstances of the United States — I will not say he could deserve more from his distressed country, but he would crown a life of patriotic labors and render an essential additional service to the world.

While America enjoys the peculiar felicity of seeing those who have conducted her councils and her battles, retire, like Cincinnatus, to the humble labors of the plow, it must be remembered that she there expects a continuance of their patriotic exertions. The Society of the Cincinnati, established upon the most benevolent principles, will never lose sight of their duty, in rendering every possible aid, as citizens, to that community which they have defended as soldiers. . . .

The present is an age of philosophy, and America the empire of reason. Here neither the pageantry of courts nor the glooms of superstition have dazzled or beclouded the mind. Our duty calls us to act worthy of the age and the country that gave us birth. Though inexperience may have betrayed us into errors, yet they have not been fatal; and our own discernment will point us to their proper remedy.

However defective the present confederated system may appear, yet a due consideration of the circumstances under which it was framed will teach us rather to admire its wisdom than to murmur at its faults. The same political abilities which were displayed in that institution, united with the experience we have had of its operation, will doubtless produce a system which will stand the test of ages in forming a powerful and happy people.

Elevated with the extensive prospect, we may consider present inconveniences as unworthy of regret. At the close of the war, an uncommon plenty of circulating specie and a universal passion for trade tempted many individuals to involve themselves in ruin and injure the credit of their country. But these are evils which work their own remedy. The paroxysm is already over. Industry is increasing faster than ever it declined; and, with some exceptions, where legislative authority has sanctioned fraud, the people are honestly discharging their private debts and increasing the resources of their wealth.

Every possible encouragement for great and generous exertions is now presented before us. Under the idea of a permanent and happy government, every point of view in which the future situation of America can be placed fills the mind with peculiar dignity and opens an unbounded field of thought. The natural resources of the country are inconceivably various and great. The enterprising genius of the people promises a most rapid improvement in all the arts that embellish human nature. The blessings of a rational government will invite emigrations from the rest of the world and fill the empire with the worthiest and happiest of mankind; while the example of political wisdom and felicity, here to be displayed, will excite emulation through the kingdoms of the earth and meliorate the condition of the human race.

27.

## THOMAS JEFFERSON: On the Necessity for a Separate Executive

*As Minister to France, Jefferson remained in Paris while the great debate was waged in Philadelphia over what kind of government America should have. Yet his interest was such that he wrote incessantly to American leaders advocating his own views. In the following letter of August 4, 1787, to Colonel Edward Carrington, a member of Congress, Jefferson emphasized the need for an executive authority in the government to cope with the administrative details that a Congress by virtue of its size could not handle.*

Source: H. A. Washington, II, pp. 217-218.

I AM HAPPY TO FIND that the states have come so generally into the schemes of the federal Convention, from which, I am sure, we shall see wise propositions. I confess I do not go as far in the reforms thought necessary as some of my correspondents in America; but if the Convention should adopt such propositions, I shall suppose them necessary. My general plan would be to make the states one as to everything connected with foreign nations, and several as to everything purely domestic.

But with all the imperfections of our present government, it is without comparison the best existing, or that ever did exist. Its greatest defect is the imperfect manner in which matters of commerce have been provided for. It has been so often said as to be generally believed that Congress have no power by the Confederation to enforce anything; for example, contributions of money. It was not necessary to give them that power expressly; they have it by the law of nature. When two parties make a compact, there results to each a power of compelling the other to execute it. Compulsion was never so easy as in our case, where a single frigate would soon levy on the commerce of any state the deficiency of its contributions; nor more safe than in the hands of Congress, which has always shown that it would wait, as it ought to do, to the last extremities, before it would execute any of its powers which are disagreeable. I think it very material to separate, in the hands of Congress, the executive and legislative powers, as the judiciary already are in some degree. This, I hope, will be done. The want of it has been the source of more evil than we have experienced from any other cause. Nothing is so embarrassing nor so mischievous, in a great assembly, as the details of execution. The smallest trifle of that kind occupies as long as the most important act of legislation and takes place of everything else.

Let any man recollect, or look over, the files of Congress; he will observe the most important propositions hanging over, from week to week and month to month, till the occasions have passed them, and the things never done. I have ever viewed the executive details as the greatest cause of evil to us, because they in fact place us as if we had no federal head, by diverting the attention of that head from great to small objects. And should this division of power not be recommended by the Convention, it is my opinion Congress should make it itself, by establishing an executive committee.

28.

## James Madison: The Federal Convention of 1787

*In* The Supreme Court and the Constitution, *Charles A. Beard remarks of the federal convention of 1787 that "never in the history of assemblies has there been a convention of men richer in political experience and in practical knowledge, or endowed with a profounder insight into the springs of human action and the intimate essence of government." This opinion was shared by many of the members themselves, which may have prompted Franklin's quip to his fellow delegates: "I cannot help expressing a wish that every member . . . doubt a little of his own infallibility"; but it was also shared by noted contemporaries who were not members of the convention, among them Jefferson, who called the convention "an assembly of demi-gods." It is true enough that, with few exceptions, nearly every American who was well versed in political science was present in Philadelphia from May through September 1787. (Among the exceptions, besides Jefferson, were John Adams and John Jay.) The delegates were men who had been active in every phase of American political, social, and economic life during and since the Revolution. Now they were assembled to terminate what Joel Barlow had called the "unfinished revolution," and to create an adequate instrument of government for a new and growing nation. Their greatest task was to harmonize through judicious compromise their widely divergent views and to design a workable, not an ideal, constitution. The divergence of views resulted not only from differing political theories but also from sectional loyalty, unequal financial status and social position, vested interest, and numerous other motives. Once it had been decided that a mere revision of the Articles of Confederation would not be adequate to the needs of the nation, the real work of the convention began, continuing through the hot summer until September 17, by which time a constitution had been drafted that thirty-nine of the fifty-five were willing to sign. During these months several delegates left the convention, owing to their complete opposition to what was going on. Other recalcitrants stayed on, in the hope of obtaining a document more to their liking. The majority continued to work together to produce the constitution that was presented to the states for their approval. The proceedings were secret and no official report was made. But James Madison acted as secretary and kept notes that enable modern readers to glimpse the drama that unfolded behind closed doors. His record, unpublished until 1840, is the most complete account of the convention; portions are reprinted below.*

Source: *Documents Illustrative of the Formation of the Union of the American States,* Charles C. Tansill, ed., Washington, 1927.

### THE VIRGINIA (RANDOLPH) PLAN: MAY 29

1. *Resolved,* that the Articles of Confederation ought to be so corrected and enlarged as to accomplish the objects proposed by their institution; namely, "common defense, security of liberty, and general welfare."

2. *Resolved,* therefore, that the rights of

suffrage in the national legislature ought to be proportioned to the quotas of contribution or to the number of free inhabitants, as the one or the other rule may seem best in different cases.

3. *Resolved,* that the national legislature ought to consist of two branches.

4. *Resolved,* that the members of the first branch of the national legislature ought to be elected by the people of the several states every ——— for the term of ———; to be of the age of ——— years at least; to receive liberal stipends by which they may be compensated for the devotion of their time to public service; to be ineligible to any office established by a particular state, or under the authority of the United States, except those peculiarly belonging to the functions of the first branch, during the term of service and for the space of ——— after its expiration; to be incapable of reelection for the space of ——— after the expiration of their term of service, and to be subject to recall.

5. *Resolved,* that the members of the second branch of the national legislature ought to be elected by those of the first, out of a proper number of persons nominated by the individual legislatures, to be of the age of ——— years at least; to hold their offices for a term sufficient to insure their independency; to receive liberal stipends, by which they may be compensated for the devotion of their time to public service; and to be ineligible to any office established by a particular state, or under the authority of the United States, except those peculiarly belonging to the functions of the second branch, during the term of service and for the space of ——— after the expiration thereof.

6. *Resolved,* that each branch ought to possess the right of originating acts; that the national legislature ought to be empowered to enjoy the legislative rights vested in Congress by the Confederation and moreover to legislate in all cases to which the separate states are incompetent, or in which the harmony of the United States may be interrupted by the exercise of individual legislation; to negative all laws passed by the several states contravening, in the opinion of the national legislature, the Articles of Union; and to call forth the force of the Union against any member of the Union failing to fulfill its duty under the articles thereof.

7. *Resolved,* that a national executive be instituted; to be chosen by the national legislature for the term of ——— years, to receive punctually at stated times a fixed compensation for the services rendered, in which no increase or diminution shall be made so as to affect the magistracy existing at the time of increase or diminution, and to be ineligible a second time; and that, besides a general authority to execute the national laws, it ought to enjoy the executive rights vested in Congress by the Confederation.

8. *Resolved,* that the executive and a convenient number of the national judiciary ought to compose a council of revision with authority to examine every act of the national legislature before it shall operate, and every act of a particular legislature before a negative thereon shall be final; and that the dissent of the said council shall amount to a rejection, unless the act of the national legislature be again passed or that of a particular legislature be again negatived by ——— of the members of each branch.

9. *Resolved,* that a national judiciary be established to consist of one or more supreme tribunals, and of inferior tribunals to be chosen by the national legislature, to hold their offices during good behavior; and to receive punctually, at stated times, fixed compensation for their services, in which no increase or diminution shall be made so as to affect the persons actually in office at the time of such increase or diminution. That the jurisdiction of the inferior tribunals shall be to hear and determine in the first instance, and of the supreme tribunal to hear and determine in the *dernier* [last] resort, all piracies and felonies on the high seas, cap-

tures from an enemy; cases in which foreigners or citizens of other states applying to such jurisdictions may be interested, or which respect the collection of the national revenue; impeachments of any national officers, and questions which may involve the national peace and harmony.

10. *Resolved,* that provision ought to be made for the admission of states lawfully arising within the limits of the United States, whether from a voluntary junction of government and territory or otherwise, with the consent of a number of voices in the national legislature less than the whole.

11. *Resolved,* that a republican government and the territory of each state, except in the instance of a voluntary junction of government and territory, ought to be guaranteed by the United States to each state.

12. *Resolved,* that provision ought to be made for the continuance of Congress and their authorities and privileges until a given day after the reform of the Articles of Union shall be adopted, and for the completion of all their engagements.

13. *Resolved,* that provision ought to be made for the amendment of the Articles of Union whensoever it shall seem necessary and that the assent of the national legislature ought not to be required thereto.

14. *Resolved,* that the legislative, executive, and judiciary powers within the several states ought to be bound by oath to support the Articles of Union.

15. *Resolved,* that the amendments which shall be offered to the Confederation by the Convention ought, at a proper time or times, after the approbation of Congress, to be submitted to an assembly or assemblies of representatives recommended by the several legislatures to be expressly chosen by the people to consider and decide thereon.

## DEBATE OF JUNE 6

MR. PINCKNEY [S.C.], according to previous notice and rule obtained, moved "that the first branch of the national legislature be elected by the state legislatures, and not by the people," contending that the people were less fit judges in such a case, and that the legislatures would be less likely to promote the adoption of the new government if they were to be excluded from all share in it.

MR. RUTLEDGE [S.C.] seconded the motion.

MR. GERRY [Mass.]: Much depends on the mode of election. In England the people will probably lose their liberty from the smallness of the proportion having a right of suffrage. Our danger arises from the opposite extreme; hence in Massachusetts the worst men get into the legislature. Several members of that body had lately been convicted of infamous crimes. Men of indigence, ignorance, and baseness spare no pains, however dirty, to carry their point against men who are superior to the artifices practised. He was not disposed to run into extremes. He was as much principled as ever against aristocracy and monarchy. It was necessary, on the one hand, that the people should appoint one branch of the government in order to inspire them with the necessary confidence. But he wished the election, on the other, to be so modified as to secure more effectually a just preference of merit. His idea was that the people should nominate certain persons in certain districts, out of whom the state legislatures should make the appointment.

MR. WILSON [Pa.]: He wished for vigor in the government, but he wished that vigorous authority to flow immediately from the legitimate source of all authority. The government ought to possess not only, first, the *force* but, second, the *mind or sense* of the people at large. The legislature ought to be the most exact transcript of the whole society. Representation is made necessary only because it is impossible for the people to act collectively. The opposition was to be expected, he said, from the *governments,* not from the citizens of the states. The latter had parted, as was observed (by Mr.

King), with all the necessary powers; and it was immaterial to them by whom they were exercised, if well exercised. The state officers were to be the losers of power. The people, he supposed, would be rather more attached to the national government than to the state governments as being more important in itself and more flattering to their pride. There is no danger of improper elections if made by *large* districts. Bad elections proceed from the smallness of the districts which give an opportunity to bad men to intrigue themselves into office.

Mr. Sherman [Conn.]: If it were in view to abolish the state governments, the elections ought to be by the people. If the state governments are to be continued, it is necessary, in order to preserve harmony between the national and state governments, that the elections to the former should be made by the latter. The right of participating in the national government would be sufficiently secured to the people by their election of the state legislatures. The objects of the Union, he thought, were few: (1) defense against foreign danger; (2) against internal disputes and a resort to force; (3) treaties with foreign nations; (4) regulating foreign commerce and drawing revenue from it. These, and perhaps a few lesser objects, alone rendered a confederation of the states necessary. All other matters, civil and criminal, would be much better in the hands of the states. The people are more happy in small than large states. States may indeed be too small, as Rhode Island, and thereby be too subject to faction. Some others were perhaps too large, the powers of government not being able to pervade them. He was for giving the general government power to legislate and execute within a defined province.

Colonel Mason [Va.]: Under the existing Confederacy, Congress represent the *states,* not the *people* of the states; their acts operate on the *states,* not on the individuals. The case will be changed in the new plan of government. The people will be represented; they ought therefore to choose the representatives. The requisites in actual representation are that the representatives should sympathize with their constituents, should think as they think and feel as they feel, and that, for these purposes, [they] should even be residents among them. Much, he said, had been alleged against democratic elections. He admitted that much might be said; but it was to be considered that no government was free from imperfections and evils and that improper elections, in many instances, were inseparable from republican governments. But compare these with the advantage of this form in favor of the rights of the people, in favor of human nature. He was persuaded there was a better chance for proper elections by the people, if divided into large districts, than by the state legislatures. Paper money had been issued by the latter when the former were against it. Was it to be supposed that the state legislatures then would not send to the national legislature patrons of such projects if the choice depended on them?

Mr. Madison [Va.] considered an election of one branch, at least, of the legislature by the people immediately as a clear principle of free government, and that this mode, under proper regulations, had the additional advantage of securing better representatives as well as of avoiding too great an agency of the state governments in the general one. He differed from the member from Connecticut (Mr. Sherman) in thinking the objects mentioned to be all the principal ones that required a national government. Those were certainly important and necessary objects; but he combined with them the necessity of providing more effectually for the security of private rights and the steady dispensation of justice.

Interferences with these were evils which had more, perhaps, than anything else produced this Convention. Was it to be supposed that republican liberty could long exist under the abuses of it practised in some of the states? The gentleman (Mr. Sherman) had admitted that, in a very small state, faction and oppression would prevail. It was to be inferred then that, wherever these prevailed, the state was too small. Had they not prevailed in the largest as well as the smallest — though less than in the smallest; and were we not thence admonished to enlarge the sphere as far as the nature of the government would admit? This was the only defense against the inconveniencies of democracy consistent with the democratic form of government.

All civilized societies would be divided into different sects, factions, and interests, as they happened to consist of rich and poor, debtors and creditors, the landed, the manufacturing, the commercial interests, the inhabitants of this district or that district, the followers of this political leader or that political leader, the disciples of this religious sect or that religious sect. In all cases where a majority are united by a common interest or passion, the rights of the minority are in danger. What motives are to restrain them? A prudent regard to the maxim that honesty is the best policy is found by experience to be as little regarded by bodies of men as by individuals. Respect for character is always diminished in proportion to the number among whom the blame or praise is to be divided.

Conscience, the only remaining tie, is known to be inadequate in individuals; in large numbers, little is to be expected from it. Besides, religion itself may become a motive to persecution and oppression. These observations are verified by the histories of every country, ancient and modern. . . . Why was America so justly apprehensive of parliamentary injustice? Because Great Britain had a separate interest, real or supposed, and, if her authority had been admitted, could have pursued that interest at our expense.

We have seen the mere distinction of color made, in the most enlightened period of time, a ground of the most oppressive dominion ever exercised by man over man. What has been the source of those unjust laws complained of among ourselves? Has it not been the real or supposed interest of the major number? Debtors have defrauded their creditors. The landed interest has borne hard on the mercantile interest. The holders of one species of property have thrown a disproportion of taxes on the holders of another species.

The lesson we are to draw from the whole is that where a majority are united by a common sentiment, and have an opportunity, the rights of the minor party become insecure. In a republican government the majority, if united, have always an opportunity. The only remedy is to enlarge the sphere and thereby divide the community into so great a number of interests and parties that, in the first place, a majority will not be likely at the same moment to have a common interest separate from that of the whole or of the minority; and, in the second place, that, in case they should have such an interest, they may not be apt to unite in the pursuit of it. It was incumbent on us then to try this remedy, and with that view to frame a republican system on such a scale and in such a form as will control all the evils which have been experienced.

Mr. Dickinson [Del.] considered it as essential that one branch of the legislature should be drawn immediately from the people and as expedient that the other should be chosen by the legislatures of the states. This combination of the state governments with the national government was as politic as it was unavoidable. In the formation of the Senate, we ought to carry it through such a refining process as will assimilate it as near as may be to the House of Lords in England. He repeated his warm eulogiums on the British constitution. He was for a strong national government but for leaving the states a considerable agency in the system. The objection against making the former dependent on the latter might be obviated by giving to the Senate an authority permanent and irrevocable for three, five, or seven years. Being thus independent, they will speak and decide with becoming freedom.

Mr. Read [Del.]: Too much attachment is betrayed to the state governments. We must look beyond their continuance. A national government must soon of necessity swallow all of them up. They will soon be reduced to the mere office of electing the national Senate. He was against patching up the old federal system; he hoped the idea would be dismissed. It would be like putting new cloth on an old garment. The Confederation was founded on temporary principles. It cannot last; it cannot be amended. If we do not establish a good government on new principles, we must either go to ruin or have the work to do over again. The people at large are wrongly suspected of being averse to a general government. The aversion lies among interested men who possess their confidence.

Mr. Pierce [Ga.] was for an election by the people as to the first branch and by the states as to the second branch, by which means the citizens of the states would be represented both *individually* and *collectively*.

General Pinckney wished to have a good national government and at the same time to leave a considerable share of power in the states. An election of either branch by the people, scattered as they are in many states, particularly in South Carolina, was totally impracticable. He differed from gentlemen who thought that a choice by the people would be a better guard against bad measures than by the legislatures. A majority of the people in South Carolina were notoriously for paper money as a legal tender; the legislature had refused to make it a legal tender. The reason was that the latter had some sense of character and were restrained by that consideration. The state legislatures also, he said, would be more jealous and more ready to thwart the national government if excluded from a participation in it. The idea of abolishing these legislatures would never go down.

Mr. Wilson would not have spoken again but for what had fallen from Mr. Read; namely, that the idea of preserving the state governments ought to be abandoned. He saw no incompatibility between the national and state governments, provided the latter were restrained to certain local purposes; nor any probability of their being devoured by the former. In all confederated systems, ancient and modern, the reverse had happened; the generality being destroyed gradually by the usurpations of the parts composing it.

On the question for electing the first branch by the state legislatures as moved by Mr. Pinckney, it was negatived.

## THE NEW JERSEY (PATERSON) PLAN: JUNE 15

1. *Resolved*, that the Articles of Confederation ought to be so revised, corrected, and enlarged as to render the federal constitution adequate to the exigencies of government and the preservation of the Union.

2. *Resolved*, that in addition to the powers vested in the United States in Congress by the present existing Articles of Confederation, they be authorized to pass acts for raising a revenue, by levying a duty or duties on all goods or merchandises of foreign growth or manufacture, imported into any part of the United States, by stamps on paper, vellum, or parchment, and by a postage on all letters or packages passing through the general post office, to be applied to such federal purposes as they shall deem proper and expedient; to make rules and regulations for the collection thereof, and

the same, from time to time, to alter and amend in such manner as they shall think proper; to pass acts for the regulation of trade and commerce as well with foreign nations as with each other, provided that all punishments, fines, forfeitures, and penalties to be incurred for contravening such acts, rules, and regulations shall be adjudged by the common-law judiciaries of the state in which any offense contrary to the true intent and meaning of such acts, rules, and regulations shall have been committed or perpetrated, with liberty of commencing in the first instance all suits and prosecutions for that purpose in the superior common-law judiciary in such state, subject nevertheless, for the correction of all errors, both in law and fact, in rendering judgment, to an appeal to the judiciary of the United States.

3. *Resolved,* that whenever requisitions shall be necessary, instead of the rule for making requisitions mentioned in the Articles of Confederation, the United States in Congress be authorized to make such requisitions in proportion to the whole number of white and other free citizens and inhabitants of every age, sex, and condition, including those bound to servitude for a term of years and three-fifths of all other persons not comprehended in the foregoing description, except Indians not paying taxes; that if such requisitions be not complied with, in the time specified therein, to direct the collection thereof in the noncomplying states and for that purpose to devise and pass acts directing and authorizing the same; provided that none of the powers hereby vested in the United States in Congress shall be exercised without the consent of at least ——— states, and in that proportion if the number of confederated states should hereafter be increased or diminished.

4. *Resolved,* that the United States in Congress be authorized to elect a federal executive to consist of ——— persons, to continue in office for the term of ——— years, to receive punctually, at stated times, a fixed compensation for their services, in which no increase or diminution shall be made so as to affect the persons composing the executive at the time of such increase or diminution, to be paid out of the federal Treasury; to be incapable of holding any other office or appointment during their time of service and for ——— years thereafter; to be ineligible a second time, and removable by Congress on application by a majority of the executives of the several states, that the executives, besides their general authority to execute the federal acts, ought to appoint all federal officers not otherwise provided for and to direct all military operations, provided that none of the persons composing the federal executive shall on any occasion take command of any troops so as personally to conduct any enterprise as general or in other capacity.

5. *Resolved,* that a federal judiciary be established to consist of a supreme tribunal, the judges of which to be appointed by the executive and to hold their offices during good behavior, to receive punctually, at stated times, a fixed compensation for their services, in which no increase or diminution shall be made so as to affect the persons actually in office at the time of such increase or diminution; that the judiciary so established shall have authority to hear and determine in the first instance on all impeachments of federal officers, and by way of appeal in the *dernier* resort in all cases touching the rights of ambassadors, in all cases of captures from an enemy, in all cases of piracies and felonies on the high seas, in all cases in which foreigners may be interested, in the construction of any treaty or treaties, or which may arise on any of the acts for regulation of trade or the collection of the federal revenue. That none of the judiciary shall during the time they remain in office be capable of receiving or holding any other office or appointment during their time of service or for ——— thereafter.

6. *Resolved,* that all acts of the United

States in Congress made by virtue and in pursuance of the powers hereby and by the Articles of Confederation vested in them, and all treaties made and ratified under the authority of the United States, shall be the supreme law of the respective states so far forth as those acts or treaties shall relate to the said states or their citizens, and that the judiciary of the several states shall be bound thereby in their decisions, anything in the respective laws of the individual states to the contrary notwithstanding; and that if any state, or any body of men in any state, shall oppose or prevent the carrying into execution such acts or treaties, the federal executive shall be authorized to call forth the power of the confederated states, or so much thereof as may be necessary to enforce and compel an obedience to such acts or an observance of such treaties.

7. *Resolved,* that provision be made for the admission of new states into the Union.

8. *Resolved,* that the rule for naturalization ought to be the same in every state.

9. *Resolved,* that a citizen of one state committing an offense in another state of the Union shall be deemed guilty of the same offense as if it had been committed by a citizen of the state in which the offense was committed.

## DEBATES ON THE VIRGINIA AND NEW JERSEY PLANS; HAMILTON'S PLAN: JUNE 16, 18, 19

*June 16.* MR. LANSING [N.Y.] called for the reading of the first resolution of each plan which he considered as involving principles directly in contrast. That of Mr. Paterson says he sustains the sovereignty of the respective states; that of Mr. Randolph destroys it. The latter requires a negative on all the laws of the particular states; the former, only certain general powers for the general good. The plan of Mr. Randolph, in short, absorbs all power except what may be exercised in the little local matters of the states which are not objects worthy of the supreme cognizance. He grounded his preference of Mr. Paterson's plan chiefly on two objections against that of Mr. Randolph's: (1) want of power in the Convention to discuss and propose it; (2) the improbability of its being adopted.

1. He was decidedly of opinion that the power of the Convention was restrained to amendments of a federal nature and having for their basis the Confederacy in being. The act of Congress, the tenor of the acts of the states, the commissions produced by the several deputations all proved this. And this limitation of the power to an amendment of the Confederacy marked the opinion of the states that it was unnecessary and improper to farther. He was sure that this was the case with his state. New York would never have concurred in sending deputies to the Convention if she had supposed the deliberations were to turn on a consolidation of the states and a national government.

2. Was it probable that the states would adopt and ratify a scheme which they had never authorized us to propose and which so far exceeded what they regarded as sufficient? We see by their several acts, particularly in relation to the plan of revenue proposed by Congress in 1783, not authorized by the Articles of Confederation, what were the ideas they then entertained. Can so great a change be supposed to have already taken place? To rely on any change which is hereafter to take place in the sentiments of the people would be trusting to too great an uncertainty. We know only what their present sentiments are. And it is vain to propose what will not accord with these. The states will never feel a sufficient confidence in a general government to give it a negative on their laws. The scheme is itself totally novel; there is no parallel to it to be found. The authority of Congress is familiar

to the people, and an augmentation of the powers of Congress will be readily approved by them.

Mr. Paterson [N.J.] said, as he had on a former occasion given his sentiments on the plan proposed by Mr. Randolph, he would now, avoiding repetition as much as possible, give his reasons in favor of that proposed by himself. He preferred it because it accorded (1) with the powers of the Convention; (2) with the sentiments of the people. If the Confederacy was radically wrong, let us return to our states and obtain larger powers, not assume them of ourselves.

I came here not to speak my own sentiments but the sentiments of those who sent me. Our object is not such a government as may be best in itself but such a one as our constituents have authorized us to prepare, and as they will approve. If we argue the matter on the supposition that no Confederacy at present exists, it cannot be denied that all the states stand on the footing of equal sovereignty. All, therefore, must concur before any can be bound. If a proportional representation be right, why do we not vote so here? If we argue on the fact that a federal compact actually exists, and consult the articles of it, we still find an equal sovereignty to be the basis of it. (He reads the 5th Article of Confederation giving each state a vote, and the 13th, declaring that no alteration shall be made without unanimous consent.) This is the nature of all treaties. What is unanimously done must be unanimously undone.

It was observed (by Mr. Wilson) that the larger states gave up the point, not because it was right but because the circumstances of the moment urged the concession. Be it so. Are they for that reason at liberty to take it back? Can the donor resume his gift without the consent of the donee? This doctrine may be convenient, but it is a doctrine that will sacrifice the lesser states. The large states acceded readily to the Confederacy. It was the small ones that came in reluctantly and slowly. New Jersey and Maryland were the two last, the former objecting to the want of power in Congress over trade; both of them to the want of power to appropriate the vacant territory to the benefit of the whole.

If the sovereignty of the states is to be maintained, the representatives must be drawn immediately from the states, not from the people; and we have no power to vary the idea of equal sovereignty. The only expedient that will cure the difficulty is that of throwing the states into hotchpot. To say that this is impracticable will not make it so. Let it be tried, and we shall see whether the citizens of Massachusetts, Pennsylvania, and Vermont accede to it. It will be objected that coercion will be impracticable. But will it be more so in one plan than the other? Its efficacy will depend on the quantum of power collected, not on its being drawn from the states or from the individuals; and according to his plan it may be exerted on individuals as well as according that of Mr. Randolph.

A distinct executive and judiciary also were equally provided by his plan. It is urged that two branches in the legislature are necessary. Why? For the purpose of a check. But the reason of the precaution is not applicable to this case. Within a particular state, where party heats prevail, such a check may be necessary. In such a body as Congress, it is less necessary, and, besides, the delegations of the different states are checks on each other. Do the people at large complain of Congress? No. What they wish is that Congress may have more power. If the power now proposed be not enough, the people hereafter will make additions to it. With proper powers, Congress will act with more energy and wisdom than the proposed national legislature; being fewer in number, and more secreted and refined by the mode of election.

The plan of Mr. Randolph will also be

enormously expensive. Allowing Georgia and Delaware two representatives each in the popular branch, the aggregate number of that branch will be 180. Add to it half as many for the other branch and you have 270 members coming once at least a year from the most distant as well as the most central parts of the republic. In the present deranged state of our finances, can so expensive a system be seriously thought of? By enlarging the powers of Congress, the greatest part of this expense will be saved and all purposes will be answered. At least a trial ought to be made.

MR. WILSON entered into a contrast of the principal points of the two plans so far, he said, as there had been time to examine the one last proposed. These points were: (1) in the Virginia plan there are two, and in some degree three, branches in the legislature; in the plan from New Jersey there is to be a *single* legislature only; (2) representation of the people at large is the basis of the one; the state legislatures, the pillars of the other; (3) proportional representation prevails in one; equality of suffrage in the other; (4) a single executive magistrate is at the head of the one; a plurality is held out in the other; (5) in the one, the majority of the people of the United States must prevail; in the other, a minority may prevail; (6) the national legislature is to make laws in all cases to which the separate states are incompetent and, in place of this, Congress are to have additional power in a few cases only; (7) a negative on the laws of the states in place of this coercion to be substituted; (8) the executive to be removable on impeachment and conviction, in one plan; in the other, to be removable at the instance of majority of the executives of the states; (9) revision of the laws provided for in one; no such check in the other; (10) inferior national tribunals in one; none such in the other; (11) in the one, jurisdiction of national tribunals to extend, etc.; an appellate jurisdiction only allowed, in the other; (12) here, the jurisdiction is to extend to all cases affecting the national peace and harmony; there, a few cases only are marked out; (13) finally, the ratification is, in this, to be by the people themselves; in that, by the legislative authorities according to the 13th Article of Confederation.

With regard to the *power of the Convention,* he conceived himself authorized to *conclude nothing,* but to be at liberty to *propose anything.* In this particular he felt himself perfectly indifferent to the two plans.

With *regard to the sentiments of the people,* he conceived it difficult to know precisely what they are. Those of the particular circle in which one moved were commonly mistaken for the general voice. He could not persuade himself that the state governments and sovereignties were so much the idols of the people, nor a national government so obnoxious to them as some supposed. Why should a national government be unpopular? Has it less dignity? Will each citizen enjoy under it less liberty or protection? Will a citizen of *Delaware* be degraded by becoming a citizen of the *United States*? Where do the people look at present for relief from the evils of which they complain? Is it from an internal reform of their governments? No, sir. It is from the national councils that relief is expected. For these reasons he did not fear that the people would not follow us into a national government, and it will be a further recommendation of Mr. Randolph's plan that it is to be submitted to *them* and not to the *legislatures* for ratification.

Proceeding now to the first point on which he had contrasted the two plans, he observed that, anxious as he was for some augmentation of the federal powers, it would be with extreme reluctance indeed that he could ever consent to give powers to Congress. He had two reasons, either of which was sufficient: (1) Congress as a legislative body does not stand on the people; (2) it is a *single* body.

1. He would not repeat the remarks he had formerly made on the principles of representation. He would only say that an inequality in it has ever been a poison contaminating every branch of government. In Great Britain, where this poison has had a full operation, the security of private rights is owing entirely to the purity of her tribunals of justice, the judges of which are neither appointed nor paid by a venal Parliament. The political liberty of that nation, owing to the inequality of representation, is at the mercy of its rulers. He means not to insinuate that there is any parallel between the situation of that country and ours at present. But it is a lesson we ought not to disregard, that the smallest bodies in Great Britain are notoriously the most corrupt. Every other source of influence must also be stronger in small than large bodies of men. When Lord Chesterfield had told us that one of the Dutch provinces had been seduced into the views of France, he need not have added that it was not Holland but one of the *smallest* of them. There are facts among ourselves which are known to all. Passing over others, he will only remark that the *impost*, so anxiously wished for by the public, was defeated, not by any of the *larger* states in the Union.

2. *Congress is a single legislature.* Despotism comes on mankind in different shapes, sometimes in an executive, sometimes in a military, one. Is there no danger of a legislative despotism? Theory and practice both proclaim it. If the legislative authority be not restrained, there can be neither liberty nor stability; and it can only be restrained by dividing it within itself, into distinct and independent branches. In a single house there is no check but the inadequate one of the virtue and good sense of those who compose it.

On another great point, the contrast was equally favorable to the plan reported by the Committee of the Whole. It vested the executive powers in a single magistrate. The plan of New Jersey vested them in a plurality. In order to control the legislative authority, you must divide it. In order to control the executive, you must unite it. One man will be more responsible than three; three will contend among themselves till one becomes the master of his colleagues. . . .

Having already taken up so much time, he would not, he said, proceed to any of the other points. Those on which he had dwelt are sufficient of themselves; and on a decision of them, the fate of the others will depend.

Mr. Pinckney: The whole comes to this, as he conceived. Give New Jersey an equal vote and she will dismiss her scruples and concur in the national system. He thought the Convention authorized to go any length in recommending which they found necessary to remedy the evils which produced this Convention.

Mr. Ellsworth [Conn.] proposed, as a more distinctive form of collecting the mind of the Committee on the subject, "that the legislative power of the United States should remain in Congress." This was not seconded, though it seemed better calculated for the purpose than the first proposition of Mr. Paterson, in place of which Mr. Ellsworth wished to substitute it.

Mr. Randolph [Va.] was not scrupulous on the point of power. When the salvation of the republic was at stake, it would be treason to our trust not to propose what we found necessary. He painted in strong colors the imbecility of the existing Confederacy and the danger of delaying a substantial reform. In answer to the objection drawn from the sense of our constituents as denoted by their acts relating to the Convention and the objects of their deliberation, he observed that as each state acted separately in the case, it would have been indecent for it to have charged the existing constitution with all the vices which it might have perceived in it. The first state that set on foot this experiment would not have been justified in going so far, ignorant as it was of the opinion of others and sensible as it must have been of the uncertainty of a successful issue to the experiment. There are certainly seasons of a peculiar nature where the ordinary cautions must be dispensed with, and this is certainly one of them. He would not, as far as depended on him, leave anything that seemed necessary undone. The present moment is favorable and is probably the last that will offer.

The true question is whether we shall adhere to thc federal plan or introduce the national plan. The insufficiency of the former has been fully displayed by the trial already made. There are but two modes by which the end of a general government can be attained: (1) by coercion as proposed by Mr. Paterson's plan; (2) by real legislation as proposed by the other plan. Coercion he pronounced to be *impracticable, expensive, cruel to individuals.* It tended also to habituate the instruments of it to shed the blood and riot in the spoils of their fellow citizens, and consequently trained them up for the service of ambition. We must resort, therefore, to a national *legislation over individuals,* for which Congress are unfit. To vest such power in them would be blending the legislative with the executive, contrary to the received maxim on this subject. If the union of these powers heretofore in Congress has been safe, it has been owing to the general impotency of that body.

Congress are, moreover, not elected by the people but by the legislatures who retain even a power of recall. They have, therefore, no will of their own; they are a mere diplomatic body and are always obsequious to the views of the states, who are always encroaching on the authority of the United States. A provision for harmony among the states, as in trade, naturalization, etc., for crushing rebellion whenever it may rear its crest, and for certain other general benefits must be made. The powers for these purposes can never be given to a body inadequate as Congress are in point of representation, elected in the mode in which they are, and possessing no more confidence than they do; for, notwithstanding what has been said to the contrary, his own experience satisfied him that a rooted distrust of Congress pretty generally prevailed. A national government alone, properly constituted, will answer the purpose; and he begged it to be considered that the present is the last moment for establishing one. After this select experiment, the people will yield to despair.

*June 18.* Mr. Hamilton [N.Y.] had been hitherto silent on the business before the Convention, partly from respect to others whose superior abilities, age, and experience rendered him unwilling to bring forward ideas dissimilar to theirs, and partly from his delicate situation with respect to his own state, to whose sentiments as expressed by his colleagues he could by no means accede. The crisis, however, which now marked our affairs was too serious to permit any scruples whatever to prevail over the duty imposed on every man to contribute his efforts for the public safety and happiness. He was obliged, therefore, to declare himself unfriendly to both plans.

He was particularly opposed to that from New Jersey, being fully convinced that no amendment of the Confederation leaving the states in possession of their sovereignty could possibly answer the purpose. On the other hand, he confessed he was much discouraged by the amazing extent of country in expecting the desired blessings from any general sovereignty that could be substituted. As to the powers of the Convention, he thought the doubts started on that subject had arisen from distinctions and reasonings too subtle. A *federal* government he conceived to mean an association of independent communities into one. . . .

The great question is — What provision shall we make for the happiness of our country? He would first make a comparative examination of the two plans — prove that there were essential defects in both and point out such changes as might render a *national one* efficacious. The great and essential principles necessary for the support of government are:

1. An active and constant interest in supporting it. This principle does not exist in the states in favor of the federal government. They have evidently, in a high degree, the esprit de corps. They constantly pursue internal interests adverse to those of the whole. They have their particular debts, their particular plans of finance, etc. All these, when opposed to, invariably prevail over the requisitions and plans of Congress.

2. The love of power. Men love power. The same remarks are applicable to this principle. The states have constantly shown a disposition rather to regain the powers delegated by them than to part with more, or to give effect to what they had parted with. The ambition of their demagogues is known to hate the control of the general government. It may be remarked too that the citizens have not that anxiety to prevent a dissolution of the general government as of the particular governments. A dissolution of the latter would be fatal; of the former, would still leave the purposes of government attainable to a considerable degree. Consider what such a state as Virginia will be in a few years, a few compared with the life of nations. How strongly will it feel its importance and self-sufficiency?

3. An habitual attachment of the people. The whole force of this tie is on the side of the state government. Its sovereignty is immediately before the eyes of the people; its protection is immediately enjoyed by them. From its hand, distributive justice, and all those acts which familiarize and endear government to a people, are dispensed to them.

4. *Force*, by which may be understood a *coercion of laws* or *coercion of arms*. Congress have not the former, except in few cases. In particular states, this coercion is nearly sufficient; though he held it in most cases not entirely so. A certain portion of military force is absolutely necessary in large communities. Massachusetts is now feeling this necessity and making provision for it. But how can this force be exerted on the states collectively? It is impossible. It amounts to a war between the parties. Foreign powers also will not be idle spectators. They will interpose, the confusion will increase, and a dissolution of the Union ensue.

5. *Influence*. He did not mean corruption but a dispensation of those regular honors and emoluments which produce an attachment to the government. Almost all the weight of these is on the side of the states; and must continue so as long as the states continue to exist. . . .

Two sovereignties cannot coexist within the same limits. Giving powers to Congress must eventuate in a bad government or in no government. The plan of New Jersey, therefore, will not do. What then is to be done? Here he was embarrassed. The extent of the country to be governed, discouraged him. . . . In every community where industry is encouraged, there will be a division of it into the few and the many. Hence, separate interests will arise. There will be debtors and creditors, etc. Give all power to the many, they will oppress the few. Give all power to the few, they will oppress the many. Both, therefore, ought to have power that each may defend itself against the other. . . .

As to the executive, it seemed to be admitted that no good one could be established on republican principles. Was not this giving up the merits of the question; for can there be a good government without a good executive? The English model was the only good one on this subject. The hereditary interest of the king was so interwoven with that of the nation, and his personal emoluments so great, that he was placed above the danger of being corrupted from abroad — and at the same time was both sufficiently independent and sufficiently controlled to answer the purpose of the institution at home. . . .

What is the inference from all these observations? That we ought to go as far in order to attain stability and permanency as republican principles will admit. Let one branch of the legislature hold their places for life, or at least during good behavior. Let the executive also be for life. He appealed to the feelings of the members present whether a term of seven years would induce the sacrifices of private affairs which an acceptance of public trust would require, so as to ensure the services of the best citizens. On this plan we should have in the Senate a permanent will, a weighty interest which would answer essential purposes. But is this a republican government, it will be asked? Yes, if all the magistrates are appointed and vacancies are filled by the people, or a process of election originating with the people.

He was sensible that an executive constituted as he proposed would have in fact but little of the power and independence that might be necessary. On the other plan of appointing him for seven years, he thought the executive ought to have but little power. He would be ambitious, with the means of making creatures; and as the object of his ambition would be to *prolong* his power, it is probable that in case of a war he would avail himself of the emergency to evade or refuse a degradation from his place. An executive for life has not this motive for forgetting his fidelity, and will therefore be a safer depository of power.

It will be objected, probably, that such an executive will be an *elective monarch* and will give birth to the tumults which characterize that form of government. He would reply that "monarch" is an indefinite term. It marks not either the degree or duration of power. If this executive magistrate would be a monarch for life, the other proposed by the report from the Committee of the Whole would be a monarch for seven years. The circumstance of being elective was also applicable to both. It had been observed by judicious writers that elective monarchies would be the best if they could be guarded against the tumults excited by the ambition and intrigues of competitors. . . .

Having made these observations, he would read to the Committee a sketch of a plan which he should prefer to either of those under consideration. . . .

I. The supreme legislative power of the United States of America to be vested in two different bodies of men; the one to be called the Assembly, the other the Senate, who together shall form the legislature of the United States with power to pass all laws whatsoever subject to the negative hereafter mentioned.

II. The Assembly to consist of persons elected by the people to serve for three years.

III. The Senate to consist of persons elected to serve during good behavior; their election to be made by electors chosen for that purpose by the people. In order to this, the states to be divided into election districts. On the death, removal, or resignation of any senator, his place to be filled out of the district from which he came.

IV. The supreme executive authority of the United States to be vested in a governor to be elected to serve during good behavior, the election to be made by electors chosen by the people in the election districts aforesaid. The authorities and functions of the executive to be as follows: to have a negative on all laws about to be passed and the execution of all laws passed; to have the direction of war when authorized or begun; to have with the advice and approbation of the Senate, the power of making all treaties; to have the sole appointment of the heads or chief officers of the departments of finance, war, and foreign affairs; to have the nomination of all other officers (ambassadors to foreign nations included), subject to the approbation or rejection of the Senate; to have the power of pardoning all offenses except treason, which he shall not pardon without the approbation of the Senate.

V. On the death, resignation, or removal of the governor, his authorities to be exercised by the president of the Senate till a successor be appointed.

VI. The Senate to have the sole power of declaring war, the power of advising and approving all treaties, the power of approving or rejecting all appointments of officers, except the heads or chiefs of the departments of finance, war, and foreign affairs.

VII. The supreme judicial authority to be vested in judges to hold their offices during good behavior with adequate and permanent salaries. This court to have original jurisdiction in all causes of capture, and an appellative jurisdiction in all causes in which the revenues of the general government or the citizens of foreign nations are concerned.

VIII. The legislature of the United States to have power to institute courts in each state for the determination of all matters of general concern.

IX. The governor, senators, and all officers of the United States to be liable to impeachment for mal- and corrupt conduct; and, upon conviction, to be removed from office and disqualified for holding any place of trust or profit. All impeachments to be tried by a court to consist of the chief ——— or judge of the superior court of law of each state, provided such judge shall hold his place during good behavior and have a permanent salary.

X. All laws of the particular states contrary to the constitution or laws of the United States to be utterly void; and, the better to prevent such laws being passed, the governor or president of each state shall be appointed by the general government and shall have a negative upon the laws about to be passed in the state of which he is governor or president.

XI. No state to have any forces, land or naval; and the militia of all the states to be under the sole and exclusive direction of the United States, the officers of which to be appointed and commissioned by them.

*June 19.* MR. MADISON: Proceeding to the consideration of Mr. Paterson's plan, he stated the object of a proper plan to be twofold: (1) to preserve the Union; (2) to provide a government that will remedy the evils felt by the states, both in their united and individual capacities. Examine Mr. Paterson's plan and say whether it promises satisfaction in these respects.

1. Will it prevent those violations of the law of nations and of treaties which, if not prevented, must involve us in the calamities of foreign wars? The tendency of the states to these violations has been manifested in sundry instances. The files of Congress contain complaints already from almost every nation with which treaties have been formed. Hitherto, indulgence has been shown to us. This cannot be the permanent disposition of foreign nations. A rupture with other powers is among the greatest of national calamities. It ought, therefore, to be effectually provided that no part of a nation shall have it in its power to bring them on the whole. The existing Confederacy does not sufficiently provide against this evil. The proposed amendment to it does not supply the omission; it leaves the will of the states as uncontrolled as ever.

2. Will it prevent encroachments on the federal authority? A tendency to such encroachments has been sufficiently exemplified among ourselves as well in every other confederated republic, ancient and modern. By the federal Articles, transactions with the Indians appertain to Congress; yet, in several instances, the states have entered into treaties and wars with them. In like manner, no two or more states can form among themselves any treaties, etc. without

the consent of Congress; yet Virginia and Maryland, in one instance, Pennsylvania and New Jersey in another, have entered into compacts without previous application or subsequent apology. No state again can of right raise troops in time of peace without the like consent. Of all cases of the league, this seems to require the most scrupulous observance.

Has not Massachusetts, notwithstanding, the most powerful member of the Union, already raised a body of troops? Is she not now augmenting them, without having even deigned to apprise Congress of her intention? In fine, have we not seen the public land dealt out to Connecticut to bribe her acquiescence in the decree constitutionally awarded against her claim on the territory of Pennsylvania; for no other possible motive can account for the policy of Congress in that measure? . . .

He observed that the plan of Mr. Paterson, besides omitting a control over the states as a general defense of the federal prerogatives, was particularly defective in two of its provisions: (1) its ratification was not to be by the people at large but by the *legislatures.* It could not, therefore, render the acts of Congress in pursuance of their powers, even legally *paramount* to the acts of the states; (2) it gave to the federal tribunal an appellate jurisdiction only — even in the criminal cases enumerated, the necessity of any such provision supposed a danger of undue acquittals in the state tribunals. Of what avail could an appellate tribunal be after an acquittal? Besides, in most if not all of the states, the executives have by their respective constitutions the right of pardon. How could this be taken from them by a legislative ratification only?

3. Will it prevent trespasses of the states on each other? Of these, enough has been already seen. He instanced acts of Virginia and Maryland, which give a preference to their own citizens in cases where the citizens of other states are entitled to equality of privileges by the Articles of Confederation. He considered the emissions of paper money and other kindred measures as also aggressions. The states relatively to one another being each of them either debtor or creditor, the creditor states must suffer unjustly from every emission by the debtor states. We have seen retaliating acts on this subject which threatened danger, not to the harmony only but the tranquillity of the Union. The plan of Mr. Paterson, not giving even a negative on the acts of the states, left them as much at liberty as ever to execute their unrighteous projects against each other.

4. Will it secure the internal tranquillity of the states themselves? The insurrections in Massachusetts admonished all the states of the danger to which they were exposed. Yet the plan of Mr. Paterson contained no provisions for supplying the defect of the Confederation on this point. According to the republican theory, indeed, right and power, being both vested in the majority, are held to be synonymous. According to fact and experience, a minority may in an appeal to force be an overmatch for the majority: (1) if the minority happen to include all such as possess the skill and habits of military life, with such as possess the great pecuniary resources, one-third may conquer the remaining two-thirds; (2) one-third of those who participate in the choice of rulers may be rendered a majority by the accession of those whose poverty disqualifies them from a suffrage and who, for obvious reasons, may be more ready to join the standard of sedition than that of the established government; (3) where slavery exists, the republican theory becomes still more fallacious.

5. Will it secure a good internal legislation and administration to the particular states? In developing the evils which vitiate the political system of the United States, it is proper to take into view those which prevail within the states individually as well as

those which affect them collectively, since the former indirectly affect the whole, and there is great reason to believe that the pressure of them had a full share in the motives which produced the present Convention. Under this head he enumerated and animadverted on (1) the multiplicity of the laws passed by the several states; (2) the mutability of their laws; (3) the injustice of them; (4) the impotence of them; observing that Mr. Paterson's plan contained no remedy for this dreadful class of evils, and could not, therefore, be received as an adequate provision for the exigencies of the community.

6. Will it secure the Union against the influence of foreign powers over its members? He pretended not to say that any such influence had yet been tried; but it was naturally to be expected that occasions would produce it. . . . The plan of Mr. Paterson, not giving to the general councils any negative on the will of the particular states, left the door open for . . . pernicious machinations among ourselves.

7. He begged the smaller states which were most attached to Mr. Paterson's plan to consider the situation in which it would leave them. In the first place, they would continue to bear the whole expense of maintaining their delegates in Congress. It ought not to be said that if they were willing to bear this burden no others had a right to complain. As far as it led the small states to forbear keeping up a representation by which the public business was delayed, it was evidently a matter of common concern. An examination of the minutes of Congress would satisfy everyone that the public business had been frequently delayed by this cause; and that the states most frequently unrepresented in Congress were not the larger states.

He reminded the Convention of another consequence of leaving on a small state the burden of maintaining a representation in Congress. During a considerable period of the war, one of the representatives of Delaware, in whom alone before the signing of the Confederation the entire vote of that state and after that event one-half of its vote frequently resided, was a citizen and resident of Pennsylvania and held an office in his own state incompatible with an appointment from it to Congress. During another period, the same state was represented by three delegates, two of whom were citizens of Pennsylvania and the third a citizen of New Jersey. These expedients must have been intended to avoid the burden of supporting delegates from their own state. But whatever might have been the cause, was not in effect the vote of one state doubled and the influence of another increased by it? In the second place, the coercion on which the efficacy of the plan depends can never be exerted but on themselves. The larger states will be impregnable, the smaller only can feel the vengeance of it. . . .

8. He begged them to consider the situation in which they would remain in case their pertinacious adherence to an inadmissible plan should prevent the adoption of any plan. The contemplation of such an event was painful; but it would be prudent to submit to the task of examining it at a distance that the means of escaping it might be the more readily embraced. Let the Union of the states be dissolved, and one of two consequences must happen — either the states must remain individually independent and sovereign; or two or more confederacies must be formed among them.

In the first event, would the small states be more secure against the ambition and power of their larger neighbors than they would be under a general government pervading with equal energy every part of the empire, and having an equal interest in protecting every part against every other part? In the second, can the smaller expect that their larger neighbors would confederate with them on the principle of the present Confederacy, which gives to each member an equal suffrage; or that they would exact less severe concessions from the smaller states than are proposed in the scheme of Mr. Randolph?

The great difficulty lies in the affair of representation; and if this could be adjusted, all others would be surmountable. It was admitted by both the gentlemen from New Jersey (Mr. Brearly and Mr. Paterson) that it would not be *just to allow Virginia,* which was sixteen times as large as Delaware, an equal vote only. Their language was that it would not be *safe for Delaware* to allow Virginia sixteen times as many votes. The expedient proposed by them was that all the states should be thrown into one mass and a new partition be made into thirteen equal parts. Would such a scheme be practicable? The dissimilarities existing in the rules of property as well as in the manners, habits, and prejudices of the different states amounted to a prohibition of the attempt. . . .

But admitting a general amalgamation and repartition of the states to be practicable, and the danger apprehended by the smaller states from a proportional representation to be real, would not a particular and voluntary coalition of these with their neighbors be less inconvenient to the whole community and equally effectual for their own safety? If New Jersey or Delaware conceived that an advantage would accrue to them from an equalization of the states, in which case they would necessarily form a junction with their neighbors, why might not this end be attained by leaving them at liberty by the constitution to form such a junction whenever they pleased? And why should they wish to obtrude a like arrangement on all the states when it was, to say the least, extremely difficult, would be obnoxious to many of the states, and when neither the inconveniency nor the benefit of the expedient to themselves would be lessened by confining it to themselves.

The prospect of many new states to the westward was another consideration of importance. If they should come into the Union at all, they would come when they contained but few inhabitants. If they should be entitled to vote according to their proportions of inhabitants, all would be right and safe. Let them have an equal vote and a more objectionable minority than ever might give law to the whole.

## DEBATE OF JULY 14

Mr. L. Martin [Md.] called for the question on the whole report, including the parts relating to the origination of money bills, and the equality of votes in the second branch.

Mr. Gerry wished, before the question should be put, that the attention of the House might be turned to the dangers apprehended from Western states. He was for admitting them on liberal terms, but not for putting ourselves into their hands. They will, if they acquire power like all men, abuse it. They will oppress commerce and drain our wealth into the Western country. To guard against these consequences, he thought it necessary to limit the number of new states to be admitted into the Union in such a manner that they should never be able to outnumber the Atlantic states. He accordingly moved that in order to secure the liberties of the states already confederated, the number of representatives in the first branch of the states which shall hereafter be established shall never exceed in number the representatives from such of the states as shall accede to this Confederation.

Mr. King [Mass.] seconded the motion.

Mr. Sherman thought there was no probability that the number of future states would exceed that of the existing states. If the event should ever happen, it was too remote to be taken into consideration at this time. Besides, we are providing for our posterity, for our children and our grandchildren, who would be as likely to be citizens of new Western states as of the old states. On this consideration alone, we ought to make no such discrimination as was proposed by the motion.

Mr. Gerry: If some of our children should remove, others will stay behind, and he thought it incumbent on us to provide for their interests. There was a rage for emigration from the Eastern states to the Western country, and he did not wish those remaining behind to be at the mercy of the emigrants. Besides, foreigners are resorting to that country, and it is uncertain what turn things may take there.

On the question for agreeing to the motion of Mr. Gerry, it passed in the negative. . . .

Mr. Pinckney moved that, instead of an equality of votes, the states should be represented in the second branch as follows: New Hampshire by 2 members; Massachusetts, 4; Rhode Island, 1; Connecticut, 3; New York, 3; New Jersey, 2; Pennsylvania, 4; Delaware, 1; Maryland, 3; Virginia, 5; North Carolina, 3; South Carolina, 3; Georgia, 2; making, in the whole, 36.

Mr. Dayton [N.J.]: The smaller states can never give up their equality. For himself, he would in no event yield that security for their rights.

Mr. Sherman urged the equality of votes, not so much as a security for the small states as for the state governments which could not be preserved unless they were represented and had a negative in the general government. He had no objection to the members in the second branch voting per capita, as had been suggested by Mr. Gerry.

Mr. Madison concurred in this motion of Mr. Pinckney as a reasonable compromise.

Mr. Gerry said he should like the motion, but could see no hope of success. An accommodation must take place, and it was apparent from what had been seen that it could not do so on the ground of the motion. He was utterly against a partial confederacy, leaving other states to accede or not accede, as had been intimated.

Mr. King said it was always with regret that he differed from his colleagues, but it was his duty to differ from Mr. Gerry on this occasion. He considered the proposed government as substantially and formally a general and national government over the people of America. There never will be a case in which it will act as a federal government on the states and not on the individual citizens. And is it not a clear principle that in a free government those who are to be the objects of a government ought to influence the operations of it? What reason can be assigned why the same rule of representation should not prevail in the second branch as in the first? He could conceive none. On the contrary, every view of the subject that presented itself seemed to require it.

Two objections had been raised against it, drawn (1) from the terms of the existing compact; (2) from a supposed danger to the smaller states. As to the first objection, he thought it inapplicable. According to the existing Confederation, the rule by which the public burdens is to be apportioned is *fixed* and must be pursued. In the proposed government it cannot be fixed because indirect taxation is to be substituted. The legislature, therefore, will have full discretion to impose taxes in such modes and proportions as they may judge expedient. As to the second objection, he thought it of as little weight. The general government can never wish to intrude on the state governments. There could be no temptation; none had been pointed out. In order to prevent the interference of measures which seemed most likely to happen, he would have no objection to throwing all the state debts into the federal debt, making one aggregate debt of about $70 million and leaving it to be discharged by the general government.

According to the idea of securing the

state governments, there ought to be three distinct legislative branches. The second was admitted to be necessary, and was actually meant to check the first branch, to give more wisdom, system, and stability to the government and ought clearly as it was to operate on the people to be proportioned to them. For the third purpose of securing the states, there ought then to be a third branch representing the states as such, and guarding by equal votes their rights and dignities.

He would not pretend to be as thoroughly acquainted with his immediate constituents as his colleagues, but it was his firm belief that Massachusetts would never be prevailed on to yield to an equality of votes. In New York (he was sorry to be obliged to say anything relative to that state in the absence of its representatives, but the occasion required it), in New York he had seen that the most powerful argument used by the considerate opponents to the grant of the impost to Congress was pointed against the vicious constitution of Congress with regard to representation and suffrage. He was sure that no government could last that was not founded on just principles. He preferred the doing of nothing to an allowance of an equal vote to all the states. It would be better, he thought, to submit to a little more confusion and convulsion than to submit to such an evil. It was difficult to say what the views of different gentlemen might be. Perhaps there might be some who thought no government coextensive with the United States could be established with a hope of its answering the purpose. Perhaps there might be other fixed opinions incompatible with the object we were pursuing. If there were, he thought it but candid that gentlemen would speak out that we might understand one another.

Mr. Strong [Mass.]: The Convention had been much divided in opinion. In order to avoid the consequences of it, an accommodation had been proposed. A committee had been appointed; and though some of the members of it were averse to an equality of votes, a report has been made in favor of it. It is agreed on all hands that Congress are nearly at an end. If no accommodation takes place, the Union itself must soon be dissolved. It has been suggested that if we cannot come to any general agreement, the principal states may form and recommend a scheme of government. But will the small states in that case ever accede it? Is it probable that the large states themselves will, under such circumstances, embrace and ratify it? He thought the small states had made a considerable concession in the article of money bills; and that they might naturally expect some concessions on the other side. From this view of the matter, he was compelled to give his vote for the report taken all together.

Mr. Madison expressed his apprehensions that if the proper foundation of government was destroyed by substituting an equality in place of a proportional representation, no proper superstructure would be raised. If the small states really wish for a government armed with the powers necessary to secure their liberties, and to enforce obedience on the larger members as well as on themselves, he could not help thinking them extremely mistaken in their means. He reminded them of the consequences of laying the existing Confederation on improper principles. All the principal parties to its compilation joined immediately in mutilating and fettering the government in such a manner that it has disappointed every hope placed on it. He appealed to the doctrine and arguments used by themselves on a former occasion.

It had been very properly observed by Mr. Paterson that representation was an expedient by which the meeting of the people themselves was rendered unnecessary; and that the representatives ought therefore to bear a proportion to the votes which their constituents, if convened, would respectively have. Was not this remark as applicable to one branch of the representation as to the other? But it had been said that the government would in its operation be partly federal, partly national; that although in the latter respect the representatives of the people ought to be in proportion to the people, yet in the former it ought to be according to the number of states. If there was any solidity in this distinction, he was ready to abide by it; if there was none, it ought to be abandoned. In all cases where the general government is to act on the people, let the people be represented and the votes be proportional. In all cases where the government is to act on the states as such, in like manner as Congress now act on them, let the states be represented and the votes be equal.

This was the true ground of compromise, if there was any ground at all; but he denied that there was any ground. He called for a single instance in which the general government was not to operate on the people individually. The practicability of making laws, with coercive sanctions, for the states as political bodies had been exploded on all hands. He observed that the people of the large states would in some way or other secure to themselves a weight proportioned to the importance accruing from their superior numbers. If they could not effect it by a proportional representation in the government, they would probably accede to no government which did not in great measure depend for its efficacy on their voluntary cooperation; in which case they would indirectly secure their object.

The existing Confederacy proved that where the acts of the general government were to be executed by the particular governments the latter had a weight in proportion to their importance. No one would say that either in Congress or out of Congress Delaware had equal weight with Pennsylvania. If the latter was to supply ten times as much money as the former, and no compulsion could be used, it was of ten times more importance that she should voluntarily furnish the supply. . . .

He enumerated the objections against an equality of votes in the second branch, notwithstanding the proportional representation in the first.

1. The minority could negative the will of the majority of the people.

2. They could extort measures by making them a condition of their assent to other necessary measures.

3. They could obtrude measures on the majority by virtue of the peculiar powers which would be vested in the Senate.

4. The evil, instead of being cured by time, would increase with every new state that should be admitted, as they must all be admitted on the principle of equality.

5. The perpetuity it would give to the preponderance of the Northern against the Southern scale was a serious consideration.

It seemed now to be pretty well understood that the real difference of interests lay not between the large and small but between the Northern and Southern states. The institution of slavery and its consequences formed the line of discrimination. There were five states on the south, eight on the northern side of this line. Should a proportional representation take place, it was true the northern side would still outnumber the other; but not in the same degree, at this time; and every day would tend toward an equilibrium.

Mr. Wilson would add a few words only. If equality in the second branch was an error that time would correct, he should be less anxious to exclude it being sensible that perfection was unattainable in any plan; but being a fundamental and a perpetual error, it ought by all means to be avoided. A vice in the representation, like an error in the first concoction, must be followed by disease, convulsions, and finally death itself. The justice of the general principle of proportional representation has not, in argument at least, been yet contradicted. But it is said that a departure from it so far as to give the states an equal vote in one branch of the legislature is essential to their preservation. He had considered this position maturely, but could not see its application. That the states ought to be preserved he admitted. But does it follow that an equality of votes is necessary for the purpose? Is there any reason to suppose that if their preservation should depend more on the large than on the small states the security of the states against the general government would be diminished? Are the large states less attached to their existence, more likely to commit suicide, than the small? An equal vote, then, is not necessary as far as he can conceive; and is liable, among other objections, to this insuperable one: The great fault of the existing Confederacy is its inactivity.

It has never been a complaint against Congress that they governed overmuch. The complaint has been that they have governed too little. To remedy this defect we were sent here. Shall we effect the cure by establishing an equality of votes as is proposed? No, this very equality carries us directly to Congress — to the system which it is our duty to rectify. The small states cannot, indeed, act by virtue of this equality, but they may control the government as they have done in Congress. This very measure is here prosecuted by a minority of the people of America. Is, then, the object of the Convention likely to be accomplished in this way? Will not our constituents say — We sent you to form an efficient government and you have given us one more complex indeed, but having all the weakness of the former government.

He was anxious for uniting all the states under one government. He knew there were some respectable men who preferred three confederacies, united by offensive and defensive alliances. Many things may be plausibly said, some things may be justly said, in favor of such a project. He could not, however, concur in it himself; but he thought nothing so pernicious as bad first principles.

Mr. Ellsworth asked two questions, one of Mr. Wilson — Whether he had ever seen a good measure fail in Congress for want of a majority of states in its favor? He had himself never known such an instance. The other of Mr. Madison — Whether a negative lodged with the majority of the states, even the smallest, could be more dangerous than the qualified negative proposed to be lodged in a single executive magistrate who must be taken from some one state?

Mr. Sherman signified that his expectation was that the general legislature would in some cases act on the *federal principle* of requiring quotas. But he thought it ought to be empowered to carry their own plans into execution if the states should fail to supply their respective quotas.

On the question for agreeing to Mr. Pinckney's motion . . . it passed in the negative.

## AUGUST 18

Mr. Madison submitted, in order to be referred to the Committee of Detail, the following powers as proper to be added to those of the general legislature:

To dispose of the unappropriated lands of the United States.

To institute temporary governments for new states arising therein.

To regulate affairs with the Indians as well within as without the limits of the United States.

To exercise exclusively legislative authority at the seat of the general government, and over a district around the same, not exceeding ——— square miles; the consent of the legislature of the state or states comprising the same being first obtained.

To grant charters of incorporation in cases where the public good may require them and the authority of a single state may be incompetent.

To secure to literary authors their copyrights for a limited time.

To establish a university.

To encourage by premiums and provisions the advancement of useful knowledge and discoveries.

To authorize the executive to procure and hold for the use of the United States landed property for the erection of forts, magazines, and other necessary buildings.

These propositions were referred to the Committee of Detail which had prepared the report, and at the same time the following which were moved by Mr. Pinckney; in both cases, unanimously.

To fix and permanently establish the seat of government of the United States in which they shall possess the exclusive right of soil and jurisdiction.

To establish seminaries for the promotion of literature and the arts and sciences.

To grant charters of incorporation.

To grant patents for useful inventions.

To secure to authors exclusive rights for a certain time.

To establish public institutions, rewards, and immunities for the promotion of agriculture, commerce, trades, and manufactures.

That funds which shall be appropriated for payment of public creditors shall not, during the time of such appropriation, be diverted or applied to any other purpose, and that the Committee prepare a clause or clauses for restraining the legislature of the United States from establishing a perpetual revenue.

To secure the payment of the public debt.

To secure all creditors under the new constitution from a violation of the public faith when pledged by the authority of the legislature.

To grant letters of mark and reprisal.

To regulate stages on the postroads.

AUGUST 20

Mr. Pinckney submitted to the House, in order to be referred to the Committee of Detail, the following propositions:

Each house shall be the judge of its own privileges and shall have authority to punish by imprisonment every person violating the same; or who, in the place where the legislature may be sitting and during the time of its session, shall threaten any of its members for anything said or done on the House; or who shall assault any of them therefor; or who shall assault or arrest any witness or other person ordered to attend either of the houses in his way going or returning; or who shall rescue any person arrested by their order.

Each branch of the legislature, as well as the supreme executive, shall have authority to require the opinions of the supreme judicial court upon important questions of law and upon solemn occasions.

The privileges and benefit of the writ of habeas corpus shall be enjoyed in this government in the most expeditious and ample manner; and shall not be suspended by the legislature except upon the most urgent and pressing occasions, and for a limited time not exceeding ——— months.

The liberty of the press shall be inviolably preserved.

No troops shall be kept up in time of peace but by consent of the legislature.

The military shall always be subordinate to the civil power, and no grants of money shall be made by the legislature for supporting military land forces for more than one year at a time.

No soldier shall be quartered in any house in time of peace without consent of the owner.

No person holding the office of President of the United States, a judge of their Supreme Court, secretary for the Department of Foreign Affairs, of Finance, of Marine, of War, or of ———, shall be capable of holding at the same time any other office of trust or emolument under the United States or an individual state.

No religious test or qualification shall ever be annexed to any oath of office under the authority of the United States.

The United States shall be forever considered as one body corporate and politic in law, and entitled to all the rights, privileges, and immunities which to bodies corporate do or ought to appertain.

The legislature of the United States shall have the power of making the great seal, which shall be kept by the President of the United States, or, in his absence, by the president of the Senate, to be used by them as the occasion may require. It shall be called the great seal of the United States and shall be affixed to all laws.

All commissions and writs shall run in the name of the United States.

The jurisdiction of the Supreme Court shall be extended to all controversies between the United States and an individual state, or the United States and the citizens of an individual state.

## THE CLOSING DAY, SEPTEMBER 17

DR. FRANKLIN rose with a speech in his hand, which he had reduced to writing for his own convenience, and which Mr. Wilson read in the words following:

> Mr. President, I confess that there are several parts of this Constitution which I do not at present approve, but I am not sure I shall never approve them. For, having lived long, I have experienced many instances of being obliged, by better information or fuller consideration, to change opinions, even on important subjects, which I once thought right but found to be otherwise. It is therefore that the older I grow the more apt I am to doubt my own judgment and to pay more respect to the judgment of others. Most men, indeed, as well as most sects in religion, think themselves in possession of all truth, and that wherever others differ from them it is so far error. Steele, a Protestant, in a dedication, tells the Pope that the only difference between our churches in their opinions of the certainty of their doctrines is [that] the Church of Rome is infallible and the Church of England is never in the wrong. But though many private persons think almost as highly of their own infallibility as that of their sect, few express it so naturally as a certain French lady who, in a dispute with her sister, said, "I don't know how it happens, sister, but I meet with nobody but myself that's always in the right — *Il n'y a que moi qui a toujours raison.*"
>
> In these sentiments, sir, I agree to this Constitution with all its faults, if they are such; because I think a general government necessary for us, and there is no form of government but what may be a blessing to the people if well administered, and believe farther that this is likely to be well administered for a course of years, and can only end in despotism, as other forms have done before it, when the people shall become so corrupted as to need despotic government, being incapable of any other. I doubt, too, whether any other convention we can obtain may be able to make a better Constitution; for when you assemble a number of men to have the advantage of their joint wisdom, you inevitably assemble with those men all their prejudices, their passions, their errors of opinion, their local interests, and their selfish views. From such an assembly can a perfect production be expected?
>
> It therefore astonishes me, sir, to find this system approaching so near to perfection as it does; and I think it will astonish our enemies, who are waiting with confidence to hear that our councils are confounded like those of the builders of Babel; and that our states are on the point of separation, only to meet hereafter for the purpose of cutting one another's throats. Thus I consent, sir, to this Constitution because I expect no better, and because I am not sure that it is not the best. The opinions I have had of its errors I sacrifice to the public good. I have never whispered a syllable of them abroad. Within these walls they were born, and here they shall die.

If every one of us, in returning to our constituents, were to report the objections he has had to it, and endeavor to gain partisans in support of them, we might prevent its being generally received and thereby lose all the salutary effects and great advantages resulting naturally in our favor among foreign nations as well as among ourselves, from our real or apparent unanimity. Much of the strength and efficiency of any government in procuring and securing happiness to the people depends on opinion, on the general opinion of the goodness of the government as well as of the wisdom and integrity of its governors. I hope, therefore, that for our own sakes as a part of the people, and for the sake of posterity, we shall act heartily and unanimously in recommending this Constitution (if approved by Congress and confirmed by the conventions) wherever our influence may extend, and turn our future thoughts and endeavors to the means of having it well administered.

On the whole, sir, I cannot help expressing a wish that every member of the Convention who may still have objections to it would, with me, on this occasion doubt a little of his own infallibility and, to make manifest our unanimity, put his name to this instrument.

He then moved that the Constitution be signed by the members and offered the following as a convenient form, viz.: "Done in Convention by unanimous consent of *the states* present the 17th of September, etc. In witness whereof we have hereunto subscribed our names."

This ambiguous form had been drawn up by Mr. Gouverneur Morris in order to gain the dissenting members, and put into the hands of Dr. Franklin that it might have the better chance of success. . . .

Mr. Randolph then rose and, with an allusion to the observations of Dr. Franklin, apologized for his refusing to sign the Constitution, notwithstanding the vast majority and venerable names that would give sanction to its wisdom and its worth. He said, however, that he did not mean by this refusal to decide that he should oppose the Constitution without doors. He meant only to keep himself free to be governed by his duty as it should be prescribed by his future judgment. He refused to sign because he thought the object of the Convention would be frustrated by the alternative which it presented to the people. Nine states will fail to ratify the plan and confusion must ensue. With such a view of the subject, he ought not, he could not, by pledging himself to support the plan, restrain himself from taking such steps as might appear to him most consistent with the public good.

Mr. Gouverneur Morris [Pa.] said that he too had objections, but, considering the present plan as the best that was to be attained, he should take it with all its faults. The majority had determined in its favor, and by that determination he should abide. The moment this plan goes forth all other considerations will be laid aside, and the great question will be: Shall there be a national government or not? And this must take place or a general anarchy will be the alternative. He remarked that the signing in the form proposed related only to the fact that the *states* present were unanimous.

Mr. Williamson [N.C.] suggested that the signing should be confined to the letter accompanying the Constitution to Congress, which might perhaps do nearly as well, and would, he found, be satisfactory to some members who disliked the Constitution. For himself he did not think a better plan was to be expected and had no scruples against putting his name to it.

Mr. Hamilton expressed his anxiety that every member should sign. A few characters of consequence, by opposing or even refusing to sign the Constitution, might do infinite mischief by kindling the latent sparks which lurk under an enthusiasm in favor of the Convention which may soon subside. No man's ideas were more remote from the plan than his were known to be; but is it possible to deliberate between anarchy and convulsion, on one side, and the chance of good to be expected from the plan, on the other?

Mr. Blount [N.C.] said he had declared that he would not sign so as to pledge himself in support of the plan, but he was relieved by the form proposed and would, without committing himself, attest the fact that the plan was the unanimous act of the states in Convention.

Dr. Franklin expressed his fears from what Mr. Randolph had said that he thought himself alluded to in the remarks offered this morning to the House. He declared that when drawing up that paper he did not know that any particular member would refuse to sign his name to the instrument and hoped to be so understood. He professed a high sense of obligation to Mr. Randolph for having brought forward the plan in the first instance, and for the assistance he had given in its progress, and hoped that he would yet lay aside his objections and, by concurring with his brethren, prevent the great mischief which the refusal of his name might produce.

Mr. Randolph could not but regard the signing in the proposed form as the same with signing the Constitution. The change of form therefore could make no difference with him. He repeated that, in refusing to sign the Constitution, he took a step which might be the most awful of his life but it was dictated by his conscience, and it was not possible for him to hesitate, much less to change. He repeated also his persuasion that the holding out this plan with a final alternative to the people, of accepting or rejecting it *in toto*, would really produce the anarchy and civil convulsions which were apprehended from the refusal of individuals to sign it.

Mr. Gerry described the painful feelings of his situation, and the embarrassment under which he rose to offer any further observations on the subject which had been finally decided. While the plan was depending, he had treated it with all the freedom he thought it deserved. He now felt himself, bound as he was, disposed to treat it with the respect due to the act of the Convention. He hoped he should not violate that respect in declaring on this occasion his fears that a civil war may result from the present crisis of the United States.

In Massachusetts, particularly, he saw the danger of this calamitous event. In that state there are two parties, one devoted to democracy, the worst, he thought, of all political evils; the other, as violent in the opposite extreme. From the collision of these in opposing and resisting the Constitution, confusion was greatly to be feared. He had thought it necessary, for this and other reasons, that the plan should have been proposed in a more mediating shape in order to abate the heat and opposition of parties. As it has been passed by the Convention, he was persuaded it would have a contrary effect. He could not, therefore, by signing the Constitution, pledge himself to abide by it at all events. The proposed form made no difference with him. But if it were not otherwise apparent, the refusals to sign should never be known from him. Alluding to the remarks of Dr. Franklin, he could not, he said, but view them as leveled at himself and the other gentlemen who meant not to sign.

General Pinckney: We are not likely to gain many converts by the ambiguity of the proposed form of signing. He thought it best to be candid and let the form speak the substance. If the meaning of the signers be left in doubt, his purpose would not be answered. He should sign the Constitution with a view to support it with all his influence and wished to pledge himself accordingly.

Dr. Franklin: It is too soon to pledge ourselves before Congress and our constituents shall have approved the plan.

Mr. Ingersoll [Pa.] did not consider the signing either as a mere attestation of the fact or as pledging the signers to support the Constitution at all events, but as a recommendation of what, all things considered, was the most eligible.

On the motion of Dr. Franklin: New Hampshire, Massachusetts, Connecticut, New Jersey, Pennsylvania, Delaware, Maryland, Virginia, North Carolina, Georgia, aye— 10; South Carolina, divided.

Mr. King suggested that the Journals of the Convention should be either destroyed or deposited in the custody of the President. He thought, if suffered to be made public, a bad use would be made of them by those who would wish to prevent the adoption of the Constitution.

Mr. Wilson preferred the second expedient; he had at one time liked the first best; but as false suggestions may be propagated, it should not be made impossible to contradict them.

A question was then put on depositing the Journals and other papers of the Convention .in the hands of the President, on which: New Hampshire, Massachusetts, Connecticut, New Jersey, Pennsylvania, Delaware, Virginia, North Carolina, South Carolina, Georgia, aye — 10; Maryland, no — 1.

The President, having asked what the Convention meant should be done with the Journals, etc., whether copies were to be allowed to the members if applied for, it was resolved, *nem. con.*, "that he retain the Journal and other papers, subject to the order of the Congress, if ever formed under the Constitution."

The members then proceeded to sign the instrument.

While the last members were signing it, Dr. Franklin, looking toward the President's chair, at the back of which a rising sun happened to be painted, observed to a few members near him that painters had found it difficult to distinguish in their art a rising from a setting sun. "I have," said he, "often, and often in the course of the session, and the vicissitudes of my hopes and fears as to its issue, looked at that behind the President without being able to tell whether it was rising or setting. But now at length I have the happiness to know that it is a rising and not a setting sun."

The Constitution, being signed by all members except Mr. Randolph, Mr. Mason, and Mr. Gerry, who declined giving it the sanction of their names, the Convention dissolved itself by an adjournment *sine die.*

---

*It is too probable that no plan we propose will be adopted. Perhaps another dreadful conflict is to be sustained. If to please the people, we offer what we ourselves disapprove, how can we afterwards defend our work? Let us raise a standard to which the wise and honest can repair. The event is in the hand of God.*

George Washington, speech at the Federal Convention, 1787, as quoted by Gouverneur Morris in his funeral oration, Dec. 31, 1799

29.

# The Constitution of the United States

*On September 17, 1787, the United States Constitution — the oldest written constitution still in effect today — was approved and signed in Philadelphia by thirty-nine delegates to the federal convention. The document has been hailed as the most successful work of its kind in modern history. William Gladstone, prime minister of Great Britain at the height of the British Empire, went further, saying of the Constitution that it is "the most wonderful work ever struck off at a given time by the brain and purpose of man." Despite such encomiums, it should not be forgotten that the U. S. Constitution is also, as Clinton Rossiter puts it, "a bundle of compromises and a mosaic of second choices." The delegates to the convention had widely differing views about the form that a central government should take. Perhaps the convention's genius was its ability to frame a single document that men of different political principles could agree to accept. Accept it they did, if not always with enthusiasm. Witness Franklin's remark at the end of the convention: "I doubt . . . whether any other Convention we can obtain, may be able to make a better Constitution . . . Thus I consent . . . to this Constitution because I expect no better, and because I am not sure, that it is not the best." The language of the Constitution, as Rossiter says, is both "precise" and "vague." These two qualities, apparently contradictory, may be the secret of the document's long life. "The Constitution of the United States was made not merely for the generation that then existed," Henry Clay observed in 1850, "but for posterity — unlimited, undefined, endless, perpetual posterity." The founding fathers were well aware that they were acting for future generations and that certain phrases in the Constitution would have to be left open for future interpretation. Succeeding generations of Americans have not been hesitant to do so. This view of the document is reflected in a remark of Charles Evans Hughes — that "we are under a Constitution, but the Constitution is what the judges say it is." This is perhaps an exaggeration; nevertheless, recognition of the Constitution as the supreme law of the land, on the whole, has not been lacking even from those who, in time of crisis, have had diametrically opposed views of its meaning and intent. As Franklin D. Roosevelt said in his First Inaugural Address, in 1933, "our Constitution is so simple and practical that it is possible always to meet extraordinary needs by changes in emphasis and arrangement without loss of essential form. That is why," he declared, "our constitutional system has proved itself the most superbly enduring political mechanism the modern world has produced."*

## PREAMBLE

WE THE PEOPLE OF THE UNITED STATES, in order to form a more perfect Union, establish justice, insure domestic tranquility, provide for the common defense, promote the general welfare, and secure the blessings of liberty to ourselves and our posterity, do ordain and establish this Constitution for the United States of America.

## ARTICLE I

Section 1. All legislative powers herein granted shall be vested in a Congress of the United States, which shall consist of a Senate and House of Representatives.

Section 2. The House of Representatives shall be composed of members chosen every second year by the people of the several states, and the electors in each state shall have the qualifications requisite for electors of the most numerous branch of the state legislature.

No person shall be a representative who shall not have attained to the age of twenty-five years, and been seven years a citizen of the United States, and who shall not, when elected, be an inhabitant of that state in which he shall be chosen.

Representatives and direct taxes shall be apportioned among the several states which may be included within this Union, according to their respective numbers, which shall be determined by adding to the whole number of free persons, including those bound to service for a term of years, and excluding Indians not taxed, three-fifths of all other persons. The actual enumeration shall be made within three years after the first meeting of the Congress of the United States, and within every subsequent term of ten years, in such manner as they shall by law direct. The number of representatives shall not exceed one for every thirty thousand, but each state shall have at least one representative; and until such enumeration shall be made, the state of New Hampshire shall be entitled to choose three, Massachusetts eight, Rhode Island and Providence Plantations one, Connecticut five, New York six, New Jersey four, Pennsylvania eight, Delaware one, Maryland six, Virginia ten, North Carolina five, South Carolina five, and Georgia three.

When vacancies happen in the representation from any state, the executive authority thereof shall issue writs of election to fill such vacancies.

The House of Representatives shall choose their speaker and other officers, and shall have the sole power of impeachment.

Section 3. The Senate of the United States shall be composed of two senators from each state, chosen by the legislature thereof, for six years; and each senator shall have one vote.

Immediately after they shall be assembled in consequence of the first election, they shall be divided as equally as may be into three classes. The seats of the senators of the first class shall be vacated at the expiration of the second year, of the second class at the expiration of the fourth year, and of the third class at the expiration of the sixth year, so that one-third may be chosen every second year; and if vacancies happen by resignation, or otherwise, during the recess of the legislature of any state, the executive thereof may make temporary appointments until the next meeting of the legislature, which shall then fill such vacancies.

No person shall be a senator who shall not have attained to the age of thirty years, and been nine years a citizen of the United States, and who shall not, when elected, be an inhabitant of that state for which he shall be chosen.

The vice-president of the United States shall be president of the Senate, but shall have no vote, unless they be equally divided.

The Senate shall choose their other officers and also a president pro tempore, in the absence of the vice-president, or when he shall exercise the office of President of the United States.

The Senate shall have the sole power to try all impeachments. When sitting for that purpose, they shall be on oath or affirmation. When the President of the United States is tried, the chief justice shall preside. And no person shall be convicted without the concurrence of two-thirds of the members present.

Judgment in cases of impeachment shall not extend further than to removal from office, and disqualification to hold and enjoy any office of honor, trust, or profit under the United States; but the party convicted shall nevertheless be liable and subject to indictment, trial, judgment, and punishment according to law.

Section 4. The times, places, and manner of holding elections for senators and representatives shall be prescribed in each state by the legislature thereof; but the Congress may at any time by law make or alter such regulations, except as to the places of choosing senators.

The Congress shall assemble at least once in every year, and such meeting shall be on the first Monday in December, unless they shall by law appoint a different day.

Section 5. Each house shall be the judge of the elections, returns, and qualifications of its own members, and a majority of each shall constitute a quorum to do business; but a smaller number may adjourn from day to day, and may be authorized to compel the attendance of absent members, in such manner and under such penalties as each house may provide.

Each house may determine the rules of its proceedings, punish its members for disorderly behavior, and, with the concurrence of two-thirds, expel a member.

Each house shall keep a journal of its proceedings and from time to time publish the same, excepting such parts as may in their judgment require secrecy; and the yeas and nays of the members of either house on any question shall, at the desire of one-fifth of those present, be entered on the journal.

Neither house, during the session of Congress, shall, without the consent of the other, adjourn for more than three days, nor to any other place than that in which the two houses shall be sitting.

Section 6. The senators and representatives shall receive a compensation for their services, to be ascertained by law, and paid out of the Treasury of the United States. They shall in all cases, except treason, felony, and breach of the peace, be privileged from arrest during their attendance at the session of their respective houses, and in going to and returning from the same; and for any speech or debate in either house, they shall not be questioned in any other place.

No senator or representative shall, during the time for which he was elected, be appointed to any civil office under the authority of the United States which shall have been created, or the emoluments whereof shall have been increased, during such time; and no person holding any office under the United States shall be a member of either house during his continuance in office.

Section 7. All bills for raising revenue shall originate in the House of Representatives; but the Senate may propose or concur with amendments as on other bills.

Every bill which shall have passed the House of Representatives and the Senate shall, before it become a law, be presented to the President of the United States. If he approve he shall sign it, but if not, he shall return it, with his objections, to that house in which it shall have originated, who shall enter the objections at large on their journal and proceed to reconsider it. If, after such reconsideration, two-thirds of that house shall agree to pass the bill, it shall be sent, together with the objections, to the other house, by which it shall likewise be reconsidered, and, if approved by two-thirds of that house, it shall become a law. But in all such cases the votes of both houses shall be determined by yeas and nays, and the names of the persons voting for and against the bill shall be entered on the journal of each house respectively. If any bill shall not be returned by the President within ten days (Sundays excepted) after it shall have been presented to him, the same shall be a law, in like manner as if he had signed it, unless the Congress by their adjournment prevent its return, in which case it shall not be a law.

Every order, resolution, or vote to which the concurrence of the Senate and House of Representatives may be necessary (except on a question of adjournment) shall be presented to the President of the United States; and before the same shall take effect, shall be approved by him, or being disapproved by him, shall be repassed by two-thirds of the Senate and House of Representatives, according to the rules and limitations prescribed in the case of a bill.

Section 8. The Congress shall have power to lay and collect taxes, duties, imposts, and excises, to pay the debts and provide for the common defense and general welfare of the United States; but all duties, imposts, and excises shall be uniform throughout the United States;

To borrow money on the credit of the United States;

To regulate commerce with foreign nations, and among the several states, and with the Indian tribes;

To establish a uniform rule of naturalization and uniform laws on the subject of bankruptcies throughout the United States;

To coin money, regulate the value thereof, and of foreign coin, and fix the standard of weights and measures;

To provide for the punishment of counterfeiting the securities and current coin of the United States;

To establish post offices and post roads;

To promote the progress of science and useful arts, by securing for limited times to authors and inventors the exclusive right to their respective writings and discoveries;

To constitute tribunals inferior to the Supreme Court;

To define and punish piracies and felonies committed on the high seas and offenses against the law of nations;

To declare war, grant letters of marque and reprisal, and make rules concerning captures on land and water;

To raise and support armies, but no appropriation of money to that use shall be for a longer term than two years;

To provide and maintain a navy;

To make rules for the government and regulation of the land and naval forces;

To provide for calling forth the militia to execute the laws of the Union, suppress insurrections, and repel invasions;

To provide for organizing, arming, and disciplining the militia, and for governing such part of them as may be employed in the service of the United States, reserving to the states respectively the appointment of the officers and the authority of training the militia according to the discipline prescribed by Congress;

To exercise exclusive legislation in all cases whatsoever over such district (not exceeding ten miles square) as may, by cession of particular states and the acceptance of Congress, become the seat of the government of the United States, and to exercise like authority over all places purchased by the consent of the legislature of the state in which the same shall be for the erection of forts, magazines, arsenals, dockyards, and other needful buildings; and

To make all laws which shall be necessary and proper for carrying into execution the foregoing powers and all other powers vested by this Constitution in the government of the United States, or in any department or officer thereof.

Section 9. The migration or importation of such persons as any of the states now existing shall think proper to admit shall not be prohibited by the Congress prior to the year 1808, but a tax or duty may be imposed on such importation, not exceeding ten dollars for each person.

The privilege of the writ of habeas corpus shall not be suspended, unless, when in cases of rebellion or invasion, the public safety may require it.

No bill of attainder or ex post facto law shall be passed.

No capitation or other direct tax shall be laid, unless in proportion to the census or enumeration hereinbefore directed to be taken.

No tax or duty shall be laid on articles exported from any state.

No preference shall be given by any regulation of commerce or revenue to the ports of one state over those of another; nor shall vessels bound to or from one state be obliged to enter, clear, or pay duties in another.

No money shall be drawn from the Treasury but in consequence of appropriations made by law; and a regular statement and account of the receipts and expenditures of all public money shall be published from time to time.

No title of nobility shall be granted by the United States. And no person holding any office of profit or trust under them shall, without the consent of the Congress, accept of any present, emolument, office, or title of any kind whatever from any king, prince, or foreign state.

Section 10. No state shall enter into any treaty, alliance, or confederation; grant letters of marque and reprisal; coin money; emit bills of credit; make anything but gold and silver coin a tender in payment of debts; pass any bill of attainder, ex post facto law, or law impairing the obligation of contracts, or grant any title of nobility.

No state shall, without the consent of the Congress, lay any imposts or duties on imports or exports, except what may be absolutely necessary for executing its inspection laws; and the net produce of all duties and imposts laid by any state on imports or exports shall be for the use of the Treasury of the United States; and all such laws shall be subject to the revision and control of the Congress.

No state shall, without the consent of Congress, lay any duty of tonnage; keep troops or ships of war in time of peace; enter into any agreement or compact with another state or with a foreign power, or engage in war, unless actually invaded, or in such imminent danger as will not admit of delay.

## ARTICLE II

Section 1. The executive power shall be vested in a President of the United States of America. He shall hold his office during the term of four years, and, together with the vice-president, chosen for the same term, be elected as follows:

Each state shall appoint, in such manner as the legislature thereof may direct, a number of electors, equal to the whole number of senators and representatives to which the state may be entitled in the Congress; but no senator or representative, or person holding an office of trust or profit under the United States, shall be appointed an elector.

The electors shall meet in their respective states and vote by ballot for two persons, of whom one at least shall not be an inhabitant of the same state with themselves. And they shall make a list of all the persons voted for and of the number of votes for each; which list they shall sign and certify, and transmit sealed to the seat of the government of the United States, directed to the president of the Senate. The president of the Senate shall, in the presence of the Senate and House of Representatives, open all the certificates, and the votes shall then be counted. The person having the greatest number of votes shall be the President, if such number be a majority of the whole number of electors appointed; and if there be more than one who have such majority, and have an equal number of votes, then the House of Representatives shall immediately choose by ballot one of them for President; and if no person have a majority, then from the five highest on the list the said house shall in like manner choose the

President. But in choosing the President, the votes shall be taken by states, the representation from each state having one vote; a quorum for this purpose shall consist of a member or members from two-thirds of the states, and a majority of all the states shall be necessary to a choice. In every case, after the choice of the President, the person having the greatest number of votes of the electors shall be the vice-president. But if there should remain two or more who have equal votes, the Senate shall choose from them by ballot the vice-president.

The Congress may determine the time of choosing the electors and the day on which they shall give their votes, which day shall be the same throughout the United States.

No person except a natural-born citizen, or a citizen of the United States at the time of the adoption of this Constitution, shall be eligible to the office of President; neither shall any person be eligible to that office who shall not have attained to the age of thirty-five years and been fourteen years a resident within the United States.

In case of the removal of the President from office, or of his death, resignation, or inability to discharge the powers and duties of the said office, the same shall devolve on the vice-president, and the Congress may by law provide for the case of removal, death, resignation, or inability, both of the President and vice-president, declaring what officer shall then act as President; and such officer shall act accordingly until the disability be removed or a President shall be elected.

The President shall, at stated times, receive for his services a compensation, which shall neither be increased nor diminished during the period for which he shall have been elected; and he shall not receive within that period any other emolument from the United States or any of them.

Before he enter on the execution of his office, he shall take the following oath or affirmation: "I do solemnly swear (or affirm) that I will faithfully execute the office of President of the United States, and will, to the best of my ability, preserve, protect, and defend the Constitution of the United States."

Section 2. The President shall be commander in chief of the Army and Navy of the United States, and of the militia of the several states when called into the actual service of the United States. He may require the opinion, in writing, of the principal officer in each of the executive departments upon any subject relating to the duties of their respective offices. And he shall have power to grant reprieves and pardons for offenses against the United States, except in cases of impeachment.

He shall have power, by and with the advice and consent of the Senate, to make treaties, provided two-thirds of the senators present concur; and he shall nominate, and by and with the advice and consent of the Senate, shall appoint ambassadors, other public ministers and consuls, judges of the Supreme Court, and all other officers of the United States whose appointments are not herein otherwise provided for, and which shall be established by law; but the Congress may by law vest the appointment of such inferior officers as they think proper in the President alone, in the courts of law, or in the heads of departments.

The President shall have power to fill up all vacancies that may happen during the recess of the Senate, by granting commissions which shall expire at the end of their next session.

Section 3. He shall from time to time give to the Congress information of the state of the Union, and recommend to their consideration such measures as he shall judge necessary and expedient; he may, on extraordinary occasions, convene both houses, or either of them, and in case of disagreement between them with respect to the time of adjournment, he may adjourn them to such time as he shall think proper; he shall receive ambassadors and other public ministers; he shall take care that the laws be faithfully executed; and shall commission all the officers of the United States.

Section 4. The President, vice-president, and all civil officers of the United States shall be removed from office on impeachment for, and conviction of, treason, bribery, or other high crimes and misdemeanors.

ARTICLE III

Section 1. The judicial power of the United States shall be vested in one Supreme Court, and in such inferior courts as the Congress may from time to time ordain and establish. The judges, both of the Supreme and inferior courts, shall hold their offices during good behavior, and shall, at stated times, receive for their services a compensation which shall not be diminished during their continuance in office.

Section 2. The judicial power shall extend to all cases, in law and equity, arising under this Constitution, the laws of the United States, and treaties made, or which shall be made, under their authority; to all cases affecting ambassadors, other public ministers and consuls; to all cases of Admiralty and maritime jurisdiction; to controversies to which the United States shall be a party; to controversies between two or more states; between a state and citizens of another state; between citizens of different states; between citizens of the same state claiming lands under grants of different states; and between a state, or the citizens thereof, and foreign states, citizens, or subjects.

In all cases affecting ambassadors, other public ministers, and consuls, and those in which a state shall be party, the Supreme Court shall have original jurisdiction. In all the other cases beforementioned, the Supreme Court shall have appellate jurisdiction, both as to law and fact, with such exceptions and under such regulations as the Congress shall make.

The trial of all crimes, except in cases of impeachment, shall be by jury; and such trial shall be held in the state where the said crimes shall have been committed; but when not committed within any state, the trial shall be at such place or places as the Congress may by law have directed.

Section 3. Treason against the United States shall consist only in levying war against them, or in adhering to their enemies, giving them aid and comfort. No person shall be convicted of treason unless on the testimony of two witnesses to the same overt act, or on confession in open court.

The Congress shall have power to declare the punishment of treason, but no attainder of treason shall work corruption of blood or forfeiture except during the life of the person attainted.

ARTICLE IV

Section 1. Full faith and credit shall be given in each state to the public acts, records, and judicial proceedings of every other state. And the Congress may by general laws prescribe the manner in which such acts, records, and proceedings shall be proved, and the effect thereof.

Section 2. The citizens of each state shall be entitled to all privileges and immunities of citizens in the several states.

A person charged in any state with treason, felony, or other crime, who shall flee from justice and be found in another state, shall, on demand of the executive authority of the state from which he fled, be delivered up to be removed to the state having jurisdiction of the crime.

No person held to service or labor in one state under the laws thereof, escaping into another, shall, in consequence of any law or regulation therein, be discharged from such service or labor, but shall be delivered up on claim of the party to whom such service or labor may be due.

Section 3. New states may be admitted by the Congress into this Union; but no new state shall be formed or erected within the jurisdiction of any other state; nor any state be formed by the junction of two or more states, or parts of states, without the consent of the legislatures of the states concerned as well as of the Congress.

The Congress shall have power to dispose of and make all needful rules and regulations respecting the territory or other property belonging to the United States; and nothing in this Constitution shall be so construed as to prejudice any claims of the United States, or of any particular state.

Section 4. The United States shall guarantee to every state in this Union a republican form of government, and shall protect each of them against invasion, and, on application of the legislature or of the executive (when the legislature cannot be convened), against domestic violence.

## ARTICLE V

The Congress, whenever two-thirds of both houses shall deem it necessary, shall propose amendments to this Constitution or, on the application of the legislatures of two-thirds of the several states, shall call a convention for proposing amendments, which, in either case, shall be valid, to all intents and purposes, as part of this Constitution when ratified by the legislatures of three-fourths of the several states, or by conventions in three-fourths thereof, as the one or the other mode of ratification may be proposed by the Congress; provided that no amendment which may be made prior to the year 1808 shall in any manner affect the first and fourth clauses in the 9th Section of the 1st Article; and that no state, without its consent, shall be deprived of its equal suffrage in the Senate.

## ARTICLE VI

All debts contracted and engagements entered into before the adoption of this Constitution shall be as valid against the United States under this Constitution as under the Confederation.

This Constitution and the laws of the United States which shall be made in pursuance thereof, and all treaties made, or which shall be made, under the authority of the United States, shall be the supreme law of the land; and the judges in every state shall be bound thereby, anything in the constitution or laws of any state to the contrary notwithstanding.

The senators and representatives beforementioned, and the members of the several state legislatures, and all executive and judicial officers, both of the United States and of the several states, shall be bound by oath or affirmation to support this Constitution; but no religious test shall ever be required as a qualification to any office or public trust under the United States.

## ARTICLE VII

The ratification of the conventions of nine states shall be sufficient for the establishment of this Constitution between the states so ratifying the same.

30.

# Richard Henry Lee: On the Rights that Must Be Preserved in the New Constitution

*Among the most distinguished and influential opponents of the new Constitution was Richard Henry Lee of Virginia. Though he sensed grave defects in the Articles of Confederation, he feared any revision of them that would increase the powers of Congress. "The first maxim of a man who loves liberty," he declared, "should be never to grant to rulers an atom of power that is not most clearly and indispensably necessary for the safety and well being of society." He opposed the Constitution and argued that the Convention, authorized only to* amend *the Articles, had exceeded its powers in writing a new constitution; that the Constitution lacked a bill of rights; and that the Constitution created a "consolidated" rather than a federal government, paving the way to an "elective despotism." In the* Letters from the Federal Farmer to the Republican, *Lee wrote a series of essays that became the best-known anti-Federalist tract of the times. The selection printed below is taken from the letters of October 8 through October 15, 1787.*

Source: *Pamphlets:* Letters I-V, pp. 279-325.

## LETTER I

*Oct. 8, 1787*

The present moment discovers a new face in our affairs. Our object has been all along to reform our federal system and to strengthen our governments — to establish peace, order, and justice in the community — but a new object now presents. The plan of government now proposed is evidently calculated totally to change, in time, our condition as a people. Instead of being thirteen republics under a federal head, it is clearly designed to make us one consolidated government. Of this, I think, I shall fully convince you in my following letters on the subject. This consolidation of the states has been the object of several men in this country for some time past. Whether such a change can ever be effected, in any manner; whether it can be effected without convulsions and civil wars; whether such a change will not totally destroy the liberties of this country, time only can determine.

To have a just idea of the government before us, and to show that a consolidated one is the object in view, it is necessary not only to examine the plan but also its history and the politics of its particular friends.

The Confederation was formed when great confidence was placed in the voluntary exertions of individuals and of the respective states; and the framers of it, to guard against usurpation, so limited and checked the powers that, in many respects, they are inadequate to the exigencies of the Union. We find, therefore, members of Congress urging alterations in the federal system almost as soon as it was adopted. It was early proposed to vest Congress with powers to levy an impost, to regulate trade, etc.; but such was known to be the caution of the states in parting with power that the vestment even of these was proposed to be under several checks and limitations. During the war, the general confusion and the introduction of paper money infused in the minds of people vague ideas respecting government and credit.

We expected too much from the return of peace, and, of course, we have been disappointed. Our governments have been new and unsettled; and several legislatures, by making tender, suspension, and paper-money laws, have given just cause of uneasiness to creditors. By these and other causes, several orders of men in the community have been prepared, by degrees, for a change of government; and this very abuse of power in the legislatures, which in some cases has been charged upon the democratic part of the community, has furnished aristocratical men with those very weapons and those very means with which, in great measure, they are rapidly effecting their favorite object. And should an oppressive government be the consequence of the proposed change, prosperity may reproach not only a few overbearing, unprincipled men but those parties in the states which have misused their powers.

The conduct of several legislatures touching paper-money and tender laws has prepared many honest men for changes in government, which otherwise they would not have thought of — when by the evils, on the one hand, and by the secret instigations of artful men, on the other, the minds of men were become sufficiently uneasy, a bold step was taken, which is usually followed by a revolution or a civil war. A general convention for mere commercial purposes was moved for — the authors of this measure saw that the people's attention was turned solely to the amendment of the federal system; and that, had the idea of a total change been started, probably no state would have appointed members to the Convention. The idea of destroying, ultimately, the state government and forming one consolidated system could not have been admitted. A convention, therefore, merely for vesting in Congress power to regulate trade was proposed. . . .

The plan proposed appears to be partly federal, but principally, however, calculated ultimately to make the states one consolidated government.

The first interesting question therefore suggested is how far the states can be consolidated into one entire government on free principles. In considering this question, extensive objects are to be taken into view, and important changes in the forms of government to be carefully attended to in all their consequences. The happiness of the people at large must be the great object with every honest statesman, and he will direct every movement to this point. If we are so situated as a people as not to be able to enjoy equal happiness and advantages under one government, the consolidation of the states cannot be admitted.

## LETTER II

*Oct. 9, 1787*

The essential parts of a free and good government are a full and equal representation of the people in the legislature, and the jury trial of the vicinage in the administration of justice — a full and equal representation is that which possesses the same interests, feelings, opinions, and views the people themselves would were they all assembled. . . .

If it were possible to consolidate the states and preserve the features of a free government, still it is evident that the middle states, the parts of the Union about the seat of government, would enjoy great advantages, while the remote states would experience the many inconveniences of remote provinces. Wealth, offices, and the benefits of government would collect in the center; and the extreme states and their principal towns become much less important. . . .

There are certain unalienable and fundamental rights, which in forming the social compact ought to be explicitly ascertained and fixed. A free and enlightened people, in forming this compact, will not resign all their rights to those who govern, and they will fix limits to their legislators and rulers, which will soon be plainly seen by those who are governed, as well as by those who govern; and the latter will know they cannot be passed unperceived by the former and without giving a general alarm. These rights should be made the basis of every constitution; and if a people be so situated, or have such different opinions, that they cannot agree in ascertaining and fixing them, it is a very strong argument against their attempting to form one entire society, to live under one system of laws only.

I confess I never thought the people of these states differed essentially in these respects, they having derived all these rights from one common source — the British systems — and having in the formation of their state constitutions discovered that their ideas relative to these rights are very similar. However, it is now said that the states differ so essentially in these respects, and even in the important article of the trial by jury, that, when assembled in convention, they can agree to no words by which to establish that trial, or by which to ascertain and establish many other of these rights, as fundamental articles in the social compact. If so, we proceed to consolidate the states on no solid basis whatever.

But I do not pay much regard to the reasons given for not bottoming the new Constitution on a better Bill of Rights. I still believe a complete federal Bill of Rights to be very practicable. Nevertheless, I acknowledge the proceedings of the Convention furnish my mind with many new and strong reasons against a complete consolidation of the states. They tend to convince me that it cannot be carried with propriety very far — that the Convention have gone much further in one respect than they found it practicable to go in another; that is, they propose to lodge in the general government very extensive powers — *powers* nearly, if not altogether, complete and unlimited over the purse and the sword. But, in its organization, they furnish the strongest proof that the proper limbs, or parts of a government to support and execute those powers on proper principles (or in which they can be safely lodged) cannot be formed.

These powers must be lodged somewhere in every society; but then they should be lodged where the strength and guardians of the people are collected. They can be wielded, or safely used, in a free country only by an able executive and judiciary, a respectable senate, and a secure, full, and equal representation of the people.

## LETTER III

*Oct. 10, 1787*

The great object of a free people must be so to form their government and laws, and so to administer them, as to create a confidence in and respect for the laws; and thereby induce the sensible and virtuous part of the community to declare in favor of the laws, and to support them without an expensive military force. I wish, though I confess I have not much hope, that this may be the case with the laws of Congress under the new Constitution. I am fully convinced that we must organize the national government on different principles, and make the parts of it more efficient, and secure in it more effectually the different interests in the community; or else leave in the state governments some powers proposed to be lodged in it — at least till such an organization shall be found to be practicable. . . .

Impressed as I am with a sense of the difficulties there are in the way of forming the parts of a federal government on proper principles, and seeing a government so unsubstantially organized, after so arduous an attempt has been made, I am led to believe that powers ought to be given to it with great care and caution. . . .

These powers — legislative, executive, and judicial — respect internal as well as external objects. Those respecting external objects, as all foreign concerns, commerce, imposts, all causes arising on the seas, peace and war, and Indian affairs, can be lodged nowhere else, with any propriety, but in this government. Many powers that respect internal objects ought clearly to be lodged in it; as those to regulate trade between the states, weights and measures, the coin or current monies, post offices, naturalization, etc. These powers may be exercised without essentially affecting the internal police of the respective states.

But powers to lay and collect internal taxes, to form the militia, to make bankrupt laws, and to decide on appeals, questions arising on the internal laws of the respective states, are of a very serious nature, and carry with them almost all other powers. These taken in connection with the others, and powers to raise armies and build navies, proposed to be lodged in this government, appear to me to comprehend all the essential powers in this community, and those which will be left to the states will be of no great importance.

## LETTER IV

*Oct. 12, 1787*

There appears to me to be not only a premature deposit of some important powers in the general government, but many of those deposited there are undefined and may be used to good or bad purposes as honest or designing men shall prevail. By Article I, Section 2, representatives and direct taxes shall be apportioned among the several states, etc.; same Article, Section 8, the Congress shall have powers to lay and collect taxes, duties, etc., for the common defense and general welfare, but all duties, imposts, and excises shall be uniform throughout the United States.

By the first recited clause, direct taxes shall be apportioned on the states. This seems to favor the idea suggested by some sensible men and writers that Congress, as to direct taxes, will only have power to make requisitions; but the latter clause, power to lay and collect taxes, etc., seems clearly to favor the contrary opinion and in my mind the true one — the Congress shall have power to tax immediately individuals, without the intervention of the state legislatures. In fact, the first clause appears to me only to provide that each state shall pay a certain portion of the tax, and the latter to provide that Congress shall have power to lay and collect taxes, that is to assess upon and to collect of the individuals in the state the state's quota; but these still I consider as undefined powers, because judicious men understand them differently.

It is doubtful whether the vice-president is to have any qualifications. None are mentioned; but he may serve as president, and it may be inferred, he ought to be qualified, therefore, as the president; but the qualifications of the president are required only of the person to be elected president. . . .

There are certain rights which we have always held sacred in the United States, and recognized in all our constitutions, and which, by the adoption of the new Constitution in its present form, will be left unsecured. By Article VI, the proposed Constitution and the laws of the United States, which shall be made in pursuance thereof, and all treaties made, or which shall be made, under the authority of the United States, shall be the supreme law of the land; and the judges in every state shall be bound thereby, anything in the Constitution or laws of any state to the contrary notwithstanding.

It is to be observed that when the people shall adopt the proposed Constitution it will be their last and supreme act; it will be adopted not by the people of New Hampshire, Massachusetts, etc., but by the people of the United States; and wherever this Constitution, or any part of it, shall be incompatible with the ancient customs, rights, the laws, or the constitutions heretofore established in the United States, it will entirely abolish them and do them away. And not only this, but the laws of the United States which shall be made in pursuance of the federal Constitution will be also supreme laws, and wherever they shall be incompatible with those customs, rights, laws, or constitutions heretofore established, they will also entirely abolish them and do them away. . . .

The federal Constitution, the laws of Congress made in pursuance of the Constitution, and all treaties must have full force and effect in all parts of the United States; and all other laws, rights, and constitutions which stand in their way must yield. It is proper the national laws should be supreme and superior to state or district laws; but then the national laws ought to yield to unalienable or fundamental rights; and national laws, made by a few men, should extend only to a few national objects. This will not be the case with the laws of Congress. To have any proper idea of their extent, we must carefully examine the legislative, executive, and judicial powers proposed to be lodged in the general government, and consider them in connection with a general clause in Article I, Section 8 in these words (after enumerating a number of powers): "To make all laws which shall be necessary and proper for carrying into execution the foregoing powers, and all other powers vested by this Constitution in the government of the United States, or in any department or officer thereof." . . .

The people of the United States made a federal Constitution, which is a fundamental compact between them and their federal rulers; these rulers, in the nature of things, cannot be bound to take notice of any other compact. It would be absurd for them, in making laws, to look over thirteen, fifteen, or twenty state constitutions to see what rights are established as fundamental and must not be infringed upon, in making laws in the society. It is true, they would be bound to do it if the people, in their federal compact, should refer to the state constitutions, recognize all parts not inconsistent with the federal Constitution, and direct their federal rulers to take notice of them accordingly; but this is not the case, as the plan stands proposed at present; and it is absurd to suppose so unnatural an idea is intended or implied. I think my opinion is not only founded in reason but I think it is supported by the report of the Convention itself. If there are a number of rights established by the state constitutions, and which will remain sacred, and the general government is bound to take notice of them, it must take notice of one as well as another; and if unnecessary to recognize or establish one by the federal Constitution, it would be unnecessary to recognize or establish another by it.

If the federal Constitution is to be construed so far in connection with the state constitution as to leave the trial by jury in civil cases, for instance, secured, on the same principles it would have left the trial by jury in criminal cases, the benefits of the writ of habeas corpus, etc., secured; they all stand on the same footing; they are the common rights of Americans, and have been recognized by the state constitutions. But the Convention found it necessary to recognize or reestablish the benefits of that writ, and the jury trial in criminal cases.

As to ex post facto laws, the Convention

has done the same in one case and gone further in another. It is a part of the compact between the people of each state and their rulers that no ex post facto laws shall be made. But the Convention, by Article I, Section 10 have put a sanction upon this part even of the state compacts. In fact, the 9th and 10th Sections in Article I in the proposed Constitution are no more nor less than a partial Bill of Rights; they establish certain principles as part of the compact upon which the federal legislators and officers can never infringe. It is here wisely stipulated that the federal legislature shall never pass a bill of attainder, or ex post facto law; that no tax shall be laid on articles exported, etc. The establishing of one right implies the necessity of establishing another and similar one.

On the whole, the position appears to me to be undeniable — that this Bill of Rights ought to be carried further, and some other principles established as a part of this fundamental compact between the people of the United States and their federal rulers.

It is true, we are not disposed to differ much, at present, about religion; but when we are making a constitution, it is to be hoped, for ages and millions yet unborn, why not establish the free exercise of religion as a part of the national compact. There are other essential rights which we have justly understood to be the rights of freemen — as freedom from hasty and unreasonable search warrants, warrants not founded on oath and not issued with due caution, for searching and seizing men's papers, property, and persons. The trials by jury in civil cases, it is said, varies so much in the several states, that no words could be found for the uniform establishment of it. If so, the federal legislation will not be able to establish it by any general laws. I confess I am of opinion it may be established, but not in that beneficial manner in which we may enjoy it, for the reasons beforementioned.

When I speak of the jury trial of the vicinage, or the trial of the fact in the neighborhood, I do not lay so much stress upon the circumstance of our being tried by our neighbors. In this enlightened country, men may be probably impartially tried by those who do not live very near them; but the trial of facts in the neighborhood is of great importance in other respects. Nothing can be more essential than the cross-examining witnesses, and generally before the triers of the facts in question. The common people can establish facts with much more ease with oral than written evidence. When trials of facts are removed to a distance from the homes of the parties and witnesses, oral evidence becomes intolerably expensive, and the parties must depend on written evidence, which to the common people is expensive and almost useless; it must be frequently taken *ex parte,* and but very seldom leads to the proper discovery of truth.

The trial by jury is very important in another point of view. It is essential in every free country that common people should have a part and share of influence in the judicial as well as in the legislative department. To hold open to them the offices of senators, judges, and offices to fill which an expensive education is required cannot answer any valuable purposes for them; they are not in a situation to be brought forward and to fill those offices; these, and most other offices of any considerable importance, will be occupied by the few. The few, the wellborn, etc., as Mr. Adams calls them, in judicial decisions as well as in legislation, are generally disposed, and very naturally too, to favor those of their own description.

The trial by jury in the judicial department, and the collection of the people by their representatives in the legislature, are those fortunate inventions which have procured for them, in this country, their true proportion of influence, and the wisest and most fit means of protecting themselves in the community. Their situation, as jurors and representatives, enables them to acquire information and knowledge in the affairs and government of the society, and to come forward, in turn, as the sentinels and guardians of each other. I am very sorry that even a few of our countrymen should consider jurors and representatives in a different point of view, as ignorant, troublesome bodies which ought not to have any share in the concerns of government.

I confess I do not see in what cases the Congress can, with any pretense of right, make a law to suppress the freedom of the press; though I am not clear that Congress is restrained from laying any duties whatever on printing, and from laying duties particularly heavy on certain pieces printed; and perhaps Congress may require large bonds for the payment of these duties. Should the printer say the freedom of the press was secured by the constitution of the state in which he lived, Congress might, and perhaps, with great propriety, answer that the federal Constitution is the only compact existing between them and the people. In this compact the people have named no others, and, therefore, Congress, in exercising the powers assigned them and in making laws to carry them into execution, are restrained by nothing beside the federal Constitution, any more than a state legislature is restrained by a compact between the magistrates and people of a county, city, or town of which the people, in forming the state constitution, have taken no notice. . . .

It may also be worthy our examination how far the provision for amending this plan, when it shall be adopted, is of any importance. No measures can be taken toward amendments unless two-thirds of the Congress, or two-thirds of the legislature of the several states, shall agree. While power is in the hands of the people, or democratic part of the community, more especially as at present, it is easy, according to the general course of human affairs, for the few influential men in the community to obtain conventions, alterations in government, and to persuade the common people that they may change for the better, and to get from them a part of the power. But when power is once transferred from the many to the few, all changes become extremely difficult; the government in this case being beneficial to the few, they will be exceedingly artful and adroit in preventing any measures which may lead to a change; and nothing will produce it but great exertions and severe struggles on the part of the common people. Every man of reflection must see that the change now proposed is a transfer of power from the many to the few, and the probability is the artful and ever active aristocracy will prevent all peaceful measures for changes, unless when they shall discover some favorable moment to increase their own influence.

I am sensible [that] thousands of men in the United States are disposed to adopt the proposed Constitution, though they perceive it to be essentially defective, under an idea that amendments of it may be obtained when necessary. This is a pernicious idea; it argues a servility of character totally unfit for the support of free government; it is very repugnant to that perpetual jealousy respecting liberty, so absolutely necessary in all free states, spoken of by Mr. Dickinson. However, if our countrymen are so soon changed, and the language of 1774 is become odious to them, it will be in vain to use the language of freedom, or to attempt to rouse them to free inquiries. But I shall never believe this is the case with them, whatever present appearances may be, till I shall have very strong evidence indeed of it.

## LETTER V

*Oct. 15, 1787*

Thus I have examined the federal Constitution as far as a few days leisure would permit. . . . There are, in my opinion, many good things in the proposed system. It is founded on elective principles, and the deposits of powers in different hands is essentially right. The guards against those evils we have experienced in some states in legislation are valuable indeed; but the value of every feature in this system is vastly lessened for the want of that one important feature in a free government — a representation of the people. Because we have sometimes abused democracy, I am not among those men who think a democratic branch a nuisance; which branch shall be sufficiently numerous to admit some of the best informed men of each order in the community into the administration of government.

While the radical defects in the proposed system are not so soon discovered, some temptations to each state, and to many classes of men, to adopt it are very visible. It uses the democratic language of several of the state constitutions, particularly that of Massachusetts; the eastern states will receive advantages so far as the regulation of trade, by a bare majority, is committed to it: Connecticut and New Jersey will receive their share of a general impost. The middle states will receive the advantages surrounding the seat of government. The southern states will receive protection, and have their Negroes represented in the legislature, and large back countries will soon have a majority in it. This system promises a large field of employment to military gentlemen and gentlemen of the law; and in case the government shall be executed without convulsions, it will afford security to creditors, to the clergy, salary-men, and others depending on money payments. So far as the system promises justice and reasonable advantages, in these respects, it ought to be supported by all honest men; but whenever it promises unequal and improper advantages to any particular states, or orders of men, it ought to be opposed.

I have, in the course of these letters, observed that there are many good things in the proposed Constitution, and I have endeavored to point out many important defects in it. I have admitted that we want a federal system — that we have a system presented, which, with several alterations, may be made a tolerable good one. I have admitted there is a well-founded uneasiness among creditors and mercantile men. In this situation of things, you ask me what I think ought to be done? My opinion in this case is only the opinion of an individual, and so far only as it corresponds with the opinions of the honest and substantial part of the community is it entitled to consideration.

Though I am fully satisfied that the state conventions ought most seriously to direct their exertions to altering and amending the system proposed before they shall adopt it, yet I have not sufficiently examined the subject, or formed an opinion, how far it will be practicable for those conventions to carry their amendments. As to the idea that it will be in vain for those conventions to attempt amendments, it cannot be admitted; it is impossible to say whether they can or not until the attempt shall be made; and when it shall be determined, by experience, that the conventions cannot agree in amendments, it will then be an important question before the people of the United States, whether they will adopt or not the system proposed in its present form. This subject of consolidating the states is new; and because forty or fifty men have agreed in a system, to suppose the good sense of this country, an enlightened nation, must adopt it without examination, and though in a state of profound peace, without endeavoring to amend those parts they perceive are defective, dangerous to freedom, and destructive of the valuable principles of republican government is truly humiliating.

It is true there may be danger in delay; but there is danger in adopting the system in its present form. And I see the danger in either case will arise principally from the conduct and views of two very unprincipled parties in the United States — two fires, between which the honest and substantial people have long found themselves situated. One party is composed of little insurgents, men in debt, who want no law and who want a share of the property of others — these are called levelers, Shayites, etc. The other party is composed of a few but more dangerous men, with their servile dependents; these avariciously grasp at all power and property. You may discover in all the actions of these men an evident dislike to free and equal government, and they will go systematically to work to change, essentially, the forms of government in this country — these are called aristocrats, m —— ites, etc. Between these two parties is the weight of the community; the men of middling property, men not in debt on the one hand, and men, on the other, content with republican governments, and not aiming at immense fortunes, offices, and power.

In 1786, the little insurgents, the levelers, came forth, invaded the rights of others, and attempted to establish governments according to their wills. Their movements evidently gave encouragement to the other party, which, in 1787, has taken the political field, and with its fashionable dependents, and the tongue and the pen, is endeavoring to establish, in a great haste, a politer kind of government. These two parties, which will probably be opposed or united as it may suit their interests and views, are really insignificant compared with the solid, free, and independent part of the community. It is not my intention to suggest that either of these parties and the real friends of the proposed Constitution are the same men. The fact is, these aristocrats support and hasten the adoption of the proposed Constitution merely because they think it is a stepping-stone to their favorite object. I think I am well-founded in this idea; I think the general politics of these men support it, as well as the common observation among them that the proffered plan is the best that can be got at present; it will do for a few years, and lead to something better. The sensible and judicious part of the community will carefully weigh all these circumstances; they will view the late Convention as a respectable body of men — America probably never will see an assembly of men, of a like number, more respectable.

But the members of the Convention met without knowing the sentiments of one man in ten thousand in these states respecting the new ground taken. Their doings are but the first attempts in the most important scene ever opened. Though each individual in the state conventions will not, probably, be so respectable as each individual in the federal Convention, yet as the state conventions will probably consist of 1,500 or 2,000 men of abilities and versed in the science of government, collected from all parts of the community and from all orders of men, it must be acknowledged that the weight of respectability will be in them. In them will be collected the solid sense and the real political character of the country. Being revisers of the subject, they will possess peculiar advantages.

To say that these conventions ought not to attempt, coolly and deliberately, the revision of the system, or that they cannot amend it, is very foolish or very assuming. If these conventions, after examining the system, adopt it, I shall be perfectly satisfied, and wish to see men make the administration of the government an equal blessing to all orders of men.

31.

# Debate on the Ratification of the Constitution in New York

*After adopting the Constitution, Congress submitted the document to the states for ratification. Though the approval of only nine states out of the thirteen was needed to establish the new government legally, and this number was attained by June 21, 1788, in fact, the consent of Virginia and New York, the two most populous, wealthy, and powerful states, was essential. Opposition to ratification by New York was led by the state's governor, George Clinton, who wished to maintain the power of his office as well as the sovereignty of his state. Alexander Hamilton led the fight for ratification by New York. Clinton and Hamilton debated the issue in an exchange of letters. Clinton's appeared in the* New-York Journal *over the pseudonym "Cato" and were addressed to the people of the state. Hamilton addressed his letters to Francis Childs, publisher of the* New York Daily Advertiser *and, aware that the historical Cato had committed suicide before a victorious Caesar, signed them "Caesar." The following letters appeared on October 11 and 17, 1787, respectively. New York ratified the Constitution on July 26, 1788.*

Source: Scott, II, pp. 617-622, 644-648.

I.

## George Clinton: Against the Adoption of the Constitution

> Remember, O my friends! the laws, the rights,
> The generous plan of power deliver'd down
> By your renown'd forefathers;
> So dearly bought, the price of so much blood!
> O let it never perish in your hands!
> But piously transmit it to your children.

The object of my last address to you was to engage your dispassionate consideration of the new federal government; to caution you against precipitancy in the adoption of it; to recommend a correction of its errors, if it contained any; to hint to you the danger of an easy perversion of some of its powers; to solicit you to separate yourselves from party, and to be independent of and uninfluenced by any in your principles of politics; and that address was closed with a promise of future observations on the same subject, which should be justified by reason and truth. Here I intended to have rested the introduction; but a writer under the signature of "Caesar," in Mr. Childs's paper of the first instant, who treats you with passion, insult, and threat, has anticipated those observations which would otherwise have remained in silence until a future period.

It would be criminal in me to hesitate a

moment to appear as your advocate in so interesting a cause, and to resist the influence of such doctrines as this "Caesar" holds. I shall take no other cognizance of his remarks on the questionable shape of my future, or the equivocal appearance of my past reflections, than to declare that in my past I did not mean to be misunderstood (for "Caesar" himself declares that it is obviously the language of distrust), and that in my future there will not be the semblance of doubt. But what is the language of "Caesar"? He ridicules your prerogative, power, and majesty. He talks of this *proffered constitution* as the tender mercy of a benevolent sovereign to deluded subjects, or, as his tyrant namesake, of his proffered grace to the virtuous Cato. He shuts the door of free deliberation and discussion, and declares that you must receive this government in manner and form as it is *proffered*: that you cannot revise or amend it. And, lastly, to close the scene, he insinuates that it will be more healthy for you that the American Fabius [Washington] should be induced to accept of the presidency of this new government than that, in case you do not acquiesce, he should be solicited to command an army to impose it on you.

Is not your indignation roused at this absolute, imperious style? For what did you open the veins of your citizens and expend their treasure? For what did you throw off the yoke of Britain and call yourselves independent? Was it from a disposition fond of change, or to procure new masters? If those were your motives, you have reward before you. Go, retire into silent obscurity, and kiss the rod that scourges you, bury the prospects you had in store, that you and your posterity would participate in the blessings of freedom and the employments of your country. Let the rich and insolent alone be your rulers.

Perhaps you are designed by Providence as an emphatic evidence of the mutability of human affairs, to have the show of happiness only, that your misery may seem the sharper, and if so, you must submit. But if you had nobler views, and you are not designed by Heaven as an example, are you now to be derided and insulted? Is the power of thinking, on the only subject important to you, to be taken away? And if perchance you should happen to differ from "Caesar," are you to have "Caesar's" principles crammed down your throats with an army? God forbid!

In democratic republics the people collectively are considered as the sovereign: all legislative, judicial, and executive power is inherent in and derived from them. As a people, your power and authority have sanctioned and established the present government. Your executive, legislative, and judicial acknowledge it by their public acts. You are again solicited to sanction and establish the future one. Yet this "Caesar" mocks your dignity and laughs at the majesty of the people. "Caesar," with his usual dogmatism, inquires, if I had talents to throw light on the subject of legislation, why did I not offer them when the Convention was in session? He is answered in a moment.

I thought with him and you that the wisdom of America, in that Convention, was drawn, as it were, to a focus. I placed an unbounded confidence in some of the characters who were members of it, from the services they had rendered their country without adverting to the ambitious and interested views of others. I was willingly led to expect a model of perfection and security that would have astonished the world. Therefore to have offered observation on the subject of legislation under these impressions would have discovered no less arrogance than "Caesar."

The Convention, too, when in session, shut their doors to the observations of the community, and their members were under an obligation of secrecy. Nothing transpired. To have suggested remarks on unknown and anticipated principles would have been like a man groping in the dark, and folly in the extreme. I confess, however, I have been disappointed, and "Caesar" is candid enough to make the same declaration, for he thinks it might have been more perfect.

But to call in dispute, at this time, and in the manner "Caesar" does, the right of free deliberation on this subject is like a man's propounding a question to another, and telling him at the same [time] that if he does not answer agreeable to the opinion of the propounder, he will exert force to make him of the same sentiment.

To exemplify this, it will be necessary to give you a short history of the rise and progress of the Convention, and the conduct of Congress thereon. The states in Congress suggested that the Articles of Confederation had provided for making alterations in the Confederation. That there were defects therein, and as a means to remedy which, a convention of delegates, appointed by the different states, was resolved expedient to be held for the sole and express purpose of revising it, and reporting to Congress and the different legislatures such alterations and provisions therein as should (when agreed to in Congress and confirmed by the several states) render the federal Constitution adequate to the exigencies of government.

This resolution is sent to the different states, and the legislature of this state, with others, appoint, in conformity thereto, delegates for the purpose; and in the words mentioned in that resolve, as by the resolution of Congress and the concurrent resolutions of the Senate and Assembly of this state, subjoined, will appear. For the sole and express purpose aforesaid, a Convention of delegates is formed at Philadelphia: What have they done? Have they revised the Confederation, and has Congress agreed to their report? Neither is the fact. This Convention have exceeded the authority given to them and have transmitted to Congress a new political fabric, essentially and fundamentally distinct and different from it, in which the different states do not retain separately their sovereignty and independency, united by a confederate league, but one entire sovereignty, a consolidation of them into one government, in which new provisions and powers are not made and vested in Congress but in an assembly, Senate, and President, who are not known in the Articles of Confederation.

Congress, without agreeing to or approving of this system proffered by the Convention, have sent it to the different legislatures, not for their confirmation but to submit it to the people; not in conformity to their own resolution but in conformity to the resolution of the Convention made and provided in that case. Was it, then, from the face of the foregoing facts, the intention of Congress and of this and the other states that the essence of our present national government should be annihilated, or that it should be retained and only have an increase of substantial necessary powers?

Congress, sensible of this latter principle, and that the Convention had taken on themselves a power which neither they nor the other states had a right to delegate to them, and that they could not agree to and approve of this consolidated system, nor the states confirm it, have been silent on its character; and although many have dwelt on their unanimity, it is no less than the unanimity of opinion that it originated in an assumption of power which your voice alone can sanctify. This new government, therefore, founded in usurpation, is referred to your opinion as the origin of power not heretofore delegated, and, to this end, the exercise of the prerogative of free examination is essentially necessary. And yet you are unhesitatingly to acquiesce, and if you do not, the American Fabius, if we may believe "Caesar," is to command an army to impose it.

It is not my view to rouse your passions.

I only wish to excite you to, and assist you in, a cool and deliberate discussion of the subject, to urge you to behave like sensible freemen. Think, speak, act, and assert your opinions and rights. Let the same good sense govern you with respect to the adoption of a future system for the administration of your public affairs that influenced you in the formation of the present. Hereafter I do not intend to be diverted by "Caesar," or any other. My object is to take up this new form of national government, compare it with the experience and opinions of the most sensible and approved political authors, and to show that its principles, and the exercise of them, will be dangerous to your liberty and happiness.

Cato

## II.

## Alexander Hamilton: For the Adoption of the Constitution

> The great source of all the evils which afflict republics is that the people are too apt to make choice of rulers who are either politicians without being patriots, or patriots without being politicians.

When I took notice of "Cato's" prefatory address to the citizens of the state of New York in your paper of the first instant, I had no serious intention of becoming a controversial defendant of the new Constitution. Indeed, if the system required defense, I was neither so weak nor so vain as to suppose myself competent to the task. To obviate difficulties which may arise when such weighty affairs as the principles of legislation are under discussion, I am sensible requires talents far beyond my limited abilities. When I offered a few remarks on "Cato's" introduction, I was strongly impressed with the idea that even the most substantial criticisms, promulgated by the most influential *avowed citizens,* could have no good tendency at this time. I viewed the public mind as wound up to a great pitch of dissatisfaction by the inadequacy of the powers of the present Congress to the general good and conversation of the Union. I believed then, as I do now, that the people were determined and prepared for a change.

I conceived, therefore, that the wish of every good man would be that *this change might be peaceably effected.* With this view, I opposed myself to "Cato." I asserted, in my last, *that the door of recommendation was shut, and cannot be opened by the same men — that the Convention was dissolved.* If I am wrong, it will be of great importance to "Cato's" future remarks that he make it appear. If he will declare from sufficient authority that the members of the late Convention have only adjourned to give time to hear the sentiments of every political disputant, that after the numerous presses of America have groaned with the heavy productions of speculative politicians, they will again meet, weigh their respective merits, and accommodate accordingly — I say if "Cato" can do this, I make no hesitation in acknowledging the utility of his plan.

In the meantime, I positively deny having the most distant desire of shutting the door of free discussion on any subject which may benefit the people; but I maintain (until "Cato's" better information refutes me) that the door, as far as relates to this subject, is already shut, not by me but by the highest possible authority which the case admits, even by those great patriots who were delegated by the people of the United States to open such a door, as might enable them to escape from impending calamities and political shipwreck. This distinction is clear, I conceive, and ought to have some weight even with "Cato," as well as those for whom he writes. I am not one of those who gain an influence by cajoling the unthinking mass (though I pity their delusions) and ringing in their ears the gracious sound of their *absolute sovereignty.* I despise the trick of such dirty policy. I know there are citizens who, to gain their own private ends, inflame the minds of the well-meaning though less intelligent parts of the community by sating their vanity with that cordial and unfailing specific that *all power is seated in the people.*

For my part, I am not much attached to the *majesty of the multitude,* and therefore waive all pretensions (founded on such conduct) to their countenance. I consider them in general as very ill-qualified to judge for themselves what government will best suit their peculiar situations; nor is this to be wondered at. The science of government is not easily understood. "Cato" will admit, I presume, that men of good education and deep reflection, only, are judges of the *form* of a government; whether it is constituted on such principles as will restrain arbitrary power, on the one hand, and equal to the exclusion of corruption and the destruction of licentiousness, on the other. Whether the new Constitution, if adopted, will prove adequate to such desirable ends, time, the mother of events, will show.

For my own part, I sincerely esteem it a system which, without the finger of God, never could have been suggested and agreed upon by such a diversity of interests. I will not presume to say that a more perfect system might not have been fabricated; but who expects perfection at once? And it may be asked — *Who are judges of it*? Few, I believe, who have leisure to study the nature of government scientifically but will frequently disagree about the quantum of power to be delegated to rulers, and the different modifications of it. Ingenious men will give every plausible, and, it may be, pretty substantial reasons for the adoption of two plans of government, which shall be fundamentally different in their construction and not less so in their operation; yet both, if honestly administered, might operate with safety and advantage. When a new form of government is fabricated, it lies with the people at large to receive or reject it — that is their *inherent right.*

Now, I would ask (without intending to triumph over the weaknesses or follies of any men) how are the people to profit by this inherent right? By what conduct do they discover that they are sensible of their own interests in this situation? Is it by the exercise of a well-disciplined reason and a correspondent education? I believe not. How then? As I humbly conceive, by a tractable and docile disposition, and by honest men endeavoring to keep their minds easy, while others of the same disposition, with the advantages of genius and learning, are constructing the bark that may, by the blessing of Heaven, carry them to the port of rest and happiness if they will embark without diffidence and proceed without mutiny. I know this is blunt and ungracious reasoning; it is the best, however, which I am prepared to offer on this momentous business; and, since my own heart does not reproach me, I shall not be very solicitous about its reception.

If truth, then, is permitted to speak, the mass of the people of America (any more than the mass of other countries) cannot judge with any degree of precision concerning the fitness of this new Constitution to the peculiar situation of America; they have, however, done wisely in delegating the power of framing a government to those every way worthy and well-qualified. And if this government is snatched, untasted, from them, it may not be amiss to inquire into the causes which will probably occasion their disappointment. Out of several which present to my mind, I shall venture to select one, baneful enough, in my opinion, to work this dreadful evil. There are always men in society of some talents but more ambition, in quest of that which it would be impossible for them to obtain in any other way than by working on the passions and prejudices of the less discerning classes of citizens and yeomanry. It is the plan of men of this stamp to frighten the people with ideal bugbears in order to mold them to their own purposes. The unceasing cry of these designing croakers is: My friends, your liberty is invaded! Have you thrown off the yoke of one tyrant to invest yourselves with that of another? Have you fought, bled, and conquered for such a change? If you have, go — retire into silent obscurity, and kiss the rod that scourges you.

To be serious: these state empirics leave no species of deceit untried to convince the unthinking people that they have power to do — what? Why, truly, to do much mischief and to occasion anarchy and wild uproar. And for what reason do these political jugglers incite the peaceably disposed to such extravagant commotions? Because, until the people really discover that they have power, by some outrageous act, they never can become of any importance. The misguided people never reflect during this frenzy that the moment they become riotous they renounce, from that moment, their independence and commence vassals to their ambitious leaders, who instantly, and with a high hand, rob them of their consequence and apply it to their own present or future aggrandizement. Nor will these tyrants over the people stick at sacrificing their good if an advantageous compromise can be effected for themselves.

Before I conclude, I cannot refrain from observing that "Cato" states very disingenuously the manner in which the federal system came abroad. He tells us Congress were sensible that the late Convention exercised a power which no authority could delegate to them. The Convention, says "Cato," have taken upon them to make a perfectly new system, which by its operations will absorb the sovereignties of the individual states. This new government founded on *usurpation* ("Cato," this expression is very indecent, but I will rouse no passions against you), this consolidated system Congress did not approve and therefore have been silent on its character.

That Congress were silent on its character is true; but could Cato find no other reason for their silence than that of disapprobation? I believe Congress were by no means dissatisfied with the freedom the Convention took with the Articles of Confederation; I believe further that with very few exceptions, that honorable body approves of the new Constitution. That they did not accompany it to the states with a recommendatory capitation or circular letter proceeded from a delicate attention to the members of the late Convention, to a few of their own body, and to the people of America at large. That the Convention went so earnestly into the business committed to their care ought, instead of being matter of chagrin, to occasion the liveliest expression of approbation and gratitude, as matters stand just now.

I think it may be fairly said that no *generous plan of government* for the *United States* has ever been constructed (the plan only excepted which is under consideration), so that it seems quite unnecessary in "Cato" to disturb the peace of society by a bombast appeal to their feelings, on the *generous plan of power delivered down by their renowned forefathers.* I venerate the memory of the slaughtered patriots of America, and rejoice as much as "Cato" that they did not bleed in vain, but I would have America profit by their death in a different manner from him. I believe they sought to obtain liberty for no particular state but for the whole Union, indissolubly connected under one controlling and supreme head.

"Cato" complains of my anticipating parts of his subject which he intended for future periods. I shall break in no more upon his *arrangements.* All he can say against the new Constitution has been already disseminated in a neighboring state by the glorious defenders of *Shaysism.* I shall therefore leave "Cato" to the wicked influences of his own heart, in the fullest persuasion that all good citizens will combine their influence to establish the fair fabric of American liberty beyond the reach of suspicion, violence, anarchy, and tyranny.

When this glorious work is accomplished, what may America not hope to arrive at? I will venture to prophesy that the day on which the Union under the new government shall be ratified by the American states, that *that day* will begin an era which will be recorded and observed by future ages as a day which the Americans had marked by their wisdom in circumscribing the power and ascertaining the decline of the ancient nations in Christendom.

CAESAR

---

32.

## JAMES MADISON: A Plurality of Interests and a Balance of Powers

*In the federal Convention of 1787, James Madison was the acknowledged leader of the group favoring a strong central government. The final draft of the Constitution did not fully satisfy Madison, for he thought the proposed government neither strong enough in itself nor able to "prevent . . . local mischiefs," such as Shays's Rebellion. Writing from New York on October 24, 1787, he sent a copy of the Constitution along with the following letter to Thomas Jefferson, in Paris, in which he gave a summary of his impressions of the work of the Convention. In Jefferson's words the letter revealed "the rich resources of his [Madison's] luminous and discriminating mind." Madison's statements in this letter substantially foreshadowed the arguments he was to make in favor of the Constitution in his famous tenth* Federalist.

Source: *Madison Letters,* I, pp. 343-358.

YOU WILL HEREWITH RECEIVE the result of the Convention, which continued its session till the 17th of September. I take the liberty of making some observations on the subject, which will help to make up a letter if they should answer no other purpose.

It appeared to be the sincere and unanimous wish of the Convention to cherish and preserve the Union of the states. No proposition was made, no suggestion was thrown out in favor of a partition of the empire into two or more confederacies.

It was generally agreed that the objects of the Union could not be secured by any system founded on the principle of a confederation of sovereign states. A *voluntary* observance of the federal law by all the members could never be hoped for. A *compulsive* one could evidently never be reduced to practice; and if it could, involved equal calamities to the innocent and the guilty, the necessity of a military force, both obnoxious and dangerous, and, in general, a scene resembling much more a civil war than the administration of a regular government.

Hence was embraced the alternative of a

government which, instead of operating on the states, should operate without their intervention on the individuals composing them; and hence the change in the principle and proportion of representation.

This groundwork being laid, the great objects which presented themselves were: (1) To unite a proper energy in the executive and a proper stability in the legislative departments, with the essential characters of republican government. (2) To draw a line of demarcation which would give to the general government every power requisite for general purposes, and leave to the states every power which might be most beneficially administered by them. (3) To provide for the different interests of different parts of the Union. (4) To adjust the clashing pretensions of the large and small states.

Each of these objects was pregnant with difficulties. The whole of them together formed a task more difficult than can be well-conceived by those who were not concerned in the execution of it. Adding to these considerations the natural diversity of human opinions on all new and complicated subjects, it is impossible to consider the degree of concord which ultimately prevailed as less than a miracle.

The first of these objects, as respects the executive, was peculiarly embarrassing. On the question whether it should consist of a single person or a plurality of coordinate members, on the mode of appointment, on the duration in office, on the degree of power, on the reeligibility — tedious and reiterated discussions took place. The plurality of coordinate members had finally but few advocates. Governor Randolph was at the head of them. The modes of appointment proposed were various: as by the people at large, by electors chosen by the people, by the executives of the states, by the Congress; some preferring a joint ballot of the two houses; some, a separate concurrent ballot, allowing to each a negative on the other house; some, a nomination of several candidates by one house, out of whom a choice should be made by the other. Several other modifications were started. The expedient at length adopted seemed to give pretty general satisfaction to the members. As to the duration in office, a few would have preferred a tenure during good behavior; a considerable number would have done so in case an easy and effectual removal by impeachment could be settled.

It was much agitated whether a long term, seven years for example, with a subsequent and perpetual ineligibility, or a short term, with a capacity to be reelected, should be fixed. In favor of the first opinion were urged the danger of a gradual degeneracy of reelections from time to time, into first a life and then a hereditary tenure, and the favorable effect of an incapacity to be reappointed on the independent exercise of the executive authority. On the other side, it was contended that the prospect of necessary degradation would discourage the most dignified characters from aspiring to the office; would take away the principal motive to the faithful discharge of its duties — the hope of being rewarded with a reappointment; would stimulate ambition to violent efforts for holding over the constitutional term; and instead of producing an independent administration and a firmer defense of the constitutional rights of the department would render the officer more indifferent to the importance of a place which he would soon be obliged to quit forever, and more ready to yield to the encroachments of the legislature, of which he might again be a member.

The questions concerning the degree of power turned chiefly on the appointment to offices and the control on the legislature. An *absolute* appointment to all offices, to some offices, to no offices formed the scale of opinions on the first point. On the second, some contended for an absolute negative as the only possible means of reducing to practice the theory of a free government, which forbids a mixture of the legislative and executive powers. Others would be content with a revisionary power to be overruled by three-fourths of both houses. It was warmly urged that the judiciary department should be associated in the revision. The idea of some was that a separate revision should be given to the two departments; that if either objected, two-thirds, if both, three-fourths, should be necessary to overrule. . . .

The second object, the due partition of power between the general and local governments was, perhaps of all, the most nice and difficult. A few contended for an entire abolition of the states, some, for indefinite power of legislation in the Congress, with a negative on the laws of the states; some, for such a power without a negative; some, for a limited power of legislation, with such a negative; the majority, finally, for a limited power without the negative. The question with regard to the negative underwent repeated discussions, and was finally rejected by a bare majority. As I formerly intimated to you my opinion in favor of this ingredient, I will take this occasion of explaining myself on the subject. Such a check on the states appears to me necessary (1) to prevent encroachments on the general authority; (2) to prevent instability and injustice in the legislation of the states.

1. Without such a check in the whole over the parts, our system involves the evil of *imperia in imperio* [governments within a government]. If a complete supremacy somewhere is not necessary in every society, a controlling power at least is so, by which the general authority may be defended against encroachments of the subordinate authorities, and by which the latter may be restrained from encroachments on each other. . . .

We find the representatives of counties and corporations in the legislatures of the states much more disposed to sacrifice the aggregate interest, and even authority, to the local views of their constituents than the latter to the former. I mean not by these remarks to insinuate that an esprit de corps will not exist in the national government, or that opportunities may not occur of extending its jurisdiction in some points. I mean only that the danger of encroachments is much greater from the other side, and that the impossibility of dividing powers of legislation in such a manner as to be free from different constructions by different interests, or even from ambiguity in the judgment of the impartial, requires some such expedient as I contend for. . . .

2. A constitutional negative on the laws of the states seems equally necessary to secure individuals against encroachments on their rights. The mutability of the laws of the states is found to be a serious evil. The injustice of them has been so frequent and so flagrant as to alarm the most steadfast friends of republicanism. I am persuaded I do not err in saying that the evils issuing from these sources contributed more to that uneasiness which produced the Convention, and prepared the public mind for a general reform, than those which accrued to our national character and interest from the inadequacy of the Confederation to its immediate objects. A reform, therefore, which does not make provision for private rights must be materially defective. The restraints against paper emissions and violations of contracts are not sufficient. Supposing them to be effectual as far as they go, they are short of the mark. Injustice may be effected by such an infinitude of legislative expedients that, where the disposition exists, it can only be controlled by some provision which reaches all cases whatsoever. The partial provision made supposes the disposition which will evade it.

It may be asked how private rights will be more secure under the guardianship of the general government than under the state governments, since they are both founded on the republican principle which refers the ultimate decision to the will of the majority, and are distinguished rather by the extent within which they will operate than by any material difference in their structure. A full discussion of this question would, if I mistake not, unfold the true principles of republican government and prove, in contradiction to the concurrent opinions of the theoretical writers, that this form of government, in order to effect its purposes, must operate not within a small but an extensive sphere. I will state some of the ideas which have occurred to me on this subject.

Those who contend for a simple democracy, or a pure republic, actuated by the sense of the majority and operating within narrow limits, assume or suppose a case which is altogether fictitious. They found their reasoning on the idea that the people composing the society enjoy not only an equality of political rights but that they have all precisely the same interests and the same feelings in every respect. Were this in reality the case, their reasoning would be conclusive. The interest of the majority would be that of the minority, also; the decisions could only turn on mere opinion concerning the good of the whole, of which the major voice would be the safest criterion; and within a small sphere, this voice could be most easily collected and the public affairs most accurately managed.

We know, however, that no society ever did, or can, consist of so homogeneous a mass of citizens. In the savage state, indeed, an approach is made toward it, but in that state little or no government is necessary. In all civilized societies distinctions are various and unavoidable. A distinction of property results from that very protection which a free government gives to unequal faculties of acquiring it. There will be rich and poor; creditors and debtors; a landed interest, a monied interest, a mercantile interest, a manufacturing interest. These classes may again be subdivided according to the different productions of different situations and soils, and according to different branches of commerce and of manufactures. In addition to these natural distinctions, artificial ones will be founded on accidental differences in political, religious, or other opinions, or an attachment to the persons of leading individuals. However erroneous or ridiculous these grounds of dissension and faction may appear to the enlightened statesman or the benevolent philosopher, the bulk of mankind, who are neither statesmen nor philosophers, will continue to view them in a different light.

It remains, then, to be inquired whether a majority having any common interest, or feeling any common passion, will find sufficient motives to restrain them from oppressing the minority. An individual is never allowed to be a judge, or even a witness, in his own cause. If two individuals are under the bias of interest or enmity against a third, the rights of the latter could never be safely referred to the majority of the three. Will 2,000 individuals be less apt to oppress 1,000, or 200,000, 100,000?

Three motives only can restrain in such cases. (1) A prudent regard to private or partial good, as essentially involved in the general and permanent good of the whole. This ought, no doubt, to be sufficient of itself. Experience, however, shows that it has little effect on individuals, and perhaps still less on a collection of individuals, and least of all on a majority with the public authority in their hands. If the former are ready to forget that honesty is the best policy, the last do more; they often proceed on the converse of the maxim that whatever is politic is honest. (2) Respect for character. This motive is not found sufficient to restrain individuals from injustice, and loses its efficacy in proportion to the number which is to divide the pain or the blame. Besides, as it has reference to public opinion, which is that of the majority, the standard is fixed by those whose conduct is to be measured by it. (3) Religion. The inefficacy of this restraint on individuals is well-known. The conduct of every popular assembly, acting on oath, the strongest of religious ties, shows that individuals join without remorse in acts against which their consciences would revolt if proposed to them separately in their closets. When, indeed, religion is kindled into enthusiasm, its force, like that of other passions, is increased by the sympathy of a multitude. But enthusiasm is only a temporary state of religion, and while it lasts will hardly be seen with pleasure at the helm. Even in its coolest state, it has been much oftener a motive to oppression than a restraint from it.

If, then, there must be different interests and parties in society, and a majority, when united by a common interest or passion, cannot be restrained from oppressing the minority, what remedy can be found in a republican government where the majority must ultimately decide, but that of giving such an extent to its sphere that no common interest or passion will be likely to unite a majority of the whole number in an unjust pursuit? In a large society, the people are broken into so many interests and parties that a common sentiment is less likely to be felt, and the requisite concert less likely to be formed by a majority of the whole. The same security seems requisite for the civil as for the religious rights of individuals. If the same sect form a majority and have the power, other sects will be sure to be depressed. *Divide et impera* [divide and conquer], the reprobated axiom of tyranny, is, under certain qualifications, the only policy by which a republic can be administered on just principles.

It must be observed, however, that this doctrine can only hold within a sphere of a mean extent. As in too small a sphere oppressive combinations may be too easily formed against the weaker party, so in too extensive a one a defensive concert may be rendered too difficult against the oppression of those entrusted with the administration. The great desideratum in government is so to modify the sovereignty as that it may be sufficiently neutral between different parts of the society to control one part from invading the rights of another, and at the same time sufficiently controlled itself from setting up an interest adverse to that of the entire society. . . .

Begging pardon for this immoderate digression, I return to the third object above mentioned: the adjustments of the different interests of different parts of the continent. Some contended for an unlimited power over trade, including exports as well as imports, and over slaves as well as other imports; some, for such a power, provided the concurrence of two-thirds of both houses were required; some, for such a qualification of the power, with an exemption of exports and slaves; others, for an exemption of exports only. The result is seen in the Constitution. South Carolina and Georgia were inflexible on the point of the slaves.

The remaining object created more embarrassment and a greater alarm for the issue of the Convention than all the rest put together. The little states insisted on retaining their equality in both branches, unless a complete abolition of the state governments should take place, and made an equality in the Senate a *sine qua non.* The large states, on the other hand, urged that as the new government was to be drawn principally from the people immediately, and was to operate directly on them not on the states; and, consequently, as the states would lose that importance which is now proportioned to the importance of their voluntary compliance with the requisitions of Congress, it was necessary that the representation in both houses should be in proportion to their size. It ended in the compromise which you will see, but very much to the dissatisfaction of several members from the large states.

33.

# Anonymous: Anti-Federalist Arguments from Pennsylvania

*The debate over the ratification of the Constitution brought forth an abundance of anti-Federalist literature from every section of the country. The critics argued variously that the document was secretly designed by a propertied aristocracy; that the Constitution contained no bill of rights; that the Convention had gone beyond its authorized power to amend the Articles of Confederation, thereby illegally framing a new government; and that the states' powers would be completely subordinate to the national power. Furthermore, the anti-Federalists admonished the framers for not dividing power equally among the three branches of the national government. The first of the following two essays deals mainly with this last theme; the second selection illustrates the anti-Federalist fears about giving the central government the power to regulate commerce. Both selections are taken from letters that appeared in the* Philadelphia Independent Gazetteer *on October 5 and November 30, 1787. The letters were signed by the unknown author, "Centinel."*

Source: McMaster, pp. 565-576, 601-608.

## I.

## On the Balance of Powers

The late Convention have submitted to your consideration a plan of a new federal government. The subject is highly interesting to your future welfare. Whether it be calculated to promote the great ends of civil society, viz., the happiness and prosperity of the community, it behooves you well to consider, uninfluenced by the authority of names. Instead of that frenzy of enthusiasm that has actuated the citizens of Philadelphia in their approbation of the proposed plan, before it was possible that it could be the result of a rational investigation into its principles, it ought to be dispassionately and deliberately examined on its own intrinsic merit, the only criterion of your patronage. If ever free and unbiased discussion was proper or necessary, it is on such an occasion. All the blessings of liberty and the dearest privileges of freemen are now at stake and dependent on your present conduct.

Those who are competent to the task of developing the principles of government ought to be encouraged to come forward and, thereby, the better enable the people to make a proper judgment; for the science of government is so abstruse that few are able to judge for themselves. Without such assistance the people are too apt to yield an implicit assent to the opinions of those characters whose abilities are held in the highest esteem, and to those in whose integrity and patriotism they can confide; not considering that the love of domination is generally in proportion to talents, abilities, and superior requirements, and that the men of the greatest purity of intention may be made instruments of despotism in the hands of the *artful and designing*. If it were not for the stability and attachment which time and habit gives to forms of government, it would be in the power of the enlightened and aspiring few, if they should combine, at any time to destroy the best establishments, and even make the people the instruments of their own subjugation.

The late Revolution having effaced in a great measure all former habits, and the present institutions are so recent that there exists not that great reluctance to innovation so remarkable in old communities, and which accords with reason, for the most comprehensive mind cannot foresee the full operation of material changes on civil polity; it is the genius of the common law to resist innovation.

The wealthy and ambitious, who in every community think they have a right to lord it over their fellow creatures, have availed themselves very successfully of this favorable disposition; for the people thus unsettled in their sentiments have been prepared to accede to any extreme of government. All the distresses and difficulties they experience, proceeding from various causes, have been ascribed to the impotency of the present Confederation, and thence they have been led to expect full relief from the adoption of the proposed system of government; and, in the other event, immediately ruin and annihilation as a nation. These characters flatter themselves that they have lulled all distrust and jealousy of their new plan by gaining the concurrence of the two men in whom America has the highest confidence, and now triumphantly exult in the completion of their long meditated schemes of power and aggrandizement. I would be very far from insinuating that the two illustrious personages alluded to have not the welfare of their country at heart; but that the unsuspecting goodness and zeal of the one has been imposed on, in a subject of which he must be necessarily inexperienced, from his other arduous engagements; and that the weakness and indecision attendant on old age has been practised on in the other.

I am fearful that the principles of government inculcated in Mr. John Adams' treatise [*Defence of the Constitutions of Government of the United States of America*], and enforced in the numerous essays and paragraphs in the newspapers, have misled some well-designing members of the late Convention. But it will appear in the sequel that the construction of the proposed plan of government is infinitely more extravagant.

I have been anxiously expecting that some enlightened patriot would, ere this, have taken up the pen to expose the futility and counteract the baneful tendency of such principles. Mr. Adams' *sine qua non* of a good government is three balancing powers, whose repelling qualities are to produce an equilibrium of interests and thereby promote the happiness of the whole community. He asserts that the administrators of every government will ever be actuated by views of private interest and ambition, to the prejudice of the public good; that therefore the only effectual method to secure the rights of the people and promote their welfare is to create an opposition of interests between the members of two distinct bodies in the exercise of the powers of government, and balanced by those of a third. This hypothesis supposes human wisdom competent to the task of instituting three coequal orders in government, and a corresponding weight in the community to enable them respectively to exercise their several parts, and whose views and interests should be so distinct as to prevent a coalition of any two of them for the destruction of the third.

Mr. Adams, although he has traced the constitution of every form of government that ever existed as far as history affords materials, has not been able to adduce a single instance of such a government. He, indeed, says that the British constitution is such in theory, but this is rather a confirmation that his principles are chimerical and not to be reduced to practice. If such an organization of power were practicable, how long would it continue? Not a day — for there is so great a disparity in the talents, wisdom, and industry of mankind that the scale would presently preponderate to one or the other body, and with every accession of power the means of further increase would be greatly extended. The state of society in England is much more favorable to such a scheme of government than that of America. There they have a powerful hereditary nobility, and real distinctions of rank and interests; but even there, for want of that perfect equality of power and distinction of interests in the three orders of government, they exist but in name. The only operative and efficient check upon the conduct of administration is the sense of the people at large.

Suppose a government could be formed and supported on such principles, would it answer the great purposes of civil society? If the administrators of every government are actuated by views of private interest and ambition, how is the welfare and happiness of the community to be the result of such jarring adverse interests?

Therefore, as different orders in government will not produce the good of the whole, we must recur to other principles. I believe it will be found that the form of government which holds those entrusted with power in the greatest responsibility to their constituents is the best calculated for freemen. A republican or free government can only exist where the body of the people are virtuous, and where property is pretty equally divided. In such a government the people are the sovereign and their sense or opinion is the criterion of every public measure. For when this ceases to be the case, the nature of the government is changed, and an aristocracy, monarchy, or despotism will rise on its ruin. The highest responsibility is to be attained in a simple structure of government, for the great body of the people never steadily attend to the operations of government, and for want of due information are liable to be imposed on. If you complicate the plan by various orders, the people will be perplexed and divided in their sentiment about the source of abuses or misconduct; some will impute it to the Senate, others to the House of Representatives, and so on, that the interposition of the people may be rendered imperfect or perhaps wholly abortive.

But if, imitating the constitution of Pennsylvania, you vest all the legislative power in one body of men (separating the executive and judicial) elected for a short period, and necessarily excluded by rotation from permanency, and guarded from precipitancy and surprise by delays imposed on its proceedings, you will create the most perfect responsibility. For then, whenever the people feel a grievance, they cannot mistake the authors, and will apply the remedy with certainty and effect, discarding them at the next election. This tie of responsibility will obviate all the dangers apprehended from a single legislature, and will the best secure the rights of the people.

Having premised this much, I shall now proceed to the examination of the proposed plan of government and, I trust, shall make it appear to the meanest capacity that it has none of the essential requisites of a free government; that it is neither founded on those balancing restraining powers recommended by Mr. Adams and attempted in the British constitution, or possessed of that responsibility to its constituents which, in my opinion, is the only effectual security for the liberties and happiness of the people. But on the contrary, that it is a most daring attempt to establish a despotic aristocracy among freemen that the world has ever witnessed. . . .

If the united states are to be melted down into one empire, it becomes you to consider whether such a government, however constructed, would be eligible in so extended a territory; and whether it would be practicable, consistent with freedom? It is the opinion of the greatest writers that a very extensive country cannot be governed on democratical principles, on any other plan than a confederation of a number of small republics, possessing all the powers of internal government, but united in the management of their foreign and general concerns. It would not be difficult to prove, that anything short of despotism could not bind so great a country under one government; and that whatever plan you might, at the first setting out, establish, it would issue in a despotism.

If one general government could be instituted and maintained on principles of freedom, it would not be so competent to attend to the various local concerns and wants, of every particular district, as well as the peculiar governments, who are nearer the scene, and possessed of superior means of information; besides, if the business of the *whole* union is to be managed by one government, there would not be time. Do we not already see, that the inhabitants in a number of larger states, who are remote from the seat of government, are loudly complaining of the inconveniences and disadvantages they are subjected to on this account, and that, to enjoy the comforts of local government, they are separating into smaller divisions? . . .

We see the House of Representatives are on the part of the people to balance the Senate, who I suppose will be composed of the *better sort,* the *wellborn,* etc. The number of the representatives (being only 1 for every 30,000 inhabitants) appears to be too few either to communicate the requisite information of the wants, local circumstances, and sentiments of so extensive an empire or to prevent corruption and undue influence in the exercise of such great powers; the term for which they are to be chosen, too long to preserve a due dependence and accountability to their constituents; and the mode and places of their election not sufficiently ascertained, for as Congress have the control over both, they may govern the choice by ordering the representatives of a whole state to be elected in one place, and that too may be the most inconvenient.

The Senate, the great efficient body in this plan of government, is constituted on the most unequal principles. The smallest state in the Union has equal weight with the great states of Virginia, Massachusetts, or Pennsylvania. The Senate, besides its legislative functions, has a very considerable share in the executive; none of the principal appointments to office can be made without its advice and consent. The term and mode of its appointment will lead to permanency. The members are chosen for six years, the mode is under the control of Congress, and as there is no exclusion by rotation, they may be continued for life, which, from their extensive means of influence, would follow of course. The President, who would be a mere pageant of state unless he coincides with the views of the Senate, would either become the head of the aristocratic junto in that body, or its minion; besides, their influence being the most predominant could the best secure his reelection to office. And from his power of granting pardons, he might screen from punishment the most treasonable attempts on the liberties of the people when instigated by the Senate.

From this investigation into the organization of this government, it appears that it is devoid of all responsibility or accountability to the great body of the people, and that, so far from being a regular balanced government, it would be in practice a *permanent* ARISTOCRACY.

## II.

## Against the Federal Commerce Power

THAT THE PRESENT CONFEDERATION is inadequate to the objects of the Union seems to be universally allowed. The only question is — What additional powers are wanting to give due energy to the federal government?

We should, however, be careful, in forming our opinion on this subject, not to impute the temporary and extraordinary difficulties that have hitherto impeded the execution of the Confederation to defects in the system itself.

Taxation is in every government a very delicate and difficult subject. Hence it has been the policy of all wise statesmen, as far as circumstances permitted, to lead the people by small beginnings and almost imperceptible degrees into the habits of taxation. Where the contrary conduct has been pursued, it has ever failed of full success, not infrequently proving the ruin of the projectors. The imposing of a burdensome tax at once on a people, without the usual gradations, is the severest test that any government can be put to; despotism itself has often proved unequal to the attempt. Under this conviction, let us take a review of our situation before and since the Revolution. From the first settlement of this country until the commencement of the late war, the taxes were so light and trivial as to be scarcely felt by the people. When we engaged in the expensive contest with Great Britain, the Congress, sensible of the difficulty of levying the moneys necessary to its support by *direct* taxation, had resource to an anticipation of the public resources by emitting bills of credit, and thus postponed the necessity of taxation for several years. This means was pursued to a most ruinous length.

But about the year '80 or '81, it was wholly exhausted, the bills of credit had suffered such a depreciation from the excessive quantities in circulation that they ceased to be useful as a medium. The country at this period was very much impoverished and exhausted; commerce had been suspended for near six years; the husbandman, for want of a market, limited his crops to his own subsistence; the frequent calls of the militia and long continuance in actual service, the devastations of the enemy, the subsistence of our own armies, the evils of the depreciation of the paper money, which fell chiefly upon the patriotic and virtuous part of the community, had all concurred to produce great distress throughout America. In this situation of affairs, we still had the same powerful enemy to contend with, who had even more numerous and better appointed armies in the field than at any former time. Our allies were applied to in this exigency, but the pecuniary assistance that we could procure from them was soon exhausted. The only resource now remaining was to obtain by direct taxation the moneys necessary for our defense.

The history of mankind does not furnish a similar instance of an attempt to levy such enormous taxes at once, nor of a people so wholly unprepared and uninured to them — the lamp of sacred liberty must indeed have burned with unsullied luster, every sordid principle of the mind must have been then extinct, when the people not only submitted to the grievous impositions but cheerfully exerted themselves to comply with the calls of their country. Their abilities, however, were not equal to furnish the necessary sums — indeed, the requisition of the year 1782 amounted to the whole income of their farms and other property, including the means of their subsistence. Perhaps the strained exertions of two years would not have sufficed to the discharge of this requisition. How then can we impute the difficulties of the people to a due compliance with the requisitions of Congress to a defect in the Confederation? Any government, however energetic in similar circumstances, would have experienced the same fate. If we review the proceedings of the states, we shall find that they gave every sanction and authority to the requisitions of Congress that their laws could confer, that they attempted to collect the sums called for in the same manner as is proposed to be done in future by the general government instead of the state legislatures.

It is a maxim that a government ought to be cautious not to govern overmuch, for, when the cord of power is drawn too tight, it generally proves its destruction. The impracticability of complying with the requisitions of Congress has lessened the sense of obligation and duty in the people and thus weakened the ties of the Union; the opinion of power in a free government is much more efficacious than the exercise of it; it requires the maturity of time and repeated practice to give due energy and certainty to the operations of government. . . .

I am persuaded that a due consideration will evince that the present inefficacy of the requisitions of Congress is not owing to a defect in the Confederation but the peculiar circumstances of the times.

The wheels of the general government having been thus clogged, and the arrearages of taxes still accumulating, it may be asked: What prospect is there of the government resuming its proper tone unless more compulsory powers are granted? To this it may be answered that the produce of imposts on commerce, which all agree to vest in Congress, together with the immense tracts of land at their disposal, will rapidly lessen and eventually discharge the present encumbrances. When this takes place, the mode by requisition will be found perfectly adequate to the extraordinary exigencies of the Union. Congress have lately sold land to the amount of $8,000,000, which is a considerable portion of the whole debt.

It is to be lamented that the interested and designing have availed themselves so successfully of the present crisis, and under the specious pretense of having discovered a panacea for all the ills of the people, they are about establishing a system of government that will prove more destructive to them than the wooden horse filled with soldiers did in ancient times to the city of Troy. This horse was introduced by their hostile enemy the Grecians by a prostitution of the sacred rites of their religion; in like manner, my fellow citizens, are aspiring despots among yourselves prostituting the name of a Washington to cloak their designs upon your liberties.

I would ask: How was the proposed Constitution to have showered down those treasures upon every class of citizens, as has been so industriously inculcated and so fondly believed by some? Would it have been by the addition of numerous and expensive establishments? By doubling our judiciaries, instituting federal courts in every county of every state? By a superb presidential court? By a large standing army? In short, by putting it in the power of the future government to levy money at pleasure, and placing this government so independent of the people as to enable the administration to gratify every corrupt passion of the mind, to riot on your spoils, without check or control?

A transfer to Congress of the power of imposing imposts on commerce, the unlimited regulation of trade, and to make treaties — I believe is all that is wanting to render America as prosperous as it is in the power of any form of government to render her; this properly understood would meet the views of all the honest and well-meaning.

What gave birth to the late Continental Convention? Was it not the situation of our commerce, which lay at the mercy of every foreign power who, from motives of interest or enmity, could restrict and control it without risking a retaliation on the part of America, as Congress was impotent on this subject? Such indeed was the case with respect to Britain, whose hostile regulations gave such a stab to our navigation as to threaten its annihilation. It became the interest of even the American merchant to give a preference to foreign bottoms; hence the distress of our seamen, shipwrights, and every mechanic art dependent on navigation.

By these regulations, too, we were limited in markets for our produce; our vessels were excluded from their West India islands; many of our staple commodities were denied entrance in Britain. Hence the husbandmen were distressed by the demand for their crops being lessened and their prices reduced. This is the source to which may be traced every evil we experience, that can be relieved by a more energetic government. Recollect the language of complaint for years past; compare the recommendations of Congress, founded on such complaints, pointing out the remedy; examine the reasons assigned by the different states for appointing delegates to the late Convention; view the powers vested in that body — they all harmonize in the sentiment that the due regulation of trade and navigation was the anxious wish of every class of citizens, was the great object of calling the Convention.

This object being provided for by the Constitution proposed by the general Convention, people overlooked and were not sensible of the needless sacrifice they were making for it. Allowing for a moment that it would be possible for trade to flourish under a despotic government, of what avail would be a prosperous state of commerce? When the produce of it would be at the absolute disposal of an arbitrary unchecked general government, who may levy at pleasure the most oppressive taxes; who may destroy every principle of freedom; who may even destroy the privilege of complaining.

If you are in doubt about the nature and principles of the proposed government, view the conduct of its authors and patrons: that affords the best explanation, the most striking comment.

The evil genius of darkness presided at its birth, it came forth under the veil of mystery, its true features being carefully concealed, and every deceptive art has been and is practising to have this spurious brat received as the genuine offspring of heaven-born liberty. So fearful are its patrons that you should discern the imposition that they have hurried on its adoption, with the greatest precipitation. They have endeavored also to preclude all investigation; they have endeavored to intimidate all opposition. By such means as these have they surreptitiously procured a Convention in this state, favorable to their views; and here again investigation and discussion are abridged, the final question is moved before the subject has been under consideration, an appeal to the people is precluded even in the last resort, lest their eyes should be opened; the Convention have denied the minority the privilege of entering the reasons of their dissent on its journals. Thus despotism is already triumphant, and the genius of liberty is on the eve of her exit, is about bidding an eternal adieu to this once happy people.

After so recent a triumph over British despots, after such torrents of blood and treasure have been spent, after involving ourselves in the distresses of an arduous war and incurring such a debt for the express purpose of asserting the rights of humanity, it is truly astonishing that a set of men among ourselves should have had the effrontery to attempt the destruction of our liberties. But in this enlightened age, to dupe the people by the arts they are practising is still more extraordinary. . . .

That the powers of Congress ought to be strengthened, all allow; but is this a conclusive proof of the necessity to adopt the proposed plan? Is it a proof that because the late Convention, in the first essay upon so arduous and difficult a subject, harmonized in their ideas, that a future convention will not, or that after a full investigation and mature consideration of the objections, they will not plan a better government and one more agreeable to the sentiments of America, or is it any proof that they can never again agree in any plan? The late Convention must indeed have been inspired, as some of its advocates have asserted, to admit the truth of these positions, or even to admit the possibility of the proposed government being such a one as America ought to adopt; for this body went upon original ground, foreign from their intentions or powers. They must therefore have been wholly uninformed of the sentiments of their constituents in respect to this form of government, as it was not in their contemplation when the Convention was appointed to erect a new government but to strengthen the old one. Indeed, they seem to have been determined to monopolize the exclusive merit of the discovery, or rather, as if darkness was essential to its success, they precluded all communication with the people by closing their doors. Thus the well-disposed members, unassisted by public information and opinion, were induced by those arts that are now practising on the people to give their sanction to this system of despotism.

---

34.

## James Wilson: A Defense of the Constitution

*William Pierce, a Georgia delegate to the Constitutional Convention, wrote that James Wilson ranked "among the foremost in legal and political knowledge." Indeed, next to James Madison, scholars have spoken of Wilson as the most effective member of the Constitutional Convention. Throughout the Convention's debates he maintained constitutional positions that were either basic to the finished document or, as in the case of his advocacy of the popular election of both the President and the whole Congress, prophetic of later amendments. He dominated the Pennsylvania Ratifying Convention, where his remarks, in part reprinted here, revealed his fervent nationalism. His reasoned defense of the original omission of a bill of rights was widely adopted by supporters of the Constitution in other states and was incorporated by Hamilton into* Federalist, *Number 84.*

Source. McMaster, pp. 218-231.

As the only member of this respectable body who had the honor of a seat in the late federal Convention, it is peculiarly my duty, Mr. President, to submit to your consideration the general principles that have produced the national Constitution, which has been framed and proposed by the assembled delegates of the United States, and which must finally stand or fall by the concurrent decision of this Convention and of others acting upon the same subject, under similar powers and authority. To frame a government for a single city or state is a business, both in its importance and facility, widely different from the task entrusted to the federal Convention, whose prospects were extended not only to thirteen independent and sovereign states, some of which in territorial jurisdiction, population, and resource, equal the most respectable nations of Europe, but likewise to innumerable states yet unformed, and to myriads of citizens who in future ages shall inhabit the vast uncultivated regions of the continent. The duties of that body, therefore, were not limited to local or partial considerations but to the formation of a plan commensurate with a great and valuable portion of the globe.

I confess, sir, that the magnitude of the object before us filled our minds with awe and apprehension. In Europe, the opening and extending the navigation of a single river has been deemed an act of imperial merit and importance; but how insignificant does it seem when we contemplate the scene that nature here exhibits, pouring forth the Potomac, the Rappahannock, the Susquehanna, and other innumerable rivers to dignify, adorn, and enrich our soil. But the magnitude of the object was equaled by the difficulty of accomplishing it, when we considered the uncommon dexterity and address that were necessary to combat and reconcile the jarring interests that seemed naturally to prevail, in a country which, presenting a coast of 1,500 miles to the Atlantic, is composed of thirteen distinct and independent states, varying essentially in their situation and dimensions, and in the number and habits of their citizens — their interests, too, in some respects really different, and in many apparently so; but whether really or apparently, such is the constitution of the human mind, they make the same impression, and are prosecuted with equal vigor and perseverance.

Can it then be a subject for surprise that with the sensations indispensably excited by so comprehensive and so arduous an undertaking, we should for a moment yield to despondency, and at length, influenced by the spirit of conciliation, resort to mutual concession as the only means to obtain the great end for which we were convened? Is it a matter of surprise that where the springs of dissension were so numerous and so powerful, some force was requisite to impel them to take, in a collected state, a direction different from that which separately they would have pursued?

There was another reason that, in this respect, increased the difficulties of the federal Convention — the different tempers and dispositions of the people for whom they acted. But, however widely they may differ upon other topics, they cordially agree in that keen and elevated sense of freedom and independence which has been manifested in their united and successful opposition to one of the most powerful kingdoms of the world. Still, it was apprehended by some that their abhorrence of constraint would be the source of objection and opposition; but I confess that my opinion, formed upon a knowledge of the good sense as well as the high spirit of my constituents, made me confident that they would esteem that government to be the best which was best calculated eventually to establish and secure the dignity and happiness of their country.

Upon this ground, I have occasionally supposed that my constituents have asked the reason of my assent to the several propositions contained in the plan before us. My answer, though concise, is a candid and, I think, a satisfactory one — because I thought them right; and thinking them right, it would be a poor compliment indeed to presume they could be disagreeable to my constituents — a presumption that might occasion a retort to which I wish not to expose myself as it would again be asked, "Is this the opinion you entertain of those who have confided in your judgment? From what ground do you infer that a vote right in itself would be disagreeble to us?" and it might with justice be added, "this sentiment evinces that you deserved not the trust which we reposed in you." No, sir! I have no right to imagine that the reflected rays of delegated power can displease by a brightness that proves the superior splendor of the luminary from which they proceed.

The extent of country for which the new Constitution was required produced another difficulty in the business of the federal Convention. It is the opinion of some celebrated writers that to a small territory the democratical, to a middling territory (as Montesquieu has termed it) the monarchical, and to an extensive territory the despotic form of government is best adapted. Regarding, then, the wide and almost unbounded jurisdiction of the United States, at first view the hand of despotism seemed necessary to control, connect, and protect it; and hence the chief embarrassment arose. For we knew that, although our constituents would cheerfully submit to the legislative restraints of a free government, they would spurn at every attempt to shackle them with despotic power.

In this dilemma, a federal republic naturally presented itself to our observation as a species of government which secured all the internal advantages of a republic, at the same time that it maintained the external dignity and force of a monarchy. The definition of this form of government may be found in Montesquieu, who says, I believe, that it consists in assembling distinct societies which are consolidated into a new body, capable of being increased by the addition of other members — an expanding quality peculiarly fitted to the circumstances of America.

But while a federal republic removed one difficulty, it introduced another, since there existed not any precedent to assist our deliberations; for, though there are many single governments, both ancient and modern, the history and principles of which are faithfully preserved and well understood, a perfect confederation of independent states is a system hitherto unknown. . . .

Another, and perhaps the most important obstacle to the proceedings of the federal Convention, arose in drawing the line between the national and the individual governments of the states. On this point, a general principle readily occurred that whatever object was confined in its nature and operation to a particular state ought to be subject to the separate government of the states; but whatever in its nature and operation extended beyond a particular state ought to be comprehended within the federal jurisdiction. The great difficulty, therefore, was the application of this general principle, for it was found impracticable to enumerate and distinguish the various objects to which it extended; and as the mathematics only are capable of demonstration, it ought not to be thought extraordinary that the Convention could not develop a subject involved in such endless perplexity. If, however, the proposed Constitution should be adopted, I trust that in the theory there will be found such harmony, and in the practice such mutual confidence between the national and individual governments, that every sentiment of jealousy and apprehension will be effectually destroyed. But, sir, permit me to ask whether, on the ground of a union, the individual or the national government ought most to be trusted? For my part, I think it more natural to presume that the interest of each would be pursued by the whole, than the reverse of the proposition that the several states would prefer the interest of the confederated body; for in the general government each is represented, but in the separate governments only the separate states.

These difficulties, Mr. President, which embarrassed the federal Convention, are not represented to enhance the merit of surmounting them but with a more important view to show how unreasonable it is to expect that the plan of government should correspond with the wishes of all the states, of all the citizens of any one state, or of all the citizens of the united continent. I remember well, sir, the effect of those surrounding difficulties in the late Convention.

At one time the great and interesting work seemed to be at a stand, at another it proceeded with energy and rapidity, and when at last it was accomplished, many respectable members beheld it with wonder and admiration. But having pointed out the obstacles which they had to encounter, I shall now beg leave to direct your attention to the end which the Convention proposed.

Our wants, imperfections, and weaknesses, Mr. President, naturally incline us to society; but it is certain society cannot exist without some restraints. In a state of nature each individual has a right, uncontrolled, to act as his pleasure or his interest may prevail; but it must be observed that this license extends to every individual, and hence the state of nature is rendered insupportable by the interfering claims and the consequent animosities of men who are independent of every power and influence but their passions and their will. On the other hand, in entering into the social compact, though the individual parts with a portion of his natural rights, yet it is evident that he gains more by the limitation of the liberty of others than he loses by the limitations of his own; so that in truth, the aggregate of liberty is more in society than it is in a state of nature.

It is, then, sir, a fundamental principle of society that the welfare of the whole shall be pursued and not of a part, and the measures necessary to the good of the community must consequently be binding upon the individuals that compose it. This principle is universally allowed to be just with respect to single governments, and there are instances in which it applies with equal force to independent communities; for the situation and circumstances of states may make it as necessary for them as for individuals to associate. Hence, Mr. President, the important question arises: Are such the situation and circumstances of the American States?

At this period, America has it in her power to adopt either of the following modes of government: she may dissolve the individual sovereignty of the states and become one consolidated empire; she may be divided into thirteen separate, independent, and unconnected commonwealths; she may be erected into two or more confederacies; or, lastly, she may become one comprehensive federal republic.

Allow me, sir, to take a short view of each of these suppositions. Is it probable that the dissolution of the state governments and the establishment of one consolidated empire would be eligible in its nature, and satisfactory to the people in its administration? I think not, as I have given reasons to show that so extensive a territory could not be governed, connected, and preserved but by the supremacy of despotic power. All the exertions of the most potent emperors of Rome were not capable of keeping that empire together, which in extent was far inferior to the dominion of America. Would an independent, an unconnected situation, without any associating head, be advantageous or satisfactory? The consequences of this system would at one time expose the states to foreign insult and depredations, and at another, to internal jealousy, contention, and war.

Then let us consider the plan of two or more confederacies, which has often been suggested and which certainly presents some aspects more inviting than either of the preceding modes, since the subjects of strife would not be so numerous, the strength of the confederates would be greater, and their interests more united. But even here, when we fairly weigh the advantages and the disadvantages, we shall find the last greatly preponderating; the expenses of government would be considerably multiplied, the seeds of rivalship and animosity would spring up, and spread the calamities of war and tumult through the country; for though the sources of rancor might be diminished, their strength and virulence would probably be increased.

Of these three species of government, however, I must observe that they obtained no advocates in the federal Convention, nor can I presume that they will find advocates here or in any of our sister states. The general sentiment in that body, and, I believe, the general sentiment of the citizens of America, is expressed in the motto which some of them have chosen, "Unite or Die"; and while we consider the extent of the country, so intersected and almost surrounded with navigable rivers, so separated and detached from the rest of the world, it is natural to presume that Providence has designed us for a united people, under one great political compact. If this is a just and reasonable conclusion, supported by the wishes of the people, the Convention did right in proposing a single, confederated republic. But in proposing it they were necessary led, not only to consider the situation, circumstances, and interests of one, two, or three states but of the collective body; and as it is essential to society that the welfare of the whole should be preferred to the accommodation of a part, they followed the same rule in promoting the national advantages of the Union in preference to the separate advantages of the states. A principle of candor, as well as duty, led to this conduct; for, as I have said before, no government, either single or confederated, can exist unless private and individual rights are subservient to the public and general happiness of the nation. It was not alone the state of Pennsylvania, however important she may be as a constituent part of the Union, that could influence the deliberations of a convention formed by a delegation from all the United States to devise a government adequate to their common exigencies and impartial in its influence and operation. In the spirit of union, inculcated by the nature of their commission, they framed the Constitution before us, and in the same spirit they submit it to the candid consideration of the constituents.

Having made some remarks upon the nature and principles of civil society, I shall now take a cursory notice of civil liberty, which is essential to the well-being of civil government. The definition of civil liberty is, briefly, that portion of natural liberty which men resign to the government, and which then produces more happiness than it would have produced if retained by the individuals who resign it, still, however, leaving to the human mind the full enjoyment of every privilege that is not incompatible with the peace and order of society. Here I am easily led to the consideration of another species of liberty, which has not yet received a discriminating name, but which I will venture to term "federal liberty." This, sir, consists in the aggregate of the civil liberty which is surrendered by each state to the national government; and the same principles that operate in the establishment of a single society, with respect to the rights reserved or resigned by the individuals that compose it, will justly apply in the case of a confederation of distinct and independent states.

These observations have been made, Mr. President, in order to preface a representation of the state of the Union as it appeared to the late convention. We all know, and we have all felt, that the present system of confederation is inadequate to the government and the exigencies of the United States. Need I describe the contrasted scene which the Revolution has presented to our view? On the one hand, the arduous struggle in the cause of liberty terminated by a glorious and triumphant peace; on the other, contention and poverty at home, discredit and disgrace abroad. Do we not remember what high expectations were formed by others and by ourselves on the return of peace? And have those honorable expectations from our national character been realized? No! What then has been the cause of disappointment? Has America lost her magnanimity or perseverance? No! Has she been subdued by any high-handed invasion of her liberties? Still I answer, no; for dangers of that kind were no sooner seen than they were repelled. But the evil has stolen in from a quarter little suspected, and the rock of freedom, which stood firm against the attacks of a foreign foe, has been sapped and undermined by the licentiousness of our own citizens. Private calamity and public anarchy have prevailed; and even the blessing of independency has been scarcely felt or understood by a people who have dearly achieved it.

Shall I, sir, be more particular in this lamentable history? The commencement of peace was likewise the commencement of our distresses and disgrace. Devoid of power, we could neither prevent the excessive importations which lately deluged the country, nor even raise from that excess a contribution to the public revenue; devoid of importance, we were unable to command a sale for our commodities in a foreign market; devoid of credit, our public securities were melting in the hands of their deluded owners like snow before the sun; devoid of dignity, we were inadequate to perform treaties on our own part, or to compel a performance on the part of a contracting nation. In short, sir, the tedious tale disgusts me, and I fondly hope it is unnecessary to proceed.

The years of languor are over. We have seen dishonor and destruction, it is true, but we have at length penetrated the cause, and are now anxious to obtain the cure. The cause need not be specified by a recapitulation of facts; every act of Congress, and the proceedings of every state, are replete with proofs in that respect, and all point to the weakness and imbecility of the existing confederation; while the loud and concurrent voice of the people proclaims an efficient national government to be the only cure. Under these impressions, and with these views, the late Convention were appointed and met; the end which they proposed to accomplish being to frame one national and efficient government, in which the exercise of beneficence, correcting the jarring interests of every part, should pervade the whole, and by which the peace, freedom, and happiness of the United States should be permanently ensured. The principles and means that were adopted by the Convention to obtain that end are now before us, and will become the great object of our discussion. But on this point, as upon others, permit me to make a few general observations.

In all governments, whatever is their form, however they may be constituted, there must be a power established from which there is no appeal, and which is, therefore, called absolute, supreme, and uncontrollable. The only question is where that power is lodged — a question that will receive different answers. . . .

But were we to ask some politicians who have taken a faint and inaccurate view of our establishments where does this supreme power reside in the United States, they would probably answer, in their constitutions. This, however, though a step nearer to the fact is not a just opinion; for, in truth, it remains and flourishes with the people; and under the influence of that truth we, at this moment, sit, deliberate, and speak. In other countries, indeed, the revolutions of government are connected with war and all its concomitant calamities. But with us, they are considered as the means of obtaining a superior knowledge of the nature of government, and of accomplishing its end. That the supreme power, therefore, should be vested in the people is, in my judgment, the great panacea of human politics. It is a power paramount to every constitution, inalienable in its nature, and indefinite in its extent. For I insist, if there are errors in government, the people have the right not only to correct and amend them but, likewise, totally to change and reject its form; and under the operation of that right, the citizens of the United States can never be wretched beyond retrieve, unless they are wanting to themselves.

Then let us examine, Mr. President, the three species of simple government, which, as I have already mentioned, are the monarchical, aristocratical, and democratical. In a monarchy, the supreme power is vested in a single person; in an aristocracy, it is possessed by a body not formed upon the principle of representation but enjoying their station by descent, by election among themselves, or in right of some personal or territorial qualification; and lastly, in a democracy, it is inherent in the people, and is either exercised by themselves or by their representatives. Each of these systems has its advantages and its disadvantages. The advantages of a monarchy are strength, dispatch, and unity; its disadvantages are expense, tyranny, and war. The advantages of an aristocracy are experience and the wisdom resulting from education; its disadvantages are the dissension of the governors and the oppression of the people. The advantages of a democracy are liberty, caution, industry, fidelity, and an opportunity of bringing forward the talents and abilities of the citizens, without regard to birth or fortune; its disadvantages are dissension and imbecility, for the assent of many being required, their exertions will be feeble and their counsels too soon discovered.

To obtain all the advantages and to avoid all the inconveniences of these governments, was the leading object of the late Convention. Having therefore considered the formation and principles of other systems, it is natural to inquire — Of what description is the Constitution before us? In its principles, sir, it is purely democratical; varying, indeed, in its form in order to admit all the advantages and to exclude all the disadvantages which are incidental to the known and established constitutions of government. But when we take an extensive and accurate view of the streams of power that appear through this great and comprehensive plan, when we contemplate the variety of their directions, the force and dignity of their currents, when we behold them intersecting, embracing, and surrounding the vast possessions and interests of the continent, and when we see them distributing on all hands beauty, energy, and riches, still, however numerous and wide their courses, however diversified and remote the blessings they diffuse, we shall be able to trace them all to one great and noble source, THE PEOPLE.

Such, Mr. President, are the general observations with which I have thought it necessary to trouble you. In discussing the distinct propositions of the federal plan, I shall have occasion to apply them more particularly to that subject; but at present I shall conclude with requesting the pardon of the Convention for having so long intruded upon their patience.

---

*I cannot help expressing a wish that every member . . . doubt a little of his own infallibility.*

BENJAMIN FRANKLIN, speech to Constitutional Convention, Sept. 17, 1787

35.

## Anonymous: The Constitution as an Instrument of Aristocracy

*Prior to the selection of delegates to the Massachusetts Ratifying Convention, an essay appeared in the* Boston Gazette and the Country Journal, *vehemently opposing the Constitution. Written under the pseudonym, "A Federalist," it exemplified the anti-Federalist belief that those who favored the new Constitution were self-interested aristocrats. The essay first appeared on November 26, 1787.*

Source: *Boston Gazette and the Country Journal*, November 26, 1787.

I AM PLEASED TO SEE a spirit of inquiry burst the band of constraint upon the subject of the new plan for consolidating the governments of the United States as recommended by the late Convention. If it is suitable to the genius and habits of the citizens of these states, it will bear the strictest scrutiny. The people are the grand inquest who have a right to judge of its merits. The hideous demon of aristocracy has hitherto had so much influence as to bar the channels of investigation, preclude the people from inquiry, and extinguish every spark of liberal information of its qualities.

At length the luminary of intelligence begins to beam its effulgent rays upon this important production; the deceptive mists cast before the eyes of the people by the delusive machinations of its interested advocates begins to dissipate, as darkness flies before the burning taper; and I dare venture to predict that, in spite of those mercenary declaimers, the plan will have a candid and complete examination. Those furious zealots who are for cramming it down the throats of the people without allowing them either time or opportunity to scan or weigh it in the balance of their understandings bear the same marks in their features as those who have been long wishing to erect an aristocracy in this commonwealth. Their menacing cry is for a rigid government; it matters little to them of what kind, provided it answers that description.

As the plan now offered comes something near their wishes, and is the most consonant to their views of any they can hope for, they come boldly forward and demand its adoption. They brand with infamy every man who is not as determined and zealous in its favor as themselves. They cry aloud the whole must be swallowed or none at all, thinking thereby to preclude any amendment; they are afraid of having it abated of its present rigid aspect. They have striven to overawe or seduce printers to stifle and obstruct a free discussion, and have endeavored to hasten it to a decision before the people can duly reflect upon its properties.

In order to deceive them, they incessantly declare that none can discover any defect in the system but bankrupts who wish no government, and officers of the present government who fear to lose a part of their power. These zealous partisans may injure their own cause, and endanger the public tranquillity by impeding a proper inquiry; the people may suspect the whole to be a dangerous plan, from such covered and designing schemes to enforce it upon them. Compulsive or treacherous measures to establish any government whatever will always excite jealousy among a free people. Better remain single and alone than blindly adopt whatever a few individuals shall demand, be they ever so wise. I had rather be a free citizen of the small republic of Massachusetts than an oppressed subject of the great American empire. Let all act understandingly or not at all.

If we can confederate upon terms that will secure to us our liberties, it is an object highly desirable because of its additional security to the whole. If the proposed plan proves such a one, I hope it will be adopted; but if it will endanger our liberties as it stands, let it be amended; in order to which it must and ought to be open to inspection and free inquiry. The inundation of abuse that has been thrown out upon the heads of those who have had any doubts of its universal good qualities have been so redundant that it may not be improper to scan the characters of its most strenuous advocates.

It will first be allowed that many undesigning citizens may wish its adoption from the best motives, but these are modest and silent when compared to the greater number who endeavor to suppress all attempts for investigation. These violent partisans are for having the people gulp down the gilded pill blindfolded, whole and without any qualification whatever. These consist generally of the noble order of Cincinnatus, holders of public securities, men of great wealth and expectations of public office, bankers and lawyers. These, with their train of dependents, form the aristocratic combination. The lawyers in particular keep up an incessant declamation for its adoption; like greedy gudgeons they long to satiate their voracious stomachs with the golden bait. The numerous tribunals to be erected by the new plan of consolidated empire will find employment for ten times their present numbers; these are the loaves and fishes for which they hunger. They will probably find it suited to their habits, if not to the habits of the people.

There may be reasons for having but few of them in the state convention, lest their "own" interest should be too strongly considered. The time draws near for the choice of delegates. I hope my fellow citizens will look well to the characters of their preference, and remember the old patriots of '75; they have never led them astray, nor need they fear to try them on this momentous occasion.

A FEDERALIST

---

*Those Who Own the Country Ought to Govern It.*

JOHN JAY, slogan of the Federalist Party

36.

## LUTHER MARTIN: The People Versus The States

*Luther Martin had been a delegate to the Constitutional Convention, where he opposed a strong central government and finally quit the convention before it adjourned. He became the leading anti-Federalist in Maryland. Speaking before the Maryland state legislature on November 29, 1787, he presented his case for states' rights and against the Constitution. Martin felt that he could not accept the document because it premised that the United States government was formed by a compact between the people as individuals. He believed that any federal government could only be a compact between the states as separate sovereignties. In his speech,* Genuine Information . . . Relative to the Proceedings of the General Convention, etc., etc., *Martin argued that adequate state governments* did *exist.*

Source: Elliot, I, pp. 344-389.

BY THE PRINCIPLES of the American Revolution, arbitrary power may, and ought to be resisted even by arms, if necessary. The time may come when it shall be the duty of a state, in order to preserve itself from the oppression of the general government, to have recourse to the sword; in which case, the proposed form of government declares that the state, and every one of its citizens who acts under its authority, are guilty of a direct act of treason; reducing, by this provision, the different states to this alternative — that they must tamely and passively yield to despotism, or their citizens must oppose it at the hazard of the halter, if unsuccessful; and reducing the citizens of the state which shall take arms to a situation in which they must be exposed to punishment, let them act as they will; since, if they obey the authority of their state government, they will be guilty of treason against the United States; if they join the general government, they will be guilty of treason against their own state.

To save the citizens of the respective states from this disagreeable dilemma, and to secure them from being punishable as traitors to the United States, when acting expressly in obedience to the authority of their own state, I wished to have obtained, as an amendment to Section 3 of this Article, the following clause:

> *Provided,* that no act or acts done by one or more of the states against the United States, or by any citizen of any one of the United States, under the authority of one or more of the said states, shall be deemed treason, or punished as such; but in case of war being levied by one or more of the states against the United States, the conduct of each party toward the other, and their adherents respectively, shall be regulated by the laws of war and of nations. . . .

I was of opinion that the states, considered as states in their political capacity, are the members of a federal government; that the states in their political capacity or as sovereignties, are entitled, and only entitled, originally to agree upon the form of, and submit themselves to, a federal government, and afterward, by mutual consent, to dissolve or alter it; that everything which relates to the formation, the dissolution, or the alteration of a federal government over states equally free, sovereign, and independent is the peculiar province of the states in their sovereign or political capacity, in the same manner as what relates to forming alliances or treaties of peace, amity, or commerce; and that the people at large, in their individual capacity, have no more right to interfere in the one case than in the other — that according to these principles we originally acted in forming our Confederation.

It was the states as states, by their representatives in Congress, that formed the Articles of Confederation; it was the states as states, by their legislatures, who ratified those Articles; and it was there established and provided that the states as states (that is, by their legislatures) should agree to any alterations that should hereafter be proposed in the federal government, before they should be binding; and any alterations agreed to in any other manner cannot release the states from the obligation they are under to each other by virtue of the original Articles of Confederation. The people of the different states never made any objection to the manner in which the Articles of Confederation were formed or ratified, or to the mode by which alterations were to be made in that government — with the rights of their respective states they wished not to interfere. Nor do I believe the people, in their individual capacity, would ever have expected or desired to have been appealed to on the present occasion, in violation of the rights of their respective states, if the favorers of the proposed Constitution, imagining they had a better chance of forcing it to be adopted by a hasty appeal to the people at large (who could not be so good judges of the dangerous consequence), had not insisted upon this mode. Nor do these positions in the least interfere with the principle that all power originates from the people; because, when once the people have exercised their power in establishing and forming themselves into a state government, it never devolves back to them; nor have they a right to resume or again to exercise that power until such events take place as will amount to a dissolution of their state government. And it is an established principle that a dissolution or alteration of a federal government does not dissolve the state governments which compose it.

It was also my opinion that, upon principles of sound policy, the agreement or disagreement to the proposed system ought to have been by the state legislatures; in which case, let the event have been what it would, there would have been but little prospect of the public peace being disturbed thereby; whereas the attempt to force down this system, although Congress and the respective state legislatures should disapprove, by appealing to the people and to procure its establishment in a manner totally unconstitutional, has a tendency to set the state governments and their subjects at variance with each other, to lessen the obligations of government, to weaken the bands of society, to introduce anarchy and confusion, and to light the torch of discord and civil war throughout this continent. All these considerations weighed with me most forcibly against giving my assent to the mode by which it is resolved that this system is to be ratified, and were urged by me in opposition to the measure.

I have now, sir, in discharge of the duty I owe to this House, given such information as has occurred to me, which I consider most material for them to know. And you will easily perceive, from this detail, that a great portion of that time which ought to have been devoted calmly and impartially to consider what alterations in our federal gov-

Library of Congress
Engraving of Luther Martin

ernment would be most likely to procure and preserve the happiness of the Union was employed in a violent struggle on the one side to obtain all power and dominion in their own hands, and on the other to prevent it; and that the aggrandizement of particular states, and particular individuals, appears to have been much more the subject sought after than the welfare of our country.

The interest of this state, not confined merely to itself, abstracted from all others, but considered relatively as far as was consistent with the common interest of the other states, I thought it my duty to pursue according to the best opinion I could form of it.

When I took my seat in the Convention, I found them attempting to bring forward a system which, I was sure, never had entered into the contemplation of those I had the honor to represent, and which, upon the fullest consideration, I considered not only injurious to the interest and rights of this state but also incompatible with the political happiness and freedom of the states in general. From that time until my business compelled me to leave the Convention, I gave it every possible opposition, in every stage of its progression. I opposed the system there with the same explicit frankness with which I have here given you a history of our proceedings, an account of my own conduct, which in a particular manner I consider you as having a right to know. While there, I endeavored to act as became a freeman and the delegate of a free state. Should my conduct obtain the approbation of those who appointed me, I will not deny it would afford me satisfaction; but to me that approbation was at most no more than a secondary consideration — my first was to deserve it. Left to myself to act according to the best of my discretion, my conduct should have been the same had I been even sure your censure would have been my only reward, since I hold it sacredly my duty to dash the cup of poison, if possible, from the hand of a state or an individual, however anxious the one or the other might be to swallow it.

Indulge me, sir, in a single observation further: There are persons who endeavor to hold up the idea that this system is only opposed by the officers of government. I, sir, am in that predicament. I have the honor to hold an appointment in this state. Had it been considered any objection, I presume I should not have been appointed to the Convention. If it could have had any effect on my mind, it would only be that of warming my heart with gratitude, and rendering me more anxious to promote the true interest of that state which has conferred on me the obligation, and to heighten my guilt had I joined in sacrificing its essential rights. But, sir, it would be well to remember that this system is not calculated to diminish the number or the value of offices. On the contrary, if adopted, it will be productive of an enormous increase in their number. Many of them will also be of great honor and emoluments.

Whether, sir, in this variety of appointments and in the scramble for them, I might not have as good a prospect to advantage myself as many others is not for me to say. But this, sir, I can say with truth, that, so far was I from being influenced in my conduct by interest or the consideration of office, that I would cheerfully resign the appointment I now hold; I would bind myself never to accept another, either under the general government or that of my own state; I would do more, sir — so destructive do I consider the present system to the happiness of my country — I would cheerfully sacrifice that share of property with which Heaven has blessed a life of industry; I would reduce myself to indigence and poverty; and those who are dearer to me than my own existence I would entrust to the care and protection of that Providence who has so kindly protected myself — if on those terms only I could procure my country to reject those chains which are forged for it.

---

37.

# Oliver Ellsworth: On a Religious Test for Holding Public Office

*Oliver Ellsworth is best known for his activities as a Connecticut delegate to the Convention of 1787. He worked diligently to arrange the great mutual concession known as the Connecticut Compromise. When the Constitution was approved by the Philadelphia delegates on September 17, 1787, Ellsworth continued his efforts on its behalf by explaining the document to the people of his state. The following selection, written on December 17, 1787, is one of several "Letters to a Landholder" by Ellsworth that were printed in the* Connecticut Courant *and in the* American Mercury. *Aimed at influencing the landholders and farmers of the region, the letter attempted to explain the constitutional clause that prohibits any religious test for public office.*

Source: Scott, II, pp. 580-583.

I have often admired the spirit of candor, liberality, and justice with which the Convention began and completed the important object of their mission. "In all our deliberation on this subject," say they, "we kept steadily in our view that which appears to us the greatest interest of every true American, the consolidation of our Union, in which is involved our prosperity, felicity, safety, perhaps our national existence. This important consideration, seriously and deeply impressed on our minds, led each state in the Convention to be less rigid on points of inferior magnitude than might otherwise have been expected; and thus the Constitution which we now present is the result of a spirit of amity, and of that mutual deference and concession which the peculiarity of our political situation rendered indispensable."

Let us, my fellow citizens, take up this Constitution with the same spirit of candor and liberality; consider it in all its parts; consider the important advantages which may be derived from it; let us obtain full information on the subject, and then weigh these objections in the balance of cool, impartial reason. Let us see if they be not wholly groundless; but if upon the whole they appear to have some weight, let us

Yale University Art Gallery

Portrait of Oliver Ellsworth by John Trumbull, 1792

consider well whether they be so important that we ought on account of them to reject the whole Constitution. Perfection is not the lot of human institutions; that which has the most excellences and fewest faults is the best that we can expect.

Some very worthy persons who have not had great advantages for information have objected against that clause in the Constitution which provides that no religious test shall ever be required as a qualification to any office or public trust under the United States. They have been afraid that this clause is unfavorable to religion. But, my countrymen, the sole purpose and effect of it is to exclude persecution and to secure to you the important right of religious liberty. We are almost the only people in the world who have a full enjoyment of this important right of human nature. In our country every man has a right to worship God in that way which is most agreeable to his conscience. If he be a good and peaceable person, he is liable to no penalties or incapacities on account of his religious sentiments; or, in other words, he is not subject to persecution.

But in other parts of the world it has been, and still is, far different. Systems of religious error have been adopted in times of ignorance. It has been the interest of tyrannical kings, popes, and prelates to maintain these errors. When the clouds of ignorance began to vanish and the people grew more enlightened, there was no other way to keep them in error but to prohibit their altering their religious opinions by severe persecuting laws. In this way persecution became general throughout Europe. It was the universal opinion that one religion must be established by law; and that all who differed in their religious opinions must suffer the vengeance of persecution. In pursuance of this opinion, when popery was abolished in England and the Church of England was established in its stead, severe penalties were inflicted upon all who dissented from the established church. In the time of the civil wars, in the reign of Charles I, the Presbyterians got the upper hand and inflicted legal penalties upon all who differed from them in their sentiments respecting religious doctrines and discipline. When Charles II was restored, the Church of England was likewise restored, and the Presbyterians and other dissenters were laid under legal penalties and incapacities.

It was in this reign that a religious test was established as a qualification for office; that is, a law was made requiring all officers, civil and military (among other things), to receive the sacrament of the Lord's Supper, according to the usage of the Church of England, within six months after their admission to office, under the penalty of £500 and disability to hold the office. And by another statute of the same reign, no person was capable of being elected to any office relating to the government of any city or corporation unless, within a twelvemonth before, he had received the sacrament according to the rites of the Church of England. The pretense for making these severe laws, by which all but churchmen were made incapable of any office, civil or military, was to exclude the Papists; but the real design was to exclude the Protestant dissenters. From this account of test laws, there arises an unfavorable presumption against them. But if we consider the nature of them and the effects which they are calculated to produce, we shall find that they are useless, tyrannical, and peculiarly unfit for the people of this country.

A religious test is an act to be done or profession to be made relating to religion (such as partaking of the sacrament according to certain rites and forms, or declaring one's belief of certain doctrines) for the purpose of determining whether his religious opinions are such that he is admissible to a public office. A test in favor of any one denomination of Christians would be to the last degree absurd in the United States. If it were in favor of either Congregationalists, Presbyterians, Episcopalians, Baptists, or Quakers, it would incapacitate more than three-fourths of the American citizens for any public office and thus degrade them from the rank of freemen. There need be no argument to prove that the majority of our citizens would never submit to this indignity.

If any test act were to be made, perhaps the least exceptionable would be one requiring all persons appointed to office to declare, at the time of their admission, their belief in the being of a God, and in the divine authority of the Scriptures. In favor of such a test, it may be said that one who believes these great truths will not be so likely to violate his obligations to his country as one who disbelieves them; we may have greater confidence in his integrity. But I answer: His making a declaration of such a belief is no security at all. For suppose him to be an unprincipled man who believes neither the Word nor the being of God, and to be governed merely by selfish motives; how easy is it for him to dissemble! How easy is it for him to make a public declaration of his belief in the creed which the law prescribes and excuse himself by calling it a mere formality.

This is the case with the test laws and creeds in England. The most abandoned characters partake of the sacrament in order to qualify themselves for public employments. The clergy are obliged by law to administer the ordinance unto them, and thus prostitute the most sacred office of religion, for it is a civil right in the party to receive the sacrament. In that country, subscribing to the Thirty-Nine Articles is a test for administration into Holy Orders. And it is a fact that many of the clergy do this, when at the same time they totally disbelieve several of the doctrines contained in them. In short, test laws are utterly ineffectual; they are no security at all, because men of loose principles will, by an external compliance, evade them. If they exclude any persons, it will be honest men, men of principle who will rather suffer an injury than act contrary to the dictates of their consciences. If we mean to have those appointed to public offices who are sincere friends to religion, we, the people who appoint them, must take care to choose such characters, and not rely upon such cobweb barriers as test laws are.

But to come to the true principle by which this question ought to be determined: The business of a civil government is to protect the citizen in his rights, to defend the community from hostile powers, and to promote the general welfare. Civil government has no business to meddle with the private opinions of the people. If I demean myself as a good citizen, I am accountable not to man but to God for the religious opinions which I embrace and the manner in which I worship the Supreme Being. If such had been the universal sentiments of mankind and they had acted accordingly, persecution, the bane of truth and nurse of error, with her bloody axe and flaming brand, would never have turned so great a part of the world into a field of blood.

But while I assert the rights of religious liberty, I would not deny that the civil power has a right, in some cases, to interfere in matters of religion. It has a right to prohibit and punish gross immoralities and impieties; because the open practice of these is of evil example and detriment. For this reason, I heartily approve of our laws against drunkenness, profane swearing, blasphemy, and professed atheism. But in this state, we have never thought it expedient to adopt a test law; and yet I sincerely believe we have as great a proportion of religion and morality as they have in England, where every person who holds a public office must either be a saint by law or a hypocrite by practice. A test law is the parent of hypocrisy, and the offspring of error and the spirit of persecution. Legislatures have no right to set up an inquisition and examine into the private opinions of men. Test laws are useless and ineffectual, unjust and tyrannical; therefore the Convention have done wisely in excluding this engine of persecution, and providing that no religious test shall ever be required.

38.

## Reasons for Dissent by the Anti-Federalists of Pennsylvania

*On December 12, 1787, Pennsylvania became the second state to ratify the Constitution. However, the haste in which the state gave its approval did not reflect unanimity at the Pennsylvania convention. Partly because the Federalists hoped to gain the new federal capital for their state, they pushed for a prompt acceptance of the Constitution. Their opponents were scarcely heard amidst the political maneuvering for fast action. Recommendations from the anti-Federalists to amend the Constitution were rejected without discussion and were not even entered into the convention's journal. Nevertheless, under the leadership of William Findley, Robert Whitehill, and John Smilie, the anti-Federalists continued to oppose the Constitution. On December 18, 1787, they published "The Address and Reasons of Dissent of the Minority of the Convention of the State of Pennsylvania to their Constituents," in the* Pennsylvania Packet and Daily Advertiser.

Source: McMaster, pp. 454-482.

The Continental Convention met in the city of Philadelphia at the time appointed. It was composed of some men of excellent character; of others who were more remarkable for their ambition and cunning than their patriotism; and of some who had been opponents to the independence of the United States. The delegates from Pennsylvania were, six of them, uniform and decided opponents to the constitution of this commonwealth. The convention sat upward of four months. The doors were kept shut, and the members brought under the most solemn engagements of secrecy. Some of those who opposed their going so far beyond their powers, retired, hopeless, from the convention; others had the firmness to refuse signing the plan altogether; and many who did sign it, did it not as a system they wholly approved but as the best that could be then obtained; and notwithstanding the time spent on this subject, it is agreed on all hands to be a work of haste and accommodation.

While the gilded chains were forging in the secret conclave, the meaner instruments of the despotism without were busily employed in alarming the fears of the people with dangers which did not exist, and exciting their hopes of greater advantages from the expected plan than even the best government on earth could produce. The proposed plan had not many hours issued forth from the womb of suspicious secrecy until such as were prepared for the purpose were carrying about petitions for people to sign, signifying their approbation of the system, and requesting the legislature to call a convention. While every measure was taken to intimidate the people against opposing it, the public papers teemed with the most violent threats against those who should dare to think for themselves, and *tar and feathers* were liberally promised to all those who would not immediately join in supporting the proposed government, be it what it would. Under such circumstances petitions in favor of calling a convention were signed by great numbers in and about the city before they had leisure to read and examine the system, many of whom — now they are better acquainted with it and have had time to investigate its principles — are heartily opposed to it. The petitions were speedily handed in to the legislature.

Affairs were in this situation when on the 28th of September last a resolution was proposed to the assembly by a member of the House, who had been also a member of the federal Convention, for calling a state convention to be elected within *ten* days for the purpose of examining and adopting the proposed Constitution of the United States, though at this time the House had not received it from Congress. This attempt was opposed by a minority, who, after offering every argument in their power to prevent the precipitate measure, without effect, absented themselves from the House as the only alternative left them, to prevent the measures taking place previous to their constituents being acquainted with the business. That violence and outrage which had been so often threatened was now practised; some of the members were seized the next day by a mob collected for the purpose, and forcibly dragged to the house, and there detained by force while the quorum of the legislature *so formed,* completed their resolution.

We shall dwell no longer on this subject: the people of Pennsylvania have been already acquainted therewith. We would only further observe that every member of the legislature, previously to taking his seat, by solemn oath or affirmation, declares "that he will not do or consent to any act or thing whatever that will have a tendency to lessen or abridge their rights and privileges, as declared in the constitution of this state." And that constitution which they are so solemnly sworn to support cannot legally be altered but by a recommendation of the council of censors, who alone are authorized to propose alterations and amendments, and even these must be published at least *six months* for the consideration of the people.

The proposed system of government for the United States, if adopted, will alter and may annihilate the constitution of Pennsylvania; and therefore the legislature had no authority whatever to recommend the calling a convention for that purpose. This proceeding could not be considered as binding on the people of this commonwealth. The House was formed by violence, some of the members composing it were detained there by force, which alone would have vitiated any proceedings to which they were otherwise competent; but had the legislature been legally formed, this business was absolutely without their power.

In this situation of affairs were the subscribers elected members of the convention of Pennsylvania — a convention called by a legislature in direct violation of their duty, and composed in part of members who were compelled to attend for that purpose to consider of a Constitution proposed by a Convention of the United States, who were not appointed for the purpose of framing a new form of government but whose powers were expressly confined to altering and amending the present Articles of Confederation. Therefore, the members of the Continental Convention in proposing the plan acted as individuals and not as deputies from Pennsylvania.[1] The assembly who called the state convention acted as individuals, and not as the legislature of Pennsylvania; nor could they or the convention chosen on their recommendation have authority to do any act or thing that can alter or annihilate the constitution of Pennsylvania (both of which will be done by the new Constitution), nor are their proceedings, in our opinion, at all binding on the people.

The election for members of the convention was held at so early a period, and the want of information was so great, that some of us did not know of it until after it was over; and we have reason to believe that great numbers of the people of Pennsylvania have not yet had an opportunity of sufficiently examining the proposed Constitution. We apprehend that no change can take place that will affect the internal government or constitution of this commonwealth, unless a majority of the people should evidence a wish for such a change; but on examining the number of votes given for members of the present state convention, we find that of upward of *70,000* freemen who are entitled to vote in Pennsylvania, the whole convention has been elected by about *13,000* voters, and though *two-thirds* of the members of the convention have thought proper to ratify the proposed Constitution, yet those *two-thirds* were elected by the votes of only *6,800* freemen.

In the city of Philadelphia and some of the eastern counties the junto that took the lead in the business agreed to vote for none but such as would solemnly promise to adopt the system *in toto,* without exercising their judgment. In many of the counties the people did not attend the elections, as they had not an opportunity of judging of the plan. Others did not consider themselves bound by the call of a set of men who assembled at the statehouse in Philadelphia and assumed the name of the legislature of Pennsylvania; and some were prevented from voting by the violence of the party, who were determined at all events to force down the measure. To such lengths did the tools of despotism carry their outrage that on the night of the election for members of convention, in the city of Philadelphia, several of the subscribers (being then in the city to transact your business) were grossly abused, ill-treated, and insulted while they were quiet in their lodgings, though they did not interfere nor had anything to do with the said election, but, as they apprehend, because they were supposed to be adverse to the proposed Constitution, and would not tamely surrender those sacred rights which you had committed to their charge.

The convention met, and the same disposition was soon manifest in considering the proposed Constitution that had been exhibited in every other stage of the business. We were prohibited by an express vote of the convention from taking any questions on the separate articles of the plan, and reduced to the necessity of adopting or rejecting *in toto.* It is true the majority permitted us to debate on each article, but restrained

1. The Continental Convention, in direct violation of the 13th Article of the Confederation, have declared "that the ratification of nine states shall be sufficient for the establishment of this Constitution, between the states so ratifying the same." Thus has the plighted faith of the states been sported with! They had solemnly engaged that the Confederation now subsisting should be inviolably preserved by each of them, and the Union thereby formed should be perpetual, unless the same should be altered by mutual consent.

us from proposing amendments. They also determined not to permit us to enter on the minutes our reasons of dissent against any of the articles, nor even on the final question our reasons of dissent against the whole. Thus situated, we entered on the examination of the proposed system of government, and found it to be such as we could not adopt without, as we conceived, surrendering up your dearest rights. We offered our objections to the convention, and opposed those parts of the plan which, in our opinion, would be injurious to you, in the best manner we were able; and closed our arguments by offering the following propositions to the convention.

1. The right of conscience shall be held inviolable; and neither the legislative, executive, nor judicial powers of the United States shall have authority to alter, abrogate, or infringe any part of the constitution of the several states which provide for the preservation of liberty in matter of religion.

2. That in controversies respecting property, and in suits between man and man, trial by jury shall remain as heretofore, as well in the federal courts as in those of the several states.

3. That in all capital and criminal prosecutions, a man has a right to demand the cause and nature of his accusation, as well in the federal courts as in those of the several states; to be heard by himself and his counsel; to be confronted with the accusers and witnesses; to call for evidence in his favor, and a speedy trial by an impartial jury of his vicinage, without whose unanimous consent he cannot be found guilty, nor can he be compelled to give evidence against himself; and, that no man be deprived of his liberty, except by the law of the land or the judgment of his peers.

4. That excessive bail ought not to be required, nor excessive fines imposed, nor cruel nor unusual punishments inflicted.

5. That warrants unsupported by evidence, whereby any officer or messenger may be commanded or required to search suspected places, or to seize any person or persons, his or their property not particularly described, are grievous and oppressive, and shall not be granted either by the magistrates of the federal government or others.

6. That the people have a right to the freedom of speech, of writing and publishing their sentiments; therefore, the freedom of the press shall not be restrained by any law of the United States.

7. That the people have a right to bear arms for the defense of themselves and their own state or the United States, or for the purpose of killing game; and no law shall be passed for disarming the people or any of them unless for crimes committed, or real danger of public injury from individuals; and as standing armies in the time of peace are dangerous to liberty, they ought not to be kept up; and that the military shall be kept under strict subordination to and be governed by the civil powers.

8. The inhabitants of the several states shall have liberty to fowl and hunt in seasonable time on the lands they hold, and on all other lands in the United States not enclosed, and in like manner to fish in all navigable waters, and others not private property, without being restrained therein by any laws to be passed by the legislature of the United States.

9. That no law shall be passed to restrain the legislatures of the several states from enacting laws for imposing taxes, except imposts and duties on goods imported or exported, and that no taxes, except imposts and duties upon goods imported and exported, and postage on letters shall be levied by the authority of Congress.

10. That the House of Representatives be properly increased in number; that elections shall remain free; that the several states shall have power to regulate the elections for senators and representatives without being controlled either directly or indirectly by any interference on the part of the

Congress; and that the elections of representatives be annual.

11. That the power of organizing, arming, and disciplining the militia (the manner of disciplining the militia to be prescribed by Congress) remain with the individual states; and that Congress shall not have authority to call or march any of the militia out of their own state without the consent of such state, and for such length of time only as such state shall agree.

That the sovereignty, freedom and independency of the several states shall be retained, and every power, jurisdiction, and right which is not by this Constitution expressly delegated to the United States in Congress assembled.

12. That the legislative, executive, and judicial powers be kept separate; and to this end that a constitutional council be appointed to advise and assist the President, who shall be responsible for the advice they give — hereby the senators would be relieved from almost constant attendance; and also that the judges be made completely independent.

13. That no treaty which shall be directly opposed to the existing laws of the United States in Congress assembled shall be valid until such laws shall be repealed or made conformable to such treaty; neither shall any treaties be valid which are in contradiction to the Constitution of the United States, or the constitution of the several states.

14. That the judiciary power of the United States shall be confined to cases affecting ambassadors, other public ministers and consuls, to cases of admiralty and maritime jurisdiction; to controversies to which the United States shall be a party; to controversies between two or more states, between a state and citizens of different states, between citizens claiming lands under grants of different states, and between a state, or the citizens thereof, and foreign states; and in criminal cases to such only as are expressly enumerated in the Constitution; and that the United States in Congress assembled shall not have power to enact laws which shall alter the laws of descent and distribution of the effects of deceased persons, the titles of lands or goods, or the regulation of contracts in the individual states.

After reading these propositions, we declared our willingness to agree to the plan, provided it was so amended as to meet those propositions or something similar to them, and finally moved the convention to adjourn, to give the people of Pennsylvania time to consider the subject and determine for themselves; but these were all rejected and the final vote taken, when our duty to you induced us to vote against the proposed plan and to decline signing the ratification of the same.

During the discussion, we met with many insults and some personal abuse. We were not even treated with decency during the sitting of the convention by the persons in the gallery of the House. However, we flatter ourselves that in contending for the preservation of those invaluable rights you have thought proper to commit to our charge, we acted with a spirit becoming freemen; and being desirous that you might know the principles which actuated our conduct, and being prohibited from inserting our reasons of dissent on the minutes of the convention, we have subjoined them for your consideration, as to you alone we are accountable. It remains with you whether you will think those inestimable privileges, which you have so ably contended for, should be sacrificed at the shrine of despotism, or whether you mean to contend for them with the same spirit that has so often baffled the attempts of an aristocratic faction to rivet the shackles of slavery on you and your unborn posterity.

Our objections are comprised under three general heads of dissent, viz.:

We dissent, first, because it is the opinion

of the most celebrated writers on government, and confirmed by uniform experience, that a very extensive territory cannot be governed on the principles of freedom otherwise than by a confederation of republics, possessing all the powers of internal government but united in the management of their general and foreign concerns.

If any doubt could have been entertained of the truth of the foregoing principle, it has been fully removed by the concession of Mr. Wilson, one of the majority on this question, and who was one of the deputies in the late general Convention. In justice to him, we will give his own words; they are as follows, viz.:

> The extent of country for which the new Constitution was required, produced another difficulty in the business of the federal Convention. It is the opinion of some celebrated writers that to a small territory, the democratical; to a middling territory (as Montesquieu has termed it), the monarchical; and to an extensive territory, the despotic form of government is best adapted. Regarding then the wide and almost unbounded jurisdiction of the United States, at first view, the hand of despotism seemed necessary to control, connect, and protect it; and hence the chief embarrassment rose. For we know that although our constituents would cheerfully submit to the legislative restraints of a free government, they would spurn at every attempt to shackle them with despotic power.

And, again, in another part of his speech, he continues:

> Is it probable that the dissolution of the state governments, and the establishment of one *consolidated empire* would be eligible in its nature, and satisfactory to the people in its administration? I think not, as I have given reasons to show that so extensive a territory could not be governed, connected, and preserved but by the *supremacy of despotic power.* All the exertions of the most potent emperors of Rome were not capable of keeping that Empire together, which in extent was far inferior to the dominion of America.

We dissent, secondly, because the powers vested in Congress by this Constitution must necessarily annihilate and absorb the legislative, executive, and judicial powers of the several states, and produce from their ruins one consolidated government, which from the nature of things will be *an iron-banded despotism,* as nothing short of the supremacy of despotic sway could connect and govern these United States under one government.

As the truth of this position is of such decisive importance, it ought to be fully investigated, and if it is founded, to be clearly ascertained; for, should it be demonstrated that the powers vested by this Constitution in Congress will have such an effect as necessarily to produce one consolidated government, the question then will be reduced to this short issue, viz.: whether satiated with the blessings of liberty, whether repenting of the folly of so recently asserting their unalienable rights against foreign despots at the expense of so much blood and treasure, and such painful and arduous struggles, the people of America are now willing to resign every privilege of freemen, and submit to the dominion of an absolute government that will embrace all America in one chain of despotism; or whether they will, with virtuous indignation, spurn at the shackles prepared for them, and confirm their liberties by a conduct becoming freemen.

That the new government will not be a confederacy of states, as it ought, but one consolidated government, founded upon the destruction of the several governments of the states, we shall now show.

The powers of Congress under the new Constitution are complete and unlimited over the *purse* and the *sword,* and are perfectly independent of and supreme over the state governments, whose intervention in these great points is entirely destroyed. By virtue of their power of taxation, Congress may command the whole or any part of the property of the people. They may impose what imposts upon commerce, they may impose what land taxes, poll taxes, excises, duties on all written instruments and duties on every other article that they may judge proper; in short, every species of taxation, whether of an external or internal nature, is comprised in Article I, Section 8, viz.:

> The Congress shall have power to lay and collect taxes, duties, imposts, and excises, to pay the debts, and provide for the common defense and general welfare of the United States.

As there is no one article of taxation reserved to the state governments, the Congress may monopolize every source of revenue, and thus indirectly demolish the state governments, for without funds they could not exist. The taxes, duties and excises imposed by Congress may be so high as to render it impracticable to levy further sums on the same articles; but whether this should be the case or not, if the state governments should presume to impose taxes, duties, or excises on the same articles with Congress, the latter may abrogate and repeal the laws whereby they are imposed, upon the allegation that they interfere with the due collection of their taxes, duties, or excises, by virtue of the following clause, part of Article I, Section 8, viz.:

> To make all laws which shall be necessary and proper for carrying into execution the foregoing powers, and all other powers vested by this Constitution in the government of the United States, or in any department or officer thereof.

The Congress might gloss over this conduct by construing every purpose for which the state legislatures now lay taxes, to be for the "general welfare," and therefore as of their jurisdiction.

And the supremacy of the laws of the United States is established by Article VI, viz.:

> That this Constitution and the laws of the United States which shall be made in pursuance thereof, and *all treaties* made, or which shall be made under the authority of the United States, shall be the *supreme law* of the *land*; and *the judges in every state shall be bound thereby; anything in the constitution or laws of any state to the contrary notwithstanding.*

It has been alleged that the words "pursuant to the Constitution" are a restriction upon the authority of Congress; but when it is considered that by other sections they are invested with every efficient power of government, and which may be exercised to the absolute destruction of the state governments, without any violation of even the forms of the Constitution, this seeming restriction, as well as every other restriction in it, appears to us to be nugatory and delusive, and only introduced as a blind upon the real nature of the government. In our opinion, "pursuant to the Constitution" will be coextensive with the *will* and *pleasure* of Congress, which, indeed, will be the only limitation of their powers.

We apprehend that two coordinate sovereignties would be a solecism in politics; that, therefore, as there is no line of distinction drawn between the general and state governments, as the sphere of their jurisdiction is undefined, it would be contrary to the nature of things that both should exist together — one or the other would necessarily triumph in the fullness of dominion. However, the contest could not be of long continuance, as the state governments are divested of every means of defense, and will be obliged by "the supreme law of the land" *to yield at discretion.*

It has been objected to this total destruction of the state governments that the existence of their legislatures is made essential to the organization of Congress; that they must assemble for the appointment of the senators and President General of the United States. True, the state legislatures may be continued for some years, as boards of appointment merely, after they are divested of every other function; but the framers of the Constitution, foreseeing that the people will soon become disgusted with this solemn mockery of a government without power and usefulness, have made a provision for relieving them from the imposition in Article I, Section 4, viz.:

> The times, places, and manner of holding elections for senators and representatives shall be prescribed in each state by the legislature thereof; *but the Congress may at any time by law make or alter such regulations, except as to the place of choosing senators.*

As Congress have the control over the time of the appointment of the President General, of the senators, and of the representatives of the United States, they may prolong their existence in office for life by postponing the time of their election and appointment from period to period under various pretenses, such as an apprehension of invasion, the factious disposition of the people, or any other plausible pretense that the occasion may suggest; and having thus obtained life estates in the government, they may fill up the vacancies themselves by their control over the mode of appointment; with this exception in regard to the senators that as the place of appointment for them must, by the Constitution, be in the particular state, they may depute some body in the respective states to fill up the vacancies in the Senate occasioned by death until they can venture to assume it themselves. In this manner may the only restriction in this clause be evaded. By virtue of the foregoing section, when the spirit of the people shall be gradually broken, when the general government shall be firmly established, and when a numerous standing army shall render opposition vain, the Congress may complete the system of despotism in renouncing all dependence on the people by continuing themselves and children in the government. . . .

The *time, mode,* and *place* of the election of representatives, senators, and President General of the United States ought not to be under the control of Congress but fundamentally ascertained and established.

The new Constitution, consistently with the plan of consolidation, contains no reservation of the rights and privileges of the state governments, which was made in the Confederation of the year 1778, by Article II, viz.:

> That each state retains its sovereignty, freedom, and independence, and every power, jurisdiction, and right which is not by this Confederation expressly delegated to the United States in Congress assembled.

The legislative power vested in Congress by the foregoing recited sections is so unlimited in its nature, may be so comprehensive and boundless in its exercise that this alone would be amply sufficient to annihilate the state governments, and swallow them up in the grand vortex of general empire.

The judicial powers vested in Congress are also so various and extensive that by legal ingenuity they may be extended to every case, and thus absorb the state judiciaries, and when we consider the decisive influence that a general judiciary would have over the civil polity of the several states, we do not hesitate to pronounce that this power, unaided by the legislative, would effect a consolidation of the states under one government.

The powers of a court of equity, vested by this Constitution in the tribunals of Congress — powers which do not exist in Pennsylvania, unless so far as they can be incorporated with jury trial — would, in this state, greatly contribute to this event. The rich and wealthy suitors would eagerly lay hold of the infinite mazes, perplexities, and delays which a court of chancery, with the appellate powers of the Supreme Court in fact as well as law would furnish him with, and thus the poor man being plunged in the bottomless pit of legal discussion, would drop his demand in despair.

In short, consolidation pervades the whole Constitution. It begins with an annunciation that such was the intention. The main pillars of the fabric correspond with it, and the concluding paragraph is a confirmation of it. The Preamble begins with the words, "We the people of the United States," which is the style of a compact between individuals entering into a state of society and not that of a confederation of states. The other features of consolidation we have before noticed.

Thus we have fully established the position that the powers vested by this Constitution in Congress will effect a consolidation of the states under one government, which even the advocates of this Constitution admit could not be done without the sacrifice of all liberty.

We dissent, thirdly, because if it were practicable to govern so extensive a territory as these United States include, on the plan of a consolidated government, consistent with the principles of liberty and the happiness of the people, yet the construction of this Constitution is not calculated to attain the object; for independent of the nature of the case, it would of itself necessarily produce a despotism, and that not by the usual gradations but with the celerity that has hitherto only attended revolutions effected by the sword.

To establish the truth of this position, a cursory investigation of the principles and form of this Constitution will suffice.

The first consideration that this review suggests is the omission of a *Bill of Rights* ascertaining and fundamentally establishing those unalienable and personal rights of men, without the full, free, and secure enjoyment of which there can be no liberty, and over which it is not necessary for a good government to have the control — the principal of which are the rights of conscience, personal liberty by the clear and unequivocal establishment of the writ of habeas corpus, jury trial in criminal and civil cases, by an impartial jury of the vicinage or county, with the common law proceedings for the safety of the accused in criminal prosecutions; and the liberty of the press, that scourge of tyrants, and the grand bulwark of every other liberty and privilege. The stipulations heretofore made in favor of them in the state constitutions are entirely superseded by this Constitution.

The legislature of a free country should be so formed as to have a competent knowledge of its constituents, and enjoy their confidence. To produce these essential requisites, the representation ought to be fair, equal, and sufficiently numerous to possess the same interests, feelings, opinions, and views which the people themselves would possess, were they all assembled; and so numerous as to prevent bribery and undue influence, and so responsible to the people, by frequent and fair elections, as to prevent their neglecting or sacrificing the views and interests of their constituents to their own pursuits.

We will now bring the legislature under this Constitution to the test of the foregoing principles, which will demonstrate that it is deficient in every essential quality of a just and safe representation.

The House of Representatives is to consist of 65 members; that is, 1 for about every 50,000 inhabitants, to be chosen every two years. Thirty-three members will form a quorum for doing business, and 17 of these, being the majority, determine the sense of the House.

The Senate, the other constituent branch of the legislature, consists of 26 members, being 2 from each state, appointed by their legislatures every six years; 14 senators make a quorum — the majority of whom, 8, determines the sense of that body, except in judging on impeachments, or in making treaties, or in expelling a member, when two-thirds of the senators present must concur.

The President is to have the control over the enacting of laws, so far as to make the concurrence of two-thirds of the representatives and senators present necessary, if he should object to the laws.

Thus it appears that the liberties, happiness, interests, and great concerns of the whole United States may be dependent upon the integrity, virtue, wisdom, and knowledge of 25 or 26 men. How inadequate and unsafe a representation! Inadequate because the sense and views of 3,000,000 or 4,000,000 people, diffused over so extensive a territory, comprising such various climates, products, habits, interests, and opinions, cannot be collected in so small a body; and, besides, it is not a fair and equal representation of the people even in proportion to its number, for the smallest state has as much weight in the Senate as the largest; and from the smallness of the number to be chosen for both branches of the legislature, and from the mode of election and appointment, which is under the control of Congress, and from the nature of the thing, men of the most elevated rank in life will alone be chosen. The other orders in the society, such as farmers, traders, and mechanics, who all ought to have a competent number of their best-informed men in the legislature, shall be totally unrepresented.

The representation is unsafe because in the exercise of such great powers and trusts, it is so exposed to corruption and undue influence, by the gift of the numerous places of honor and emolument at the disposal of the executive, by the arts and address of the great and designing, and by direct bribery.

The representation is moreover inadequate and unsafe because of the long terms for which it is appointed, and the mode of its appointment, by which Congress may not only control the choice of the people but may so manage as to divest the people of this fundamental right, and become self-elected.

The number of members in the House of Representatives *may* be increased to 1 for every 30,000 inhabitants. But when we consider that this cannot be done without the consent of the Senate, who from their share in the legislative, in the executive, and judicial departments, and permanency of appointment, will be the great efficient body in this government, and whose weight and predominancy would be abridged by an increase of the representatives, we are persuaded that this is a circumstance that cannot be expected. On the contrary, the number of representatives will probably be continued at 65, although the population of the country may swell to treble what it now is, unless a revolution should effect a change.

We have before noticed the judicial power as it would affect a consolidation of the states into one government; we will now examine it as it would affect the liberties and welfare of the people, supposing such a government were practicable and proper.

The judicial power, under the proposed Constitution, is founded on well-known principles of the *civil law*, by which the judge determines both on law and fact, and appeals are allowed from the inferior tribunals to the superior upon the whole question; so that *facts* as well as *law* would be reexamined, and even new facts brought forward in the Court of Appeals; and to use the words of a very eminent civilian —

> The cause is many times another thing before the Court of Appeals than what it was at the time of the first sentence.

That this mode of proceeding is the one which must be adopted under this Constitution is evident from the following circumstances: (1) That the trial by jury, which is the grand characteristic of the common law, is secured by the Constitution only in criminal cases. (2) That the appeal from both *law* and *fact* is expressly established, which is utterly inconsistent with the principles of the common law and trials by jury. The only mode in which an appeal from law and fact can be established is by adopting the principles and practice of the civil law, unless the United States should be drawn into the absurdity of calling and swearing juries merely for the purpose of contradicting their verdicts, which would render juries contemptible and worse than useless. (3) That the courts to be established would decide on all cases of *law and equity,* which is a well-known characteristic of the civil law, and these courts would have conusance [cognizance] not only of the laws of the United States, and of treaties, and of cases affecting ambassadors but of all cases of *admiralty and maritime jurisdiction,* which last are matters belonging exclusively to the civil law, in every nation in Christendom.

Not to enlarge upon the loss of the invaluable right of trial by an unbiased jury, so dear to every friend of liberty, the monstrous expense and inconveniences of the mode of proceeding to be adopted are such as will prove intolerable to the people of this country. . . .

We abhor the idea of losing the transcendent privilege of trial by jury. . . . At the same time we regret the intolerable delay, the enormous expense, and infinite vexation to which the people of this country will be exposed from the voluminous proceedings of the courts of civil law, and especially from the appellate jurisdiction, by means of which a man may be drawn from the utmost boundaries of this extensive country to the seat of the Supreme Court of the nation to contend, perhaps, with a wealthy and powerful adversary. The consequence of this establishment will be an absolute confirmation of the power of aristocratical influence in the courts of justice; for the common people will not be able to contend or struggle against it.

Trial by jury in criminal cases may also be excluded by declaring that the libeler, for instance, shall be liable to an action of debt for a specified sum, thus evading the common-law prosecution by indictment and trial by jury. And the common course of proceeding against a ship for breach of revenue laws by informa (which will be classed among civil causes) will at the civil law be within the resort of a court, where no jury intervenes. Besides, the benefit of jury trial, in cases of a criminal nature, which cannot be evaded, will be rendered of little value by calling the accused to answer far from home, there being no provision that the trial be by a jury of the neighborhood or country. Thus, an inhabitant of Pittsburgh, on a charge of crime committed on the banks of the Ohio, may be obliged to defend himself at the side of the Delaware, and so *vice versa.* To conclude this head: we observe that the judges of the courts of Congress would not be independent as they are not debarred from holding other offices, during the pleasure of the President and Senate, and as they may derive their support in part from fees, alterable by the legislature.

The next consideration that the Constitution presents is the undue and dangerous mixture of the powers of government; the same body possessing legislative, executive, and judicial powers. The Senate is a constituent branch of the legislature; it has judicial power in judging on impeachments; and, in this case, unites in some measure the characters of judge and party, as all the principal officers are appointed by the President General, with the concurrence of the Senate, and, therefore, they derive their offices in part from the Senate. This may bias the judgments of the senators and tend to screen great delinquents from punishment.

And the Senate has, moreover, various and great executive powers, viz., in concurrence with the President General, they form treaties with foreign nations that may control and abrogate the constitutions and laws of the several states. Indeed, there is no power, privilege, or liberty of the state governments, or of the people, but what may be affected by virtue of this power. For all treaties made by them are to be the "supreme law of the land; anything in the constitution or laws of any state, to the contrary notwithstanding."

And this great power may be exercised by the President and ten senators (being two-thirds of fourteen, which is a quorum of that body). What an inducement would this offer to the ministers of foreign powers to compass by bribery *such concessions* as could not otherwise be obtained. It is the unvaried usage of all free states, whenever treaties interfere with the positive laws of the land, to make the intervention of the legislature necessary to give them operation. This became necessary, and was afforded by the Parliament of Great Britain, in consequence of the late commercial treaty between that kingdom and France. As the Senate judges on impeachments, who is to try the members of the Senate for the abuse of this power! And none of the great appointments to office can be made without the consent of the Senate.

Such various, extensive, and important powers combined in one body of men are inconsistent with all freedom. The celebrated Montesquieu tells us that

> when the legislative and executive powers are united in the same person, or in the same body of magistrates, there can be no liberty, because apprehensions may arise, lest the same monarch or *senate* should enact tyrannical laws, to execute them in a tyrannical manner.
>
> Again, there is no liberty, if the power of judging be not separated from the legislative and executive powers. Were it joined with the legislative, the life and liberty of the subject would be exposed to arbitrary control; for the judge would then be legislator. Were it joined to the executive power, the judge might behave with all the violence of an oppressor. There would be an end of everything were the same man, or the same body of the nobles, or of the people to exercise those three powers: that of enacting laws, that of executing the public resolutions, and that of judging the crimes or differences of individuals.

The President General is dangerously connected with the Senate; his coincidence with the views of the ruling junto in that body is made essential to his weight and importance in the government, which will destroy all independency and purity in the executive department; and having the power of pardoning without the concurrence of a council, he may screen from punishment the most treasonable attempts that may be made on the liberties of the people when instigated by his coadjutors in the Senate. Instead of this dangerous and improper mixture of the executive with the legislative and judicial, the supreme executive powers ought to have been placed in the President, with a small independent council made personally responsible for every appointment to office or other act by having their opinions recorded; and that without the concurrence of the majority of the quorum of this council, the President should not be capable of taking any step.

We have before considered internal taxation as it would effect the destruction of the state governments and produce one consolidated government. We will now consider that subject as it affects the personal concerns of the people.

The power of direct taxation applies to every individual, as Congress, under this government, is expressly vested with the authority of laying a capitation or poll tax upon every person to any amount. This is a tax that, however oppressive in its nature and unequal in its operation, is certain as to its produce and simple in its collection; it cannot be evaded like the objects of imposts or excise, and will be paid, because all that a man has will he give for his head. This tax is so congenial to the nature of despotism that it has ever been a favorite under such governments. Some of those who were in the late general Convention from this state have labored to introduce a poll tax among us.

The power of direct taxation will further apply to every individual, as Congress may tax land, cattle, trades, occupations, etc., to any amount, and every object of internal taxation is of that nature that, however oppressive, the people will have but this alternative — either to pay the tax or let their property be taken, for all resistance will be vain. The standing army and select militia would enforce the collection.

For the moderate exercise of this power, there is no control left in the state governments, whose intervention is destroyed. No relief or redress of grievances can be extended as heretofore by them. There is not even a declaration of *rights* to which the people may appeal for the vindication of their wrongs in the court of justice. They must, therefore, implicitly obey the most arbitrary laws, as the most of them will be pursuant to the principles and form of the Constitution, and that strongest of all checks upon the conduct of administration, *responsibility to the people,* will not exist in this government.

The permanency of the appointments of senators and representatives, and the control the Congress have over their election, will place them independent of the sentiments and resentment of the people, and the administration having a greater interest in the government than in the community, there will be no consideration to restrain them from oppression and tyranny. In the government of this state, under the old Confederation, the members of the legislature are taken from among the people, and their interests and welfare are so inseparably connected with those of their constituents that they can derive no advantage from oppressive laws and taxes, for they would suffer in common with their fellow citizens, would participate in the burdens they impose on the community, as they must return to the common level after a short period; and notwithstanding every exertion of influence, every means of corruption, a necessary rotation excludes them from permanency in the legislature.

This large state is to have but ten members in that Congress which is to have the liberty, property, and dearest concerns of every individual in this vast country at absolute command; and even these ten persons, who are to be our only guardians, who are to supersede the legislature of Pennsylvania, will not be of the choice of the people, nor amenable to them. From the mode of their election and appointment, they will consist of the lordly and high-minded; of men who will have no congenial feelings with the people, but a perfect indifference for, and contempt of them; they will consist of those harpies of power that prey upon the very vitals that riot on the miseries of the community. But we will suppose, although in all probability it may never be realized in fact, that our deputies in Congress have the welfare of their constituents at heart, and will exert themselves in their behalf, what security could even this afford? What relief could they extend to their oppressed constituents? To attain this, the majority of the deputies of the twelve other states in Congress must be alike well disposed; must alike forego the sweets of power, and relinquish the pursuits of ambition, which, from the nature of things, is not to be expected.

If the people part with a responsible representation in the legislature, founded upon fair, certain, and frequent elections, they have nothing left they can call their own. Miserable is the lot of that people whose every concern depends on the will and pleasure of their rulers. Our soldiers will become Janissaries, and our officers of government, Bashaws; in short, the system of despotism will soon be completed.

39.

## Thomas Jefferson: On the Omission of a Bill of Rights from the Constitution

*One of the main grievances of the anti-Federalists was the omission of a bill of rights from the Constitution. The framers had briefly discussed such an addition but rejected the idea for a number of reasons. First, each state had its own declaration of rights that it considered sufficient protection for the people. A second, and even more pertinent, objection was the belief that every man has certain natural inalienable rights that need not be enumerated. In contrast to the Federalist viewpoint, those who supported a list of fundamental rights believed that such an enumeration would provide a needed restraint on the powers of the government. In addition, the courts would have a basis for decisions when a person's rights were infringed upon. Though Thomas Jefferson was not an anti-Federalist, as he himself insisted, and though he highly praised the Constitution, he agreed with those who advocated a bill of rights. The following letter of December 20, 1787, to James Madison, helped to convince the latter that the Constitution needed such an addition.*

Source: H. A. Washington, II, pp. 327-333.

I like much the general idea of framing a government which should go on of itself peaceably, without needing continual recurrence to the state legislatures. I like the organization of the government into legislative, judiciary, and executive. I like the power given the legislature to levy taxes, and for that reason solely I approve of the greater House being chosen by the people directly. For though I think a House so chosen will be very far inferior to the present Congress, will be very illy qualified to legislate for the Union, for foreign nations, etc., yet this evil does not weigh against the good of preserving inviolate the fundamental principle that the people are not to be taxed but by representatives chosen immediately by themselves. I am captivated by the compromise of the opposite claims of the great and little states, of the latter to equal, and the former to proportional influence. I am much pleased, too, with the substitution of the method of voting by person, instead of that of voting by states, and I like the negative given to the executive, conjointly with a third of either House; though I should have liked it better had the judiciary been associated for that purpose, or invested separately with a similar power. There are other good things of less moment.

I will now tell you what I do not like. First, the omission of a bill of rights, providing clearly and without the aid of sophism for freedom of religion, freedom of the press, protection against standing armies, restriction of monopolies, the eternal and unremitting force of the habeas corpus laws, and trials by jury in all matters of fact triable by the laws of the land and not by the laws of nations. To say, as Mr. Wilson does, that a bill of rights was not necessary because all is reserved in the case of the general government, which is not given, while in the particular ones, all is given which is not reserved, might do for the audience to which it was addressed, but it is surely a *gratis dictum* [a mere assertion], the reverse of which might just as well be said; and it is opposed by strong inferences from the body of the instrument as well as from the omission of the clause of our present Confederation, which had made the reservation in express terms.

It was hard to conclude because there has been a want of uniformity among the states as to the cases triable by jury, because some have been so incautious as to dispense with this mode of trial in certain cases, therefore, the more prudent states shall be reduced to the same level of calamity. It would have been much more just and wise to have concluded the other way, that as most of the states had preserved with jealousy this sacred palladium of liberty, those who had wandered should be brought back to it; and to have established general right rather than general wrong. For I consider all the ill as established which may be established. I have a right to nothing which another has a right to take away; and Congress will have a right to take away trials by jury in all civil cases. Let me add that a bill of rights is what the people are entitled to against every government on earth, general or particular; and what no just government should refuse or rest on inference.

---

40.

## Anonymous: The Commerce Power Under the New Constitution

*The clause in the new Constitution giving Congress the power "to regulate commerce with foreign nations, and among the several states, and with Indian tribes" disturbed many anti-Federalists. The strictly partisan commercial interests of a Massachusetts anti-Federalist are reflected in the following letter, which first appeared in the* Massachusetts Gazette, *Tuesday, December 18, 1787. The letter was one of a series of eighteen that were printed in the same newspaper between November 23, 1787, and February 5, 1788. The anonymous author "Agrippa" has been uncertainly identified as James Winthrop of Cambridge.*

Source: *Essays on the Constitution of the United States, etc., etc.,* Paul L. Ford, ed., Brooklyn, 1892, pp. 72-75.

There cannot be a doubt that, while the trade of this continent remains free, the activity of our countrymen will secure their full share. All the estimates for the present year, let them be made by what party they may, suppose the balance of trade to be largely in our favor. The credit of our merchants is, therefore, fully established in foreign countries. This is a sufficient proof that, when business is unshackled, it will find out that channel which is most friendly to its course. We ought, therefore, to be exceedingly cautious about diverting or restraining it. Every day produces fresh proofs that people, under the immediate pressure of difficulties, do not, at first glance, discover the proper relief.

The last year, a desire to get rid of embarrassments induced many honest people to agree to a tender act, and many others, of a different description, to obstruct the courts of justice. Both these methods only increased the evil they were intended to cure. Experience has since shown that, instead of trying to lessen an evil by altering the present course of things, that every endeavor should have been applied to facilitate the course of law, and thus to encourage a mutual confidence among the citizens, which increases the resources of them all and renders easy the payment of debts. By this means, one does not grow rich at the expense of another, but all are benefited.

The case is the same with the states. Pennsylvania, with one port and a large territory, is less favorably situated for trade than the Massachusetts, which has an extensive coast in proportion to its limits of jurisdiction. Accordingly, a much larger proportion of our people are engaged in maritime affairs. We ought, therefore, to be particularly attentive to securing so great an interest. It is vain to tell us that we ought to overlook local interests. It is only by protecting local concerns that the interest of the whole is preserved. No man when he enters into society does it from a view to promote the good of others, but he does it for his own good. All men having the same view are bound equally to promote the welfare of the whole. To recur, then, to such a principle as that local interests must be disregarded is requiring of one man to do more than another and is subverting the foundation of a free government. The Philadelphians would be shocked with a proposition to place the seat of general government and the unlimited right to regulate trade in the Massachusetts. There can be no greater reason for our surrendering the preference to them. Such sacrifices, however we may delude ourselves with the form of words, always originate in folly and not in generosity.

Let me now request your attention a little while to the actual state of public credit, that we may see whether it has not been as much misrepresented as the state of our trade.

At the beginning of the present year, the whole Continental debt was about £12,000,000 in our money. About one-quarter part of this sum was due to our foreign creditors. Of these, France was the principal, and called for the arrears of interest. A new loan of £120,000 was negotiated in Holland, at 5 percent, to pay the arrears due to France. At first sight this has the appearance of bad economy and has been used for the villainous purpose of disaffecting the people. But, in the course of this same year, Congress have negotiated the sale of as much of their Western lands on the Ohio and Mississippi as amount nearly to the whole sum of the foreign debt; and instead of a dead loss by borrowing money at 5 percent to the amount of £120,000 in one sum, they make a saving of the interest at 6 percent on £3,000,000 of their domestic debt, which is an annual saving of £180,000. It is easy to see how such an immense fund as the Western territory may be applied to the payment of the foreign debt. Purchasers of the land would as willingly procure any kind of the produce of the United States as they would buy loan-office certificates to pay for the land. The produce thus procured would easily be negotiated for the benefit of our foreign creditors. I do not mean to insinuate that no other provision should be made for our creditors but only to show that our credit is not so bad in other countries as has been represented, and that our resources are fully equal to the pressure.

The perfection of government depends on the equality of its operation, as far as human affairs will admit, upon all parts of the empire and upon all the citizens. Some inequalities, indeed, will necessarily take place. One man will be obliged to travel a few miles farther than another man to procure justice. But, when he has traveled, the poor man ought to have the same measure of justice as the rich one. Small inequalities may be easily compensated. There ought, however, to be no inequality in the law itself, and the government ought to have the same authority in one place as in another.

Evident as this truth is, the most plausible argument in favor of the new plan is drawn from the inequality of its operation in different states. In Connecticut, they have been told that the bulk of the revenue will be raised by impost and excise, and, therefore, they need not be afraid to trust Congress with the power of levying a dry tax at pleasure. New York and Massachusetts are both more commercial states than Connecticut. The latter, therefore, hopes that the other two will pay the bulk of the Continental expense. The argument is, in itself, delusive. If the trade is not overtaxed, the consumer pays it. If the trade is overtaxed, it languishes, and, by the ruin of trade, the farmer loses his market. The farmer has, in truth, no other advantage from imposts than that they save him the trouble of collecting money for the government. He neither gets nor loses money by changing the mode of taxation. The government indeed finds it the easiest way to raise the revenue; and the reason is that the tax is by this means collected where the money circulates most freely. But if the argument was not delusive, it ought to conclude against the plan, because it would prove the unequal operation of it; and, if any saving is to be made by the mode of taxing, the saving should be applied toward our own debt and not to the payment of that part of the Continental burden which Connecticut ought to discharge.

It would be impossible to refute in writing all the delusions made use of to force this system through. Those respecting the public debt, and the benefit of imposts, are the most important, and these I have taken pains to explain. In one instance, indeed, the impost does raise money at the direct expense of the seaports. This is when goods are imported subject to a duty, and reexported without a drawback. Whatever benefit is derived from this source, surely should not be transferred to another state, at least till our own debts are cleared.

Another instance of unequal operation is that it establishes different degrees of authority in different states and thus creates different interests. The lands in New Hampshire having been formerly granted by this state, and afterward by that state to private persons, the whole authority of trying titles becomes vested in a Continental court, and that state loses a branch of authority which the others retain over their own citizens.

I have now gone through two parts of my argument and have proved the efficiency of the state governments for internal regulation, and the disadvantages of the new system, at least some of the principal. The argument has been much longer than I at first apprehended, or possibly I should have been deterred from it. The importance of the question has, however, prevented me from relinquishing it.

AGRIPPA

---

*To adopt the laws of God . . . until there is time to frame better.*

First legislative measure passed by the state of Vermont

41.

## Robert Yates and John Lansing: Arguments Against Consolidating the States into One Government

*Robert Yates and John Lansing, New York delegates to the Convention of 1787, were strongly in favor of the Articles of Confederation, and thus were among the bitterest foes of the Constitution. When they realized that their colleagues were determined to frame an entirely new government, Yates and Lansing left Philadelphia. In the following letter to Governor Clinton, they give their reasons for boycotting the Convention, stressing the familiar anti-Federalist theme, the evils of consolidated government.*

Source: Elliot, I, pp. 480-482.

We do ourselves the honor to advise Your Excellency that in pursuance to concurrent resolutions of the honorable Senate and Assembly we have, together with Mr. Hamilton, attended the Convention appointed for revising the Articles of Confederation, and reporting amendments to the same.

It is with the sincerest concern we observe that, in the prosecution of the important objects of our mission, we have been reduced to the disagreeable alternative of either exceeding the powers delegated to us, and giving assent to measures which we conceive destructive to the political happiness of the citizens of the United States, or opposing our opinions to that of a body of respectable men to whom those citizens had given the most unequivocal proofs of confidence. Thus circumstanced, under these impressions, to have hesitated would have been to be culpable. We therefore gave the principles of the Constitution which has received the sanction of a majority of the Convention our decided and unreserved dissent; but we must candidly confess that we should have been equally opposed to any system, however modified, which had in object the consolidation of the United States into one government.

We beg leave, briefly, to state some cogent reasons which, among others, influenced us to decide against a consolidation of the states. These are reducible into two heads:

1. The limited and well-defined powers under which we acted and which could not, on any possible construction, embrace an idea of such magnitude as to assent to a general Constitution, in subversion of that of the state.

2. A conviction of the impracticability of establishing a general government, pervading every part of the United States, and extending essential benefits to all.

Our powers were explicit and confined to the sole and express purpose of revising the Articles of Confederation, and reporting such alterations and provisions therein as should render the federal Constitution adequate to the exigencies of government and the preservation of the Union.

From these expressions, we were led to believe that a system of consolidated government could not in the remotest degree have been in contemplation of the legislature of this state; for that so important a trust as the adopting measures which tended to deprive the state government of its most essential rights of sovereignty, and to place it in a dependent situation, could not have been confided by implication; and the circumstance, that the acts of the Convention were to receive a state approbation in the last resort, forcibly corroborated the opinion that our powers could not involve the subversion of a Constitution which, being immediately derived from the people, could only be abolished by their express consent, and not by a legislature possessing authority vested in them for its preservation. Nor could we suppose that, if it had been the intention of the legislature to abrogate the existing Confederation, they would, in such pointed terms, have directed the attention of their delegates to the revision and amendment of it in total exclusion of every other idea.

Reasoning in this manner, we were of opinion that the leading feature of every amendment ought to be the preservation of the individual states in their uncontrolled constitutional rights; and that, in reserving these, a mode might have been devised of granting to the Confederacy the moneys arising from a general system of revenue, the power of regulating commerce and enforcing the observance of foreign treaties, and other necessary matters of less moment.

Exclusive of our objections originating from the want of power, we entertained an opinion that a general government, however guarded by declarations of rights or cautionary provisions, must unavoidably, in a short time, be productive of the destruction of the civil liberty of such citizens who could be effectually coerced by it, by reason of the extensive territory of the United States, the dispersed situation of its inhabitants, and the insuperable difficulty of controlling or counteracting the views of a set of men (however unconstitutional and oppressive their acts might be) possessed of all the powers of government, and who, from their remoteness from their constituents, and necessary permanency of office, could not be supposed to be uniformly actuated by an attention to their welfare and happiness; that, however wise and energetic the principles of the general government might be, the extremities of the United States could not be kept in due submission and obedience to its laws, at the distance of many hundred miles from the seat of government; that, if the general legislature was composed of so numerous a body of men as to represent the interests of all the inhabitants of the United States in the usual and true ideas of representation, the expense of supporting it would become intolerably burdensome; and that if a few only were vested with a power of legislation, the interests of a great majority of the inhabitants of the United States must necessarily be unknown, or, if known, even in the first stages of the operations of the new government, unattended to.

These reasons were, in our opinion, conclusive against any system of consolidated government; to that recommended by the Convention, we suppose most of them very forcibly apply.

It is not our intention to pursue this subject further than merely to explain our conduct in the discharge of the trust which the honorable the legislature reposed in us. Interested, however, as we are, in common with our fellow citizens, in the result, we cannot forbear to declare that we have the strongest apprehensions that a government so organized as that recommended by the Convention cannot afford that security to equal and permanent liberty which we wished to make an invariable object of our pursuit.

We were not present at the completion of the new Constitution; but before we left the Convention, its principles were so well established as to convince us that no alteration was to be expected to conform it to our ideas of expediency and safety. A persuasion that our further attendance would be fruitless and unavailing rendered us less solicitous to return.

We have thus explained our motives for opposing the adoption of the national Constitution, which we conceived it our duty to communicate to Your Excellency, to be submitted to the consideration of the honorable legislature.

42.

# The Northwest Ordinance

*The lands west of the Alleghenies, now the states of Ohio, Indiana, Illinois, Michigan, and Wisconsin, attracted a great number of settlers and land speculators. The area became the responsibility of Congress when Virginia and other states ceded their holdings to the Confederation. The demand for a well-defined policy in the territories came primarily from the Ohio Land Company that was soon to obtain vast holdings in the Northwest. In reply to this, Congress passed several ordinances, the most important being the Northwest Ordinance of July 13, 1787, which organized the northern portion of the Ohio Valley on lines laid out originally by Thomas Jefferson in his* Report of Government for Western Lands *(1784). Considered to be one of the most significant accomplishments of the Congress of the Confederation, it provided for the formation of new states; not less than three nor more than five states were to be carved out of the area. In addition, it contained provisions for the advancement of education, the maintenance of civil liberties, and the exclusion of slavery.*

Source: Poore, 2nd edition, I, pp. 429-432.

Section 1. *Be it ordained by the United States in Congress assembled,* that the said territory, for the purpose of temporary government, be one district, subject, however, to be divided into two districts as future circumstances may, in the opinion of Congress, make it expedient.

Section 2. *Be it ordained by the authority aforesaid,* that the estates both of resident and nonresident proprietors in the said territory, dying intestate, shall descend to, and be distributed among, their children and the descendants of a deceased child in equal parts, the descendants of a deceased child or grandchild to take the share of their deceased parent in equal parts among them; and where there shall be no children or descendants, then in equal parts to the next of kin, in equal degree. And among collaterals, the children of a deceased brother or sister of the intestate shall have, in equal parts among them, their deceased parent's share; and there shall in no case be a distinction between kindred of the whole and half blood; saving in all cases to the widow of the intestate her third part of the real estate for life, and one-third part of the personal estate; and this law relative to descents and dower shall remain in full force until altered by the legislature of the district. And until the governor and judges shall adopt laws as hereinafter mentioned, estates in the said territory may be devised or bequeathed by wills in writing, signed and sealed by him

Harvard University Law School

Portrait of Nathan Dane, co-drafter of the Northwest Ordinance, by Chester Harding

or her in whom the estate may be (being of full age), and attested by three witnesses; and real estates may be conveyed by lease and release, or bargain and sale, signed, sealed, and delivered by the person, being of full age, in whom the estate may be, and attested by two witnesses, provided such wills be duly proved, and such conveyances be acknowledged, or the execution thereof duly proved, and be recorded within one year after proper magistrates, courts, and registers shall be appointed for that purpose; and personal property may be transferred by delivery, saving, however, to the French and Canadian inhabitants, and other settlers of the Kaskaskies (Kaskaskia), Saint Vincents (Vincennes), and the neighboring villages, who have heretofore professed themselves citizens of Virginia, their laws and customs now in force among them, relative to the descent and conveyance of property.

Section 3. *Be it ordained by the authority aforesaid,* that there shall be appointed, from time to time, by Congress, a governor whose commission shall continue in force for the term of three years, unless sooner revoked by Congress; he shall reside in the district, and have a freehold estate therein, in 1,000 acres of land, while in the exercise of his office.

Section 4. There shall be appointed, from time to time, by Congress, a secretary whose commission shall continue in force for four years, unless sooner revoked; he shall reside in the districts, and have a freehold estate therein, in 500 acres of land, while in the exercise of his office. It shall be his duty to keep and preserve the acts and laws passed by the legislature, and the public records of the district, and the proceedings of the governor in his executive department, and transmit authentic copies of such acts and proceedings every six months to the secretary of Congress. There shall also be appointed a court to consist of three judges, any two of whom to form a court, who shall have a common-law jurisdiction and reside in the district, and have each therein a freehold estate, in 500 acres of land, while in the exercise of their offices; and their commissions shall continue in force during good behavior.

Section 5. The governor and judges, or a majority of them, shall adopt and publish in the district such laws of the original states, criminal and civil, as may be necessary, and best suited to the circumstances of the district, and report them to Congress from time to time, which laws shall be in force in the district until the organization of the general assembly therein, unless disapproved of by Congress; but afterward the legislature shall have authority to alter them as they shall think fit.

Section 6. The governor, for the time being, shall be commander in chief of the militia, appoint and commission all officers in the same below the rank of general officers; all general officers shall be appointed and commissioned by Congress.

Section 7. Previous to the organization of the general assembly, the governor shall appoint such magistrates and other civil officers in each county or township as he shall find necessary for the preservation of the peace and good order in the same. After the general assembly shall be organized, the powers and duties of magistrates and other civil officers shall be regulated and defined by the said assembly; but all magistrates and other civil officers not herein otherwise directed shall, during the continuance of this temporary government, be appointed by the governor.

Section 8. For the prevention of crimes and injuries, the laws to be adopted or made shall have force in all parts of the district, and for the execution of process, criminal and civil, the governor shall make proper divisions thereof; and he shall proceed, from time to time, as circumstances may require, to lay out the parts of the district in which the Indian titles shall have been extinguished into counties and townships, subject, however, to such alterations as may thereafter be made by the legislature.

Section 9. So soon as there shall be 5,000 free male inhabitants of full age in the district, upon giving proof thereof to the governor, they shall receive authority, with time and place, to elect representatives from their counties or townships to represent them in the general assembly: *provided,* that for every 500 free male inhabitants there shall be one representative, and so on, progressively, with the number of free male inhabitants shall the right of representation increase, until the number of representatives shall amount to 25; after which the number and proportion of representatives shall be regulated by the legislature: *provided,* that no person be eligible or qualified to act as a representative unless he shall have been a citizen of one of the United States three years, and be a resident in the district, or unless he shall have resided in the district three years; and, in either case, shall likewise hold in his own right, in fee simple, 200 acres of land within the same: *provided also,* that a freehold in 50 acres of land in the district, having been a citizen of one of the states, and being resident in the district, or the like freehold and two years' residence in the district, shall be necessary to qualify a man as an elector of a representative.

Section 10. The representatives thus elected shall serve for the term of two years; and in case of the death of a representative, or removal from office, the governor shall issue a writ to the county or township for which he was a member to elect another in his stead to serve for the residue of the term.

Section 11. The general assembly, or legislature, shall consist of the governor, legislative council, and a house of representatives. The legislative council shall consist of five members, to continue in office five years, unless sooner removed by Congress; any three of them to be a quorum; and the members of the council shall be nominated and appointed in the following manner, to wit: As soon as representatives shall be elected, the governor shall appoint a time and place for them to meet together, and when met they shall nominate ten persons, resident in the district and each possessed of a freehold in 500 acres of land, and return their names to Congress, five of whom Congress shall appoint and commission to serve as aforesaid; and whenever a vacancy shall happen in the council, by death or removal from office, the house of representatives shall nominate two persons, qualified as aforesaid, for each vacancy, and return their names to Congress, one of whom Congress shall appoint and commission for the residue of the term; and every five years, four months at least before the expiration of the time of service of the members of the council, the said house shall nominate ten persons, qualified as aforesaid, and return their names to Congress, five of whom Congress shall appoint and commission to serve as members of the council five years, unless sooner removed. And the governor, legislative council, and house of representatives shall have authority to make laws in all cases for the good government of the district not repugnant to the principles and articles in this ordinance established and declared. And all bills, having passed by a majority in the house and by a majority in the council, shall be referred to the governor for his assent; but no bill or legislative act whatever shall be of any force without his assent. The governor shall have power to convene, prorogue, and dissolve the general assembly when, in his opinion, it shall be expedient.

Section 12. The governor, judges, legislative council, secretary, and such other officers as Congress shall appoint in the district shall take an oath or affirmation of fidelity and of office; the governor before the president of Congress, and all other officers before the governor. As soon as a legislature shall be formed in the district, the council and house assembled in one room shall have authority, by joint ballot, to elect a delegate to Congress, who shall have a seat in Congress, with a right of debating but not of voting, during this temporary government.

Section 13. And for extending the fundamental principles of civil and religious liberty which form the basis whereon these republics, their laws, and constitutions are erected; to fix and establish those principles as the basis of all laws, constitutions, and governments, which forever hereafter shall be formed in the said territory; to provide, also, for the establishment of states, and permanent government therein, and for their admission to a share in the federal councils on an equal footing with the original states, at as early periods as may be consistent with the general interest.

Section 14. *It is hereby ordained and declared, by the authority aforesaid,* that the following articles shall be considered as articles of compact between the original states and the people and states in the said territory, and forever remain unalterable, unless by common consent, to wit:

## ARTICLE I

No person demeaning himself in a peaceable and orderly manner shall ever be molested on account of his mode of worship or religious sentiments in the said territory.

## ARTICLE II

The inhabitants of the said territory shall always be entitled to the benefits of the writs of habeas corpus and of the trial by jury, of a proportionate representation of the people in the legislature, and of judicial proceedings according to the course of the common law. All persons shall be bailable, unless for capital offenses, where the proof shall be evident, or the presumption great. All fines shall be moderate; and no cruel or unusual punishment shall be inflicted. No man shall be deprived of his liberty or property but by the judgment of his peers or the law of the land; and, should the public exigencies make it necessary for the common preservation to take any person's property, or to demand his particular services, full compensation shall be made for the same. And, in the just preservation of rights and property, it is understood and declared that no law ought ever to be made or have force in the said territory that shall, in any manner whatever, interfere with or affect private contracts, or engagements, bona fide, and without fraud previously formed.

## ARTICLE III

Religion, morality, and knowledge being necessary to good government and the happiness of mankind, schools and the means of education shall forever be encouraged. The utmost good faith shall always be observed toward the Indians; their lands and property shall never be taken from them without their consent; and in their property, rights, and liberty they never shall be invaded or disturbed unless in just and lawful wars authorized by Congress; but laws founded in justice and humanity shall, from time to time, be made for preventing wrongs being done to them and for preserving peace and friendship with them.

## ARTICLE IV

THE SAID TERRITORY, and the states which may be formed therein, shall forever remain a part of this Confederacy of the United States of America, subject to the Articles of Confederation, and to such alterations therein as shall be constitutionally made; and to all the acts and ordinances of the United States in Congress assembled, conformable thereto. The inhabitants and settlers in the said territory shall be subject to pay a part of the federal debts contracted, or to be contracted, and a proportional part of the expenses of government to be apportioned on them by Congress, according to the same common rule and measure by which apportionments thereof shall be made on the other states; and the taxes for paying their proportion shall be laid and levied by the authority and direction of the legislatures of the district, or districts, or new states, as in the original states, within the time agreed upon by the United States in Congress assembled. The legislatures of those districts or new states shall never interfere with the primary disposal of the soil by the United States in Congress assembled, nor with any regulations Congress may find necessary for securing the title in such soil to the bona fide purchasers. No tax shall be imposed on lands the property of the United States; and in no case shall nonresident proprietors be taxed higher than residents. The navigable waters leading into the Mississippi and St. Lawrence, and the carrying places between the same, shall be common highways, and forever free, as well to the inhabitants of the said territory as to the citizens of the United States, and those of any other states that may be admitted into the Confederacy, without any tax, impost, or duty therefor.

## ARTICLE V

THERE SHALL BE FORMED in the said territory not less than three nor more than five states; and the boundaries of the states, as soon as Virginia shall alter her act of cession and consent to the same, shall become fixed and established as follows, to wit: the Western state, in the said territory, shall be bounded by the Mississippi, the Ohio, and the Wabash rivers; a direct line drawn from the Wabash and Post Vincents (Fort Vincennes) due north to the territorial line between the United States and Canada; and by the said territorial line to the Lake of the Woods and Mississippi. The middle state shall be bounded by the said direct line, the Wabash from Post Vincents to the Ohio, by the Ohio, by a direct line drawn due north from the mouth of the Great Miami to the said territorial line, and by the said territorial line. The Eastern state shall be bounded by the last-mentioned direct line, the Ohio, Pennsylvania, and the said territorial line: *provided, however,* and it is further understood and declared, that the boundaries of these three states shall be subject so far to be altered that, if Congress shall hereafter find it expedient, they shall have authority to form one or two states in that part of the said territory which lies north of an east and west line drawn through the southerly bend or extreme of Lake Michigan. And whenever any of the said states shall have 60,000 free inhabitants therein, such state shall be admitted by its delegates into the Congress of the United States, on an equal footing with the original states, in all respects whatever; and shall be at liberty to form a permanent constitution and state government: *provided,* the constitution and government so to be formed shall be republican, and in conformity to the principles contained in these Articles, and, so far as it can be consistent with the general interest of the Confederacy, such admission shall be allowed at an earlier period, and when there may be a less number of free inhabitants in the state than 60,000.

ARTICLE VI

There shall be neither slavery nor involuntary servitude in the said territory, otherwise than in the punishment of crimes, whereof the party shall have been duly convicted: *provided always,* that any person escaping into the same, from whom labor or service is lawfully claimed in any one of the original states, such fugitive may be lawfully reclaimed and conveyed to the person claiming his or her labor or service as aforesaid.

*Be it ordained by the authority aforesaid,* that the resolutions of the 23rd of April, 1784, relative to the subject of this ordinance be, and the same are, hereby repealed and declared null and void.

Done by the United States in Congress assembled, the 13th day of July, in the year of our Lord 1787, and of their sovereignty and independence the twelfth.

---

43.

## Tench Coxe: Prospects for American Manufacturing

*Tench Coxe, a political economist and Philadelphia merchant, was among the first Americans to recognize the significance of the new machine technology being used by manufacturers. He was concerned for the post-Revolution economic state of America and, consequently, took a deep interest in the Convention of 1787. In the eighteenth century, the American economy was primarily based on agriculture, and while always aware of the farmers' claims, Coxe thought their interests would best be served by developing manufactures that would provide a domestic market for their products. On August 9, 1787, he gave the following speech to the first meeting of the Pennsylvania Society for the Encouragement of Manufactures and Useful Arts.*

Source: *A View of the United States of America, etc., etc.,* Philadelphia, 1794, pp. 35-56.

While I obey with sincere pleasure the commands of the respectable assembly whom I have now the honor to address, I feel the most trying emotions of anxiety and apprehension in attempting to perform so difficult and serious a duty as that prescribed to me at our last meeting. The importance and novelty of the subject, the injurious consequences of mistaken opinions on it, and your presence necessarily excite feelings such as these. They are lessened, however, by the hope of some benefit to that part of my fellow citizens who depend for comfort on our native manufactures, and by an ardent wish to promote every measure that will give to our newborn states the strength of manhood. Supported by these considerations and relying on the kind indulgence which is ever shown to well-meant endeavors, however unsuccessful, I shall venture to proceed.

Providence has bestowed upon the United States of America means of happiness as great and numerous as are enjoyed by any country in the world. A soil fruitful and diversified — a healthful climate — mighty rivers and adjacent seas abounding with fish are the great advantages for which we are indebted to a beneficent Creator. Agriculture, manufactures, and commerce, naturally arising from these sources, afford to our industrious citizens certain subsistence and innumerable opportunities of acquiring wealth. To arrange our affairs in salutary and well-digested systems, by which the fruits of industry, in every line, may be most easily attained, and the possession of property and the blessings of liberty may be completely secured — these are the important objects that should engross our present attention. The interests of commerce and the establishment of a just and effective government are already committed to the care of the august body now sitting in our capital. The importance of agriculture has long since recommended it to the patronage of numerous associations and the attention of all the legislatures; but manufactures, at least in Pennsylvania, have had but few unconnected friends, till sound policy and public spirit gave a late but auspicious birth to this society.

The situation of America before the Revolution was very unfavorable to the objects of this institution. The prohibition of most foreign raw materials — considerable bounties in England for carrying away the unwrought productions of this country to that, as well as on exporting British goods from their markets — the preference for those goods which habit carried much beyond what their excellence would justify, and many other circumstances created artificial impediments which appeared almost insuperable. Several branches, however, were carried on with great advantage. But as long as we remained in our colonial situation, our progress was very slow; and, indeed, the necessity of attention to manufactures was not so urgent as it has become since our assuming an independent station. The employment of those whom the decline of navigation has deprived of their usual occupations, the consumption of the increasing produce of our lands and fisheries, and the certainty of supplies in the time of war, are very weighty reasons for establishing new manufactories now, which existed but in a small degree or not at all before the Revolution.

While we readily admit that in taking measures to promote the objects of this society, nothing should be attempted which may injure our agricultural interests, they being undoubtedly the most important, we must observe, in justice to ourselves, that very many of our citizens who are expert at manufactures and the useful arts are entirely unacquainted with rural affairs, or unequal to the expenses of a new settlement. And many, we may believe, will come among us, invited to our shores from foreign countries by the blessings of liberty, civil and religious. We may venture to assert, too, that more profit to the individual and riches to the nation will be derived from some manufactures which promote agriculture than from any species of cultivation whatever. The truth of this remark, however, will be better determined when the subject shall be further considered.

Let us first endeavor to disencumber manufactures of the objections that appear against them, the principal of which are the high rate of labor, which involves the price of provisions; the want of a sufficient number of hands on any terms; the scarcity and dearness of raw materials; want of skill in the business itself; and its unfavorable effects on the health of the people.

Factories which can be carried on by watermills, windmills, fire, horses, and machines ingeniously contrived are not burdened with any heavy expense of boarding, lodging, clothing, and paying workmen; and they supply the force of hands to a great extent without taking our people from agriculture. By wind and water machines we can make pig and bar iron, nail rods, tire, sheet-iron, sheet-copper, sheet-brass, anchors, meal of all kinds, gunpowder, writing, printing and hanging paper, snuff, linseed oil, boards, plank, and scantling; and they assist us in finishing scythes, sickles, and woolen cloths. Strange as it may appear, they also card, spin, and even weave, it is said, by water in the European factories. Bleaching and tanning must not be omitted, while we are speaking of the usefulness of water.

By fire we conduct our breweries, distilleries, salt and potash works, sugar houses, potteries, casting and steel furnaces, works for animal and vegetable oils and refining drugs. Steam mills have not yet been adopted in America, but we shall probably see them after a short time in places where there are few mill seats and in this and other great towns of the United States. The city of Philadelphia, by adopting the use of them, might make a great saving on all the grain brought hither by water, which is afterward manufactured into meal, and they might be usefully applied to many other valuable purposes.

Horses give us, in some instances, a relief from the difficulties we are endeavoring to obviate. They grind the tanners' bark and potters' clay; they work the brewers' and distillers' pumps, and might be applied, by an inventive mind, as the moving principle of many kinds of mills.

Machines ingeniously constructed will give us immense assistance. The cotton and silk manufacturers in Europe are possessed of some that are invaluable to them. Several instances have been ascertained, in which a few hundreds of women and children perform the work of thousands of carders, spinners, and winders. In short, combinations of machines with fire and water have already accomplished much more than was formerly expected from them by the most visionary enthusiast on the subject. Perhaps I may be too sanguine, but they appear to me fraught with immense advantages to us, and not a little dangerous to the manufacturing nations of Europe; for should they continue to use and improve them, as they have heretofore done, their people may be driven to us for want of employment; and if, on the other hand, they should return to manual labor, we may underwork them by these invaluable engines. We may certainly borrow some of their inventions, and others of the same nature we may strike out ourselves; for on the subject of mechanism America may justly pride herself. Every combination of machinery may be expected from a country, a native son of which, reaching this inestimable object at its highest point, has epitomized the motions of the spheres that roll throughout the universe.

The lovers of mankind, supported by experienced physicians and the opinions of enlightened politicians, have objected to manufactures as unfavorable to the health of the people. Giving to this humane and important consideration its full weight, it furnishes an equal argument against several other occupations by which we obtain our comforts and promote our agriculture. The painting business, for instance, reclaiming marshes, clearing swamps, the culture of rice and indigo, and some other employments are even more fatal to those who are engaged in them. But this objection is urged principally against carding, spinning, and weaving, which formerly were entirely manual and sedentary occupations. Our plan, as we have already shown, is not to pursue those modes unless in cases particularly circumstanced, for we are sensible that our people must not be diverted from their farms. Horses, and the potent elements of fire and water, aided by the faculties of the human mind, are to be, in many instances, our daily laborers. After giving immediate relief to the industrious poor, these unhurtful means will be pursued and will procure us private wealth and national prosperity.

Emigration from Europe will also assist us. The blessings of civil and religious liberty in America and the oppressions of most foreign governments, the want of employment at home and the expectations of profit here, curiosity, domestic unhappiness, civil wars, and various other circumstances will bring many manufacturers to this asylum for mankind. Ours will be their industry, and, what is of still more consequence, ours will be their skill. Interest and necessity, with such instructors, will teach us quickly. In the last century the manufactures of France were next to none; they are now worth millions to her yearly. Those of England have been more improved within the last twelve years than in the preceding fifty. At the peace of 1763, the useful arts and manufactures were scarcely known in America. How great has been their progress since, unaided, undirected, and discouraged. Countenanced by your patronage and promoted by your assistance what may they not be ere such another space of time shall elapse?

Wonderful as it must appear, the manufacturers of beer, that best of all our commodities, have lately been obliged to import malt from England. Here must be inexcusable neglect or a strange blindness to our most obvious interests. The cultivation of barley should certainly be more attended to, and, if I mistake not exceedingly, the present abundant crop of wheat will so fill our markets that the farmer, who shall reap barley the ensuing year, will find it the most profitable of all the grains. We cannot, however, have any permanent difficulty on this article.

Of flax and hemp, little need be said but that we can increase them as we please, which we shall do according to the demand.

Wool must become much more abundant as our country populates. Mutton is the best meat for cities, manufactories, seminaries of learning, and poorhouses and should be given by rule, as in England. The settlement of our new lands, remote from water carriage, must introduce much more pasturage and grazing than has been heretofore necessary, as sheep, horses, and horned cattle will carry themselves to market through roads impassable by wagons. The foreign restrictions on our trade will also tend to increase the number of sheep.

Horses and horned cattle used to form a great part of the New England cargoes for the English West India islands. These animals are exported to those places, now, in smaller numbers, as our vessels are excluded from their ports. The farms, capital, and men which were formerly employed in raising them will want a market for their usual quantity, and the nature of that country being unfit for grain, sheep must occupy a great proportion of their lands.

Cotton thrives as well in the Southern states as in any part of the world. The West India Islands and those states raised it formerly, when the price was not half what it has been for years past in Europe. It is also worth double the money in America which it sold for before the Revolution, all the European nations having prohibited the exportation of it from their respective colonies to any foreign country. It is much to be desired that the Southern planters would adopt the cultivation of an article from which the best informed manufacturers calculate the greatest profits, and on which some established factories depend.

Silk has long been a profitable production of Georgia and other parts of the United

States and may be increased, it is presumed, as fast as the demand will rise. This is the strongest of all raw materials, and the great empire of China, though abounding with cotton, finds it the cheapest clothing for her people.

Iron we have in great abundance, and a sufficiency of lead and copper, were labor low enough to extract them from the bowels of the earth.

Madder has scarcely been attempted, but this and many other dyestuffs may be cultivated to advantage or found in America.

Under all the disadvantages which have attended manufactures and the useful arts, it must afford the most comfortable reflection to every patriotic mind to observe their progress in the United States and particularly in Pennsylvania. For a long time after our forefathers sought an establishment in this place, then a dreary wilderness, everything necessary for their simple wants was the work of European hands. How great — how happy is the change! The list of articles we now make ourselves, if particularly enumerated, would fatigue the ear and waste your valuable time. Permit me, however, to mention them under their general heads: meal of all kinds, ships and boats, malt liquors, distilled spirits, potash, gunpowder, cordage, loaf sugar, pasteboard, cards and paper of every kind, books in various languages, snuff, tobacco, starch, cannon, muskets, anchors, nails and very many other articles of iron, bricks, tiles, pottersware, millstones and other stonework, cabinetwork, trunks and Windsor chairs, carriages and harness of all kinds, corn fans, plows and many other implements of husbandry, sadlery and whips, shoes and boots, leather of various kinds, hosiery, hats and gloves, wearing apparel, coarse linens and woolens and some cotton goods, linseed and fish oil, wares of gold, silver, tin, pewter, lead, brass and copper, clocks and watches, wool and cotton cards, printing types, glass, and stoneware, candles, soap, and several other . . . articles with which the memory cannot furnish us at once.

If the nations of Europe possess some great advantages over us in manufacturing for the rest of the world, it is, however, clear that there are some capital circumstances in our favor when they meet us in our own markets. The expenses of importing raw materials, which in some instances they labor under, while we do not; the same charges in bringing their commodities hither; the duties we must lay on their goods for the purposes of revenue; the additional duties which we may venture to impose without risking the corruption of morals or the loss of the revenue by smuggling; the prompt payment our workmen receive; the long credits they give on their goods; the sale of our articles by the piece to the consumer, while they sell theirs by great invoices to intermediate purchasers; the durable nature of some American manufactures, especially of linens; the injuries theirs often sustain from their mode of bleaching — these things taken together will give us an advantage of 25 to 50 percent on many articles, and must work the total exclusion of several others.

Besides the difference in the qualities of American and European linens, arising from the mode of bleaching, there is a very considerable saving of expense from the same cause. So much and so powerful a sunshine saves a great loss of time and expense of bleaching stuffs and preparations, and this will be sensibly felt in our manufactures of linen and cotton.

We must carefully examine the conduct of other countries in order to possess ourselves of their methods of encouraging manufactories and pursue such of them as apply to our situation, so far as it may be in our power; exempting raw materials, dyestuffs, and certain implements for manufacturing from duty on importation is a very proper measure. Premiums for useful inventions and improvements, whether foreign or

American, for the best experiments in any unknown matter, and for the largest quantity of any valuable raw material, must have an excellent effect. They would assist the efforts of industry and hold out the noble incentive of honorable distinction to merit and genius. The state might with great convenience enable an enlightened society, established for the purpose, to offer liberal rewards in land for a number of objects of this nature. Our funds of that kind are considerable and almost dormant. An unsettled tract of 1,000 acres, as it may be paid for at this time, yields little money to the state. By offering these premiums for useful inventions to any citizen of the Union, or to any foreigner who would become a citizen, we might often acquire in the man a compensation for the land, independently of the merit which gave it to him. If he should be induced to settle among us with a family and property, it would be of more consequence to the state than all the purchase money.

It might answer a useful purpose if a committee of this society should have it in charge to visit every ship arriving with passengers from any foreign country, in order to inquire what persons they may have on board capable of constructing useful machines, qualified to carry on manufacture, or coming among us with a view to that kind of employment. It would be a great relief and encouragement to those friendless people in a land of strangers, and would fix many among us whom little difficulties might incline to return.

Extreme poverty and idleness in the citizens of a free government will ever produce vicious habits and disobedience to the laws, and must render the people fit instruments for the dangerous purposes of ambitious men. In this light the employment, in manufactures, of such of our poor as cannot find other honest means of subsistence is of the utmost consequence. A man oppressed by extreme want is prepared for all evil, and the idler is ever prone to wickedness; while the habits of industry, filling the mind with honest thoughts and requiring the time for better purposes, do not leave leisure for meditating or executing mischief.

An extravagant and wasteful use of foreign manufactures has been too just a charge against the people of America since the close of the war. They have been so cheap, so plenty, and so easily obtained on credit that the consumption of them has been absolutely wanton. To such an excess has it been carried that the importation of the finer kinds of coat, vest, and sleeve buttons, buckles, broaches, breastpins, and other trinkets into this port only is supposed to have amounted in a single year to £10,000 sterling, which cost wearers above $60,000. This lamentable evil has suggested to many enlightened minds a wish for sumptuary regulations, and even for an unchanging national dress suitable to the climate and the other circumstances of the country. A more general use of such manufactures as we can make ourselves would wean us from the folly we have just now spoken of, and would produce, in a less exceptionable way, some of the best effects of sumptuary laws. Our dresses, furniture, and carriages would be fashionable, because they were American and proper in our situation, not because they were foreign, showy, or expensive.

Our farmers, to their great honor and advantage, have been long in the excellent economical practice of domestic manufactures for their own use, at least in many parts of the Union. It is chiefly in the towns that this madness for foreign finery rages and destroys. There, unfortunately, the disorder is epidemical. It behooves us to consider our untimely passion for European luxuries as a malignant and alarming symptom, threatening convulsions and dissolution to the political body. Let us hasten then to apply the most effectual remedies, ere the disease becomes inveterate, lest unhappily we should find it incurable.

I cannot conclude this address, gentlemen, without taking notice of the very favorable and prodigious effects upon the landed interest which may result from manufactures. The breweries of Philadelphia, in their present infant state, require 40,000 bushels of barley annually, and when the stock on hand of English beer shall be consumed, will call for a much larger quantity. Could the use of malt liquors be more generally introduced, it would be, for many reasons, a most fortunate circumstance. Without insisting on the pernicious effects of distilled spirits, it is sufficient for our present purpose to observe that 1,000 hogsheads of rum and brandy, mixed with water for common use, will make as much strong drink as will require 120,000 bushels of grain to make an equivalent quantity of beer, besides the horses, fuel, hops, and other articles of the country which a brewery employs.

The fruits of the earth and the productions of nature in America are also required by various other manufacturers, whom you will remember without enumeration. But it is not in their occupations only that these valuable citizens demand our native commodities. They and their brethren, who work in foreign articles, with their wives, children, and servants, necessarily consume in food and raiment a prodigious quantity of our produce, and the buildings for the accommodation of their families and business are principally drawn from our lands. Their effects upon agriculture are of more consequence than has ever been supposed by those who have not made the necessary estimates. So great are the benefits to the landed interest, which are derived from them, that I venture to assert without apprehension of mistake that the value of American productions annually applied to their various uses as above stated, without including the manufacturers of flour, lumber, and bar-iron, is double the aggregate amount of all our exports in the most plentiful year with which Providence has ever blessed this fruitful country. How valuable is this market for our increasing produce — how clearly does it evince the importance of our present plan?

But we may venture to proceed a step further; without manufactures the progress of agriculture would be arrested on the frontiers of Pennsylvania. Though we have a country practicable for roads, some of our Western counties are yet unable to support them, and too remote perhaps to use land carriage of the most easy kind. Providence has given them, in certain prospect, a passage by water; but the natural impediments, though very inconsiderable, and the more cruel obstructions arising from political circumstances, are yet to be removed. The inhabitants of the fertile tracts adjacent to the waters of the Ohio, Potomac, and Susquehanna, besides the cultivation of grain, must extend their views immediately to pasturage and grazing and even to manufactures. Foreign trade will not soon take off the fruits of their labor in their native state. They must manufacture first for their own consumption, and when the advantages of their mighty waters shall be no longer suspended, they must become the greatest factory of American raw materials for the United States. Their resources in wood and water are very great, as are their mines of coal. As they do not sell much grain, but for home consumption, and must propagate sheep and cattle for the reasons above stated, their country will in a short time be the cheapest upon earth.

How numerous and important then do the benefits appear which may be expected from this salutary design! It will consume our native productions, now increasing to super-abundance; it will improve our agriculture, and teach us to explore the fossil and vegetable kingdoms, into which few researches have heretofore been made; it will accelerate the improvement of our internal navigation and bring into action the dormant powers of nature and the elements; it will lead us once more into the paths of public virtue by restoring frugality and industry, those potent antidotes to the vices of mankind; and will give us real independence by rescuing us from the tyranny of foreign fashions and the destructive torrent of luxury.

Should these blessed consequences ensue, those severe restrictions of the European nations which have already impelled us to visit the most distant regions of the Eastern Hemisphere, defeating the schemes of short-sighted politicians, will prove, through the wisdom and goodness of Providence, the means of our political salvation.

Opinions had prevailed in America, that manufacturing employments were injurious to the best interests of the country, that the pursuit of agriculture should occupy all our citizens, and that labor was so dear as to preclude all chances of success. Yet it was observed that many emigrators and others in the manufacturing branches had actually succeeded, and it was manifest that the civil and religious freedom of the country, and the low price of food, of fuel, and of raw materials would continue to attract persons of that description. Further investigation and reflection threw new and pleasing lights upon the subject. It was perceived that children too young for labor could be kept from idleness and rambling, and of course from early temptations to vice, by placing them for a time in manufactories, and that the means of their parents to clothe, feed, and educate them could be thereby increased; that women, valetudinarians, and old men could be employed; that the portions of time of housewives and young women which were not occupied in family affairs could be profitably filled up. . . .

It has been ascertained on further examination that wages in several parts of the United States are not higher than in parts of Britain, as had been erroneously supposed, especially taking into consideration the prices of provisions and the same degree of comfortable living. It was therefore confidently expected by many who carefully examined the subject that great advantages would result from a rational and steady course of attention, private and public, to the advancement of manufactures. It will appear in the sequel that the prudent exertions which have been incessantly made have been crowned accordingly with abundant success, considering the shortness of the time and how many other matters of great importance have called for attention, industry, and capital in the United States.

44.

# Judicial Review in a Southern Court

*Land which had been confiscated from Loyalists during the Revolutionary War was, in North Carolina, sold to new owners through state-appointed commissioners. The only way the original owner could recover his property was through a lawsuit. In 1785, the legislature of North Carolina passed a law stating that such suits could be dismissed on a motion from the defendants, the new owners, if they had proof of purchase from an authorized state commissioner. In* Bayard v. Singleton *(1787), a North Carolina court declared this piece of legislation unconstitutional. The court felt that every citizen had the right to a jury trial in a question of property rights. This was the first case of judicial review under a written constitution in which a law was declared unconstitutional. The implication of the court's decision was that no legislature can be allowed to alter the constitution under which it operates. A portion of the court's decision is reprinted below.*

Source: *North Carolina Reports,* François X. Martin, ed., 2nd edition, Raleigh, N.C., 1843, Vol. I, pp. 42-48.

The Court recommended to the parties to consent to a fair decision of the property in question by a jury, according to the common law of the land, and pointed out to the defendant the uncertainty that would always attend his title if this case should be dismissed without a trial; as upon a repeal of the present act (which would probably happen sooner or later), suit might be again commenced against him for the same property at the time when evidences, which at present were easy to be had, might be wanting. But this recommendation was without effect.

Another mode was proposed for putting the matter in controversy on a more constitutional footing for a decision than that of the motion under the aforesaid act. The Court then, after every reasonable endeavor had been used in vain for avoiding a disagreeable difference between the legislature and the judicial powers of the state, at length, with much apparent reluctance, but with great deliberation and firmness, gave their opinion separately but unanimously for overruling the aforementioned motion for the dismission of the said suits.

In the course of which the judges observed that the obligation of their oaths and the duty of their office required them in that situation to give their opinion on that important and momentous subject; and that notwithstanding the great reluctance they might feel against involving themselves in a dispute with the legislature of the state, yet no object of concern or respect could come in competition or authorize them to dispense with the duty they owed the public, in consequence of the trust they were invested with under the solemnity of their oaths.

That they therefore were bound to declare that they considered that whatever disabilities the persons under whom the plaintiffs were said to derive their titles might justly have incurred, against their maintaining or prosecuting any suits in the courts of this state; yet that such disabilities in their nature were merely personal, and not by any means capable of being transferred to the present plaintiffs, either by descent or purchase; and that these plaintiffs, being citizens of one of the United States, are citizens of this state, by the confederation of all the states; which is to be taken as a part of the law of the land, unrepealable by any act of the General Assembly.

That, by the constitution, every citizen had undoubtedly a right to a decision of his property by a trial by jury. For that if the legislature could take away this right and require him to stand condemned in his property without a trial, it might with as much authority require his life to be taken away without a trial by jury, and that he should stand condemned to die without the formality of any trial at all; that if the members of the General Assembly could do this, they might with equal authority not only render themselves the legislators of the state for life, without any further election of the people, but from thence transmit the dignity and authority of legislation down to their heirs male forever.

But that it was clear that no act they could pass could by any means repeal or alter the constitution, because if they could do this, they would at the same instant of time destroy their own existence as a legislature and dissolve the government thereby established. Consequently, the constitution (which the judicial was bound to take notice of as much as of any other law whatever) standing in full force as the fundamental law of the land, notwithstanding the act on which the present motion was grounded, the same act must of course, in that instance, stand as abrogated and without any effect.

45.

## Philip Freneau: "The Indian Burying Ground"

*Philip Freneau has been called the "poet of the American Revolution" because of his many ballads and satires on this period. Combining the talents of poet, journalist, and seaman, he spent alternate periods at sea as a captain and at his desk writing verse, prose, and partisan essays for Jeffersonian Republicanism. For more than half a century his writings appeared in a number of periodicals, and several volumes of his collected works were published during his lifetime. Upon visiting an Indian burying ground, Freneau was inspired to write the following poem, which is generally considered to be one of the first to idealize the Indians. "The Indian Burying Ground" was first published in the* American Museum, *November 1787.*

Source: *The Miscellaneous Works of Mr. Philip Freneau, etc., etc.,* Philadelphia, 1788.

### THE INDIAN BURYING GROUND

In spite of all the learned have said,
I still my old opinion keep;
The posture that we give the dead,
Points out the soul's eternal sleep.

Not so the ancients of these lands —
The Indian, when from life released,
Again is seated with his friends,
And shares again the joyous feast.

His imaged birds, and painted bowl,
And venison, for a journey dressed,
Bespeak the nature of the soul,
Activity, that knows no rest.

His bow, for action ready bent,
And arrows, with a head of bone,
Can only mean that life is spent,
And not the finer essence gone.

Thou, stranger, that shalt come this way,
No fraud upon the dead commit,
Yet, mark the swelling turf, and say,
They do not lie, but here they sit.

Here, still a lofty rock remains,
On which the curious eye may trace
(Now wasted half by wearing rains)
The fancies of a ruder race.

Here, still an aged elm aspires,
Beneath whose far-projecting shade
(And which the shepherd still admires)
The children of the forest played.

There oft a restless Indian queen,
(Pale Marian, with her braided hair)
And many a barbarous form is seen
To chide the man that lingers there.

By midnight moons, o'er moistening dews,
In habit for the chase arrayed,
The hunter still the deer pursues,
The hunter and the deer — a shade.

And long shall timorous fancy see
The painted chief, and pointed spear,
And reason's self shall bow the knee
To shadows and delusions here.

46.

# Benjamin Rush: Thoughts on Female Education

*According to Benjamin Rush, American political society necessitated a good educational system not only for men, but also a program attuned to the needs of women. His* Thoughts upon Female Education, *published in 1787, was first an address by Rush to the Visitors of the Young Ladies' Academy in Philadelphia, on July 28 of the same year.*

Source: *Essays, Literary, Moral and Philosophical,* Philadelphia, 1806, pp. 75-92.

I have yielded with diffidence to the solicitations of the principal of the Academy, in undertaking to express my regard for the prosperity of this seminary of learning by submitting to your candor a few thoughts upon female education.

The first remark that I shall make upon this subject is that female education should be accommodated to the state of society, manners, and government of the country in which it is conducted.

This remark leads me at once to add that the education of young ladies in this country should be conducted upon principles very different from what it is in Great Britain, and in some respects different from what it was when we were a part of a monarchical empire.

There are several circumstances in the situation, employments, and duties of women in America which require a peculiar mode of education.

I. The early marriages of our women, by contracting the time allowed for education, renders it necessary to contract its plan and to confine it chiefly to the more useful branches of literature.

II. The state of property in America renders it necessary for the greatest part of our citizens to employ themselves in different occupations for the advancement of their fortunes. This cannot be done without the assistance of the female members of the community. They must be the stewards and guardians of their husbands' property. That education, therefore, will be most proper for our women which teaches them to discharge the duties of those offices with the most success and reputation.

III. From the numerous avocations from their families to which a professional life exposes gentlemen in America, a principal share of the instruction of children naturally devolves upon the women. It becomes us therefore to prepare them, by a suitable education, for the discharge of this most important duty of mothers.

IV. The equal share that every citizen has in the liberty and the possible share he may have in the government of our country make it necessary that our ladies should be qualified to a certain degree by a peculiar and suitable education, to concur in instructing their sons in the principles of liberty and government.

V. In Great Britain the business of servants is a regular occupation, but in America this humble station is the usual retreat of unexpected indigence; hence the servants in this country possess less knowledge and subordination than are required from them; and hence our ladies are obliged to attend more to the private affairs of their families than ladies generally do of the same rank in

Great Britain. "They are good servants," said an American lady of distinguished merit in a letter to a favorite daughter, "who will do well with good looking after." This circumstance should have great influence upon the nature and extent of female education in America.

The branches of literature most essential for a young lady in this country appear to be:

I. A knowledge of the English language. She should not only read but speak and spell it correctly. And to enable her to do this, she should be taught the English grammar and be frequently examined in applying its rules in common conversation.

II. Pleasure and interest conspire to make the writing of a fair and legible hand a necessary branch of a lady's education. For this purpose she should be taught not only to shape every letter properly, but to pay the strictest regard to points and capitals.[1]

I once heard of a man who professed to discover the temper and disposition of persons by looking at their handwriting. Without inquiring into the probability of this story, I shall only remark that there is one thing in which all mankind agree upon this subject, and that is in considering writing that is blotted, crooked, or illegible as a mark of a vulgar education. I know of few things more rude or illiberal than to obtrude a letter upon a person of rank or business which cannot be easily read. Peculiar care should be taken to avoid every kind of ambiguity and affectation in writing *names.*

I have now a letter in my possession upon business, from a gentleman of a liberal profession in a neighboring state, which I am unable to answer because I cannot discover the name which is subscribed to it. For obvious reasons I would recommend the writing of the first or Christian name at full length, where it does not consist of more than two syllables. Abbreviations of all kinds in letter writing, which always denote either haste or carelessness, should likewise be avoided. I have only to add under this head that the Italian and inverted hands, which are read with difficulty, are by no means accommodated to the active state of business in America or to the simplicity of the citizens of a republic.

III. Some knowledge of figures and bookkeeping is absolutely necessary to qualify a young lady for the duties which await her in this country. There are certain occupations in which she may assist her husband with this knowledge, and should she survive him and agreeably to the custom of our country be the executrix of his will, she cannot fail of deriving immense advantages from it.

IV. An acquaintance with geography and some instruction in chronology will enable a young lady to read history, biography, and travels, with advantage, and thereby qualify her not only for a general intercourse with the world, but to be an agreeable companion for a sensible man. To these branches of knowledge may be added, in some instances, a general acquaintance with the first principles of astronomy, natural philosophy and chemistry, particularly with such parts of them as are calculated to prevent superstition, by explaining the causes or obviating the effects of natural evil, and such as are capable of being applied to domestic and culinary purposes.

V. Vocal music should never be neglected in the education of a young lady in this country. Besides preparing her to join in that part of public worship which consists in psalmody, it will enable her to soothe the cares of domestic life. The distress and

1. The present mode of writing among persons of taste is to use a capital letter only for the first word of a sentence, and for names of persons, places, and months, and for the first word of every line in poetry. The words should be so shaped that a straight line may be drawn between two lines without touching the extremities of the words in either of them.

vexation of a husband, the noise of a nursery, and even the sorrows that will sometimes intrude into her own bosom may all be relieved by a song, where sound and sentiment unite to act upon the mind. I hope it will not be thought foreign to this part of our subject to introduce a fact here which has been suggested to me by my profession, and that is, that the exercise of the organs of the breast by singing contributes very much to defend them from those diseases to which our climate and other causes have of late exposed them. Our German fellow citizens are seldom afflicted with consumptions, nor have I ever known but one instance of a spitting of blood among them. This, I believe, is in part occasioned by the strength which their lungs acquire by exercising them frequently in vocal music, for this constitutes an essential branch of their education. The music master of our Academy has furnished me with an observation still more in favor of this opinion. He informed me that he had known several instances of persons who were strongly disposed to the consumption who were restored to health by the moderate exercise of their lungs in singing.

VI. Dancing is by no means an improper branch of education for an American lady. It promotes health and renders the figure and motions of the body easy and agreeable. I anticipate the time when the resources of conversation shall be so far multiplied that the amusement of dancing shall be wholly confined to children. But in our present state of society and knowledge, I conceive it to be an agreeable substitute for the ignoble pleasures of drinking and gaming in our assemblies of grown people.

VII. The attention of our young ladies should be directed as soon as they are prepared for it to the reading of history, travels, poetry, and moral essays. These studies are accommodated, in a peculiar manner, to the present state of society in America, and when a relish is excited for them in early life, they subdue that passion for reading novels which so generally prevails among the fair sex. I cannot dismiss this species of writing and reading without observing that the subjects of novels are by no means accommodated to our present manners. They hold up *life*, it is true, but it is not yet *life* in America. Our passions have not as yet "overstepped the modesty of nature," nor are they "torn to tatters," to use the expressions of the poet, by extravagant love, jealousy, ambition, or revenge. As yet the intrigues of a British novel are as foreign to our manners as the refinements of Asiatic vice. Let it not be said that the tales of distress which fill modern novels have a tendency to soften the female heart into acts of humanity. The fact is the reverse of this. The abortive sympathy which is excited by the recital of imaginary distress blunts the heart to that which is real; and, hence, we sometimes see instances of young ladies who weep away a whole forenoon over the criminal sorrows of a fictitious Charlotte or Werter, turning with disdain at three o'clock from the sight of a beggar who solicits in feeble accents or signs a small portion only of the crumbs which fall from their fathers' tables.

VIII. It will be necessary to connect all these branches of education with regular instruction in the Christian religion. For this purpose the principles of the different sects of Christians should be taught and explained, and our pupils should early be furnished with some of the most simple arguments in favor of the truth of Christianity. A portion of the Bible (of late improperly banished from our schools) should be read by them every day and such questions should be asked, after reading it, as are calculated to imprint upon their minds the interesting stories contained in it.

IX. If the measures that have been recommended for inspiring our pupils with a sense of religious and moral obligation be adopted, the government of them will be easy and agreeable. I shall only remark under this head that *strictness* of discipline will always render *severity* unnecessary and that there will be the most instruction in that school where there is the most order.

I have said nothing in favor of instrumental music as a branch of female education because I conceive it is by no means accommodated to the present state of society and manners in America. The price of musical instruments and the extravagant fees demanded by the teachers of instrumental music form but a small part of my objections to it.

To perform well upon a musical instrument requires much time and long practice. From two to four hours in a day, for three or four years, appropriated to music are an immense deduction from that short period of time which is allowed by the peculiar circumstances of our country for the acquisition of the useful branches of literature that have been mentioned. How many useful ideas might be picked up in these hours from history, philosophy, poetry, and the numerous moral essays with which our language abounds, and how much more would the knowledge acquired upon these subjects add to the consequence of a lady with her husband and with society than the best performed pieces of music upon a harpsichord or a guitar! Of the many ladies whom we have known who have spent the most important years of their lives in learning to play upon instruments of music, how few of them do we see amuse themselves or their friends with them after they become mistresses of families! Their harpsichords serve only as sideboards for their parlors and prove by their silence that necessity and circumstances will always prevail over fashion and false maxims of education.

Let it not be supposed from these observations that I am insensible of the charms of instrumental music or that I wish to exclude it from the education of a lady where a musical ear irresistibly disposes to it, and affluence at the same time affords a prospect of such an exemption from the usual cares and duties of the mistress of a family as will enable her to practice it. These circumstances form an exception to the general conduct that should arise upon this subject, from the present state of society and manners in America.

It is agreeable to observe how differently modern writers and the inspired author of the *Proverbs* describe a fine woman. The former confine their praises chiefly to personal charms, and ornamental accomplishments, while the latter celebrates only the virtues of a valuable mistress of a family and a useful member of society. The one is perfectly acquainted with all the fashionable languages of Europe; the other "opens her mouth with wisdom" and is perfectly acquainted with all the uses of the needle, the distaff, and the loom. The business of the one is pleasure; the pleasure of the other is business. The one is admired abroad; the other is honored and beloved at home. "Her children arise up and call her blessed, her husband also, and he praiseth her." There is no fame in the world equal to this, nor is there a note in music half so delightful as the respectful language with which a grateful son or daughter perpetuates the memory of a sensible and affectionate mother.

It should not surprise us that British customs with respect to female education have been transplanted into our American schools and families. We see marks of the same incongruity of time and place in many other things. We behold our houses accommodated to the climate of Great Britain by eastern and western directions. We behold our ladies panting in a heat of ninety degrees, under a hat and cushion which were calculated for the temperature of a British summer. We behold our citizens condemned and punished by a criminal law which was copied from a country where maturity in corruption renders public executions a part of the amusements of the nation. It is high time to awake from this servility — to study our own character — to examine the age of our country — and to adopt manners in everything that shall be accommodated to our state of society and to the forms of our government. In particular it is incumbent upon us to make ornamental accomplishments yield to principles and knowledge in the education of our women.

A philosopher once said, "let me make all the ballads of a country and I care not who makes its laws." He might with more propriety have said, let the ladies of a country be educated properly, and they will not only make and administer its laws, but form its manners and character. It would require a lively imagination to describe, or even to comprehend, the happiness of a country where knowledge and virtue were generally diffused among the female sex. Our young men would then be restrained from vice by the terror of being banished from their company. The loud laugh and the malignant smile, at the expense of innocence or of personal infirmities — the feats of successful mimicry and the low priced wit which is borrowed from a misapplication of scripture phrases — would no more be considered as recommendations to the society of the ladies. A double entendre in their presence would then exclude a gentleman forever from the company of both sexes and probably oblige him to seek an asylum from contempt in a foreign country.

The influence of female education would be still more extensive and useful in domestic life. The obligations of gentlemen to qualify themselves by knowledge and industry to discharge the duties of benevolence would be increased by marriage; and the patriot — the hero — and the legislator would find the sweetest reward of their toils in the approbation and applause of their wives. Children would discover the marks of maternal prudence and wisdom in every station of life, for it has been remarked that there have been few great or good men who have not been blessed with wife and prudent mothers. Cyrus was taught to revere the gods by his mother Mandane; Samuel was devoted to his prophetic office before he was born by his mother Hannah; Constantine was rescued from paganism by his mother Constantia; and Edward VI inherited those great and excellent qualities which made him the delight of the age in which he lived from his mother, Lady Jane Seymour. Many other instances might be mentioned, if necessary, from ancient and modern history, to establish the truth of this proposition.

I am not enthusiastic upon the subject of education. In the ordinary course of human affairs we shall probably too soon follow the footsteps of the nations of Europe in manners and vices. The first marks we shall perceive of our declension will appear among our women. Their idleness, ignorance, and profligacy will be the harbingers of our ruin. Then will the character and performance of a buffoon on the theater be the subject of more conversation and praise than the patriot or the minister of the gospel; then will our language and pronunciation be enfeebled and corrupted by a flood of French and Italian words; then will the history of romantic amours be preferred to the pure and immortal writings of Addison, Hawkesworth, and Johnson; then will our churches be neglected and the name of the Supreme Being never be called upon but in profane exclamations; then will our Sundays be appropriated only to feasts and concerts; and then will begin all that train of domestic and political calamities.

But, I forbear. The prospect is so painful that I cannot help silently imploring the great Arbiter of human affairs to interpose His almighty goodness and to deliver us from these evils, that at least one spot of the earth may be reserved as a monument of the effects of good education, in order to show in some degree what our species was before the fall and what it shall be after its restoration.

Thus, gentlemen, I have briefly finished what I proposed. If I am wrong in those opinions in which I have taken the liberty of departing from the general and fashionable habits of thinking, I am sure you will discover and pardon my mistakes. But, if I am right, I am equally sure you will adopt my opinions; for to enlightened minds truth is alike acceptable, whether it comes from the lips of age or the hand of antiquity or whether it be obtruded by a person who has no other claim to attention than a desire of adding to the stock of human happiness.

I cannot dismiss the subject of female education without remarking that the city of Philadelphia first saw a number of gentlemen associated for the purpose of directing the education of young ladies. By means of this plan the power of teachers is regulated and restrained and the objects of education are extended. By the separation of the sexes in the unformed state of their manners, female delicacy is cherished and preserved. Here the young ladies may enjoy all the literary advantages of a boarding school and at the same time live under the protection of their parents. Here emulation may be excited without jealousy, ambition without envy, and competition without strife.

The attempt to establish this new mode of education for young ladies was an experiment, and the success of it hath answered our expectations. Too much praise cannot be given to our principal and his assistants, for the abilities and fidelity with which they have carried the plan into execution. The proficiency which the young ladies have discovered in reading, writing, spelling, arithmetic, grammar, geography, music, and their different catechisms since the last examination is a less equivocal mark of the merits of our teachers than anything I am able to express in their favor.

But the reputation of the academy must be suspended till the public are convinced by the future conduct and character of our pupils of the advantages of the institution. To you, therefore, young ladies, an important problem is committed for solution; and that is, whether our present plan of education be a wise one and whether it be calculated to prepare you for the duties of social and domestic life. I know that the elevation of the female mind, by means of moral, physical, and religious truth, is considered by some men as unfriendly to the domestic character of a woman. But this is the prejudice of little minds and springs from the same spirit which opposes the general diffusion of knowledge among the citizens of our republics. If men believe that ignorance is favorable to the government of the female sex, they are certainly deceived, for a weak and ignorant woman will always be governed with the greatest difficulty.

I have sometimes been led to ascribe the invention of ridiculous and expensive fashions in female dress entirely to the gentlemen in order to divert the ladies from improving their minds and thereby to secure a more arbitrary and unlimited authority over them. It will be in your power, ladies, to correct the mistakes and practice of our sex upon these subjects by demonstrating that the female temper can only be governed by reason and that the cultivation of reason in women is alike friendly to the order of nature and to private as well as public happiness.

# 1787 - 1788

47.

## Alexander Hamilton and James Madison: Federalist Papers

*Between October 1787 and August 1788, Alexander Hamilton, John Jay, and James Madison wrote a series of essays that appeared in various New York newspapers under the pseudonym "Publius."* The Federalist, *as the combined essays are called, was written to combat anti-federalism. Hoping to persuade the public of the necessity for the Constitution, Publius gave excellent arguments for adopting it and discarding the Articles.* The Federalist *stresses the urgent need for an adequate central government and the ease with which the republican form of government would be adapted to the large expanse of territory and widely divergent interests found in the United States. It was immediately recognized as the most powerful defense of the new Constitution and hailed as a classic in constitutional theory. Jefferson called* The Federalist *"the best commentary on the principles of government which ever was written." Of the eighty-five essays, John Jay definitely wrote five, Madison twenty-six, and Hamilton fifty-one. The authorship of the other three is in doubt. The following selection includes essays by Hamilton and Madison.*

Source: *The Federalist,* Henry Cabot Lodge, ed., New York, 1888.

### THE FEDERALIST NO. 1 (HAMILTON)

After an unequivocal experience of the inefficiency of the subsisting federal government, you are called upon to deliberate on a new Constitution for the United States of America. The subject speaks its own importance; comprehending in its consequences nothing less than the existence of the Union, the safety and welfare of the parts of which it is composed, the fate of an empire in many respects the most interesting in the world. It has been frequently remarked that it seems to have been reserved to the people of this country, by their conduct and example, to decide the important question, whether societies of men are really capable or not of establishing good government from reflection and choice, or whether they are forever destined to depend for their political constitutions on accident and force. If there be any truth in the remark, the crisis at which we are arrived may with propriety be regarded as the era in which that decision is to be made; and a wrong election of the part we shall act may, in this view, deserve to be considered as the general misfortune of mankind.

This idea will add the inducements of philanthropy to those of patriotism, to heighten the solicitude which all considerate and good men must feel for the event. Happy will it be if our choice should be directed by a judicious estimate of our true interests, unperplexed and unbiased by considerations not connected with the public good. But this is a thing more ardently to be wished than seriously to be expected. The plan offered to our deliberations affects too many particular interests, innovates upon too many local institutions, not to involve in its discussion a variety of objects foreign to its merits, and of views, passions, and prejudices little favorable to the discovery of truth.

Among the most formidable of the obstacles which the new Constitution will have to encounter may readily be distinguished the obvious interest of a certain class of men in every state to resist all changes which may hazard a diminution of the power, emolument, and consequence of the offices they hold under the state establishments; and the perverted ambition of another class of men who will either hope to aggrandize themselves by the confusions of their country or will flatter themselves with fairer prospects of elevation from the subdivision of the empire into several partial confederacies than from its union under one government.

It is not, however, my design to dwell upon observations of this nature. I am well aware that it would be disingenuous to resolve indiscriminately the opposition of any set of men (merely because their situations might subject them to suspicion) into interested or ambitious views. Candor will oblige us to admit that even such men may be actuated by upright intentions; and it cannot be doubted that much of the opposition which has made its appearance, or may hereafter make its appearance, will spring from sources, blameless at least, if not respectable — the honest errors of minds led astray by preconceived jealousies and fears.

So numerous, indeed, and so powerful are the causes which serve to give a false bias to the judgment that we, upon many occasions, see wise and good men on the wrong as well as on the right side of questions of the first magnitude to society. This circumstance, if duly attended to, would furnish a lesson of moderation to those who are ever so much persuaded of their being in the right in any controversy. And a further reason for caution, in this respect, might be drawn from the reflection that we are not always sure that those who advocate the truth are influenced by purer principles than their antagonists. Ambition, avarice, personal animosity, party opposition, and many other motives not more laudable than these, are apt to operate as well upon those who support as those who oppose the right side of a question. Were there not even these inducements to moderation, nothing could be more ill judged than that intolerant spirit which has, at all times, characterized political parties. For in politics, as in religion, it is equally absurd to aim at making proselytes by fire and sword. Heresies in either can rarely be cured by persecution.

And yet, however just these sentiments will be allowed to be, we have already sufficient indications that it will happen in this as in all former cases of great national discussion. A torrent of angry and malignant passions will be let loose. To judge from the conduct of the opposite parties, we shall be led to conclude that they will mutually hope to evince the justness of their opinions, and to increase the number of their converts by the loudness of their declamations and the bitterness of their invectives. An enlightened zeal for the energy and efficiency of government will be stigmatized as the offspring of a temper fond of despotic power and hostile to the principles of liberty.

An overscrupulous jealousy of danger to

the rights of the people, which is more commonly the fault of the head than of the heart, will be represented as mere pretense and artifice, the stale bait for popularity at the expense of public good. It will be forgotten, on the one hand, that jealousy is the usual concomitant of love, and that the noble enthusiasm of liberty is apt to be infected with a spirit of narrow and illiberal distrust. On the other hand, it will be equally forgotten that the vigor of government is essential to the security of liberty; that, in the contemplation of a sound and well-informed judgment, their interest can never be separated; and that a dangerous ambition more often lurks behind the specious mask of zeal for the rights of the people than under the forbidding appearance of zeal for the firmness and efficiency of government. History will teach us that the former has been found a much more certain road to the introduction of despotism than the latter, and that of those men who have overturned the liberties of republics, the greatest number have begun their career by paying an obsequious court to the people, commencing demagogues and ending tyrants.

In the course of the preceding observations, I have had an eye, my fellow citizens, to putting you upon your guard against all attempts, from whatever quarter, to influence your decision in a matter of the utmost moment to your welfare, by any impressions other than those which may result from the evidence of truth. You will, no doubt, at the same time, have collected from the general scope of them that they proceed from a source not unfriendly to the new Constitution. Yes, my countrymen, I own to you that, after having given it an attentive consideration, I am clearly of opinion it is your interest to adopt it. I am convinced that this is the safest course for your liberty, your dignity, and your happiness. I affect not reserves which I do not feel. I will not amuse you with an appearance of deliberation when I have decided. I frankly acknowledge to you my convictions, and I will freely lay before you the reasons on which they are founded. The consciousness of good intentions disdains ambiguity. I shall not, however, multiply professions on this head. My motives must remain in the depository of my own breast. My arguments will be open to all, and may be judged of by all. They shall at least be offered in a spirit which will not disgrace the cause of truth.

I propose, in a series of papers, to discuss the following interesting particulars: *the utility of the Union to your political prosperity; the insufficiency of the present Confederation to preserve that Union; the necessity of a government at least equally energetic with the one proposed, to the attainment of this object; the conformity of the proposed Constitution to the true principles of republican government; its analogy to your own state constitution; and, lastly, the additional security which its adoption will afford to the preservation of that species of government, to liberty, and to property.*

In the progress of this discussion I shall endeavor to give a satisfactory answer to all the objections, which shall have made their appearance, that may seem to have any claim to your attention.

It may perhaps be thought superfluous to offer arguments to prove the utility of the Union, a point, no doubt, deeply engraved on the hearts of the great body of the people in every state, and one which, it may be imagined, has no adversaries. But the fact is that we already hear it whispered in the private circles of those who oppose the new Constitution that the thirteen states are of too great extent for any general system, and that we must of necessity resort to separate confederacies of distinct portions of the whole. This doctrine will, in all probability, be gradually propagated, till it has votaries enough to countenance an open avowal of it. For nothing can be more evident, to those who are able to take an enlarged view of the subject, than the alternative of an adoption of the new Constitution or a dismemberment of the Union.

## THE FEDERALIST NO. 10 (MADISON)

Among the numerous advantages promised by a well-constructed Union, none deserves to be more accurately developed than its tendency to break and control the violence of faction. The friend of popular governments never finds himself so much alarmed for their character and fate as when he contemplates their propensity to this dangerous vice. He will not fail, therefore, to set a due value on any plan which, without violating the principles to which he is attached, provides a proper cure for it. The instability, injustice, and confusion introduced into the public councils have, in truth, been the mortal diseases under which popular governments have everywhere perished; as they continue to be the favorite and fruitful topics from which the adversaries to liberty derive their most specious declamations.

The valuable improvements made by the American constitutions on the popular models, both ancient and modern, cannot certainly be too much admired; but it would be an unwarrantable partiality to contend that they have as effectually obviated the danger on this side, as was wished and expected. Complaints are everywhere heard from our most considerate and virtuous citizens, equally the friends of public and private faith, and of public and personal liberty, that our governments are too unstable, that the public good is disregarded in the conflicts of rival parties, and that measures are too often decided, not according to the rules of justice and the rights of the minor party, but by the superior force of an interested and overbearing majority. However anxiously we may wish that these complaints had no foundation, the evidence of known facts will not permit us to deny that they are in some degree true.

It will be found, indeed, on a candid review of our situation, that some of the distresses under which we labor have been erroneously charged on the operation of our governments; but it will be found, at the same time, that other causes will not alone account for many of our heaviest misfortunes; and, particularly, for that prevailing and increasing distrust of public engagements, and alarm for private rights, which are echoed from one end of the continent to the other. These must be chiefly, if not wholly, effects of the unsteadiness and injustice with which a factious spirit has tainted our public administrations.

By a faction, I understand a number of citizens, whether amounting to a majority or minority of the whole, who are united and actuated by some common impulse of passion, or of interest, adverse to the rights of other citizens, or to the permanent and aggregate interests of the community.

There are two methods of curing the mischiefs of faction: the one, by removing its causes; the other, by controlling its effects.

There are again two methods of removing the causes of faction: the one, by destroying the liberty which is essential to its existence; the other, by giving to every citizen the same opinions, the same passions, and the same interests.

It could never be more truly said than of the first remedy that it was worse than the disease. Liberty is to faction what air is to fire, an aliment without which it instantly expires. But it could not be less folly to abolish liberty, which is essential to political life, because it nourishes faction, than it would be to wish the annihilation of air, which is essential to animal life, because it imparts to fire its destructive agency.

The second expedient is as impracticable as the first would be unwise. As long as the reason of man continues fallible, and he is at liberty to exercise it, different opinions will be formed. As long as the connection subsists between his reason and his self-love, his opinions and his passions will have a reciprocal influence on each other; and the former will be objects to which the latter will attach themselves. The diversity in the faculties of men, from which the rights of property originate, is not less an insuperable obstacle to a uniformity of interests. The protection of these faculties is the first object of government. From the protection of different and unequal faculties of acquiring property, the possession of different degrees and kinds of property immediately results; and from the influence of these on the sentiments and views of the respective proprietors ensues a division of the society into different interests and parties.

The latent causes of faction are thus sown in the nature of man; and we see them everywhere brought into different degrees of activity, according to the different circumstances of civil society. A zeal for different opinions concerning religion, concerning government, and many other points, as well of speculation as of practice; an attachment of different leaders ambitiously contending for preeminence and power; or to persons of other descriptions whose fortunes have been interesting to the human passions, have, in turn, divided mankind into parties, inflamed them with mutual animosity, and rendered them much more disposed to vex and oppress each other than to cooperate for their common good. So strong is this propensity of mankind to fall into mutual animosities that, where no substantial occasion presents itself, the most frivolous and fanciful distinctions have been sufficient to kindle their unfriendly passions and excite their most violent conflicts. But the most common and durable source of factions has been the various and unequal distribution of property.

Those who hold and those who are without property have ever formed distinct interests in society. Those who are creditors and those who are debtors fall under a like discrimination. A landed interest, a manufacturing interest, a mercantile interest, a moneyed interest, with many lesser interests, grow up of necessity in civilized nations and divide them into different classes, actuated by different sentiments and views. The regulation of these various and interfering interests forms the principal task of modern legislation and involves the spirit of party and faction in the necessary and ordinary operations of the government.

No man is allowed to be a judge in his own cause, because his interest would certainly bias his judgment and, not improbably, corrupt his integrity. With equal, nay, with greater reason, a body of men are unfit to be both judges and parties at the same time; yet what are many of the most important acts of legislation but so many judicial determinations, not indeed concerning the rights of single persons, but concerning the rights of large bodies of citizens? And what are the different classes of legislators but advocates and parties to the causes which they determine? Is a law proposed concerning private debts? It is a question to which the creditors are parties on one side and the debtors on the other. Justice ought to hold the balance between them. Yet the parties are, and must be, themselves the judges; and the most numerous party or, in other words, the most powerful faction must be expected to prevail.

Shall domestic manufactures be encouraged, and in what degree, by restrictions on foreign manufactures? [These] are questions which would be differently decided by the landed and the manufacturing classes, and probably by neither with a sole regard to justice and the public good. The apportionment of taxes on the various descriptions of property is an act which seems to require the most exact impartiality; yet there is, perhaps, no legislative act in which greater opportunity and temptation are given to a predominant party to trample on the rules of justice. Every shilling with which they overburden the inferior number is a shilling saved to their own pockets.

It is in vain to say that enlightened statesmen will be able to adjust these clashing interests and render them all subservient to the public good. Enlightened statesmen will not always be at the helm. Nor, in many cases, can such an adjustment be made at all without taking into view indirect and remote considerations, which will rarely prevail over the immediate interest which one party may find in disregarding the rights of another or the good of the whole.

The inference to which we are brought is that the *causes* of faction cannot be removed and that relief is only to be sought in the means of controlling its *effects.*

If a faction consists of less than a majority, relief is supplied by the republican principle, which enables the majority to defeat its sinister views by regular vote. It may clog the administration, it may convulse the society; but it will be unable to execute and mask its violence under the forms of the Constitution. When a majority is included in a faction, the form of popular government, on the other hand, enables it to sacrifice to its ruling passion or interest both the public good and the rights of other citizens. To secure the public good and private rights against the danger of such a faction, and at the same time to preserve the spirit and the form of popular government, is then the great object to which our inquiries are directed. Let me add that it is the great desideratum by which this form of government can be rescued from the opprobrium under which it has so long labored and be recommended to the esteem and adoption of mankind.

By what means is this object attainable? Evidently by one of two only. Either the existence of the same passion or interest in a majority at the same time must be prevented, or the majority, having such coexistent passion or interest, must be rendered, by their number and local situation, unable to concert and carry into effect schemes of oppression. If the impulse and the opportunity be suffered to coincide, we well know that neither moral nor religious motives can be relied on as an adequate control. They are not found to be such on the injustice and violence of individuals and lose their efficacy in proportion to the number combined together, that is, in proportion as their efficacy becomes needful.

From this view of the subject it may be concluded that a pure democracy, by which I mean a society consisting of a small number of citizens who assemble and administer the government in person, can admit of no cure for the mischiefs of faction. A common passion or interest will, in almost every case, be felt by a majority of the whole; a communication and concert result from the form of government itself; and there is nothing to check the inducements to sacrifice the weaker party or an obnoxious individual. Hence it is that such democracies have ever been spectacles of turbulence and contention; have ever been found incompatible with personal security or the rights of property; and have in general been as short in their lives as they have been violent in their deaths. Theoretic politicians, who have patronized this species of government, have erroneously supposed that by reducing mankind to a perfect equality in their political rights, they would, at the same time, be perfectly equalized and assimilated in their possessions, their opinions, and their passions.

A republic, by which I mean a government in which the scheme of representation takes place, opens a different prospect and promises the cure for which we are seeking. Let us examine the points in which it varies from pure democracy, and we shall comprehend both the nature of the cure and the efficacy which it must derive from the Union.

The two great points of difference between a democracy and a republic are: first, the delegation of the government, in the latter, to a small number of citizens elected by the rest; secondly, the greater number of citizens, and greater sphere of country, over which the latter may be extended.

The effect of the first difference is, on the one hand, to refine and enlarge the public views by passing them through the medium of a chosen body of citizens, whose wisdom may best discern the true interest of their country, and whose patriotism and love of justice will be least likely to sacrifice it to temporary or partial considerations. Under such a regulation, it may well happen that the public voice, pronounced by the representatives of the people, will be more consonant to the public good than if pronounced by the people themselves, convened for the purpose. On the other hand, the effect may be inverted. Men of factious tempers, of local prejudices, or of sinister designs may, by intrigue, by corruption, or by other means, first obtain the suffrages, and then betray the interests of the people. The question resulting is, whether small or extensive republics are more favorable to the election of proper guardians of the public weal; and it is clearly decided in favor of the latter by two obvious considerations:

In the first place, it is to be remarked that, however small the republic may be, the representatives must be raised to a certain number, in order to guard against the cabals of a few; and that, however large it may be, they must be limited to a certain number, in order to guard against the confusion of a multitude. Hence, the number of representatives in the two cases not being in proportion to that of the two constituents, and being proportionally greater in the small republic, it follows that, if the proportion of fit characters be not less in the large than in the small republic, the former will present a greater option, and consequently a greater probability of a fit choice.

In the next place, as each representative will be chosen by a greater number of citizens in the large than in the small republic, it will be more difficult for unworthy candidates to practice with success the vicious arts by which elections are too often carried; and the suffrages of the people being more free, will be more likely to center in men who possess the most attractive merit and the most diffusive and established character.

It must be confessed that in this, as in most other cases, there is a mean, on both sides of which inconveniences will be found to lie. By enlarging too much the number of electors, you render the representative too little acquainted with all their local circumstances and lesser interests; as by reducing it too much, you render him unduly attached to these and too little fit to comprehend and pursue great and national objects. The federal Constitution forms a happy combination in this respect: the great and aggregate interests being referred to the national, the local and particular to the state legislatures.

The other point of difference is the greater number of citizens and extent of territory which may be brought within the compass of republican than of democratic government; and it is this circumstance principally which renders factious combinations less to be dreaded in the former than in the latter. The smaller the society, the fewer probably will be the distinct parties and interests composing it; the fewer the distinct parties and interests, the more frequently will a majority be found of the same party; and the smaller the number of individuals composing a majority, and the smaller the compass within which they are placed, the more easily will they concert and execute their plans of oppression. Extend the sphere and you take in a greater variety of parties and interests; you make it less probable that a majority of the whole will have a common motive to invade the rights of other citizens; or if such a common motive exists, it will be more difficult for all who feel it to discover their own strength and to act in unison with each other. Besides other impediments, it may be remarked that, where there is a consciousness of unjust or dishonorable purposes, communication is always checked by distrust in proportion to the number whose concurrence is necessary.

Hence, it clearly appears that the same advantage which a republic has over a democracy, in controlling the effects of factions, is enjoyed by a large over a small republic — is enjoyed by the Union over the states composing it. Does the advantage consist in the substitution of representatives whose enlightened views and virtuous sentiments render them superior to local prejudices and to schemes of injustice? It will not be denied that the representation of the Union will be most likely to possess these requisite endowments. Does it consist in the greater security afforded by a greater variety of parties, against the event of any one party being able to outnumber and oppress the rest? In an equal degree does the increased variety of parties comprised within the Union increase this security? Does it, in fine, consist in the greater obstacles opposed to the concert and accomplishment of the secret wishes of an unjust and interested majority? Here, again, the extent of the Union gives it the most palpable advantage.

The influence of factious leaders may kindle a flame within their particular states but will be unable to spread a general conflagration through the other states. A religious sect may degenerate into a political faction in a part of the Confederacy; but the variety of sects dispersed over the entire face of it must secure the national councils against any danger from that source. A rage for paper money, for an abolition of debts, for an equal division of property, or for any other improper or wicked project will be less apt to pervade the whole body of the Union than a particular member of it; in the same proportion as such a malady is more likely to taint a particular county or district than an entire state.

In the extent, and proper structure of the Union, therefore, we behold a republican remedy for the diseases most incident to republican government. And according to the degree of pleasure and pride we feel in being republicans, ought to be our zeal in cherishing the spirit and supporting the character of Federalists.

## THE FEDERALIST NO. 14 (MADISON)

We have seen the necessity of the Union, as our bulwark against foreign danger, as the conservator of peace among ourselves, as the guardian of our commerce and other common interests, as the only substitute for those military establishments which have subverted the liberties of the Old World, and as the proper antidote for the diseases of faction, which have proved fatal to other popular governments, and of which alarming symptoms have been betrayed by our own. All that remains, within this branch of our inquiries, is to take notice of an objection that may be drawn from the great extent of country which the Union embraces. A few observations on this subject will be the more proper, as it is perceived that the adversaries of the new Constitution are availing themselves of a prevailing prejudice with regard to the practicable sphere of republican administration, in order to supply, by imaginary difficulties, the want of those solid objections which they endeavor in vain to find.

The error which limits republican government to a narrow district has been unfolded and refuted in preceding papers. I remark here only that it seems to owe its rise and prevalence chiefly to the confounding of a republic with a democracy, applying to the former reasonings drawn from the nature of the latter. The true distinction between these forms was also adverted to on a former occasion. It is that, in a democracy, the people meet and exercise the government in person; in a republic, they assemble and administer it by their representatives and agents. A democracy, consequently, will be confined to a small spot. A republic may be extended over a large region.

To this accidental source of the error may be added the artifice of some celebrated authors, whose writings have had a great share in forming the modern standard of political opinions. Being subjects either of an absolute or limited monarchy, they have endeavored to heighten the advantages, or palliate the evils of those forms by placing in comparison the vices and defects of the republican, and by citing as specimens of the latter the turbulent democracies of ancient Greece and modern Italy. Under the confusion of names, it has been an easy task to transfer to a republic observations applicable to a democracy only; and, among others, the observation that it can never be established but among a small number of people, living within a small compass of territory.

Such a fallacy may have been the less perceived, as most of the popular governments of antiquity were of the democratic species; and even in modern Europe, to which we owe the great principle of representation, no example is seen of a government wholly popular, and founded, at the same time, wholly on that principle. If Europe has the merit of discovering this great mechanical power in government by the simple agency of which the will of the largest political body may be concentrated, and its force directed to any object which the public good requires, America can claim the merit of making the discovery the basis of unmixed and extensive republics. It is only to be lamented that any of her citizens should wish to deprive her of the additional merit of displaying its full efficacy in the establishment of the comprehensive system now under her consideration.

As the natural limit of a democracy is that distance from the central point which will just permit the most remote citizens to assemble as often as their public functions demand, and will include no greater number than can join in those functions; so the natural limit of a republic is that distance from the center which will barely allow the representatives to meet as often as may be necessary for the administration of public affairs. Can it be said that the limits of the United States exceed this distance? It will not be said by those who recollect that the Atlantic coast is the longest side of the Union, that during the term of thirteen years the representatives of the states have been almost continually assembled, and that the members from the most distant states are not chargeable with greater intermissions of attendance than those from the states in the neighborhood of Congress.

That we may form a juster estimate with regard to this interesting subject, let us resort to the actual dimensions of the Union. The limits, as fixed by the treaty of peace, are: on the east the Atlantic, on the south the latitude of 31°, on the west the Mississippi, and on the north an irregular line running in some instances beyond 45°, in others falling as low as 42°. The southern shore of Lake Erie lies below that latitude. Computing the distance between 31° and 45°, it amounts to 973 common miles; computing it from 31° to 42°, to 764½ miles. Taking the mean for the distance, the amount will be 868¾ miles. The mean distance from the Atlantic to the Mississippi does not probably exceed 750 miles.

On a comparison of this extent with that of several countries in Europe, the practicability of rendering our system commensurate to it appears to be demonstrable. It is not a great deal larger than Germany, where a diet representing the whole empire is continually assembled; or than Poland before the late dismemberment, where another national diet was the depositary of the supreme power. Passing by France and Spain, we find that in Great Britain, inferior as it may be in size, the representatives of the northern extremity of the island have as far to travel to the national council as will be required of those of the most remote parts of the Union.

## THE FEDERALIST NO. 39 (MADISON)

THE LAST PAPER HAVING CONCLUDED the observations which were meant to introduce a candid survey of the plan of government reported by the convention, we now proceed to the execution of that part of our undertaking.

The first question that offers itself is whether the general form and aspect of the government be strictly republican. It is evident that no other form would be reconcilable with the genius of the people of America; with the fundamental principles of the Revolution; or with that honorable determination which animates every votary of freedom, to rest all our political experiments on the capacity of mankind for self-government. If the plan of the convention, therefore, be found to depart from the republican character, its advocates must abandon it as no longer defensible.

What, then, are the distinctive characters of the republican form? Were an answer to this question to be sought, not by recurring to principles, but in the application of the term by political writers to the constitutions of different states, no satisfactory one would ever be found. Holland, in which no particle of the supreme authority is derived from the people, has passed almost universally under the denomination of a republic. The same title has been bestowed on Venice, where absolute power over the great body of the people is exercised in the most absolute manner by a small body of hereditary nobles. Poland, which is a mixture of aristocracy and of monarchy in their worst forms, has been dignified with the same appellation. The government of England, which has one republican branch only, combined with a hereditary aristocracy and monarchy, has, with equal impropriety, been frequently placed on the list of republics. These examples, which are nearly as dissimilar to each other as to a genuine republic, show the extreme inaccuracy with which the term has been used in political disquisitions.

If we resort for a criterion to the different principles on which different forms of government are established, we may define a republic to be, or at least may bestow that name on, a government which derives all its powers directly or indirectly from the great body of the people, and is administered by persons holding their offices during pleasure, for a limited period, or during good behavior. It is essential to such a government that it be derived from the great body of the society, not from an inconsiderable proportion or a favored class of it; otherwise a handful of tyrannical nobles, exercising their oppressions by a delegation of their powers, might aspire to the rank of republicans and claim for their government the honorable title of republic. It is sufficient for such a government that the persons administering it be appointed, either directly or indirectly, by the people; and that they hold their appointments by either of the tenures just specified; otherwise every government in the United States, as well as every other popular government that has been or can be well organized or well executed, would be degraded from the republican character.

According to the constitution of every state in the Union, some or other of the officers of government are appointed indirectly only by the people. According to most of them, the chief magistrate himself is so appointed. And according to one, this mode of appointment is extended to one of the coordinate branches of the legislature. According to all the constitutions, also, the tenure of the highest offices is extended to a definite period, and in many instances, both within the legislative and executive departments, to a period of years. According to the provisions of most of the constitutions, again, as well as according to the most respectable and received opinions on the subject, the members of the judiciary department are to retain their offices by the firm tenure of good behavior.

On comparing the Constitution planned by the convention with the standard here fixed, we perceive at once that it is, in the most rigid sense, conformable to it. The House of Representatives, like that of one branch at least of all the state legislatures, is elected immediately by the great body of the people. The Senate, like the present Congress and the senate of Maryland, derives its appointment indirectly from the people. The president is indirectly derived from the choice of the people, according to the example in most of the states. Even the judges, with all other officers of the Union, will, as in the several states, be the choice, though a remote choice, of the people themselves.

The duration of the appointments is equally conformable to the republican standard and to the model of state constitutions. The House of Representatives is periodically elective, as in all the states; and for the period of two years as in the state of South Carolina. The Senate is elective, for the period of six years; which is but one year more than the period of the senate of Maryland, and but two more than that of the senates of New York and Virginia. The President is to continue in office for the period of four years; as in New York and Delaware the chief magistrate is elected for three years, and in South Carolina for two years. In the other states the election is annual.

In several of the states, however, no constitutional provision is made for the impeachment of the chief magistrate. And in Delaware and Virginia he is not impeachable till out of office. The President of the United States is impeachable at any time during his continuance in office. The tenure by which the judges are to hold their places is, as it unquestionably ought to be, that of good behavior. The tenure of the ministerial offices generally will be a subject of legal regulation, conformably to the reason of the case and the example of the state constitutions.

Could any further proof be required of the republican complexion of this system, the most decisive one might be found in its absolute prohibition of titles of nobility, both under the federal and the state governments; and in its express guaranty of the republican form to each of the latter.

"But it was not sufficient," say the adversaries of the proposed Constitution, "for the convention to adhere to the republican form. They ought, with equal care, to have preserved the federal form, which regards the Union as a Confederacy of sovereign states; instead of which, they have framed a national government, which regards the Union as a consolidation of the states." And it is asked by what authority this bold and radical innovation was undertaken? The handle which has been made of this objection requires that it should be examined with some precision.

Without inquiring into the accuracy of the distinction on which the objection is founded, it will be necessary to a just estimate of its force, first, to ascertain the real character of the government in question; secondly, to inquire how far the convention were authorized to propose such a government; and, thirdly, how far the duty they owed to their country could supply any defect of regular authority.

First, in order to ascertain the real character of the government, it may be considered in relation to the foundation on which it is to be established; to the sources from which its ordinary powers are to be drawn; to the operation of those powers; to the extent of them; and to the authority by which future changes in the government are to be introduced.

On examining the first relation, it appears, on one hand, that the Constitution is to be founded on the assent and ratification of the people of America, given by deputies elected for the special purpose; but, on the other, that this assent and ratification is to be given by the people, not as individuals composing one entire nation, but as composing the distinct and independent states to which they respectively belong. It is to be the assent and ratification of the several states, derived from the supreme authority in each state — the authority of the people themselves. The act, therefore, establishing the Constitution will not be a *national* but a *federal* act.

That it will be a federal and not a national act, as these terms are understood by the objectors; the act of the people, as forming so many independent states, not as forming one aggregate nation, is obvious from this single consideration, that it is to result neither from the decision of a majority of the people of the Union nor from that of a majority of the states. It must result from the unanimous assent of the several states that are parties to it, differing no otherwise from their ordinary assent than in its being expressed, not by the legislative authority, but by that of the people themselves.

Were the people regarded in this transaction as forming one nation, the will of the majority of the whole people of the United States would bind the minority, in the same manner as the majority in each state must bind the minority; and the will of the majority must be determined either by a comparison of the individual votes, or by considering the will of the majority of the states as evidence of the will of a majority of the people of the United States. Neither of these rules has been adopted. Each state, in ratifying the Constitution, is considered as a sovereign body, independent of all others, and only to be bound by its own voluntary act. In this relation, then, the new Constitution will, if established, be a *federal*, and not a *national* constitution.

The next relation is to the sources from which the ordinary powers of government are to be derived. The House of Representatives will derive its powers from the people of America; and the people will be represented in the same proportion, and on the same principle, as they are in the legislature of a particular state. So far the government is *national*, not *federal*. The Senate, on the other hand, will derive its powers from the states, as political and coequal societies; and these will be represented on the principle of equality in the Senate, as they now are in the existing Congress. So far the government is *federal*, not *national*. The executive power will be derived from a very compound source. The immediate election of the President is to be made by the states in their political characters. The votes allotted to them are in a compound ratio, which considers them partly as distinct and coequal societies, partly as unequal members of the same society. The eventual election, again, is to be made by that branch of the legislature which consists of the national representatives; but in this particular act they are to be thrown into the form of individual delegations from so many distinct and coequal bodies politic. From this aspect of the government, it appears to be of a mixed character, presenting at least as many *federal* as *national* features.

The difference between a federal and national government, as it relates to the operation of the government, is supposed to consist in this, that in the former the powers operate on the political bodies composing the Confederacy, in their political capacities; in the latter, on the individual citizens composing the nation, in their individual capacities. On trying the Constitution by this criterion, it falls under the *national*, not the *federal* character; though perhaps not so completely as has been understood. In several cases, and particularly in the trial of controversies to which states may be parties, they must be viewed and proceeded against in their collective and political capacities only. So far the national countenance of the government on this side seems to be disfigured by a few federal features. But this blemish is perhaps unavoidable in any plan; and the operation of the government on the people, in their individual capacities, in its ordinary and most essential proceedings, may, on the whole, designate it, in this relation, a *national* government.

But if the government be national with regard to the operation of its powers, it changes its aspect again when we contemplate it in relation to the extent of its powers. The idea of a national government involves in it not only an authority over the individual citizens but an indefinite supremacy over all persons and things so far as they are objects of lawful government. Among a people consolidated into one nation, this supremacy is completely vested in the national legislature. Among communities united for particular purposes, it is vested partly in the general and partly in the municipal legislatures. In the former case, all local authorities are subordinate to the supreme; and may be controlled, directed, or abolished by it at pleasure. In the latter, the local or municipal authorities form distinct and independent portions of the supremacy, no more subject, within their respective spheres, to the general authority than the general authority is subject to them within its own sphere. In this relation, then, the proposed government cannot be deemed a *national* one, since its jurisdiction extends to certain enumerated objects only, and leaves to the several states a residuary and inviolable sovereignty over all other objects.

It is true that in controversies relating to the boundary between the two jurisdictions, the tribunal which is ultimately to decide is to be established under the general government. But this does not change the principle of the case. The decision is to be impartially made according to the rules of the Constitution; and all the usual and most effectual precautions are taken to secure this impartiality. Some such tribunal is clearly essential to prevent an appeal to the sword and a dissolution of the compact; and that it ought to be established under the general rather than under the local governments, or, to speak more properly, that it could be safely established under the first alone, is a position not likely to be combated.

If we try the Constitution by its last relation to the authority by which amendments are to be made, we find it neither wholly *national* nor wholly *federal.* Were it wholly national, the supreme and ultimate authority would reside in the majority of the people of the Union; and this authority would be competent at all times, like that of a majority of every national society, to alter or abolish its established government. Were it wholly federal, on the other hand, the concurrence of each state in the Union would be essential to every alteration that would be binding on all. The mode provided by the plan of the convention is not founded on either of these principles. In requiring more than a majority, and particularly in computing the proportion by states, not by citizens, it departs from the *national* and advances toward the *federal* character; in rendering the concurrence of less than the whole number of states sufficient, it loses again the *federal* and partakes of the *national* character.

The proposed Constitution, therefore, is, in strictness, neither a national nor a federal Constitution but a composition of both. In its foundation it is federal, not national; in the sources from which the ordinary powers of the government are drawn, it is partly federal and partly national; in the operation of these powers, it is national, not federal;

in the extent of them, again, it is federal, not national; and, finally, in the authoritative mode of introducing amendments, it is neither wholly federal nor wholly national.

## THE FEDERALIST NO. 49 (MADISON)

THE AUTHOR [JEFFERSON] of the *Notes on the State of Virginia,* quoted in the last paper, has subjoined to that valuable work the draft of a constitution which had been prepared in order to be laid before a convention expected to be called in 1783, by the legislature, for the establishment of a constitution for that commonwealth. The plan, like everything from the same pen, marks a turn of thinking original, comprehensive, and accurate; and is the more worthy of attention as it equally displays a fervent attachment to republican government and an enlightened view of the dangerous propensities against which it ought to be guarded. One of the precautions which he proposes, and on which he appears ultimately to rely as a palladium to the weaker departments of power against the invasions of the stronger, is perhaps altogether his own and, as it immediately relates to the subject of our present inquiry, ought not to be overlooked.

His proposition is: "that whenever any two of the three branches of government shall concur in opinion, each by the voices of two-thirds of their whole number, that a convention is necessary for altering the constitution, or *correcting breaches of it,* a convention shall be called for the purpose."

As the people are the only legitimate fountain of power, and it is from them that the constitutional charter, under which the several branches of government hold their power, is derived, it seems strictly consonant to the republican theory to recur to the same original authority, not only whenever it may be necessary to enlarge, diminish, or new-model the powers of the government, but also whenever any one of the departments may commit encroachments on the chartered authorities of the others. The several departments being perfectly coordinate by the terms of their common commission, neither of them, it is evident, can pretend to an exclusive or superior right of settling the boundaries between their respective powers; and how are the encroachments of the stronger to be prevented, or the wrongs of the weaker to be redressed, without an appeal to the people themselves, who, as the grantors of the commission, can alone declare its true meaning, and enforce its observance?

There is certainly great force in this reasoning, and it must be allowed to prove that a constitutional road to the decision of the people ought to be marked out and kept open, for certain great and extraordinary occasions. But there appear to be insuperable objections against the proposed recurrence to the people, as a provision in all cases for keeping the several departments of power within their constitutional limits.

In the first place, the provision does not reach the case of a combination of two of the departments against the third. If the legislative authority, which possesses so many means of operating on the motives of the other departments, should be able to gain to its interest either of the others, or even one-third of its members, the remaining department could derive no advantage from its remedial provision. I do not dwell, however, on this objection, because it may be thought to be rather against the modification of the principle than against the principle itself.

In the next place, it may be considered as an objection inherent in the principle that, as every appeal to the people would carry an implication of some defect in the government, frequent appeals would, in a great measure, deprive the government of that veneration which time bestows on everything, and without which perhaps the wisest and freest governments would not possess the requisite stability.

If it be true that all governments rest on opinion, it is no less true that the strength of opinion in each individual, and its practical influence on his conduct, depend much on the number which he supposes to have entertained the same opinion. The reason of man, like man himself, is timid and cautious when left alone, and acquires firmness and confidence in proportion to the number with which it is associated. When the examples which fortify opinion are *ancient* as well as *numerous,* they are known to have a double effect. In a nation of philosophers, this consideration ought to be disregarded. A reverence for the laws would be sufficiently inculcated by the voice of an enlightened reason. But a nation of philosophers is as little to be expected as the philosophical race of kings wished for by Plato. And in every other nation, the most rational government will not find it a superfluous advantage to have the prejudices of the community on its side.

The danger of disturbing the public tranquillity by interesting too strongly the public passions is a still more serious objection against a frequent reference of constitutional questions to the decision of the whole society. Notwithstanding the success which has attended the revisions of our established forms of government, and which does so much honor to the virtue and intelligence of the people of America, it must be confessed that the experiments are of too ticklish a nature to be unnecessarily multiplied. We are to recollect that all the existing constitutions were formed in the midst of a danger which repressed the passions most unfriendly to order and concord; of an enthusiastic confidence of the people in their patriotic leaders, which stifled the ordinary diversity of opinions on great national questions; of a universal ardor for new and opposite forms, produced by a universal resentment and indignation against the ancient government; and whilst no spirit of party connected with the changes to be made or the abuses to be reformed could mingle its leaven in the operation. The future situations in which we must expect to be usually placed do not present any equivalent security against the danger which is apprehended.

But the greatest objection of all is that the decisions which would probably result from such appeals would not answer the purpose of maintaining the constitutional equilibrium of the government. We have seen that the tendency of republican governments is to an aggrandizement of the legislative at the expense of the other departments. The appeals to the people, therefore, would usually be made by the executive and judiciary departments. But whether made by one side or the other, would each side enjoy equal advantages on the trial? Let us view their different situations.

The members of the executive and judiciary departments are few in number and can be personally known to a small part only of the people. The latter, by the mode of their appointment, as well as by the nature and permanency of it, are too far removed from the people to share much in their prepossessions. The former are generally the objects of jealousy, and their administration is always liable to be discolored and rendered unpopular. The members of the legislative department, on the other hand, are numerous. They are distributed and dwell among the people at large. Their connections of blood, of friendship, and of acquaintance embrace a great proportion of the most influential part of the society. The nature of their public trust implies a personal influence among the people, and that they are more immediately the confidential guardians of the rights and liberties of the people. With these advantages, it can hardly be supposed that the adverse party would have an equal chance for a favorable issue.

But the legislative party would not only

be able to plead their cause most successfully with the people. They would probably be constituted themselves the judges. The same influence which had gained them an election into the legislature would gain them a seat in the convention. If this should not be the case with all, it would probably be the case with many, and pretty certainly with those leading characters on whom everything depends in such bodies. The convention, in short, would be composed chiefly of men who had been, who actually were, or who expected to be, members of the department whose conduct was arraigned. They would consequently be parties to the very question to be decided by them.

It might, however, sometimes happen that appeals would be made under circumstances less adverse to the executive and judiciary departments. The usurpations of the legislature might be so flagrant and so sudden as to admit of no specious coloring. A strong party among themselves might take side with the other branches. The executive power might be in the hands of a peculiar favorite of the people. In such a posture of things, the public decision might be less swayed by prepossessions in favor of the legislative party. But still it could never be expected to turn on the true merits of the question. It would inevitably be connected with the spirit of preexisting parties, or of parties springing out of the question itself. It would be connected with persons of distinguished character and extensive influence in the community. It would be pronounced by the very men who had been agents in, or opponents of, the measures to which the decision would relate. The *passions,* therefore, not the *reason,* of the public would sit in judgment. But it is the reason, alone, of the public that ought to control and regulate the government. The passions ought to be controlled and regulated by the government.

## THE FEDERALIST NO. 78 (HAMILTON)

WE PROCEED NOW to an examination of the judiciary department of the proposed government.

In unfolding the defects of the existing Confederation, the utility and necessity of a federal judicature have been clearly pointed out. It is the less necessary to recapitulate the considerations there urged, as the propriety of the institution in the abstract is not disputed; the only questions which have been raised being relative to the manner of constituting it and to its extent. To these points, therefore, our observations shall be confined.

The manner of constituting it seems to embrace these several objects: first, the mode of appointing the judges; second, the tenure by which they are to hold their places; third, the partition of the judiciary authority between different courts, and their relations to each other.

First, as to the mode of appointing the judges: this is the same with that of appointing the officers of the Union in general, and has been so fully discussed in the last two numbers that nothing can be said here which would not be useless repetition.

Second, as to the tenure by which the judges are to hold their places: this chiefly concerns their duration in office; the provisions for their support; the precautions for their responsibility.

According to the plan of the Convention, all judges who may be appointed by the United States are to hold their offices *during good behavior;* which is conformable to the most approved of the state constitutions, and among the rest, to that of this state. Its propriety having been drawn into question by the adversaries of that plan is no light symptom of the rage for objection which disorders their imaginations and judgments. The standard of good behavior for the continuance in office of the judicial magistracy is certainly one of the most valuable of the modern improvements in the practice of government. In a monarchy it is an excellent barrier to the despotism of the prince; in a republic it is a no less excellent barrier to the encroachments and oppressions of the representative body. And it is the best expedient which can be devised in any government to secure a steady, upright, and impartial administration of the laws.

Whoever attentively considers the different departments of power must perceive that, in a government in which they are separated from each other, the judiciary, from the nature of its functions, will always be the least dangerous to the political rights of the Constitution, because it will be least in a capacity to annoy or injure them. The executive not only dispenses the honors but holds the sword of the community. The legislature not only commands the purse but prescribes the rules by which the duties and rights of every citizen are to be regulated. The judiciary, on the contrary, has no influence over either the sword or the purse; no direction either of the strength or of the wealth of the society; and can take no active resolution whatever. It may be truly said to have neither force nor will, but merely judgment; and must ultimately depend upon the aid of the executive arm even for the efficacy of its judgments.

This simple view of the matter suggests several important consequences. It proves incontestably that the judiciary is beyond comparison the weakest of the three departments of power; that it can never attack with success either of the other two; and that all possible care is requisite to enable it to defend itself against their attacks. It equally proves that, though individual oppression may now and then proceed from the courts of justice, the general liberty of the people can never be endangered from that quarter; I mean so long as the judiciary remains truly distinct from both the legislature and the executive.

For I agree that "there is no liberty, if the power of judging be not separated from the legislative and executive powers." And it proves, in the last place, that as liberty can have nothing to fear from the judiciary alone but would have everything to fear from its union with either of the other departments; that as all the effects of such a union must ensue from a dependence of the former on the latter, notwithstanding a nominal and apparent separation; that as, from the natural feebleness of the judiciary, it is in continual jeopardy of being overpowered, awed, or influenced by its coordinate branches; and that as nothing can contribute so much to its firmness and independence as permanency in office, this quality may therefore be justly regarded as an indispensable ingredient in its constitution and, in a great measure, as the citadel of the public justice and the public security.

The complete independence of the courts of justice is peculiarly essential in a limited constitution. By a limited constitution, I understand one which contains certain specified exceptions to the legislative authority; such, for instance, as that it shall pass no bills of attainder, no ex post facto laws, and the like. Limitations of this kind can be preserved in practice no other way than through the medium of courts of justice, whose duty it must be to declare all acts contrary to the manifest tenor of the constitution void. Without this, all the reservations of particular rights or privileges would amount to nothing.

Some perplexity respecting the rights of the courts to pronounce legislative acts void, because contrary to the Constitution, has arisen from an imagination that the doctrine would imply a superiority of the judiciary to the legislative power. It is urged that the authority which can declare the acts of another void must necessarily be superior to the one whose acts may be declared void. As this doctrine is of great importance in all the American constitutions, a brief discussion of the ground on which it rests cannot be unacceptable.

There is no position which depends on clearer principles than that every act of a delegated authority, contrary to the tenor of the commission under which it is exercised, is void. No legislative act, therefore, contrary to the Constitution, can be valid. To deny this would be to affirm that the deputy is greater than his principal; that the servant is above his master; that the representatives of the people are superior to the people themselves; that men acting by virtue of powers may do not only what their powers do not authorize but what they forbid.

If it be said that the legislative body are themselves the constitutional judges of their own powers, and that the construction they put upon them is conclusive upon the other departments, it may be answered that this cannot be the natural presumption, where it is not to be collected from any particular provisions in the Constitution. It is not otherwise to be supposed that the Constitution could intend to enable the representatives of the people to substitute their *will* to that of their constituents. It is far more rational to suppose that the courts were designed to be an intermediate body between the people and the legislature, in order, among other things, to keep the latter within the limits assigned to their authority. The interpretation of the laws is the proper and peculiar province of the courts. A constitution is in fact — and must be regarded by the judges as — a fundamental law. It therefore belongs to them to ascertain its meaning, as well as the meaning of any particular act proceeding from the legislative body. If there should happen to be an irreconcilable variance between the two, that which has the superior obligation and validity ought, of course, to be preferred; or, in other words, the Constitution ought to be preferred to the statute; the intention of the people to the intention of their agents.

Nor does this conclusion by any means suppose a superiority of the judicial to the legislative power. It only supposes that the power of the people is superior to both; and that where the will of the legislature, declared in its statutes, stands in opposition to that of the people, declared in the Constitution, the judges ought to be governed by the latter rather than the former. They ought to regulate their decisions by the fundamental laws, rather than by those which are not fundamental.

This exercise of judicial discretion in determining between two contradictory laws is exemplified in a familiar instance. It not uncommonly happens that there are two statutes existing at one time, clashing in whole or in part with each other, and neither of them containing any repealing clause or expression. In such a case, it is the province of the courts to liquidate and fix their meaning and operation. So far as they can, by any fair construction, be reconciled to each other, reason and law conspire to dictate that this should be done; where this is impracticable, it becomes a matter of necessity to give effect to one, in exclusion of the other. The rule which has obtained in the courts for determining their relative validity is that the last in order of time shall be preferred to the first. But this is a mere rule of construction, not derived from any positive law but from the nature and reason of the thing. It is a rule not enjoined upon the courts by legislative provision but adopted by themselves, as consonant to truth and propriety, for the direction of their conduct as interpreters of the law. They thought it reasonable that, between the interfering acts of an *equal* authority, that which was the last indication of its will should have the preference.

But in regard to the interfering acts of a superior and subordinate authority, of an original and derivative power, the nature and reason of the thing indicate the converse of that rule as proper to be followed. They teach us that the prior act of a superior ought to be preferred to the subsequent act of an inferior and subordinate authority; and that accordingly, whenever a particular statute contravenes the Constitution, it will be the duty of the judicial tribunals to adhere to the latter and disregard the former.

It can be of no weight to say that the courts, on the pretense of a repugnancy, may substitute their own pleasure to the constitutional intentions of the legislature. This might as well happen in the case of two contradictory statutes; or it might as well happen in every adjudication upon any single statute. The courts must declare the sense of the law; and if they should be disposed to exercise will instead of judgment, the consequence would equally be the substitution of their pleasure to that of the legislative body. The observation, if it prove anything, would prove that there ought to be no judges distinct from that body.

If, then, the courts of justice are to be considered as the bulwarks of a limited constitution against legislative encroachments, this consideration will afford a strong argument for the permanent tenure of judicial offices, since nothing will contribute so much as this to that independent spirit in the judges which must be essential to the faithful performance of so arduous a duty.

This independence of the judges is equally requisite to guard the Constitution and the rights of individuals from the effects of those ill humors which the arts of designing men, or the influence of particular conjunctures, sometimes disseminate among the people themselves, and which, though they speedily give place to better information and more deliberate reflection, have a tendency, in the meantime, to occasion dangerous innovations in the government and serious oppressions of the minor party in the community.

Though I trust the friends of the proposed Constitution will never concur with its enemies in questioning that fundamental principle of republican government which admits the right of the people to alter or abolish the established Constitution, whenever they find it inconsistent with their happiness, yet it is not to be inferred from this principle that the representatives of the people, whenever a momentary inclination happens to lay hold of the majority of their constituents, incompatible with the provisions in the existing Constitution, would, on that account, be justifiable in a violation of those provisions; or that the courts would be under a greater obligation to connive at infractions in this shape than when they had proceeded wholly from the cabals of the representative body.

Until the people have, by some solemn and authoritative act, annulled or changed the established form, it is binding upon themselves collectively, as well as individually; and no presumption, or even knowledge, of their sentiments can warrant their representatives in a departure from it prior to such an act. But it is easy to see that it would require an uncommon portion of fortitude in the judges to do their duty as faithful guardians of the Constitution, where the legislative invasions of it had been instigated by the major voice of the community.

But it is not with a view to infractions of the Constitution only that the independence of the judges may be an essential safeguard against the effects of occasional ill humors in the society. These sometimes extend no farther than to the injury of the private rights of particular classes of citizens by unjust and partial laws. Here also the firmness of the judicial magistracy is of vast importance in mitigating the severity and confining the operation of such laws. It not only serves to moderate the immediate mischiefs of those which may have been passed, but it operates as a check upon the legislative body in passing them; who, perceiving that obstacles to the success of iniquitous intention are to be expected from the scruples of the courts, are in a manner compelled, by the very motives of the injustice they meditate, to qualify their attempts. This is a circumstance calculated to have more influence upon the character of our governments than but few may be aware of.

The benefits of the integrity and moderation of the judiciary have already been felt in more states than one; and though they may have displeased those whose sinister expectations they may have disappointed, they must have commanded the esteem and applause of all the virtuous and disinterested. Considerate men of every description ought to prize whatever will tend to beget or fortify that temper in the courts; as no man can be sure that he may not be tomorrow the victim of a spirit of injustice by which he may be a gainer today. And every man must now feel that the inevitable tendency of such a spirit is to sap the foundations of the public and private confidence, and to introduce in its stead universal distrust and distress.

That inflexible and uniform adherence to the rights of the Constitution and of individuals, which we perceive to be indispensable in the courts of justice, can certainly not be expected from judges who hold their offices by a temporary commission. Periodical appointments, however regulated or by whomsoever made, would, in some way or other, be fatal to their necessary independence. If the power of making them was committed either to the executive or legislature, there would be danger of an improper complaisance to the branch which possessed it; if to both, there would be an unwillingness to hazard the displeasure of either; if to the people, or to persons chosen by them for the special purpose, there would be too great a disposition to consult popularity to justify a reliance that nothing would be consulted but the Constitution and the laws.

There is yet a further and a weightier reason for the permanency of the judicial offices, which is deducible from the nature of the qualifications they require. It has been frequently remarked, with great propriety, that a voluminous code of laws is one of the inconveniences necessarily connected with the advantages of a free government. To avoid an arbitrary discretion in the courts, it is indispensable that they should be bound down by strict rules and precedents, which serve to define and point out their duty in every particular case that comes before them; and it will readily be conceived from the variety of controversies which grow out of the folly and wickedness of mankind that the records of those precedents must unavoidably swell to a very considerable bulk, and must demand long and laborious study to acquire a competent knowledge of them.

Hence it is that there can be but few men in the society who will have sufficient skill in the laws to qualify them for the stations of judges. And making the proper deductions for the ordinary depravity of human nature, the number must be still smaller of those who unite the requisite integrity with the requisite knowledge. These considerations apprise us that the government can have no great option between fit character; and that a temporary duration in office, which would naturally discourage such characters from quitting a lucrative line of practice to accept a seat on the bench, would have a tendency to throw the administration of justice into hands less able, and less well qualified, to conduct it with utility and dignity. In the present circumstances of this country, and in those in which it is likely to be for a long time to come, the disadvantages on this score would be greater than they may at first sight appear; but it must be confessed that they are far inferior to those which present themselves under the other aspects of the subject.

Upon the whole, there can be no room to doubt that the Convention acted wisely in copying from the models of those constitutions which have established *good behavior* as the tenure of their judicial offices in point of duration; and that so far from being blamable on this account, their plan would have been inexcusably defective if it had wanted this important feature of good government. The experience of Great Britain affords an illustrious comment on the excellence of the institution.

### THE FEDERALIST NO. 84 (HAMILTON)

THE MOST CONSIDERABLE of the remaining objections is that the plan of the Convention contains no bill of rights. Among other answers given to this, it has been upon different occasions remarked that the constitutions of several of the states are in a similar predicament. I add that New York is of the number. And yet the opposers of the new system, in this state, who profess an unlimited admiration for its Constitution, are among the most intemperate partisans of a bill of rights. To justify their zeal in this matter, they allege two things: one is that, though the constitution of New York has no bill of rights prefixed to it, yet it contains in the body of it various provisions in favor of particular privileges and rights, which, in substance, amount to the same thing; the other is that the Constitution adopts, in their full extent, the common and statute law of Great Britain, by which many other rights, not expressed in it, are equally secured.

To the first, I answer that the Constitution proposed by the Convention contains, as well as the constitution of this state, a number of such provisions.

Independent of those which relate to the structure of the government, we find the following: Article I, Section 3, clause 7 — "Judgment in cases of impeachment shall not extend further than to removal from office, and disqualification to hold and enjoy any office of honor, trust, or profit under the United States; but the party convicted shall, nevertheless, be liable and subject to indictment, trial, judgment, and punishment according to law." Section 9 of the same article, clause 2 — "The privilege of the writ of habeas corpus shall not be suspended, unless when in cases of rebellion or invasion the public safety may require it." Clause 3 — "No bill of attainder or ex post facto law shall be passed." Clause 7 — "No title of nobility shall be granted by the United States; and no person holding any office of profit or trust under them, shall, without the consent of the Congress, accept of any present, emolument, office, or title of any kind whatever from any king, prince, or foreign state." Article III, Section 2, clause 3 — "The trial of all crimes, except in cases of impeachment, shall be by jury; and such trial shall be held in the state where the said crimes shall have been committed; but when not committed within any state, the trial shall be at such place or places as the Congress may by law have directed." Section 3 of the same article — "Treason against the United States shall consist only in levying war against them, or in adhering to their enemies, giving them aid and comfort. No person shall be convicted of treason, unless on the testimony of two witnesses to the same overt act, or on confession in open court." And clause 3 of the same section — "The Congress shall have power to declare the punishment of treason; but no attainder of treason shall work corruption of blood, or forfeiture, except during the life of the person attainted."

It may well be a question whether these are not, upon the whole, of equal importance with any which are to be found in the constitution of this state. The establishment of the writ of habeas corpus, the prohibition of ex post facto laws, and of TITLES OF NOBILITY, *to which we have no corresponding provision in our Constitution,* are perhaps greater securities to liberty and republicanism than any it contains. The creation of crimes after the commission of the fact, or, in other words, the subjecting of men to punishment for things which, when they were done, were breaches of no law, and the practice of arbitrary imprisonments have been, in all ages, the favorite and most formidable instruments of tyranny. The observations of the judicious Blackstone in reference to the latter are well worthy of recital: "To bereave a man of life or by violence to confiscate his estate, without accusation or trial would be so gross and notorious an act of despotism as must at once convey the alarm of tyranny throughout the whole nation; but confinement of the person by secretly hurrying him to jail, where his sufferings are unknown or forgotten, is a less public, a less striking, and, therefore, *a more dangerous engine* of arbitrary government." And as a remedy for this fatal evil he is everywhere peculiarly emphatical in his encomiums on the habeas corpus act, which in one place he calls "the *bulwark* of the British Constitution."

Nothing need be said to illustrate the importance of the prohibition of titles of nobility. This may truly be denominated the cornerstone of republican government; for so long as they are excluded there can never be serious danger that the government will be any other than that of the people.

To the second — that is, to the pretended establishment of the common and statute law by the Constitution — I answer that they are expressly made subject "to such alterations and provisions as the legislature shall from time to time make concerning the same." They are therefore at any moment liable to repeal by the ordinary legislative power, and, of course, have no constitutional sanction. The only use of the declaration was to recognize the ancient law and to remove doubts which might have been occasioned by the Revolution. This consequently can be considered as no part of a declaration of rights, which under our constitutions must be intended as limitations of the power of the government itself.

It has been several times truly remarked that bills of rights are, in their origin, stipulations between kings and their subjects, abridgments of prerogative in favor of privilege, reservations of rights not surrendered to the prince. Such was Magna Carta, obtained by the barons, sword in hand, from King John. Such were the subsequent confirmations of that charter by succeeding princes. Such was the Petition of Right assented to by Charles I in the beginning of his reign. Such, also, was the Declaration of Right presented by the Lords and Commons to the Prince of Orange in 1688 and afterward thrown into the form of an act of Parliament called the Bill of Rights. It is evident, therefore, that, according to their primitive signification, they have no application to constitutions professedly founded upon the power of the people and executed by their immediate representatives and servants. Here, in strictness, the people surrender nothing; and as they retain everything they have no need of particular reservations.

"We the people of the United States, to secure the blessings of liberty to ourselves and our posterity, do *ordain* and *establish* this Constitution for the United States of America." Here is a better recognition of popular rights than volumes of those aphorisms which make the principal figure in several of our state bills of rights, and which would sound much better in a treatise of ethics than in a constitution of government.

But a minute detail of particular rights is certainly far less applicable to a constitution like that under consideration, which is merely intended to regulate the general political interests of the nation, than to a constitution which has the regulation of every species of personal and private concerns. If, therefore, the loud clamors against the plan of the Convention on this score are well founded, no epithets of reprobation will be too strong for the constitution of this state. But the truth is that both of them contain all which, in relation to their objects, is reasonably to be desired.

I go further and affirm that bills of rights, in the sense and to the extent in which they are contended for, are not only unnecessary in the proposed Constitution but would even be dangerous. They would contain various exceptions to powers not granted;

and, on this very account, would afford a colorable pretext to claim more than were granted. For why declare that things shall not be done which there is no power to do? Why, for instance, should it be said that the liberty of the press shall not be restrained when no power is given by which restrictions may be imposed? I will not contend that such a provision would confer a regulating power; but it is evident that it would furnish to men disposed to usurp a plausible pretense for claiming that power. They might urge with a semblance of reason that the Constitution ought not to be charged with the absurdity of providing against the abuse of an authority which was not given, and that the provision against restraining the liberty of the press afforded a clear implication that a power to prescribe proper regulations concerning it was intended to be vested in the national government. This may serve as a specimen of the numerous handles which would be given to the doctrine of constructive powers by the indulgence of an injudicious zeal for bills of rights.

On the subject of the liberty of the press, as much as has been said, I cannot forbear adding a remark or two. In the first place, I observe, that there is not a syllable concerning it in the constitution of this state; in the next, I contend that whatever has been said about it in that of any other state amounts to nothing. What signifies a declaration, that "the liberty of the press shall be inviolably preserved?" What is the liberty of the press? Who can give it any definition which would not leave the utmost latitude for evasion? I hold it to be impracticable; and from this I infer that its security, whatever fine declarations may be inserted in any constitution respecting it, must altogether depend on public opinion, and on the general spirit of the people and of the government. And here, after all, as is intimated upon another occasion, must we seek for the only solid basis of all our rights.

There remains but one other view of this matter to conclude the point. The truth is, after all the declamations we have heard, that the Constitution is itself, in every rational sense and to every useful purpose, A BILL OF RIGHTS. The several bills of rights in Great Britain form its constitution, and, conversely, the constitution of each state is its bill of rights. And the proposed Constitution, if adopted, will be the bill of rights of the Union. Is it one object of a bill of rights to declare and specify the political privileges of the citizens in the structure and administration of the government? This is done in the most ample and precise manner in the plan of the Convention; comprehending various precautions for the public security which are not to be found in any of the state constitutions. Is another object of a bill of rights to define certain immunities and modes of proceeding which are relative to personal and private concerns? This we have seen has also been attended to, in a variety of cases, in the same plan.

Adverting, therefore, to the substantial meaning of a bill of rights, it is absurd to allege that it is not to be found in the work of the Convention. It may be said that it does not go far enough, though it will not be easy to make this appear; but it can, with no propriety, be contended that there is no such thing. It certainly must be immaterial what mode is observed as to the order of declaring the rights of the citizens, if they are to be found in any part of the instrument which establishes the government. And hence it must be apparent that much of what has been said on this subject rests merely on verbal and nominal distinctions, entirely foreign from the substance of the thing.

Another objection which has been made, and which, from the frequency of its repetition, it is to be presumed is relied on, is of this nature: "It is improper [say the objectors] to confer such large powers as are proposed upon the national government, because the seat of that government must of necessity be too remote from many of the states to admit of a proper knowledge on the part of the constituent of the conduct of the representative body." This argument, if it proves anything, proves that there ought to be no general government whatever. For the powers which, it seems to be agreed on all hands, ought to be vested in the Union cannot be safely entrusted to a body which is not under every requisite control. But there are satisfactory reasons to show that the objection is in reality not well founded. There is in most of the arguments which relate to distance a palpable illusion of the imagination.

What are the sources of information by which the people in Montgomery County must regulate their judgment of the conduct of their representatives in the state legislature? Of personal observation they can have no benefit. This is confined to the citizens on the spot. They must, therefore, depend on the information of intelligent men, in whom they confide; and how must these men obtain their information? Evidently from the complexion of public measures, from the public prints, from correspondences with their representatives, and with other persons who reside at the place of their deliberations. This does not apply to Montgomery County only, but to all the counties at any considerable distance from the seat of government.

It is equally evident that the same sources of information would be open to the people in relation to the conduct of their representatives in the general government, and the impediments to a prompt communication which distance may be supposed to create will be overbalanced by the effects of the vigilance of the state governments. The executive and legislative bodies of each state will be so many sentinels over the persons employed in every department of the national administration; and as it will be in their power to adopt and pursue a regular and effectual system of intelligence, they can never be at a loss to know the behavior of those who represent their constituents in the national councils and can readily communicate the same knowledge to the people. Their disposition to apprise the community of whatever may prejudice its interests from another quarter may be relied upon, if it were only from the rivalship of power. And we may conclude with the fullest assurance that the people, through that channel, will be better informed of the conduct of their national representatives than they can be by any means they now possess of that of their state representatives.

It ought also to be remembered that the citizens who inhabit the country at and near the seat of government will, in all questions that affect the general liberty and prosperity, have the same interest with those who are at a distance, and that they will stand ready to sound the alarm when necessary and to point out the actors in any pernicious project. The public papers will be expeditious messengers of intelligence to the most remote inhabitants of the Union.

Among the many curious objections which have appeared against the proposed Constitution, the most extraordinary and the least colorable is derived from the want of some provision respecting the debts due *to* the United States. This has been represented as a tacit relinquishment of those debts and as a wicked contrivance to screen public defaulters. The newspapers have teemed with the most inflammatory railings on this head; yet there is nothing clearer than that the suggestion is entirely void of foundation, the offspring of extreme ignorance or extreme dishonesty. In addition to the remarks I have made upon the subject in another place, I shall only observe that as it is a plain dictate of common sense, so it is also an established doctrine of political law, that "*states neither lose any of their rights, nor are discharged from any of their obligations, by a change in the form of their civil government.*"

The last objection of any consequence, which I at present recollect, turns upon the article of expense. If it were even true that the adoption of the proposed government would occasion a considerable increase of expense, it would be an objection that ought to have no weight against the plan.

The great bulk of the citizens of America are with reason convinced that Union is the basis of their political happiness. Men of sense of all parties now, with few exceptions, agree that it cannot be preserved under the present system, nor without radical alterations; that new and extensive powers ought to be granted to the national head, and that these require a different organization of the federal government — a single body being an unsafe depositary of such ample authorities. In conceding all this, the question of expense must be given up; for it is impossible, with any degree of safety, to narrow the foundation upon which the system is to stand. The two branches of the legislature are, in the first instance, to consist of only sixty-five persons, which is the same number of which Congress, under the existing Confederation, may be composed. It is true that this number is intended to be increased, but this is to keep pace with the progress of the population and resources of the country. It is evident that a less number would, even in the first instance, have been unsafe, and that a continuance of the present number would, in a more advanced stage of population, be a very inadequate representation of the people.

Whence is the dreaded augmentation of expense to spring? One source indicated is the multiplication of offices under the new government. Let us examine this a little.

It is evident that the principal departments of the administration under the present government are the same which will be required under the new. There are now a secretary of war, a secretary of foreign affairs, a secretary for domestic affairs, a Board of Treasury, consisting of three persons, a treasurer, assistants, clerks, etc. These officers are indispensable under any system and will suffice under the new as well as the old. As to ambassadors and other ministers and agents in foreign countries the proposed Constitution can make no other difference than to render their characters, where they reside, more respectable, and their services more useful. As to persons to be employed in the collection of the revenues, it is unquestionably true that these will form a very considerable addition to the number of federal officers; but it will not follow that this will occasion an increase of public expense. It will be in most cases nothing more than an exchange of state for national officers. In the collection of all duties, for instance, the persons employed will be wholly of the latter description. The states individually will stand in no need of any for this purpose. What difference can it make in point of expense to pay officers of the customs appointed by the state or by the United States? There is no good reason to suppose that either the number or the salaries of the latter will be greater than those of the former.

Where, then, are we to seek for those additional articles of expense which are to swell the account to the enormous size that has been represented to us? The chief item which occurs to me respects the support of the judges of the United States. I do not add the President, because there is now a president of Congress, whose expenses may not be far, if anything, short of those which will be incurred on account of the President of the United States. The support of the judges will clearly be an extra expense, but to what extent will depend on the particular plan which may be adopted in regard to this matter. But upon no reasonable plan can it amount to a sum which will be an object of material consequence.

Let us now see what there is to counterbalance any extra expense that may attend the establishment of the proposed government. The first thing which presents itself is that a great part of the business which now keeps Congress sitting through the year will be transacted by the President. Even the management of foreign negotiations will naturally devolve upon him, according to general principles concerted with the Senate and subject to their final concurrence. Hence it is evident that a portion of the year will suffice for the session of both the Senate and the House of Representatives; we may suppose about a fourth for the latter and a third, or perhaps half, for the former. The extra business of treaties and appointments may give this extra occupation to the Senate. From this circumstance we may infer that, until the House of Representatives shall be increased greatly beyond its present number, there will be a considerable saving of expense from the difference between the constant session of the present and the temporary session of the future Congress.

But there is another circumstance of great importance in the view of economy. The business of the United States has hitherto occupied the state legislatures, as well as Congress. The latter has made requisitions which the former have had to provide for. Hence it has happened that the sessions of the state legislatures have been protracted greatly beyond what was necessary for the execution of the mere local business of the states. More than half their time has been frequently employed in matters which related to the United States. Now the members who compose the legislatures of the several states amount to 2,000 and upward, which number has hitherto performed what under the new system will be done in the first instance by sixty-five persons, and probably at no future period by above a fourth or a fifth of that number. The Congress, under the proposed government, will do all the business of the United States themselves, without the intervention of the state legislatures, who thenceforth will have only to attend to the affairs of their particular states and will not have to sit in any proportion as long as they have heretofore done. This difference in the time of the sessions of the state legislatures will be clear gain and will alone form an article of saving which may be regarded as an equivalent for any additional objects of expense that may be occasioned by the adoption of the new system.

The result from these observations is that the sources of additional expense from the establishment of the proposed Constitution are much fewer than may have been imagined; that they are counterbalanced by considerable objects of saving; and that, while it is questionable on which side the scale will preponderate, it is certain that a government less expensive would be incompetent to the purposes of the Union.

---

*The warmest friends and the best supporters the Constitution has, do not contend that it is free from imperfections; but they found them unavoidable and are sensible, if evil is likely to arise therefrom, the remedy must come hereafter; for in the present moment, it is not to be obtained; and, as there is a Constitutional door open for it, I think the people (for it is with them to judge) can as they will have the advantage of experience on their side, decide with as much propriety on the alterations and amendments which are necessary as ourselves. I do not think we are more inspired, have more wisdom, or possess more virtue than those who will come after us.*

George Washington, letter to Bushrod Washington, Nov. 10, 1787

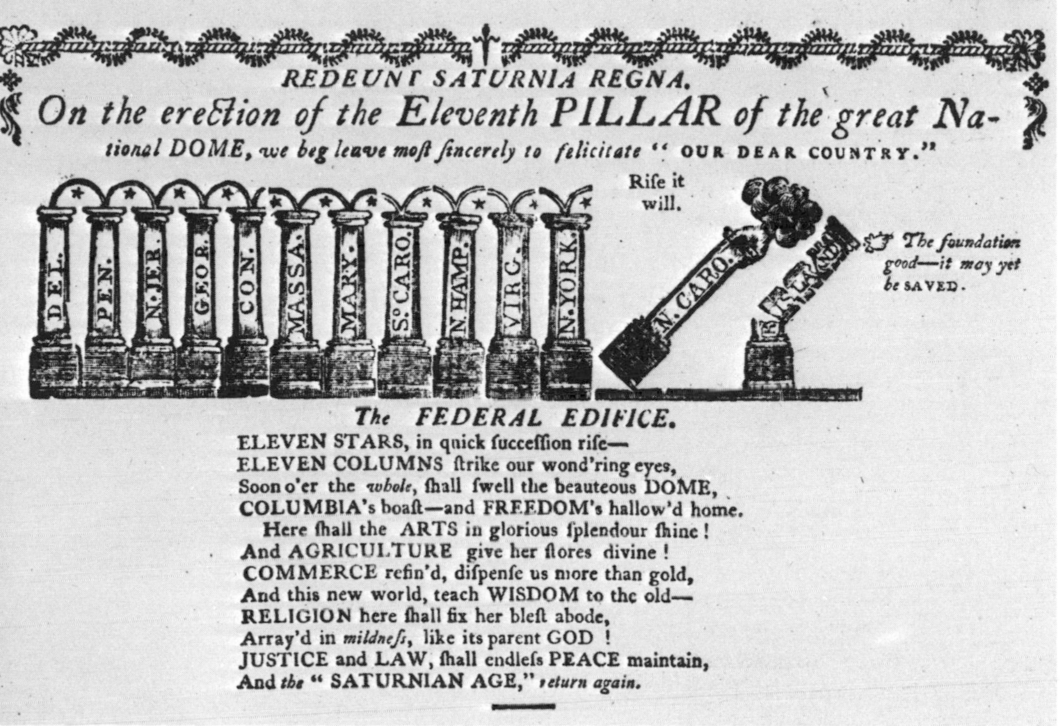

The CENTINEL. VOL IX

REDEUNT SATURNIA REGNA.

*On the erection of the Eleventh PILLAR of the great National DOME, we beg leave moſt ſincerely to felicitate "OUR DEAR COUNTRY."*



The FEDERAL EDIFICE.

ELEVEN STARS, in quick ſucceſſion riſe—<br>
ELEVEN COLUMNS ſtrike our wond'ring eyes,<br>
Soon o'er the *whole*, ſhall ſwell the beauteous DOME,<br>
COLUMBIA's boaſt—and FREEDOM's hallow'd home.<br>
Here ſhall the ARTS in glorious ſplendour ſhine!<br>
And AGRICULTURE give her ſtores divine!<br>
COMMERCE refin'd, diſpenſe us more than gold,<br>
And this new world, teach WISDOM to the old—<br>
RELIGION here ſhall fix her bleſt abode,<br>
Array'd in *mildneſs*, like its parent GOD!<br>
JUSTICE and LAW, ſhall endleſs PEACE maintain,<br>
And *the* "SATURNIAN AGE," *return again.*

New York Historical Society

**This representation of the "Federal Edifice" from the Massachusetts "Centinel" commemorates the ratification of the Constitution by eleven states and calls for erection of the final pillars**

# THE RATIFICATION DEBATE

Drafting of the Constitution at the Convention in Philadelphia was only the first step toward enactment. It remained to secure the approval of at least nine states. Though the proceedings of the Convention were technically secret, many of the basic arguments appeared in print even before the draft Constitution was approved and sent to the states, as champions and critics sought to acquaint the public with their particular interpretations of the document.

As analysis and debate accelerated during the ratification process, the major criticism turned on the absence of a Bill of Rights explicitly assuring individuals protection from their government. The fears aroused were symptomatic of a more general distrust of or distaste for a strong central government with authority over the states.

This sentiment was strongest in New York, Massachusetts, and Virginia, where state leaders, directing a unified opposition, were intent on protecting the advantage that strong, independent state governments and larger populations gave them.

Delaware became the first state to ratify in December 1787, voting unanimous approval. Pennsylvania followed almost immediately, but it was not until June 1788, when New Hampshire became the ninth state to ratify, that the necessary majority was achieved. By the end of July, New York and Virginia added their essential support to the new government, and the process of organization began. The remaining two states, North Carolina and Rhode Island, did not join the union until after Washington's inauguration.

THE BOSTON AND COUNTRY GAZETTE, THE JOURNAL.

No. 1739.]

Containing the latest Occurrences, Foreign and Domestic:

MONDAY, November 26, 1787.



Printed by BENJAMIN EDES and SON, No. 49, Marlborough-Street, BOSTON.

A FREE PRESS MAINTAINS THE MAJESTY OF THE PEOPLE.

Mess'rs. EDES',

I AM pleased to see a spirit of inquiry burst the band of constraint upon the subject of the NEW PLAN for consolidating the governments of the United States, as recommended by the late Convention. If it is suitable to the GENIUS and HABITS of the citizens of these states, it will bear the strictest scrutiny. The PEOPLE are the grand inquest who have a RIGHT to judge of its merits. The hideous dæmon of Aristocracy has hitherto had so much influence as to bar the channels of investigation, preclude the people from inquiry and extinguish every spark of liberal information of its qualities. At length the luminary of intelligence begins to beam its effulgent rays upon this important production; the deceptive mists cast before the eyes of the people by the delusive machinations of its INTERESTED advocates begins to dissipate, as darkness flies before the burning taper; and I dare venture to predict, that in spite of those mercenary declaimers, the plan will have a candid and complete examination—those furious zealots who are for cramming it down the throats of the people, without allowing them either time or opportunity to scan or weigh it in the balance of their understandings, bear the same marks in their features as those who have been long wishing to erect an aristocracy in THIS COMMONWEALTH—their menacing cry is for a RIGID government, it matters little to them of what kind, provided it answers THAT description—As the plan now offered comes something near their wishes, and is the most consonant to their views of any they can hope for, they come boldly forward and DEMAND its adoption—they brand with infamy every man who is not as determined and zealous in its favour as themselves—they cry aloud the whole must be swallowed or none at all, thinking thereby to preclude any amendment; they are afraid of having it abated of its present RIGID aspect—they have strived to overawe or seduce printers to stifle and obstruct a free discussion, and have endeavoured to hasten it to a decision before the people can duly reflect upon its properties,—in order to deceive them, they incessantly declare that none can discover any defect in the system but bankrupts who wish no government, and officers of the present government who fear to lose a part of their power.—These zealous partizans may injure their own cause, and endanger the public tranquility by impeding a proper inquiry; the people may suspect the WHOLE to be a dangerous plan, from such COVERED & DESIGNING schemes to enforce it upon them: compulsive or treacherous measures to establish any government whatever, will always excite jealousy among a free people: better remain single and alone, than blindly adopt whatever a few individuals shall demand, be they ever so wise; I had rather be a free citizen of the small republic of Massachusetts, than an oppressed subject of the great American empire: let all act understandingly or not at all—If we can confederate upon terms that will secure to us our liberties, it is an object highly desirable, because of its additional security to the whole—if the proposed plan proves such an one, I hope it will be adopted, but if it will endanger our liberties as it stands, let it be amended; in order to which it must and ought to be open to inspection and free inquiry—the inundation of abuse that has been thrown out upon the heads of those who have had any doubts of its universal good qualities, have been so redundant, that it may not be improper to scan the characters of its most strenuous advocates: it will first be allowed that many undesigning citizens may wish its adoption from the best motives, but these are modest and silent, when compared to the greater number, who endeavour to suppress all attempts for investigation; these violent partizans are for having the people gulp down the gilded pill blind-folded, whole, & without any qualification whatever, these consist generally of the NOBLE order of C s, holders of public securities, men of great wealth and expectations of public office, B---k--s and L--y--s: these with their train of dependents from the Aristocratick combination---the L--y-r in particular, keep up an incessant declamation for its adoption, like greedy gudgeons they long to satiate their voracious stomacks with the golden bait---The numerous tribunals to be erected by the new plan of consolidated empire, will find employment for ten times their present numbers; these are the LOAVES AND FISHES for which they hunger; they will probably find it suited to THEIR HABITS, if not to the HABITS OF the PEOPLE---There may be reasons for having but few of them in the State Convention, lest THEIR 'OWN' INTEREST should be too strongly considered.---The time draws near for the choice of Delegates, I hope my fellow-citizens will look well to the characters of their preference, and remember the Old Patriots of 75; they have never led them astray, nor need they fear to try them on this momentous occasion.

A FEDERALIST.

Library of Congress

Charles M. Eaton Collection; photo, Frick

Independence National Historical Park

(Top left) Article urging ratification of the Constitution; (above) James Madison, co-author of "The Federalist"; (left) John Dickinson, author of a series of letters calling for adoption of the Constitution

(Right) George Clinton; (far right) letter in the "New York Journal" from two of Clinton's supporters giving their reasons for opposition to the Constitution; (below) Samuel Chase, opponent of the new government

New York Historical Society

# Campaign in the Press

During the course of the ratification debates newspapers and periodicals were flooded with articles, ranging from closely reasoned analysis to polemical character assassination. By and large, however, the problems of self-government after independence and the difficulties encountered under the Articles of Confederation provided experiences that gave the analysis of the ratification period a clear sense of the problems of representative government.

"The Federalist," a series of articles by Madison, Hamilton, and John Jay growing out of the impasse in the New York convention, constituted the most thorough explication of the philosophy of government represented by the Constitution. The articles candidly discussed the basic recurring problems inherent in federal government and urged strongly that the proposed Constitution dealt judiciously with these problems.

Independence National Historical Park

Library of Congress

Late yeſterday evening we were favored, by a correſpondent, with the following COPY *of a* LETTER from the Hon. ROBERT YATES, jun. and JOHN LANSING, Eſquires, members of the general convention, lately held in the city of Philadelphia, aſſigning their reaſons for giving their diſſent to the conſtitution, agreed upon by that body, and which was laid before the legiſlature by his excellency the Governor, at the opening of the ſeſſion, on Friday laſt.——From a conſideration of the *very intereſting nature* of this LETTER to the public, notwithſtanding the late hour of its receipt, the editor thus expeditiouſly preſents it to the public view.

REASONS OF DISSENT.

Albany, Dec. 21, 1787.

SIR,

WE do ourſelves the honor to adviſe your excellency, that in purſuance of concurrent reſolutions of the honorable ſenate and aſſembly, we have, together with Mr. Hamilton, attended the convention, appointed for reviſing the articles of confederation, and reporting amendments to the ſame.

It is with the ſincereſt concern we obſerve, that in the proſecution of the important objects of our miſſion, we have been reduced to the diſagreeable alternative, of either exceeding the powers delegated to us, and giving our aſſent to meaſures which we conceived diſtructive of the political happineſs of the citizens of the United States, or oppoſing our opinion to that of a body of reſpectable men, to whom thoſe citizens had given the moſt unequivocal proofs of confidence.—Thus circumſtanced, under theſe impreſſions, to have heſitated, would have been to be culpable: we therefore, gave the principles of the conſtitutio, which has received the ſanction of a majority of the convention, our decided and unreſerved diſſent: but we muſt candidly confeſs, that we ſhould have been equally oppoſed to any ſyſtem, however modified, which had in object the conſolidation of the United States into one government.

We beg leave briefly to ſtate ſome cogent reaſons, which, among others, influenced us to decide againſt a conſolidation of the ſtates. Theſe are reducible into two heads.

1ſt. The limited and well-defined powers under which we acted, and which could not, on any poſſible conſtruction, embrace an idea of ſuch magnitude, as to aſſent to a general conſtitution, in ſubverſion of that of the ſtate.

2dly. A conviction of the impracticability of eſtabliſhing a general government, pervading every part of the United States, and extending eſſential benefits to all.

Our powers were explicit, and confined to the *ſole and expreſs purpoſe of reviſing the articles of confederation*, and reporting ſuch alterations and proviſions therein, as ſhould render the federal conſtitution adequate to the exigencies of government, and the preſervation of the Union.

From theſe expreſſions we were led to believe, that a ſyſtem of conſolidated government could not, in the remoteſt degree, have been in contemplation of the legiſlature of this ſtate; for that ſo important a truſt as the adopting meaſures which tended to deprive the ſtate government of its moſt eſſential rights of ſovereignty, and to place it in a dependent ſituation, could not have been confided by implication; and the circumſtance, that the acts of the convention were to receive a ſtate approbation in the laſt reſort, forcibly corroborated the opinion, that our powers could not involve the ſubverſion of a conſtitution, which, being immediately derived from the people, could only be aboliſhed by their expreſs conſent, and not by a legiſlature, poſſeſſing authority veſted in them for its preſervation. Nor could we ſuppoſe, that if it had been the intention of the legiſlature, to abrogate the exiſting confederation, they would, in ſuch pointed terms, have directed the attention of their delegates to the reviſion and amendment of it, in total excluſion of every other idea.

Reaſoning in this manner, we were of opinion, that the leading feature of every amendment, ought to be the preſervation of the individual ſtates, in their uncontrouled conſtitutional rights, and that in reſerving theſe, a mode might have been deviſed of granting to the confederacy, the monies ariſing from a general ſyſtem of revenue; the power of regulating commerce, and enforcing the obſervance of foreign treaties, and other neceſſary matters of leſs moment.

Excluſive of our objections, originating from the want of power, we entertained an opinion, that a general government, however guarded by declarations of rights, or cautionary proviſions, muſt unavoidably, in a ſhort time, be productive of the deſtruction of the civil liberty of ſuch citizens who could be effectually coerced by it; by reaſon of the extenſive territory of the United States, the diſperſed ſituation of its inhabitants, and the inſuperable difficulty of controuling or counteracting the views of a ſet of men (however unconſtitutional and oppreſſive their acts might be) poſſeſſed of all the powers of government; and who, from their remoteneſs from their conſtituents, and neceſſary permanency of office, could not be ſuppoſed to be uniformly actuated by an attention to their welfare and happineſs; that however wiſe and energetic, the principles of the general government might be, the extremities of the United States could not be kept in due ſubmiſſion and obedience to its laws, at the diſtance of many hundred miles from the ſeat of government; that if the general legiſlature was compoſed of ſo numerous a body of men, as to repreſent the intereſts of all the inhabitants of the United States, in the uſual and true ideas of repreſentation, the expence of ſupporting it would become intolerably burthenſome; and that, if a few only were veſted with a power of legiſlation, the intereſts of a great majority of the inhabitants of the United States, muſt neceſſarily be unknown; or if known, even in the firſt ſtages of the operations of the new government, unattended to.

Theſe reaſons were, in our opinion, concluſive againſt any ſyſtem of conſolidated government: To that recommended by the convention, we ſuppoſe moſt of them very forcibly apply.

It is not our intention to purſue this ſubject farther than merely to explain our conduct in the diſcharge of the truſt which the honorable the legiſlature repoſed in us—Intereſted, however, as we are, in common with our fellow citizens, in the reſult, we cannot forbear to declare, that we have the ſtrongeſt apprehenſions, that a government ſo organized, as that recommended by the convention, cannot afford that ſecurity to equal and permanent liberty which we wiſhed to make an invariable object of our purſuit.

We were not preſent at the completion of the new conſtitution; but before we left the convention, its principles were ſo well eſtabliſhed as to convince us, that no alteration was to be expected to conform it to our ideas of expediency and ſafety. A perſuaſion, that our further attendance would be fruitleſs, and unavailing, rendered us leſs ſolicitous to return.

We have thus explained our motives for oppoſing the adoption of the national conſtitution, which we conceived it our duty to communicate to your Excellency, to be ſubmitted to the conſideration of the honorable legiſlature.

We have the honor to be,
With the greateſt reſpect,
Your Excellency's
Moſt obedient, and
Very humble ſervant,
ROBERT YATES,
JOHN LANSING, jun.

*His Excellency* GOVERNOR CLINTON.

---

On Saturday evening his excellency the Governor arrived in this city from Poughkeepſie.

PEACE.——FRANCE and ENGLAND have "FROWN'D *their rage away*." See foreign intelligence.

We learn from Connecticut, that their convention have reſolved to adopt the new conſtitution, 120 yeas, 40 nays, 160 being preſent.

A brig from Jamaica is on ſhore, between South and Eaſt-Hampton, bound to Philadelphia; the people, veſſel, and principal part of the cargo, loſt.

The King of Pruſſia will not accept the mediation of France in the affairs of Holland; but on

We the Deputies of the People of the Delaware State, in Convention met, having taken into our serious consideration the Federal Constitution proposed and agreed upon by the Deputies of the United States in a General Convention held at the City of Philadelphia on the seventeenth day of September in the year of our Lord one thousand seven hundred and eighty seven. Have approved, assented to, ratified, and confirmed, and by these Presents, Do, in virtue of the Power and Authority to us given for that purpose, for and in behalf of ourselves and our Constituents, fully, freely, and entirely approve of, assent to, ratify, and confirm the said Constitution.

Done in Convention at Dover this seventh day of December in the year aforesaid, and in the year of the Independence of the United States of America the twelfth. In Testimony whereof we have hereunto subscribed our Names.

| Sussex County | Kent County | New Castle County |
|---|---|---|
| John Ingram | Nicholas Ridgely | Jas. Latimer, President |
| John Jones | Richard Smith | James Black |
| William Moore | George Truitt | Jno. James |
| William Hall | Richard Bassett | Gunning Bedford Sr. |
| Thomas Laws | James Sykes | Kensey Johns |
| Isaac Cooper | Allen McLane | Thomas Watson |
| Woodman Stockly | Daniel Cummins Sr. | Solomon Maxwell |
| John Laws | Joseph Barker | Nicholas Way |
| Thomas Evans | Edward White | Thomas Duff |
| Israel Holland | George Manlove | Gunning Bedford Jr. |

To all whom these Presents shall come Greeting. I Thomas Collins President of the Delaware State do hereby certify, that the above instrument of writing is a true copy of the original ratification of the Federal Constitution by the Convention of the Delaware State, which original ratification is now in my possession. In Testimony whereof I have caused the seal of the Delaware State to be hereunto annexed.

Tho. Collins

National Archives

# The States Take Action

On the whole, the smaller states tended to favor the Constitution, for they had more to gain and less to lose under its provisions. Ratification in Delaware, New Jersey, and Georgia was unanimous; in Connecticut and Maryland, it carried by large majorities. In Pennsylvania, the Federalists, who had a commanding majority around Philadelphia, hoped to make their state the first to ratify the Constitution. They rushed together a ratifying convention before the frontier Republicans could muster a unified group of delegates. As a result, the Constitution was approved with only minimum debate.

Connecticut State Library

Peabody Institute Collection; photo, Frick

OPPOSITE PAGE: (Top) Delaware ratification statement signed by the delegates, Dec. 7, 1787; (bottom) Oliver Wolcott II, governor of Connecticut who directed ratification in his state. THIS PAGE: (Left) Gov. William Paca of Maryland, chairman of his state's ratification convention; the cartoon portrays attacks on the Pennsylvania state constitution by self-interest groups, suggesting that the Federalist control was not as strong as it tried to appear at the ratifying convention

Library of Congress

CONGRESS OF THE UNITED STATES.

*In the House of Representatives,*

*Monday, 24th August, 1789,*

RESOLVED, BY THE SENATE AND HOUSE OF REPRESENTATIVES OF THE UNITED STATES OF AMERICA IN CONGRESS ASSEMBLED, two thirds of both Houses ~~deeming it necessary~~, That the following Articles be proposed to the Legislatures of the several States, as Amendments to the Constitution of the United States, all or any of which Articles, when ratified by three fourths of the said Legislatures, to be valid to all intents and purposes as part of the said Constitution—Viz.

concurring

ARTICLES in addition to, and amendment of, the Constitution of the United States of America, proposed by Congress, and ratified by the Legislatures of the several States, pursuant to the fifth Article of the original Constitution.

ARTICLE THE FIRST.

After the first enumeration, required by the first Article of the Constitution, there shall be one Representative for every thirty thousand, until the number shall amount to one hundred, after which the proportion shall be so regulated by Congress, that there shall be not less than one hundred Representatives, nor less than one Representative for every forty thousand persons, until the number of Representatives shall amount to two hundred, after which the proportion shall be so regulated by Congress, that there shall not be less than two hundred Representatives, nor less than one Representative for every fifty thousand persons.

amendment

ARTICLE THE SECOND.

No law varying the compensation ~~to the members of Congress~~, shall take effect, until an election of Representatives shall have intervened.

ARTICLE THE THIRD.

Congress shall make no law establishing ~~religion or prohibiting the free exercise thereof, nor shall the rights of Conscience be infringed.~~

ARTICLE THE FOURTH.

The Freedom of Speech, and of the Press, and the right of the

National Archives

# Virginia and the Bill of Rights

National Archives

[ 2 ]

ARTICLE THE FIFTH.

A well regulated militia, composed of the body of the People, being the best security of a free State, the right of the People to keep and bear arms, shall not be infringed, but no one religiously scrupulous of bearing arms, shall be compelled to render military service in person.

ARTICLE THE SIXTH.

No soldier shall, in time of peace, be quartered in any house without the consent of the owner, nor in time of war, but in a manner to be prescribed by law.

ARTICLE THE SEVENTH.

The right of the People to be secure in their persons, houses, papers and effects, against unreasonable searches and seizures, shall not be violated, and no warrants shall issue, but upon probable cause supported by oath or affirmation, and particularly describing the place to be searched, and the persons or things to be seized.

ARTICLE THE EIGHTH.

No person shall be subject, ~~except in case of impeachment, to more than one trial, or one punishment~~ for the same offense, nor shall be compelled in any criminal case, to be a witness against himself, nor be deprived of life, liberty or property, without due process of law; nor shall private property be taken for public use without just compensation.

ARTICLE THE NINTH.

In all criminal prosecutions, the accused shall enjoy the right to a speedy and public trial, to be informed of the nature and cause of the accusation, to be confronted with the witnesses against him, to have compulsory process for obtaining witnesses in his favor, and to have the assistance of counsel for his defence.

ARTICLE THE TENTH.

The trial of all crimes (except in cases of impeachment, and in cases arising in the land or naval forces, or in the militia when in actual service in time of war or public danger) shall be by an Impartial Jury of the Vicinage, with the requisite of unanimity for conviction, the right of challenge, and other accustomed requisites; and no person shall be held to answer for a capital, or otherways infamous crime, unless on a presentment or indictment by a Grand Jury; ~~but if a crime be committed in a place in the possession of an enemy, or in which an insurrection may prevail, the indictment and trial may by law be authorised in some other place within the same State.~~

(Left and opposite page) Senate's work ing draft of the Bill of Rights; (below Richard Henry Lee, supporter of th Constitution at the state ratification co vention

Independence National Historical Park

Gunston Hall

(Far left) Patrick Henry and (left) George Mason, leaders of opposition in Virginia; (below) Edmund Pendleton, chairman of the ratification convention and supporter of the new plan of government

Colonial Williamsburg

Virginia Historical Society

In the Virginia convention the absence of a Bill of Rights in the Constitution was particularly worrisome since these guarantees had already been incorporated into the state constitution. Several of the Virginia delegates at the Constitutional Convention had refused to approve the draft without a Bill of Rights. This absence, combined with a suspicion of central authority, formed the basis of the opposition to ratification articulated by George Mason and Patrick Henry.

James Madison, a principal author of the Constitution, was the chief advocate for ratification, and his success in converting Edmund Randolph to the Federalist position was the key development insuring passage. As a compromise, a call for the first Congress to pass a Bill of Rights accompanied Virginia's ratification.

National Archives

[ 3 ]

ARTICLE THE ELEVENTH.

No appeal to the Supreme Court of the United States, ſhall be allowed, where the value in controverſy ſhall not amount to one thouſand dollars, nor ſhall any fact, triable by a Jury according to the courſe of the common law, be otherwiſe re-examinable, than according to the rules of common law.

ARTICLE THE TWELFTH.

In ſuits at common law, the right of trial by Jury ſhall be preſerved.

ARTICLE THE THIRTEENTH.

Exceſſive bail ſhall not be required, nor exceſſive fines impoſed, nor cruel and unuſual puniſhments inflicted.

ARTICLE THE FOURTEENTH.

No State ſhall infringe the right of trial by Jury in criminal caſes, nor the rights of conſcience, nor the freedom of ſpeech, or of the preſs.

ARTICLE THE FIFTEENTH.

The enumeration in the Conſtitution of certain rights, ſhall not be conſtrued to deny or diſparage others retained by the people.

ARTICLE THE SIXTEENTH.

The powers delegated by the Conſtitution to the government of the United States, ſhall be exerciſed as therein appropriated, ſo that the Legiſlative ſhall never exerciſe the powers veſted in the Executive or Judicial; nor the Executive the powers veſted in the Legiſlative or Judicial; nor the Judicial the powers veſted in the Legiſlative or Executive.

ARTICLE THE SEVENTEENTH.

The powers not delegated by the Conſtitution, nor prohibited by it, to the States, are reſerved to the States reſpectively.

Teſte,

JOHN BECKLEY, Clerk.

*In* Senate, *Auguſt* 25, 1789.

Read and ordered to be printed for the conſideration of the Senate.

New York Public Library

# Massachusetts and New York

Yale Art Gallery

As the Massachusetts ratification convention opened, the memory of Shays's Rebellion indicated the need for a strong central government to insure order. However, John Hancock and Samuel Adams opposed ratification, and only skillful maneuvering by the Federalists brought about passage of a compromise similar to that in Virginia.

In New York, Gov. George Clinton controlled two-thirds of the delegates and as chairman of the convention his opposition seemed decisive. Hamilton succeeded in having each section examined before voting, which delayed immediate rejection. His politicking and news that Virginia had ratified changed enough votes to give ratification a majority.

**(Top left) A representation of Shays's Rebellion; (top right) John Hancock, chairman of the Massachusetts convention; (bottom left) Robert R. Livingston, Hamilton's assistant in the New York convention; (bottom right) Alexander Hamilton, Federalist leader in New York**

Independence National Historical Park

New York Historical Society

# 1788

48.

## JAMES IREDELL: Some Objections to the Constitution Answered

*James Iredell, a North Carolina delegate to the Convention of 1787, was a highly respected and influential defender of the Constitution. After a careful study of the document, he wrote a pamphlet, part of which is reprinted here, entitled "Answers to Mr. [George] Mason's Objections to the New Constitution." His argument, which was written under the pseudonym, "Marcus," attracted much national attention when it was first published in January 1788.*

Source: *Pamphlets,* pp. 335-370.

*Objection:* There is no declaration of rights, and the laws of the general government being paramount to the laws and constitutions of the several states, the declarations of rights in the separate states are no security. Nor are the people secured even in the enjoyment of the benefit of the common law, which stands here upon no other foundation than its having been adopted by the respective acts forming the constitutions of the several states.

*Answer:* 1. As to the want of a declaration of rights. The introduction of these in England, from which the idea was originally taken, was in consequence of usurpations of the Crown, contrary, as was conceived, to the principles of their government. But there no original constitution is to be found, and the only meaning of a declaration of rights in that country is that in certain particulars specified, the Crown had no authority to act. Could this have been necessary had there been a constitution in being by which it could have been clearly discerned whether the Crown had such authority or not? Had the people, by a solemn instrument, delegated particular powers to the Crown at the formation of their government, surely the Crown, which in that case could claim under that instrument only, could not have contended for more power than was conveyed by it.

So it is in regard to the new Constitution here: the future government which may be formed under that authority certainly cannot act beyond the warrant of that authority. As well might they attempt to impose a king upon America as go one step in any other respect beyond the terms of their institution. The question then only is whether more power will be vested in the future government than is necessary for the general purposes of the Union. This may occasion a ground of dispute; but after expressly defining the powers that are to be exercised, to say that they shall exercise no other powers (either by a general or particular enumeration) would seem to me both nugatory and ridiculous. As well might a judge, when he condemns a man to be hanged, give strong injunctions to the sheriff that he should not be beheaded.[1]

2. As to the common law, it is difficult to know what is meant by that part of the objection. So far as the people are now entitled to the benefit of the common law, they certainly will have a right to enjoy it under the new Constitution until altered by the general legislature, which even in this point has some cardinal limits assigned to it. What are most acts of assembly but a deviation in some degree from the principles of the common law? The people are expressly secured (contrary to Mr. Mason's wishes) against ex post facto laws; so that the tenure of any property at anytime held under the principles of the common law, cannot be altered by any future act of the general legislature. The principles of the common law, as they now apply, must surely always hereafter apply, except in those particulars in which express authority is given by this Constitution. In no other particulars can the Congress have authority to change it; and I believe it cannot be shown that any one power of this kind given is unnecessarily given, or that the power would answer its proper purpose if the legislature was restricted from any innovations on the principles of the common law, which would not in all cases suit the vast variety of incidents that might arise out of it.

1. It appears to me a very just remark of Mr. Wilson's, in his celebrated speech, that a bill of rights would have been dangerous, as implying that without such a reservation the Congress would have had authority in the cases enumerated, so that if any had been omitted (and who would undertake to recite all the state and individual rights not relinquished by the new Constitution?) they might have been considered at the mercy of the general legislature.

*Objection:* In the House of Representatives there is not the substance but the shadow only of representation, which can never produce proper information in the legislature, or inspire confidence in the people; the laws will, therefore, generally, be made by men little concerned in and unacquainted with their effects and consequences.

*Answer:* This is a mere matter of calculation. It is said the weight of this objection was in a great measure removed by altering the number of 40,000 to 30,000 constituents. To show the discontented nature of man, some have objected to the number of representatives as being too large. I leave to every man's judgment whether the number is not sufficiently respectable, and whether, if that number be sufficient, it would have been right, in the very infancy of this government, to burden the people with a great additional expense to answer no good purpose. . . .

*Objection:* The judiciary of the United States is so constructed and extended as to absorb and destroy the judiciaries of the several states, thereby rendering law as tedious, intricate, and expensive; and justice as unattainable by a great part of the community, as in England; and enabling the rich to oppress and ruin the poor.

*Answer:* Mr. Mason has here asserted, "That the judiciary of the United States is so constructed and extended as to absorb and destroy the judiciaries of the several states." How is this the case? Are not the state judiciaries left uncontrolled as to the affairs of that *state* only? In this as in all other cases where there is a wise distribution, power is commensurate to its object. With the mere internal concerns of a state, Congress are to have nothing to do. In no case, but where the Union is in some measure concerned, are the federal courts to have any jurisdiction. The state judiciary will be a satellite waiting upon its proper

James Iredell

planet — that of the Union, like the sun, cherishing and preserving a whole planetary system.

In regard to a possible ill construction of this authority, we must depend upon our future legislature in this case as well as others, in respect to which it is impracticable to define everything, that it will be provided for so as to occasion as little expense and distress to individuals as can be. *In parting with the coercive authority over the states as states, there must be a coercion allowed as to individuals. The former power no man of common sense can any longer seriously contend for; the latter is the only alternative.* Suppose an objection should be made that the future legislature should not ascertain salaries, because they might divide among themselves and their officers all the revenue of the Union. Will not every man see how irrational it is to expect that any government can exist which is to be fettered in its most necessary operations for fear of abuse? . . .

*Objection:* Under their own construction of the general clause at the end of the enumerated powers, the Congress may grant monopolies in trade and commerce, constitute new crimes, inflict unusual and severe punishment, and extend their power as far as they shall think proper; so that the state legislatures have no security for the powers now presumed to remain to them, or the people for their rights. There is no declaration of any kind for preserving the liberty of the press, the trial by jury in civil causes, nor against the danger of standing armies in time of peace.

*Answer:* The general clause at the end of the enumerated powers is as follows:

> To make all laws which shall be necessary and proper for carrying into execution the *foregoing powers, and all other powers vested by this Constitution in the United States, or in any department or office thereof.*

Those powers would be useless except acts of legislation could be exercised upon them. It was not possible for the Convention, nor is it for any human body, to foresee and provide for all contingent cases that may arise. Such cases must therefore be left to be provided for by the general legislature as they shall happen to come into existence. If Congress, under pretense of exercising the power delegated to them, should in fact, by the exercise of any other power, usurp upon the rights of the different legislatures or of any private citizens, the people will be exactly in the same situation as if there had been an express provision against such power in particular, and yet they had presumed to exercise it. It would be an act of tyranny against which no parchment stipulations can guard; and the Convention surely can be only answerable for the propriety of the powers given, not for the future virtues of all with whom those powers may be entrusted. It does not, therefore, appear to me that there is any weight in this objection more than in others. . . .

*Objection:* The general legislature is restrained from prohibiting the further importation of slaves for twenty-odd years, though such importation renders the United States weaker, more vulnerable, and less capable of defense.

*Answer:* If all the states had been willing to adopt this regulation, I should as an individual most heartily have approved of it, because even if the importation of slaves in fact rendered us stronger, less vulnerable and more capable of defense, I should rejoice in the prohibition of it as putting an end to a trade which has already continued too long for the honor and humanity of those concerned in it. But as it was well known that South Carolina and Georgia thought a further continuance of such importations useful to them, and would not perhaps otherwise have agreed to the new Constitution, those states which had been importing till they were satisfied could not with decency have insisted upon their relinquishing advantages themselves had already enjoyed. Our situation makes it necessary to bear the evil as it is. It will be left to the future legislatures to allow such importations or not. If any, in violation of their clear conviction of the injustice of this trade, persist in pursuing it, this is a matter between God and their own consciences. The interests of humanity will, however, have gained something by the prohibition of this inhuman trade, though at a distance of twenty-odd years.

---

49.

## Reservations of the Massachusetts Ratifying Convention

*On February 6, 1788, the Massachusetts Ratifying Convention accepted the Constitution by a vote of 187 to 168. The story behind this vote is one of excellent leadership provided by the Federalists, a minority at the Boston convention. Of paramount importance to gaining ratification was their influence on two anti-Federalists, Samuel Adams and John Hancock, the president of the convention. Federalist leaders suggested that the president offer the assembly a compromise, a "conciliatory proposition" as it was called, stating that if Massachusetts approved the Constitution certain amendments would be attached to it for future consideration. Partly because Hancock was seeking Federalist support in his bid for the governorship, he joined the pro-Constitutional ranks and presented the proposition to the convention. Under the president's leadership, Adams and a number of other anti-Federalists were persuaded to vote for the Constitution. This key Federalist victory in Massachusetts was certain to have an influence over other states. The selection below is taken from the debates of the convention.*

Source: Elliot, II, pp. 122-125, 176-178.

Hon. Mr. Hancock: When the Convention met in the afternoon, His Excellency the President observed that a motion had been made and seconded that this Convention do assent to and ratify the Constitution which had been under consideration; and that he had . . . intimated his intention of submitting a proposition to the Convention. "My motive," says he, "arises from my earnest desire to this Convention, my fellow citizens, and the public at large that this Convention may adopt such a form of government as may extend its good influence to every part of the United States, and advance the prosperity of the whole world." His situation, His Excellency said, had not permitted him to enter into the debates of this Convention; it however, appeared to him necessary, from what had been advanced in them to adopt the form of government proposed. But, observing a diversity of sentiment in the gentlemen of the Convention, he had frequently had conversation with them on the subject, and from this conversation he was induced to propose to them whether the introduction of some general amendments would not be attended with the happiest consequences.

For that purpose, he should, with the leave of the honorable Convention, submit to their consideration a proposition in order to remove the doubts and quiet the apprehensions of gentlemen; and if in any degree the object should be acquired, he should feel himself perfectly satisfied. He should therefore submit them; for he was, he said, unable to go more largely into the subject, if his abilities would permit him; relying on the candor of the Convention to bear him witness that his wishes for a good constitution were sincere. [His Excellency then read his proposition.] "This, gentlemen," concluded His Excellency, "is the proposition which I had to make; and I submit it to your consideration, with the sincere wish that it may have a tendency to promote a spirit of union." . . .

HON. MR. ADAMS: Mr. President, I feel myself happy in contemplating the idea that many benefits will result from Your Excellency's conciliatory proposition to this commonwealth and to the United States; and I think it ought to precede the motion made by the gentleman from Newburyport, and to be at this time considered by the Convention. I have said that I have had my doubts of this Constitution. I could not digest every part of it as readily as some gentlemen; but this, sir, is my misfortune, not my fault. Other gentlemen have had their doubts; but in my opinion the proposition submitted will have a tendency to remove such doubts, and to conciliate the minds of the Convention and the people without doors.

This subject, sir, is of the greatest magnitude and has employed the attention of every rational man in the United States; but the minds of the people are not so well agreed on it as all of us could wish. A proposal of this sort coming from Massachusetts, from her importance, will have its weight. Four or five states have considered and ratified the Constitution as it stands; but we know there is a diversity of opinion even in these states, and one of them is greatly agitated. If this Convention should particularize the amendments necessary to be proposed, it appears to me it must have weight in other states where conventions have not yet met. I have observed the sentiments of gentlemen on the subject as far as Virginia, and I have found that the objections were similar, in the newspapers, and in some of the conventions. Considering these circumstances, it appears to me that such a measure will have the most salutary effect throughout the Union.

It is of the greatest importance that *America* should still be united in sentiment. I think I have not heretofore been unmindful of the advantage of such a union. It is essential that the people should be united in the federal government, to withstand the common enemy and to preserve their valuable rights and liberties. We find, in the great state of Pennsylvania, one-third of the Convention are opposed to it; should, then, there be large minorities in the several states, I should fear the consequences of such disunion.

Sir, there are many parts of it I esteem as highly valuable, particularly the article which empowers Congress to regulate commerce, to form treaties, etc. For want of this power in our national head, our friends are grieved and our enemies insult us. Our ambassador at the Court of London is considered as a mere cipher instead of the representative of the United States. Therefore it appears to me that a power to remedy this evil should be given to Congress, and the remedy applied as soon as possible.

The only difficulty on gentlemen's minds is whether it is best to accept this Constitution on conditional amendments, or to rely on amendments in future, as the Constitution provides. When I look over the article which provides for a revision, I have my doubts. Suppose, sir, nine states accept the Constitution without any conditions at all, and the four states should wish to have amendments — where will you find nine states to propose, and the legislatures of nine states to agree to the introduction of amendments? Therefore it seems to me that the expectation of amendments taking place at some future time will be frustrated. This method, if we take it, will be the most likely to bring about the amendments, as the conventions of New Hampshire, Rhode Island, New York, Maryland, Virginia, and South Carolina have not yet met. I apprehend, sir, that these states will be influenced by the proposition which Your Excellency has submitted, as the resolutions of Massachusetts have ever had their influence. If this should be the case, the necessary amendments would be introduced more early and more safely. From these considerations, as Your Excellency did not think it proper to make a motion, with submission, I move that the paper read by Your Excellency be now taken under consideration by the Convention. . . .

The question now before you is such as no nation on earth without the limits of America has ever had the privilege of deciding upon. As the Supreme Ruler of the universe has seen fit to bestow upon us this glorious opportunity, let us decide upon it; appealing to Him for the rectitude of our intentions, and in humble confidence that He will yet continue to bless and save our country.

The question being put, whether this Convention will accept of the report of the committee, as follows:

## COMMONWEALTH OF MASSACHUSETTS

*In Convention of the Delegates of the People of the Commonwealth of Massachusetts, 1788.*

The Convention, having impartially discussed and fully considered the Constitution for the United States of America, reported to Congress by the Convention of delegates from the United States of America, and submitted to us by a resolution of the General Court of the said Commonwealth, passed the 25th day of October last past; and acknowledging with grateful hearts the goodness of the Supreme Ruler of the universe in affording the people of the United States, in the course of His providence, an opportunity, deliberately and peaceably without fraud or surprise, of entering into an explicit and solemn compact with each other by assenting to and ratifying a new Constitution, in order to form a more perfect Union, establish justice, ensure domestic tranquillity, provide for the common defense, promote the general welfare, and secure the blessings of liberty to themselves and their posterity, *do,* in the name and in behalf of the people of the Commonwealth of Massachusetts, assent to and ratify the said Constitution for the United States of America.

And as it is the opinion of this Convention that certain amendments and alterations in the said Constitution would remove the fears and quiet the apprehensions of many of the good people of the Commonwealth, and more effectually guard against an undue administration of the federal government, the Convention do therefore recommend that the following alterations and provisions be introduced into the said Constitution:

*First.* That it be explicitly declared, that all powers not expressly delegated by the aforesaid Constitution are reserved to the several states, to be by them exercised.

*Second.* That there shall be one representative to every 30,000 persons, according to the census mentioned in the Constitution, until the whole number of representatives amounts to 200.

*Third.* That Congress do not exercise the powers vested in them by the 4th Section of the 1st Article, but in cases where a state shall neglect or refuse to make the regulations therein mentioned, or shall make regulations subversive of the rights of the people to a free and equal representation in Congress, agreeably to the Constitution.

*Fourth.* That Congress do not lay direct taxes, but when the moneys arising from the impost and excise are insufficient for the public exigencies, nor then, until Congress shall have first made a requisition upon the states, to assess, levy, and pay their respective proportion of such requisitions, agreeably to the census fixed in the said Constitution, in such way and manner as the legislatures of the states shall think best, and, in such case, if any state shall neglect or refuse to pay its proportion, pursuant to such requisition, then Congress may assess and levy such state's proportion, together with interest thereon, at the rate of 6 percent per annum, from the time of payment prescribed in such requisitions.

*Fifth.* That Congress erect no company with exclusive advantages of commerce.

*Sixth.* That no person shall be tried for any crime by which he may incur an infamous punishment, or loss of life, until he be first indicted by a grand jury, except in such cases as may arise in the government and regulation of the land and naval forces.

*Seventh.* The Supreme Judicial Federal Court shall have no jurisdiction of causes between citizens of different states, unless the matter in dispute, whether it concern the realty or personalty, be of the value of $3,000 at the least; nor shall the federal judicial powers extend to any action between citizens of different states where the matter in dispute, whether it concern the realty or personalty, is not of the value of $1,500 at the least.

*Eighth.* In civil actions between citizens of different states, every issue of fact arising in actions at common law shall be tried by a jury, if the parties, or either of them request it.

*Ninth.* Congress shall at no time consent that any person holding an office of trust or profit, under the United States, shall accept of a title of nobility, or any other title or office, from any king, prince, or foreign state.

And the Convention do, in the name and in the behalf of the people of this Commonwealth, enjoin it upon their representatives in Congress, at all times, until the alterations and provisions aforesaid have been considered, agreeably to the 5th Article of the said Constitution, to exert all their influence, and use all reasonable and legal methods, to obtain a ratification of the said alterations and provisions, in such manner as is provided in the said article.

50.

# MELANCTON SMITH: Changes Needed Before Ratifying the Constitution

*Among the foremost New York anti-Federalists was Melancton Smith, who spoke against the proposed Constitution in the New York Ratifying Convention. However, news that Virginia had already ratified, coupled with Hamilton's eloquence, finally won Smith's support for the Constitution. New York was thus able to ratify the Constitution by the narrow margin of three votes. In 1788, Smith wrote a pamphlet entitled* An Address to the People of the State of New-York Showing the Necessity of Making Amendments to the Constitution, Proposed for the United States Previous to its Adoption. *In the following excerpts from this pamphlet, Smith, writing under the pseudonym "A Plebeian," argued for a revision of the Constitution.*

Source: *Pamphlets,* pp. 91-111.

THE ADVOCATES FOR THE PROPOSED NEW Constitution, having been beaten off the field of argument, on its merits, have now taken new ground. They admit it is liable to well-founded objections — that a number of its articles ought to be amended; that if alterations do not take place, a door will be left open for an undue administration and encroachments on the liberties of the people; and many of them go so far as to say if it should continue for any considerable period, in its present form, it will lead to a subversion of our equal republican forms of government. But, still, although they admit this, they urge that it ought to be adopted, and that we should confide in procuring the necessary alterations after we have received it. Most of the leading characters who advocate its reception now profess their readiness to concur with those who oppose, in bringing about the most material amendments contended for, provided they will first agree to accept the proffered system as it is. . . .

It is agreed, the plan is defective; that some of the powers granted are dangerous; others not well defined; and amendments are necessary. Why, then, not amend it? Why not remove the cause of danger and, if possible, even the apprehension of it? The instrument is yet in the hands of the people; it is not signed, sealed, and delivered, and they have power to give it any form they please.

But it is contended — adopt it first and then amend it. I ask: Why not amend and then adopt it? Most certainly the latter mode of proceeding is more consistent with our ideas of prudence in the ordinary concerns of life. If men were about entering into a contract respecting their private concerns, it would be highly absurd in them to sign and seal an instrument containing stipulations which are contrary to their interests and wishes, under the expectation that the parties, after its execution, would agree to make alterations agreeable to their desire. They would insist upon the exceptionable clauses being altered before they would ratify the contract. And is a compact for the government of ourselves and our posterity of less moment than contracts between individuals? Certainly not. But to this reasoning, which at first view would appear to admit of no reply, a variety of objections are made and a number of reasons urged for adopting the system and afterward proposing amendments. Such as have come under my observation I shall state and remark upon.

It is insisted that the present situation of our country is such as not to admit of a delay in forming a new government, or of time sufficient to deliberate and agree upon the amendments which are proper without involving ourselves in a state of anarchy and confusion.

On this head, all the powers of rhetoric and arts of description are employed to paint the condition of this country in the most hideous and frightful colors. We are told that agriculture is without encouragement; trade is languishing; private faith and credit are disregarded and public credit is prostrate; that the laws and magistrates are contemned and set at naught; that a spirit of licentiousness is rampant and ready to break over every bound set to it by the government; that private embarrassments and distresses invade the house of every man of middling property, and insecurity threatens every man in affluent circumstances: in short, that we are in a state of the most grievous calamity at home and that we are contemptible abroad, the scorn of foreign nations, and the ridicule of the world.

From this high-wrought picture, one would suppose that we were in a condition the most deplorable of any people upon earth. But suffer me, my countrymen, to call your attention to a serious and sober estimate of the situation in which you are placed, while I trace the embarrassments under which you labor to their true sources. What is your condition? Does not every man sit under his own vine and under his own fig tree, having none to make him afraid? Does not everyone follow his calling without impediments and receive the reward of his well-earned industry? The farmer cultivates his land and reaps the fruit which the bounty of Heaven bestows on his honest toil. The mechanic is exercised in his art and receives the reward of his labor. The merchant drives his commerce and none can deprive him of the gain he honestly acquires; all classes and callings of men among us are protected in their various pursuits and secured by the laws in the possession and enjoyment of the property obtained in those pursuits. The laws are as well executed as they ever were in this or any other country. Neither the hand of private violence nor the more to be dreaded hand of legal oppression are reached out to distress us.

It is true many individuals labor under embarrassments, but these are to be imputed to the unavoidable circumstances of things rather than to any defect in our governments. We have just emerged from a long and expensive war. During its existence few people were in a situation to increase their fortunes, but many to diminish them. Debts contracted before the war were left unpaid while it existed, and these were left a burden too heavy to be borne at the commencement of peace.

Add to these that, when the war was over, too many of us, instead of reassuming our old habits of frugality and industry, by which alone every country must be placed in a prosperous condition, took up the profuse use of foreign commodities. The country was deluged with articles imported from abroad, and the cash of the country has been sent to pay for them, and still left us laboring under the weight of a huge debt to persons abroad. These are the true sources to which we are to trace all the private difficulties of individuals. But will a new government relieve you from these? The advocates for it have not yet told you how it will do it. And I will venture to pronounce that there is but one way in which it can be effected, and that is by industry and economy; limit your expenses within your earnings; sell more than you buy and everything will be well on this score. . . .

With regard to our public and national concerns, what is there in our condition that threatens us with any immediate danger? We are at peace with all the world; no nation menaces us with war; nor are we called upon by any cause of sufficient importance to attack any nation. The state governments answer the purposes of preserving the peace and providing for present exigencies. Our condition as a nation is in no respect worse than it has been for several years past. Our public debt has been lessened in various ways, and the western territory, which has been relied upon as a productive fund to discharge the national debt, has at length been brought to market and a considerable part actually applied to its reduction.

I mention these things to show that there is nothing special, in our present situation, as it respects our national affairs, that should induce us to accept the proffered system without taking sufficient time to consider and amend it. I do not mean by this to insinuate that our government does not stand in need of reform. It is admitted by all parties that alterations are necessary in our federal Constitution, but the circumstances of our case do by no means oblige us to precipitate this business or require that we should adopt a system materially defective. We may safely take time to deliberate and amend without in the meantime hazarding a condition in any considerable degree worse than the present.

But it is said that if we postpone the ratification of this system until the necessary amendments are first incorporated, the consequence will be a civil war among the states. On this head weak minds are alarmed with being told that the militia of Connecticut and Massachusetts, on the one side, and of New Jersey and Pennsylvania on the other, will attack us with hostile fury; and either destroy us from the face of the earth, or at best divide us between the two states adjoining on either side. The apprehension of danger is one of the most powerful incentives to human action, and is therefore generally excited on political questions. But, still, a prudent man, though he foresees the evil and avoids it, yet he will not be terrified by imaginary dangers. We ought, therefore, to inquire what ground there is to fear such an event? . . .

As to the inclination of the states to make war with us for declining to accede until it is amended, this is highly improbable, not only because such a procedure would be most unjust and unreasonable in itself but for various other reasons.

The idea of a civil war among the states is abhorrent to the principles and feelings of almost every man of every rank in the Union. It is so obvious to everyone of the least reflection that in such an event we should hazard the loss of all things without the hope of gaining anything that the man who should entertain a thought of this kind would be justly deemed more fit to be shut up in Bedlam than to be reasoned with. But the idea of one or more states attacking another for insisting upon alterations upon the system before it is adopted is more extravagant still; it is contradicting every principle of liberty which has been entertained by the states, violating the most solemn compact, and taking from the states the right of deliberation. Indeed, to suppose that a people, entertaining such refined ideas of the rights of human nature as to be induced to wage war with the most powerful nation on earth, upon a speculative point, and from the mere apprehension of danger only, should be so far lost to their own feelings and principles as to deny to their brethren, who were associated with them in the arduous conflict, the right of deliberation on a question of the first importance to their political happiness and safety, is equally an insult to the character of the people of America and to common sense, and could only be suggested by a vicious heart and a corrupt mind.

The idea of being attacked by the other states will appear visionary and chimerical if we consider that, though several of them have adopted the new Constitution, yet the opposition to it has been numerous and formidable. The Eastern states, from whom we are told we have most to fear should a civil war be blown up, would have full employ to keep in awe those who are opposed to it in their own governments. Massachusetts, after a long and dubious contest in their convention, has adopted it by an inconsiderable majority and in the very act has marked it with a stigma in its present form. No man of candor, judging from their public proceedings, will undertake to say on which side the majority of the people are. Connecticut, it is true, has acceded to it by a large majority of its convention; but it is a fact well known that a large proportion of the yeomanry of the country are against it. And it is equally true that a considerable part of those who voted for it in the Convention wish to see it altered.

In both these states the body of the common people, who always do the fighting of a country, would be more likely to fight against than for it. Can it then be presumed that a country divided among themselves, upon a question where even the advocates for it admit the system they contend for needs amendments, would make war upon a sister state who only insist that that should be done before they receive it, which it is granted ought to be done after, and where it is confessed no obligation lies upon them by compact to do it? Can it, I say, be imagined, that in such case, they would make war on a sister state? The idea is preposterous and chimerical.

It is further urged we must adopt this plan because we have no chance of getting a better. This idea is inconsistent with the principles of those who advance it. They say it must be altered, but it should be left until after it is put in operation. But if this objection is valid, the proposal of altering, after it is received, is mere delusion. . . .

The reasonings made use of to persuade us that no alterations can be agreed upon previous to the adoption of the system are as curious as they are futile. It is alleged that there was great diversity of sentiments in forming the proposed Constitution; that it was the effect of mutual concessions and a spirit of accommodation, and from hence it is inferred that further changes cannot be hoped for. I should suppose that the contrary inference was the fair one. If the Convention who framed this plan were possessed of such a spirit of moderation and condescension as to be induced to yield to each other certain points, and to accommodate themselves to each other's opinions and even prejudices, there is reason to expect that this same spirit will continue and prevail in a future convention and produce a union of sentiments on the points objected to. There is more reason to hope for this because the subject has received a full discussion and the minds of the people much better known than they were when the Convention sat.

Previous to the meeting of the Convention, the subject of a new form of government had been little thought of and scarcely written upon at all. It is true it was the general opinion that some alterations were requisite in the federal system. This subject had been contemplated by almost every thinking man in the Union. It had been the subject of many well-written essays, and it was the anxious wish of every true friend to America. But it was never in the contemplation of one in a thousand of those who had reflected on the matter to have an entire change in the nature of our federal government; to alter it from a confederation of states to that of one entire government which will swallow up that of the individual states. I will venture to say that the idea of a government similar to the one proposed never entered the minds of the legislatures who appointed the Convention, and of but very few of the members who composed it until they had assembled and heard it proposed in that body. Much less had the people any conception of such a plan until after it was promulgated.

While it was agitated, the debates of the Convention were kept an impenetrable secret, and no opportunity was given for well-informed men to offer their sentiments upon the subject. The system was therefore never publicly discussed, nor indeed could be, because it was not known to the people until after it was proposed. Since that, it has been the object of universal attention — it has been thought of by every reflecting man — been discussed in a public and private manner, in conversation and in print; its defects have been pointed out, and every objection to it stated; able advocates have written in its favor, and able opponents have written against it. And what is the result? It cannot be denied but that the general opinion is that it contains material errors and requires important amendments. This then being the general sentiment, both of the friends and foes of the system, can it be doubted that another convention would concur in such amendments as would quiet the fears of the opposers and effect a great degree of union on the subject? — an event most devoutly to be wished.

But it is further said that there can be no prospect of procuring alterations before it is acceded to because those who oppose it do not agree among themselves with respect to the amendments that are necessary. To this I reply that this may be urged against attempting alterations after it is received with as much force as before; and, therefore, if it concludes anything, it is that we must receive any system of government proposed to us because those who object to it do not entirely concur in their objections. But the assertion is not true to any considerable extent. There is a remarkable uniformity in the objections made to the Constitution on the most important points. It is also worthy of notice that very few of the matters found fault with in it are of a local nature, or such as affect any particular state; on the contrary, they are such as concern the principles of general liberty in which the people of New Hampshire, New York, and Georgia are equally interested.

It would be easy to show that in the leading and most important objections that have been made to the plan there has been and is an entire concurrence of opinion among writers and in public bodies throughout the United States. . . .

It has been objected to that the new system, that it is calculated to, and will effect such a consolidation of the states, as to supplant and overturn the state governments. In this the minority of Pennsylvania, the opposition in Massachusetts, and all the writers of any ability or note in Philadelphia, New York, and Boston concur. It may be added, that this appears to have been the opinion of the Massachusetts convention, and gave rise to that article in the amendments proposed which confines the general government to the exercise only of powers expressly given.

It has been said that the representation in the general legislature is too small to secure liberty or to answer the intention of representation. In this there is a union of sentiments in the opposers.

The Constitution has been opposed because it gives to the legislature an unlimited power of taxation, both with respect to direct and indirect taxes; a right to lay and collect taxes, duties, imposts, and excises of every kind and description, and to any amount. In this there has been as general a concurrence of opinion as in the former.

The opposers to the Constitution have said that it is dangerous because the judicial power may extend to many cases which ought to be reserved to the decision of the state courts, and because the right of trial by jury is not secured in the judicial courts of the general government in civil cases. All the opposers are agreed in this objection.

The power of the general legislature to alter and regulate the time, place, and manner of holding elections has been stated as an argument against the adoption of the system. It has been argued that this power will place in the hands of the general government the authority, whenever they shall be disposed and a favorable opportunity offers, to deprive the body of the people, in effect, of all share in the government. The opposers to the Constitution universally agree in this objection, and of such force is it that most of its ardent advocates admit its validity, and those who have made attempts to vindicate it have been reduced to the necessity of using the most trifling arguments to justify it.

The mixture of legislative, judicial, and executive powers in the Senate; the little degree of responsibility under which the great officers of government will be held; and the liberty granted by the system to establish and maintain a standing army without any limitation or restriction are also objections to the Constitution; and in these there is a great degree of unanimity of sentiment in the opposers. . . .

Friends, countrymen, and fellow citizens: the present is the most important crisis at which you ever have arrived. You have before you a question big with consequences, unutterably important to yourselves, to your children, to generations yet unborn, to the cause of liberty and of mankind; every motive of religion and virtue, of private happiness and public good, of honor and dignity should urge you to consider coolly and determine wisely.

Almost all the governments that have arisen among mankind have sprung from force and violence. The records of history inform us of none that have been the result of cool and dispassionate reason and reflection. It is reserved for this favored country to exhibit to mankind the first example. This opportunity is now given us, and we are to exercise our rights in the choice of persons to represent us in convention, to deliberate and determine upon the Constitution proposed. It will be to our everlasting disgrace to be indifferent on such a subject; for it is impossible we can contemplate anything that relates to the affairs of this life of half the importance.

You have heard that both sides on this great question agree that there are in it great defects; yet the one side tell you, choose such men as will adopt it, and then amend it — while the other say, amend previous to its adoption. I have stated to you my reasons for the latter and I think they are unanswerable. Consider, you the common people, the yeomanry of the country, for to such I principally address myself — you are to be the principal losers if the Constitution should prove oppressive. When a tyranny is established, there are always masters as well as slaves; the great and wellborn are generally the former and the middling class the latter. Attempts have been made, and will be repeated, to alarm you with the fear of consequences; but reflect there are consequences on both sides; and none can be apprehended more dreadful than entailing on ourselves and posterity a government which will raise a few to the height of human greatness and wealth, while it will depress the many to the extreme of poverty and wretchedness. Consequences are under the control of that all-wise and all-powerful Being, whose providence conducts the affairs of all men.

Our part is to act right and we may then have confidence that the consequences will be favorable. The path in which you should walk is plain and open before you; be united as one man and direct your choice to such men as have been uniform in their opposition to the proposed system in its present form or without proper alterations. In men of this description you have reason to place confidence, while, on the other hand, you have just cause to distrust those who urge the adoption of a bad Constitution under the delusive expectation of making amendments after it is acceded to. Your jealousy of such characters should be the more excited when you consider that the advocates for the Constitution have shifted their ground. When men are uniform in their opinions, it affords evidence that they are sincere. When they are shifting, it gives reason to believe they do not change from conviction.

It must be recollected that when this plan was first announced to the public its supporters cried it up as the most perfect production of human wisdom. It was represented either as having no defects or, if it had, they were so trifling and inconsiderable that they served only as the shades in a fine picture, to set off the piece to the greater advantage. One gentleman in Philadelphia went so far in the ardor of his enthusiasm in its favor as to pronounce that the men who formed it were as really under the guidance of Divine Revelation as was Moses, the Jewish lawgiver. Their language is now changed; the question has been discussed; the objections to the plan ably stated; and they are admitted to be unanswerable. The same men who held it almost perfect now admit it is very imperfect, that it is necessary it should be amended.

The only question between us is simply this — Shall we accede to a bad Constitution under the uncertain prospect of getting it amended after we have received it, or shall we amend it before we adopt it? Common sense will point out which is the most rational, which is the most secure line of conduct. May Heaven inspire you with wisdom, union, moderation, and firmness, and give you hearts to make a proper estimate of your invaluable privileges and preserve them to you, to be transmitted to your posterity unimpaired; and may they be maintained in this, our country, while sun and moon endure.

A Plebeian

---

*You will permit me to say, that a greater drama is now acting on this theatre than has heretofore been brought on the American stage, or any other in the world. We exhibit at present the novel and astonishing spectacle of a whole people deliberating calmly on what form of government will be most conducive to their happiness; and deciding with an unexpected degree of unanimity in favour of a system which they conceive calculated to answer the purpose.*

George Washington, letter to Sir Edward Newenham, Aug. 29, 1788

51.

# Anonymous: On the Power of the Judiciary

*A series of anti-Federalist letters, written under the pseudonym "Brutus," appeared in the* New-York Journal and Weekly Register *during the winter of 1787-1788. Generally attributed to Robert Yates of New York, though some scholars have credited Thomas Treadwell with them, the Brutus letters stand among the most clearly stated rebuttals to the famous remarks of Alexander Hamilton in* The Federalist. *Even before the Constitution was ratified, Brutus foresaw that it would be loosely interpreted to give the national government maximum power over the states. The selection below, which appeared on January 31, 1788, is a lucid interpretation of the powers granted the three branches of the national government, paying particular attention to the judiciary. The Constitution, as proposed, left the judicial branch unchecked. Brutus felt that it could therefore exert control over the entire government.*

Source: *New-York Journal and Weekly Register,* January 31, 1788: "Brutus, No. 11."

Much has been said and written upon the subject of this new system, on both sides, but I have not met with any writer who has discussed the judicial powers with any degree of accuracy. And yet it is obvious that we can form but very imperfect ideas of the manner in which this government will work or the effect it will have in changing the internal police and mode of distributing justice at present subsisting in the respective states without a thorough investigation of the powers of the judiciary and of the manner in which they will operate. This government is a complete system, not only for making but for executing laws. And the courts of law which will be constituted by it are not only to decide upon the Constitution and the laws made in pursuance of it but by officers subordinate to them to execute all their decisions. The real effect of this system of government will therefore be brought home to the feelings of the people through the medium of the judicial power. It is, moreover, of great importance to examine with care the nature and extent of the judicial power, because those who are to be vested with it are to be placed in a situation altogether unprecedented in a free country. They are to be rendered totally independent, both of the people and the legislature, both with respect to their offices and salaries. No errors they may commit can be corrected by any power above them, if any such power there be, nor can they be removed from office for making ever so many erroneous adjudications.

The only causes for which they can be displaced [are] conviction of treason, bribery, and high crimes and misdemeanors.

This part of the plan is so modeled as to authorize the courts not only to carry into execution the powers expressly given but, where these are wanting or ambiguously expressed, to supply what is wanting by their own decisions.

That we may be enabled to form a just opinion on this subject, I shall, in considering it, (1) examine the nature and extent of the judicial powers; and (2) inquire whether the courts who are to exercise them are so constituted as to afford reasonable ground of confidence that they will exercise them for the general good.

With a regard to the nature and extent of the judicial powers, I have to regret my want of capacity to give that full and minute explanation of them that the subject merits. To be able to do this, a man should be possessed of a degree of law knowledge far beyond what I pretend to. A number of hard words and technical phrases are used in this part of the system, about the meaning of which gentlemen learned in the law differ.

Its advocates know how to avail themselves of these phrases. In a number of instances, where objections are made to the powers given to the judicial, they give such an explanation to the technical terms as to avoid them.

Though I am not competent to give a perfect explanation of the powers granted to this department of the government, I shall yet attempt to trace some of the leading features of it, from which I presume it will appear that they will operate to a total subversion of the state judiciaries, if not to the legislative authority of the states.

In Article III, Section 2, it is said, "The judicial power shall extend to all cases in law and equity arising under this Constitution, the laws of the United States, and treaties made, or which shall be made, under their authority, etc."

The first article to which this power extends is all cases in law and equity arising under this Constitution.

What latitude of construction this clause should receive, it is not easy to say. At first view, one would suppose that it meant no more than this — that the courts under the general government should exercise, not only the powers of courts of law but also that of courts of equity, in the manner in which those powers are usually exercised in the different states. But this cannot be the meaning, because the next clause authorizes the courts to take cognizance of all cases in law and equity arising under the laws of the United States; this last article, I conceive, conveys as much power to the general judicial as any of the state courts possess.

The cases arising under the Constitution must be different from those arising under the laws, or else the two clauses mean exactly the same thing. The cases arising under the Constitution must include such as bring into question its meaning, and will require an explanation of the nature and extent of the powers of the different departments under it. This article, therefore, vests the judicial with a power to resolve all questions that may arise on any case on the construction of the Constitution, either in law or in equity.

First, they are authorized to determine all questions that may arise upon the meaning of the Constitution either in law or in equity. This article vests the courts with authority to give the Constitution a legal construction, or to explain it according to the rules laid down for construing a law. These rules give a certain degree of latitude of explanation. According to this mode of construction, the courts are to give such meaning to the Constitution as comports best with the common, and generally received acceptation of the words in which it is expressed, regarding their ordinary and popular use, rather than their grammatical propriety. Where words are dubious, they will be explained by the context. The end of the clause will be attended to, and the words will be understood, as having a view to it; and the words will not be so understood as to bear no meaning or a very absurd one.

Second, the judicial are not only to decide questions arising upon the meaning of the Constitution in law but also in equity. By this they are empowered to explain the Constitution according to the reasoning spirit of it, without being confined to the words or letter. . . .

They will give the sense of every article of the Constitution that may from time to time come before them. And in their decisions they will not confine themselves to any fixed or established rules, but will determine, according to what appears to them, the reason and spirit of the Constitution. The opinions of the Supreme Court, whatever they may be, will have the force of law because there is no power provided in the Constitution that can correct their errors or control their adjudications. From this court there is no appeal. And I conceive the legislature themselves cannot set aside a judgment of this court because they are authorized by the Constitution to decide in the last resort. The legislature must be controlled by the Constitution, and not the Constitution by them. They have therefore no more right to set aside any judgment pronounced upon the construction of the Constitution than they have to take from the President the chief command of the Army and Navy and commit it to some other person. The reason is plain — the judicial and executive derive their authority from the same source that the legislature do theirs; and, therefore, in all cases where the Constitution does not make the one responsible to or controllable by the other, they are altogether independent of each other

The judicial power will operate to effect, in the most certain but yet silent and imperceptible manner, what is evidently the tendency of the Constitution: I mean, an entire subversion of the legislative, executive, and judicial powers of the individual states. Every adjudication of the Supreme Court on any question that may arise upon the nature and extent of the general government will affect the limits of the state jurisdiction. In proportion as the former enlarge the exercise of their powers will that of the latter be restricted.

That the judicial power of the United States will lean strongly in favor of the general government, and will give such an explanation to the Constitution as will favor an extension of its jurisdiction, is very evident from a variety of considerations.

First, the Constitution itself strongly countenances such a mode of construction. Most of the articles in this system which convey powers of any considerable importance are conceived in general and indefinite terms, which are either equivocal, ambiguous, or which require long definitions to unfold the extent of their meaning. The two most important powers committed to any government, those of raising money and of raising and keeping up troops, have already been considered and shown to be unlimited by anything but the discretion of the legislature. The clause which vests the power to pass all laws which are proper and necessary to carry the powers given into execution, it has been shown, leaves the legislature at liberty to do everything which in their judgment is best. It is said, I know, that this clause confers no power on the legislature which they would not have had without it — though I believe this is not the fact. Yet, admitting it to be, it implies that the Constitution is not to receive an explanation strictly according to its letter; but more power is implied than is expressed. And this clause, if it is to be considered as explanatory of the extent of the powers given rather than giving a new power, is to be understood as declaring that, in construing any of the articles conveying power, the spirit, intent, and design of the clause should be attended to as well as the words in their common acceptation.

This Constitution gives sufficient color for adopting an equitable construction if we consider the great end and design it professedly has in view. There appears from its Preamble to be, "to form a more perfect union, establish justice, insure domestic tranquillity, provide for the common defense, promote the general welfare, and secure the blessings of liberty to ourselves and posterity." The design of this system is here expressed, and it is proper to give such a meaning to the various parts as will best promote the accomplishment of the end; this idea suggests itself naturally upon reading the Preamble, and will countenance the court in giving the several articles such a sense as will the most effectually promote the ends the Constitution had in view. . . .

Second, not only will the Constitution justify the courts in inclining to this mode of explaining it but they will be interested in using this latitude of interpretation. Every body of men invested with office are tenacious of power; they feel interested, and hence it has become a kind of maxim to hand down their offices, with all its rights and privileges unimpaired, to their successors. The same principle will influence them to extend their power and increase their rights; this of itself will operate strongly upon the courts to give such a meaning to the Constitution, in all cases where it can possibly be done, as will enlarge the sphere of their own authority. Every extension of the power of the general legislature, as well as of the judicial powers, will increase the powers of the courts; and the dignity and importance of the judges will be in proportion to the extent and magnitude of the powers they exercise. I add, it is highly probable the emolument of the judges will be increased with the increase of the business they will have to transact and its importance. From these considerations the judges will be interested to extend the powers of the courts, and to construe the Constitution as much as possible in such a way as to favor it; and that they will do it appears probable.

Third, because they will have precedent to plead, to justify them in it. . . .

When the courts will have a precedent before them of a court which extended its jurisdiction in opposition to an act of the legislature, is it not to be expected that they will extend theirs, especially when there is nothing in the Constitution expressly against it? And they are authorized to construe its meaning, and are not under any control?

This power in the judicial will enable them to mold the government into almost any shape they please.

BRUTUS

---

52.

## OLIVER ELLSWORTH: The Economic Advantages of a Federal Union

*In March 1788, only six of the nine states required had ratified the proposed Constitution. Oliver Ellsworth of Connecticut, the constant champion of the document, directed a defense of it to the reluctant citizens of New Hampshire. In an open letter to the citizens of New Hampshire of March 10, 1788, he attempted to explain the economic advantages that a new Constitution would have for the people. New Hampshire became the ninth state to ratify on June 21, 1788.*

Source: Scott, II, pp. 596-599.

THOSE WHO WISH TO ENJOY THE BLESSINGS of society must be willing to suffer some restraint of personal liberty, and devote some part of their property to the public that the remainder may be secured and protected. The cheapest form of government is not always best, for parsimony, though it spends little, generally gains nothing. Neither is that the best government which imposes the least restraint on its subjects; for the benefit of having others restrained may be greater than the disadvantage of being restrained ourselves. That is the best form of government which returns the greatest number of advantages in proportion to the disadvantages with which it is attended.

Measured by this rule, the state of New Hampshire cannot expect a Constitution preferable to that now proposed for the Union. In point of defense it gives you the whole force of the empire, so arranged as to act speedily and in concert, which is an article of greatest importance to the frontier states. With the present generation of men, national interest is the measure by which war or peace are determined; and when we see the British nation by a late treaty paying an enormous annual subsidy to the little principality of Hesse Cassel for the purpose of retaining her in military alliance, it should teach us the necessity of those parts in the Constitution which enable the efficient force of the whole to be opposed to an invasion of any part.

A national revenue and the manner of collecting it is another very interesting matter, and here the citizens of New Hampshire have better terms offered them than their local situation can ever enable them to demand or enforce. Impost and duties on trade, which must be collected in the great importing towns, are the means by which an American revenue will be principally, and perhaps wholly, raised. But a point of your state comes near the sea, and that point so situated that it never can collect commerce and become an emporium for the whole state. Nineteen parts in twenty of New Hampshire are greatly inland, so that local situation necessitates you to be an agricultural people; and this is not a hard necessity if you now form such a political connection with other states as will entitle you to a just share in that revenue they raise on commerce. New York, the trading towns on Connecticut River, and Boston are the sources from which a great part of your foreign supplies will be obtained, and where your produce will be exposed for market.

In all these places an impost is collected, of which, as consumers, you pay a share without deriving any public benefit. You cannot expect any alteration in the private systems of these states, unless effected by the proposed governments; neither to remedy the evil can you command trade from the natural channels, but must sit down contented under the burden, if the present hour of deliverance be not accepted. This argument alone, if there were no other, ought to decide you in favor of adoption.

It has been said that you object to the number of inhabitants being a ratio to determine your proportion of the national expense — that your lands are poor but the climate favorable to population, which will draw a share of expense beyond your ability to pay. I do not think this objection well-founded. Long experience has taught that the number of industrious inhabitants in any climate is not only the strength but the wealth of a state, and very justly measures their ability of defraying public expenses without encroaching on the necessary support of life.

If a great proportion of your lands are barren, you ought likewise to remember another rule of nature; that the population and fertility in many tracts of country will be proportioned to each other. Accidental causes for a short time may interrupt the rule, but they cannot be of dangerous continuance. Force may control a despotic government, and commerce may interrupt it in an advantageous situation for trade; but from the first of these causes you have no reason to fear, and the last, should it happen, will increase wealth with numbers.

The fishery is a source of wealth and an object of immense consequence to all the eastern coasts. The jealousy of European nations ought to teach us its value. So far as you become a navigating people, the fishery should be an object of your first attention. It cannot flourish until patronized and protected by the general government. All the interests of navigation and commerce must be protected by the Union or come to ruin, and in our present system where is the power to do it?

When Americans are debarred [from] the fishery, as will soon be the case unless a remedy is provided, all the eastern shores will become miserably poor.

Your forests embosom an immense quantity of timber for shipbuilding and the lumber trade, but of how little value at present you cannot be ignorant, and the value cannot increase until American navigation and commerce are placed on a respectable footing which no single state can do for itself. The embarrassments of trade lower the price of your produce, which with the distance of transportation almost absorbs the value, and when by a long journey we have arrived at the place of market, even the finest of your grain will not command cash at that season of the year most convenient for you to transport. Hence arises that scarcity of specie of which you complain. Your interest is intimately connected with that of the most commercial states, and you cannot separate it. When trade is embarrassed the merchant is the first to complain, but the farmer in event bears more than his share of the loss.

Let the citizens of New Hampshire candidly consider these facts and they must be convinced that no other state is so much interested in adopting that system of government now under consideration.

---

53.

## Anonymous: Factions and Public Liberty

*Both Federalists and anti-Federalists were concerned with the threat to liberty posed by factionalism. In* Federalist, *Number 10, one of the best-known treatments of the subject, James Madison contended that a republican form of government had the tendency "to break and control the violence of faction." In contrast to Madison's views, the anonymous author "A Farmer" expressed his fear in the essay reprinted below, that the problem of factions could be* intensified *by the form of government outlined in the proposed Constitution. Though poorly written, it is a noteworthy example of the anti-Federalist cure for the "mischiefs of factions." It first appeared in a Maryland newspaper in March 1788.*

Source: *Baltimore General Advertiser,* March 18, 1788.

The opposite qualities of the first Confederation were rather caused by, than the cause of, two parties, which from its first existence began and have continued their operations, I believe, unknown to their country and almost unknown to themselves — as really but few men have the capacity or resolution to develop the secret causes which influence their daily conduct. The old Congress was a national government and a union of states, both brought into one political body, as these opposite powers — I do not mean parties — were so exactly blended and very nearly balanced, like every artificial, operative machine where action is equal to reaction. It stood perfectly still. It would not move at all. Those who were merely confederal in their views were for dividing the public debt. Those who were for national government were for increasing of it. Those who thought any national government would be destructive to the liberties of America, as I imagine, assisted those who thought it our only safety — to put everything as wrong as possible. Requisitions were made, which everybody knew it was impossible to comply with. Either in '82 or '83, ten millions of hard dollars, if not thirteen, were called into the Continental Treasury, when there could not be half that sum in the whole tract of territory between Nova Scotia and Florida. The states neglected them in despair. The public honor was tarnished and our governments abused by their servants and best friends. In fine, it became a cant word — things are not yet bad enough to mend.

However, as great part of the important objects of society were entrusted to this mongrel species of general government, the sentiment of pushing it forward became general throughout America, and the late Convention met at Philadelphia under the uniform impression that such was the desire of their constituents. But even then the advantages and disadvantages of national government operated so strongly, although silently, on each individual that the conflict was nearly equal. A third or middle opinion, which always arises in such cases, broke off and took the lead. The national party assisted, pursued steadily their object; the federal party dropped off, one by one; and, finally, when the middle party came to view the offspring which they had given birth to, and in a great measure reared, several of them immediately disowned the child.

Such has been hitherto the progress of party, or rather of the human mind, dispassionately contemplating our separate and relative situation, and aiming at that perfect completion of social happiness and grandeur, which perhaps can be combined only in idea. Every description of men entertain the same wishes (excepting perhaps a few very bad men of each); they forever will differ about the mode of accomplishment; and some must be permitted to doubt the practicability.

As our citizens are now apprised of the progress of parties or political opinions on the continent, it is fit they should also be informed of the present state, force, and designs of each, in order that they may form their decisions with safety to the public and themselves. This shall be given with all the precision and impartiality the author is capable of.

America is at present divided into three classes or descriptions of men, and in a few years there will be but two.

The first class comprehends all those men of fortune and reputation who stepped forward in the late Revolution from opposition to the administration rather than the government of Great Britain: all those aristocrats whose pride disdains equal law; many men of very large fortune, who entertain real or imaginary fears for the security of property; those young men who have sacrificed their time and their talents to public service without any prospect of an adequate pecuniary or honorary reward; all your people of fashion and pleasure who are corrupted by the dissipation of the French, English, and American armies, and a love of European manners and luxury; the public creditors of the continent, whose interest has been heretofore sacrificed by their friends in order to retain their services on this occasion; a large majority of the mercantile people, which is at present a very unformed and consequently dangerous interest.

Our old native merchants have been almost universally ruined by the receipt of their debts in paper during the war, and the payment in hard money of what they owed their British correspondents since peace. Those who are not bankrupts have generally retired and given place to a set of young men who, conducting themselves as rashly as ignorantly, have embarrassed their affairs and lay the blame on the government, and who are really unacquainted with the true mercantile interest of the country — which is perplexed from circumstances rather temporary than permanent. The foreign merchants are generally not to be trusted with influence in our government — they are most of them birds of passage. Some, perhaps British emissaries increasing and rejoicing in our political mistakes, and even those who have settled among us with an intention to fix themselves and their posterity in our soil, have brought with them more foreign prejudices than wealth. Time must elapse before the mercantile interest will be so organized as to govern themselves, much less others, with propriety.

And, lastly, to this class I suppose we may ultimately add the Tory interest, with the exception of very many respectable characters, who reflect with a gratification mixed with disdain that those principles are now become fashionable for which they have been persecuted and hunted down — which, although by no means so formidable as is generally imagined, is still considerable. They are at present wavering. They are generally, though with very many exceptions, openly for the proposed, but secretly against any, American government. *A burnt child dreads the fire.* But should they see any fair prospect of confusion arise, these gentry will be off at any moment for these five and twenty years to come. Ultimately, should the administration promise stability to the new government, they may be counted on as the Janizaries of power, ready to efface all suspicion by the violence of their zeal.

In general, all these various people would prefer a government as nearly copied after that of Great Britain as our circumstances will permit. Some would strain these circumstances. Others still retain a deep-rooted jealousy of the executive branch and strong republican prejudices, as they are called. Finally, this class contains more aggregate wisdom and moral virtue than both the other two together. It commands nearly two-thirds of the property and almost one-half the numbers of America, and has at present become almost irresistible from the name of the truly great and amiable man who, it has been said, is disposed to patronize it, and from the influence which it has over the second class. This class is nearly at the height of their power; they must decline or moderate, or another revolution will ensue, for the opinion of America is becoming daily more unfavorable to those radical changes which high-toned government requires. A conflict would terminate in the destruction of this class or the liberties of their country. May the Guardian Angel of America prevent both!

The second class is composed of those descriptions of men who are certainly more numerous with us than in any other part of the globe. First, those men who are so wise as to discover that their ancestors and indeed all the rest of mankind were and are fools. We have a vast overproportion of these great men who, when you tell them that from the earliest period at which mankind devoted their attention to social happiness, it has been their uniform judgment that a government over governments cannot exist — that is, two governments operating on the same individual — assume the smile of confidence and tell you of two people traveling the same road — of a perfect and precise division of the duties of the individual. Still, however, the political apothegm is as old as the proverb that no man can serve two masters; and whoever will run their noddles against old proverbs will be sure to break them, however hard they may be. And if they broke only their own, all would be right; but it is very horrible to reflect that all our numbskulls must be cracked in concert. Second, the trimmers, who from sympathetic indecision are always united with, and when not regularly employed always fight under the banners of, these great men. These people are forever at market, and when parties are nearly equally divided, they get very well paid for their services. Third, the indolent, that is, almost every second man of independent fortune you meet with in America — these are quite easy and can live under any government — if men can be said to live who scarcely breathe; and if breathing was attended with any bodily exertion, would give up their small portion of life in despair. These men do not swim with the stream as the trimmers do, but are dragged like mud at the bottom. As they have no other weight than their fat flesh, they are hardly worth mentioning when we speak of the sentiments and opinions of America.

As this second class never can include any of the yeomanry of the Union, who never affect superior wisdom, and can have no interest but the public good, it can be only said to exist at the birth of government, and as soon as the first and third classes become more decided in their views, this will divide with each and dissipate like a mist, or sink down into what are called moderate men, and become the tools and instruments of others. These people are prevented by a cloud from having *any* view; and if they are not virtuous, they at least preserve the appearance, which in this world amounts to the same thing.

At the head of the third class appear the old rigid republicans, who, although few in number, are still formidable. Reverence will follow these men in spite of detraction, as long as wisdom and virtue are esteemed among mankind. They are joined by the true *democrats,* who are in general fanatics and enthusiasts, and some few sensible, charming madmen. A decided majority of the *yeomanry* of America will, for a length of years, be ready to support these two descriptions of men. But as this last class is forced to act as a residuary legatee and receive all the trash and filth, it is in some measure disgraced and its influence weakened by, third, the freebooters and plunderers, who infest all countries, and ours perhaps as little as any other whatever. These men have that natural antipathy to any kind or sort of government that a rogue has to a halter. In number they are few indeed — such characters are the offspring of dissipation and want, and there is not that country in the world where so much real property is shared so equally among so few citizens, for where property is as easily acquired by fair means, very few indeed will resort to foul.

Lastly, by the poor mob, *infoelix pecus* [unhappy cattle]! — the property of whoever will feed them and take care of them. Let them be spared; let the burden of taxation sit lightly on their shoulders. But alas! This is not their fate. It is here that government forever falls with all its weight. It is here that the proposed government will press where it should scarcely be felt. . . .

If ever a direct tax is laid by the general government, it must, if not from necessity at least from propriety, be laid on polls; it is the only one I believe to be practicable. There ought then to be some security that they avoid direct taxation where not absolutely indispensable. . . .

In this class may be counted men of the greatest mental powers and of as sublime virtue as any in America. They at present command nearly one-third of the property and above half the numbers of the United States, and in either event they must continue to increase in influence by great desertions from both the other classes. If the government is adopted, by the numerous, discontented, and disappointed, and from that natural jealousy which Englishmen and their descendants always will retain, of their government and governors; if the government is not adopted, theirs will be the prevalent opinion. The object of this class either is or will be purely federal — a union of independent states, not a government of individuals. And should the proposed federal plan fail, from the obstinacy of those who will listen to no *conditional* amendments, although such as they cannot disapprove; or should it ultimately, in its execution upon a fair trial, disappoint the wishes and expectations of our country — a union purely federal is what the reasonable and dispassionate patriots of America must bend their views to.

My countrymen, preserve your jealousy — reject suspicion, it is the fiend that destroys public and private happiness. I know some weak, but very few if any wicked, men in public confidence. And *learn* this most difficult and necessary lesson: That on the preservation of parties, public liberty depends. Whenever men are unanimous on great public questions, whenever there is but one party, freedom ceases and despotism commences. The object of a free and wise people should be so to balance parties that from the weakness of all you may be governed by the moderation of the combined judgments of the whole, not tyrannized over by the blind passions of a few individuals.

A Farmer

---

54.

## John Jay: Arguments for Adopting the Proposed Federal Constitution

*By September 17, 1787, the final draft of the Constitution was ready for presentation to the states for ratification. However, the existence of widespread anti-Federalist sentiment made a heated struggle for state approval appear likely. In New York, an anti-Federalist stronghold, John Jay was concerned over the criticism heaped upon the Constitution. With the hope of converting his New York opponents, Jay wrote a pamphlet reciting the merits of the Constitution and the arguments for its ratification. His pamphlet, a portion of which is reprinted below, brought praise from many of his contemporaries when it was published in April 1788. "The good sense, forcible observations, temper and moderation with which the pamphlet is written," said George Washington, "cannot fail, I should think, of making a serious impression upon the anti-federal mind, where it is not under the influence of such local views as will yield to no argument, no proof."*

Source: *Pamphlets:* "An address to the people of the State of New-York on the Subject of the Constitution, Agreed upon at Philadelphia, the 17th of September, 1787."

The question now before us now naturally leads to three inquiries:

1. Whether it is probable that a better plan can be obtained?
2. Whether, if attainable, it is likely to be in season?
3. What would be our situation if, after rejecting this, all our efforts to obtain a better should prove fruitless?

The men who formed this plan are Americans who had long deserved and enjoyed our confidence, and who are as much interested in having a good government as any of us are or can be. They were appointed to that business at a time when the states had become very sensible of the derangement of our national affairs and of the impossibility of retrieving them under the existing Confederation. Although well persuaded that nothing but a good national government could oppose and divert the tide of evils that was flowing upon us, yet those gentlemen met in Convention with minds perfectly unprejudiced in favor of any particular plan. The minds of their constituents were at the time equally unbiased, cool, and dispassionate. All agreed in the necessity of doing something, but no one ventured to say decidedly what precisely ought to be done; opinions were then fluctuating and unfixed, and whatever might have been the wishes of a few individuals, yet, while the Convention deliberated, the people remained in silent suspense. Neither wedded to favorite systems of their own nor influenced by popular ones abroad, the members were more desirous to receive light from, than to impress their private sentiments on, one another. These circumstances naturally opened the door to that spirit of candor, of calm inquiry, of mutual accommodation, and mutual respect which entered into the Convention with them and regulated their debates and proceedings.

The impossibility of agreeing upon any plan that would exactly quadrate with the local policy and objects of every state soon became evident; and they wisely thought it better mutually to concede and accommodate, and in that way to fashion their system as much as possible by the circumstances and wishes of different states, than by pertinaciously adhering each to his own ideas, oblige the Convention to rise without doing anything. They were sensible that obstacles arising from local circumstances would not cease while those circumstances continued to exist; and so far as those circumstances depended on differences of climate, productions, and commerce, that no change was to be expected. They were likewise sensible that on a subject so comprehensive, and involving such a variety of points and questions, the most able, the most candid, and the most honest men will differ in opinion.

The same proposition seldom strikes many minds exactly in the same point of light; different habits of thinking, different degrees and modes of education, different prejudices and opinions early formed and long entertained conspire with a multitude of other circumstances to produce among men a diversity and contrariety of opinions on questions of difficulty. Liberality, therefore, as well as prudence, induced them to treat each other's opinions with tenderness, to argue without asperity, and to endeavor to convince the judgment without hurting the feelings of each other. Although many weeks were passed in these discussions, some points remained on which a unison of opinions could not be effected. Here again that same happy disposition to unite and conciliate induced them to meet each other; and enabled them, by mutual concessions, finally to complete and agree to the plan they have recommended, and that too with a degree of unanimity which, considering the variety of discordant views and ideas they had to reconcile, is really astonishing.

They tell us very honestly that this plan is the result of accommodation: they do not hold it up as the best of all possible ones, but only as the best which they could unite in and agree to. If such men, appointed and meeting under such auspicious circumstances, and so sincerely disposed to conciliation, could go no further in their endeavors to please every state and everybody, what reason have we at present to expect any system that would give more general satisfaction?

Suppose this plan to be rejected, what measures would you propose for obtaining a better? Some will answer — let us appoint another Convention; and as everything has been said and written that can well be said and written on the subject, they will be better informed than the former one was, and consequently be better able to make and agree upon a more eligible one.

This reasoning is fair, and, as far as it goes, has weight; but it nevertheless takes one thing for granted which appears very doubtful; for although the new convention might have more information and perhaps equal abilities, yet it does not from thence follow that they would be equally disposed to agree. The contrary of this position is the most probable. You must have observed that the same temper and equanimity which prevailed among the people on the former occasion no longer exists. We have unhappily become divided into parties; and this important subject has been handled with such indiscreet and offensive acrimony, and with so many little unhandsome artifices and misrepresentations, that pernicious heats and animosities have been kindled and spread their flames far and wide among us.

When, therefore, it becomes a question who shall be deputed to the new convention, we cannot flatter ourselves that the talents and integrity of the candidates will determine who shall be elected. Federal electors will vote for Federal deputies, and anti-Federal electors for anti-Federal ones. Nor will either party prefer the most moderate of their adherents, for as the most staunch and active partisians will be the most popular, so the men most willing and able to carry points, to oppose, and divide, and embarrass their opponents, will be chosen. A convention formed at such a season, and of such men, would be but too exact an epitome of the great body that named them. The same party views, the same propensity to opposition, the same distrusts and jealousies, and the same unaccommodating spirit which prevail without would be concentered and ferment with still greater violence within. Each deputy would recollect *who* sent him and *why* he was sent, and be too apt to consider himself bound in honor to contend and act vigorously under the standard of his party and not hazard their displeasure by preferring compromise to victory.

As vice does not sow the seeds of virtue, so neither does passion cultivate the fruits of reason. Suspicions and resentments create no disposition to conciliate, nor do they infuse a desire of making partial and personal objects bend to general union and the common good. The utmost efforts of that excellent disposition were necessary to enable the late Convention to perform their task; and although contrary causes sometimes operate similar effects, yet to expect that discord and animosity should produce the fruits of confidence and agreement is to expect "grapes from thorns, and figs from thistles."

The states of Georgia, Delaware, Jersey, and Connecticut have adopted the present plan with unexampled unanimity; they are content with it as it is, and consequently their deputies, being apprised of the sentiments of their constituents, will be little inclined to make alterations, and cannot be otherwise than averse to changes which they have no reason to think would be agreeable to their people. Some other states, though less unanimous, have nevertheless adopted it by very respectable majorities; and for reasons so evidently cogent that even the minority in one of them have nobly pledged themselves for its promotion and support.

From these circumstances, the new convention would derive and experience difficulties unknown to the former. Nor are these the only additional difficulties they would have to encounter. Few are ignorant that there has lately sprung up a sect of politicians who teach and profess to believe that the extent of our nation is too great for the superintendence of one national government, and on that principle argue that it ought to be divided into two or three. This doctrine, however mischievous in its tendency and consequences, has its advocates; and, should any of them be sent to the convention, it will naturally be their policy rather to cherish than to prevent divisions. For well knowing that the institution of any national government would blast their favorite system, no measures that lead to it can meet with their aid or approbation.

Nor can we be certain whether or not any and what foreign influence would, on such an occasion, be indirectly exerted, nor for what purposes: delicacy forbids an ample discussion of this question. Thus much may be said without error or offense, viz.: that such foreign nations as desire the prosperity of America and would rejoice to see her become great and powerful, under the auspices of a government wisely calculated to extend her commerce, to encourage her navigation and marine, and to direct the whole weight of her power and resources as her interest and honor may require, will doubtless be friendly to the Union of the states, and to the establishment of a government able to perpetuate, protect, and dignify it. Such other foreign nations, if any such there be, who, jealous of our growing importance, and fearful that our commerce and navigation should impair their own; who behold our rapid population with regret, and apprehend that the enterprising spirit of our people, when seconded by power and probability of success, may be directed to objects not consistent with their policy or interests, cannot fail to wish that we may continue a weak and a divided people.

These considerations merit much attention, and candid men will judge how far they render it probable that a new convention would be able either to agree in a better plan or, with tolerable unanimity, in any plan at all. Any plan forcibly carried by a slender majority must expect numerous opponents among the people, who, especially in their present temper, would be more inclined to reject than adopt any system so made and carried. We should in such case again see the press teeming with publications for and against it; for as the minority would take pains to justify their dissent, so would the majority be industrious to display the wisdom of their proceedings. Hence new divisions, new parties, and new distractions would ensue, and no one can foresee or conjecture when or how they would terminate.

Let those who are sanguine in their expectations of a better plan from a new convention also reflect on the delays and risk to which it would expose us. Let them consider whether we ought, by continuing much longer in our present humiliated condition, to give other nations further time to perfect their restrictive systems of commerce, to reconcile their own people to them, and to fence and guard and strengthen them by all those regulations and contrivances in which a jealous policy is ever fruitful. Let them consider whether we ought to give further opportunities to discord to alienate the hearts of our citizens from one another, and thereby encourage new Cromwells to bold exploits. Are we certain that our foreign creditors will continue patient and ready to proportion their forbearance to our delays? Are we sure that our distresses, dissensions, and weakness will neither invite hostility nor insult? If they should, how ill prepared shall we be for defense! Without union, without government, without money, and without credit!

It seems necessary to remind you that some time must yet elapse before all the states will have decided on the present plan. If they reject it, some time must also pass before the measure of a new convention can be brought about and generally agreed to. A further space of time will then be requisite to elect their deputies and send them on to convention. What time they may expend when met cannot be divined, and it is equally uncertain how much time the several states may take to deliberate and decide on any plan they may recommend. If adopted, still a further space of time will be necessary to organize and set it in motion. In the meantime our affairs are daily going on from bad to worse, and it is not rash to say that our distresses are accumulating like compound interest.

But if for the reasons already mentioned, and others that we cannot now perceive, the new convention, instead of producing a better plan, should give us only a history of their disputes, or should offer us one still less pleasing than the present, where should we be then? The old Confederation has done its best and cannot help us; and is now so relaxed and feeble that in all probability it would not survive so violent a shock. Then "to your tents Oh Israel!" would be the word. Then every band of union would be severed. Then every state would be a little nation, jealous of its neighbors and anxious to strengthen itself by foreign alliances against its former friends. Then farewell to fraternal affection, unsuspecting intercourse, and mutual participation in commerce, navigation, and citizenship. Then would arise mutual restrictions and fears, mutual garrisons, and standing armies. . . .

Consider, my fellow citizens, what you are about before it is too late; consider what in such an event would be your particular case. You know the geography of your state and the consequences of your local position. Jersey and Connecticut, to whom your impost laws have been unkind — Jersey and Connecticut, who have adopted the present plan and expect much good from it — will impute its miscarriage and all the consequent evils to you. They now consider your opposition as dictated more by your fondness for your impost than for those rights to which they have never been behind you in attachment. They cannot, they will not love you. They border upon you and are your neighbors; but you will soon cease to regard their neighborhood as a blessing. You have but one port and outlet to your commerce, and how you are to keep that outlet free and uninterrupted merits consideration. What advantage Vermont in combination with others might take of you may easily be conjectured; nor will you be at a loss to perceive how much reason the people of Long Island, whom you cannot protect, have to deprecate being constantly exposed to the depredations of every invader.

These are short hints (they ought not to be more developed); you can easily in your own mind dilate and trace them through all their relative circumstances and connections. Pause then for a moment and reflect whether the matters you are disputing about are of sufficient moment to justify your running such extravagant risks.

Reflect that the present plan comes recommended to you by men and fellow citizens who have given you the highest proofs that men can give of their justice, their love for liberty and their country; of their prudence; of their application; and of their talents. They tell you it is the best that they could form; and that in their opinion it is necessary to redeem you from those calamities which already begin to be heavy upon us all. You find that not only those men but others of similar characters, and of whom you have also had very ample experience, advise you to adopt it. You find that whole states concur in the sentiment, and among them are your next neighbors; both whom have shed much blood in the cause of liberty and have manifested as strong and constant a predilection for a free republican government as any state in the Union, and perhaps in the world. They perceive not those latent mischiefs in it, with which some double-sighted politicians endeavor to alarm you.

You cannot but be sensible that this plan

or constitution will always be in the hands and power of the people, and that if on experiment it should be found defective or incompetent, they may either remedy its defects or substitute another in its room. The objectionable parts of it are certainly very questionable, for otherwise there would not be such a contrariety of opinions about them. Experience will better determine such questions than theoretical arguments, and so far as the danger of abuses is urged against the institution of a government, remember that a power to do good always involves a power to do harm. We must in the business of government, as well as in all other business, have some degree of confidence as well as a great degree of caution. Who on a sick bed would refuse medicines from a physician merely because it is as much in his power to administer deadly poisons as salutary remedies?

You cannot be certain that by rejecting the proposed plan you would not place yourself in a very awkward situation. Suppose nine states should nevertheless adopt it, would you not in that case be obliged either to separate from the Union or rescind your dissent? The first would not be eligible, nor could the latter be pleasant (a mere hint is sufficient on this topic). You cannot but be aware of the consequences.

Consider, then, how weighty and how many considerations advise and persuade the people of America to remain in the safe and easy path of union; to continue to move and act as they hitherto have done, as a *band of brothers*; to have confidence in themselves and in one another; and since all cannot see with the same eyes, at least to give the proposed Constitution a fair trial, and to mend it as time, occasion, and experience may dictate. It would little become us to verify the predictions of those who ventured to prophesy that *peace*, instead of blessing us with happiness and tranquillity, would serve only as the signal for factions, discords, and civil contentions to rage in our land and overwhelm it with misery and distress.

Let us also be mindful that the cause of freedom greatly depends on the use we make of the singular opportunities we enjoy of governing ourselves wisely; for if the event should prove that the people of this country either cannot or will not govern themselves, who will hereafter be advocates for systems which, however charming in theory and prospect, are not reducible to practice. If the people of our nation, instead of consenting to be governed by laws of their own making and rulers of their own choosing, should let licentiousness, disorder, and confusion reign over them, the minds of men everywhere will insensibly become alienated from republican forms, and prepared to prefer and acquiesce in governments which, though less friendly to liberty, afford more peace and security.

*Receive this address with the same candor with which it is written; and may the spirit of wisdom and patriotism direct and distinguish your councils and your conduct.*

*Constitutions should consist only of general provisions; the reason is that they must necessarily be permanent, and that they cannot calculate for the possible change of things.*

ALEXANDER HAMILTON, speech, 1788

55.

# The Interest of the Few and the Rights of the Many

*John F. Mercer of Maryland spent only two weeks at the Philadelphia Convention and returned home a determined anti-Federalist. He was not present during the debates in which many of the doubts about the proposed form of government were whittled away, and he remained a rigid opponent of the new Constitution. According to Madison's notes, Mercer expressed to the convention "his dislike of the whole plan, and his opinion that it could never succeed." The following selection, an effort to dissuade the states from ratifying the Constitution, is possibly by Mercer, although doubt has recently been thrown on his authorship of it. In any event, it reflects his views and those of others who flatly opposed the Constitution.*

Source: Historical Society of Pennsylvania, Etting Collection, "Members of Old Congress," Vol. II, p. 93.

*To the Members of the Conventions of New York and Virginia*

Gentlemen:

The galling chains of despotism under the oppressive weight of which nine-tenths of our fellow mortals groan — the tortures which unfeeling tyranny has invented and fearlessly practised in every age and every clime — are melancholy and terrifying proofs of the incapacity of the many to defend those rights which God and nature gave them from the artful and unceasing usurpations of the few. And they are frightful lessons to teach us a watchful jealousy of great and unnecessary grants of power and of changes in a state of society which we know to be mild and free. Still there are moments of national languor and lethargy which the ambitious, ever enterprising, mark with alacrity and use with success.

The people, long unaccustomed, in a good and guarded government, to bold and selfish designs in their rulers, look up with an unsuspicious confidence to any alteration which those entrusted with power may propose. However unconstitutional the changes, if recommended by men used to govern them, they seem to come forward under the sanction of legal authority. [This is especially so if the changes are] prepared in secrecy, the public mind taken by surprise and every engine previously set in motion, [and if] the unconceited and unconnected defense of individuals is branded with the opprobrious epithet of opposition and overwhelmed in the directed tide of popular clamor — a clamor which a number of wealthy men may at all times command at a small expense from the most indigent of the populace.

We forbear to remark on the manner in which the Constitution proposed for the United States came forward. As the circumstances are known to you, your own feelings will render any observations unnecessary.

The object of our present address is to prevent your forming unjust conclusions from the adoption of the Constitution in the state of Maryland by so large a majority of the convention and the subsequent dissolution of that body without proposing any amendments.

Permit us to assure you that the torrent which burst forth at the birth of the Constitution had but little effect on the minds of many of us. And although it might prevent our having that weight with our countrymen, in the first paroxysms of frenzy which forever accompany great and sudden revolutions in government, we were yet determined not to be wanting in our duty to the republic at that moment when reason should resume her empire over the unagitated minds of our fellow citizens. From many circumstances we despaired of this in Maryland until the adoption of the Constitution. At that period, when our efforts could not be subjected to calumniating misrepresentation, we expected that an appeal to the reflection of our countrymen would be listened to with attention and produce those effects which unanswered and unanswerable reasons ought to command.

All opposition being thus postponed and every necessary step to inform the minds of our citizens on one side neglected, while unremitting exertions by a number of wealthy and respectable characters were continued on the other, it cannot be surprising that the elections were generally favorable to the Constitution. In a very few of the counties did any candidates propose themselves against it. Very few voted and, even in those counties where the opposition succeeded by such a decided majority, those gentlemen's offering was merely accidental. They had refused every solicitation of the people and had actually determined not to serve in convention until within six days before the election.

That the people of the state would have made alterations and amendments a condition of adoption is a question which, from the above circumstances, it is impossible to decide; but that four-fifths of the people of Maryland are now in favor of considerable alterations and amendments, and will insist on them, we don't hesitate to declare (as our opinion) to you and the world. . . .

We are persuaded that the people of so large a continent, so different in interests, so distinct in habits, cannot in all cases legislate in one body by themselves or their representatives. By themselves, it is obviously impracticable. By their representatives, it will be found, on investigation, equally so; for if these representatives are to pursue the general interest without constitutional checks and restraints, it must be done by a mutual sacrifice of the interests, wishes, and prejudices of the parts they represent — and then they cannot be said to represent those parts, but to misrepresent them. Besides, as their constituents cannot judge of their conduct by their own sense of what is right and proper, and as a representative can always in this view screen his abuse of trust under the cloak of compromise, we do not see what check can remain in the hands of the constituents — for they cannot know how far the compromise was necessary and the representative wrong. And to turn out and disgrace a man when they cannot prove him wrong, and when he will have of course the voice of the body he is a member of in his favor, would in the event be found subversive of the principles of good government.

Thus, then, the pursuit of the general interest produces an unchecked misrepresentation; but if representatives are to pursue the partial interests of the districts they represent (which to recommend themselves to their constituents it is most probable they will do), then the majority must ruin the minority, for the majority will be found interested to throw the burdens of government upon that minority, which in these states present a fair opening by difference of cultivation, importation, and property.

In such extensive territories, governed by one legislature, the experience of mankind tells us that, if not by preference, the people will at least be led gradually to confide the legislative power to the hands of one man and his family who alone can represent the whole, without partial interests, and this is or leads to unlimited despotism.

56.

# Debates in the Virginia Ratifying Convention

*Of the special conventions called in the states to ratify or reject the new Constitution, none was more fateful than the Virginia Convention that met in June 1788. As the largest, wealthiest, and most populous of the states, Virginia's support was indispensable to the success of the proposed federal government. In the end, she gave that support by the narrow vote of 89 to 79. Among the convention's most influential men were Patrick Henry and George Mason, who feared the power of such a central authority and who finally accepted it only with the conviction that it should be amended by what has come to be known as the Bill of Rights. Edmund Pendleton emerged from retirement to be elected unanimously to the presidency of the convention, despite his well-known position in favor of the Constitution. Though his official position would normally restrain the president from taking a stand on the issues before the assembly, Pendleton spoke on several occasions in behalf of the document. Speeches of these three orators are presented in the following selection.*

Source: Elliot, III, pp. 21-23, 29-41, 156-162, 445-449.

## I.

## George Mason: Against Imposing Direct Taxes

Mr. Chairman, whether the Constitution be good or bad, the present clause clearly discovers that it is a national government and no longer a confederation. I mean that clause which gives the first hint of the general government laying direct taxes. The assumption of this power of laying direct taxes does, of itself, entirely change the confederation of the states into one consolidated government. This power, being at discretion, unconfined and without any kind of control must carry everything before it. The very idea of converting what was formerly a confederation to a consolidated government is totally subversive of every principle which has hitherto governed us.

This power is calculated to annihilate totally the state governments. Will the people of this great community submit to be individually taxed by two different and distinct powers? Will they suffer themselves to be doubly harassed? These two concurrent powers cannot exist long together; the one will destroy the other: the general government being paramount to and in every respect more powerful than the state governments, the latter must give way to the former. Is it to be supposed that one national government will suit so extensive a country, embracing so many climates and containing inhabitants so very different in manners, habits, and customs?

It is ascertained by history that there never was a government over a very extensive country without destroying the liberties of the people. History also, supported by the opinions of the best writers, shows us that monarchy may suit a large territory, and despotic governments over so extensive a country, but that popular governments can only exist in small territories. Is there a single example on the face of the earth to support a contrary opinion? Where is there one exception to this general rule? Was there ever an instance of a general national government extending over so extensive a country, abounding in such a variety of climates, etc., where the people retained their liberty?

I solemnly declare that no man is a greater friend to a firm union of the American states than I am; but, sir, if this great end can be obtained without hazarding the rights of the people, why should we recur to such dangerous principles? Requisitions have been often refused, sometimes from an impossibility of complying with them; often from that great variety of circumstances which retards the collection of moneys; and perhaps sometimes from a willful design of procrastinating. But why shall we give up to the national government this power, so dangerous in its nature, and for which its members will not have sufficient information? Is it not well known that what would be a proper tax in one state would be grievous in another?

The gentleman who has favored us with a eulogium in favor of this system must, after all the encomiums he has been pleased to bestow upon it, acknowledge that our federal representatives must be unacquainted with the situation of their constituents. Sixty-five members cannot possibly know the situation and circumstances of all the inhabitants of this immense continent. When a certain sum comes to be taxed, and the mode of levying to be fixed, they will lay the tax on that article which will be most productive and easiest in the collection, without consulting the real circumstances or convenience of a country with which, in fact, they cannot be sufficiently acquainted.

The mode of levying taxes is of the utmost consequence; and yet here it is to be determined by those who have neither knowledge of our situation, nor a common interest with us, nor a fellow feeling for us. The subject of taxation differs in three-fourths, nay, I might say with truth, in four-fifths of the states. If we trust the national government with an effectual way of raising the necessary sums, it is sufficient; everything we do further is trusting the happiness and rights of the people. Why, then, should we give up this dangerous power of individual taxation? Why leave the manner of laying taxes to those who, in the nature of things, cannot be acquainted with the situation of those on whom they are to impose them, when it can be done by those who are well acquainted with it?

If, instead of giving this oppressive power, we give them such an effectual alternative as will answer the purpose, without encountering the evil and danger that might arise from it, then I would cheerfully acquiesce. And would it not be far more eligible? I candidly acknowledge the inefficacy of the Confederation; but requisitions have been made which were impossible to be complied with — requisitions for more gold and silver than were in the United States. If we give the general government the power of demanding their quotas of the states, with an alternative of laying direct taxes in case of noncompliance, then the mischief would be avoided; and the certainty of this conditional power would, in all human probability, prevent the application, and the sums necessary for the Union would be then laid by the states by those who know how it can best be raised, by those who have a fellow feeling for us.

Give me leave to say that the sum raised one way with convenience and ease would be very oppressive another way. Why, then, not leave this power to be exercised by those who know the mode most convenient for the inhabitants, and not by those who must necessarily apportion it in such a manner as shall be oppressive? . . .

An indispensable amendment . . . is that

Congress shall not exercise the power of raising direct taxes till the states shall have refused to comply with the requisitions of Congress. On this condition it may be granted; but I see no reason to grant it unconditionally, as the states can raise the taxes with more ease, and lay them on the inhabitants with more propriety, than it is possible for the general government to do. If Congress has this power without control, the taxes will be laid by those who have no fellow feeling or acquaintance with the people. This is my objection to the article now under consideration. It is a very great and important one. I therefore beg gentlemen to consider it. Should this power be restrained, I shall withdraw my objections to this part of the Constitution; but as it stands, it is an objection so strong in my mind, that its amendment is with me a *sine qua non* of its adoption. I wish for such amendments, and such only, as are necessary to secure the dearest rights of the people.

## II.

## Patrick Henry: Against Ratification

Mr. Chairman, the public mind, as well as my own, is extremely uneasy at the proposed change of government. Give me leave to form one of the number of those who wish to be thoroughly acquainted with the reasons of this perilous and uneasy situation, and why we are brought hither to decide on this great national question. I consider myself as the servant of the people of this Commonwealth, as a sentinel over their rights, liberty, and happiness. I represent their feelings when I say that they are exceedingly uneasy at being brought from that state of full security, which they enjoyed, to the present delusive appearance of things. A year ago, the minds of our citizens were at perfect repose. Before the meeting of the late federal Convention at Philadelphia, a general peace and a universal tranquillity prevailed in this country; but, since that period, they are exceedingly uneasy and disquieted.

When I wished for an appointment to this Convention, my mind was extremely agitated for the situation of public affairs. I conceived the republic to be in extreme danger. If our situation be thus uneasy, whence has arisen this fearful jeopardy? It arises from this fatal system; it arises from a proposal to change our government — a proposal that goes to the utter annihilation of the most solemn engagements of the states — a proposal of establishing nine states into a confederacy, to the eventual exclusion of four states. It goes to the annihilation of those solemn treaties we have formed with foreign nations.

The present circumstances of France — the good offices rendered us by that kingdom — require our most faithful and most punctual adherence to our treaty with her. We are in alliance with the Spaniards, the Dutch, the Prussians; those treaties bound us as thirteen states confederated together. Yet here is a proposal to sever that confederacy. Is it possible that we shall abandon all our treaties and national engagements? — and for what? I expected to hear the reasons for an event so unexpected to my mind and many others. Was our civil polity, or public justice, endangered or sapped? Was the real existence of the country threatened, or was this preceded by a mournful progression of events?

This proposal of altering our federal government is of a most alarming nature! Make the best of this new government — say it is composed by anything but inspiration — you ought to be extremely cautious, watchful, jealous of your liberty; for, instead of securing your rights, you may lose them forever. If a wrong step be now made, the republic may be lost forever. If this new government will not come up to the expectation of the people and they shall be disappointed, their liberty will be lost, and tyranny must and will arise. I repeat it again, and I beg gentlemen to consider that a wrong step made now will plunge us into misery, and our republic will be lost. It will be necessary for this Convention to have a faithful historical detail of the facts that preceded the session of the federal Convention, and the reasons that actuated its members in proposing an entire alteration of government, and to demonstrate the dangers that awaited us. If they were of such awful magnitude as to warrant a proposal so extremely perilous as this, I must assert that this Convention has an absolute right to a thorough discovery of every circumstance relative to this great event.

And here I would make this inquiry of those worthy characters who composed a part of the late federal Convention. I am sure they were fully impressed with the necessity of forming a great consolidated government instead of a confederation. That this is a consolidated government is demonstrably clear; and the danger of such a government is, to my mind, very striking. I have the highest veneration for those gentlemen; but, sir, give me leave to demand — What right had they to say, "We, the people"? My political curiosity, exclusive of my anxious solicitude for the public welfare, leads me to ask — Who authorized them to speak the language of "We, the people," instead of, "We, the states"? States are the characteristics and the soul of a confederation. If the states be not the agents of this compact, it must be one great, consolidated, national government of the people of all the states. I have the highest respect for those gentlemen who formed the Convention, and, were some of them not here, I would express some testimonial of esteem for them. America had, on a former occasion, put the utmost confidence in them — a confidence which was well placed; and I am sure, sir, I would give up anything to them; I would cheerfully confide in them as my representatives. But, sir, on this great occasion, I would demand the cause of their conduct.

Even from that illustrious man who saved us by his valor, I would have a reason for his conduct; that liberty which he has given us by his valor tells me to ask this reason; and sure I am, were he here, he would give us that reason. But there are other gentlemen here who can give us this information. The people gave them no power to use their name. That they exceeded their power is perfectly clear. It is not mere curiosity that actuates me: I wish to hear the real, actual, existing danger, which should lead us to take those steps, so dangerous in my conception.

Disorders have arisen in other parts of America; but here, sir, no dangers, no insurrection or tumult have happened; everything has been calm and tranquil. But, notwithstanding this, we are wandering on the great ocean of human affairs. I see no landmark to guide us. We are running we know not whither. Difference of opinion has gone to a degree of inflammatory resentment in different parts of the country which has been occasioned by this perilous innovation. The federal Convention ought to have amended the old system; for this purpose they were solely delegated; the object of their mission extended to no other consideration. You must, therefore, forgive the solicitation of one unworthy member to know what danger could have arisen under the present Confederation, and what are the causes of this proposal to change our government. . . .

A number of characters of the greatest eminence in this country object to this government for its consolidating tendency. This is not imaginary. It is a formidable reality. If consolidation proves to be as mischievous to this country as it has been to other countries, what will the poor inhabitants of this country do? This government will operate like an ambuscade. It will destroy the state governments and swallow the liberties of the people, without giving previous notice. If gentlemen are willing to run the hazard, let them run it; but I shall exculpate myself by my opposition and monitory warnings within these walls.

But then comes paper money. We are at peace on this subject. Though this is a thing which that mighty federal Convention had no business with, yet I acknowledge that paper money would be the bane of this country. I detest it. Nothing can justify a people in resorting to it but extreme necessity. It is at rest, however, in this Commonwealth. It is no longer solicited or advocated.

Sir, I ask you, and every other gentleman who hears me, if he can retain his indignation at a system which takes from the state legislatures the care and preservation of the interest of the people. One hundred and eighty representatives, the choice of the people of Virginia, cannot be trusted with their interests. They are a mobbish, suspected *herd.* This country has not virtue enough to manage its own internal interests. These must be referred to the chosen ten. If we cannot be trusted with the private contracts of the citizens, we must be depraved indeed. If he can prove that by one uniform system of abandoned principles the legislature has betrayed the rights of the people, then let us seek another shelter. So degrading an indignity, so flagrant an outrage on the states, so vile a suspicion is humiliating to my mind, and many others.

Will the adoption of this new plan pay our debts? This, sir, is a plain question. It is inferred that our grievances are to be redressed, and the evils of the existing system to be removed by the new Constitution. Let me inform the honorable gentleman that no nation ever paid its debts by a change of government without the aid of industry. You never will pay your debts but by a radical change of domestic economy. At present you buy too much, and make too little, to pay. Will this new system promote manufactures, industry, and frugality? If, instead of this, your hopes and designs will be disappointed, you relinquish a great deal, and hazard indefinitely more, for nothing. Will it enhance the value of your lands? Will it lessen your burdens? Will your looms and wheels go to work by the act of adoption? If it will, in its consequence, produce these things, it will consequently produce a reform and enable you to pay your debts. Gentlemen must prove it. I am a skeptic, an infidel, on this point. I cannot conceive that it will have these happy consequences. I cannot confide in assertions and allegations. The evils that attend us lie in extravagance and want of industry, and can only be removed by assiduity and economy. Perhaps we shall be told by gentlemen that these things will happen because the administration is to be taken from us and placed in the hands of the few who will pay greater attention, and be more studiously careful than we can be supposed to be.

With respect to the economical operation of the new government, I will only remark that the national expenses will be increased; if not doubled, it will approach it very nearly. I might, without incurring the imputation of illiberality or extravagance, say that the expense will be multiplied tenfold. I might tell you of a numerous standing army, a great, powerful navy, a long and rapacious train of officers and dependents, independent of the president, senators, and representatives, whose compensations are without limitation. How are our debts to be discharged unless the taxes are increased, when the expenses of the government are so greatly augmented?

The defects of this system are so numerous and palpable, and so many states object to it, that no union can be expected unless it be amended. Let us take a review of the facts. New Hampshire and Rhode Island have rejected it. They have refused to become federal. New York and North Carolina are reported to be strongly against it. From high authority give me leave to tell that New York is in high opposition. Will any gentleman say that North Carolina is not against it? They may say so; but I say that the adoption of it in those two states amounts to entire uncertainty. The system must be amended before these four states will accede to it; besides, there are several other states which are dissatisfied and wish alterations. Massachusetts has, in decided terms, proposed amendments; but, by her previous ratification, has put the cart before the horse. Maryland instituted a committee to propose amendments. It then appears that two states have actually refused to adopt; two of those who have adopted have a desire of amending; and there is a probability of its being rejected by New York and North Carolina. The other states have acceded without proposing amendments. With respect to them, local circumstances have, in my judgment, operated to produce its unconditional, instantaneous adoption. The locality of the seat of government, ten miles square, and the seat of justice, with all their concomitant emoluments, operated so powerfully with the first adopting state that it was adopted without taking time to reflect.

We are told that numerous advantages will result from the concentration of the wealth and grandeur of the United States in one happy spot to those who will reside in or near it. Prospects of profits and emoluments have a powerful influence on the human mind. We, sir, have no such projects as that of a grand seat of government for thirteen states, and perhaps for one hundred states hereafter. Connecticut and New Jersey have their localities also. New York lies between them. They have no ports and are not importing states. New York is an importing state, and, taking advantage of its situation, makes them pay duties for all the articles of their consumption; thus these two states, being obliged to import all they want through the medium of New York, pay the particular taxes of that state. I know the force and effect of reasoning of this sort by experience. When the impost was proposed, some years ago, those states which were not importing states readily agreed to concede to Congress the power of laying an impost on all goods imported for the use of the Continental treasury. Connecticut and New Jersey, therefore, are influenced by advantages of trade in their adoption. The amount of all imposts is to go into one common treasury. This favors adoption by the nonimporting states, as they participate in the profits which were before exclusively enjoyed by the importing states. Notwithstanding this obvious advantage to Connecticut, there is a formidable minority there against it.

After taking this general view of American affairs as respecting federalism, will the honorable gentleman tell me that he can expect union in America? When so many states are pointedly against it; when two adopting states have pointed out, in express terms, their dissatisfaction as it stands; and when there is so respectable a body of men discontented in every state, can the honorable gentleman promise himself harmony, of which he is so fond? If he can, I cannot. To me it appears unequivocally clear that we shall not have that harmony. If it appears to the other states that our aversion is founded on just grounds, will they not be willing to indulge us? If disunion will really result from Virginia's proposing amendments, will they not wish the reestablishment of the Union, and admit us, if not on such terms as we prescribe, yet on advantageous terms? Is not union as essential to their happiness as to ours? Sir, without a radical alteration, the states will never be embraced in one federal pale. If you attempt to force it down men's throats and call it union, dreadful consequences must follow. . . .

I am persuaded of the rectitude of my honorable friend's [Mr. Mason] opinion that one government cannot reign over so extensive a country as this is without absolute despotism. Compared to such a consolidation, small confederacies are little evils; though they ought to be recurred to but in case of necessity. Virginia and North Carolina are despised. They could exist separated from the rest of America. Maryland and Vermont were not overrun when out of the Confederacy. Though it is not a desirable object, yet I trust that, on examination, it will be found that Virginia and North Carolina would not be swallowed up in case it was necessary for them to be joined together.

When we come to the spirit of domestic peace, the humble genius of Virginia has formed a government suitable to the genius of her people. I believe the hands that formed the American Constitution triumph in the experiment. It proves that the man who formed it, and perhaps by accident, did what design could not do in other parts of the world. After all your reforms in government, unless you consult the genius of its inhabitants, you will never succeed; your system can have no duration.

Let me appeal to the candor of the committee if the want of money be not the source of all our misfortunes. We cannot be blamed for not making dollars. This want of money cannot be supplied by changes in government. The only possible remedy, as I have before asserted, is industry aided by economy. . . .

Mr. Chairman, the necessity of a Bill of Rights appears to me to be greater in this government than ever it was in any government before. . . . All rights not expressly and unequivocally reserved to the people are impliedly and incidentally relinquished to rulers, as necessarily inseparable from the delegated powers. . . . Let us consider the sentiments which have been entertained by the people of America on this subject. At the Revolution, it must be admitted that it was their sense to set down those great rights which ought, in all countries, to be held inviolable and sacred. Virginia did so, we all remember. She made a compact to reserve, expressly, certain rights.

When fortified with full, adequate, and abundant representation, was she satisfied with that representation? No. She most cautiously and guardedly reserved and secured those invaluable, inestimable rights and privileges which no people, inspired with the least glow of patriotic liberty, ever did, or ever can, abandon. She is called upon now to abandon them and dissolve that compact which secured them to her. She is called upon to accede to another compact, which most infallibly supersedes and annihilates her present one. Will she do it? This is the question. If you intend to reserve your unalienable rights, you must have the most express stipulation; for, if implication be allowed, you are ousted of those rights. If the people do not think it necessary to reserve them, they will be supposed to be given up.

How were the congressional rights defined when the people of America united by a confederacy to defend their liberties and rights against the tyrannical attempts of Great Britain? The states were not then contented with implied reservation. No, Mr. Chairman. It was expressly declared in our Confederation that every right was retained by the states, respectively, which was not given up to the government of the United States. But there is no such thing here. You, therefore, by a natural and unavoidable implication, give up your rights to the general government.

Your own example furnishes an argument against it. If you give up these powers, without a Bill of Rights, you will exhibit the most absurd thing to mankind that ever the world saw — a government that has abandoned all its powers — the powers of direct taxation, the sword, and the purse. You have disposed of them to Congress, without a Bill of Rights — without check, limitation, or control. And still you have checks and guards; still you keep barriers — pointed where? Pointed against your weakened, prostrated, enervated state government! You have a Bill of Rights to defend you against the state government, which is bereaved of all power, and yet you have none against Congress, though in full and exclusive possession of all power!

By this Constitution, some of the best barriers of human rights are thrown away. Is there not an additional reason to have a Bill of Rights? By the ancient common law, the trial of all facts is decided by a jury of impartial men from the immediate vicinage. This paper speaks of different juries from the common law in criminal cases, and, in civil controversies, excludes trial by jury altogether. There is, therefore, more occasion for the supplementary check of a Bill of Rights now than then.

Congress, from their general powers, may fully go into business of human legislation. They may legislate, in criminal cases, from treason to the lowest offense — petty larceny. They may define crimes and prescribe punishments. In the definition of crimes, I trust they will be directed by what wise representatives ought to be governed by. But when we come to punishments, no latitude ought to be left, nor dependence put on the virtue of representatives. What says our Bill of Rights? "That excessive bail ought not to be required, nor excessive fines imposed, nor cruel and unusual punishments inflicted." Are you not, therefore, now calling on those gentlemen who are to compose Congress to prescribe trials and define punishments without this control? Will they find sentiments there similar to this Bill of Rights? You let them loose; you do more — you depart from the genius of your country.

That paper tells you that the trial of crimes shall be by jury and held in the state where the crime shall have been committed. Under this extensive provision, they may proceed in a manner extremely dangerous to liberty. A person accused may be carried from one extremity of the state to another, and be tried, not by an impartial jury of the vicinage acquainted with his character and the circumstances of the fact, but by a jury unacquainted with both, and who may be biased against him. Is not this sufficient to alarm men? . . .

In this business of legislation, your members of Congress will loose the restriction of not imposing excessive fines, demanding excessive bail, and inflicting cruel and unusual punishments. These are prohibited by your declaration of rights. What has distinguished our ancestors? — that they would not admit of tortures or cruel and barbarous punishment. But Congress may introduce the practice of the civil law, in preference to that of the common law. They may introduce the practice of France, Spain, and Germany — of torturing to extort a confession of the crime. They will say that they might as well draw examples from those countries as from Great Britain, and they will tell you that there is such a necessity of strengthening the arm of government, that they must have a criminal equity, and extort confession by torture in order to punish with still more relentless severity.

We are then lost and undone. And can any man think it troublesome when we can, by a small interference, prevent our rights from being lost? If you will, like the Virginian government, give them knowledge of the extent of the rights retained by the people and the powers of themselves, they will, if they be honest men, thank you for it. Will they not wish to go on sure grounds? But if you leave them otherwise, they will not know how to proceed; and, being in a state of uncertainty, they will assume rather than give up powers by implication. . . .

In the present Constitution, they are restrained from issuing general warrants to search suspected places, or seize persons not named, without evidence of the commission of a fact, etc. There was certainly some celestial influence governing those who deliberated on that Constitution; for they have, with the most cautious and enlightened circumspection, guarded those indefeasible rights which ought ever to be held sacred! The officers of Congress may come upon you now, fortified with all the terrors of paramount federal authority. Excisemen may come in multitudes, for the limitation of their numbers no man knows. They may, unless the general government be restrained by a Bill of Rights, or some similar restriction, go into your cellars and rooms, and search, ransack, and measure everything you eat, drink, and wear. They ought to be restrained within proper bounds.

With respect to the freedom of the press, I need say nothing; for it is hoped that the gentlemen who shall compose Congress will take care to infringe as little as possible the rights of human nature. This will result from their integrity. They should, from prudence, abstain from violating the rights of their constituents. They are not, however, expressly restrained. But whether they will intermeddle with that palladium of our liberties or not, I leave you to determine.

## III.

### Edmund Pendleton: For Ratification

Mr. Chairman, my worthy friend [Mr. Henry] has expressed great uneasiness in his mind and informed us that a great many of our citizens are also extremely uneasy at the proposal of changing our government; but that, a year ago, before this fatal system was thought of, the public mind was at perfect repose. It is necessary to inquire whether the public mind was at ease on the subject, and if it be since disturbed, what was the cause. What was the situation of this country before the meeting of the federal Convention? Our general government was totally inadequate to the purpose of its institution; our commerce decayed; our finances deranged; public and private credit destroyed. These and many other national evils rendered necessary the meeting of that Convention. If the public mind was then at ease, it did not result from a conviction of being in a happy and easy situation; it must have been an inactive, unaccountable stupor.

The federal Convention devised the paper on your table as a remedy to remove our political diseases. What has created the public uneasiness since? Not public reports, which are not to be depended upon but mistaken apprehensions of danger, drawn from observations on government which do not apply to us. When we come to inquire into the origin of most governments of the world, we shall find that they are generally dictated by a conqueror, at the point of the sword, or are the offspring of confusion, when a great popular leader, taking advantage of circumstances, if not producing them, restores order at the expense of liberty and becomes the tyrant over the people. It may well be supposed that, in forming a government of this sort, it will not be favorable to liberty; the conqueror will take care of his own emoluments and have little concern for the interest of the people. In either case, the interest and ambition of a despot, and not the good of the people, have given the tone to the government. A government thus formed must necessarily create a continual war between the governors and governed.

Writers consider the two parties (the people and tyrants) as in a state of perpetual warfare, and sound the alarm to the people. But what is our case? We are perfectly free from sedition and war; we are not yet in confusion; we are left to consider our real happiness and security; we want to secure these objects; we know they cannot be attained without government. Is there a single man in this committee of a contrary opinion? What was it that brought us from a state of nature to society, but to secure happiness? And can society be formed without government? Personify government; apply to it as a friend to assist you, and it will grant your request. This is the only government founded in real compact. There is no quarrel between government and liberty; the former is the shield and protector of the latter. The war is between government and licentiousness, faction, turbulence, and other violations of the rules of society to preserve liberty. Where is the cause of alarm? We, the people, possessing all power, form a government such as we think will secure happiness; and suppose, in adopting this plan, we should be mistaken in the end — where is the cause of alarm on that quarter?

In the same plan we point out an easy and quiet method of reforming what may be found amiss. No, but, say gentlemen, we have put the introduction of that method in the hands of our servants, who will interrupt it from motives of self-interest. What then? We will resist, did my friend say, conveying an idea of force? Who shall dare to resist the people? No, we will assemble in Convention; wholly recall our delegated powers, or reform them so as to prevent such abuse; and punish those servants who have perverted powers, designed for our happiness, to their own emolument. We ought to be extremely cautious not to be drawn into dispute with regular government by faction and turbulence, its natural enemies. Here, then, sir, there is no cause of alarm on this side; but on the other side, rejecting of government and dissolving of the Union produce confusion and despotism.

But an objection is made to the form: the expression "We, the people" is thought improper. Permit me to ask the gentleman who made this objection, who but the people can delegate powers? Who but the people have a right to form government? The expression is a common one, and a favorite one with me. The representatives of the people, by their authority, is a mode wholly inessential. If the objection be that the Union ought to be not of the people but of the state governments, then I think the choice of the former very happy and proper. What have the state governments to do with it? Were they to determine, the people would not, in that case, be the judges upon what terms it was adopted.

But the power of the Convention is doubted. What is the power? To propose, not to determine. This power of proposing was very broad; it extended to remove all defects in government; the members of that Convention, who were to consider all the defects in our general government, were not confined to any particular plan. Were they deceived? This is the proper question here. Suppose the paper on your table dropped from one of the planets; the people found it, and sent us here to consider whether it was proper for their adoption. Must we not obey them? Then the question must be between this government and the Confederation.

The latter is no government at all. It has been said that it has carried us through a dangerous war to a happy issue.

Not that Confederation but common danger, and the spirit of America, were bonds of our Union. Union and unanimity, and not that insignificant paper, carried us through that dangerous war. "United, we stand — divided, we fall!" echoed and re-echoed through America — from Congress to the drunken carpenter — was effectual, and procured the end of our wishes, though now forgotten by gentlemen, if such there be, who incline to let go this stronghold to catch at feathers; for such all substituted projects may prove.

This spirit had nearly reached the end of its power when relieved by peace. It was the spirit of America, and not the Confederation, that carried us through the war: thus I prove it. The moment of peace showed the imbecility of the federal government.

Congress was empowered to make war and peace; a peace they made, giving us the great object, independence, and yielding us a territory that exceeded my most sanguine expectations. Unfortunately, a single disagreeable clause, not the object of the war, has retarded the performance of the treaty on our part. Congress could only recommend its performance, not enforce it; our last Assembly (to their honor be it said) put this on its proper grounds, on honorable grounds; it was as much as they ought to have done. This single instance shows the imbecility of the Confederation; the debts contracted by the war were unpaid; demands were made on Congress; all that Congress was able to do was to make an estimate of the debt and proportion it among the several states; they sent on the requisitions, from time to time, to the states, for their respective quotas. These were either complied with partially or not at all. Repeated demands on Congress distressed that honorable body; but they were unable to fulfill those engagements, as they so earnestly wished.

What was the idea of other nations respecting America? What was the idea entertained of us by those nations to whom we were so much indebted? The inefficacy of the general government warranted an idea that we had no government at all. Improvements were proposed and agreed to by twelve states, but were interrupted because the little state of Rhode Island refused to accede to them. This was a further proof of the imbecility of that government. Need I multiply instances to show that it is wholly ineffectual for the purposes of its institution? Its whole progress since the peace proves it.

Shall we then, sir, continue under such a government, or shall we introduce that kind of government which shall produce the real happiness and security of the people? When gentlemen say that we ought not to introduce this new government but strengthen the hands of Congress, they ought to be explicit. In what manner shall this be done? If the union of the states be necessary, government must be equally so; for without the latter, the former cannot be effected. Government must then have its complete powers, or be ineffectual; a legislature to fix rules, impose sanctions, and point out the punishment of the transgressors of these rules; an executive to watch over officers and bring them to punishment; a judiciary to guard the innocent, and fix the guilty, by a fair trial. Without an executive, offenders would not be brought to punishment; without a judiciary, any man might be taken up, convicted, and punished without a trial. Hence the necessity of having these three branches.

Would any gentleman in this committee agree to vest these three powers in one body: Congress? No. Hence the necessity of a new organization and distribution of those powers. If there be any feature in this government which is not republican, it would be exceptionable. From all the public servants responsibility is secured by their being representatives, mediate or immediate, for short terms, and their powers defined. It is, on the whole complexion of it, a government of laws, not of men.

But it is represented to be a consolidated government, annihilating that of the states — a consolidated government, which so extensive a territory as the United States cannot admit of without terminating in despotism. If this be such a government, I will confess, with my worthy friend, that it is inadmissible over such a territory as this country. Let us consider whether it be such a government or not. I should understand a consolidated government to be that which should have the sole and exclusive power, legislative, executive, and judicial, without any limitation. Is this such a government? Or can it be changed to such a one? It only extends to the general purposes of the Union. It does not intermeddle with the local, particular affairs of the states. Can Congress legislate for the state of Virginia? Can they make a law altering the form of transferring property, or the rule of descents, in Virginia? In one word, can they make a single law for the individual, exclusive purpose of any one state?

It is the interest of the federal to preserve the state governments; upon the latter the existence of the former depends. The Senate derives its existence immediately from the state legislatures; and the representatives and the president are elected under their direction and control; they also preserve order among the citizens of their respective states, and without order and peace no society can possibly exist. Unless, therefore, there be state legislatures to continue the existence of Congress, and preserve order and peace among the inhabitants, this general government, which gentlemen suppose will annihilate the state governments, must itself be destroyed. When, therefore, the federal government is, in so many respects, so absolutely dependent on the state governments, I wonder how any gentleman, reflecting on the subject, could have conceived an idea of a possibility of the former destroying the latter.

But the power of laying direct taxes is objected to. Government must be supported; this cannot be done without a revenue: if a sufficient revenue be not otherwise raised, recurrence must be had to direct taxation; gentlemen admit this, but insist on the propriety of first applying to the state legislatures.

Let us consider the consequence that would result from this. In the first place, time would be lost by it. Congress would make requisitions in December; our legislature does not meet till October. Here would be a considerable loss of time, admitting the requisitions to be fully complied with. But suppose the requisitions to be refused; would it not be dangerous to send a collector to collect the congressional taxes after the state legislature had absolutely refused to comply with the demands of Congress? Would not resistance to collectors be the probable consequence? Would not this resistance terminate in confusion and a dissolution of the Union? The concurrent power of two different bodies laying direct taxes is objected to. These taxes are for two different purposes, and cannot interfere with one another. I can see no danger resulting from this; and we must suppose that a very small sum more than the impost would be sufficient. But the representation is supposed too small. I confess, I think with the gentleman who opened the debate [Mr. Nicholas] on this subject; and I think he gave a very satisfactory answer to this objection when he observed that, though the number might be insufficient to convey information of necessary local interests to a state legislature, yet it was sufficient for the federal legislature, who are to act only on general subjects, in which this state is concerned in common with other states.

The apportionment of representation and taxation by the same scale is just; it removes the objection that, while Virginia paid one-sixth part of the expenses of the Union, she had no more weight in public counsels than Delaware, which paid but a very small portion. By this just apportionment she is put on a footing with the small states, in point of representation and influence in councils. I cannot imagine a more judicious principle than is here fixed by the Constitution — the number shall not exceed 1 for every 30,000. But it is objected that the number may be less. If Virginia sends in that proportion, I ask, where is the power in Congress to reject them? States might incline to send too many; they are therefore restrained; but can it be doubted that they will send the number they are entitled to? We may be, therefore, sure, from this principle unequivocally fixed in the Constitution, that the number of our representatives will be in proportion to the increase or decrease of our population. I can truly say that I am of no party, nor actuated by any influence, but the true interest and real happiness of those whom I represent; and my age and situation, I trust, will sufficiently demonstrate the truth of this assertion. I cannot conclude without adding that I am perfectly satisfied with this part of the system.

57.

# Virginia's Recommended Amendments to the Constitution

*Virginia's ratification of the Constitution was announced on June 25, 1788, with the stipulation that amendments would be considered immediately for presentation to the first Congress. A committee was appointed for the purpose of drafting recommendations, several of which were later included in the Bill of Rights. The suggested amendments, reprinted below, are largely based on demands originally made by Patrick Henry in the Virginia Convention.*

Source: Elliot, III, pp. 657-661.

MR. WYTHE REPORTED, from the committee appointed, such amendments to the proposed Constitution of government for the United States as were by them deemed necessary to be recommended to the consideration of the Congress which shall first assemble under the said Constitution, to be acted upon according to the mode prescribed in the 5th Article thereof; and he read the same in his place, and afterward delivered them in at the clerk's table, where the same were again read, and are as follows:

That there be a declaration or bill of rights asserting, and securing from encroachment, the essential and unalienable rights of the people, in some such manner as the following:

1. That there are certain natural rights, of which men, when they form a social compact, cannot deprive or divest their posterity; among which are the enjoyment of life and liberty, with the means of acquiring, possessing, and protecting property, and pursuing and obtaining happiness and safety.

2. That all power is naturally invested in, and consequently derived from, the people; that magistrates therefore are their trustees and agents, at all times amenable to them.

3. That government ought to be instituted for the common benefit, protection, and security of the people; and that the doctrine of nonresistance against arbitrary power and oppression is absurd, slavish, and destructive to the good and happiness of mankind.

4. That no man or set of men are entitled to separate or exclusive public emoluments or privileges from the community, but in consideration of public services,

which not being descendible, neither ought the offices of magistrate, legislator, or judge, or any other public office to be hereditary.

5. That the legislative, executive, and judicial powers of government should be separate and distinct; and, that the members of the two first may be restrained from oppression by feeling and participating [in] the public burdens, they should, at fixed periods, be reduced to a private station, return into the mass of the people, and the vacancies be supplied by certain and regular elections in which all or any part of the former members to be eligible or ineligible, as the rules of the Constitution of government and the laws shall direct.

6. That the elections of representatives in the legislature ought to be free and frequent, and all men having sufficient evidence of permanent common interest with, and attachment to, the community, ought to have the right of suffrage; and no aid, charge, tax, or fee can be set, rated, or levied upon the people without their own consent, or that of their representatives, so elected; nor can they be bound by any law to which they have not in like manner assented, for the public good.

7. That all power of suspending laws, or the execution of laws, by any authority, without the consent of the representatives of the people in the legislature, is injurious to their rights and ought not to be exercised.

8. That in all criminal and capital prosecutions a man has a right to demand the cause and nature of his accusation, to be confronted with the accusers and witnesses, to call for evidence, and be allowed counsel in his favor, and to a fair and speedy trial by an impartial jury of his vicinage, without whose unanimous consent he cannot be found guilty (except in the government of the land and naval forces); nor can he be compelled to give evidence against himself.

9. That no freeman ought to be taken, imprisoned, or disseized of his freehold, liberties, privileges, or franchises, or outlawed or exiled, or in any manner destroyed or deprived of his life, liberty, or property but by the law of the land.

10. That every freeman restrained of his liberty is entitled to a remedy, to inquire into the lawfulness thereof, and to remove the same, if unlawful, and that such remedy ought not to be denied nor delayed.

11. That in controversies respecting property, and in suits between man and man, the ancient trial by jury is one of the greatest securities to the rights of the people and [is] to remain sacred and inviolable.

12. That every freeman ought to find a certain remedy, by recourse to the laws, for all injuries and wrongs he may receive in his person, property, or character. He ought to obtain right and justice freely, without sale, completely and without denial, promptly and without delay, and that all establishments or regulations contravening these rights are oppressive and unjust.

13. That excessive bail ought not to be required, nor excessive fines imposed, nor cruel and unusual punishments inflicted.

14. That every freeman has a right to be secure from all unreasonable searches and seizures of his person, his papers, and property. All warrants, therefore, to search suspected places or seize any freeman, his papers, or property, without information on oath (or affirmation of a person religiously scrupulous of taking an oath) of legal and sufficient cause, are grievous and oppressive; and all general warrants to search suspected places, or to apprehend any suspected person, without specially naming or describing the place or person, are dangerous and ought not to be granted.

15. That the people have a right peaceably to assemble together to consult for the common good or to instruct their representatives; and that every freeman has a right to petition or apply to the legislature for redress of grievances.

16. That the people have a right to free-

Library of Congress
Engraving of George Wythe by J. B. Longacre

dom of speech and of writing and publishing their sentiments; that the freedom of the press is one of the greatest bulwarks of liberty and ought not to be violated.

17. That the people have a right to keep and bear arms; that a well-regulated militia, composed of the body of the people trained to arms, is the proper, natural, and safe defense of a free state; that standing armies, in time of peace, are dangerous to liberty and therefore ought to be avoided as far as the circumstances and protection of the community will admit; and that, in all cases, the military should be under strict subordination to, and governed by, the civil power.

18. That no soldier in time of peace ought to be quartered in any house without the consent of the owner, and in time of war in such manner only as the law directs.

19. That any person religiously scrupulous of bearing arms ought to be exempted, upon payment of an equivalent to employ another to bear arms in his stead.

20. That religion, or the duty which we owe to our Creator, and the manner of discharging it, can be directed only by reason and conviction, not by force or violence; and therefore all men have an equal, natural, and unalienable right to the free exercise of religion, according to the dictates of conscience, and that no particular religious sect or society ought to be favored or established by law in preference to others.

AMENDMENTS TO THE CONSTITUTION

1. That each state in the Union shall respectively retain every power, jurisdiction, and right which is not by this Constitution delegated to the Congress of the United States, or to the departments of the federal government.

2. That there shall be 1 representative for every 30,000, according to the enumeration or census mentioned in the Constitution, until the whole number of representatives amounts to 200; after which, that number shall be continued or increased, as Congress shall direct, upon the principles fixed in the Constitution, by apportioning the representatives of each state to some greater number of people, from time to time, as population increases.

3. When the Congress shall lay direct taxes or excises, they shall immediately inform the executive power of each state of the quota of such state, according to the census herein directed, which is proposed to be thereby raised; and if the legislature of any state shall pass a law which shall be effectual for raising such quota at the time required by Congress, the taxes and excises laid by Congress shall not be collected in such state.

4. That the members of the Senate and House of Representatives shall be ineligible to, and incapable of holding, any civil office under the authority of the United States during the time for which they shall respectively be elected.

5. That the journals of the proceedings of the Senate and House of Representatives shall be published at least once every year,

except such parts thereof relating to treaties, alliances, or military operations, as in their judgment require secrecy.

6. That a regular statement and account of the receipts and expenditures of public money shall be published at least once a year.

7. That no commercial treaty shall be ratified without the concurrence of two-thirds of the whole number of the members of the Senate; and no treaty ceding, contracting, restraining, or suspending the territorial rights or claims of the United States, or any of them, or their, or any of their rights or claims to fishing in the American seas or navigating the American rivers, shall be made, but in cases of the most urgent and extreme necessity; nor shall any such treaty be ratified without the concurrence of three-fourths of the whole number of the members of both houses respectively.

8. That no navigation law, or law regulating commerce, shall be passed without the consent of two-thirds of the members present, in both houses.

9. That no standing army, or regular troops, shall be raised, or kept up, in time of peace, without the consent of two-thirds of the members present, in both houses.

10. That no soldier shall be enlisted for any longer term than four years, except in time of war, and then for no longer term than the continuance of the war.

11. That each state respectively shall have the power to provide for organizing, arming, and disciplining its own militia, whensoever Congress shall omit or neglect to provide for the same. That the militia shall not be subject to martial law; except when in actual service, in time of war, invasion, or rebellion; and when not in the actual service of the United States, shall be subject only to such fines, penalties, and punishments as shall be directed or inflicted by the laws of its own state.

12. That the exclusive power of legislation given to Congress over the federal town and its adjacent district, and other places, purchased or to be purchased by Congress of any of the states, shall extend only to such regulations as respect the police and good government thereof.

13. That no person shall be capable of being President of the United States for more than eight years in any term of sixteen years.

14. That the judicial power of the United States shall be vested in one Supreme Court, and in such courts of admiralty as Congress may from time to time ordain and establish in any of the different states. The judicial power shall extend to all cases in law and equity arising under treaties made, or which shall be made, under the authority of the United States; to all cases affecting ambassadors, other foreign ministers, and consuls; to all cases of admiralty and maritime jurisdiction; to controversies to which the United States shall be a party; to controversies between two or more states, and between parties claiming lands under the grants of different states. In all cases affecting ambassadors, other foreign ministers, and consuls, and those in which a state shall be a party, the Supreme Court shall have original jurisdiction; in all other cases before mentioned, the Supreme Court shall have appellate jurisdiction, as to matters of law only, except in cases of equity, and of admiralty and maritime jurisdiction, in which the Supreme Court shall have appellate jurisdiction both as to law and fact, with such exceptions and under such regulations as the Congress shall make. But the judicial power of the United States shall extend to no case where the cause of action shall have originated before the ratification of the Constitution, except in disputes between states about their territory, disputes between persons claiming lands under the grants of different states, and suits for debts due to the United States.

15. That in criminal prosecutions no man shall be restrained in the exercise of the

usual and accustomed right of challenging or excepting to the jury.

16. That Congress shall not alter, modify, or interfere in the times, places, or manner of holding elections for senators and representatives, or either of them, except when the legislature of any state shall neglect, refuse, or be disabled by invasion or rebellion to prescribe the same.

17. That those clauses which declare that Congress shall not exercise certain powers be not interpreted, in any manner whatsoever, to extend the powers of Congress; but that they be construed either as making exceptions to the specified powers where this shall be the case, or, otherwise, as inserted merely for greater caution.

18. That the laws ascertaining the compensation of senators and representatives for their services be postponed in their operation until after the election of representatives immediately succeeding the passing thereof; that excepted which shall first be passed on the subject.

19. That some tribunal other than the Senate be provided for trying impeachments of senators.

20. That the salary of a judge shall not be increased or diminished during his continuance in office, otherwise than by general regulations of salary, which may take place on a revision of the subject at stated periods of not less than seven years, to commence from the time such salaries shall be first ascertained by Congress.

---

58.

## Anonymous: The Constitution Attacked as Setting Up Government by the Few

*Among the many arguments against the Constitution, one embodied a major concern expressed by both the anti-Federalists and their opponents alike: the question of legislative power. For the Federalists, the bicameral legislature of the Connecticut Compromise had given an adequate solution to the problem of popular representation. But the anti-Federalists viewed the Senate as a potentially aristocratic body and the House of Representatives, according to one Bostonian, as an "assistant aristocratical branch." The following satiric essay, authored anonymously by "Aristocrotis," is one of many writings portraying the anti-Federalist fear of aristocratic rule.*

Source: *The Government of Nature Delineated; or An Exact Picture of the New Federal Constitution,* Carlisle, Pa., 1788.

The present is an active period. Europe is in a ferment breaking their constitutions; America is in a similar state, making a constitution. For this valuable purpose a convention was appointed, consisting of such as excelled in wisdom and knowledge, who met in Philadelphia last May. For my own part, I was so smitten with the character of the members that I had assented to their production while it was yet in embryo. And I make no doubt but every good republican did so too. But how great was my surprise, when it appeared with such a venerable train of names annexed to its tail, to find some of the people under different signatures, such as "Centinel," "Old Whig," "Brutus," etc. — daring to oppose it, and that too with barefaced arguments, obstinate reason, and stubborn truth. This is certainly a piece of the most extravagant impudence to presume to contradict the collected wisdom of the United States; or to suppose a body, who engrossed the whole wisdom of the continent, was capable of erring. I expected the superior character of the Convention would have secured it from profane sallies of a plebeian's pen; and its inherent infallibility debarred the interference of impertinent reason or truth.

It was too great an act of condescension to permit the people, by their state conventions, "to assent and ratify" what the grand Convention prescribed to them; but to inquire into its principles or investigate its properties was a presumption too daring to escape resentment. Such licentious conduct practised by the people is a striking proof of our feeble governments and calls aloud for the pruning knife, viz., the establishment of some proper plan of discipline.

This the Convention, in the depth of their united wisdom, has prescribed, which, when established, will certainly put a stop to the growing evil. A consciousness of this is, no doubt, the cause which stimulates the people to oppose it with so much vehemence. They deprecate the idea of being confined within their proper sphere. They cannot endure the thoughts of being obliged to mind their own business and leave the affairs of government to those whom nature has destined to rule. I say nature, for it is a fundamental principle, as clear as an axiom, that nature has placed proper degrees and subordinations among mankind and ordained a few to rule and many to obey. I am not obliged to prove this principle because it would be madness in the extreme to attempt to prove a self-evident truth. But with all due submission to the infallible wisdom of the grand Convention, let me presume to examine whether they have not, in the new plan of government, inviolably adhered to this supreme principle.

The exorbitant power, which the people of this country possess, of electing their rulers is directly repugnant to this superlative principle of nature and tends to the subversion of all order and good government; for they may, and often do, advance those men to be rulers whom nature had ordained for subjects, and to neglect the natural rulers. This is a gross inversion of the law of nature and ought to be cashiered; but the vulgar opinion is so strong in favor of this unnatural practice that it would be dangerous to divest them of it all at once. It might inflame their turbulent minds and excite them to commit some outrageous action in support of what they have been taught to consider as their "natural, inherent, and unalienable rights." The venerable Convention foresaw this and accommodated their plan to humor these mistaken notions of the people, so far as was consistent with the honor, dignity, and rights of the more illustrious descended, whose title to rule is founded on the law of nature.

In Article I, Section 1, of the new plan, it is declared that "all legislative powers herein granted shall be vested in a Congress of the United States, which shall consist of a Senate" (very right, quite agreeable to nature) "and House of Representatives" (not quite so right). This is a palpable compliance with the humors and corrupt practices of the times. But what follows in Section 2 is still worse: "The House of Representatives shall be composed of members chosen every second year by the people of the several states." This is a most dangerous power and must soon produce fatal and pernicious consequences were it not circumscribed and poised by proper checks and balances. But in this is displayed the unparalleled sagacity of the august Convention: that when such bulwarks of prejudice surrounded the evil, so as to render it both difficult and dangerous to attack it by assault and storm, they have invested and barricaded it so closely as will certainly deprive it of its baneful influence and prevent its usual encroachments. They have likewise stationed their miners and sappers so judiciously that they will certainly, in process of time, entirely reduce and demolish this obnoxious practice of popular election.

There is a small thrust given to it in the body of the conveyance itself. The term of holding elections is every two years; this is much better than the detestable mode of *annual* elections, so fatal to energy. However, if nothing more than this were done, it would still remain an insupportable inconvenience. But in Section 4 it is provided that Congress by law may alter and make such regulations with respect to the times, places, and manner of holding elections as to them seem fit and proper. This is certainly a very salutary provision, most excellently adapted to counterbalance the great and apparently dangerous concessions made to the plebeians in the first and second sections. With such a prudent restriction as this they are quite harmless. No evil can arise from them if Congress have only the sagacity and fortitude to avail themselves of the power they possess by this section; for when the stated term (for which the primary members were elected) is nigh expired, Congress may appoint [the] next election to be held in one place in each state; and so as not to give the rabble needless disgust, they may appoint the most central place for that purpose.

They can never be at a loss for an ostensible reason to vary and shift from place to place until they may fix it at any extremity of the state it suits. This will be the business of the Senate, to observe the particular places in each state where their influence is most extensive and where the inhabitants are most obsequious to the will of their superiors, and there appoint the elections to be held. By this means, such members will be returned to the House of Representatives (as it is called) as the President and Senate shall be pleased to recommend; and they no doubt will recommend such gentlemen only as are distinguished by some peculiar federal feature, so that unanimity and concord will shine conspicuous through every branch of government.

This section is ingeniously calculated and must have been intended by the Convention to exterminate electioneering entirely; for by putting the time of election in the hands of Congress they have thereby given them a power to perpetuate themselves when they shall find it safe and convenient to make the experiment. For though a preceding clause says "that representatives shall be chosen for two years, and senators for six years," yet this clause being subsequent annuls the former, and puts it in the power of Congress (when some favorable juncture intervenes) to alter the time to four and twelve years. This cannot be deemed an unconstitutional stretch of power, for the Constitution in express terms puts the time of holding elections in their power, and certainly they are the proper judges when to exert that power. Thus, by doubling the period from time to time, its extent will soon be rendered coeval with the life of man. And it is but a very short and easy transition from this to hereditary succession. . . .

The next object that presents itself is the power which the new Constitution gives to Congress to regulate the manner of elections. The common practice of voting at present is by ballot. By this mode it is impossible for a gentleman to know how he is served by his dependent, who may be possessed of a vote. Therefore this mode must be speedily altered for that *viva voce*, which will secure to a rich man all the votes of his numerous dependents and friends and their dependents. By this means he may command any office in the gift of the people which he pleases to set up for. This will answer a good end while electioneering exists, and will likewise contribute something toward its destruction. A government founded agreeable to nature must be entirely independent; that is, it must be beyond the reach of annoyance or control from every power on earth.

Now, in order to render it thus, several things are necessary. First, the means of their own support must be within the immediate reach of the rulers. For this purpose they must possess the sole power of taxation. As this is a principal article, it ought, in all things, to have preeminence; and therefore the Convention has placed it in front. "The Congress shall have power to lay and collect taxes, duties, imposts, and excises," so that they shall never be at a loss for money while there is a shilling on the continent, for their power to procure it is as extensive as their desires. And so it ought, because they can never desire anything but is good and salutary; for there is no doubt but the Convention will transfer their infallibility to the new Congress, and so secure them from doing evil.

This power of taxation will answer many valuable purposes besides the support of government. In the first place, in the course of its operation it will annihilate the relics of the several state legislators. For every tax which they may lay will be deemed by Congress an infringement upon the federal Constitution, which Constitution and the laws of Congress being paramount to all other authority will of consequence nullify every inferior law which the several states may think proper to enact, particularly such as relate to taxes; so that they being deprived of the means of existence, their pretended sovereignties will gradually linger away.

Second, it will create and diffuse a spirit of industry among the people. They will then be obliged to labor for money to pay their taxes. There will be no trifling from time to time as is done now. The new government will have energy sufficient to compel immediate payment.

Third, this will make the people attend to their own business, and not be dabbling in politics — things they are entirely ignorant of; nor is it proper they should understand. But it is very probable that the exercise of this power may be opposed by the refractory plebeians, who (such is the perverseness of their natures) often refuse to comply with what is manifestly for their advantage. But to prevent all inconvenience from this quarter the Congress have power to raise and support armies. This is the second thing necessary to render government independent. The creatures who compose these armies are a species of animals wholly at the disposal of government. What others call their natural rights they resign into the hands of their superiors. Even the right of self-preservation (so precious to all other beings) they entirely surrender, and put their very lives in the power of their masters; so that, having no rights of their own to care for, they become naturally jealous and envious of those possessed by others. They are therefore proper instruments in the hands of government to divest the people of their usurped rights. But the capital business of these armies will be to assist the collectors of taxes, imposts, and excise in raising the revenue; and this they will perform with the greatest alacrity, as it is by this they are supported; but for this they would be in a great measure useless; and without this they could not exist.

To render government entirely independent, they must have the sole and absolute command of the militia, without restriction or reserve, either as to time or place, principle or conscience; and with this power the Constitution has amply furnished them — see Article I, Section 8. "The Congress shall have power to provide for calling forth the militia to execute the laws of the Union, suppress insurrections, and repel invasions, to provide for organizing, arming, and disciplining the militia, and for governing such part of them as may be employed in the service of the United States." By this clause the militia is divided into two classes, viz., active and inactive. The active militia will be those employed "in the service of the United States," or in other words in the service of Congress; they will consist of young men chiefly, who will not be attached to any particular place on account of their families; or such eccentric geniuses as by their superior address or daring spirit may gain an ascendancy over the minds of the vulgar, and so become the heads of liberty factions. . . .

Another privilege which the people possess at present, and which the new Congress will find it their interest to deprive them of, is trial by jury; for, of all the powers which the people have wrested from government, this is the most absurd; it is even a gross violation of common sense and most destructive to energy. In the first place, it is absurd that twelve ignorant plebeians should be constituted judges of a law which passed through so many learned hands — first, a learned legislature, after many learned animadversions and criticisms have enacted it; second, learned writers have explained and commented on it; third, learned lawyers twisted, turned, and new modeled it; and, lastly, a learned judge opened up and explained it. Yet after all these learned discussions, an illiterate jury (who have scarce a right to think for themselves instead of judging for others) must determine whether it applies to the fact or not; and by their verdict the learned judge must be governed in passing sentence; and perhaps a learned gentleman be cast in an action with an insignificant cottager. . . .

There have been but few nations in the world where the people possessed the privilege of electing their rulers; of prefixing a bill of rights to their constitutions, enjoyed a free press, or trial by jury; but there was never a nation in the world whose government was not circumscribed by religion. . . . What the world could not accomplish from the commencement of time till now, they easily performed in a few moments by declaring that "no religious test shall ever be required as a qualification to any office or public trust under the United States." This is laying the ax to the root of the tree, whereas other nations only lopped off a few noxious branches. This is purifying the fountain — the streams must of course be pure. . . .

From these remarks, I think it is evident that the grand Convention has dexterously provided for the removal of everything that has ever operated as a restraint upon government in any place or age of the world. But perhaps some weak heads may think that the Constitution itself will be a check upon the new Congress. But this I deny, for the Convention has so happily worded themselves that every part of this Constitution either bears double meaning or no meaning at all; and if any concessions are made to the people in one place, it is effectually canceled in another, so that in fact this Constitution is much better and gives more scope to the rulers than they dared safely take if there was no constitution at all. For then the people might contend that the power was inherent in them and that they had made some implied reserves in the original grant. But now they cannot, for everything is expressly given away to government in this plan.

Perhaps some people may think that power which the House of Representatives possesses, of impeaching the officers of government, will be a restraint upon them. But this entirely vanishes when it is considered that the Senate has the principal say in appointing these officers and that they are the sole judges of all impeachments. Now it would be absurd to suppose that they would remove their own servants for performing their secret orders, perhaps, for the interest of rulers and the ruled will then be two distinct things.

The mode of electing the President is another excellent regulation, most wisely calculated to render him the obsequious machine of Congress. He is to be chosen by electors appointed in such manner as the state legislators shall direct. But then the highest in votes cannot be President unless he has the majority of all the electors; and if none have this majority, then the Congress is to choose the President out of the five highest on the return. By this means the Congress will always have the making of the President after the first election; so that if the reigning President pleases his masters, he need be under no apprehensions of being turned out for any severities used to the people; for, though the Congress may not have influence enough to procure him the majority of the votes of the electoral college, yet they will always be able to prevent any other from having such a majority and to have him returned among the five highest, so that they may have the appointing of him themselves.

All these wise regulations prove to a demonstration that the grand Convention was infallible. The Congress having thus disentangled themselves from all popular checks and choices, and being supported by a well-disciplined army and active militia, will certainly command dread and respect abroad, obedience and submission at home. They will then look down with awful dignity and tremendous majesty, from the pinnacle of glory to which fortune has raised them, upon the insignificant creatures, their subjects, whom they have reduced to that state of vassalage and servile submission for which they were primarily destined by nature.

America will then be great among the nations and princess among the provinces. Her fleets will cover the deserts of the ocean and convert it into a popular city, and her invincible armies overturn the thrones of princes. The glory of Britain shall fall like lightning before her puissant arm when she arises to shake the nations and take vengeance on all who dare oppose her.

O! thou most venerable and august Congress! With what astonishing ideas my mind is ravished when I contemplate thy rising grandeur and anticipate thy future glory! Happy thy servants! Happy thy vassals! And happy thy slaves which sit under the shade of thy omnipotent authority and behold the glory of thy majesty! For such a state, who would not part with ideal blessings of liberty? Who would not cheerfully resign the nominal advantages of freedom? The dazzling splendor of Assyrian, Persian, Macedonian, and Roman greatness will then be totally eclipsed by the radiant blaze of this glorious Western luminary! These beautiful expressions, aristocracy and oligarchy, upon which the popular odium has fixed derision and contempt, will then resume their natural emphasis; their genuine signification will be perfectly understood, and no more perverted or abused.

ARISTOCROTIS

---

*The sober second thought of the people shall be law.*

FISHER AMES, speech in Congress, 1788

59.

## William Lenoir: The Interest of the Few and the Liberties of the People

*Another anti-Federalist, William Lenoir, speaking in the North Carolina Ratifying Convention, gave arguments similar to those of his colleagues against the Constitution. Attacking the aristocratic tendencies that he felt were inherent in the document, Lenoir gave a forceful rebuttal to North Carolina Federalists such as James Iredell. The following speech is extracted from the debates of the convention, which met in August and again in November of 1788. North Carolina finally ratified on November 21, 1789, becoming the twelfth state to do so.*

Source: Elliot, IV, pp. 201-206.

Mr. Chairman I conceive that I shall not be out of order to make some observations on this last part of the system, and take some retrospective view of some other parts of it. I think it not proper for our adoption as I consider that it endangers our liberties. When we consider this system collectively, we must be surprised to think that any set of men who were delegated to amend the Confederation should propose to annihilate it; for that and this system are utterly different and cannot exist together. It has been said that the fullest confidence should be put in those characters who formed this Constitution. We will admit them, in private and public transactions, to be good characters. But, sir, it appears to me and every other member of this committee that they exceeded their powers. Those gentlemen had no sort of power to form a new constitution altogether; neither had the citizens of this country such an idea in their view.

I cannot undertake to say what principles actuated them. I must conceive they were mistaken in their politics, and that this system does not secure the unalienable rights of freemen. It has some aristocratical and some monarchical features, and perhaps some of them intended the establishment of one of these governments. Whatever might be their intent, according to my views, it will lead to the most dangerous aristocracy that ever was thought of — an aristocracy established on a constitutional bottom! I conceive (and I believe most of this committee will likewise) that this is so dangerous that I should like as well to have no constitution at all. Their powers are almost unlimited.

A constitution ought to be understood by everyone. The most humble and trifling characters in the country have a right to know what foundation they stand upon. I confess I do not see the end of the powers here proposed, nor the reasons for granting them. The principal end of a constitution is to set forth what must be given up for the community at large, and to secure those rights which ought never to be infringed.

The proposed plan secures no right; or, if it does, it is in so vague and undeterminate a manner that we do not understand it.

My constituents instructed me to oppose the adoption of this Constitution. The principal reasons are as follow:

The right of representation is not fairly and explicitly preserved to the people, it being easy to evade that privilege as provided in this system, and the terms of election being too long. If our General Assembly be corrupt, at the end of the year we can make new men of them by sending others in their stead. It is not so here. If there be any reason to think that human nature is corrupt, and that there is a disposition in men to aspire to power, they may embrace an opportunity, during their long continuance in office, by means of their powers, to take away the rights of the people. The senators are chosen for six years, and two-thirds of them, with the president, have most extensive powers. They may enter into a dangerous combination. And they may be continually reelected. The president may be as good a man as any in existence, but he is but a man. He may be corrupt. He has an opportunity of forming plans dangerous to the community at large.

I shall not enter into the minutiae of this system, but I conceive, whatever may have been the intention of its framers, that it leads to a most dangerous aristocracy. It appears to me that, instead of securing the sovereignty of the states, it is calculated to melt them down into one solid empire. If the citizens of this state like a consolidated government, I hope they will have virtue enough to secure their rights. I am sorry to make use of the expression, but it appears to me to be a scheme to reduce this government to an aristocracy. It guarantees a republican form of government to the states; when all these powers are in Congress, it will only be a form. It will be past recovery, when Congress has the power of the purse and the sword. The power of the sword is in explicit terms given to it. The power of direct taxation gives the purse. They may prohibit the trial by jury, which is a most sacred and valuable right. There is nothing contained in this Constitution to bar them from it. The federal courts have also appellate cognizance of law and fact; the sole cause of which is to deprive the people of that trial, which it is optional in them to grant or not. We find no provision against infringement on the rights of conscience. Ecclesiastical courts may be established which will be destructive to our citizens. They may make any establishment they think proper. They have also an exclusive legislation in their ten miles square, to which may be added their power over the militia, who may be carried thither and kept there for life. Should any one grumble at their acts, he would be deemed a traitor, and perhaps taken up and carried to the exclusive legislation, and there tried without a jury.

We are told there is no cause to fear. When we consider the great powers of Congress, there is great cause of alarm. They can disarm the militia. If they were alarmed, they would be a resource against great oppressions. The laws of a great empire are difficult to be executed. If the laws of the Union were oppressive, they could not carry them into effect if the people were possessed of proper means of defense. It was cried out that we were in a most desperate situation, and that Congress could not discharge any of their most sacred contracts. I believe it to be the case. But why give more power than is necessary?

The men who went to the federal Convention went for the express purpose of amending the government, by giving it such additional powers as were necessary. If we should accede to this system, it may be thought proper by a few designing persons to destroy it, in a future age, in the same manner that the old system is laid aside. The Confederation was binding on all the states. It could not be destroyed but with the consent of all the states. There was an express article to that purpose. The men who were deputed to the Convention, instead of amending the old, as they were solely empowered and directed to do, proposed a new system. If the best characters departed so far from their authority, what may not be apprehended from others, who may be agents in the new government?

It is natural for men to aspire to power — it is the nature of mankind to be tyrannical; therefore, it is necessary for us to secure our rights and liberties as far as we can. But it is asked why we should suspect men who are to be chosen by ourselves, while it is their interest to act justly, and while men have self-interest at heart. I think the reasons which I have given are sufficient to answer that question. We ought to consider the depravity of human nature, the predominant thirst of power which is in the breast of everyone, the temptations our rulers may have, and the unlimited confidence placed in them by this system. These are the foundation of my fears. They would be so long in the general government that they would forget the grievances of the people of the states.

But it is said we shall be ruined if separated from the other states, which will be the case if we do not adopt. If so, I would put less confidence in those states. The states are all bound together by the Confederation, and the rest cannot break from us without violating the most solemn compact. If they break that, they will this.

But it is urged that we ought to adopt, because so many other states have. In those states which have patronized and ratified it, many great men have opposed it. The motives of those states I know not. It is the goodness of the Constitution we are to examine. We are to exercise our own judgments and act independently. And as I conceive we are not out of the Union, I hope this Constitution will not be adopted till amendments are made. Amendments are wished for by the other states.

It was urged here that the president should have power to grant reprieves and pardons. This power is necessary with proper restrictions. But the president may be at the head of a combination against the rights of the people, and may reprieve or pardon the whole. It is answered to this that he cannot pardon in cases of impeachment. What is the punishment in such cases? Only removal from office and future disqualification. It does not touch life or property. He has power to do away punishment in every other case. It is too unlimited, in my opinion. It may be exercised to the public good, but may also be perverted to a different purpose. Should we get those who will attend to our interest, we should be safe under any constitution, or without any. If we send men of a different disposition, we shall be in danger. Let us give them only such powers as are necessary for the good of the community.

The president has other great powers. He has the nomination of all officers, and a qualified negative on the laws. He may delay the wheels of government. He may drive the Senate to concur with his proposal. He has other extensive powers. There is no assurance of the liberty of the press. They may make it treason to write against the most arbitrary proceedings. They have power to control our elections as much as they please. It may be very oppressive on this state, and all the Southern states.

Much has been said of taxation and the inequality of it on the states. But nothing has been said of the mode of furnishing men. In what proportion are the states to furnish men? Is it in proportion to the whites and blacks? I presume it is. This state has 100,000 blacks. By this Constitution, 50 Negroes are equal to 30 whites. This state, therefore, besides the proportion she must raise for her white people, must furnish an additional number for her blacks, in proportion as 30 is to 50. Suppose there be a state to the northward that has 60,000 persons; this state must furnish as many men for the blacks as that whole state, exclusive of those she must furnish for her whites. Slaves, instead of strengthening, weaken the state; the regulation, therefore, will greatly injure it, and the other Southern states.

There is another clause which I do not, perhaps, understand. The power of taxation seems to me not to extend to the lands of the people of the United States; for the rule of taxation is the number of the whites and three-fifths of the blacks. Should it be the case that they have no power of taxing this object, must not direct taxation be hard upon the greater part of this state? I am not confident that it is so, but it appears to me that they cannot lay taxes on this object. This will oppress the poor people who have large families of whites, and no slaves to assist them in cultivating the soil, although the taxes are to be laid in proportion to three-fifths of the Negroes, and all the whites.

Another disadvantage to this state will arise from it. This state has made a contract with its citizens. The public securities and certificates I allude to. These may be negotiated to men who live in other states. Should that be the case, these gentlemen will have demands against this state on that account. The Constitution points out the mode of recovery; it must be in the federal court only, because controversies between a state and the citizens of another state are cognizable only in the federal courts. They cannot be paid but in gold and silver. Actual specie will be recovered in that court. This would be an intolerable grievance without remedy.

I wish not to be so understood as to be so averse to this system as that I should object to all parts of it, or attempt to reflect on the reputation of those gentlemen who formed it; though it appears to me that I would not have agreed to any proposal but the amendment of the Confederation. If there were any security for the liberty of the people, I would, for my own part, agree to it. But in this case, as millions yet unborn are concerned and deeply interested in our decision, I would have the most positive and pointed security. I shall, therefore, hope that, before this house will proceed to adopt this Constitution, they will propose such amendments to it as will make it complete; and when amendments are adopted, perhaps I will be as ready to accede to it as any man. One thing will make it aristocratical. Its powers are very indefinite. There was a very necessary clause in the Confederation, which is omitted in this system. That was a clause declaring that every power, etc., not given to Congress was reserved to the states. The omission of this clause makes the power so much greater. Men will naturally put the fullest construction on the power given them. Therefore, lay all restraint on them, and form a plan to be understood by every gentleman of this committee and every individual of the community.

60.

# Consideration of a Bill of Rights

*The support of the New York Ratifying Convention was given to the new government on July 26, 1788, leaving only two states, North Carolina and Rhode Island, left to approve the Constitution. The framers were confident that the government would surely succeed, but their work was still not completed. The Federalists had won several key states with the promise that amendments concerning individual liberties would be presented to the first session of Congress. On July 31, 1788, Thomas Jefferson wrote a letter to his friend James Madison, praising the document as well as enumerating the points that he felt should be included in a bill of rights. Madison was not eager to have qualifying amendments added to the Constitution he had done so much to create; he had fought diligently for its ratification without such limitations. However, a letter written on October 17, 1788, to Jefferson, indicates that Madison was becoming convinced that he should support a bill of rights. The following selection contains a portion of this correspondence.*

Source: Ford, V, pp. 43-48. *Madison Letters,* I, pp. 421-427.

I.

## Thomas Jefferson to James Madison

I sincerely rejoice at the acceptance of our new Constitution by nine states. (It is a good canvas on which some strokes only want retouching.) What these are, I think are sufficiently manifested by the general voice from North to South which calls for a Bill of Rights. It seems pretty generally understood that this should go to juries, habeas corpus, standing armies, printing, religion, and monopolies. I conceive there may be difficulty in finding general modification of these suited to the habits of all the states. But if such cannot be found then it is better to establish trials by jury, the right of habeas corpus, freedom of the press, and freedom of religion in all cases, and to abolish standing armies in time of peace, and monopolies, in all cases, than not to do it in any. The few cases wherein these things may do evil cannot be weighed against the multitude wherein the want of them will do evil. In disputes between a foreigner and a native, a trial by jury may be improper. But if this exception cannot be agreed to, the remedy will be to model the jury by giving the *medietas linguae* [jury half aliens, half citizens] in civil as well as criminal cases.

Why suspend the habeas corpus in insurrections and rebellions? The parties who may be arrested may be charged instantly with a well-defined crime. Of course the judge will remand them. If the public safety requires that the government should have a man imprisoned on less probable testimony in those than in other emergencies, let him be taken and tried, retaken and retried, while the necessity continues, only giving him redress against the government for damages. Examine the history of England: see how few of the cases of the suspension of the habeas corpus law have been worthy of that suspension. They have been either real treasons, wherein the parties might as well have been charged at once, or sham plots, where it was shameful they should ever have been suspected. Yet for the few cases wherein the suspension of the habeas corpus has done real good, that operation is now become habitual, and the minds of the nation almost prepared to live under its constant suspension.

A declaration that the federal government will never restrain the presses from printing anything they please will not take away the liability of the printers for false facts printed. The declaration that religious faith shall be unpunished does not give impunity to criminal acts dictated by religious error.

The saying there shall be no monopolies lessens the incitements to ingenuity which is spurred on by the hope of a monopoly for a limited time, as of fourteen years; but the benefit even of limited monopolies is too doubtful to be opposed to that of their general suppression.

If no check can be found to keep the number of standing troops within safe bounds while they are tolerated as far as necessary, abandon them altogether, discipline well the militia, and guard the magazines with them. More than magazine guards will be useless if few, and dangerous if many. No European nation can ever send against us such a regular army as we need fear, and it is hard if our militia are not equal to those of Canada or Florida. My idea then is that, though proper exceptions to these general rules are desirable and probably practicable, yet, if the exceptions cannot be agreed on, the establishment of the rules in all cases will do ill in very few. I hope, therefore, a Bill of Rights will be formed to guard the people against the federal government as they are already guarded against their state governments in most instances.

The abandoning the principle of necessary rotation in the Senate has, I see, been disapproved by many; in the case of the president, by none. I readily, therefore, suppose my opinion wrong, when opposed by the majority, as in the former instance, and the totality, as in the latter. In this, however, I should have done it with more complete satisfaction had we all judged from the same position.

II.

## Madison to Jefferson

The states which have adopted the new Constitution are all proceeding to the arrangements for putting it into action in March next. Pennsylvania alone has as yet actually appointed deputies, and that only for the Senate. My last mentioned that these were Mr. R. Morris and a Mr. McClay. How the other elections there and elsewhere will run is matter of uncertainty. The presidency alone unites the conjectures of the public. The vice-president is not at all marked out by the general voice. As the president will be from a Southern state, it falls almost of course for the other part of the continent to supply the next in rank. South Carolina may, however, think of Mr. Rutledge, unless it should be previously discovered that votes will be wasted on him.

The only candidates in the Northern states brought forward with their known consent are Hancock and Adams. Between these it seems probable the question will lie. Both of them are objectionable, and would, I think, be postponed by the general suffrage to several others, if they would accept the place. Hancock is weak, ambitious, a courtier of popularity, given to low intrigue, and lately reunited by a factious friendship with S. Adams. J. Adams has made himself obnoxious to many, particularly in the Southern states, by the political principles avowed in his book. Others, recollecting his cabal during the war against General Washington, knowing his extravagant self-importance, and considering his preference of an unprofitable dignity to some place of emolument better adapted to his private fortune as a proof of his having an eye to the presidency, conclude that he would not be a very cordial second to the General, and that an impatient ambition might even intrigue for a premature advancement. The danger would be the greater if factious characters, as may be the case, should get into the public councils. Adams, it appears, is not unaware of some of the obstacles to his wish, and through a letter to Smith has thrown out popular sentiments as to the proposed president.

The little pamphlet herewith enclosed will give you a collective view of the alterations which have been proposed by the state conventions for the new Constitution. Various and numerous as they appear, they certainly omit many of the true grounds of opposition. The articles relating to treaties, to paper money, and to contracts created more enemies than all the errors in the system, positive and negative, put together. It is true, nevertheless, that not a few, particularly in Virginia, have contended for the proposed alterations from the most honorable and patriotic motives; and that among the advocates for the Constitution there are some who wish for further guards to public liberty and individual rights. As far as these may consist of a constitutional declaration of the most essential rights, it is probable they will be added; though there are many who think such addition unnecessary, and not a few who think it misplaced in such a Constitution. There is scarce any point on which the party in opposition is so much divided as to its importance and its propriety.

My own opinion has always been in favor of a Bill of Rights, provided it be so framed as not to imply powers not meant to be included in the enumeration. At the same time I have never thought the omission a material defect, nor been anxious to supply it even by subsequent amendment for any other reason than that it is anxiously desired by others. I have favored it because I supposed it might be of use, and if properly executed could not be of disservice.

I have not viewed it in an important light: 1. Because I conceive that in a certain degree, though not in the extent argued by Mr. Wilson, the rights in question are reserved by the manner in which the federal powers are granted. 2. Because there is great reason to fear that a positive declaration of some of the most essential rights could not be obtained in the requisite latitude. I am sure that the rights of conscience in particular, if submitted to public definition, would be narrowed much more than they are likely ever to be by an assumed power. One of the objections in New England was that the Constitution, by prohibiting religious tests, opened a door for Jews, Turks, and infidels. 3. Because the limited powers of the federal government and the jealousy of the subordinate governments afford a security which has not existed in the case of the state governments and exists in no other. 4. Because experience proves the inefficacy of a Bill of Rights on those occasions when its control is most needed. Repeated violations of these parchment barriers have been committed by overbearing majorities in every state.

In Virginia I have seen the Bill of Rights violated in every instance where it has been opposed to a popular current. Notwithstanding the explicit provision contained in that instrument for the rights of conscience, it is well known that a religious establishment would have taken place in that state if the legislative majority had found, as they expected, a majority of the people in favor of the measure; and I am persuaded that if a majority of the people were now of one sect, the measure would still take place, and on narrower ground than was then proposed, notwithstanding the additional obstacle which the law has since created.

Wherever the real power in a government lies, there is the danger of oppression. In our governments the real power lies in the majority of the community, and the invasion of private rights is chiefly to be apprehended, not from acts of government contrary to the sense of its constituents but from acts in which the government is the mere instrument of the major number of the constituents. This is a truth of great importance but not yet sufficiently attended to; and is probably more strongly impressed on my mind by facts, and reflections suggested by them, than on yours, which has contemplated abuses of power issuing from a very different quarter. Wherever there is an interest and power to do wrong, wrong will generally be done, and not less readily by a powerful and interested party than by a powerful and interested prince. The difference, so far as it relates to the superiority of republics over monarchies, lies in the less degree of probability that interest may prompt abuses of power in the former than in the latter; and in the security in the former against an oppression of more than the smaller part of the society, whereas in the latter it may be extended in a manner to the whole.

The difference so far as it relates to the point in question, the efficacy of a Bill of Rights in controlling abuses of power, lies in this: that in a monarchy the latent force of the nation is superior to that of the sovereign, and a solemn charter of popular rights must have a great effect as a standard for trying the validity of public acts and a signal for rousing and uniting the superior force of the community. Whereas, in a popular government, the political and physical power may be considered as vested in the same hands, that is, in a majority of the people; and consequently the tyrannical will of the sovereign is not to be controlled by the dread of an appeal to any other force within the community.

What use then, it may be asked, can a Bill of Rights serve in popular governments? I answer: The two following, which, though less essential than in other governments, sufficiently recommend the precaution: 1. The political truths declared in that solemn manner acquire by degrees the character of fundamental maxims of free government, and, as they become incorporated with the national sentiment, counteract the impulses of interest and passion. 2. Although it be generally true, as above stated, that the danger of oppression lies in the interested majorities of the people rather than in usurped acts of the government, yet there may be occasions on which the evil may spring from the latter source; and, on such, a Bill of Rights will be a good ground for an appeal to the sense of the community. Perhaps, too, there may be a certain degree of danger that a succession of artful and ambitious rulers may, by gradual and well-timed advances, finally erect an independent government on the subversion of liberty. Should this danger exist at all, it is prudent to guard against it, especially when the precaution can do no injury.

At the same time I must own that I see no tendency in our governments to danger on that side. It has been remarked that there is a tendency in *all* governments to an augmentation of power at the expense of liberty. But the remark as usually understood does not appear to me well-founded. Power, when it has attained a certain degree of energy and independence, goes on generally to further degrees. But when below that degree, the direct tendency is to further degrees of relaxation, until the abuses of liberty beget a sudden transition to an undue degree of power. With this explanation the remark may be true; and in the latter sense only is it, in my opinion, applicable to the existing governments in America. It is a melancholy reflection that liberty should be equally exposed to danger whether the government have too much or too little power; and that the line which divides these extremes should be so inaccurately defined by experience.

Supposing a Bill of Rights to be proper, the articles which ought to compose it admit of much discussion. I am inclined to think that *absolute* restrictions in cases that are doubtful, or where emergencies may overrule them, ought to be avoided. The restrictions, however strongly marked on paper, will never be regarded when opposed to the decided sense of the public; and, after repeated violations, in extraordinary cases they will lose even their ordinary efficacy. Should a rebellion or insurrection alarm the people as well as the government, and a suspension of the habeas corpus be dictated by the alarm, no written prohibitions on earth would prevent the measure. Should an army in time of peace be gradually established in our neighborhood by Britain or Spain, declarations on paper would have as little effect in preventing a standing force for the public safety. The best security against these evils is to remove the pretext for them.

With regard to monopolies, they are justly classed among the greatest nuisances in government. But is it clear that, as encouragements to literary works and ingenious discoveries, they are not too valuable to be wholly renounced? Would it not suffice to reserve in all cases a right to the public to abolish the privilege at a price to be specified in the grant of it? Is there not, also, infinitely less danger of this abuse in our governments than in most others? Monopolies are sacrifices of the many to the few. Where the power is in the few it is natural for them to sacrifice the many to their own partialities and corruptions. Where the power, as with us, is in the many not in the few, the danger cannot be very great that the few will be thus favored. It is much more to be dreaded that the few will be unnecessarily sacrificed to the many.

---

61.

## An Orderly Transition to a New Government

*In the summer of 1788, the Congress of the Confederation prepared to set in motion the machinery of the new government. The second stage of the Revolution would be completed with the installation of the President and Congress under The Constitution of the United States. Officially, the dates for the presidential election and the first meeting of Congress were set by the following resolution of the Confederate Congress made on September 13, 1788. Mainly owing to bad roads and weather conditions, a quorum had not reached New York by the March date cited in the resolution. By April 6, 1789, enough Congressmen had assembled to begin preliminary business. George Washington was officially notified of his election on April 23; on April 30 he was sworn into office and the United States made an unprecedented orderly transition to its new federal government under the Constitution.*

Source: *Documents Illustrative of the Formation of the Union of the American States*, Charles C. Tansill, ed., Washington, 1927, p. 1062.

Congress assembled. Present: New Hampshire, Massachusetts, Connecticut, New York, New Jersey, Pennsylvania, Virginia, North Carolina, South Carolina, and Georgia; and from Rhode Island, Mr. Arnold, and from Delaware, Mr. Kearney. . . .

*Whereas* the Convention assembled in Philadelphia pursuant to the resolution of Congress of the 21st of February, 1787, did on the 17th of September in the same year report to the United States in Congress assembled a constitution for the people of the United States. Whereupon Congress on the 28th of the same September did resolve unanimously, "That the said report with the resolutions and letter accompanying the same be transmitted to the several legislatures in order to be submitted to a convention of delegates chosen in each state by the people thereof in conformity to the resolves of the convention made and provided in that case." And whereas the constitution so reported by the Convention and by Congress transmitted to the several legislatures has been ratified in the manner therein declared to be sufficient for the establishment of the same and such ratifications duly authenticated have been received by Congress and are filed in the Office of the Secretary; therefore, *Resolved* that the first Wednesday in January next be the day for appointing electors in the several states, which before the said day shall have ratified the said constitution; that the first Wednesday in February next be the day for the electors to assemble in their respective states and vote for a president; and that the first Wednesday in March next be the time and the present seat of Congress the place for commencing proceedings under the said constitution.

---

62.

## Rufus Putnam: On a Treaty with the Indians

*After the Revolution, the land in the Ohio Valley was primarily under the jurisdiction of the Confederation. The ailing financial situation of the Confederation presented an excellent opportunity for land speculation. Under the leadership of Rufus Putnam, a general in the Revolutionary War, the Ohio Land Company was formed in 1786. Negotiations with Congress were to be carried on by Reverend Manasseh Cutler, an Ipswich clergyman who, through a questionable deal with the secretary of the Board of Treasury, secured the authorization of Congress to sell large areas of land to private companies. During the first year, the company attracted fewer settlers than it had hoped; rumors of Indian attacks had reached the ears of many potential buyers. In a letter to Cutler on May 16, 1788, Putnam stressed the urgency of a treaty with the Indians, hoping thereby to encourage further migration to the Ohio Valley area.*

Source: William Parker Cutler and Julia Perkins Cutler, *Life, Journal, and Correspondence of Rev. Manasseh Cutler,* Cincinnati, 1888, Vol. I, pp. 376-380.

Your favor of the 20th of February came to hand a few days since, and I find by its contents that Mr. Plummer has alarmed the people with respect to the Indians very much. And perhaps he is not to blame; for had I given heed to the opinion, at least the pretended opinion, of people at Pittsburgh and vicinity, I certainly should not have come down without an army for my protection. However, we made no delay on that account. That the Indians are dissatisfied, on account of Congress or the commissioners of Congress (at the several treaties which have been held with them) considering these lands as the property of the United States, in consequence of the part the Indians took in the war and the treaty of peace with Great Britain, is true. They have told Congress so in a spirited, manly letter addressed to that honorable body by Joseph Brant, in which he assures them that unless these wrongs are redressed and the lands fairly purchased, the Indians will certainly go to war (and I believe they will be as good as their word).

In consequence of this application of Brant, Congress has promised them a treaty, which was to have been held about this time; but I am told that the Indians have informed Governor St. Clair that they are to hold a great council among themselves about the middle of June, near Sandusky. From these circumstances, it is probable Governor St. Clair will not be able to see them till July, when I have no doubt everything will be settled to general satisfaction. At present, we do not think ourselves perfectly secure from them on account of a few lawless bandits made up of Mingos, Shawnees, and Cherokees, who reside at present on the waters of the Scioto. These are a set of thievish, murdering rascals; but from any other quarter we are under no apprehension at present. The Delawares and Wyandots visit us almost every day and appear very friendly; relying on it, as I believe, that Governor St. Clair, at the treaty, will have power and inclination to do them complete justice.

You wish to be informed if it will be prudent for families to move on in the spring and summer? I answer, by all means; for let the treaty end how it may, the sooner they come on the better; the sooner they get in a way of cultivating their lands and raising provisions, the better. The constant coming in of new settlers, and the troops which will be kept in the country by Congress, will give us a good market for many years; and these little skulking parties of Indians, if they are never won over to be our friends, can never do us any considerable injury. On the other hand, should there be a general Indian war, this will be a place of general rendezvous for an army. So that, in all human probability, the settlement can never fail of the protection of government.

It will be inquired, I presume, why we laid out some of the 8-acre lots so far from the city plat? To which I answer, 4,000 acres for city and commons take up a large tract of land. In Township No. 2, and 8th Range, the lots No. 8, 16, and 29 are public lots, which otherwise would have been laid out into 8-acre lots. Again, it was the original design to have them as nearly equal as possible in quality and situation, and so situated that the produce might, in case of necessity, be brought to the city. This, I conceive, may better be done ten miles by water than two by land, where the country is more than commonly hilly (which is ever the case near large rivers) and roads to make.

But you, perhaps, will inquire why all the margins of the River Ohio and Muskingum are not taken up so far as we extend these lots on either of them? Answer: They are so where there is any considerable body of interval or second bottom bordering on them. In some places, the hill shuts down to the river bank; in others, the bottom is narrow and ought to be laid out with the adjoining hill country. But another circumstance, attended to, will perhaps satisfy you and every other person. It will be only on extraordinary occasions, and which I hope will never happen, that it will be necessary to bring the produce of any lots that lie remote to the city of Adelphia. Nothing but a general war, and a war in which we must be very unfortunate, can prevent . . . settlements being established, in the course of one year, which are so situated in point of distance, and suitable grounds for building and other purposes, as will undoubtedly recommend them to their present owners, or others, to erect houses on immediately, which it will be prudent to stockade for a few years. . . .

It would give you pain, and me no pleasure, to detail our march over the mountains, or our delays afterward on account of bad weather, or other misfortunes. I shall only observe that I arrived at Major White's party on the Youghiogheny River the 14th of February. No boats built, boards or planks in readiness, or person capable of building a canoe, much less a boat, among the party. Mill frozen up and no boards to be had; he had, however, three canoes, such as they were, on the stocks; and five of his men sick with the smallpox, which they took by inoculation.

On the 1st day of April, in the afternoon, we left the Youghiogheny and arrived at Fort Harmar on the 7th, being obliged to stop at Harmon and Buffalo Creek on our way to take in provisions, etc. Our whole fleet consisted of the Union galley of forty-five tons burden, designed to pass and repass between this and Buffalo, or Short Creek, to bring down settlers; the Adelphia ferryboat, burden, three tons, for the use of the settlers at the Post; and three log canoes of different sizes.

On our arrival here the surveys commenced immediately; but a series of rains, and being obliged to survey so much more land than was expected in order to obtain lands suitable to our purpose, prevented our completing our plans till yesterday. The city lots will be ready to draw by the first Wednesday of July, as proposed at the meeting in Providence, but the others will not. It was General Knox's advice that I shall not presume to survey more till after the treaty.

The men have most of them been employed these ten days in clearing land for themselves, which they will plant next week, and the rest are doing the same for the company. Several proprietors have come on this spring and are doing the same. They all work on the city plat, and the whole quantity of corn planted, I expect, will be about 100 acres. As soon as this work is over, we shall turn our attention to building houses and boats suitable to prosecute the surveys with.

Independence National Historical Park

Portrait of Rufus Putnam, artist unknown

As to the mode of conveying letters, I have hit on none yet to convey from this place to Philadelphia, or from thence to this place, that could be depended upon. Perhaps we may find out some way in the course of the summer.

The expense has risen much beyond our calculation, and if the treaty concludes favorably, the surveys must no doubt be pushed till late in the fall; of consequence, more money will be wanted. But I expect Generals Parsons and Varnum will be on soon; [I] will therefore not propose anything at present on that subject.

The men are generally in good health and I believe much pleased with the country; that I am so myself, you may rest assured.

The accounts of Moulton and others I will attend to. The winter in this quarter was severe indeed, the most so known for many years. But I can only add, the situation of the city plat is the most delightful of any I ever saw, and those traces of ancient walls, mounds, etc., are truly surprising. Mr. Sargent's painting gives but a faint idea of what is to be seen on the spot.

63.

## Benjamin Rush: Plan of a Federal University

*During the 1700s, several schools for higher education were formed under the auspices of local religious groups, colonial governments, and private donors. However, a number of men, including members of the Philadelphia convention and several of the first Presidents, envisioned a national university that would bring together young persons from all parts of the country in the common pursuit of learning. On October 29, 1788, Benjamin Rush published an essay that advocated a federal university in which education would be "adapted to the new and peculiar situation of our country." Excerpts from this article, which first appeared in the* Federal Gazette, *signed "Citizen of Pennsylvania," are reprinted here.*

Source: *American Museum,* October 1788.

"Your government cannot be executed. It is too extensive for a republic. It is contrary to the habits of the people," say the enemies of the Constitution of the United States. However opposite to the opinions and wishes of a majority of the citizens of the United States these declarations and predictions may be, the latter will certainly be verified unless the people are prepared for our new form of government by an education adapted to the new and peculiar situation of our country. To effect this great and necessary work, let one of the first acts of the new Congress be to establish, within the district to be allotted for them, a federal university, into which the youth of the United States shall be received after they have finished their studies and taken their degrees in the colleges of their respective states. In this university, let those branches of literature only be taught which are calculated to prepare our youth for civil and public life. These branches should be taught by means of lectures, and the following arts and sciences should be the subjects of them.

1. The principles and forms of government, applied in a particular manner to the explanation of every part of the Constitution and laws of the United States, together with the laws of nature and nations, which last should include everything that relates to peace, war, treaties, ambassadors, and the like.

2. History, both ancient and modern, and chronology.

3. Agriculture in all its numerous and extensive branches.

4. The principles and practice of manufactures.

5. The history, principles, objects, and channels of commerce.

6. Those parts of mathematics which are necessary to the division of property, to finance, and to the principles and practice of war, for there is too much reason to fear that war will continue, for some time to come, to be the un-Christian mode of deciding disputes between Christian nations.

7. Those parts of natural philosophy and chemistry which admit of an application to agriculture, manufactures, commerce, and war.

8. Natural history, which includes the history of animals, vegetables, and fossils.

To render instruction in these branches of science easy, it will be necessary to establish a museum, as also a garden, in which not only all the shrubs, etc., but all the forest trees of the United States should be cultivated. . . .

9. Philology, which should include, besides rhetoric and criticism, lectures upon the construction and pronunciation of the English language. Instruction in this branch of literature will become the more necessary in America as our intercourse must soon cease with the bar, the stage, and the pulpits of Great Britain, from whence we received our knowledge of the pronunciation of the English language. Even modern English books should cease to be the models of style in the United States. The present is the age of simplicity in writing in America. The turgid style of Johnson, the purple glare of Gibbon, and even the studied and thickset metaphors of Junius, are all equally unnatural and should not be admitted into our country.

The cultivation and perfection of our language becomes a matter of consequence when viewed in another light. It will probably be spoken by more people in the course of two or three centuries than ever spoke any one language at one time since the creation of the world. When we consider the influence which the prevalence of only two languages, viz., the English and the Spanish, in the extensive regions of North and South America will have upon manners, commerce, knowledge, and civilization, scenes of human happiness and glory open before us, which elude from their magnitude the utmost grasp of the human understanding.

10. The German and French languages should be taught in this university. The many excellent books which are written in both these languages upon all subjects, more especially upon those which relate to the advancement of national improvements of all kinds, will render a knowledge of them an essential part of the education of a legislator of the United States.

11. All those athletic and manly exercises should likewise be taught in the university which are calculated to impart health, strength, and elegance to the human body.

To render the instruction of our youth as easy and extensive as possible in several of the above-mentioned branches of literature, let four young men of good education and active minds be sent abroad at the public expense to collect and transmit to the professors of the said branches all the improvements that are daily made in Europe, in agriculture, manufactures, and commerce, and in the art of war and practical government. This measure is rendered the more necessary from the distance of the United States from Europe, by which means the rays of knowledge strike the United States so partially that they can be brought to a useful focus only by employing suitable persons to collect and transmit them to our country. . . .

Besides sending four young men abroad to collect and transmit knowledge for the benefit of our country, two young men of suitable capacities should be employed at the public expense in exploring the vegetable, mineral, and animal productions of our country, in procuring histories and samples of each of them, and in transmitting them to the professor of natural history. It is in consequence of the discoveries made by young gentlemen employed for these purposes that Sweden, Denmark, and Russia have extended their manufactures and commerce, so as to rival in both the oldest nations in Europe.

Let the Congress allow a liberal salary to the principal of this university. Let it be his business to govern the students, and to inspire them by his conversation and by occasional public discourses with federal and patriotic sentiments. Let this principal be a man of extensive education, liberal manners, and dignified deportment.

Let the professors of each of the branches that have been mentioned have a moderate salary of £150 or £200 a year, and let them depend upon the number of their pupils to supply the deficiency of their maintenance from their salaries. Let each pupil pay for each course of lectures two or three guineas.

Let the degrees conferred in this university receive a new name that shall designate the design of an education for civil and public life.

In thirty years after this university is established, let an act of Congress be passed to prevent any person being chosen or appointed into power or office who has not taken a degree in the federal university. We require certain qualifications in lawyers, physicians, and clergymen before we commit our property, our lives, or our souls to their care. We even refuse to commit the charge of a ship to a pilot who cannot produce a certificate of his education and knowledge in his business. Why then should we commit our country, which includes liberty, property, life, wives, and children, to men who cannot produce vouchers of their qualifications for the important trust? We are restrained from injuring ourselves by employing quacks in law; why should we not be restrained in like manner, by law, from employing quacks in government?

Should this plan of a federal university, or one like it, be adopted, then will begin the golden age of the United States. While the business of education in Europe consists in lectures upon the ruins of Palmyra and the antiquities of Herculaneum, or in disputes about Hebrew points, Greek particles, or the accent and quantity of the Roman language, the youth of America will be employed in acquiring those branches of knowledge which increase the conveniences of life, lessen human misery, improve our country, promote population, exalt the human understanding, and establish domestic, social, and political happiness.

Let it not be said "that this is not the time for such a literary and political establishment. Let us first restore public credit by funding or paying our debts, let us regulate our militia, let us build a navy, and let us protect and extend our commerce. After this, we shall have leisure and money to establish a university for the purposes that have been mentioned." This is false reasoning. We shall never restore public credit, regulate our militia, build a navy, or revive our commerce until we remove the ignorance and prejudices and change the habits of our citizens; and this can never be done till we inspire them with federal principles, which can only be effected by our young men meeting and spending two or three years together in a national university, and afterward disseminating their knowledge and principles through every county, township, and village of the United States.

Till this is done, senators and representatives of the United States, you will undertake to make bricks without straw. Your supposed union in Congress will be a rope of sand. The inhabitants of Massachusetts began the business of government by establishing the University of Cambridge, and the wisest kings in Europe have always found their literary institutions the surest means of establishing their power as well as of promoting the prosperity of their people.

These hints for establishing the Constitution and happiness of the United States upon a permanent foundation are submitted to the friends of the federal government in each of the states by a private

Citizen of Pennsylvania

64.

## Philip Freneau: "The Indian Student"

*Freneau, the "poet of the American Revolution," was best known during his own time for his patriotic writings in behalf of independence and for his vitriolic attacks on Tories and the British generally. However, he is known today for his lifelong search for an unmistakably American idiom in verse, a search that failed in all but a few poems. "The Indian Student" was one of his successes; in it he managed to satirize the efforts of learned Easterners to civilize the primitive, savage Indians of the West, at the same time that he expressed the student's — and probably Freneau's own — special feeling for "Nature's ancient forests" and for his "native shades." The poem was not new in tone, however; the cults of nature and of the noble savage were well established both in England and in America by the last third of the eighteenth century.*

Source: *The Miscellaneous Works of Mr. Philip Freneau, etc., etc.,* Philadelphia, 1788.

### THE INDIAN STUDENT

From Susquehanna's utmost springs
Where savage tribes pursue their game,
His blanket tied with yellow strings,
A shepherd of the forest came.

Not long before, a wandering priest
Expressed his wish, with visage sad —
"Ah, why (he cried) in Satan's waste,
Ah, why detain so fine a lad?

In Yanky land there stands a town
Where learning may be purchased low —
Exchange his blanket for a gown,
And let the lad to college go."

From long debate the council rose,
And viewing *Shalum's* tricks with joy
To *Harvard Hall,* o'er wastes of snows,
They sent the copper-colored boy.

One generous chief a bow supplied,
This gave a shaft, and that a skin;
The feathers, in vermilion dyed,
Himself did from a turkey win.

Thus dressed so gay, he took his way
O'er barren hills, alone, alone!
His guide a star, he wandered far,
His pillow every night a stone.

At last he came, with leg so lame,
Where learned men talk heathen Greek,
And Hebrew lore is gabbled o'er,
To please the Muses, twice a week.

Awhile he writ, awhile he read,
Awhile he learned the grammar rules —
An Indian savage so well bred,
Great credit promised to their schools.

Some thought he would in *law* excel,
Some said in *physic* he would shine;
And one that knew him passing well,
Beheld in him a sound Divine.

But those of more discerning eye
Even then could other prospects show,
And saw him lay his *Virgil* by
To wander with his dearer bow.

The tedious hours of study spent,
The heavy-molded lecture done,
He to the woods a-hunting went,
But sighed to see the setting sun.

No mystic wonders fired his mind;
He sought to gain no learned degree,
But only sense enough to find
The squirrel in the hollow tree.

The shady bank, the purling stream,
The woody wild his heart possessed,
The dewy lawn his morning dream
In Fancy's gayest colors dressed.

"And why (he cried) did I forsake
My native wood for gloomy walls;
The silver stream, the limpid lake
For musty books and college halls.

A little could my wants supply —
Can wealth and honor give me more;
Or will the sylvan god deny
The humble treat he gave before?

Let seraphs reach the bright abode,
And heaven's sublimest mansions see —
I only bow to Nature's God —
The Land of Shades will do for me.

These dreadful secrets of the sky
Alarm my soul with chilling fear —
Do planets in their orbits fly,
And is the earth, indeed, a sphere?

Let planets still their aims pursue,
And comets round creation run—
In Him my faithful friend I view,
The image of my God — the Sun.

Where Nature's ancient forests grow,
And mingled laurel never fades,
My heart is fixed; and I must go
To die among my native shades."

He spoke and to the western springs
(His gown discharged, his money spent),
His blanket tied with yellow strings,
The shepherd of the forest went.

Returning to the rural reign
The Indians welcomed him with joy;
The council took him home again,
And blessed the copper-colored boy.

65.

# Benjamin Rush: Recommendations for Publishing a Newspaper

*In the summer of 1788, Andrew Brown announced that his paper, the* Federal Gazette, *which he had published for a short time during the previous spring, would be revived. The first issue appeared on October 1, 1788, and included the following letter from Brown's friend, Benjamin Rush. The letter was anonymously signed "A Friend to the Union," and contained suggested guidelines for the content and context of an "innocent, useful, and entertaining" paper for Americans.*

Source: *Federal Gazette,* October 1, 1788.

I have read your proposals for printing a newspaper and feel a disposition to subscribe for it, but shall delay to do so until I am satisfied that you conduct it upon the principles you have promised. In the meanwhile, I shall take the liberty of suggesting a few directions for conducting a paper in such a manner as to make it innocent, useful, and entertaining.

1. Consider that we live 3,000 miles from the nations of Europe and that we have but little interest in their domestic parties or national quarrels. The less, therefore, you publish of them, the better.

2. Avoid filling your paper with anecdotes of British vices and follies. What have the citizens of the United States to do with the duels, the elopements, the criminal consortings, the kept mistresses, the murders, the suicides, the thefts, the forgeries, the boxing matches, the wagers for eating, drinking, and walking, etc., etc., of the people of Great Britain? Such stuff, when circulated through our country by means of a newspaper, is calculated to destroy that delicacy in the mind which is one of the safeguards of the virtue of a young country.

3. If any of the above-named vices should ever be committed in the United States, the less that is said about it the better. What have the citizens of Philadelphia to do with the criminal amours of Mr. M —— of Boston? The frequent and minute histories of such gross vices take off from the horror they would otherwise excite in the mind.

4. Never suffer your paper to be a vehicle of private scandal or of personal disputes. If the faults of public officers are exposed, let it be done with decency. No man has a right to attack the vices or follies of private citizens in a newspaper. Should you, under a false idea of preserving the liberty of the press, lay open the secrets of families and thereby wound female honor and delicacy, I hope our legislature will repeal the law that relates to assault and battery, and that the *liberty of the bludgeon* will be as sacred and universal in Pennsylvania as your *liberty of the press.*

5. Never publish an article in your paper that you would not wish your wife and

daughter (if you have any) should read or understand.

6. The less you publish about yourself the better. What have your readers to do with the neglects or insults that are offered to you by your fellow citizens? If a printer offends you, attack him in your paper, because he can defend himself with the same weapons with which you wound him. Type against type is fair play; but to attack a man who has no types nor printing press, or who does not know anything about the manual of using them, is cowardly in the highest degree. If you had been in twenty Bunker Hill battles instead of one, and had fought forty duels into the bargain, and were afterwards to revenge an affront upon a man who was not a printer in your newspaper, I would not believe that you possessed a particle of true courage. If such a person injures you, if you are a Christian, you may forgive him or sue him. If you are a savage, you may challenge him to fight a duel. And if you are a wild beast, you may tear him to pieces with your claws or kick him into the gutter.

7. Publish as often as you can obtain them an exact but short account of all the laws that are passed in all the states in the Union.

8. Furnish your customers if possible with the future debates of the Senate and House of Representatives of the United States.

9. Let the advancement of agriculture, manufactures, and commerce be the principal objects of your paper. A receipt to destroy the insects that feed upon turnips or to prevent the rot in sheep will be more useful in America than all the inventions for destroying the human species which so often fill the columns of European newspapers.

10. Publish a price-current and a state of the weather once a week; and once a month publish a list of all the deaths in the city and, if possible, the names of the diseases which occasioned them.

11. Do not neglect to insert a good essay or paragraph because it has been published in another newspaper. Extracts from modern publications upon useful subjects will at all times be acceptable to your readers.

Wishing you success in your undertaking only in proportion as you comply with these directions, I am your humble servant.

---

*The basis of our governments being the opinion of the people, the very first object should be to keep that right; and were it left to me to decide whether we should have a government without newspapers, or newspapers without a government, I should not hesitate a moment to prefer the latter. But I should mean that every man should receive those papers, and be capable of reading them.*

THOMAS JEFFERSON, letter to Colonel Edward Carrington, Paris, Jan. 16, 1787

66.

# Philip Freneau: The Past and Future of America

*Awed by the sea that, as a ship's captain, had been his home for many years, and by the splendors of America's lands, Philip Freneau romanticized the wonders of nature in his verse and prose. His concern for America's future and for the proper use of her natural resources — the resources of the land and the resources of men's minds — is reflected in the poetically written essay reprinted here in part. It is one of his patriotic contributions, a version of which appeared in the [Philadelphia]* Freeman's Journal, *a paper which Freneau had helped to publish between 1781 and 1783. He included this piece in his* Works *of 1788 under the title "The Philosopher of the Forest, Number X."*

Source: *The Miscellaneous Works of Mr. Philip Freneau, etc., etc.,* Philadelphia, 1788.

When nature first brought forth her infant, the American world, to enjoy the blessings and vivifying influences of the new created sun, as if conscious of the injuries this part of her creation was to suffer in future ages, she seemed particularly industrious, she took especial care to plant it in such a situation that many hundreds of centuries, an immense numbers of years, must elapse before it could possibly be discovered by the greedy natives of the eastern continent. "Till more than five thousand years have passed away (said she) it shall be inaccessible to all, except a few tribes of wandering Tartars, who from time to time may find their way thither by accident; literally the children of nature, wild as the wind and waves, and free as the animals that wander in the woody or the watery waste.

"The magnet alone," continued she, "shall enable the polished people of the eastern regions to discover and ravage the delectable lands I have formed in the opposite hemisphere; but that fossil, the invaluable lodestone, I will bury deep in the earth, unobserved its wonderful properties, till destiny and overruling fate, whose decrees no one can obviate, to my extremest grief, shall disclose it to the eye of avarice, ambition, and scrutinizing curiosity, and prompt a bold and daring Columbus to go in quest of those shores which it will not be in my power any longer to conceal."

So spoke Nature, the mother of all men and all things. In the meantime, ages rolled away. The Old World was peopled, unpeopled, and peopled again. Nations grew and flourished; they quarreled, they fought, and made peace; the four great monarchies succeeded each other, and fell again into decay, with their emperors, kings, and heroes, by far less durable than the lifeless marble columns which to this day mark the spot where their proudest capitals stood, or where their most famous battles were fought. These nations had their ages of politeness and barbarism, ignorance and science, misery and felicity. The follies of one age were acted over again by another, and each retired in its turn to the receptacles of silence, solitude, and darkness, to make room for succeeding generations.

But still America lay unknown and undiscovered, with all her islands, lakes, mountains, woods, plains, capacious harbors, and extended shores. Here the fish sported in the waters, undisturbed by hooks or nets, and the beasts of the forest enjoyed a secure repose. The poets of the Eastern world were in the meantime amusing their iron-hearted contemporaries with the fictions of a golden age: their fabulous Arcadias and Saturnian kingdoms, the ideas and notions of which must have owed their existence to the magic power of fancy alone, as they were wholly ignorant that the happy scenes, the innocent people, and pastoral ages of which they sung were at that moment realizing in another quarter of the globe, as yet unexplored and unknown. But, in process of time, as Nature had foreseen, this immense continent was at length raised from its long night of obscurity to the view of astonished nations. The inhabitants, like the country, seemed to be a new race of mortals; of different natures, ideas, and inclinations from those already known. They, also, gazed at the Europeans as a species of men differing in all respects from themselves, and, as far as regarded power and abilities, beings of a superior nature.

As the Europeans had the *means,* they of course conceived they had also the *right* to extirpate the innocent natives or drive them from the seacoasts to the interior parts of the country. The most specious pretext for this procedure seems to have been that the aborigines, or old inhabitants of America, did not sufficiently exert themselves to cultivate and improve the lands Nature had so liberally bestowed upon them. They were content with the productions of the simple genius of the earth and therefore were scarcely to be considered, according to these casuists, as legal proprietors of the immense territories that were now discovered.

Full of this idea, the Europeans flocked over and carefully examined the soil and productions of this newfound region. The best lands in North America were observed to lie in a temperate climate, and the newcomers soon found it their interest to cultivate and improve a soil that promised so much to the hand of industry. This roused the jealousy of the natives, who, unwilling to part with their pleasant abodes in the neighborhood of the sea, made many attempts (and sometimes not unsuccessfully) to annihilate these intruding strangers; but, as the several divisions of the Old World were at that time overstocked with inhabitants who constantly waged bloody wars with each other, notwithstanding the devastation and destruction of the human species occasioned thereby, it became absolutely necessary that many should emigrate. Providence gave permission to the arm of tyranny to expel thousands from their native lands; and many, in hopes of bettering their fortunes, submitted to become voluntary exiles.

Among the rest, Britain seemed very busy in virtually banishing and expelling her subjects to this remote region, who chose the northern coast, as knowing of no other asylum, excepting the grave, from the scourge of oppression. These, with a mixture of adventurers from various nations, at length humbled the savage tribes, and, by the mere force of industry, rendered a large proportion of this new country rich and flourishing. Britain soon cast a greedy eye upon the hard-earned possessions of this exiled race. She claimed them as subjects and took them under her protection; but at the same time said in her heart, "They shall hereafter be my slaves."

The children of the first emigrants immediately forgot the wrongs and injuries their forefathers had experienced and strictly united themselves to her, not as yet aware of her insidious designs. But Nature disregarded the connection; and whispering in the ear of Reason was heard to say, "The union cannot be lasting."

Her words have proved true: the people of the present age have seen the unnatural bonds in a moment dissolved, the union broken, and the connection at an end! Tell me, ye advocates for the dependence of these states upon the remote island of Britain; ye who assert that their happiness, their interest, and their glory is bound up in such a dependence, would you not esteem him a madman who should attempt amid the rage of contending winds and waves to bind together two bulky ships with a single thread of silk for their mutual safety? Just as reasonable is to suppose that America and the comparatively paltry and oppositely interested island of Britain can be happily united under one and the same sovereign.

What a spectacle of derision do the infatuated Britons now exhibit to the world in seriously attempting to subjugate a country to which Nature never gave them a shadow of right, and whose immense extent is, of itself, a standing and insurmountable obstacle to their success! An island, situated on the extremities of the ocean, on the verge of polar darkness, encumbered with rugged mountains, traversed by uncouth savages of horrid mien; barren heaths and useless, broken lands; a spot whose strength is merely artificial, sending out on impracticable conquests her fleets and armies, the flower of her youth and her ablest commanders, who, the moment they come within the vortex, the sphere of attraction of this huge, unwieldy body, the American world, are instantly swallowed up, like straws in a whirlpool, and irrecoverably lost!

What a nation of numerous and ingenious mechanics and manufacturers were the English only ten years ago! With the fleeces of their sheep they warmed the inhabitants of either frigid zone, the fine linens of their island were in high estimation in every clime. But in order to prosecute their mad scheme of reducing to unconditional submission or desolating a country naturally invincible, they have taken the weaver from the loom and the cobbler from his stall; the back of the peddler is released from its burden; and he who of yore was honestly and profitably occupied in fitting garments to the shoulders of his brethren, fancying himself on a sudden an Alexander or a Hernando Cortez — in search of glory, in quest of never-fading laurels, and for the support of his idol, Royalty, traverses the wide extended ocean, and leads to imaginary conquests and devastations in the transatlantic world!

It is not easy to conceive what will be the greatness and importance of North America in a century or two to come if the present fabric of Nature is upheld, and the people retain those bold and manly sentiments of freedom which actuate them at this day. Agriculture, the basis of a nation's greatness, will here, most probably, be advanced to its summit of perfection; and its attendant, commerce, will so agreeably and usefully employ mankind that wars will be forgotten; nations, by a free intercourse with this vast and fertile continent, and this continent with the whole world, will again become brothers after so many centuries of hatred and jealousy, and no longer treat each other as savages and monsters. The iron generation will verge to decay, and those days of felicity advance which have been so often wished for by all good men and which are so beautifully described by the prophetic sages of ancient times.

My friend the clergyman informs me that after passing a ridge of lofty mountains extending on the western frontiers of these republics, a new and most enchanting region opens, of inexpressible beauty and fertility. The lands are there of a quality far superior to those situated in the neighborhood of the seacoast. The trees of the forest are stately and tall; the meadows and pastures spacious, supporting vast herds of the native animals of the country, which own no master, nor expect their sustenance from the hands of men. The climate, he says, is moderate and agreeable; there the rivers no longer bend their courses eastward to the Atlantic, but, inclining to the west and south, and moving with a gentle current through the channels that Nature has opened, fall at length into that grand repository of a thousand streams, [the] Mississippi, who, collecting his waters derived from a source remote and unknown, rolls onward through the frozen regions of the north; and, stretching his prodigiously extended arms to the east and west, embraces those savage groves and dreary solitudes as yet uninvestigated by the traveler, unsung by the poet, and unmeasured by the chain of the geometrician; till uniting with the Ohio and turning due south, receiving afterward the Missouri and a hundred others, this prince of rivers, in comparison of whom the Nile is but a small rivulet and the Danube a ditch, hurries with his immense flood of waters into the Mexican Sea, laving the shores of many fertile countries in his passage inhabited by savage nations, to this day almost unknown and without a name.

It is a standing rule in philosophy that Nature does nothing in vain. A potent nation, now at war with these republics, has proclaimed her resolution to *lay waste what she cannot reclaim by conquest, and schemes are projected to oblige such to reemigrate to Europe as shall escape the fury of the destroyers.* But if this New World was not to become at some time or another the receptacle of numerous civilized nations, from one extremity to the other, for what visible purpose could Nature have formed these vast lakes in the bosom of her infant empire, which surprise and astonish the traveler, who, leaving the salt ocean behind him to the east, finds, unexpectedly, new oceans of a prodigious extent in those tracts where Fancy would have surmised nothing but endless hills, inhospitable wilds, and dreary forests existed?

These lakes having, severally, a communication with each other, and lastly with the Atlantic Ocean, toward the northeast, approaching also very near, by the west, to several of the navigable branches of the Mississippi, from an easy communication through a long tract of country, the intercourse between the various parts of which would, in future times, at least for the purposes of commerce, be extremely difficult and laborious were it not for this continuation of waters that for ages have been waiting to receive the bark of traffic, urged forward by the sail or the stroke of the springy oar; as the soil bordering thereon has no less impatiently expected the operations of the industrious plow.

During a very considerable part of the year the southwest wind blows unremittedly on the face of this serpentine river, the Ohio, and even at other times the current of air is more prevalent in that direction than in any other; which, being directly opposed to the course of the stream moving at the rate of one mile hourly, is it not evident that Providence, Nature, or Fate has so ordered this matter that the commercial vessels hereafter sailing northward thereon may have favorable gales to make an answerable progress against a current that is still contrary and the same; and that those bound to the south may have the assistance of the ebbing stream to combat the adverse winds with more advantage?

It would carry me far beyond the bounds of a short essay to point out every particular indicating the future importance of this newly discovered country; and it is really astonishing, as I intimated before, that a nation endued with the divine gift of reason, if they would exercise that gift, should at this day entertain a serious thought of reducing, by force of arms, this immense continent to their absolute sway — a continent beholding two hemispheres, abounding with a hardy and active race of inhabitants, producing everything within itself proper for its own maintenance and defense; a continent extending through such a number of degrees of latitude and longitude, from the limits of the torrid zone, the circle of the northern tropic, to those frozen streams and icy mountains, where, chilled with the extreme rigors of perpetual winter, Nature seems to have lost her vegetative powers; and where a few of the human race, the natives of the polar regions that are found to exist in those unjoyous climes, bear so little resemblance in the features of the mind to what the civilized world calls a *man* that they scarcely deserve the name.

Stokes Collection, New York Public Library

**Inauguration of Washington; engraving by Amos Doolittle**

# THE NEW GOVERNMENT

On April 30, 1789, George Washington took the oath of office as first President of the United States. His inauguration marked the beginning of what was at the time an uncertain experiment in federal government.

The Constitution at last offered a framework for a functioning national government, but it was a spare document. It was carefully worded and unequivocal on matters of principle, but it left much of the specific detail for Congress to work out. The first deliberations of Congress, whose membership included many participants in the Constitutional Convention, often are described as a second Constitutional Convention.

In addition, as each man assumed his elected office or appointment in the various branches of government, there were few precedents to follow and few clear lines of responsibility. However, the demands for establishing the nation's credit, setting up a system of courts, and establishing international relations forced the government to forge ahead under whatever leadership revealed itself, chiefly that of Hamilton and Madison.

# Washington Takes Office

## By the United States in Congreſs aſſembled,

SEPTEMBER 13, 1788.

WHEREAS the Convention aſſembled in Philadelphia, purſuant to the Reſolution of Congreſs of the 21ſt February, 1787, did, on the 17th of September in the ſame year, report to the United States in Congreſs aſſembled, a Conſtitution for the People of the United States; whereupon Congreſs, on the 28th of the ſame September, did reſolve unanimouſly, "That the ſaid report, with the Reſolutions and Letter accompanying the ſame, be tranſmitted to the ſeveral Legiſlatures, in order to be ſubmitted to a Convention of Delegates choſen in each State by the people thereof, in conformity to the Reſolves of the Convention made and provided in that caſe:" And whereas the Conſtitution ſo reported by the Convention, and by Congreſs tranſmitted to the ſeveral Legiſlatures, has been ratified in the manner therein declared to be ſufficient for the eſtabliſhment of the ſame, and ſuch Ratifications duly authenticated have been received by Congreſs, and are filed in the Office of the Secretary--- therefore,

RESOLVED, That the firſt Wedneſday in January next, be the day for appointing Electors in the ſeveral States, which before the ſaid day ſhall have ratified the ſaid Conſtitution; that the firſt Wedneſday in February next, be the day for the Electors to aſſemble in their reſpective States, and vote for a Preſident; and that the firſt Wedneſday in March next, be the time, and the preſent Seat of Congreſs the place for commencing Proceedings under the ſaid Conſtitution.

National Archives

National Archives

Copy

New York, 6th April, 1789.

Sir,

I have the honor to transmit to your Excellency the information of your unanimous election to the office of President of the United States of America. Suffer me, Sir, to indulge the hope, that so auspicious a mark of public confidence will meet your approbation, and be considered as a sure pledge of the affection and support you are to expect from a free and an enlightened People.

I am, Sir, with sentiments of respect, Yr. obt. hble. servt.

J L

His Excellency George Washington, Esqr.

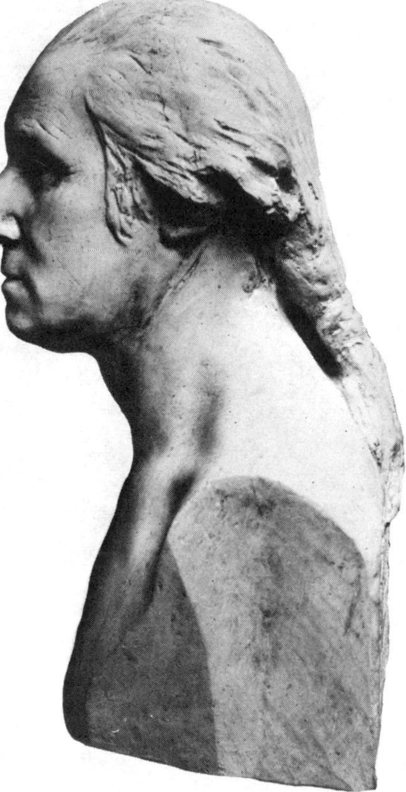

New York Historical Society

**(Top left) Call for the first presidential election; (bottom left) letter to Washington informing him of his election as president; (above) profile view of Houdon's bust of Washington**

Library of Congress

The architects of the new government considered Washington the only well-known public figure who was both uncontroversial and of sufficient stature to assume the presidency. The electors, sent by the states, chose Washington unanimously and named John Adams as vice-president.

Washington had some doubts about his political skill and proceeded cautiously in office. He knew that each of his decisions established a precedent that had implications for future interpretations of the president's role. Then as now, the question of the scope of executive power was a sensitive one. Also, each successive realization of the Constitutional outline aroused suspicion in the critics of federal power.

Library of Congress

Library of Congress

**Triumphal arches erected throughout the country to commemorate the inauguration of President Washington: (top) Grays Ferry near Philadelphia and Trenton (center) were along the route traveled by Washington from Mount Vernon to New York; (bottom) colonnade and arch in Boston**

Stokes Collection, New York Public Library

**(Above) A view of Broad Street and Wall Street, with Federal Hall, site of Washington's inauguration, in the background; (below) first page of Washington's inaugural address**

National Archives

Fellow Citizens of the Senate
and
of the House of Representatives.

Among the vicissitudes
incident to life, no event could have
filled me with greater anxieties than
that of which the notification was
transmitted by your order, and received on the fourteenth day of the
present month:— On the one hand,
I was summoned by my Country, whose
voice I can never hear but with venera
tion and love, from a retreat which
I had chosen with the fondest predilection, and, in my flattering hopes,
with an immutable decision, as the
asylum of my declining years: a re
treat which was rendered every day
more necessary as well as more dear
to me, by the addition of habit to inclination, and of frequent interruptions in my health to the gradual waste
committed on it by time.— On the
other hand, the magnitude and difficulty of the trust to which the voice
of my country called me, being sufficient to awaken in the wisest and most
experienced of her citizens, a distrust
ful

In a nation dedicated to the rule of law, an essential order of business was the organization of the formal judicial structure. The Constitution had established the Supreme Court, but the problem of lesser courts was left to Congress. The Judiciary Act of 1789 separated the state and federal court systems and divided the federal system into districts, each presided over by a justice of the Supreme Court.

The government also had to establish its foreign relations and improve its maritime position to insure domestic solvency and development. Thus, John Jay was sent to England in 1794 to negotiate various unresolved claims, but ministers of the new government still had little stature abroad, and the treaty Jay extracted from the British was considered an affront by critics in Congress. Though it arranged the return of frontier forts still held by the British and opened East Indian trade to Americans, the treaty left undefined the rights of American shipping and failed to compensate Americans for slaves taken by the British Army. Approval was finally secured in the Senate after a long delay, with the realization that it was the best arrangement possible. In 1795, Thomas Pinckney negotiated an important treaty with Spain that secured access to the port of New Orleans.

Yale Art Gallery

**John Rutledge, associate justice in the first Supreme Court appointed by Washington**

**Oliver Ellsworth, successor to Jay as chief justice of the Supreme Court**

Connecticut DAR

New York Historical Society

**John Jay, first chief justice of the Supreme Court, resigned in 1795**

**Thomas Pinckney, minister to Great Britain, 1792-96, and envoy to Spain, 1795**

Yale Art Gallery

Independence National Historical Park

**Alexander Hamilton, first secretary of the treasury; portrait by C. W. Peale**

Independence National Historical Park

**Thomas Jefferson, Washington's first secretary of state; portrait by C. W. Peale**

**General Henry Knox, secretary of war; portrait by Gilbert Stuart**

City of Boston; on deposit at the Museum of Fine Arts

**Edmund Randolph, the first attorney general**

Virginia State Library

# The Cabinet

New York Public Library

**(Above) The first presidential mansion, in New York City, occupied by Washington until 1790; (below) the executive mansion during the time that Philadelphia was the nation's capital**

The most critical problems facing the administration were financial: lack of revenue and huge debts. This, plus Hamilton's natural forcefulness, made the secretary of the treasury the central figure in the Cabinet. Hamilton's basic position was that the government could establish its credit standing, domestic and foreign, only by honoring its debts, and that this could best be done by applying a fixed portion of revenues to payment of debt interest and by federal assumption of state debts. Hamilton thus hoped to enhance the importance of the federal government, by bringing creditors into contact with the federal rather than state government, and by assuming many of the taxes formerly levied by the states. The political implications of these proposals aroused considerable opposition, but the clear need for freer trade and a greater flow of money overrode most resistance.

Library of Congress

Yale Art Gallery
Yale Art Gallery
Independence National Historical Park

**Rufus King (left), Federalist senator from N.Y., director of the Bank of the U.S.; Fisher Ames, representative from Mass., an outspoken Federalist; Robert Morris (right), Federalist senator from Pa., financial leader during the Revolution and later superintendent of finance**

# Congress

Library of Congress

Amherst College

**James Madison by Stuart; (right) Senate chambers and (below) House of Representatives, both in New York**

Library of Congress

Madison, who served in the House, was the leading figure in Congress. As both a Southerner and an architect of the Constitution, he personified the difficulty of reconciling regional needs with national policy. The revenue acts of 1789, essential to the viability of the new government, were passed only after extensive compromise efforts by Madison, since their sources of income — tariffs and tonnage duties — were regarded as disadvantageous to the South, which exported large quantities of raw materials and depended heavily on imports. Madison opposed Hamilton's credit proposals because they favored the North, which had the most debts. In the arguments over the Bill of Rights, the basically anti-federal stance of the South also made Madison's role as mediator more difficult.

**John Adams (left) and Frederick Muhlenberg, first House speaker**

Boston Athenaeum

Library of Congress

New York Historical Society

**Federalist cartoon depicting Jefferson and the Republicans hindering effective government**

# Party Politics

By the end of Washington's second term the political differences that had been put aside in favor of the larger goals of independence and national self-preservation now returned to dominate the country's politics. There was general support for the Constitution, but class, regional, and philosophical differences gradually polarized around Hamilton on one side and Jefferson on the other. The French Revolution served as a warning example to Hamilton's Federalists, who represented the commercial, banking, and property interests best served by a strong central government. To them the French experience was a cogent example of the anarchy and economic chaos inherent in the democratic and agrarian principles of the Jeffersonian Republicans who, for their part, distrusted the motives of many Federalists. Tariff policies and suffrage restrictions were the key specific issues. A strong central government versus government by the people was the general issue.

**English caricature of Tom Paine's involvement in the French Revolution represents also the Federalist attitude toward his radical democratic views**

Library of Congress

# 1789

67.

## David Ramsay: The Influence of the Revolution on the Minds and Morals of the Citizens

*David Ramsay was a physician in Charleston, South Carolina, and an ardent patriot. He is best remembered for a variety of historical works that his extraordinary energy enabled him to write in his spare time. Among these was his* History of the American Revolution, *in two volumes. It is valuable for its firsthand knowledge of the war. The following excerpt dealing with the influence of the Revolution on the "minds and morals" of the American people continues to be regarded as a perceptive account of its subject.*

Source: *The History of the American Revolution*, Philadelphia, 1789, Vol. II, Appendix, No. IV.

The great body of Tories in the southern states was among the settlers on their western frontier. Many of these were disorderly persons who had fled from the old settlements to avoid the restraints of civil government. Their numbers were increased by a set of men called "Regulators." The expense and difficulty of obtaining the decision of courts against horse thieves and other criminals had induced sundry persons, about the year 1770, to take the execution of the laws into their own hands, in some of the remote settlements, both of North and South Carolina. In punishing crimes, forms as well as substance must be regarded. From not attending to the former, some of these Regulators, though perhaps aiming at nothing but what they thought right, committed many offenses, both against law and justice. By their violent proceedings, regular government was prostrated. This drew on them the vengeance of royal governors. The Regulators, having suffered from their hands, were slow to oppose an established government, whose power to punish they had recently experienced. Apprehending that the measures of Congress were like their own regulating schemes, and fearing that they would terminate in the same disagreeable consequences, they and their adherents were generally opposed to the Revolution.

Religion also divided the inhabitants of America. The Presbyterians and Independents were almost universally attached to the measures of Congress. Their religious societies are governed on the republican plan. From independence they had much to hope, but from Great Britain, if finally successful, they had reason to fear the establishment of a church hierarchy.

Most of the Episcopal ministers of the northern provinces were pensioners on the bounty of the British government. The greatest part of their clergy, and many of their laity in these provinces, were therefore disposed to support a connection with Great Britain. The Episcopal clergy in these southern provinces, being under no such bias, were often among the warmest Whigs. Some of them, foreseeing the downfall of religious establishments from the success of the Americans, were less active, but, in general, where their church was able to support itself, their clergy and laity zealously espoused the cause of independence. Great pains were taken to persuade them that those who had been called dissenters were aiming to abolish the Episcopal establishment to make way for their own exaltation, but the good sense of the people restrained them from giving any credit to the unfounded suggestion. Religious controversy was happily kept out of view: The well informed of all denominations were convinced that the contest was for their civil rights, and therefore did not suffer any other considerations to interfere or disturb their union. . . .

The American Revolution, on the one hand, brought forth great vices; but, on the other hand, it called forth many virtues and gave occasion for the display of abilities which, but for that event, would have been lost to the world. . . . While the Americans were guided by the leading strings of the mother country, they had no scope nor encouragement for exertion. All the departments of government were established and executed for them, but not by them. In the years 1775 and 1776, the country, being suddenly thrown into a situation that needed the abilities of all its sons, these generally took their places, each according to the bent of his inclination. As they severally pursued their objects with ardor, a vast expansion of the human mind speedily followed.

This displayed itself in a variety of ways. It was found that the talents for great stations did not differ in kind, but only in degree, from those which were necessary for the proper discharge of the ordinary business of civil society. In the bustle that was occasioned by the war, few instances could be produced of any persons who made a figure, or who rendered essential services, but from among those who had given specimens of similar talents in their respective professions. Those who from indolence or dissipation had been of little service to the community in time of peace were found equally unserviceable in war. A few young men were exceptions to this general rule. Some of these, who had indulged in youthful follies, broke off from their vicious courses and, on the pressing call of their country, became useful servants of the public.

But the great bulk of those who were the active instruments of carrying on the Revolution were self-made, industrious men. These who by their own exertions had established or laid a foundation for establishing personal independence were most generally trusted and most successfully employed in establishing that of their country. In these times of action, classical education was found of less service than good natural parts, guided by common sense and sound judgment. . . .

It seemed as if the war not only required but created talents. Men whose minds were warmed with the love of liberty, and whose abilities were improved by daily exercise and sharpened with a laudable ambition to serve their distressed country, spoke, wrote, and acted with an energy far surpassing all expectations which could be reasonably founded on their previous acquirements.

The Americans knew but little of one another previous to the Revolution. Trade and business had brought the inhabitants of their seaports acquainted with each other, but the bulk of the people in the interior country were unacquainted with their fellow citizens. A Continental Army and Congress composed of men from all the states, by freely mixing together, were assimilated into one mass. Individuals of both, mingling with the citizens, disseminated principles of union among them. Local prejudices abated. By frequent collision, asperities were worn off and a foundation was laid for the establishment of a nation out of discordant materials. Intermarriages between men and women of different states were much more common than before the war, and became an additional cement to the Union. Unreasonable jealousies had existed between the inhabitants of the Eastern and of the Southern states; but, on becoming better acquainted with each other, these in a great measure subsided.

A wiser policy prevailed. Men of liberal minds led the way in discouraging local distinctions, and the great body of the people, as soon as reason got the better of prejudice, found that their best interests would be most effectually promoted by such practices and sentiments as were favorable to union.

Religious bigotry had broken in upon the peace of various sects before the American War. This was kept up by partial establishments and by a dread that the Church of England, through the power of the mother country, would be made to triumph over all other denominations. These apprehensions were done away by the Revolution. The different sects, having nothing to fear from each other, dismissed all religious controversy.

A proposal for introducing bishops into America before the war had kindled a flame among the dissenters; but the Revolution was no sooner accomplished than a scheme for that purpose was perfected, with the consent and approbation of all those sects who had previously opposed it. Pulpits, which had formerly been shut to worthy men because their heads had not been consecrated by the imposition of the hands of a bishop or of a presbytery, have, since the establishment of independence, been reciprocally opened to each other whensoever the public convenience required it. The world will soon see the result of an experiment in politics, and be able to determine whether the happiness of society is increased by religious establishments or diminished by the want of them.

Though schools and colleges were generally shut up during the war, yet many of the arts and sciences were promoted by it. The geography of the United States before the Revolution was but little known; but the marches of armies and the operations of war gave birth to many geographical inquiries and discoveries which otherwise would not have been made. A passionate fondness for studies of this kind and the growing importance of the country excited one of its sons, the Rev. Mr. Morse, to travel through every state of the Union and amass a fund of topographical knowledge far exceeding anything heretofore communicated to the public. The necessities of the states led to the study of tactics, fortification, gunnery, and a variety of other arts connected with war, and diffused a knowledge of them among a peaceable people who would otherwise have had no inducement to study them.

The abilities of ingenious men were directed to make further improvements in the art of destroying an enemy. Among these, David Bushnell of Connecticut invented a machine for submarine navigation, which was found to answer the purpose of rowing horizontally, at any given depth under water, and of rising or sinking at pleasure. To this was attached a magazine of powder, and the whole was contrived in such a manner as to make it practicable to blow up vessels by machinery under them. Mr. Bushnell also contrived sundry other curious machines for the annoyance of British shipping; but from accident they only succeeded in part. He destroyed one vessel in charge of Commodore Symonds and a second one near the shore of Long Island.

Surgery was one of the arts which was promoted by the war. From the want of hospitals and other aids, the medical men of America had few opportunities of perfecting themselves in this art, the thorough knowledge of which can only be acquired by practice and observation. The melancholy events of battles gave the American students an opportunity of seeing and learning more in one day than they could have acquired in years of peace. It was in the hospitals of the United States that Dr. Rush first discovered the method of curing the lockjaw by bark and wine added to other invigorating remedies, which has since been adopted with success in Europe as well as in the United States.

The science of government has been more generally diffused among the Americans by means of the Revolution. The policy of Great Britain in throwing them out of her protection induced a necessity of establishing independent constitutions. This led to reading and reasoning on the subject. The many errors that were at first committed by inexperienced statesmen have been a practical comment on the folly of unbalanced constitutions and injudicious laws. The discussions concerning the new Constitution gave birth to much reasoning on the subject of government, and particularly to a series of letters signed "Publius," but really the work of Alexander Hamilton, in which much political knowledge and wisdom were displayed and which will long remain a monument of the strength and acuteness of the human understanding in investigating truth.

When Great Britain first began her encroachments on the colonies, there were few natives of America who had distinguished themselves as speakers or writers, but the controversy between the two countries multiplied their number.

The Stamp Act, which was to have taken place in 1765, employed the pens and tongues of many of the colonists, and by repeated exercise improved their ability to serve their country. The duties imposed in 1767 called forth the pen of John Dickinson, who, in a series of letters signed "A Pennsylvania Farmer," may be said to have sown the seeds of the Revolution; for, being universally read by the colonists, they universally enlightened them on the dangerous consequences likely to result from their being taxed by the Parliament of Great Britain.

In establishing American independence, the pen and the press had merit equal to that of the sword. As the war was the people's war and was carried on without funds, the exertions of the army would have been insufficient to effect the Revolution unless the great body of the people had been prepared for it and also kept in a constant disposition to oppose Great Britain. To rouse and unite the inhabitants and to persuade them to patience for several years, under present sufferings, with the hope of obtaining remote advantages for their posterity, was a work of difficulty. This was effected in a great measure by the tongues and pens of the well-informed citizens; and on it depended the success of military operations.

To enumerate the names of all those who were successful laborers in this arduous business is impossible. The following list contains in nearly alphabetical order the names of the most distinguished writers in favor of the rights of America:

John Adams and Samuel Adams of Boston; Bland of Virginia; John Dickinson of Pennsylvania; Daniel Dulany of Annapolis; William Henry Drayton of South Carolina; Dr. Franklin of Philadelphia; John Jay and Alexander Hamilton of New York; Thomas Jefferson and Arthur Lee of Virginia; Jonathan Hyman of Connecticut; Governor Livingston of New Jersey; Dr. Mayhew and James Otis of Boston; Thomas Paine, Dr. Rush, Charles Thompson, and James Wilson of Philadelphia; William Tennant of South Carolina; Josiah Quincy and Dr. Warren of Boston.

These and many others labored in enlightening their countrymen on the subject of their political interests, and in animating them to a proper line of conduct in defense of their liberties. To these individuals may be added the great body of the clergy, especially in New England. The printers of newspapers had also much merit in the same way. Particularly Eedes and Gill of Boston; Holt of New York; Bradford of Philadelphia; and Timothy of South Carolina.

The early attention which had been paid to literature in New England was also eminently conducive to the success of the Americans in resisting Great Britain. The University of Cambridge was founded as early as 1636 and Yale College in 1700. It has been computed that in the year the Boston Port Act was passed there were in the four eastern colonies upward of 2,000 graduates of their colleges dispersed through their several towns, who, by their knowledge and abilities, were able to influence and direct the great body of the people to a proper line of conduct for opposing the encroachments of Great Britain on their liberties.

The colleges to the southward of New England, except that of William and Mary in Virginia, were but of modern date; but they had been of a standing sufficiently long to have trained for public service a considerable number of the youth of the country. The College of New Jersey, which was incorporated about twenty-eight years before the Revolution, had in that time educated upward of 300 persons, who, with a few exceptions, were active and useful friends of independence.

From the influence which knowledge had in securing and preserving the liberties of America, the present generation may trace the wise policy of their fathers in erecting schools and colleges. They may also learn that it is their duty to found more and support all such institutions. Without the advantages derived from these lights of this New World, the United States would probably have fallen in their unequal contest with Great Britain. Union which was essential to the success of their resistance could scarcely have taken place in the measures adopted by an ignorant multitude. Much less could wisdom in council, unity in system, or perseverance in the prosecution of a long and self-denying war be expected from an uninformed people.

It is a well-known fact that persons unfriendly to the Revolution were always most numerous in those parts of the United States which had either never been illuminated or but faintly warmed by the rays of science. The uninformed and the misinformed constituted a great proportion of those Americans who preferred the leading strings of the parent state, though encroaching on their liberties, to a government of their own countrymen and fellow citizens.

As literature had in the first instance favored the Revolution, so in its turn the Revolution promoted literature. The study of eloquence and of the *belles lettres* was more successfully prosecuted in America after the disputes between Great Britain and her colonies began to be serious than it ever had been before. The various orations, addresses, letters, dissertations, and other literary performances which the war made necessary called forth abilities where they were, and excited the rising generation to study arts, which brought with them their own reward. Many incidents afforded materials for the favorites of the Muses to display their talents. Even burlesquing royal proclamations by parodies and doggerel poetry had great effects on the minds of the people.

A celebrated historian has remarked that the song of *Lillibullero* forwarded the Revolution of 1688 in England. It may be truly affirmed that similar productions produced similar effects in America. Francis Hopkinson rendered essential service to his country by turning the artillery of wit and ridicule on the enemy. Philip Freneau labored successfully in the same way. Royal proclamations and other productions which issued from royal printing presses were, by the help of a warm imagination, arrayed in such dresses as rendered them truly ridiculous. Trumbull, with a vein of original Hudibrastic humor, diverted his countrymen so much with the follies of their enemies that for a time they forgot the calamities of war. Humphries twined the literary with the military laurel by superadding the fame of an elegant poet to that of an accomplished officer. Barlow increased the fame of his country and of the distinguished actors in the Revolution by the bold design of an epic poem ably executed on the idea that Columbus foresaw in vision the scenes that were to be transacted on the theater of that New World which he had discovered.

Dwight struck out in the same line, and at an early period of life finished an elegant work entitled *The Conquest of Canaan* on a plan which has rarely been attempted. The principles of their mother tongue were first unfolded to the Americans since the Revolution by their countryman Webster. Pursuing an unbeaten track, he has made discoveries in the genius and construction of the English language which had escaped the researches of preceding philologists. These and a group of other literary characters have been brought into view by the Revolution. It is remarkable that, of these, Connecticut has produced an unusual proportion. In that truly republican state, everything conspires to adorn human nature with its highest honors.

From the later periods of the Revolution till the present time, schools, colleges, societies and institutions for promoting literature, arts, manufactures, agriculture, and for extending human happiness have been increased far beyond anything that ever took place before the Declaration of Independence. Every state in the Union has done more or less in this way, but Pennsylvania has done the most. The following institutions have been very lately founded in that state, and most of them in the time of the war or since the peace. A university in the city of Philadelphia; a college of physicians in the same place; Dickinson College at Carlisle; Franklin College at Lancaster; the Protestant Episcopal Academy in Philadelphia; academies at Yorktown, at Germantown, at Pittsburgh and Washington; and an academy in Philadelphia for young ladies; societies for promoting political inquiries; for the medical relief of the poor, under the title of the Philadelphia Dispensary; for the promoting the abolition of slavery and the relief of free Negroes unlawfully held in bondage; for propagating the gospel among the Indians, under the direction of the United Brethren; for the encouragement of manufactures and the useful arts; for alleviating the miseries of prisons. Such have been some of the beneficial effects which have resulted from that expansion of the human mind which has been produced by the Revolution; but these have not been without alloy.

To overset an established government unhinges many of those principles which bind individuals to each other. A long time and much prudence will be necessary to reproduce a spirit of union and that reverence for government without which society is a rope of sand. The right of the people to resist their rulers when invading their liberties forms the cornerstone of the American republics. This principle, though just in itself, is not favorable to the tranquility of present establishments. The maxims and measures, which in the years 1774 and 1775 were successfully inculcated and adopted by American patriots for oversetting the established government, will answer a similar purpose when recurrence is had to them by factious demagogues for disturbing the freest governments that were ever devised. . . .

In consequence of the war, the institutions of religion have been deranged, the public worship of the Deity suspended, and a great number of the inhabitants deprived of the ordinary means of obtaining that religious knowledge which tames the fierceness and softens the rudeness of human passions and manners. Many of the temples dedicated to the service of the Most High were destroyed, and these, from a deficiency of ability and inclination, are not yet rebuilt. The clergy were left to suffer without proper support. The depreciation of the paper currency was particularly injurious to them. It reduced their salaries to a pittance so insufficient for their maintenance that several of them were obliged to lay down their profession and engage in other pursuits. Public preaching, of which many of the inhabitants were thus deprived, seldom fails of rendering essential service to society by civilizing the multitude and forming them to union.

No class of citizens have contributed more to the Revolution than the clergy, and none have hitherto suffered more in consequence of it. From the diminution of their number and the penury to which they have been subjected, civil government has lost many of the advantages it formerly derived from the public instructions of that useful order of men.

On the whole, the literary, political, and military talents of the citizens of the United States have been improved by the Revolution, but their moral character is inferior to what it formerly was. So great is the change for the worse that the friends of public order are loudly called upon to exert their utmost abilities in extirpating the vicious principles and habits which have taken deep root during the late convulsions.

---

68.

## John Trumbull: Pictures of the Revolution

*John Trumbull was the foremost member of a group of artists who painted visual representations of important American historical events. As a colonel and aide to General Washington in the American Revolution, he obtained firsthand knowledge of the war. While residing in London, he became greatly influenced by English artists as well as by the French style of Jacques Louis David and Mme Vigée-LeBrun. He eventually secured a commission to provide paintings for the Rotunda of the National Capitol. "Washington Resigning His Commission," "The Surrender of Cornwallis," "The Surrender of Burgoyne," and "The Declaration of Independence" are among his most famous efforts. In 1789, Thomas Jefferson, then minister to France, asked Trumbull to serve as his private secretary. The artist refused, explaining his reasons in the following letter, written from London on June 11, 1789.*

Source: *Autobiography, Reminiscences and Letters of John Trumbull, from 1756 to 1841*, New York, 1841, pp. 157-162.

I have received yours of the 1st by the last post, and am happy that you find the account correct; since writing that, you will have received by Mr. Broome the bill of exchange. You will receive by the diligence tomorrow, *Sterne's Sermons, Tristram Shandy,* and the *Sentimental Journey,* unbound; being all of his works which have been published by Wenman, in his very small size. They cost 8*s.* 6*d.*

If my affairs were in other respects as I could wish them, I should have given at once a positive answer to your proposition. It would have been an answer of thankfulness and acceptance, for nothing could be proposed to me more flattering to my pride or more consonant, at least for a time, to my favorite pursuit. The greatest motive I had or have for engaging in or for continuing my pursuit of painting has been the wish of commemorating the great events of our country's Revolution. I am fully sensible that the profession, as it is generally practised, is frivolous, little useful to society, and unworthy of a man who has talents for more serious pursuits.

But to preserve and diffuse the memory of the noblest series of actions which have ever presented themselves in the history of man; to give to the present and the future sons of oppression and misfortune such glorious lessons of their rights and of the spirit with which they should assert and support them, and even to transmit to their descendants the personal resemblance of those who have been the great actors in those illustrious scenes were objects which gave a dignity to the profession peculiar to my situation. And some superiority also arose from my having borne personally a humble part in the great events which I was to describe. No one lives with me possessing this advantage, and no one can come after me to divide the honor of truth and authenticity, however easily I may hereafter be exceeded in elegance.

Vanity was thus on the side of duty, and I flattered myself that by devoting a few years of life to this object I did not make an absolute waste of time, or squander uselessly talents from which my country might justly demand more valuable services; and I feel some honest pride in the prospect of accomplishing a work such as had never been done before, and in which it was not easy that I should have a rival.

With how much assiduity and with what degree of success I have pursued the studies necessarily preparatory to this purpose, the world will decide in the judgment it shall pass on the picture (of Gibraltar) which I now exhibit to them; and I need not fear that this judgment will deceive me, for it will be biased here to a favorable decision, by no partiality for me, or for my country.

But, while I have done whatever depended upon my personal exertions, I have been under the necessity of employing and relying upon the exertions of another. The two paintings which you saw in Paris three years ago "Bunker's Hill" and "Quebec" I placed in the hands of a printseller and publisher to cause to be engraved, and as the prospect of profit to him was considerable, I relied upon his using the utmost energy and dispatch; instead of which, three years have been suffered to elapse without almost the smallest progress having been made in the work. Instead, therefore, of having a work already far advanced to submit to the world and to my countrymen, I am but where I was three years since, with the deduction from my ways and means of three years' expenses, with prospects blighted, and the hope of the future damped by the experience of past mismanagement.

And the most serious reflection is that the memory and enthusiasm for actions, however great, fade daily from the human mind; that the warm attention which the nations of Europe once paid to us begins to be diverted to objects more nearly and immediately interesting to themselves; and that France, in particular, from which country I entertained peculiar hopes of patronage, is beginning to be too much occupied by her own approaching revolution to think so much of us as perhaps she did formerly.

Thus circumstanced, I foresee the utter impossibility of proceeding in my work without the warm patronage of my countrymen. Three or four years more must pass before I can reap any considerable advantage from what I am doing in this country, and, as I am far from being rich, those years must not be employed in prosecuting a plan which, without the real patronage of my country, will only involve me in new certainties of great and immediate expense with little probability of even distant recompense. I do not aim at opulence, but I must not knowingly rush into embarrassment and ruin.

I am ashamed to trouble you with such details, but without them I could not so well have explained my reason for not giving you at once a decided answer. You see, sir, that my future movements depend entirely upon my reception in America, and as that shall be cordial or cold, I am to decide whether to abandon my country or my profession. I think I shall determine without much hesitation; for although I am secure of a kind reception in any quarter of the globe if I will follow the general example of my profession by flattering the pride or apologizing for the vices of men, yet the ease, perhaps even elegance, which would be the fruit of such conduct would compensate but poorly for the contempt which I should feel for myself, and for the necessity which it would impose upon me of submitting to a voluntary sentence of perpetual exile.

I hope for better things. Monuments have been in repeated instances voted to her heroes; why then should I doubt a readiness in our country to encourage me in producing monuments, not of heroes only but of those events on which their title to the gratitude of the nation is founded, and which by being multiplied and little expensive may be diffused over the world, instead of being bounded to one narrow spot?

Immediately, therefore, upon my arrival in America, I shall offer a subscription for prints to be published from such a series of pictures as I intend, with the condition of returning their money to subscribers if the sum received shall not prove to be sufficient to justify me in proceeding with the work; and I shall first solicit the public protection of Congress.

I am told that it is a custom in France for the king to be considered as a subscriber for 100 copies of all elegant works engraved by his subjects; that these are deposited in the Bibliothèque du Roi, and distributed as presents to foreigners of distinction and taste, as specimens of the state of the fine arts in France. Would this be a mode of diffusing a knowledge of their origin and at the same time a lesson on the rights of humanity, improper to be adopted by the United States? And if the example of past greatness be a powerful incentive to emulation, would such prints be improper presents to their servants? The expense would be small and the purpose of monuments and medals as rewards of merit and confirmations of history would receive a valuable support since perhaps it may be the fate of prints sometimes to outlast either marble or bronze.

If a subscription of this sort should fill in such a manner as to justify me, I shall proceed with all possible diligence, and must of course pass some years in Europe; and as I have acquired that knowledge in this country which was my only object for residing here, and shall have many reasons for preferring Paris hereafter, I shall in that case be happy and proud to accept your flattering proposal. But if, on the contrary, my countrymen should not give me such encouragement as I wish and hope, I must give up the pursuit and of course I shall have little desire to return for any stay in Europe. In the meantime, viewing the absolute uncertainty of my situation, I must beg you not to pass by any more favorable subject which may offer before I have the happiness to meet you in America, which I hope will be ere long.

69.

## Thomas Jefferson: On the New Constitution

*Thomas Jefferson summarized his judgment of the new Constitution in a letter to Francis Hopkinson of March 13, 1789. "The great leader" to whom he refers was George Washington. Not until 1951 was an amendment passed, of the sort he wished, limiting the eligibility of the President to two terms — the precedent established by Washington when he refused to run for a third term in 1796.*

Source: H. A. Washington, II, pp. 585-587.

You say that I have been dished up to you as an Anti-Federalist, and ask me if it be just. My opinion was never worthy enough of notice to merit citing; but, since you ask it, I will tell it to you. I am not a Federalist, because I never submitted the whole system of my opinions to the creed of any party of men whatever, in religion, in philosophy, in politics, or in anything else, where I was capable of thinking for myself. Such an addiction is the last degradation of a free and moral agent. If I could not go to heaven but with a party, I would not go there at all. Therefore, I am not of the party of Federalists.

But I am much farther from that of the Anti-Federalists. I approved, from the first moment, of the great mass of what is in the new Constitution: the consolidation of the government; the organization into executive, legislative, and judiciary; the subdivision of the legislative; the happy compromise of interests between the great and little states by the different manner of voting in the different houses; the voting by persons instead of states; the qualified negative on laws given to the executive, which, however, I should have liked better if associated with the judiciary also, as in New York; and the power of taxation. I thought at first that the latter might have been limited. A little reflection soon convinced me it ought not to be.

What I disapproved from the first moment, also, was the want of a bill of rights to guard liberty against the legislative as well as the executive branches of the government; that is to say, to secure freedom in religion, freedom of the press, freedom from monopolies, freedom from unlawful imprisonment, freedom from a permanent military, and a trial by jury, in all cases determinable by the laws of the land. I disapproved, also, the perpetual reeligibility of the President. To these points of disapprobation I adhere.

My first wish was that the nine first conventions might accept the Constitution as the means of securing to us the great mass of good it contained, and that the four last might reject it as the means of obtaining amendments. But I was corrected in this wish the moment I saw the much better plan of Massachusetts, and which had never occurred to me. With the respect to the declaration of rights, I suppose the majority of the United States are of my opinion; for

I apprehend all the Anti-Federalists and a very respectable proportion of the Federalists think that such a declaration should now be annexed. The enlightened part of Europe have given us the greatest credit for inventing the instrument of security for the rights of the people and have been not a little surprised to see us so soon give it up.

With respect to the reeligibility of the President, I find myself differing from the majority of my countrymen; for I think there are but three states out of the eleven which have desired an alteration of this. And, indeed, since the thing is established, I would wish it not to be altered during the life of our great leader, whose executive talents are superior to those, I believe, of any man in the world, and who, alone, by the authority of his name and the confidence reposed in his perfect integrity, is fully qualified to put the new government so under way as to secure it against the efforts of opposition. But, having derived from our error all the good there was in it, I hope we shall correct it the moment we can no longer have the same name at the helm.

These, my dear friend, are my sentiments, by which you will see I was right in saying I am neither Federalist nor Anti-Federalist; that I am of neither party, nor yet a trimmer between parties. These, my opinions, I wrote within a few hours after I had read the Constitution to one or two friends in America. I had not then read one single word printed on the subject. I never had an opinion in politics or religion which I was afraid to own. A costive reserve on these subjects might have procured me more esteem from some people, but less from myself. My great wish is to go on in a strict but silent performance of my duty; to avoid attracting notice and to keep my name out of newspapers, because I find the pain of a little censure, even when it is unfounded, is more acute than the pleasure of much praise. The attaching circumstance of my present office is that I can do its duties un seen by those for whom they are done.

You did not think, by so short a phrase in your letter, to have drawn on yourself such an egotistical dissertation. I beg your pardon for it, and will endeavor to merit that pardon by the constant sentiments of esteem and attachment with which I am, dear sir, your sincere friend and servant.

---

***Our Constitution is in actual operation; everything appears to promise that it will last; but in this world nothing is certain but death and taxes.***

BENJAMIN FRANKLIN, letter to M. Leroy, 1789

70.

## George Washington: First Inaugural Address

*Though the formation of the Union was preceded by bitter debate, the choice of George Washington as the first President was vigorously supported by most of the public. The charismatic name of Washington was a symbol of the victorious Revolution and of national unity. At fifty-six years of age, Washington had hoped to spend his remaining years on his farm at Mount Vernon. However, the voice of his country, which he never heard "but with veneration and love," compelled him to service. The First Inaugural Address, reprinted here, was presented in the Senate chamber on April 30, 1789. It is doubtful that Washington alone wrote these famous words, as he often resorted to the more fluent styles of men like Alexander Hamilton. The address* does *express, most certainly, the first President's hopes for the new nation.*

Source: Richardson, I, pp. 51-54.

Fellow Citizens of the Senate and of the House of Representatives:

Among the vicissitudes incident to life no event could have filled me with greater anxieties than that of which the notification was transmitted by your order, and received on the 14th day of the present month. On the one hand, I was summoned by my country, whose voice I can never hear but with veneration and love, from a retreat which I had chosen with the fondest predilection, and, in my flattering hopes, with an immutable decision, as the asylum of my declining years — a retreat which was rendered every day more necessary as well as more dear to me by the addition of habit to inclination, and of frequent interruptions in my health to the gradual waste committed on it by time.

On the other hand, the magnitude and difficulty of the trust to which the voice of my country called me, being sufficient to awaken in the wisest and most experienced of her citizens a distrustful scrutiny into his qualifications, could not but overwhelm with despondence one who (inheriting inferior endowments from nature and unpractised in the duties of civil administration) ought to be peculiarly conscious of his own deficiencies.

In this conflict of emotions all I dare aver is that it has been my faithful study to collect my duty from a just appreciation of every circumstance by which it might be affected. All I dare hope is that if, in executing this task, I have been too much swayed by a grateful remembrance of former instances, or by an affectionate sensibility to this transcendent proof of the confidence of my fellow citizens, and have thence too little consulted my incapacity as well as disinclination for the weighty and untried cares before me, my error will be palliated by the motives which mislead me, and its consequences be judged by my country with some share of the partiality in which they originated.

Such being the impressions under which

I have, in obedience to the public summons, repaired to the present station, it would be peculiarly improper to omit in this first official act my fervent supplications to that Almighty Being who rules over the universe, who presides in the councils of nations, and whose providential aids can supply every human defect, that His benediction may consecrate to the liberties and happiness of the people of the United States a government instituted by themselves for these essential purposes, and may enable every instrument employed in its administration to execute with success the functions allotted to his charge. In tendering this homage to the Great Author of every public and private good, I assure myself that it expresses your sentiments not less than my own, nor those of my fellow citizens at large less than either.

No people can be bound to acknowledge and adore the Invisible Hand which conducts the affairs of men more than those of the United States. Every step by which they have advanced to the character of an independent nation seems to have been distinguished by some token of providential agency; and in the important revolution just accomplished in the system of their united government the tranquil deliberations and voluntary consent of so many distinct communities from which the event has resulted cannot be compared with the means by which most governments have been established without some return of pious gratitude, along with a humble anticipation of the future blessings which the past seem to presage. These reflections, arising out of the present crisis, have forced themselves too strongly on my mind to be suppressed. You will join with me, I trust, in thinking that there are none under the influence of which the proceedings of a new and free government can more auspiciously commence.

By the article establishing the Executive Department, it is made the duty of the President "to recommend to your consideration such measures as he shall judge necessary and expedient." The circumstances under which I now meet you will acquit me from entering into that subject further than to refer to the great constitutional charter under which you are assembled, and which, in defining your powers, designates the objects to which your attention is to be given. It will be more consistent with those circumstances, and far more congenial with the feelings which actuate me, to substitute, in place of a recommendation of particular measures, the tribute that is due to the talents, the rectitude, and the patriotism which adorn the characters selected to devise and adopt them. In these honorable qualifications I behold the surest pledges that as on one side no local prejudices or attachments, no separate views nor party animosities will misdirect the comprehensive and equal eye which ought to watch over this great assemblage of communities and interests, so, on another, that the foundation of our national policy will be laid in the pure and immutable principles of private morality, and the preeminence of free government be exemplified by all the attributes which can win the affections of its citizens and command the respect of the world.

I dwell on this prospect with every satisfaction which an ardent love for my country can inspire, since there is no truth more thoroughly established than that there exists in the economy and course of nature an indissoluble union between virtue and happiness; between duty and advantage; between the genuine maxims of an honest and magnanimous policy and the solid rewards of public prosperity and felicity; since we ought to be no less persuaded that the propitious smiles of Heaven can never be expected on a nation that disregards the eternal rules of order and right which Heaven itself has ordained; and since the preservation of the sacred fire of liberty and the destiny of the republican model of government are justly considered, perhaps, as *deep-*

*ly*, as *finally*, staked on the experiment entrusted to the hands of the American people.

Besides the ordinary objects submitted to your care, it will remain with your judgment to decide how far an exercise of the occasional power delegated by the 5th Article of the Constitution is rendered expedient at the present juncture by the nature of objections which have been urged against the system, or by the degree of inquietude which has given birth to them.

Instead of undertaking particular recommendations on this subject, in which I could be guided by no lights derived from official opportunities, I shall again give way to my entire confidence in your discernment and pursuit of the public good; for I assure myself that, while you carefully avoid every alteration which might endanger the benefits of a united and effective government, or which ought to await the future lessons of experience, a reverence for the characteristic rights of freemen and a regard for the public harmony will sufficiently influence your deliberations on the question how far the former can be impregnably fortified or the latter be safely and advantageously promoted.

To the foregoing observations I have one to add, which will be most properly addressed to the House of Representatives. It concerns myself, and will therefore be as brief as possible. When I was first honored with a call into the service of my country, then on the eve of an arduous struggle for its liberties, the light in which I contemplated my duty required that I should renounce every pecuniary compensation. From this resolution I have in no instance departed; and being still under the impressions which produced it, I must decline as inapplicable to myself any share in the personal emoluments which may be indispensably included in a permanent provision for the Executive Department, and must accordingly pray that the pecuniary estimates for the station in which I am placed may, during my continuance in it, be limited to such actual expenditures as the public good may be thought to require.

Having thus imparted to you my sentiments as they have been awakened by the occasion which brings us together, I shall take my present leave; but not without resorting once more to the benign Parent of the human race in humble supplication that, since He has been pleased to favor the American people with opportunities for deliberating in perfect tranquillity, and dispositions for deciding with unparalleled unanimity on a form of government for the security of their Union and the advancement of their happiness, so His divine blessing may be equally *conspicuous* in the enlarged views, the temperate consultations, and the wise measures on which the success of this government must depend.

---

*If to be venerated for benevolence: if to be admired for talents: if to be esteemed for patriotism: if to be beloved for philanthropy, can gratify the human mind, you must have the pleasing consolation that you have not lived in vain.*

George Washington, letter to Benjamin Franklin, 1789

71.

## WILLIAM MACLAY: Titles and Ceremonials

*William Maclay represented Pennsylvania in the Senate when the new government under the Constitution began operations in April 1789. Fortunately for posterity, he kept a journal of the proceedings in that first session of the Senate, because there was no official record prepared for public information. His journal therefore is the most complete record available of the contest between the Federalists and their opponents in the precedent-creating early years of the federal government. The following selection from Maclay's* Journal *deals with the controversy between aristocrats and democrats over the matter of titles and ceremony. The aristocrats are represented by Vice-President John Adams, while Senator Maclay leads the opposition.*

Source: *Journal of William Maclay,* Edgar S. Maclay, ed., New York, 1890, pp. 7-29.

*April 30, Thursday.* This is a great, important day. Goddess of Etiquette, assist me while I describe it. The Senate stood adjourned to half after eleven o'clock. About ten, dressed in my best clothes; went for Mr. Morris' lodgings, but met his son, who told me that his father would not be in town until Saturday. Turned into the Hall. The crowd already great. The Senate met. The Vice-President rose in the most solemn manner. This son of Adam seemed impressed with deeper gravity, yet what shall I think of him? He often, in the midst of his most important airs — I believe when he is at loss for expressions (and this he often is, wrapped up, I suppose, in the contemplation of his own importance) — suffers an unmeaning kind of vacant laugh to escape him. This was the case today, and, really, to me, bore the air of ridiculing the farce he was acting. "Gentlemen, I wish for the direction of the Senate. The President will, I suppose, address the Congress. How shall I behave? How shall we receive it? Shall it be standing or sitting?"

Here followed a considerable deal of talk from him which I could make nothing of. Mr. Lee began with the House of Commons (as is usual with him), then the House of Lords, then the king, and then back again. The result of his information was that the Lords sat and the Commons stood on the delivery of the king's speech. Mr. Izard got up and told how often he had been in the Houses of Parliament. He said a great deal of what he had seen there. [He] made, however, this sagacious discovery, that the Commons stood because they had no seats to sit on, being arrived at the bar of the House of Lords. It was discovered, after some time, that the king sat, too, and had his robes and crown on.

Mr. Adams got up again and said he had been very often indeed at the Parliament on those occasions, but there always was such a crowd, and ladies along, that for his part he could not say how it was. Mr. Carroll got up to declare that he thought it of no consequence how it was in Great Britain; they were no rule to us, etc. But, all at once, the secretary, who had been out, whispered to the Chair that the clerk from the Representatives was at the door with a communication. Gentlemen of the Senate, how shall he be received? A silly kind of resolution of the committee on that business had been laid on the table some days ago. The amount of it was that each House should communicate to the other what and how they chose; it concluded, however, something in this way: that everything should be done with all the *propriety* that was *proper*.

The question was, shall this be adopted, that we may know how to receive the clerk? It was objected [that] this will throw no light on the subject; it will leave you where you are. Mr. Lee brought the House of Commons before us again. He reprobated the rule; declared that the clerk should not come within the bar of the House; that the proper mode was for the sergeant at arms, with the mace on his shoulder, to meet the clerk at the door and receive his communication. We are not, however, provided for this ceremonious way of doing business, having neither mace nor sergeant nor masters in chancery, who carry down bills from the English Lords.

Mr. Izard got up and labored unintelligibly to show the great distinction between a communication and a delivery of a thing, but he was not minded. Mr. Elsworth showed plainly enough that if the clerk was not permitted to deliver the communication, the Speaker might as well send it enclosed. Repeated accounts came [that] the Speaker and Representatives were at the door. Confusion ensued; the members left their seats. Mr. Read rose and called the attention of the Senate to the neglect that had been shown Mr. Thompson, late secretary. Mr. Lee rose to answer him, but I could not hear one word he said. The Speaker was introduced, followed by the Representatives. Here we sat an hour and ten minutes before the President arrived — this delay was owing to Lee, Izard, and Dalton, who had stayed with us while the Speaker came in instead of going to attend the President.

The President advanced between the Senate and Representatives, bowing to each. He was placed in the chair by the Vice-President; the Senate with their president on the right, the Speaker and the Representatives on his left. The Vice-President rose and addressed a short sentence to him. The import of it was that he should now take the oath of office as president. He seemed to have forgot half what he was to say, for he made a dead pause and stood for some time, to appearance, in a vacant mood. He finished with a formal bow, and the President was conducted out of the middle window into the gallery, and the oath was administered by the chancellor. Notice that the business done was communicated to the crowd by proclamation, etc., who gave three cheers, and repeated it on the President's bowing to them.

As the company returned into the Senate chamber, the President took the chair and the senators and representatives their seats. He rose, and all arose also, and addressed them. This great man was agitated and embarrassed more than ever he was by the leveled cannon or pointed musket. He trembled, and several times could scarce make out to read, though it must be supposed he had often read it before. . . . When he came to the words "all the world," he made a flourish with his right hand, which left rather an ungainly impression. I sincerely, for my part, wished all set ceremony in the hands of the dancing masters, and that this first of men had read off his address in the plainest manner, without ever taking his eyes from the paper, for I felt hurt that he was not first in everything. . . .

From the Hall there was a grand procession to Saint Paul's Church, where prayers were said by the bishop. The procession was well conducted and without accident, as far as I have heard. The militia were all under arms, lined the street near the church, made a good figure, and behaved well.

The Senate returned to their chamber after service, formed, and took up the address.

Our Vice-President called it *his most gracious speech.* I cannot approve of this. A committee was appointed on it — Johnson, Carroll, Patterson. Adjourned.

In the evening there were grand fireworks. The Spanish ambassador's house was adorned with transparent paintings; the French minister's house was illuminated, and had some transparent pieces; the Hall was grandly illuminated; and, after all this, the people went to bed.

*May 1.* Attended at the Hall at eleven. The prayers were over and the minutes reading. When we came to the minute of the speech it stood, "His most gracious speech." I looked all around the Senate. Every countenance seemed to wear a blank. The secretary was going on. I must speak or nobody would. "Mr. President, we have lately had a hard struggle for our liberty against kingly authority. The minds of men are still heated; everything related to that species of government is odious to the people. The words prefixed to the President's speech are the same that are usually placed before the speech of His Britannic Majesty. I know they will give offense. I consider them as improper. I therefore move that they be struck out, and that it stand simply, address, or, speech, as may be judged most suitable."

Mr. Adams rose in his chair and expressed the greatest surprise that anything should be objected to on account of its being taken from the practice of that government under which we had lived so long and happily formerly; that he was for a dignified and respectable government, and, as far as he knew the sentiments of people, they thought as he did; that for his part he was one of the first in the late contest and, if he could have thought of this, he never would have drawn his sword.

Painful as it was, I had to contend with the Chair. I admitted that the people of the colonies (now states) had enjoyed formerly great happiness under that species of government, but the abuses of that government under which they had smarted had taught them what they had to fear from that kind of government; that there had been a revolution in the sentiments of people respecting government equally great as that which had happened in the government itself; that even the modes of it were now abhorred; that the enemies of the Constitution had objected to it the facility there would be of transition from it to kingly government and all the trappings and splendor of royalty; that if such a thing as this appeared on our minutes, they would not fail to represent it as the first step of the ladder in the ascent to royalty. The Vice-President rose a second time and declared that he had mentioned it to the secretary; that he could not possibly conceive that any person could take offense at it. I had to get up again and declare that, although I knew of it being mentioned from the Chair, yet my opposition did not proceed from any motive of contempt; that, although it was a painful task, it was solely a sense of duty that raised me.

The Vice-President stood during this time; said he had been long abroad and did not know how the temper of people might be now. Up now rose Mr. Read, and declared for the paragraph. He saw no reason to object to it because the British speeches were styled "most gracious." If we chose to object to words because they had been used in the same sense in Britain, we should soon be at a loss to do business. I had to reply. "It is time enough to submit to necessity when it exists. At present we are at no loss for words. The words 'speech' or 'address' without any addition will suit us well enough." The first time I was up, Mr. Lee followed me with a word or two by way of seconding me; but when the Vice-President, on being last up, declared that he was the person from whom the words were taken, Mr. Lee got up and informed the Chair that he did not know that circumstance as he had been absent when it happened. The question was put and carried for erasing the words without a division.

After the House adjourned the Vice-President took me to one side, declared how much he was for an efficient government, how much he respected General Washington, and much of that kind. I told him I would yield to no person in respect to General Washington; that our common friends would perhaps one day inform him that I was not wanting in respect to himself; that my wishes for an efficient government were as high as any man's; and begged him to believe that I did myself great violence when I opposed him in the Chair, and nothing but a sense of duty could force me to it. He got on the subject of checks to government and the balances of power. His tale was long. He seemed to expect some answer. I caught at the last word, and said undoubtedly without a balance there could be no equilibrium, and so left him hanging in geometry.

The unequivocal declaration that he would never have drawn his sword, etc., has drawn my mind to the following remarks: That the motives of the actors in the late Revolution were various cannot be doubted. The abolishing of royalty, the extinguishing of patronage and dependencies attached to that form of government were the exalted motives of many revolutionists, and these were the improvements meant by them to be made of the war which was forced on us by British aggression — in fine, the amelioration of government and bettering the condition of mankind.

These ends and none other were publicly avowed, and all our constitutions and public acts were formed in this spirit. Yet there were not wanting a party whose motives were different. They wished for the loaves and fishes of government, and cared for nothing else but a translation of the diadem and scepter from London to Boston, New York, or Philadelphia; or, in other words, the creation of a new monarchy in America, and to form niches for themselves in the temple of royalty.

This spirit manifested itself strongly among the officers at the close of the war, and I have been afraid the Army would not have been disbanded if the common soldiers could have been kept together. This spirit they developed in the Order of Cincinnati, where I trust it will spend itself in a harmless flame and soon become extinguished. That Mr. Adams should, however, so unequivocally avow this motive, at a time when a republican form of government is secured to every state in the Union, appears to me a mark of extreme folly. . . .

*May 8*. Attended a joint committee on the papers of the old Congress. Made progress in the business. Agreed to meet at half-past ten on Monday and report. Senate formed. The secretary, as usual, had made some mistakes, which were rectified, and now Mr. Elsworth moved for the report of the Joint Committee to be taken up on the subject of titles. It was accordingly done. Mr. Lee led the business. He took his old ground — all the world, civilized and savage, called for titles; that there must be something in human nature that occasioned this general consent; that, therefore, he conceived it was right. Here he began to enumerate many nations who gave titles — such as Venice, Genoa, and others. The Greeks and Romans, it was said, had no titles, "but" (making a profound bow to the Chair) "you were pleased to set us right in this with respect to the Conscript Fathers the other day." Here he repeated the Vice-President's speech of the 23rd ultimo [April], almost verbatim all over.

Mr. Elsworth rose. He had a paper in his hat, which he looked constantly at. He repeated almost all that Mr. Lee had said, but got on the subject of kings, declared that the sentence in the primer of "fear God and honor the king" was of great importance; that kings were of divine appointment; that Saul, the head and shoulders taller than the rest of the people, was elected by God and anointed by his appointment.

I sat, after he had done, for a considerable time, to see if anybody would rise. At last I got up and first answered Lee as well as I could with nearly the same arguments, drawn from the Constitution, as I had used on the 23rd ultimo. I mentioned that within the space of twenty years back more light had been thrown on the subject of governments and on human affairs in general than for several generations before; that this light of knowledge had diminished the veneration for titles, and that mankind now considered themselves as little bound to imitate the follies of civilized nations as the brutalities of savages; that the abuse of power and the fear of bloody masters had extorted titles as well as adoration, in some instances, from the trembling crowd; that the impression now on the minds of the citizens of these states was that of horror for kingly authority.

Izard got up. He dwelt almost entirely on the antiquity of kingly government. He could not, however, well get further back than Philip of Macedon. He seemed to have forgot both Homer and the Bible. He urged for something equivalent to nobility having been common among the Romans, for they had three names that seemed to answer to honorable, or something like it, before and something behind. He did not say Esquire. Mr. Carroll rose and took my side of the question. He followed nearly the track I had been in, and dwelt much on the information that was now abroad in the world. He spoke against kings. Mr. Lee and Mr. Izard were both up again. Elsworth was up again. Langdon was up several times, but spoke short each time. Patterson was up, but there was no knowing which side he was of. Mr. Lee considered him as against him and answered him, but Patterson finally voted with Lee. The Vice-President repeatedly helped the speakers for titles. Elsworth was enumerating how common the appellation of president was. The Vice-President put him in mind that there were presidents of fire companies and of a cricket club. Mr. Lee at another time was saying he believed some of the states authorized titles by their constitutions. The Vice-President, from the Chair, told him that Connecticut did it. At sundry other times he interfered in a like manner. I had been frequently up to answer new points during the debate.

I collected myself for a last effort. I read the clause in the Constitution against titles of nobility; showed that the spirit of it was against not only granting titles by Congress but against the permission of foreign potentates granting *any titles whatever;* that as to kingly government, it was equally out of the question, as a republican government was guaranteed to every state in the Union; that they were both equally forbidden fruit of the Constitution. I called the attention of the House to the consequences that were like to follow; that gentlemen seemed to court a rupture with the other House. The Representatives had adopted the report, and were this day acting on it, or according to the spirit of the report. We were proposing a title. Our conduct would mark us to the world as actuated by the spirit of dissension, and the characters of the Houses would be as aristocratic and democratical.

The report [of the Committee on Titles] was, however, rejected. "Excellency" was moved for as a title by Mr. Izard. It was withdrawn by Mr. Izard, and "highness" with some prefatory word proposed by Mr. Lee. Now, long harangues were made in favor of this title. "Elective" was placed before. It was insisted that such a dignified title would add greatly to the weight and authority of the government both at home and abroad. I declared myself totally of a different opinion; that at present it was impossible to add to the respect entertained for General Washington; that if you gave him the title of any foreign prince or potentate, a belief would follow that the manners of that prince and his modes of government would be adopted by the President. (Mr. Lee had, just before I got up, read over a list of the titles of all the princes and potentates of the earth, marking where the word "highness" occurred. The Grand Turk had it, all the princes of Germany had [it], sons and daughters of crown heads, etc.) That particularly "elective highness," which sounded nearly like "electoral highness," would have a most ungrateful sound to many thousands of industrious citizens who had fled from German oppression; that "highness" was part of the title of a prince or princes of the blood, and was often given to dukes; that it was degrading our President to place him on a par with any prince of any blood in Europe, nor was there one of them that could enter the list of true glory with him.

But I will minute no more. The debate lasted till half after three o'clock, and it ended in appointing a committee to consider of a title to be given to the President. This whole silly business is the work of Mr. Adams and Mr. Lee; Izard follows Lee, and the New England men, who always herd together, follow Mr. Adams. Mr. Thompson says this used to be the case in the old Congress. I had, to be sure, the greatest share in this debate, and must now have completely sold (no, sold is a bad word, for I have got nothing for it) every particle of court favor; for a court our House seems determined on, and to run into all the fooleries, fopperies, fineries, and pomp of royal etiquette — and all this for Mr. Adams.

*May 9.* Attended the Hall at ten o'clock to go on the Judicial Committee. Met many of the members. I know not the motive, but I never was received with more familiarity, nor quite so much, before by the members. Elsworth, in particular, seemed to show a kind of fondness. The Judicial Committee did no business. Senate formed. It took a long time to correct the minutes. Otis keeps them miserably. At length the committee came in and reported a title — "His Highness the President of the United States of America and Protector of the Rights of the Same." Mr. Few had spoken a word or two with me, and signified his unwillingness to do anything hastily. He got up and spoke a great deal against hasty measures. He did not pointedly move for postponement, but it amounted nearly to it. The clerk of the other House, in the meantime, appeared at the bar and announced the adoption of the report of the Joint Committee (rejecting titles).

I got up and expressed my opinion that what had fallen from the honorable gentleman from Georgia amounted to a motion for postponement, and asked leave to second him. I then pointed out the rupture that was likely to ensue with the other House; that this was a matter of very serious import, and I thought it our indispensable duty to avoid any inconvenience of that kind; that by the arrangement between the Houses in case of disagreement a conference might be requested; that my intention was, if the postponement was carried, to move immediately for a committee of conference to be appointed on the difference between the Houses, and I had hopes that by these means all subject of debate would be done away. Mr. Read got up and moved that the report might be adopted. He was not seconded, but the motion was in itself idle. Mr. Strong spoke in favor of the postponement, and was interrupted from the Chair. Mr. Dalton, after some time, spoke in favor of it. I could now see a visible anxiety in the Chair.

I had a fine, slack, and easy time of it today. Friends seemed to rise in succession. Lee went over his old ground twice, but owned at last there was great difficulty every way, but said plainly the best mode was for the House to adopt the report, and then the other House would follow. He found, however, the current began to turn against him, and he laid his head on his hand as if he would have slept. Mr. Strong was up again. He said, among many things, that he thought the other House would follow, but there was a risk in it.

Mr. Izard got up at last. He, too, was for a postponement. I could see the Vice-President kindled at him. Mr. Izard said we knew the other House had adopted the report [rejecting titles]. The Vice-President interrupted him and said no; we had no right to know it nor could we know it until after the clerk had this morning given official information. The members fixed themselves, and the question was called for.

Up now got the Vice-President, and for forty minutes did he harangue us from the Chair. He began first on the subject of order, and found fault with everything almost, but down he came to particulars, and pointedly blamed a member for disorderly behavior. The member had mentioned the appearance of a captious disposition in the other House. This was disorderly and spoke with asperity. The member meant was Mr. Izard. All this was only prefatory. On he got to his favorite topic of titles, and over the old ground of the immense advantage of, the absolute necessity of them. When he had exhausted this subject, he turned a new leaf, I believe, on the conviction that the postponement would be carried and perhaps the business lost by an attention to the other House.

> Gentlemen, I must tell you that it is you and the President that have the making of titles. Suppose the President to have the appointment of Mr. Jefferson at the court of France. Mr. Jefferson is, in virtue of that appointment, the most illustrious, the most powerful, and what not. But the President must be himself something that includes all the dignities of the diplomatic corps and something greater still. What will the common people of foreign countries, what will the sailors and the soldiers say, "George Washington, President of the United States?" They will despise him to all eternity. This is all nonsense to the philosopher, but so is all government whatever.

The above I recollect with great precision, but he said fifty more things, equally injudicious, which I do not think worth minuting. It is evident that he begins to despair of getting the article of titles through the House of Representatives, and has turned his eye to get it done solely by the Senate.

Having experienced relief by the interference of sundry members, I had determined not to say another word, but his new leaf appeared so absurd I could not help some animadversions on it. I rose.

> Mr. President, the Constitution of the United States has designated our chief magistrate by the appellation of the "President of the United States of America." This is his title of office, nor can we alter, add to, or diminish it without infringing the Constitution. In like manner, persons authorized to transact business with foreign powers are styled "ambassadors, public ministers," etc. To give them any other appellation would be an equal infringement. As to grades of orders or titles of nobility, nothing of the kind can be established by Congress.
>
> Can, then, the President and Senate do that which is prohibited to the United States at large? Certainly not. Let us read the Constitution: "No title of nobility shall be granted by the United States." The Constitution goes further. The servants of the public are prohibited from accepting them from any foreign state, king, or prince. So that the appellations and terms given to nobility in the Old World are contraband language in the United States, nor can we apply them to our citizens, consistent with the Constitution. As to what the common people, soldiers, and sailors of foreign countries may think of us, I do not think it imports us much. Perhaps the less they think, or have occasion to think of us, the better. . . .

After all this, he had to put the question, and the postponement was carried. I kept my word and offered the resolution for a conference on the differences, etc. It was carried, and the committee appointed. Elsworth, the most conceited man in the world, drew up a new resolution. It was to keep the differences out of sight, and to proceed *de novo* on a title for the President. I did not enter into debate, but expressed my fear that the House of Representatives would be irritated and would not meet us on that ground. And, as if they meant to provoke the other House, they insisted that the minute of rejection should go down with the appointment of the committee. Little good can come of it thus circumstanced, more especially as the old committee were reappointed.

---

72.

## JAMES MADISON: A Bill of Rights Proposed

*On June 8, 1789, the order of business before the House of Representatives was to consider the proposed amendments to the Constitution that would define individual liberties. Ironically, James Madison, who had previously given vigorous expression of his opposition to these amendments, was the representative who presented them to the House. "Without promise of a limiting Bill of Rights," Justice Robert H. Jackson observed in 1943, "it is doubtful if our Constitution would have mustered enough strength to enable its ratification." Partly to fulfill this promise, partly to enhance his own political position, and partly because he was convinced by Thomas Jefferson's arguments for a written declaration of rights, Madison had decided to sponsor the constitutional amendments. The following selection contains Madison's comments as well as the actual proposals that he made on this occasion.*

Source: *Debates,* I, pp. 424-450.

THIS DAY, MR. SPEAKER, is the day assigned for taking into consideration the subject of amendments to the Constitution. As I considered myself bound in honor and in duty to do what I have done on this subject, I shall proceed to bring the amendments before you as soon as possible and advocate them until they shall be finally adopted or rejected by a constitutional majority of this House. With a view of drawing your attention to this important object, I shall move that this House do now resolve itself into a committee of the whole on the state of the Union; by which an opportunity will be given to bring forward some propositions, which I have strong hopes will meet with the unanimous approbation of this House after the fullest discussion and most serious regard. . . .

When I first hinted to the House my intention of calling their deliberations to this object, I mentioned the pressure of other important subjects, and submitted the propriety of postponing this till the more urgent business was dispatched; but finding that business not dispatched when the order of the day for considering amendments arrived, I thought it a good reason for a further delay; I moved the postponement accordingly. I am sorry the same reason still exists in some degree, but it operates with less force when it is considered that it is not now proposed to enter into a full and minute discussion of every part of the subject but merely to bring it before the House, that our constituents may see we pay a proper attention to a subject they have much at heart; and if it does not give that full gratification which is to be wished, they will discover that it proceeds from the urgency of business of a very important nature. But if we continue to postpone from time to time, and refuse to let the subject come into view, it may occasion suspicions which, though not well founded, may tend to inflame or prejudice the public mind against our decisions. They may think we are not sincere in our desire to incorporate such amendments in the Constitution as will secure those rights, which they consider as not sufficiently guarded.

The applications for amendments come from a very respectable number of our constituents, and it is certainly proper for Congress to consider the subject in order to quiet that anxiety which prevails in the public mind. Indeed, I think it would have been of advantage to the government if it had been practicable to have made some propositions for amendments the first business we entered upon; it would have stifled the voice of complaint, and made friends of many who doubted the merits of the Constitution. Our future measures would then have been more generally agreeably supported; but the justifiable anxiety to put the government into operation prevented that; it, therefore, remains for us to take it up as soon as possible.

I wish, then, to commence the consideration at the present moment; I hold it to be my duty to unfold my ideas, and explain myself to the House in some form or other without delay. I only wish to introduce the great work, and, as I said before, I do not expect it will be decided immediately; but if some step is taken in the business, it will give reason to believe that we may come to a final result. This will inspire a reasonable hope in the advocates for amendments, that full justice will be done to the important subject; and I have reason to believe their expectation will not be defeated. I hope the House will not decline my motion for going into a committee. . . .

I will state my reasons why I think it proper to propose amendments, and state the amendments themselves so far as I think they ought to be proposed. If I thought I could fulfil the duty which I owe to myself and my constituents, to let the subject pass over in silence, I most certainly should not trespass upon the indulgence of this House. But I cannot do this, and am, therefore, compelled to beg a patient hearing to what I have to lay before you. And I do most sincerely believe that if Congress will devote but one day to this subject, so far as to satisfy the public that we do not disregard their wishes, it will have a salutary influence on the public councils, and prepare the way for a favorable reception of our future measures. It appears to me that this House is bound by every motive of prudence not to let the first session pass over without proposing to the state legislatures some things to be incorporated into the Constitution that will render it as acceptable to the whole people of the United States as it has been found acceptable to a majority of them.

I wish, among other reasons why something should be done, that those who had been friendly to the adoption of this Constitution may have the opportunity of proving to those who were opposed to it that they were as sincerely devoted to liberty and a republican government as those who charged them with wishing the adoption of this Constitution in order to lay the foundation of an aristocracy or despotism. It will be a desirable thing to extinguish from the bosom of every member of the community any apprehensions that there are those among his countrymen who wish to deprive them of the liberty for which they valiantly fought and honorably bled. And if there are amendments desired of such a nature as will not injure the Constitution, and they can be ingrafted so as to give satisfaction to the doubting part of our fellow citizens, the friends of the federal government will evince that spirit of deference and concession for which they have hitherto been distinguished.

It cannot be a secret to the gentlemen in this House that, notwithstanding the ratification of this system of government by eleven of the thirteen United States, in some cases unanimously, in others by large majorities; yet still there is a great number of our constituents who are dissatisfied with it, among whom are many respectable for their talents and patriotism, and respectable for the jealousy they have for their liberty, which, though mistaken in its object, is laudable in its motive. There is a great body of the people falling under this description, who at present feel much inclined to join their support to the cause of Federalism, if they were satisfied on this one point. We ought not to disregard their inclination, but, on principles of amity and moderation, conform to their wishes and expressly declare the great rights of mankind secured under this Constitution. The acquiescence which our fellow citizens show under the government calls upon us for a like return of moderation.

But perhaps there is a stronger motive than this for our going into a consideration of the subject. It is to provide those securities for liberty which are required by a part of the community. I allude in a particular manner to those two states that have not thought fit to throw themselves into the bosom of the Confederacy. It is a desirable thing, on our part as well as theirs, that a reunion should take place as soon as possible. I have no doubt, if we proceed to take those steps which would be prudent and requisite at this juncture, that in a short time we should see that disposition prevailing in those states which have not come in, that we have seen prevailing in those states which have embraced the Constitution.

But I will candidly acknowledge that, over and above these considerations, I do conceive that the Constitution may be amended; that is to say, if all power is subject to abuse, that then it is possible the abuse of the powers of the general government may be guarded against in a more secure manner than is now done, while no one advantage arising from the exercise of that power shall be damaged or endangered by it. We have in this way something to gain, and, if we proceed with caution, nothing to lose. And in this case it is necessary to proceed with caution; for, while we feel all these inducements to go into a revisal of the Constitution, we must feel for the Constitution itself, and make that revisal a moderate one. I should be unwilling to see a door opened for a reconsideration of the whole structure of the government — for a reconsideration of the principles and the substance of the powers given; because I doubt if such a door were opened we should be very likely to stop at that point which would be safe to the government itself. But I do wish to see a door opened to consider, so far as to incorporate those provisions for the security of rights, against which I believe no serious objection has been made by any class of our constituents, such as would be likely to meet with the concurrence of two-thirds of both houses, and the approbation of three-fourths of the state legislatures. I will not propose a single alteration which I do not wish to see take place, as intrinsically proper in itself, or proper because it is wished for by a respectable number of my fellow citizens; and, therefore, I shall not propose a single alteration but is likely to meet the concurrence required by the Constitution.

There have been objections of various

kinds made against the Constitution. Some were leveled against its structure because the president was without a council; because the Senate, which is a legislative body, had judicial powers in trials on impeachments; and because the powers of that body were compounded in other respects in a manner that did not correspond with a particular theory; because it grants more power than is supposed to be necessary for every good purpose, and controls the ordinary powers of the state governments. I know some respectable characters who opposed this government on these grounds; but I believe that the great mass of the people who opposed it disliked it because it did not contain effectual provisions against the encroachments on particular rights, and those safeguards which they have been long accustomed to have interposed between them and the magistrate who exercises the sovereign power; nor ought we to consider them safe while a great number of our fellow citizens think these securities necessary.

It is a fortunate thing that the objection to the government has been made on the ground I stated; because it will be practicable, on that ground, to obviate the objection, so far as to satisfy the public mind that their liberties will be perpetual, and this without endangering any part of the Constitution, which is considered as essential to the existence of the Government by those who promoted its adoption.

The amendments which have occurred to me, proper to be recommended by Congress to the state legislatures, are these:

First, that there be prefixed to the Constitution a declaration that all power is originally vested in, and consequently derived from, the people. That government is instituted and ought to be exercised for the benefit of the people; which consists in the enjoyment of life and liberty with the right of acquiring and using property, and generally of pursuing and obtaining happiness and safety. That the people have an indubitable, unalienable, and indefeasible right to reform or change their government whenever it be found adverse or inadequate to the purposes of its institution.

Second, that in Article I, Section 2, clause 3, these words be struck out, to wit: "The number of representatives shall not exceed 1 for every 30,000, but each state shall have at least 1 representative, and until such enumeration shall be made"; and that in place thereof be inserted these words, to wit: "After the first actual enumeration, there shall be 1 representative for every 30,000 until the number amounts to ———, after which the proportion shall be so regulated by Congress that the number shall never be less than ———, nor more than ———, but each state shall, after the first enumeration, have at least 2 representatives; and prior thereto."

Third, that in Article I, Section 6, clause 1, there be added to the end of the first sentence these words, to wit: "But no law varying the compensation last ascertained shall operate before the next ensuing election of representatives."

Fourth, that in Article I, Section 9, between clauses 3 and 4, be inserted these clauses, to wit:

The civil rights of none shall be abridged on account of religious belief or worship, nor shall any national religion be established, nor shall the full and equal rights of conscience be in any manner, or on any pretext, infringed.

The people shall not be deprived or abridged of their right to speak, to write, or to publish their sentiments; and the freedom of the press, as one of the great bulwarks of liberty, shall be inviolable.

The people shall not be restrained from peaceably assembling and consulting for their common good; nor from applying to the legislature by petitions or remonstrances for redress of their grievances.

The right of the people to keep and bear arms shall not be infringed; a well-armed and well-regulated militia being the best security of a free country; but no person religiously scrupulous of bearing arms shall be compelled to render military service in person.

No soldier shall in time of peace be quartered in any house without the consent of the owner, nor at any time, but in a manner warranted by law.

No person shall be subject, except in cases of impeachment, to more than one punishment or one trial for the same offense; nor shall be compelled to be a witness against himself; nor be deprived of life, liberty, or property without due process of law; nor be obliged to relinquish his property, where it may be necessary for public use, without a just compensation.

Excessive bail shall not be required, nor excessive fines imposed, nor cruel and unusual punishments inflicted.

The rights of the people to be secured in their persons, their houses, their papers, and their other property from all unreasonable searches and seizures shall not be violated by warrants issued without probable cause, supported by oath or affirmation, or not particularly describing the places to be searched, or the persons or things to be seized.

In all criminal prosecutions, the accused shall enjoy the right to a speedy and public trial, to be informed of the cause and nature of the accusation, to be confronted with his accusers and the witnesses against him; to have a compulsory process for obtaining witnesses in his favor; and to have the assistance of counsel for his defense.

The exceptions here or elsewhere in the Constitution made in favor of particular rights shall not be so construed as to diminish the just importance of other rights retained by the people, or as to enlarge the powers delegated by the Constitution; but either as actual limitations of such powers, or as inserted merely for greater caution.

Fifth, that in Article I, Section 10, between clauses 1 and 2, be inserted this clause, to wit:

No state shall violate the equal rights of conscience, or the freedom of the press, or the trial by jury in criminal cases.

Sixth, that, in Article III, Section 2 be annexed to the end of clause 2 these words, to wit: "But no appeal to such court shall be allowed where the value in controversy shall not amount to ——— dollars: nor shall any fact triable by jury, according to the course of common law, be otherwise reexaminable than may consist with the principles of common law."

Seventh, that in Article III, Section 2 the 3rd clause be struck out, and in its place be inserted the clauses following, to wit:

The trial of all crimes (except in cases of impeachments, and cases arising in the land or naval forces, or the militia when on actual service in time of war or public danger) shall be by an impartial jury of freeholders of the vicinage, with the requisite of unanimity for conviction, of the right of challenge, and other accustomed requisites; and in all crimes punishable with loss of life or member, presentment or indictment by a grand jury shall be an essential preliminary, provided that in cases of crimes committed within any county which may be in possession of an enemy, or in which a general insurrection may prevail, the trial may by law be authorized in some other county of the same state, as near as may be to the seat of the offense.

In cases of crimes committed not within any county, the trial may by law be in such county as the laws shall have prescribed. In suits at common law between man and man, the trial by jury, as one of the best securities to the rights of the people, ought to remain inviolate.

Eighth, that immediately after Article VI be inserted, as Article VII, the clauses following, to wit:

The powers delegated by this Constitution are appropriated to the departments to which they are respectively distributed; so that the Legislative Department shall never exercise the powers vested in the Executive or Judicial, nor the Executive exercise the powers vested in the Legislative or Judicial, nor the Judicial exercise the powers vested in the Legislative or Executive Departments.

The powers not delegated by this Constitution, nor prohibited by it to the states, are reserved to the states, respectively.

Ninth, that Article VII be numbered as Article VIII.

The first of these amendments relates to what may be called a Bill of Rights. I will own that I never considered this provision so essential to the federal Constitution as to make it improper to ratify it, until such an amendment was added; at the same time, I always conceived that, in a certain form and to a certain extent, such a provision was neither improper nor altogether useless. I am aware that a great number of the most respectable friends to the government and champions for republican liberty have thought such a provision not only unnecessary but even improper; nay, I believe some have gone so far as to think it even dangerous. Some policy has been made use of, perhaps, by gentlemen on both sides of the question.

I acknowledge the ingenuity of those arguments which were drawn against the Constitution by a comparison with the policy of Great Britain in establishing a Declaration of Rights, but there is too great a difference in the case to warrant the comparison; therefore, the arguments drawn from that source were in a great measure inapplicable. In the Declaration of Rights which that country has established, the truth is they have gone no further than to raise a barrier against the power of the Crown; the power of the legislature is left altogether indefinite. Although I know whenever the great rights — the trial by jury, freedom of the press, or liberty of conscience — come in question in that body, the invasion of them is resisted by able advocates, yet their Magna Carta does not contain any one provision for the security of those rights, respecting which the people of America are most alarmed. The freedom of the press and rights of conscience, those choicest privileges of the people, are unguarded in the British constitution.

But although the case may be widely different, and it may not be thought necessary to provide limits for the legislative power in that country, yet a different opinion prevails in the United States. The people of many states have thought it necessary to raise barriers against power in all forms and departments of government; and I am inclined to believe, if once bills of rights are established in all the states as well as the federal Constitution, we shall find that, although some of them are rather unimportant, yet, upon the whole, they will have a salutary tendency. It may be said, in some instances, they do no more than state the perfect equality of mankind. This, to be sure, is an absolute truth, yet it is not absolutely necessary to be inserted at the head of a constitution.

In some instances they assert those rights which are exercised by the people in forming and establishing a plan of government. In other instances, they specify those rights which are retained when particular powers are given up to be exercised by the legislature. In other instances, they specify positive rights, which may seem to result from the nature of the compact. Trial by jury cannot be considered as a natural right but a right resulting from a social compact which regulates the action of the community, but is as essential to secure the liberty of the people as any one of the preexistent rights of nature. In other instances, they lay down dogmatic maxims with respect to the construction of the government; declaring that the Legislative, Executive, and Judicial branches shall be kept separate and distinct. Perhaps the best way of securing this in practice is to provide such checks as will prevent the encroachment of the one upon the other.

But, whatever may be the form which

the several states have adopted in making declarations in favor of particular rights, the great object in view is to limit and qualify the powers of government by excepting out of the grant of power those cases in which the government ought not to act, or to act only in a particular mode. They point these exceptions sometimes against the abuse of the executive, and, in some cases, against the community itself; or, in other words, against the majority in favor of the minority.

In our government it is, perhaps, less necessary to guard against the abuse in the Executive Department than any other; because it is not the stronger branch of the system but the weaker. It, therefore, must be leveled against the Legislative, for it is the most powerful and most likely to be abused, because it is under the least control. Hence, so far as a declaration of rights can tend to prevent the exercise of undue power, it cannot be doubted but such declaration is proper. But I confess that I do conceive, that in a government modified like this of the United States, the great danger lies rather in the abuse of the community than in the legislative body. The prescriptions in favor of liberty ought to be leveled against that quarter where the greatest danger lies, namely, that which possesses the highest prerogative of power. But this is not found in either the Executive or Legislative departments of government but in the body of the people, operating by the majority against the minority. . . .

It has been said by way of objection to a Bill of Rights by many respectable gentlemen out of doors, and I find opposition on the same principles likely to be made by gentlemen on this floor, that they are unnecessary articles of a republican government, upon the presumption that the people have those rights in their own hands, and that is the proper place for them to rest. It would be a sufficient answer to say that this objection lies against such provisions under the state governments, as well as under the general government; and there are, I believe, but few gentlemen who are inclined to push their theory so far as to say that a declaration of rights in those cases is either ineffectual or improper. It has been said that in the federal government they are unnecessary because the powers are enumerated, and it follows that all that are not granted by the Constitution are retained; that the Constitution is a bill of powers, the great residuum being the rights of the people; and, therefore, a Bill of Rights cannot be so necessary as if the residuum was thrown into the hands of the government.

I admit that these arguments are not entirely without foundation; but they are not conclusive to the extent which has been supposed. It is true, the powers of the general government are circumscribed, they are directed to particular objects; but even if government keeps within those limits, it has certain discretionary powers with respect to the means, which may admit of abuse to a certain extent, in the same manner as the powers of the state governments under their constitutions may to an indefinite extent; because in the Constitution of the United States there is a clause granting to Congress the power to make all laws which shall be necessary and proper for carrying into execution all the powers vested in the government of the United States, or in any department or officer thereof; this enables them to fulfil every purpose for which the government was established.

Now, may not laws be considered necessary and proper by Congress (for it is for them to judge of the necessity and propriety to accomplish those special purposes which they may have in contemplation), which laws in themselves are neither necessary nor proper; as well as improper laws could be enacted by the state legislatures for fulfilling the more extended objects of those Governments? I will state an instance, which I think in point, and proves that this might be the case. The general government has a right to pass all laws which shall be necessary to collect its revenue; the means for enforcing the collection are within the direction of the legislature: may not general warrants be considered necessary for this purpose, as well as for some purposes which it was supposed at the framing of their constitutions the state governments had in view? If there was reason for restraining the state governments from exercising this power, there is like reason for restraining the federal government.

It may be said, indeed, it has been said, that a Bill of Rights is not necessary because the establishment of this government has not repealed those declarations of rights which are added to the several state constitutions; that those rights of the people which had been established by the most solemn act could not be annihilated by a subsequent act of that people who meant and declared at the head of the instrument that they ordained and established a new system for the express purpose of securing to themselves and posterity the liberties they had gained by an arduous conflict.

I admit the force of this observation, but I do not look upon it to be conclusive. In the first place, it is too uncertain ground to leave this provision upon, if a provision is at all necessary to secure rights so important as many of those I have mentioned are conceived to be, by the public in general, as well as those in particular who opposed the adoption of this Constitution. Besides, some states have no bills of rights, there are others provided with very defective ones, and there are others whose bills of rights are not only defective but absolutely improper; instead of securing some in the full extent which republican principles would require, they limit them too much to agree with the common ideas of liberty.

It has been objected also against a Bill of Rights that, by enumerating particular exceptions to the grant of power, it would disparage those rights which were not placed in that enumeration; and it might follow by implication that those rights which were not singled out were intended to be assigned into the hands of the general government, and were consequently insecure. This is one of the most plausible arguments I have ever heard urged against the admission of a Bill of Rights into this system; but, I conceive that it may be guarded against. I have attempted it, as gentlemen may see by turning to the last clause of the 4th resolution.

It has been said that it is unnecessary to load the Constitution with this provision because it was not found effectual in the constitution of the particular states. It is true there are a few particular states in which some of the most valuable articles have not, at one time or other, been violated; but it does not follow but they may have, to a certain degree, a salutary effect against the abuse of power. If they are incorporated into the Constitution, independent tribunals of justice will consider themselves in a peculiar manner the guardians of those rights; they will be an impenetrable bulwark against every assumption of power in the legislative or executive; they will be naturally led to resist every encroachment upon rights expressly stipulated for in the Constitution by the declaration of rights. Besides this security, there is a great probability that such a declaration in the federal system would be enforced; because the state legislatures will jealously and closely watch the operations of this government, and be able to resist with more effect every assumption of power than any other power on earth can do; and the greatest opponents to a federal government admit the state legislatures to be sure guardians of the people's liberty.

I conclude, from this view of the subject, that it will be proper in itself, and highly politic for the tranquility of the public mind and the stability of the government that we should offer something, in the form I have proposed, to be incorporated in the system of government as a declaration of the rights of the people.

In the next place, I wish to see that part of the Constitution revised which declares that the number of representatives shall not exceed the proportion of 1 for every 30,000 persons, and allows one representative to every state which rates below that proportion. If we attend to the discussion of this subject which has taken place in the state conventions, and even in the opinion of the friends to the Constitution, an alteration here is proper. It is the sense of the people of America that the number of representatives ought to be increased, but particularly that it should not be left in the discretion of the government to diminish them below that proportion which certainly is in the power of the legislature, as the Constitution now stands; and they may, as the population of the country increases, increase the House of Representatives to a very unwieldy degree, I confess I always thought this part of the Constitution defective, though not dangerous; and that it ought to be particularly attended to whenever Congress should go into the consideration of amendments.

There are several minor cases enumerated in my proposition, in which I wish also to see some alteration take place. That article which leaves it in the power of the legislature to ascertain its own emolument is one to which I allude. I do not believe this is a power which, in the ordinary course of government, is likely to be abused. Perhaps of all the powers granted, it is least likely to abuse; but there is a seeming impropriety in leaving any set of men without control to put their hand into the public coffers, to take out money to put in their pockets; there is a seeming indecorum in such power, which leads me to propose a change. We have a guide to this alteration in several of the amendments which the different conventions have proposed. I have gone, therefore, so far as to fix it, that no law varying the compensation shall operate until there is a change in the legislature; in which case it cannot be for the particular benefit of those who are concerned in determining the value of the service.

I wish, also, in revising the Constitution, we may throw into that section which interdicts the abuse of certain powers in the state legislatures, some other provisions of equal if not greater importance than those already made. The words "No state shall pass any bill of attainder, *ex post facto* law, etc.," were wise and proper restrictions in the Constitution. I think there is more danger of those powers being abused by the state governments than by the government of the United States. The same may be said of other powers which they possess, if not controlled by the general principle that laws are unconstitutional which infringe the rights of the community. I should, therefore, wish to extend this interdiction and add, as I have stated in the 5th resolution, that no state shall violate the equal right of conscience, freedom of the press, or trial by jury in criminal cases; because it is proper that every government should be disarmed of powers which trench upon those particular rights. I know, in some of the state constitutions, the power of the government is controlled by such a declaration; but others are not. I cannot see any reason against obtaining even a double security on those points; and nothing can give a more sincere proof of the attachment of those who opposed this Constitution to these great and important rights than to see them join in obtaining the security I have now proposed; because it must be admitted on all hands that the state governments are as liable to attack these invaluable privileges as the general government is, and, therefore ought to be as cautiously guarded against.

I think it will be proper, with respect to the judiciary powers, to satisfy the public mind on those points which I have mentioned. Great inconvenience has been apprehended to suitors from the distance they would be dragged to obtain justice in the Supreme Court of the United States upon an appeal on an action for a small debt. To remedy this, declare that no appeal shall be made unless the matter in controversy amounts to a particular sum; this, with the regulations respecting jury trials in criminal cases and suits at common law, it is to be hoped, will quiet and reconcile the minds of the people to that part of the Constitution.

I find, from looking into the amendments proposed by the state conventions, that several are particularly anxious that it should be declared in the Constitution that the powers not therein delegated should be reserved to the several states. Perhaps other words may define this more precisely than the whole of the instrument now does. I admit they may be deemed unnecessary; but there can be no harm in making such a declaration if gentlemen will allow that the fact is as stated. I am sure I understand it so, and do, therefore, propose it.

These are the points on which I wish to see a revision of the Constitution take place. How far they will accord with the sense of this body, I cannot take upon me absolutely to determine; but I believe every gentleman will readily admit that nothing is in contemplation, so far as I have mentioned, that can endanger the beauty of the government in any one important feature, even in the eyes of its most sanguine admirers. I have proposed nothing that does not appear to me as proper in itself, or eligible as patronized by a respectable number of our fellow citizens; and if we can make the Constitution better in the opinion of those who are opposed to it without weakening its frame or abridging its usefulness in the judgment of those who are attached to it, we act the part of wise and liberal men to make such alterations as shall produce that effect.

Having done what I conceived was my duty in bringing before this House the subject of amendments, and also stated such as I wish for and approve and offered the reasons which occurred to me in their support, I shall content myself, for the present, with moving "that a committee be appointed to consider of and report such amendments as ought to be proposed by Congress to the legislatures of the states to become, if ratified by three-fourths thereof, part of the Constitution of the United States." By agreeing to this motion, the subject may be going on in the committee while other important business is proceeding to a conclusion in the House. I should advocate greater dispatch in the business of amendments if I were not convinced of the absolute necessity there is of pursuing the organization of the government; because I think we should obtain the confidence of our fellow citizens in proportion as we fortify the rights of the people against the encroachments of the government.

73.

## The Bill of Rights

*In the three and a half months during which the proposed amendments to the Constitution were before Congress, only seven or eight days were actually spent in debating them. On September 25, 1789, final drafts of twelve amendments (out of the many that had been suggested by Madison and others) were passed by Congress and presented to the states for approval. Two of the twelve were never ratified; they would have limited the number of members of the House of Representatives, and prevented Congress from raising its salaries without an election intervening. On December 15, 1791, when Virginia became the eleventh state to ratify them, the other ten proposed amendments or additions to the Constitution, which are reprinted here, became part of the supreme law of the land. The so-called Bill of Rights, as finally ratified, was generally modeled after the Virginia Declaration of Rights of 1776. Its significant contribution was to put into writing as part of a constitution those protections against government encroachment that had often been assumed, but not before so explicitly defined.*

Source: Poore, 2nd edition, I, pp. 21-22.

### ARTICLE I

Congress shall make no law respecting an establishment of religion or prohibiting the free exercise thereof, or abridging the freedom of speech or of the press, or the right of the people peaceably to assemble and to petition the government for a redress of grievances.

### ARTICLE II

A well-regulated militia being necessary to the security of a free state, the right of the people to keep and bear arms shall not be infringed.

### ARTICLE III

No soldier shall, in time of peace, be quartered in any house without the consent of the owner, nor in time of war but in a manner to be prescribed by law.

### ARTICLE IV

The right of the people to be secure in their persons, houses, papers, and effects against unreasonable searches and seizures shall not be violated, and no warrants shall issue, but upon probable cause, supported by oath or affirmation, and particularly describing the place to be searched and the persons or things to be seized.

### ARTICLE V

No person shall be held to answer for a capital or otherwise infamous crime unless on a presentment or indictment of a grand jury, except in cases arising in the land or naval forces, or in the militia, when in actual service in time of war or public danger; nor shall any person be subject for the same offense to be twice put in jeopardy of life or limb; nor shall be compelled in any criminal case to be a witness against himself, nor be deprived of life, liberty, or property without due process of law; nor shall private property be taken for public use without just compensation.

ARTICLE VI

In all criminal prosecutions, the accused shall enjoy the right to a speedy and public trial by an impartial jury of the state and district wherein the crime shall have been committed, which district shall have been previously ascertained by law, and to be informed of the nature and cause of the accusation; to be confronted with the witnesses against him; to have compulsory process for obtaining witnesses in his favor, and to have the assistance of counsel for his defense.

ARTICLE VII

In suits at common law, where the value in controversy shall exceed twenty dollars, the right of trial by jury shall be preserved, and no fact tried by a jury shall be otherwise reexamined in any court of the United States than according to the rules of the common law.

ARTICLE VIII

Excessive bail shall not be required, nor excessive fines imposed, nor cruel and unusual punishments inflicted.

ARTICLE IX

The enumeration in the Constitution of certain rights shall not be construed to deny or disparage others retained by the people.

ARTICLE X

The powers not delegated to the United States by the Constitution, nor prohibited by it to the states, are reserved to the states respectively, or to the people.

---

74.

## Benjamin Franklin: On the Press as an Unofficial Tribunal

*Benjamin Franklin began his career as a printer and, though his activities branched into many other fields throughout his lifetime, he never lost interest in the press. He was not only concerned with the artistry and technicalities of the printing profession and journalism, but also with the political and social ramifications of the press. The selection reprinted here is from the* Federal Gazette, *September 12, 1789, and is one of the many essays Franklin wrote on the abuse of liberty by the press.*

Source: Sparks, II: "An Account of the Supremest Court of Judicature in Pennsylvania, viz., The Court of the Press."

### POWER OF THIS COURT

It may receive and promulgate accusations of all kinds against all persons and characters among the citizens of the state, and even against all inferior courts; and may judge, sentence, and condemn to infamy, not only private individuals but public bodies, etc., with or without inquiry or hearing, *at the court's discretion.*

## IN WHOSE FAVOR AND FOR WHOSE EMOLUMENT THIS COURT IS ESTABLISHED

It is in favor of about 1 citizen in 500, who, by education or practice in scribbling, has acquired a tolerable style as to grammar and construction so as to bear printing, or who is possessed of a press and a few types. This five-hundredth part of the citizens have the privilege of accusing and abusing the other 499 parts at their pleasure; or they may hire out their pens and press to others for that purpose.

## PRACTICE OF THE COURT

It is not governed by any of the rules of common courts of law. The accused is allowed no grand jury to judge of the truth of the accusation before it is publicly made, nor is the name of the accuser made known to him, nor has he an opportunity of confronting the witnesses against him; for they are kept in the dark as in the Spanish court of Inquisition. Nor is there any petty jury of his peers sworn to try the truth of the charges. The proceedings are also sometimes so rapid that an honest, good citizen may find himself suddenly and unexpectedly accused; and in the same morning judged and condemned and sentence pronounced against him, that he is a rogue and a villain. Yet, if an officer of this court receives the slightest check for misconduct in this, his office, he claims immediately the rights of a free citizen by the Constitution and demands to know his accuser, to confront the witnesses, and to have a fair trial by a jury of his peers.

## THE FOUNDATION OF ITS AUTHORITY

It is said to be founded on an article in the state constitution which establishes the *liberty of the press,* a liberty which every Pennsylvanian will fight and die for, though few of us, I believe, have distinct ideas of its nature and extent. It seems, indeed, somewhat like the *liberty of the press* that felons have, by the common law of England, before conviction: that is, to be *pressed* to death or hanged. If by the *liberty of the press* were understood merely the liberty of discussing the propriety of public measures and political opinions, let us have as much of it as you please; but if it means the liberty of affronting, calumniating, and defaming one another, I, for my part, own myself willing to part with my share of it whenever our legislators shall please so to alter the law, and shall cheerfully consent to exchange my *liberty* of abusing others for the *privilege* of not being abused myself.

## BY WHOM THIS COURT IS COMMISSIONED OR CONSTITUTED

It is not by any commission from the supreme executive council, who might previously judge of the abilities, integrity, knowledge, etc., of the persons to be appointed to this great trust, of deciding upon the characters and good fame of the citizens; for this court is above that council, and may *accuse, judge,* and *condemn* it at pleasure. Nor is it hereditary, as in the court of dernier resort in the peerage of England. But any man who can procure pen, ink, and paper, with a press, a few types, and a huge pair of *blacking* balls may commissionate himself; and his court is immediately established in the plenary possession and exercise of its rights. For if you make the least complaint of the judge's conduct, he daubs his blacking balls in your face wherever he meets you; and, besides tearing your private character to flitters, marks you out for the odium of the public, as an *enemy to the liberty of the press.*

## OF THE NATURAL SUPPORT OF THESE COURTS

THEIR SUPPORT is founded in the depravity of such minds as have not been mended by religion nor improved by good education:

> There is a lust in man no charm can tame,
> Of loudly publishing his neighbor's shame.

Hence,

> On eagle's wings immortal scandals fly,
> While virtuous actions are but born and die.
>
> DRYDEN

Whoever feels pain in hearing a good character of his neighbor will feel a pleasure in the reverse. And of those who, despairing to rise into distinction by their virtues, are happy if others can be depressed to a level with themselves, there are a number sufficient in every great town to maintain one of these courts by their subscriptions. A shrewd observer once said that, in walking the streets in a slippery morning, one might see where the good-natured people lived by the ashes thrown on the ice before their doors; probably he would have formed a different conjecture of the temper of those whom he might find engaged in such a subscription.

## OF THE CHECKS PROPER TO BE ESTABLISHED AGAINST THE ABUSE OF POWER IN THESE COURTS

HITHERTO there are none. But since so much has been written and published on the federal Constitution, and the necessity of checks in all other parts of good government has been so clearly and learnedly explained, I find myself so far enlightened as to suspect some check may be proper in this part also. But I have been at a loss to imagine any that may not be construed an infringement of the sacred *liberty of the press.* At length, however, I think I have found one that, instead of diminishing general liberty, shall augment it; which is, by restoring to the people a species of liberty of which they have been deprived by our laws; I mean the *liberty of the cudgel.* In the rude state of society prior to the existence of laws, if one man gave another ill language, the affronted person would return it by a box on the ear and, if repeated, by a good drubbing; and this without offending against any law. But now the right of making such returns is denied, and they are punished as breaches of the peace; while the right of abusing seems to remain in full force, the laws made against it being rendered ineffectual by the *liberty of the press.*

My proposal, then, is to leave the *liberty of the press* untouched, to be exercised in its full extent, force, and vigor; but to permit the *liberty of the cudgel* to go with it *pari passu* [on equal footing]. Thus, my fellow citizens, if an impudent writer attacks your reputation, dearer to you perhaps than your life, and puts his name to the charge, you may go to him as openly and break his head. If he conceals himself behind the printer, and you can nevertheless discover who he is, you may in like manner waylay him in the night, attack him behind, and give him a good drubbing. Thus far goes my project as to private resentment and retribution. But if the public should ever happen to be affronted, as it ought to be with the conduct of such writers, I would not advise proceeding immediately to these extremities; but that we should in moderation content ourselves with tarring and feathering, and tossing them in a blanket.

If, however, it should be thought that this proposal of mine may disturb the public peace, I would then humbly recommend to our legislators to take up the consideration of both liberties, that of the press, and that of the cudgel, and by an explicit law mark their extent and limits; and, at the same time that they secure the person of a citizen from assaults, they would likewise provide for the security of his reputation.

75.

# The Judiciary Act of 1789

*Federal judiciary power was vested by the Constitution in "one Supreme Court, and in such inferior courts as the Congress may from time to time ordain and establish." No further provisions were made for the organization or composition of the judicial branch of government. Thus, on September 24, 1789, Congress passed the first Judiciary Act, specifying the number of judges and types of courts to have federal jurisdiction. The establishment of federal judicial review over state legislation was of great significance; it was a doctrine that was to have far-reaching economic and social effects. The essential features of this architectonic act are still in force.*

Source: *Statutes*, I, pp. 73-93.

Section 1. *Be it enacted by the Senate and House of Representatives of the United States of America in Congress assembled,* that the Supreme Court of the United States shall consist of a chief justice and five associate justices, any four of whom shall be a quorum and shall hold annually at the seat of government two sessions: the one commencing the first Monday of February, and the other the first Monday of August. That the associate justices shall have precedence according to the date of their commissions, or when the commissions of two or more of them bear date on the same day according to their respective ages.

Section 2. *And be it further enacted,* that the United States shall be, and they hereby are, divided into thirteen districts. . . .

Section 3. *And be it further enacted,* that there be a court called a District Court in each of the aforementioned districts, to consist of one judge, who shall reside in the district for which he is appointed, and shall be called a district judge, and shall hold annually four sessions. . . .

Section 4. *And be it further enacted,* that the . . . districts, except those of Maine and Kentucky, shall be divided into three circuits and be called the Eastern, the Middle, and the Southern circuit. That the Eastern Circuit shall consist of the districts of New Hampshire, Massachusetts, Connecticut, and New York; that the Middle Circuit shall consist of the districts of New Jersey, Pennsylvania, Delaware, Maryland, and Virginia; and that the Southern Circuit shall consist of the districts of South Carolina and Georgia; and that there shall be held annually in each district of said circuits two courts, which shall be called circuit courts, and shall consist of any two justices of the Supreme Court and the district judge of such districts, any two of whom shall constitute a quorum. *Provided,* that no district judge shall give a vote in any case of appeal or error from his own decision; but may assign the reasons of such his decision. . . .

Section 9. *And be it further enacted,* that the district courts shall have, exclusively of the courts of the several states, cognizance of all crimes and offenses that shall be cognizable under the authority of the United States, committed within their respective districts or upon the high seas; where no other punishment than whipping, not exceeding thirty stripes, a fine not exceeding $100, or a term of imprisonment not exceeding six months, is to be inflicted; and shall also have exclusive original cognizance of all civil cases of Admiralty and maritime jurisdiction, including all seizures under laws of impost, navigation, or trade of the United States, where the seizures are made, on waters which are navigable from the sea by vessels of ten or more tons burden, within their respective districts as well as upon the high seas; saving to suitors, in all cases, the right of a common law remedy, where the common law is competent to give it; and shall also have exclusive original cognizance of all seizures on land, or other waters than as aforesaid, made, and of all suits for penalties and forfeitures incurred, under the laws of the United States.

And shall also have cognizance, concurrent with the courts of the several states, or the circuit courts, as the case may be, of all cases where an alien sues for a tort only in violation of the law of nations or a treaty of the United States. And shall also have cognizance, concurrent as last mentioned, of all suits at common law where the United States sue, and the matter in dispute amounts, exclusive of costs, to the sum or value of $100. And shall also have jurisdiction exclusively of the courts of the several states, of all suits against consuls or vice-consuls, except for offenses above the description aforesaid. And the trial of issues in fact, in the district courts, in all cases except civil cases of Admiralty and maritime jurisdiction, shall be by jury. . . .

Section 11. *And be it further enacted,* that the circuit courts shall have original cognizance, concurrent with the courts of the several states, of all suits of a civil nature at common law or in equity, where the matter in dispute exceeds, exclusive of costs, the sum or value of $500, and the United States are plaintiffs or petitioners; or an alien is a party, or the suit is between a citizen of the state where the suit is brought and a citizen of another state. And shall have exclusive cognizance of all crimes and offenses cognizable under the authority of the United States, except where this act otherwise provides, or the laws of the United States shall otherwise direct, and concurrent jurisdiction with the district courts of the crimes and offenses cognizable therein.

But no person shall be arrested in one district for trial in another, in any civil action before a circuit or district court. And no civil suit shall be brought before either of said courts against an inhabitant of the United States, by any original process in any other district than that whereof he is an inhabitant, or in which he shall be found at the time of serving the writ, nor shall any district or circuit court have cognizance of any suit to recover the contents of any promissory note or other chose in action in favor of an assignee, unless a suit might have been prosecuted in such court to recover the said contents if no assignment had been made, except in cases of foreign bills of exchange. And the circuit courts shall also have appellate jurisdiction from the district courts under the regulations and restrictions hereinafter provided. . . .

Section 13. *And be it further enacted,* that the Supreme Court shall have exclusive jurisdiction of all controversies of a civil nature, where a state is a party, except between a state and its citizens; and except also between a state and citizens of other states, or aliens, in which latter case it shall have original but not exclusive jurisdiction. And shall have exclusively all such jurisdiction of suits or proceedings against ambassadors or other public ministers, or their domestics, or domestic servants, as a court of law can have or exercise consistently with the law of nations; and original, but not exclusive, jurisdiction of all suits brought by ambassadors or other public ministers, or in which a consul or vice-consul shall be a party. And the trial of issues in fact in the Supreme Court in all actions at law against citizens of the United States shall be by jury. The Supreme Court shall also have appellate jurisdiction from the circuit courts and courts of the several states in the cases hereinafter specially provided for; and shall have power to issue writs of prohibition to the district courts, when proceeding as Court of Admiralty and maritime jurisdiction, and writs of mandamus, in cases warranted by the principles and usages of law, to any courts appointed, or persons holding office under the authority of the United States.

Section 14. *And be it further enacted,* that all the beforementioned courts of the United States shall have power to issue writs of *scire facias,* habeas corpus, and all other writs not specially provided for by statute, which may be necessary for the exercise of their respective jurisdictions, and agreeable to the principles and usages of law. And that either of the justices of the Supreme Court, as well as judges of the district courts, shall have power to grant writs of habeas corpus for the purpose of an inquiry into the cause of commitment. *Provided,* that writs of habeas corpus shall in no case extend to prisoners in gaol, unless where they are in custody, under or by color of the authority of the United States, or are committed for trial before some court of the same, or are necessary to be brought into court to testify.

Section 15. *And be it further enacted,* that all the said courts of the United States shall have power in the trial of actions at law, on motion and due notice thereof being given, to require the parties to produce books or writings in their possession or power which contain evidence pertinent to the issue, in cases and under circumstances where they might be compelled to produce the same by the ordinary rules of proceeding in chancery; and if a plaintiff shall fail to comply with such order to produce books or writings, it shall be lawful for the courts respectively, on motion, to give the like judgment for the defendant as in cases of nonsuit; and if a defendant shall fail to comply with such order to produce books or writings, it shall be lawful for the courts respectively, on motions as aforesaid, to give judgment against him or her by default.

Section 16. *And be it further enacted,* that suits in equity shall not be sustained in either of the courts of the United States, in any case where plain, adequate, and complete remedy may be had at law.

Section 17. *And be it further enacted,* that all the said courts of the United States shall have power to grant new trials in cases where there has been a trial by jury for reasons for which new trials have usually been granted in the courts of law; and shall have power to impose and administer all necessary oaths or affirmations, and to punish by fine or imprisonment, at the discretion of said courts, all contempts of authority in any case or hearing before the same; and to make and establish all necessary rules for the orderly conducting of business in the said courts, provided such rules are not repugnant to the laws. . . .

Section 25. *And be it further enacted,* that a final judgment or decree in any suit, in the highest court of law or equity of a state in which a decision in the suit could be had, where is drawn in question the validity of a treaty or statute of, or an authority exercised under, the United States, and the decision is against their validity; or where is drawn in question the validity of a statute of, or an authority exercised under, any state, on the ground of their being repugnant to the Constitution, treaties, or laws of the United States, and the decision is in favor of such their validity; or where is drawn in question the construction of any clause of the Constitution, or of a treaty, or statute of, or commission held under, the United States, and the decision is against the title, right, privilege, or exemption specially set up or claimed by either party, under such clause of the said Constitution, treaty, statute, or commission, may be reexamined, and reversed or affirmed in the Supreme Court of the United States upon a writ of error, the citation being signed by the chief justice, or judge or chancellor of the court rendering or passing the judgment or decree complained of, or by a justice of the Supreme Court of the United States, in the same manner and under the same regulations.

And the writ shall have the same effect as if the judgment or decree complained of had been rendered or passed in a circuit court, and the proceeding upon the reversal shall also be the same, except that the Supreme Court, instead of remanding the case for a final decision as before provided, may, at their discretion, if the case shall have been once remanded before, proceed to a final decision of the same and award execution. But no other error shall be assigned or regarded as a ground of reversal in any such case as aforesaid than such as appears on the face of the record, and immediately respects the beforementioned questions of validity or construction of the said Constitution, treaties, statutes, commissions, or authorities in dispute. . . .

Section 27. *And be it further enacted,* that a marshal shall be appointed in and for each district for the term of four years, but shall be removable from office at pleasure, whose duty it shall be to attend the district and circuit courts when sitting therein, and also the Supreme Court in the district in which that court shall sit. And to execute throughout the district all lawful precepts directed to him, and issued under the authority of the United States; and he shall have power to command all necessary assistance in the execution of his duty, and to appoint, as there shall be occasion, one or more deputies. . . .

Section 29. *And be it further enacted,* that, in cases punishable with death, the trial shall be had in the county where the offense was committed, or where that cannot be done without great inconvenience, twelve petit jurors at least shall be summoned from thence. . . .

Section 30. *And be it further enacted,* that the mode of proof by oral testimony and examination of witnesses in open court shall be the same in all the courts of the United States, as well in the trial of cases in equity and of Admiralty and maritime jurisdiction, as of actions at common law. And when the testimony of any person shall be necessary in any civil case depending in any district in any court of the United States, who shall live at a greater distance from the place of trial than one hundred miles, or is bound on a voyage to sea, or is about to go out of the United States, or out of such district, and to a greater distance from the place of trial than as aforesaid, before the time of trial, or is ancient or very infirm, the deposition of such person may be taken *de bene esse* before any justice or judge of any of the courts of the United States, or before any chancellor, justice, or judge of a supreme or superior court, mayor or chief magistrate of a city, or judge of a county court or court of common pleas of any of the United States, not being of counsel or attorney to either of the parties, or interested in the event of the case. . . .

Section 35. *And be it further enacted,* that, in all the courts of the United States, the parties may plead and manage their own cases personally or by the assistance of such counsel or attorneys at law as by the rules of the said courts respectively shall be permitted to manage and conduct cases therein. And there shall be appointed in each district a meet person learned in the law to act as attorney for the United States in such district, who shall be sworn or affirmed to the faithful execution of his office, whose duty it shall be to prosecute in such district all delinquents for crimes and offenses, cognizable under the authority of the United States, and all civil actions in which the United States shall be concerned, except before the Supreme Court in the district in which that court shall be held. And he shall receive as a compensation for his services such fees as shall be taxed therefor in the respective courts before which the suits or prosecutions shall be.

And there shall also be appointed a meet person, learned in the law, to act as attorney general for the United States, who shall be sworn or affirmed to a faithful execution of his office, whose duty it shall be to prosecute and conduct all suits in the Supreme Court in which the United States shall be concerned, and to give his advice and opinion upon questions of law when required by the President of the United States, or when requested by the heads of any of the departments, touching any matters that may concern their departments, and shall receive such compensation for his services as shall by law be provided.

---

76.

## Benjamin Franklin: Remarks on the Revision of the Pennsylvania Constitution

*In the fall of 1789, it was proposed that the Pennsylvania constitution be changed so as to divide the state legislature into two houses, one of which would represent the property owners and the other the non-property owners, with equal authority between them. To support this and other proposals an article, entitled "Hints for the Members of [the] Convention," appeared in the* Federal Gazette, *November 3, 1789. Among those who opposed any change in the Pennsylvania constitution was Benjamin Franklin, who, though old and dying, undertook to combat the proposals contained in the "Hints." In the text of "Queries and Remarks Respecting Alterations in the Constitution of Pennsylvania" that follows, Franklin's replies are printed in roman type. Franklin had vainly contended in the federal convention of 1787 for a single-chambered national legislature.*

Source: Sparks, V, pp. 163-169.

### OF THE EXECUTIVE BRANCH

*Your executive should consist of a single person.*

On this I would ask, is he to have no council? How is he to be informed of the state and circumstances of the different counties, their wants, their abilities, their dispositions, and the characters of the principal people, respecting their integrity, capacities, and qualifications for offices? Does not the present construction of our executive provide well for these particulars? And, during the number of years it has existed, have its errors or failures in answering the end of its appointment been more or greater than might have been expected from a single person?

*But an individual is more easily watched and controlled than any greater number.*

On this I would ask, who is to watch and control him? And by what means is he to be controlled? Will not those means, whatever they are, and in whatever body vested, be subject to the same inconveniencies of expense, delay, obstruction of good intentions, etc., which are objected to the present executive?

## THE DURATION OF THE APPOINTMENT

*This should be governed by the following principles: the independence of the magistrate and the stability of his administration; neither of which can be secured but by putting both beyond the reach of every annual gust of folly and of faction.*

On this it may be asked, ought it not also to be put beyond the reach of every triennial, quinquennial, or septennial gust of folly and of faction, and, in short, beyond the reach of folly and of faction at any period whatever? Does not this reasoning aim at establishing a monarchy at least for life, like that of Poland? Or to prevent the inconveniences such as that kingdom is subject to in a new election on every decease? Are the freemen of Pennsylvania convinced, from a view of the history of such governments, that it will be for their advantage to submit themselves to a government of such construction?

## ON THE LEGISLATIVE BRANCH

*A plural legislature is as necessary to good government as a single executive. It is not enough that your legislature should be numerous; it should also be divided. Numbers alone are not a sufficient barrier against the impulses of passion, the combination of interest, the intrigues of faction, the haste of folly, or the spirit of encroachment. One division should watch over and control the other, supply its wants, correct its blunders, and cross its designs, should they be criminal or erroneous. Wisdom is the specific quality of the legislature, grows out of the number of the body, and is made up of the portions of sense and knowledge which each member brings to it.*

On this it may be asked, may not the wisdom brought to the legislature by each member be as effectual a barrier against the impulses of passion, etc., when the members are united in one body as when they are divided? If one part of the legislature may control the operations of the other, may not the impulses of passion, the combinations of interest, the intrigues of faction, the haste of folly, or the spirit of encroachment in one of those bodies obstruct the good proposed by the other, and frustrate its advantages to the public? Have we not experienced in this state, when a province under the government of the proprietors, the mischiefs of a second branch existing in the proprietary family, countenanced and aided by an aristocratic council? How many delays and what great expenses were occasioned in carrying on the public business; and what a train of mischiefs, even to the preventing of the defense of the province during several years, when distressed by an Indian war, by the iniquitous demand that the proprietary property should be exempt from taxation!

The wisdom of a few members in one single legislative body — may it not frequently stifle bad motions in their infancy and so prevent their being adopted? Whereas, if those wise men, in case of a double legislature, should happen to be in that branch wherein the motion did not arise, may it not, after being adopted by the other, occasion long disputes and contentions between the two bodies, expensive to the public, obstructing the public business, and promoting factions among the people, many tempers naturally adhering obstinately to measures they have once publicly adopted?

Have we not seen, in one of our neighboring states, a bad measure, adopted by one branch of the legislature for want of the assistance of some more intelligent members who had been packed into the other, occasion many debates conducted with much asperity, which could not be settled but by an expensive general appeal to the public? And have we not seen, in another neighboring state, a similar difference between the two branches, occasioning long debates and contentions, whereby the state was prevented for many months enjoying the advantage of having senators in the Congress of the United States? And has our present legislative in one assembly committed any errors of importance, which they have not remedied, or may not easily remedy; more easily, probably, than if divided into two branches? And if the wisdom brought by the members to the assembly is divided into two branches, may it not be too weak in each to support a good measure or obstruct a bad one? . . .

Has not the famous political fable of the snake with two heads and one body some useful instruction contained in it? She was going to a brook to drink, and in her way was to pass through a hedge, a twig of which opposed her direct course; one head chose to go on the right side of the twig, the other on the left; so that time was spent in the contest, and, before the decision was completed, the poor snake died with thirst.

*Hence it is that the two branches should be elected by persons differently qualified; and, in short, that, as far as possible, they should be made to represent different interests. Under this reason I would establish a legislature of two houses. The upper should represent the property; the lower, the population of the state. The upper should be chosen by freemen possessing in lands and houses £1,000; the lower, by all such as had resided four years in the country and paid taxes. The first should be chosen for four, the last for two years. They should in authority be coequal.*

Several questions may arise upon this proposition. First, what is the proportion of freemen possessing lands and houses of £1,000 value compared to that of freemen whose possessions are inferior? Are they as one to ten? Are they even as one to twenty? I should doubt whether they are as one to fifty. If this minority is to choose a body expressly to control that which is to be chosen by the great majority of the freemen, what have this great majority done to forfeit so great a portion of their right in elections? Why is this power of control, contrary to the spirit of all democracies, to be vested in a minority instead of a majority? Then is it intended, or is it not, that the rich should have a vote in the choice of members for the lower house, while those of inferior property are deprived of the right of voting for members of the upper house? And why should the upper house, chosen by a minority, have equal power with the lower chosen by a majority? Is it supposed that wisdom is the necessary concomitant of riches, and that one man worth £1,000 must have as much wisdom as twenty who have each only £999? And why is property to be represented at all?

Suppose one of our Indian nations should now agree to form a civil society; each individual would bring into the stock of the society little more property than his gun and his blanket, for at present he has no other. We know that when one of them has attempted to keep a few swine, he has not been able to maintain a property in them, his neighbors thinking they have a right to kill and eat them whenever they want provision, it being one of their maxims that hunting is free for all. The accumulation, therefore, of property in such a society, and its security to individuals in every society, must be an effect of the protection afforded to it by the joint strength of the society in the execution of its laws. Private property, therefore, is a creature of society, and is subject to the calls of that society whenever its necessities shall require it, even to its last farthing. Its contributions, therefore, to the public exigencies are not to be considered as conferring a benefit on the public, entitling the contributors to the distinctions of honor and power, but as the return of an obligation previously received, or the payment of a just debt.

The combinations of civil society are not like those of a set of merchants who club their property in different proportions for building and freighting a ship, and may therefore have some right to vote in the disposition of the voyage in a greater or less degree according to their respective contributions. But the important ends of civil society, and the personal securities of life and liberty there, remain the same in every member of the society. And the poorest continues to have an equal claim to them with the most opulent, whatever difference time, chance, or industry may occasion in their circumstances.

On these considerations, I am sorry to see the signs this paper I have been considering affords, of a disposition among some of our people to commence an aristocracy, by giving the rich a predominancy in government, a choice peculiar to themselves in one-half the legislature to be proudly called the upper house, and the other branch, chosen by the majority of the people, degraded by the denomination of the lower; and giving to this upper house a permanency of four years, and but two to the lower. I hope, therefore, that our representatives in the convention will not hastily go into these innovations, but take the advice of the prophet: "Stand in the old ways, view the ancient paths, consider them well, and be not among those that are given to change."

---

77.

## Noah Webster: Toward a National Language

*As the feeling of nationalism became a factor in the new nation, the English language took on many distinctly American characteristics. The lexicographer, Noah Webster, believed that full independence from England included the development of a uniquely American culture. Thus his* American Dictionary of the English Language, *published in 1828, made use of Americanized spellings and included many new words, such as "land-office," that were peculiar to the new institutions and experience of the United States. The following selection is taken from "An Essay on the Necessity, Advantages and Practicability of Reforming the Mode of Spelling," and contains many of the principles that inspired Webster's spellers, grammars, and his famous* Dictionary. *The "Essay" first appeared in 1789; Webster's spellings are retained here.*

Source: *Dissertations on the English Language: with Notes, Historical and Critical,* Boston, 1789, Appendix.

It has been observed by all writers on the English language that the orthography or spelling of words is very irregular; the same letters often representing different sounds, and the same sounds often expressed by different letters. For this irregularity, two principal causes may be assigned.

1. The changes to which the pronunciation of a language is liable, from the progress of science and civilization.

2. The mixture of different languages, occasioned by revolutions in England, or by a predilection of the learned for words of foreign growth and ancient origin.

To the first cause may be ascribed the difference between the spelling and pronunciation of Saxon words. The northern nations of Europe originally spoke much in gutturals. This is evident from the number of aspirates and guttural letters which still remain in the orthography of words derived from those nations; and from the modern pronunciation of the collateral branches of the Teutonic, the Dutch, Scotch, and German. Thus, *k* before *n* was once pronounced as in *knave, know;* the *gh* in *might, though, daughter,* and other similar words; the *g* in *reign, feign,* etc.

But as savages proceed in forming languages, they lose the guttural sounds, in some measure, and adopt the use of labials and the more open vowels. The ease of speaking facilitates this progress, and the pronunciation of words is softened, in proportion to a national refinement of manners. This will account for the difference between the ancient and modern languages of France, Spain, and Italy; and for the difference between the soft pronunciation of the present languages of those countries and the more harsh and guttural pronunciation of the northern inhabitants of Europe.

In this progress, the English have lost the sounds of most of the guttural letters. The *k* before *n* in *know,* the *g* in *reign,* and in many other words, are become mute in practice; and the *gh* is softened into the sound of *f,* as in *laugh,* or is silent, as in *brought.*

To this practice of softening the sounds of letters, or wholly suppressing those which are harsh and disagreeable, may be added a popular tendency to abbreviate words of common use. Thus, *Southwark,* by a habit of quick pronunciation, is become *Suthark; Worcester* and *Leicester* are become *Wooster* and *Lester; business, bizness; colonel, curnel; cannot, will not, cant, wont.*[1] In this manner the final *e* is not heard in many modern words, in which it formerly made a syllable. The words *clothes, cares,* and most others of the same kind, were formerly pronounced in two syllables. . . .

When words have been introduced from a foreign language into the English, they have generally retained the orthography of the original, however ill adapted to express the English pronunciation. Thus, *fatigue, marine, chaise* retain their French dress, while, to represent the true pronunciation in English, they should be spelt *fateeg, mareen, shaze.* Thus, thro an ambition to exhibit the etymology of words, the English, in *Philip, physic, character, chorus,* and other Greek derivatives, preserve the representatives of the original Φ and X; yet these words are pronounced, and ought ever to have been spelt, *Fillip, fyzzic* or *fizzic, karacter, korus.*[2]

But such is the state of our language. The pronunciation of the words which are strictly *English* has been gradually changing for ages, and since the revival of science in Europe, the language has received a vast accession of words from other languages, many of which retain an orthography very ill suited to exhibit the true pronunciation.

The question now occurs: Ought the Americans to retain these faults which produce innumerable inconveniencies in the acquisition and use of the language, or ought they at once to reform these abuses, and introduce order and regularity into the orthography of the AMERICAN TONGUE?

Let us consider this subject with some attention.

Several attempts were formerly made in England to rectify the orthography of the

1. *Wont* is strictly a contraction of *woll not,* as the word was anciently pronounced.

2. The words *number, chamber,* and many others in English are from the French *nombre, chambre,* etc. Why was the spelling changed, or rather why is the spelling of *lustre, metre, theatre not* changed? The cases are precisely similar. The Englishman who first wrote *number* for *nombre* had no greater authority to make the change than any modern writer has to spell *lustre, metre* in a similar manner, *luster, meter.* The change in the first instance was a valuable one; it conformed the spelling to the pronunciation, and I have taken the liberty, in all my writings, to pursue the principle in *luster, meter, miter, theater, sepulcher,* etc.

language.[3] But I apprehend their schemes failed of success, rather on account of their intrinsic difficulties than on account of any necessary impracticability of a reform. It was proposed, in most of these schemes, not merely to throw out superfluous and silent letters but to introduce a number of new characters. Any attempt on such a plan must undoubtedly prove unsuccessful. It is not to be expected that an orthography, perfectly regular and simple, such as would be formed by a "synod of grammarians on principles of science," will ever be substituted for that confused mode of spelling which is now established. But it is apprehended that great improvements may be made, and an orthography almost regular, or such as shall obviate most of the present difficulties which occur in learning our language, may be introduced and established with little trouble and opposition.

The principal alterations necessary to render our orthography sufficiently regular and easy are these:

1. The omission of all superfluous or silent letters, as *a* in *bread.* Thus, *bread, head, give, breast, built, meant, realm, friend,* would be spelt *bred, hed, giv, brest, bilt, ment, relm, frend.* Would this alteration produce any inconvenience, any embarrassment or expense? By no means. On the other hand, it would lessen the trouble of writing and, much more, of learning the language; it would reduce the true pronunciation to a certainty; and while it would assist foreigners and our own children in acquiring the language, it would render the pronunciation uniform in different parts of the country, and almost prevent the possibility of changes.

2. A substitution of a character that has a certain definite sound for one that is more vague and indeterminate. Thus, by putting *ee* instead of *ea* or *ie,* the words *mean, near, speak, grieve, zeal* would become *meen, neer, speek, greev, zeel.* This alteration could not occasion a moment's trouble; at the same time it would prevent a doubt respecting the pronunciation; whereas the *ea* and *ie,* having different sounds, may give a learner much difficulty. Thus, *greef* should be substituted for *grief; kee* for *key; beleev* for *believe; laf* for *laugh; dawter* for *daughter; plow* for *plough; tuf* for *tough; proov* for *prove; blud* for *blood;* and *draft* for *draught.* In this manner *ch* in Greek derivatives should be changed into *k;* for the English *ch* has a soft sound, as in *cherish;* but *k* always a hard sound. Therefore, *character, chorus, cholic, architecture* should be written *karacter, korus, kolic, arkitecture;* and were they thus written, no person could mistake their true pronunciation.

Thus, *ch* in French derivatives should be changed into *sh; machine, chaise, chevalier* should be written *masheen, shaze, shevaleer;* and *pique, tour, oblique* should be written *peek, toor, obleek.*

3. A trifling alteration in a character or the addition of a point would distinguish different sounds without the substitution of a new character. Thus, a very small stroke across *th* would distinguish its two sounds. A point over a vowel, in this manner, *ȧ,* or *ȯ,* or *i,* might answer all the purposes of different letters. And for the diphthong *ow,* let the two letters be united by a small stroke, or both engraven on the same piece of metal, with the left hand line of the *w* united to the *o.*

These, with a few other inconsiderable alterations, would answer every purpose, and render the orthography sufficiently correct and regular.

The advantages to be derived from these alterations are numerous, great, and permanent.

1. The simplicity of the orthography would facilitate the learning of the lan-

3. The first by Sir Thomas Smith, secretary of state to Queen Elizabeth; another by Dr. Gill, a celebrated master of St. Paul's School in London; another by Mr. Charles Butler, who went so far as to print his book in his proposed orthography; several in the time of Charles I; and in the present age, Mr. Elphinstone has published a treatise in a very ridiculous orthography.

guage. It is now the work of years for children to learn to spell; and, after all, the business is rarely accomplished. A few men, who are bred to some business that requires constant exercise in writing, finally learn to spell most words without hesitation; but most people remain, all their lives, imperfect masters of spelling, and liable to make mistakes whenever they take up a pen to write a short note. Nay, many people, even of education and fashion, never attempt to write a letter without frequently consulting a dictionary.

But with the proposed orthography, a child would learn to spell, without trouble, in a very short time, and the orthography being very regular, he would ever afterwards find it difficult to make a mistake. It would, in that case, be as difficult to spell *wrong* as it is now to spell *right*.

Besides this advantage, foreigners would be able to acquire the pronunciation of English, which is now so difficult and embarrassing that they are either wholly discouraged on the first attempt, or obliged, after many years' labor, to rest contented with an imperfect knowledge of the subject.

2. A correct orthography would render the pronunciation of the language as uniform as the spelling in books. A general uniformity thro the United States would be the event of such a reformation as I am here recommending. All persons, of every rank, would speak with some degree of precision and uniformity.[4] Such a uniformity in these states is very desirable; it would remove prejudice and conciliate mutual affection and respect.

3. Such a reform would diminish the number of letters about one-sixteenth or eighteenth. This would save a page in eighteen; and a saving of an eighteenth in the expense of books is an advantage that should not be overlooked.

4. I once heard Dr. Franklin remark "that those people spell best who do not know how to spell"; that is, they spell as their ears dictate, without being guided by rules, and thus fall into a regular orthography.

4. But a capital advantage of this reform in these states would be that it would make a difference between the English orthography and the American. This will startle those who have not attended to the subject; but I am confident that such an event is an object of vast political consequence.

For the alteration, however small, would encourage the publication of books in our own country. It would render it, in some measure, necessary that all books should be printed in America. The English would never copy our orthography for their own use; and consequently the same impressions of books would not answer for both countries. The inhabitants of the present generation would read the English impressions; but posterity, being taught a different spelling, would prefer the American orthography.

Besides this, a *national language* is a band of *national union*. Every engine should be employed to render the people of this country *national;* to call their attachments home to their own country; and to inspire them with the pride of national character. However they may boast of independence, and the freedom of their government, yet their *opinions* are not sufficiently independent; an astonishing respect for the arts and literature of their parent country and a blind imitation of its manners are still prevalent among the Americans. Thus an habitual respect for another country, deserved indeed and once laudable, turns their attention from their own interests and prevents their respecting themselves. . . .

Sensible I am how much easier it is to *propose* improvements than to *introduce* them. Everything new starts the idea of difficulty; and yet it is often mere novelty that excites the appearance; for on a slight examination of the proposal, the difficulty vanishes. When we firmly believe a scheme to be practicable, the work is half accomplished. We are more frequently deterred by fear from making an attack than repulsed in the encounter.

Habit also is opposed to changes; for it

renders even our errors dear to us. Having surmounted all difficulties in childhood, we forget the labor, the fatigue, and the perplexity we suffered in the attempt, and imagine the progress of our studies to have been smooth and easy.[5] What seems intrinsically right is so merely thro habit.

Indolence is another obstacle to improvements. The most arduous task a reformer has to execute is to make people *think;* to rouse them from that lethargy which, like the mantle of sleep, covers them in repose and contentment.

But America is in a situation the most favorable for great reformations; and the present time is, in a singular degree, auspicious. The minds of men in this country have been awakened. New scenes have been, for many years, presenting new occasions for exertion; unexpected distresses have called forth the powers of invention; and the application of new expedients has demanded every possible exercise of wisdom and talents. Attention is roused; the mind expanded; and the intellectual faculties invigorated. Here men are prepared to receive improvements, which would be rejected by nations whose habits have not been shaken by similar events.

NOW is the time, and *this* the country, in which we may expect success in attempting changes favorable to language, science, and government. Delay in the plan here proposed may be fatal; under a tranquil general government the minds of men may again sink into indolence; a national acquiescence in error will follow; and posterity be doomed to struggle with difficulties, which time and accident will perpetually multiply.

Let us then seize the present moment and establish a *national language,* as well as a national government. Let us remember that there is a certain respect due to the opinions of other nations. As an independent people, our reputation abroad demands that in all things we should be federal, be national; for if we do not respect ourselves, we may be assured that other nations will not respect us. In short, let it be impressed upon the mind of every American that to neglect the means of commanding respect abroad is treason against the character and dignity of a brave, independent people.

5. Thus most people suppose the present mode of spelling to be really the easiest and best. This opinion is derived from habit; the new mode of spelling proposed would save three-fourths of the labor now bestowed in learning to write our language. A child would learn to spell as well in one year as he can now in four. This is not a supposition: it is an assertion capable of proof; and yet people, never knowing, or having forgot the labor of learning, suppose the present mode to be the easiest. No person but one who has taught children has any idea of the difficulty of learning to spell and pronounce our language in its present form.

78.

# James Wilson: The Study of Law in the United States

*James Wilson had been continually active in all phases of politics since his arrival in America in 1765. His knowledge of government was extensive, as is shown by his speeches for ratification of the Constitution in the Pennsylvania convention of 1787. However, his major pursuit was the study and practice of the law. In 1789, the College of Philadelphia opened a law school, and Wilson was invited to become its first professor. His inaugural address of December 15, 1789, was delivered before an audience of distinguished Americans, including President Washington. The text, part of which is reprinted here, gives evidence of Wilson's strong desire to create an American jurisprudence independent of European ties. Though he served on the Supreme Court as an associate justice from 1789 to 1798, he was not fated to play the creative role in American law that he had cut out for himself.*

Source: *Selected Political Essays of James Wilson*, Randolph G. Adams, ed., New York, 1930, pp. 185-214.

Were I called upon for my reasons why I deem so highly of the American character, I would assign them in a very few words: that character has been eminently distinguished by the love of liberty and the love of law. . . .

In free countries — in free countries, especially, that boast the blessing of a common law, springing warm and spontaneous from the manners of the people — law should be studied and taught as a historical science.

The eloquent Rousseau complains that the origin of nations is much concealed by the darkness or the distance of antiquity.

In many parts of the world the fact may be as he represents it; and yet his complaint may be without foundation: for, in many parts of the world, the origin of nations ought to be buried in oblivion. To succeeding ages, the knowledge of it would convey neither pleasure nor instruction.

With regard to the states of America, I am happy in saying that a complaint concerning the uncertainty of their first settlements cannot be made with propriety or truth; though I must add that, if it could be made with propriety or truth, it would be a subject of the deepest regret.

If the just and genuine principles of society can diffuse a luster round the establishment of nations, that of the states of America is indeed illustrious. Fierce oppression, rattling in her left hand the chains of tyranny and brandishing in her right hand the torch of persecution, drove our predecessors from the coasts of Europe; liberty, benevolent and serene, pointing to a cornucopia on one side and to a branch of olive on the other, invited and conducted them to the American shores.

In discharging the duties of this office, I shall have the pleasure of presenting to my hearers what, as to the nations in the transatlantic world, must be searched for in vain: an original compact of a society on its first arrival in this section of the globe. How the lawyers, and statesmen, and antiquarians, and philosophers of Europe would exult on discovering a similar monument of the Athenian commonwealth! And yet, perhaps, the historical monuments of the states of America are not, intrinsically, less important or less worthy of attention than the historical monuments of the states of Greece. The latter, indeed, are gilded with the gay decorations of fable and mythology; but the former are clothed in the neater and more simple garb of freedom and truth.

The doctrine of toleration in matters of religion, reasonable though it certainly is, has not been long known or acknowledged. For its reception and establishment, where it has been received and established, the world has been thought to owe much to the inestimable writings of the celebrated Locke. To the inestimable writings of that justly celebrated man let the tribute of applause be plenteously paid; but while immortal honors are bestowed on the name and character of Locke, why should an ungracious silence be observed with regard to the name and character of Calvert?

Let it be known that, before the doctrine of toleration was published in Europe, the practice of it was established in America. A law in favor of religious freedom was passed in Maryland as early as the year 1649.

When my Lord Baltimore was afterwards urged, not by the spirit of freedom, to consent that this law should be repealed, with the enlightened principles of a man and a Christian, he had the fortitude to declare that he never would assent to the repeal of a law which protected the natural rights of men by ensuring to every one freedom of action and thought.

Indeed, the character of this excellent man has been too little known. He was truly the father of his country. To the legislature of Maryland he often recommended a maxim which deserves to be written in letters of gold: "By concord a small colony may grow into a great and renowned nation; but, by dissensions, mighty and glorious kingdoms have declined and fallen into nothing."

Similar to that of Calvert has been the fate of many other valuable characters in America. They have been too little known. To those around them, their modest merits have been too familiar, perhaps too uniform, to attract particular and distinguished attention: by those at a distance, the mild and peaceful voice of their virtue has not been heard. But to their memories justice should be done, as far as it can be done, by a just and grateful country.

In the European temple of fame William Penn is placed by the side of Lycurgus. Will America refuse a temple to her patriots and her heroes? No; she will not. The glorious dome already rises. Its architecture is of the neatest and chastest order; its dimensions are spacious; its proportions are elegant and correct. In its front a number of niches are formed. In some of them statues are placed. On the left hand of the portal are the names and figures of Warren, Montgomery, Mercer. On the right hand, are the names and figures of Calvert, Penn, Franklin. In the middle is a niche of larger size, and decorated with peculiar ornaments. On the left side of it are sculptured the trophies of war; on the right, the more precious emblems of peace. Above it is represented the rising glory of the United States. It is without a statue and without a name. Beneath it, in letters very legible, are these words: "*for the most worthy.*" By the enraptured voice of grateful America, with the consenting plaudits of an admiring world, the designation is unanimously made. Late, very late, may the niche be filled. [President George Washington was present when this lecture was delivered.]

But while we perform the pleasing duties of gratitude, let not other duties be disregarded. Illustrious examples are displayed to our view, that we may imitate as well as admire. Before we can be distinguished by the same honors, we must be distinguished by the same virtues.

What are those virtues? They are chiefly the same virtues which we have already seen to be descriptive of the American character: the love of liberty and the love of law. But law and liberty cannot rationally become the objects of our love unless they first become the objects of our knowledge. The same course of study, properly directed, will lead us to the knowledge of both. Indeed, neither of them can be known — because neither of them can exist — without the other. Without liberty, law loses its nature and its name and becomes oppression. Without law, liberty also loses its nature and its name and becomes licentiousness. In denominating, therefore, that science by which the knowledge of both is acquired, it is unnecessary to preserve, in terms, the distinction between them. That science may be named, as it has been named, the science of law.

The science of law should in some measure, and in some degree, be the study of every free citizen and of every free man. Every free citizen and every free man has duties to perform and rights to claim. Unless, in some measure, and in some degree, he knows those duties and those rights, he can never act a just and independent part.

Happily, the general and most important principles of law are not removed to a very great distance from common apprehension. It has been said of religion that though the elephant may swim, yet the lamb may wade in it. Concerning law, the same observation may be made.

The home navigation, carried on along the shores, is more necessary, and more useful too, than that which is pursued through the deep and expanded ocean. A man may be a most excellent coaster, though he possess not the nautical accomplishments and experience of a [James] Cook.

As a science, the law is far from being so disagreeable or so perplexed a study as it is frequently supposed to be. Some, indeed, involve themselves in a thick mist of terms of art, and use a language unknown to all but those of the profession. By such, the knowledge of the law, like the mysteries of some ancient divinity, is confined to its initiated votaries, as if all others were in duty bound blindly and implicitly to obey. But this ought not to be the case. The knowledge of those rational principles on which the law is founded ought, especially in a free government, to be diffused over the whole community.

In a free country, every citizen forms a part of the sovereign power: he possesses a vote or takes a still more active part in the business of the commonwealth. The right and the duty of giving that vote, the right and the duty of taking that share, are necessarily attended with the duty of making that business the object of his study and inquiry.

In the United States, every citizen is frequently called upon to act in this great public character. He elects the legislative, and he takes a personal share in the executive and judicial departments of the nation. It is true that a man who wishes to be right will, with the official assistance afforded him, be seldom under the necessity of being wrong; but it is equally true, and it ought not to be concealed, that the public duties and the public rights of every citizen of the United States loudly demand from him all the time which he can prudently spare, and all the means which he can prudently employ, in order to learn that part which it is incumbent on him to act.

On the public mind, one great truth can never be too deeply impressed: that the weight of the government of the United States, and of each state composing the Union, rests on the shoulders of the people.

I express not this sentiment now, as I have never expressed it heretofore, with a view to flatter; I express it now, as I have always expressed it heretofore, with a far other and higher aim: with an aim to excite the people to acquire, by vigorous and manly exercise, a degree of strength sufficient to support the weighty burden which is laid upon them; with an aim to convince them that their duties rise in strict proportion to their rights; and that few are able to trace or to estimate the great danger, in a free government, when the rights of the people are unexercised; and the still greater danger, when the rights of the people are ill exercised.

At a general election, too few attend to the important consequences of voting or not voting; and to the consequences, still more important, of voting right or voting wrong.

The rights and the duties of jurors in the United States are great and extensive. No punishment can be inflicted without the intervention of one; in much the greater number of cases, without the intervention of more than one jury. Is it not of immense consequence to the public that those who have committed crimes should not escape with impunity? Is it not of immense consequence to individuals that all, except those who have committed crimes, should be secure from the punishment denounced against their commission? Is it not, then, of immense consequence to both that jurors should possess the spirit of just discernment to discriminate between the innocent and the guilty? This spirit of just discernment requires knowledge of, at least, the general principles of the law, as well as knowledge of the minute particulars concerning the facts.

It is true that, in matters of law, the jurors are entitled to the assistance of the judges; but it is also true that, after they receive it, they have the right of judging for themselves. And is there not to this right the great corresponding duty of judging properly?

Surely, therefore, those who discharge the important and, let me add, the dignified functions of jurors, should acquire, as far as they possibly can acquire, a knowledge of the laws of their country. For, let me add further, the dignity, though not the importance of their functions, will greatly depend on the abilities with which they discharge them.

But in the administration of justice, that part of government which comes home most intimately to the business and the bosoms of men, there are judges as well as jurors; those whose peculiar province it is to answer questions of law, as well as those whose peculiar province it is to answer questions of fact.

In many courts, in many respectable courts within the United States, the judges are not, and for a long time cannot be gentlemen of professional acquirements. They may, however, fill their offices usefully and honorably, the want of professional acquirements notwithstanding. But can they do this without a reasonable degree of acquaintance with the law?

We have already seen that in questions of law, the jurors are entitled to the assistance of the judges; but can the judges give assistance, without knowing what answers to make to the questions which the jury may propose? Can those direct others who themselves know not the road?

Unquestionably, then, those who fill, and those who expect to fill the offices of judges in courts not, indeed, supreme, but rising in importance and in dignity above the appellation of inferior, ought to make the strongest efforts in order to obtain a respectable degree of knowledge in the law.

Let me ascend to a station more elevated still. In the United States, the doors of public honors and public offices are, on the broad principles of equal liberty, thrown open to all. A laudable emulation, an emulation that ought to be encouraged in a free government, may prompt a man to legislate as well as to decide for his fellow citizens; to legislate, not merely for a single state, but for the most august Union that has yet been formed on the face of the globe.

Should not he who is to supply the deficiencies of the existing law know when the existing law is defective? Should not he who is to introduce alterations into the existing law know in what instances the existing law ought to be altered?

The first and governing maxim in the interpretation of a statute is to discover the meaning of those who made it. The first rule, subservient to the principle of the governing maxim, is to discover what the law was before the statute was made. The inference necessarily resulting from the joint operation of the maxim and the rule is this: that in explaining a statute, the judges ought to take it for granted that those who made it knew the antecedent law. This certainly implies that a competent knowledge of, at least, the general principles of law is of indispensable necessity to those who undertake the transcendent office of legislation. I say a knowledge of the general principles of law: for though an accurate, a minute, and an extensive knowledge of its practice and particular rules be highly useful, yet I cannot conceive it to be absolutely requisite to the able discharge of a legislative trust. . . .

A question deeply interesting to the American states now presents itself. Should the elements of a law education, particularly as it respects public law, be drawn entirely from another country? Or should they be drawn, in part at least, from the constitutions and governments and laws of the United States and of the several states composing the Union?

The subject, to one standing where I stand, is not without its delicacy. Let me, however, treat it with the decent but firm freedom which befits an independent citizen and a professor in independent states.

Surely I am justified in saying that the principles of the constitutions and governments and laws of the United States and the republics of which they are formed, are materially different from the principles of the constitution and government and laws of England; for that is the only country, from the principles of whose constitution and government and laws it will be contended, that the elements of law education ought to be drawn. I presume to go further: the principles of our constitutions and governments and laws are materially better than the principles of the constitution and government and laws of England.

Permit me to mention one great principle, the vital principle I may well call it, which diffuses animation and vigor through all the others. The principle I mean is this: that the supreme or sovereign power of the society resides in the citizens at large; and that, therefore, they always retain the right of abolishing, altering, or amending their constitution at whatever time, and in whatever manner, they shall deem it expedient. . . .

We have thought and we have acted upon revolution principles, without offering them up as sacrifices at the shrine of revolution precedents.

Why should we not teach our children those principles upon which we ourselves have thought and acted? Ought we to instill into their tender minds a theory, especially if unfounded, which is contradictory to our own practice, built on the most solid foundation? Why should we reduce them to the cruel dilemma of condemning either those principles which they have been taught to believe or those persons whom they have been taught to revere? . . .

It is the opinion of many that the revolution of 1688 did more than set a mere precedent, even in England. But be that as it may: a revolution principle certainly is, and certainly should be taught, as a principle of the constitution of the United States and of every state in the Union.

This revolution principle — that, the sovereign power residing in the people, they may change their constitution and government whenever they please — is not a principle of discord, rancor, or war; it is a principle of melioration, contentment, and peace. It is a principle not recommended merely by a flattering theory; it is a principle recommended by happy experience. To the testimony of Pennsylvania, to the testimony of the United States I appeal for the truth of what I say. . . .

Besides the reasons which I have already offered, others may be suggested why the elements of a law education ought to be drawn from our own constitutions and governments and laws.

In every government which is not altogether despotical, the institution of youth is of some public consequence. In a republican government it is of the greatest. Of no class of citizens can the education be of more public consequence than that of those who are destined to take an active part in public affairs. Those who have had the advantage of a law education are very frequently destined to take this active part. This deduction clearly shows that, in a free government, the principles of a law education are matters of the greatest public consequence.

Ought not those principles to be congenial with the principles of government? By the revolution in the United States a very great alteration, a very great improvement, as we have already seen, has taken place in our system of government. Ought not a proportioned alteration, ought not a proportioned improvement to be introduced into our system of law education?

We have passed the Red Sea in safety; we have survived a tedious and dangerous journey through the wilderness; we are now in full and peaceable possession of the promised land. Must we, after all, return to the fleshpots of Egypt? Is there not danger that when one nation teaches, it may, in some instances, give the law to another?

A foundation of human happiness, broader and deeper than any that has heretofore been laid, is now laid in the United States. On that broad and deep foundation let it be our pride, as it is our duty, to build a superstructure of adequate extent and magnificence.

But further: many parts of the laws of England can, in their own nature, have neither force nor application here. Such are all those parts which are connected with ecclesiastical jurisdiction and an ecclesiastical establishment. Such are all those parts, too, which relate to the monarchical and aristocratic branches of the English constitution. Every one who has perused the ponderous volumes of the law knows how great a proportion of them is filled with the numerous and extensive titles relating to those different subjects. Surely they need not enter into the elements of a law education in the United States.

I mean not, however, to exclude them from the subsequent investigation of those who shall aspire at the character of accomplished lawyers. I only mean that they ought not to be put into the hands of students, as deserving the same time and the same attention with other parts, which are to have a practical influence upon their future conduct in their profession.

The numerous regulations in England respecting the poor, and the more artificial refinements and distinctions concerning real estates, must be known; but known as much in order to be avoided as to be practiced. The study of them, therefore, need not be so minute here as in England.

Concerning many other titles of the English law, similar observations might be made. The force and the extent of each will increase day after day and year after year.

All combine in showing that the foundation, at least, of a separate, an unbiased, and an independent law education should be laid in the United States.

Deeply impressed with the importance of this truth, I have undertaken the difficult, the laborious, and the delicate task of contributing to lay that foundation. I feel most sensibly the weight of the duty which I have engaged to perform. I will not promise to perform it successfully, as well as it might be performed; but I will promise to perform it faithfully, as well as I can perform it. I feel its full importance.

It may be asked (I am told it has been asked), is it proper that a judge of the Supreme Court of the United States should deliver lectures on law? It will not surely be suspected that I deem too lightly of the very dignified and independent office which I have the honor to hold, in consequence of the favorable sentiments entertained concerning me by those whose favorable sentiments are indeed an honor. Had I thought that the dignity of that seat could be disparaged by an alliance with this chair, I would have spurned it from me. But I thought and I still think in a very different manner. By my acceptance of this chair, I think I shall certainly increase my usefulness, without diminishing my dignity as a judge; and I think that, with equal certainty, I shall, as a judge, increase my usefulness — I will not say my dignity — in this chair. He who is well qualified to teach is well qualified to judge; and he who is well qualified to judge is well qualified to teach. Every acquisition of knowledge, and it is my duty to acquire much, can, with equal facility, and with equal propriety, be applied to either office; for let it be remembered that both offices view the same science as their common object.

Any interference as to the times of discharging the two offices — the only one that strikes me as possible — will be carefully avoided.

But it may be further asked: ought a judge to commit himself by delivering his sentiments in a lecture? To this question I shall give a very explicit answer; and in that answer I shall include the determination which I have taken both as a professor and as a judge. When I deliver my sentiments from this chair, they shall be my honest sentiments; when I deliver them from the bench, they shall be nothing more. In both places I shall make, because I mean to support, the claim to integrity: in neither shall I make, because, in neither, can I support, the claim to infallibility.

My house of knowledge is, at present, too small. I feel it my duty, on many accounts, to enlarge it. But in this, as in every other kind of architecture, I believe it will be found that he who adds much must alter some.

When the greatest judges who ever adorned or illuminated a court of justice have candidly and cheerfully acknowledged their mistakes, shall I be afraid of committing myself?

The learned and indefatigable Spelman, after all the immense researches which enabled him to prepare and publish his *Glossary*, published it with this remarkable precaution: "under the protestation of adding, retracting, correcting, and polishing, as, upon more mature consideration, shall seem expedient."

I hope I have now shown that my acceptance of this chair, instead of diminishing, is calculated to increase my usefulness as a judge. Does it derogate from my dignity? By no means, in my opinion.

Let things be considered as they really are. As a judge, I can decide whether property in dispute belongs to the man on my right hand or to the man on my left hand. As a judge, I can pass sentence on a felon or a cheat. By doing both, a judge may be eminently useful in preserving peace and in securing property.

Property highly deserving security is, however, not an end but a means. How miserable and how contemptible is that man who inverts the order of nature, and makes his property not a means but an end!

Society ought to be preserved in peace, most unquestionably. But is this all? Ought it not to be improved as well as protected? Look at individuals: observe them from infancy to youth, from youth to manhood. Such is the order of Providence with regard to society. It is in a progressive state moving on toward perfection. How is this progressive state to be assisted and accelerated? Principally by teaching the young "ideas how to shoot," and the young affections how to move.

What intrinsically can be more dignified

than to assist in preparing tender and ingenuous minds for all the great purposes for which they are intended! What, I repeat it, can intrinsically be more dignified, than to assist in forming a future Cicero, or a future Bacon, without the vanity of one, and without the meanness of the other! . . .

I have been zealous — I hope I have not been altogether unsuccessful — in contributing the best of my endeavors toward forming a system of government; I shall rise in importance, if I can be equally successful — I will not be less zealous — in contributing the best of my endeavors toward forming a system of education, likewise, in the United States. I shall rise in importance because I shall rise in usefulness.

What are laws without manners? How can manners be formed but by a proper education?

Methinks I hear one of the female part of my audience exclaim: what is all this to us? We have heard much of societies, of states, of governments, of laws, and of a law education. Is everything made for your sex? Why should not we have a share? Is our sex less honest, or less virtuous, or less wise than yours?

Will any of my brethren be kind enough to furnish me with answers to these questions? I must answer them, it seems, myself, and I mean to answer them most sincerely.

Your sex is neither less honest, nor less virtuous, nor less wise than ours. With regard to the two first of these qualities, a superiority, on our part, will not be pretended; with regard to the last, a pretension of superiority cannot be supported.

I will name three women, and I will then challenge any of my brethren to name three men superior to them in vigor and extent of abilities. My female champions are Semiramis of Nineveh; Zenobia, the queen of the East; and Elizabeth of England. I believe it will readily be owned that three men of superior active talents cannot be named.

You will please, however, to take notice that the issue upon which I put the characters of these three ladies, is not that they were accomplished; it is, that they were able women.

This distinction immediately reminds you that a woman may be an able, without being an accomplished, female character.

In this latter view, I did not produce the three female characters I have mentioned. I produced them as women merely of distinguished abilities, of abilities equal to those displayed by the most able of our sex.

But would you wish to be tried by the qualities of our sex? I will refer you to a more proper standard: that of your own.

All the three able characters I have mentioned had, I think, too much of the masculine in them. Perhaps I can conjecture the reason. Might it not be owing in a great measure, might it not be owing altogether to the masculine employments to which they devoted themselves?

Two of them were able warriors; all of them were able queens; but in all of them we feel and we regret the loss of the lovely and accomplished woman. And let me assure you that, in the estimation of our sex, the loss of the lovely and accomplished woman is irreparable, even when she is lost in the queen.

For these reasons, I doubt much, whether it would be proper that you should undertake the management of public affairs. You have, indeed, heard much of public government and public law; but these things were not made for themselves: they were made for something better; and of that something better, you form the better part — I mean society — I mean particularly domestic society. There the lovely and accomplished woman shines with superior luster. . . .

Female beauty is the expression of female virtue. The purest complexion, the finest features, the most elegant shape are uninteresting and insipid, unless we can discover, by them, the emotions of the mind. How beautiful and engaging, on the other hand, are the features, the looks, and the gestures, while they disclose modesty, sensibility, and every sweet and tender affection! When these appear, there is a "soul upon the countenance."

These observations enhance the value of beauty and show that to possess and to admire it is to possess and to admire the exhibition of the finest qualities, intellectual and moral. These observations do more: they show how beauty may be acquired, and improved, and preserved. When the beauties of the mind are cultivated, the countenance becomes beautifully eloquent in expressing them.

I know very well that mere complexion and shape enter into the composition of beauty: but they form beauty only of a lower order. Separate them from animation, separate them from sensibility, separate them from virtue. What are they? The ingredients that compose a beautiful picture or a beautiful statue. I say too much; for the painters and the statuaries know that expression is the soul of mimic as well as of real life.

As complexion and shape will not supply the place of the higher orders of beauty, so those higher orders have an independent existence after the inferior influence of complexion and shape are gone. Though the bloom of youth be faded; though the impressions of time be distinctly marked; yet, while the countenance continues to be enlivened by the beaming emanations of the mind, it will produce, in every beholder possessed of sensibility and taste, an effect far more pleasing, and far more lasting, than can be produced by the prettiest piece of uninformed nature, however florid, however regular, and however young.

How many purposes may be served at once if things are done in the proper way! I have been giving a recipe for the improvement and preservation of female beauty; but I find that I have, at the same time, been delivering instructions for the culture and refinement of female virtue; and have been pointing at the important purposes which female virtue is fitted and intended to accomplish.

If Nature evinces her designs by her works, you were destined to embellish, to refine, and to exalt the pleasures and virtues of social life.

To protect and to improve social life is, as we have seen, the end of government and law. If, therefore, you have no share in the formation, you have a most intimate connection with the effects of a good system of law and government.

That plan of education which will produce, or promote, or preserve such a system, is, consequently, an object to you peculiarly important.

But if you would see such a plan carried into complete effect, you must, my amiable hearers, give it your powerful assistance. The pleasing task of forming your daughters is almost solely yours. In my plan of education for your sons, I must solicit you to cooperate. Their virtues in a certain proportion, the refinement of their virtues in a much greater proportion, must be molded on your example.

In your sex, too, there is a natural, an easy, and, often, a pure flow of diction, which lays the best foundation for that eloquence which, in a free country, is so important to ours.

The style of some of the finest orators of antiquity was originally formed on that of their mothers or of other ladies to whose acquaintance they had the honor of being introduced.

You see now, my fair and amiable hearers, how deeply and nearly interested you are in a proper plan of law education. By some of you, whom I know to be well qualified for taking in it the share which I have described, that share will be taken. By the younger part of you the good effects of such a plan will, I hope, be participated; for those of my pupils who themselves shall become most estimable will treat you with the highest degree of estimation.

# 1789 - 1790

79.

## That the Earth Belongs to the Living

*Though Thomas Jefferson profoundly believed in the principles of the Revolution of 1776 and of the Constitution, he did not insist that they were immutable. He believed that every man and every generation must think in relation to conditions of the times and not hold the laws, constitutions, or contracts of the past as sacred. "The earth," he said in a letter to James Madison, September 6, 1789, "belongs in usufruct to the living." The letter was sent from Paris and did not reach Madison, who was then in New York, until February 1790. On February 4, he replied with typical Madisonian clarity, expressing his disagreement with some of Jefferson's points.*

Source: Ford, V, pp. 115-124. *Madison Letters*, I, pp. 503-506.

I.

### Thomas Jefferson to James Madison

I sit down to write to you without knowing by what occasion I shall send my letter. I do it because a subject comes into my head which I would wish to develop a little more than is practicable in the hurry of the moment of making up general dispatches.

The question whether one generation of men has a right to bind another seems never to have been started either on this or our side of the water. Yet it is a question of such consequences as not only to merit decision but place also among the fundamental principles of every government. The course of reflection in which we are immersed here on the elementary principles of society has presented this question to my mind; and that no such obligation can be transmitted I think very capable of proof. I set out on this ground which I suppose to be self-evident, "that the earth belongs in usufruct to the living"; that the dead have neither powers nor rights over it. The portion occupied by any individual ceases to be his when himself ceases to be, and reverts to the society.

If the society has formed no rules for the appropriation of its lands in severalty, it will be taken by the first occupants. These will generally be the wife and children of the decedent. If they have formed rules of appropriation, those rules may give it to the wife and children, or to some one of them, or to the legatee of the deceased; so they may give it to his creditor. But the child, the legatee, or creditor takes it, not by any natural right, but by a law of the society of which they are members, and to which they are subject. Then no man can by *natural right* oblige the lands he occupied, or the persons who succeed him in that occupation to the payment of debts contracted by him. For if he could, he might during his own life eat up the usufruct of the lands for several generations to come, and then the lands would belong to the dead, and not to the living, which would be reverse of our principle.

What is true of every member of the society individually is true of them all collectively, since the rights of the whole can be no more than the sum of the rights of individuals. To keep our ideas clear when applying them to a multitude, let us suppose a whole generation of men to be born on the same day, to attain mature age on the same day, and to die on the same day, leaving a succeeding generation in the moment of attaining their mature age all together. Let the ripe age be supposed of 21 years, and their period of life 34 years more, that being the average term given by the bills of mortality to persons who have already attained 21 years of age. Each successive generation would, in this way, come on and go off the stage at a fixed moment, as individuals do now. Then I say the earth belongs to each of these generations during its course, fully, and in their own right. The second generation receives it clear of the debts and encumbrances of the first, the third of the second, and so on. For if the first could charge it with a debt, then the earth would belong to the dead and not the living generation. Then no generation can contract debts greater than may be paid during the course of its own existence. At 21 years of age they may bind themselves and their lands for 34 years to come; at 22, for 33; at 23, for 32; and at 54, for 1 year only; because these are the terms of life which remain to them at those respective epochs.

But a material difference must be noted between the succession of an individual and that of a whole generation. Individuals are parts only of a society, subject to the laws of a whole. These laws may appropriate the portion of land occupied by a decedent to his creditor rather than to any other, or to his child, on condition he satisfies his creditor. But when a whole generation, that is, the whole society dies, as in the case we have supposed, and another generation or society succeeds, this forms a whole, and there is no superior who can give their territory to a third society, who may have lent money to their predecessors beyond their faculty of paying.

What is true of a generation all arriving to self-government on the same day, and dying all on the same day, is true of those on a constant course of decay and renewal, with this only difference. A generation coming in and going out entire, as in the first case, would have a right in the first year of their self-dominion to contract a debt for 33 years; in the tenth, for 24; in the twentieth, for 14; in the thirtieth, for 4; whereas generations changing daily, by daily deaths and births, have one constant term beginning at the date of their contract and ending when a majority of those of full age at that date shall be dead. The length of that term may be estimated from the tables of mortality, corrected by the circumstances of climate, occupation, etc., peculiar to the country of the contractors.

Take, for instance, the table of M. de Buffon, wherein he states . . . 23,994 deaths, and the ages at which they happened. Suppose a society in which 23,994 persons are born every year and live to the ages stated in this table. The conditions of that society will be as follows: (1) it will consist constantly of 617,703 persons of all ages; (2) of those living at any one instant of time, one-half will be dead in 24 years, 8 months; (3) 10,675 will arrive every year at the age of 21 years complete; (4) it will constantly have 348,417 persons of all ages above 21 years; (5) and the half of those of 21 years and upwards living at any one instant of time will be dead in 18 years, 8 months, or say 19 years as the nearest integral number. Then 19 years is the term beyond which neither the representatives of a nation, nor even the whole nation itself assembled, can validly extend a debt.

To render this conclusion palpable by example, suppose that Louis XIV and XV had contracted debts in the name of the French nation to the amount of 10,000 milliards of livres and that the whole had been contracted in Genoa. The interest of this sum would be 500 milliards, which is said to be the whole rent toll, or net proceeds of the territory of France. Must the present generation of men have retired from the territory in which nature produced them, and ceded it to the Genoese creditors? No. They have the same rights over the soil on which they were produced as the preceding generations had. They derive these rights not from their predecessors, but from nature. They, then, and their soil are by nature clear of the debts of their predecessors.

Again, suppose Louis XV and his contemporary generation had said to the moneylenders of Genoa, "Give us money that we may eat, drink, and be merry in our day; and on condition you will demand no interest till the end of 19 years, you shall then forever after receive an annual interest of 12.5 percent." The money is lent on these conditions, is divided among the living, eaten, drunk, and squandered. Would the present generation be obliged to apply the produce of the earth and of their labor to replace their dissipations? Not at all.

I suppose that the received opinion that the public debts of one generation devolve on the next has been suggested by our seeing habitually in private life that he who succeeds to lands is required to pay the debts of his ancestor or testator without considering that this requisition is municipal only, not moral, flowing from the will of the society which has found it convenient to appropriate the lands become vacant by the death of their occupant on the condition of a payment of his debts; but that between society and society, or generation and generation, there is no municipal obligation, no umpire but the law of nature. We seem not to have perceived that, by the law of nature, one generation is to another as one independent nation to another.

The interest of the national debt of France being in fact but a two-thousandth part of its rent roll, the payment of it is practicable enough, and so becomes a question merely of honor or expediency. But with respect to future debts; would it not be wise and just for that nation to declare in the constitution they are forming that neither the legislature, nor the nation itself can validly contract more debt than they may pay within their own age, or within the term of 19 years? And that all future contracts shall be deemed void as to what shall remain unpaid at the end of 19 years from their date? This would put the lenders, and the borrowers also on their guard. By reducing, too, the faculty of borrowing within its natural limits, it would bridle the spirit of war, to which too free a course has been procured by the inattention of money lenders to this law of nature, that succeeding generations are not responsible for the preceding.

On similar ground it may be proved that no society can make a perpetual constitution, or even a perpetual law. The earth belongs always to the living generation. They may manage it then, and what proceeds from it, as they please, during their usufruct. They are masters too of their own persons, and, consequently, may govern them as they please. But persons and property make the sum of the objects of government. The constitution and the laws of their predecessors extinguished them, in their natural course, with those whose will gave them being. This could preserve that being till it ceased to be itself, and no longer. Every constitution, then, and every law naturally expires at the end of 19 years. If it be enforced longer, it is an act of force and not of right.

It may be said that the succeeding generation exercising in fact the power of repeal, this leaves them as free as if the constitution or law had been expressly limited to 19 years only. In the first place, this objection admits the right in proposing an equivalent. But the power of repeal is not an equivalent. It might be indeed if every form of government were so perfectly contrived that the will of the majority could always be obtained fairly and without impediment. But this is true of no form. The people cannot assemble themselves; their representation is unequal and vicious. Various checks are opposed to every legislative proposition. Factions get possession of the public councils. Bribery corrupts them. Personal interests lead them astray from the general interests of their constituents; and other impediments arise so as to prove to every practical man that a law of limited duration is much more manageable than one which needs a repeal.

This principle that the earth belongs to the living and not to the dead is of very extensive application and consequences in every country, and most especially in France. It enters into the resolution of the questions — whether the nation may change the descent of lands held entail? Whether they may change the appropriation of lands given anciently to the church, to hospitals, colleges, orders of chivalry, and otherwise in perpetuity? Whether they may abolish the charges and privileges attached on lands, including the whole catalogue ecclesiastical and feudal? It goes to hereditary offices, authorities, and jurisdictions; to hereditary orders, distinctions, and appellations; to perpetual monopolies in commerce, the arts or sciences; with a long train of *et ceteras;* and it renders the question of reimbursement a question of generosity and not of right.

In all these cases the legislature of the day could authorize such appropriations and establishments for their own time, but no longer; and the present holders, even where they or their ancestors have purchased, are in the case of bona fide purchasers of what the seller had no right to convey.

Turn this subject in your mind, my dear sir, and particularly as to the power of contracting debts, and develop it with that perspicuity and cogent logic which is so peculiarly yours. Your station in the councils of our country gives you an opportunity of producing it to public consideration, of forcing it into discussion. At first blush it may be rallied as a theoretical speculation; but examination will prove it to be solid and salutary. It would furnish matter for a fine preamble to our first law for appropriating the public revenue; and it will exclude, at the threshold of our new government, the contagious and ruinous errors of this quarter of the globe which have armed despots with means not sanctioned by nature for binding in chains their fellowmen. We have already given, in example, one effectual check to the dog of war by transferring the power of letting him loose from the executive to the legislative body, from those who are to spend to those who are to pay. I should be pleased to see this second obstacle held out by us also in the first instance.

No nation can make a declaration against the validity of long-contracted debts so disinterestedly as we since we do not owe a shilling which may not be paid with ease, principal and interest within the time of our own lives. Establish the principle also in the new law to be passed for protecting copyrights and new inventions by securing the exclusive right for 19 instead of 14 years. Besides familiarizing us to this term, it will be an instance the more of our taking reason for our guide instead of English precedents, the habit of which fetters us, with all the political heresies of a nation, equally remarkable for its encitement from some errors, as long slumbering under others. I write you no news, because when an occasion occurs I shall write a separate letter for that.

## II.

### Madison to Jefferson

Your favor of January 9, enclosing one of September last, did not get to hand till a few days ago. The idea which the latter evolves is a great one, and suggests many interesting reflections to legislators, particularly when contracting and providing for public debts. Whether it can be received in the extent to which your reasonings carry it is a question which I ought to turn more in my thoughts than I have yet been able to do before I should be justified in making up a full opinion on it. My first thoughts lead me to view the doctrine as not in *all respects* compatible with the course of human affairs. I will endeavor to sketch the grounds of my skepticism. "As the earth belongs to the living, not to the dead, a living generation can bind itself only; in every society, the will of the majority binds the whole; according to the laws of mortality, a majority of those ripe for the exercise of their will do not live beyond the term of 19 years; to this term, then, is limited the validity of every act of the society, nor can any act be continued beyond this term, without an *express* declaration of the public will." This I understand to be the outline of the argument.

The acts of a political society may be divided into three classes:

1. The fundamental constitution of the government.

2. Laws involving some stipulation which renders them irrevocable at the will of the legislature.

3. Laws involving no such irrevocable quality.

However applicable in theory the doctrine may be to a constitution, it seems liable in practice to some weighty objections. Would not a government, ceasing of necessity at the end of a given term unless prolonged by some constitutional act previous to its expiration, be too subject to the casualty and consequences of an interregnum? Would not a government so often revised become too mutable and novel to retain that share of prejudice in its favor which is a salutary aid to the most rational government? Would not such a periodical revision engender pernicious factions that might not otherwise come into existence, and agitate the public mind more frequently and more violently than might be expedient?

In the second class of acts involving stipulations, must not exceptions, at least to the doctrine, be admitted? If the earth be the gift of *nature* to the living, their title can extend to the earth in its *natural* state only. The *improvements* made by the dead form a debt against the living who take the benefit of them. This debt cannot be otherwise discharged than by a proportionate obedience to the will of the authors of the improvements.

But a case less liable to be controverted may, perhaps, be stated. Debts may be incurred with a direct view to the interests of the unborn as well as of the living. Such are debts for repelling a conquest, the evils of which descend through many generations. Debts may even be incurred principally for the benefit of posterity. Such, perhaps, is the debt incurred by the United States. In these instances the debts might not be dischargeable within the term of 19 years.

There seems, then, to be some foundation in the nature of things, in the relation which one generation bears to another, for the *descent* of obligations from one to another. Equity may require it. Mutual good may be promoted by it. And all that seems indispensable in stating the account between the dead and the living is to see that the debts against the latter do not exceed the advances made by the former. Few of the encumbrances entailed on nations by their predecessors would bear a liquidation even on this principle.

Objections to the doctrine, as applied to the third class of acts, must be merely practical. But in that view alone they appear to be material. Unless such temporary laws should be kept in force by acts regularly anticipating their expiration, all the rights depending on positive laws, that is, most of the rights of property, would become absolutely defunct, and the most violent struggles ensue between the parties interested in reviving, and those interested in reforming, the antecedent state of property. Nor does it seem improbable that such an event might be suffered to take place. The checks and difficulties opposed to the passage of laws which render the power of repeal inferior to an opportunity to reject, as a security against oppression, would here render the latter an insecure provision against anarchy.

Add to this that the very possibility of an event so hazardous to the rights of property could not but depreciate its value; that the approach of the crisis would increase the effect; that the frequent return of periods superseding all the obligations dependent on antecedent laws and usages must, by weakening the sense of them, cooperate with motives to licentiousness already too powerful; and that the general uncertainty and vicissitudes of such a state of things would, on one side, discourage every useful effort of steady industry pursued under the sanction of existing laws, and, on the other, give an immediate advantage to the more sagacious over the less sagacious part of the society.

I can find no relief from such embarrassments but in the received doctrine that a *tacit* assent may be given to established governments and laws, and that this assent is to be inferred from the omission of an express revocation.

Is it not doubtful whether it be possible to exclude wholly the idea of an implied or tacit assent without subverting the very foundation of civil society?

On what principle is it that the voice of the majority binds the minority? It does not result, I conceive, from a law of nature, but from compact founded on utility. A greater proportion might be required by the fundamental constitution of society, if, under any particular circumstances, it were judged eligible. Prior, therefore, to the establishment of this principle, *unanimity* was necessary; and rigid theory accordingly presupposes the assent of every individual to the rule which subjects the minority to the will of the majority. If this assent cannot be given tacitly, or be not implied where no positive evidence forbids, no person born in society could, on attaining ripe age, be bound by any acts of the majority, and either a unanimous renewal of every law would be necessary as often as a new member should be added to the society, or the express consent of every new member be obtained to the rule by which the majority decides for the whole.

If these observations be not misapplied, it follows that a limitation of the validity of all acts to the computed life of the generation establishing them is in some cases not required by theory, and in others not consistent with practice. They are not meant, however, to impeach either the utility of the principle as applied to the cases you have particularly in view, or the general importance of it in the eye of the philosophical legislator. On the contrary, it would give me singular pleasure to see it first announced to the world in a law of the United States, and always kept in view as a salutary restraint on living generations from unjust and unnecessary burdens on their successors. This is a pleasure, however, which I have no hope of enjoying. It is so much easier to descry the little difficulties immediately incident to every great plan than to comprehend its general and remote benefits, that further light must be added to the councils of our country before many truths which are seen through the medium of philosophy become visible to the naked eye of the ordinary politician.

# 1790

80.

## William Selby: "Ode for the New Year"

*Among the many European musicians who came to America seeking fame and fortune was the London organist and composer, William Selby. He arrived in Boston in 1771, where he became active in the city's musical affairs. In 1790, when George Washington was in the second year of his presidency, Selby wrote "Ode for the New Year" as a tribute to him.*

Source: *The American Musical Miscellany: A Collection of the Newest and Most Approved Songs, Set to Music,* Northampton, Mass., 1798, pp. 189-195.

### ODE FOR THE NEW YEAR

Hark! notes melodious fill the skies!
"From Thetis' lap, Apollo, rise!
Thy swift wheeled chariot speed amain!
O'er fleeting coursers, loose the rein,
The blushing hours impatient stand!
The virgin day waits thy command!
Awake, O Sol! and lead from ether's sphere,
In pomp of bridal joy, the wedded year!

"And as the golden car of light,
Refulgent beams on mortal sight;
As fiery steeds (which oft times lave
Their winged feet in ocean's wave)
Ascend above the mantling deep,
And rapid gain th' empyrean steep,
Let slumbering nations rise and loud prolong,
To day's celestial prince, the choral song."

Columbia heard the high behest,
Her freeborn millions smote the breast!
And silent slept the heaven-strung lyre,
Till freedom breathed impassioned fire;
Till virtue formed the hallowed sound;
And fame, enraptured, rolled it round.
"All hail to freedom's, virtue's, glory's son!
Ye worlds, repeat, repeat! 'Tis Washington."

European kingdoms caught the strain,
From mount to vale — from hill to plain,
Triumphant shouts with one acclaim,
Reechoing swelled the trump of fame;
"All Hail!" the Gallic peasant cries!
The cloistered monk, the nun replies!
"Illustrious George! Great patriot sage! 'Twas thine
To pour on France the flood of light divine!"

What notes are these? How grand! sublime!
'Tis freedom's song in Afric's clime!
The wretch, the slave whom fetters bound,
Exulting hears the joyful sound;
Ecstatic transports fire his soul,
And grateful paeans hourly roll;
For thee alone he hails the rising dawn;
The friend of man in Washington was born.

Lo, Asia joins the note of praise;
Her myriads dream of halcyon days,
When holy truth, with eagle ken,
Shall scan the rights of fellow men;
When impious tyrants, hurled from power,
No more shall spoil industry's flower;
But perfect freedom gild her evening sun,
And glow with cloudless beam — like Washington.

Hail, favored land, the pride of earth!
All nations hail Columbia's birth;
From Europe's realms to Asia's shore,
Or where the Niger's billows roar;
On eagle plume thy deeds shall fly;
And long as Sol adorns the sky,
Ten thousand thousand clarion tongues proclaim
The godlike Washington's immortal name.

# ART IN THE NEW NATION

Pennsylvania Academy of Fine Arts

## Charles Willson Peale

Of all the painters active after the Revolution, Charles Willson Peale seems to represent most fully the spirit of the times. In 1767, after working as an apprentice saddler in Maryland, he went to Benjamin West's studio in London, a pilgrimage common to aspiring American artists. Returning to America, he served in the Continental Army, and for a year in the Pennsylvania General Assembly. Peale painted more than 1,000 portraits of the leading figures of the period in direct, uncomplicated likenesses. Displaying some talent as an entrepreneur, Peale undertook a variety of projects. He organized a museum (shown above) to display both his political portraits and his natural history collection, which included, eventually, a mastodon skeleton. He was active in the establishment of the Pennsylvania Academy of Fine Arts and published books on bridge building, natural history, and ways of keeping healthy.

Independence National Historical Park

**John Adams; portrait by Peale, 1791-94**

Independence National Historical Park

**Joseph Brant; portrait painted in 1797**

**Portrait of C. W. Peale by Benjamin West**

New York Historical Society

**Self-portrait by C. W. Peale, 1824**

Pennsylvania Academy of Fine Arts

**"Staircase Group," portrait of Peale's sons**

Philadelphia Museum of Art

Lyman Allyn Museum

Litchfield Historical Society

**(Above) Amos Doolittle, the noted engraver, and Mrs. Benjamin Tallmadge with her children**

# Earl

Ralph Earl (1751-1801), sometimes described as the "most accomplished primitive," continued to paint in the severe style of traditional New England painting, even after seven years in London during the Revolution. His claims of having studied with Reynolds, as well as West, are not revealed in his work. Returning to America in 1785, Earl achieved popularity as a portraitist, in spite of intemperance with money and drink. His distinctively direct approach, which concentrated on the surroundings and dress of his subjects, apparently influenced a number of artists in western Connecticut where Earl spent most of his life. His few landscapes were ahead of their time and never earned appreciation.

**(Center right) "Looking East from Denny Hill," one of Earl's landscapes; (right) Mr. and Mrs. Oliver Ellsworth; in the background is the Ellsworth estate**

Worcester Art Museum

Wadsworth Atheneum

Museum of Fine Arts, Boston; bequest of George Black

**(Above) Self-portrait by Trumbull; (below) "Cardinal Bentivoglio," copied by Trumbull from Smibert's copy of the Van Dyck original**

Fogg Art Museum, Harvard

New York Historical Society

**Gen. Philip Schuyler; oil on mahogany panel**

# John Trumbull

John Trumbull (1756-1843), after service as an officer in the Revolution, undertook to record the war in the grand style of Benjamin West, with whom he studied for several years. In preparation for these large canvases, Trumbull painted dozens of life sketches, which together comprise his most vibrant work. Trumbull was appointed head of the American Academy of Fine Arts in 1817, where his conservative regime led to the foundation of the National Academy of Design.

**Henry Laurens, miniature painted in 1791**

Yale Art Gallery

Yale Art Gallery

"The Surrender of Burgoyne" (above) and "The Surrender of Lord Cornwallis" are from Trumbull's Revolutionary series. Engravings of the paintings, including some by Asher B. Durand, were sold well into the 19th century and as late as 1817 Trumbull was commissioned to recreate the canvases for the Capitol rotunda.

Yale Art Gallery

# Gilbert Stuart

Gilbert Stuart (1755-1828), who was born in Rhode Island, is the outstanding example of an American who profited fully from his experience in London. Between 1775, when he left America, and 1793, when he returned, Stuart established the pattern for his life and career. He absorbed the rich and vivid style that brought him success in both London and America; his extravagant debts forced him to flee London, first to Dublin and then to America. Painting successively in New York, Philadelphia, Washington, and finally in Boston, Stuart found preeminent popularity with his fluid and luminous society portraits.

Redwood Library

**Gilbert Stuart, self-portrait dated 1778**

Metropolitan Museum of Art; collection of D. K. Jay

**(Left) Portrait of John Jay as chief justice, 1794; (right) Mrs. Dolly Madison**

Library of Congress

Massachusetts Historical Society

**Study for a portrait of Abigail Adams**

National Collection of Fine Arts

**John Adams by Stuart, c. 1825**

Although his portraits were often careless flatteries for money, Stuart, in his best work, achieved much greater richness and subtlety than his predecessors and completely abandoned the austere colonial tradition. Stuart was the father of a long line of talented portraitists active in America during the early 19th century.

**Two of Stuart's portraits of Mrs. Perez Morton; the unfinished sketch (right) is dated 1802**

Museum of Fine Arts, Boston

Worcester Art Museum

New York Historical Society

**Portrait of the artist showing his first picture, a scene from "Hamlet," to his family**

# William Dunlap

William Dunlap (1766-1839), while not notably talented, lived a kind of "artistic" life not yet common in America. When his father sent him to study with West, Dunlap instead devoted most of his time to the theater. Returning to New York, he continually lost money promoting various theatrical ventures, generally staging his own plays or his translations of popular European plays. Although he was regarded highly enough to be a founding member of the National Academy of Design, Dunlap turned to painting only when forced to by poverty. He produced undistinguished portraits and miniatures as well as versions of Biblical or theatrical scenes for traveling exhibitions. In all, Dunlap wrote about 30 plays and an equal number of translations, but such success as he achieved derived from his books, particularly "The Rise and Progress of the Arts of Design in the United States."

# Edward Savage

Edward Savage (1761-1817) was another of Benjamin West's pupils whose work barely reflects his training but whose modest skills, applied straightforwardly, created portraits of considerable charm. His small success as a portraitist was enhanced by his work as a skilled engraver. In later life Savage went into business as partner in a cotton mill in Lancaster, Massachusetts.

**John Hancock and His Wife, by Savage**

Corcoran Gallery of Art

81.

## Royall Tyler: Prologue to *The Contrast*

The Contrast, *a play by Royall Tyler, was the first American comedy produced by a professional theatrical company. It is an example of the eighteenth-century American tendency to imitate European drama. Though placed in a local context and steeped in American nationalism, the drama was influenced by Sheridan's* The School for Scandal, *Vanbrugh and Cibber's* The Provoked Husband, *and John O'Keeffe's* The Poor Soldier. *The "Mr. Wignell" referred to in the Prologue is the English comedian Thomas Wignell, who first appeared in America in 1785. The play was first performed in New York in April 1787, and first published in 1790. The Prologue to the play is reprinted here.*

Source: *The Contrast*, Publications of the Dunlap Society, No. 1, New York, 1887.

### PROLOGUE

WRITTEN BY A YOUNG GENTLEMAN OF NEW YORK,
AND SPOKEN BY MR. WIGNELL

Exult, each patriot heart! This night is shown
A piece, which we may fairly call our own;
Where the proud titles of "My Lord! Your Grace!"
To humble *Mr.* and plain *Sir* give place.
Our Author pictures not from foreign climes
The fashions or the follies of the times;
But has confined the subject of his work
To the gay scenes — the circles of New York.
On native themes his Muse displays her pow'rs;
If ours the faults, the virtues too are ours.
Why should our thoughts to distant countries roam,
When each refinement may be found at home?
Who travels now to ape the rich or great,
To deck an equipage and roll in state;
To court the graces, or to dance with ease,
Or by hypocrisy to strive to please?
Our freeborn ancestors such arts despised;
Genuine sincerity alone they prized;
Their minds, with honest emulation fired,
To solid good — not ornament — aspired;
Or, if ambition roused a bolder flame,
Stern virtue throve, where indolence was shame.

But modern youths, with imitative sense,
Deem taste in dress the proof of excellence;
And spurn the meanness of your homespun arts,
Since homespun habits would obscure their parts;
Whilst all, which aims at splendor and parade,
Must come from Europe, *and be ready made.*
Strange! we should thus our native worth disclaim,
And check the progress of our rising fame.
Yet *one,* whilst imitation bears the sway,
Aspires to nobler heights, and points the way.
Be roused, my friends! his bold example view;
Let your own bards be proud to copy *you*!
Should rigid critics reprobate our play,

At least the patriotic heart will say,
"Glorious our fall, since in a noble cause.
The bold *attempt alone* demands applause."
Still may the wisdom of the Comic Muse
Exalt your merits, or your faults accuse.
But think not, 'tis her aim to be severe;
We all are mortals, and as mortals err.
If candor pleases, we are truly blest;
Vice trembles, when compelled to stand confessed.
Let not light censure on your faults offend,
Which aims not to expose them, but amend.
Thus does our Author to your candor trust;
Conscious, the *free* are generous, as just.

*A national debt, if it is not excessive, will be to us a national blessing.*

ALEXANDER HAMILTON, *c.* 1790

*The principle of spending money to be paid by posterity, under the name of funding, is but swindling futurity on a large scale.*

THOMAS JEFFERSON, *c.* 1790

82.

## ALEXANDER HAMILTON: First Report on the Public Credit

*Alexander Hamilton, as the first secretary of the treasury, was confronted with the task of establishing a stable national economy in the face of sectional interests, prejudices, and factions. His firm belief in a powerful central government went hand in hand with the financial policies he was to put into effect. On January 14, 1790, Hamilton gave his first report to Congress on the public debt. In it he emphasized the importance for the nation of good credit, especially in times of danger, and urged specific policies that he felt would lead to this goal: First, the foreign debt should be funded; second, the wartime securities that had been issued by the old Congress should be recalled; and third, the federal government should assume $25,000 in state debts. Such action, thought Hamilton, would insure the supremacy of the central government over the states. The first major political conflict in the new government, which would soon lead to the formation of political parties, was precipitated by this* Report, *part of which is reprinted here.*

Source: *American State Papers, Documents, Legislative and Executive, of the Congress of the United States, etc., etc.,* Walter Lowrie and Matthew Clarke, eds., Vol. V, Washington, 1832, pp. 15-25.

THE SECRETARY OF THE TREASURY, in obedience to the resolution of the House of Representatives of the 21st day of September last, has, during the recess of Congress, applied himself to the consideration of a proper plan for the support of the public credit, with all the attention which was due to the authority of the House and to the magnitude of the object. In the discharge of this duty, he has felt, in no small degree, the anxieties which naturally flow from a just estimate of the difficulty of the task, from a well-founded diffidence of his own qualifications for executing it with success, and from a deep and solemn conviction of the momentous nature of the truth contained in the resolution under which his investigations have been conducted, "That an adequate provision for the support of the public credit is a matter of high importance to the honor and prosperity of the United States."

With an ardent desire that his well-meant endeavors may be conducive to the real advantage of the nation; and with the utmost deference to the superior judgment of the House, he now respectfully submits the result of his inquiries and reflections to their indulgent construction.

In the opinion of the secretary, the wisdom of the House, in giving their explicit sanction to the proposition which has been stated, cannot but be applauded by all who will seriously consider and trace, through their obvious consequences, these plain and undeniable truths:

That exigencies are to be expected to occur, in the affairs of nations, in which there will be a necessity for borrowing;

That loans in times of public danger, especially from foreign war, are found an indispensable resource, even to the wealthiest of them;

And that, in a country which, like this, is possessed of little active wealth, or, in other words, little moneyed capital, the necessity for that resource must, in such emergencies, be proportionably urgent.

And as, on the one hand, the necessity for borrowing, in particular emergencies, cannot be doubted; so, on the other, it is equally evident that, to be able to borrow upon good terms, it is essential that the credit of a nation should be well established. For, when the credit of a country is in any degree questionable, it never fails to give an extravagant premium, in one shape or another, upon all the loans it has occasion to make. Nor does the evil end here; the same disadvantage must be sustained upon whatever is to be bought on terms of future payment. From this constant necessity of borrowing and buying dear, it is easy to conceive how immensely the expenses of a nation, in a course of time, will be augmented by an unsound state of the public credit.

To attempt to enumerate the complicated variety of mischiefs in the whole system of the social economy which proceed from a neglect of the maxims that uphold public credit, and justify the solicitude manifested by the House on this point, would be an improper intrusion on their time and patience. In so strong a light, nevertheless, do they appear to the Secretary that, on their due observance, at the present critical juncture, materially depends, in his judgment, the individual and aggregate prosperity of the citizens of the United States; their relief from the embarrassments they now experience; their character as a people; the cause of good government.

If the maintenance of public credit, then, be truly so important, the next inquiry which suggests itself is by what means it is to be effected. The ready answer to which question is: by good faith, by a punctual performance of contracts. States, like individuals, who observe their engagements are respected and trusted; while the reverse is the fate of those who pursue an opposite conduct.

Every breach of the public engagements, whether from choice or necessity, is, in different degrees, hurtful to public credit. When such a necessity does truly exist, the evils of it are only to be palliated by a scrupulous attention, on the part of the government, to carry the violation no further than the necessity absolutely requires, and to manifest, if the nature of the case admit of it, a sincere disposition to make reparation whenever circumstances shall permit. But, with every possible mitigation, credit must suffer and numerous mischiefs ensue. It is, therefore, highly important when an appearance of necessity seems to press upon the public councils, that they should examine well its reality and be perfectly assured that there is no method of escaping from it, before they yield to its suggestions.

For, though it cannot safely be affirmed that occasions have never existed, or may not exist, in which violations of the public faith, in this respect, are inevitable, yet there is great reason to believe that they exist far less frequently than precedents indicate and are oftenest either pretended, through levity or want of firmness, or supposed, through want of knowledge. Expedients might often have been devised to effect, consistently with good faith, what has been done in contravention of it. Those who are most commonly creditors of a nation are, generally speaking, enlightened men; and there are signal examples to warrant a conclusion that, when a candid and fair appeal is made to them, they will understand their true interest too well to refuse their concurrence in such modifications of their claims as any real necessity may demand.

While the observance of that good faith, which is the basis of public credit, is recommended by the strongest inducements of political expediency, it is enforced by considerations of still greater authority. There are arguments for it which rest on the immutable principles of moral obligation. And in proportion as the mind is disposed to contemplate, in the order of Providence, an intimate connection between public virtue and public happiness will be its repugnancy to a violation of those principles.

This reflection derives additional strength from the nature of the debt of the United States. It was the price of liberty. The faith of America has been repeatedly pledged for it, and with solemnities that give peculiar force to the obligation. There is, indeed, reason to regret that it has not hitherto been kept; that the necessities of the war, conspiring with inexperience in the subjects of finance, produced direct infractions; and that the subsequent period has been a continued scene of negative violation or noncompliance. But a diminution of this regret arises from the reflection that the last seven years have exhibited an earnest and uniform effort on the part of the government of the Union to retrieve the national credit by doing justice to the creditors of the nation; and that the embarrassments of a defective constitution, which defeated this laudable effort, have ceased.

From this evidence of a favorable disposition given by the former government, the institution of a new one, clothed with powers competent to calling forth the resources of the community, has excited correspondent expectations. A general belief accordingly prevails that the credit of the United States will quickly be established on the firm foundation of an effectual provision for the existing debt. The influence which this has had at home is witnessed by the rapid increase that has taken place in the market value of the public securities. From January to November, they rose 33⅓ percent; and from that period to this time, they have risen 50 percent more; and the intelligence from abroad announces effects proportionably favorable to our national credit and consequence.

It cannot but merit particular attention that, among ourselves, the most enlightened friends of good government are those whose expectations are the highest.

To justify and preserve their confidence; to promote the increasing respectability of the American name; to answer the calls of justice; to restore landed property to its due value; to furnish new resources both to agriculture and commerce; to cement more closely the union of the states; to add to their security against foreign attack; to establish public order on the basis of an upright and liberal policy — these are the great and invaluable ends to be secured by a proper and adequate provision, at the present period, for the support of public credit.

To this provision we are invited, not only by the general considerations which have been noticed but by others of a more particular nature. It will procure to every class of the community some important advantages, and remove some no less important disadvantages. The advantage to the public creditors from the increased value of that part of their property which constitutes the public debt needs no explanation.

But there is a consequence of this, less obvious, though not less true, in which every other citizen is interested. It is a well-known fact that in countries in which the national debt is properly funded, and an object of established confidence, it answers most of the purposes of money. Transfers of stock or public debt are there equivalent to payments in specie; or, in other words, stock, in the principal transactions of business, passes current as specie. The same thing would, in all probability, happen here under the like circumstances.

The benefits of this are various and obvious:

First, trade is extended by it, because there is a larger capital to carry it on and the merchant can, at the same time, afford to trade for smaller profits; as his stock, which, when unemployed, brings him an interest from the government, serves him also as money when he has a call for it in his commercial operations.

Second, agriculture and manufactures are also promoted by it, for the like reason that more capital can be commanded to be employed in both, and because the merchant, whose enterprise in foreign trade gives to them activity and extension, has greater means for enterprise.

Third, the interest of money will be lowered by it, for this is always in a ratio to the quantity of money and to the quickness of circulation. This circumstance will enable both the public and individuals to borrow on easier and cheaper terms.

And from the combination of these effects, additional aids will be furnished to labor, to industry, and to arts of every kind. But these good effects of a public debt are only to be looked for when, by being well funded, it has acquired an adequate and stable value; till then, it has rather a contrary tendency. The fluctuation and insecurity incident to it in an unfunded state render it a mere commodity and a precarious one. As such, being only an object of occasional and particular speculation, all the money applied to it is so much diverted from the more useful channels of circulation, for which the thing itself affords no substitute, so that, in fact, one serious inconvenience of an unfunded debt is that it contributes to the scarcity of money.

This distinction, which has been little if at all attended to, is of the greatest moment; it involves a question immediately interesting to every part of the community, which is no other than this: Whether the public debt, by a provision for it on true principles, shall be rendered a substitute for money; or whether, by being left as it is, or by being provided for in such a manner as will wound those principles and destroy confidence, it shall be suffered to continue as it is, a pernicious drain of our cash from the channels of productive industry?

The effect which the funding of the public debt, on right principles, would have upon landed property, is one of the circumstances attending such an arrangement, which has been least adverted to, though it deserves the most particular attention. The present depreciated state of that species of property is a serious calamity. The value of cultivated lands, in most of the states, has fallen, since the Revolution, from 25 to 50 percent. In those farther south, the decrease is still more considerable. Indeed, if the representations continually received from that quarter may be credited, lands there will command no price which may not be deemed an almost total sacrifice. This decrease in the value of lands, ought, in a great measure, to be attributed to the scarcity of money; consequently, whatever produces an augmentation of the moneyed capital of the country must have a proportional effect in raising that value. The beneficial tendency of a funded debt, in this respect, has been manifested by the most decisive experience in Great Britain.

The proprietors of lands would not only feel the benefit of this increase in the value of their property, and of a more prompt and better sale, when they had occasion to sell, but the necessity of selling would be itself greatly diminished. As the same cause would contribute to the facility of loans, there is reason to believe that such of them as are indebted would be able, through that resource, to satisfy their more urgent creditors.

It ought not, however, to be expected that the advantages described as likely to result from funding the public debt would be instantaneous. It might require some time to bring the value of stock to its natural level, and to attach to it that fixed confidence which is necessary to its quality as money. Yet the late rapid rise of the public securities encourages an expectation that the progress of stock, to the desirable point, will be much more expeditious than could have been foreseen. And as, in the meantime, it will be increasing in value, there is room to conclude that it will, from the outset, answer many of the purposes in contemplation. Particularly, it seems to be probable, that from creditors, who are not themselves necessitous, it will early meet with a ready reception in payment of debts, at its current price.

Having now taken a concise view of the inducements to a proper provision for the public debt, the next inquiry which presents itself is: What ought to be the nature of such a provision? This requires some preliminary discussions.

It is agreed on all hands that that part of the debt which has been contracted abroad and is denominated the foreign debt ought to be provided for according to the precise terms of the contracts relating to it. The discussions which can arise, therefore, will have reference essentially to the domestic part of it, or to that which has been contracted at home. It is to be regretted that there is not the same unanimity of sentiment on this part as on the other.

The Secretary has too much deference for the opinions of every part of the community not to have observed one, which has more than once made its appearance in the public prints, and which is occasionally to be met with in conversation. It involves this question: Whether a discrimination ought not to be made between original holders of the public securities and present possessors by purchase? Those who advocate a discrimination are for making a full provision for the securities of the former at their nominal value but contend that the latter ought to receive no more than the cost to them and the interest. And the idea is sometimes suggested of making good the difference to the primitive possessor.

In favor of this scheme, it is alleged that it would be unreasonable to pay 20*s.* in the pound to one who had not given more for it than 3 or 4. And it is added that it would be hard to aggravate the misfortune of the first owner, who, probably through necessity, parted with his property at so great a loss, by obliging him to contribute to the profit of the person who had speculated on his distresses.

The Secretary, after the most mature reflection on the force of this argument, is induced to reject the doctrine it contains as equally unjust and impolitic; as highly injurious, even to the original holders of public securities; as ruinous to public credit. It is inconsistent with justice, because, in the first place, it is a breach of contract, a violation of the rights of a fair purchaser. The nature of the contract, in its origin, is that the public will pay the sum expressed in the security to the first holder or his assignee. The intent in making the security assignable is that the proprietor may be able to make use of his property by selling it for as much as it may be worth in the market and that the buyer may be safe in the purchase.

Every buyer, therefore, stands exactly in the place of the seller, has the same right with him to the identical sum expressed in the security, and, having acquired that right by fair purchase, and in conformity to the original agreement and intention of the government, his claim cannot be disputed without manifest injustice.

That he is to be considered as a fair purchaser results from this: whatever necessity the seller may have been under was occasioned by the government in not making a proper provision for its debts. The buyer had no agency in it and therefore ought not to suffer. He is not even chargeable with having taken an undue advantage. He paid what the commodity was worth in the market and took the risks of reimbursement upon himself. He of course gave a fair equivalent and ought to reap the benefit of his hazard; a hazard which was far from inconsiderable, and which, perhaps, turned on little less than a revolution in government.

That the case of those who parted with their securities from necessity is a hard one cannot be denied; but, whatever complaint of injury or claim of redress they may have respects the government solely. They have not only nothing to object to the persons who relieved their necessities by giving them the current price of their property, but they are even under an implied condition to contribute to the reimbursement of those persons. They knew that, by the terms of the contract with themselves, the public were bound to pay to those to whom they should convey their title the sums stipulated to be paid to them; and that, as citizens of the United States, they were to bear their proportion of the contribution for that purpose. This, by the act of assignment, they tacitly engage to do; and, if they had an option, they could not, with integrity or good faith, refuse to do it without the consent of those to whom they sold.

But, though many of the original holders sold from necessity, it does not follow that this was the case with all of them. It may well be supposed that some of them did it either through want of confidence in an eventual provision or from the allurements of some profitable speculation.

How shall these different classes be discriminated from each other? How shall it be ascertained, in any case, that the money which the original holder obtained for his security was not more beneficial to him than if he had held it to the present time, to avail himself of the provision which shall be made? How shall it be known whether, if the purchaser had employed his money in some other way, he would not be in a better situation than by having applied it in the purchase of securities, though he should now receive their full amount? And, if neither of these things can be known, how shall it be determined, whether a discrimination, independent of the breach of contract, would not do a real injury to purchasers; and, if it included a compensation to the primitive proprietors, would not give them an advantage to which they had no equitable pretension? . . .

But there is still a point of view in which it will appear perhaps even more exceptionable than in either of the former. It would be repugnant to an express provision of the Constitution of the United States. This provision is that "all debts contracted, and engagements entered into, before the adoption of that Constitution, shall be as valid against the United States under it as under the Confederation"; which amounts to a constitutional ratification of the contracts respecting the debt in the state in which they existed under the Confederation; and, resorting to that standard, there can be no doubt that the rights of assignees and original holders must be considered as equal. In exploding thus fully the principle of discrimination, the Secretary is happy in reflecting that he is only the advocate of what has been already sanctioned by the formal and express authority of the government of the Union in these emphatic terms: "The remaining class of creditors," say Congress, in their circular address to the states of the 26th of April, 1783,

> is composed partly of such of our fellow citizens as originally lent to the public the use of their funds, or have since manifested most confidence in their country by receiving transfers from the lenders; and partly of those whose property has been either advanced or assumed for the public service. To discriminate the merits of these several descriptions of creditors would be a task equally unnecessary and invidious. If the voice of humanity plead more loudly in favor of some than of others, the voice of policy, no less than of justice, pleads in favor of all. A wise nation will never permit those who relieve the wants of their country, or who rely most on its faith, its firmness, and its resources, when either of them is distrusted, to suffer by the event.

The Secretary, concluding that a discrimination between the different classes of creditors of the United States cannot, with propriety, be made, proceeds to examine whether a difference ought to be permitted to remain between them and another description of public creditors: those of the states individually. The Secretary, after mature reflection on this point, entertains a full conviction that an assumption of the debts of the particular states by the Union, and a like provision for them as for those of the Union, will be a measure of sound policy and substantial justice.

It would, in the opinion of the Secretary, contribute, in an eminent degree, to an orderly, stable, and satisfactory arrangement of the national finances. Admitting, as ought to be the case, that a provision must be made, in some way or other, for the entire debt, it will follow that no greater revenues will be required, whether that provision be made wholly by the United States, or partly by them and partly by the states separately.

The principal question, then, must be whether such a provision cannot be more conveniently and effectually made, by one general plan issuing from one authority, than by different plans, originating in different authorities? In the first case, there can be no competition for resources; in the last, there must be such a competition. The consequences of this, without the greatest caution on both sides, might be interfering regulations, and thence, collision and confusion. Particular branches of industry might also be oppressed by it. The most productive objects of revenue are not numerous. Either these must be wholly engrossed by one side, which might lessen the efficacy of the provisions by the other, or both must have recourse to the same objects, in different modes, which might occasion an accumulation upon them, beyond what they could properly bear. If this should not happen, the caution requisite to avoiding it would prevent the revenue's deriving the full benefit of each object. The danger of interference and of excess would be apt to impose restraints very unfriendly to the complete command of those resources which are the most convenient, and to compel the having recourse to others, less eligible in themselves, and less agreeable to the community.

The difficulty of an effectual command of the public resources, in case of separate provisions for the debt, may be seen in another, and, perhaps, more striking light. It would naturally happen that different states, from local considerations, would, in some instances, have recourse to different objects, in others to the same objects, in different degrees, for procuring the funds of which they stood in need. It is easy to conceive how this diversity would affect the aggregate revenue of the country. By the supposition, articles which yielded a full supply in some states would yield nothing, or an insufficient product, in others. And, hence, the public revenue would not derive the full benefit of those articles from state regulations; neither could the deficiencies be made good by those of the Union. It is a provision of the national Constitution that "all duties, imposts, and excises shall be uniform throughout the United States." And, as the general government would be under a necessity, from motives of policy, of paying regard to the duty which may have been previously imposed upon any article, though but in a single state, it would be constrained either to refrain wholly from any further imposition upon such article, where it had been already rated as high as was proper, or to confine itself to the difference between the existing rate and what the article would reasonably bear. Thus the preoccupancy of an article by a single state would tend to arrest or abridge the impositions of the Union on that article. And as it is supposable that a great variety of articles might be placed in this situation, by dissimilar arrangements of the particular states, it is evident that the aggregate revenue of the country would be likely to be very materially contracted by the plan of separate provisions.

If all the public creditors receive their dues from one source, distributed with an equal hand, their interests will be the same; and, having the same interests, they will unite in the support of the fiscal arrangements of the government, as these, too, can be made with more convenience where there is no competition. These circumstances combined will insure to the revenue laws a more ready and more satisfactory execution.

If, on the contrary, there are distinct provisions, there will be distinct interest, drawing different ways. That union and concert of views among the creditors, which in every government is of great importance to their security, and to that of public credit, will not only not exist but will be likely to give place to mutual jealousy and opposition; and from this cause, the operation of the systems which may be adopted both by the particular states and by the Union, with relation to their respective debts, will be in danger of being counteracted.

There are several reasons which render it probable that the situation of the state creditors would be worse than that of the creditors of the Union, if there be not a national assumption of the state debts. Of these it will be sufficient to mention two: one, that a principal branch of revenue is exclusively vested in the Union; the other, that a state must always be checked in the imposition of taxes on articles of consumption, from the want of power to extend the same regulation to the other states, and from the tendency of partial duties to injure its industry and commerce. Should the state creditors stand upon a less eligible footing than the others, it is unnatural to expect they would see with pleasure a provision for them. The influence which their dissatisfaction might have could not but operate injuriously, both for the creditors and the credit of the United States.

Hence it is even the interest of the creditors of the Union that those of the individual states should be comprehended in a general provision. Any attempt to secure to the former either exclusive or peculiar advantages would materially hazard their interests. Neither would it be just that one class of the public creditors should be more favored than the other. The object for which both descriptions of the debt were contracted are in the main the same. Indeed, a great part of the particular debts of the states has arisen from assumptions by them on account of the Union; and it is most equitable that there should be the same measure of retribution for all. There is an objection, however, to an assumption of the state debts, which deserves particular notice. It may be supposed that it would increase the difficulty of an equitable settlement between them and the United States.

The principles of that settlement, whenever they shall be discussed, will require all the moderation and wisdom of the government. In the opinion of the Secretary, that discussion, till further lights are obtained, would be premature. All, therefore, which he would now think advisable on the point in question would be that the amount of the debts assumed and provided for should be charged to the respective states, to abide an eventual arrangement. This, the United States, as assignees to the creditors, would have an indisputable right to do. But, as it might be a satisfaction to the House to have before them some plan for the liquidation of accounts between the Union and its members, which, including the assumption of the state debts, would consist with equity, the Secretary will submit, in this place, such thoughts on the subject as have occurred to his own mind, or been suggested to him, most compatible, in his judgment, with the end proposed.

Let each state be charged with all the money advanced to it out of the Treasury of the United States, liquidated according to the specie value at the time of each advance, with interest at 6 percent.

Let it also be charged with the amount, in specie value, of all its securities which shall be assumed, with the interests upon them to the time when interest shall become payable by the United States.

Let it be credited for all moneys paid and

articles furnished to the United States, and for all other expenditures during the war, either toward general or particular defense, whether authorized or unauthorized by the United States; the whole liquidated to specie value, and bearing an interest of 6 percent from the several times at which the several payments, advances, and expenditures accrued.

And let all sums of Continental money, now in the treasuries of the respective states, which shall be paid into the Treasury of the United States, be credited at specie value.

Upon a statement of the accounts according to these principles, there can be little doubt that balances would appear in favor of all the states against the United States.

To equalize the contributions of the states, let each be then charged with its proportion of the aggregate of those balances according to some equitable ratio to be devised for that purpose.

If the contributions should be found disproportionate, the result of this adjustment would be that some states would be creditors, some debtors, to the Union. Should this be the case — as it will be attended with less inconvenience to the United States to have to pay balances to, than to receive them from, the particular states — it may, perhaps, be practicable to effect the former by a second process, in the nature of a transfer of the amount of the debts of debtor states to the credit of creditor states; observing the ratio by which the first apportionment shall have been made. This, while it would destroy the balances due from the former, would increase those due to the latter; these to be provided for by the United States at a reasonable interest but not to be transferable. The expediency of this second process must depend on a knowledge of the result of the first. If the inequalities should be too great, the arrangement may be impracticable, without unduly increasing the debt of the United States. But it is not likely that this would be the case. It is also to be remarked that, though this second process might not, upon the principle of apportionment, bring the thing to the point aimed at, yet it may approach so nearly to it as to avoid essentially the embarrassment of having considerable balances to collect from any of the states. . . .

The result of the foregoing discussions is this: that there ought to be no discrimination between the original holders of the debt and present possessors by purchase; that it is expedient there should be an assumption of the state debts by the Union; and that the arrears of interest should be provided for on an equal footing with the principal.

The next inquiry in order, toward determining the nature of a proper provision, respects the quantum of the debt and the present rates of interest.

The debt of the Union is distinguishable into foreign and domestic.

The foreign debt, as stated in Schedule B, amounts to:

| | |
|---|---|
| Principal | $10,070,307.00 |
| Bearing an interest of 4, and partly an interest of 5% | |
| Arrears of interest to the last of December 1789 | 1,640,071.62 |
| Making together | $11,710,378.62 |

The domestic debt may be sub-divided into liquidated and unliquidated; principal and interest.

| | |
|---|---|
| The principal of the liquidated part, as stated in Schedule C, amounts to | $27,383,917.74 |
| Bearing an interest of 6% | |
| The arrears of interest, as stated in Schedule D, to the end of 1790, amount to | 13,030,168.20 |
| Making together | $40,414,085.94 |

83.

# THOMAS JEFFERSON: The Hamiltonian System

*One of the fiercest opponents of Hamilton's policies was another of George Washington's appointees, Thomas Jefferson, the new secretary of state. The President had chosen these two men, who represented such divergent views, in the hope of winning support for the Union from all sections of the country. However, the opposition to Hamilton increased during the 1790s and split the Union into two political factions. During his years as secretary of state, Jefferson recorded his thoughts and impressions in notes that, collectively, are called the* Anas. *He often spoke of Hamilton's "monarchist" tendencies, and in the following selection from the* Anas, *he scathingly indicted Hamilton's financial policies. The text reprinted here reflects changes made by Jefferson some twenty-five years later, when, as he said, he had "given to the whole a calm revisal."*

Source: H. A. Washington, IX, pp. 87-99.

A SHORT REVIEW OF FACTS . . . will show that the contests of that day were contests of principle between the advocates of republican and those of kingly government and that, had not the former made the efforts they did, our government would have been, even at this early day, a very different thing from what the successful issue of those efforts has made it.

The alliance between the states under the old Articles of Confederation, for the purpose of joint defense against the aggression of Great Britain, was found insufficient, as treaties of alliance generally are, to enforce compliance with their mutual stipulations; and these, once fulfilled, that bond was to expire of itself, and each state to become sovereign and independent in all things. Yet it could not but occur to everyone that these separate independencies, like the petty states of Greece, would be eternally at war with each other and would become at length the mere partisans and satellites of the leading powers of Europe. All then must have looked forward to some further bond of union which would insure eternal peace and a political system of our own, independent of that of Europe.

Whether all should be consolidated into a single government, or each remain independent as to internal matters, and the whole form a single nation as to what was foreign only, and whether that national government should be a monarchy or republic, would of course divide opinions, according to the constitutions, the habits, and the circumstances of each individual. Some officers of the Army, as it has always been said and believed (and Steuben and Knox have ever been named as the leading agents), trained to monarchy by military habits, are understood to have proposed to General Washington to decide this great question by the Army before its disbandment and to assume himself the crown on the assurance of their support. The indignation with which he is said to have scouted this parricide proposition was equally worthy of his virtue and wisdom.

The next effort was (on suggestion of the same individuals, in the moment of their separation) the establishment of a hereditary order under the name of the Cincinnati, ready prepared by that distinction to be ingrafted into the future frame of government, and placing General Washington still at their head. The General wrote to me on this subject while I was in Congress at Annapolis . . . He afterward called on me at that place on his way to a meeting of the society, and after a whole evening of consultation, he left that place fully determined to use all his endeavors for its total suppression. But he found it so firmly riveted in the affections of the members that, strengthened as they happened to be by an adventitious occurrence of the moment, he could effect no more than the abolition of its hereditary principle. . . .

The want of some authority which should procure justice to the public creditors, and an observance of treaties with foreign nations, produced, some time after, the call of a convention of the states at Annapolis. Although, at this meeting, a difference of opinion was evident on the question of a republican or kingly government, yet so general through the states was the sentiment in favor of the former that the friends of the latter confined themselves to a course of obstruction only, and delay, to everything proposed. They hoped that, nothing being done, and all things going from bad to worse, a kingly government might be usurped and submitted to by the people as better than anarchy and wars internal and external — the certain consequences of the present want of a general government.

The effect of their maneuvers, with the defective attendance of deputies from the states, resulted in the measure of calling a more general convention, to be held at Philadelphia. At this, the same party exhibited the same practices, and with the same views of preventing a government of concord, which they foresaw would be republican, and of forcing through anarchy their way to monarchy. But the mass of that convention was too honest, too wise, and too steady to be baffled and misled by their maneuvers. One of these was a form of government proposed by Colonel Hamilton, which would have been in fact a compromise between the two parties of royalism and republicanism. According to this, the executive and one branch of the legislature were to be during good behavior, *i.e.*, for life, and the governors of the states were to be named by these two permanent organs. This, however, was rejected; on which Hamilton left the convention, as desperate, and never returned again until near its final conclusion.

These opinions and efforts, secret or avowed, of the advocates for monarchy, had begotten great jealousy through the states generally; and this jealousy it was which excited the strong opposition to the conventional constitution; a jealousy which yielded at last only to a general determination to establish certain amendments as barriers against a government either monarchical or consolidated. In what passed through the whole period of these conventions, I have gone on the information of those who were members of them, being absent myself on my mission to France.

I returned from that mission in the first year of the new government, having landed in Virginia in December 1789, and proceeded to New York in March 1790, to enter on the office of secretary of state. Here, certainly, I found a state of things which, of all I had ever contemplated, I the least expected. I had left France in the first year of her revolution, in the fervor of natural rights and zeal for reformation. My conscientious devotion to these rights could not be heightened, but it had been aroused and excited by daily exercise. The President received me cordially, and my colleagues and the circle of principal citizens apparently with welcome. The courtesies of dinner parties given me, as a stranger newly arrived among them, placed me at once in their familiar society. But I cannot describe the wonder and mortification with which the table conversations filled me.

Politics was the chief topic, and a preference of kingly over republican government was evidently the favorite sentiment. An apostate I could not be, nor yet a hypocrite; and I found myself, for the most part, the only advocate on the republican side of the question, unless among the guests there chanced to be some member of that party from the legislative houses. Hamilton's financial system had then passed. It had two objects; first, as a puzzle, to exclude popular understanding and inquiry; second, as a machine for the corruption of the legislature. For he avowed the opinion that man could be governed by one of two motives only, force or interest; force, he observed, in this country was out of the question, and the interests, therefore, of the members must be laid hold of to keep the legislative in unison with the executive. And with grief and shame it must be acknowledged that his machine was not without effect; that even in this, the birth of our government, some members were found sordid enough to bend their duty to their interest, and to look after personal rather than public good.

It is well known that during the war the greatest difficulty we encountered was the want of money or means to pay our soldiers who fought, or our farmers, manufacturers, and merchants who furnished the necessary supplies of food and clothing for them. After the expedient of paper money had exhausted itself, certificates of debt were given to the individual creditors, with assurance of payment so soon as the United States should be able. But the distresses of these people often obliged them to part with these for the half, the fifth, and even the tenth of their value; and speculators had made a trade of cozening them from the holders by the most fraudulent practices, and persuasions that they would never be paid.

In the bill for funding and paying these, Hamilton made no difference between the original holders and the fraudulent purchasers of this paper. Great and just repugnance arose at putting these two classes of creditors on the same footing, and great exertions were used to pay the former the full value, and to the latter, the price only which they had paid, with interest. But this would have prevented the game which was to be played, and for which the minds of greedy members were already tutored and prepared.

When the trial of strength on these several efforts had indicated the form in which the bill would finally pass, this being known within doors sooner than without, and especially than to those who were in distant parts of the Union, the base scramble began. Couriers and relay horses by land, and swift-sailing pilot boats by sea, were flying in all directions. Active partners and agents were associated and employed in every state, town, and country neighborhood, and this paper was bought up at *5s.*, and even as low as *2s.* in the pound, before the holder knew that Congress had already provided for its redemption at par. Immense sums were thus filched from the poor and ignorant, and fortunes accumulated by those who had themselves been poor enough before. Men thus enriched by the dexterity of a leader would follow of course the chief who was leading them to fortune and become the zealous instruments of all his enterprises.

This game was over, and another was on the carpet at the moment of my arrival; and to this I was most ignorantly and innocently made to hold the candle. This fiscal maneuver is well known by the name of the *Assumption.* Independently of the debts of Congress, the states had during the war contracted separate and heavy debts; and Massachusetts particularly, in an absurd attempt, absurdly conducted, on the British post of Penobscot; and the more debt Hamilton could rake up, the more plunder for his mercenaries. This money, whether wisely or foolishly spent, was pretended to have been spent for general purposes, and ought, therefore, to be paid from the general purse.

But it was objected that nobody knew what these debts were, what their amount, or what their proofs. No matter; we will guess them to be $20,000,000. But of these $20,000,000, we do not know how much should be reimbursed to one state, or how much to another. No matter; we will guess. And so another scramble was set on foot among the several states, and some got much, some little, some nothing. But the main object was obtained, the phalanx of the Treasury was reinforced by additional recruits. This measure produced the most bitter and angry contest ever known in Congress, before or since the union of the states. I arrived in the midst of it. But a stranger to the ground, a stranger to the actors on it, so long absent as to have lost all familiarity with the subject, and as yet unaware of its object, I took no concern in it.

The great and trying question, however, was lost in the House of Representatives. So high were the feuds excited by this subject that, on its rejection, business was suspended. Congress met and adjourned from day to day without doing anything, the parties being too much out of temper to do business together. The eastern members particularly, who, with Smith from South Carolina, were the principal gamblers in these scenes, threatened a secession and dissolution. Hamilton was in despair. As I was going to the President's one day, I met him in the street. He walked me backward and forward before the President's door for half an hour. He painted pathetically the temper into which the legislature had been wrought; the disgust of those who were called the creditor states; the danger of the *secession* of their members, and the separation of the states.

He observed that the members of the administration ought to act in concert; that though this question was not of my department, yet a common duty should make it a common concern; that the President was the center on which all administrative questions ultimately rested, and that all of us should rally around him, and support, with joint efforts, measures approved by him; and that the question having been lost by a small majority only, it was probable that an appeal from me to the judgment and discretion of some of my friends might effect a change in the vote, and the machine of government, now suspended, might be again set into motion. I told him that I was really a stranger to the whole subject; that, not having yet informed myself of the system of finances adopted, I knew not how far this was a necessary sequence; that undoubtedly, if its rejection endangered a dissolution of our Union at this incipient stage, I should deem that the most unfortunate of all consequences, to avert which all partial and temporary evils should be yielded.

I proposed to him, however, to dine with me the next day, and I would invite another friend or two, bring them into conference together, and I thought it impossible that reasonable men, consulting together coolly, could fail, by some mutual sacrifices of opinion, to form a compromise which was to save the Union. The discussion took place. I could take no part in it but an exhortatory one, because I was a stranger to the circumstances which should govern it. But it was finally agreed that, whatever importance had been attached to the rejection of this proposition, the preservation of the Union and of concord among the states was more important, and that therefore it would be better that the vote of rejection should be rescinded, to effect which some members should change their votes. But it was observed that this pill would be peculiarly bitter to the Southern states, and that some concomitant measure should be adopted to sweeten it a little to them.

There had before been propositions to fix the seat of government either at Philadelphia, or at Georgetown on the Potomac; and it was thought that by giving it to Philadelphia for ten years, and to Georgetown permanently afterward, this might, as an anodyne, calm in some degree the ferment which might be excited by the other measure alone. So two of the Potomac members (White and Lee, but White with a revulsion of stomach almost convulsive) agreed to change their votes, and Hamilton undertook to carry the other point. In doing this, the influence he had established over the eastern members, with the agency of Robert Morris with those of the middle states, effected his side of the engagement; and so the *Assumption* was passed, and $20,000,000 of stock divided among favored states, and thrown in as a pabulum to the stockjobbing herd. This added to the number of votaries to the Treasury and made its chief the master of every vote in the legislature, which might give to the government the direction suited to his political views.

I know well, and so must be understood, that nothing like a majority in Congress had yielded to this corruption. Far from it. But a division, not very unequal, had already taken place in the honest part of that body, between the parties styled Republican and Federal. The latter, being monarchists in principle, adhered to Hamilton of course, as their leader in that principle, and this mercenary phalanx, added to them, insured him always a majority in both houses, so that the whole action of legislature was now under the direction of the Treasury. Still the machine was not complete. The effect of the funding system, and of the *Assumption,* would be temporary; it would be lost with the loss of the individual members whom it has enriched, and some engine of influence more permanent must be contrived, while these myrmidons were yet in place to carry it through all opposition.

This engine was the Bank of the United States. All that history is known, so I shall say nothing about it. While the government remained at Philadelphia, a selection of members of both houses were constantly kept as directors who, on every question interesting to that institution, or to the views of the federal head, voted at the will of that head; and, together with the stockholding members, could always make the federal vote that of the majority. By this combination, legislative expositions were given to the Constitution, and all the administrative laws were shaped on the model of England, and so passed. And from this influence we were not relieved until the removal from the precincts of the bank to Washington.

Here, then, was the real ground of the opposition which was made to the course of administration. Its object was to preserve the legislature pure and independent of the executive, to restrain the administration to republican forms and principles, and not permit the Constitution to be construed into a monarchy, and to be warped, in practice, into all the principles and pollutions of their favorite English model. Nor was this an opposition to General Washington. He was true to the republican charge confided to him; and has solemnly and repeatedly protested to me, in our conversations, that he would lose the last drop of his blood in support of it; and he did this the oftener and with the more earnestness, because he knew my suspicions of Hamilton's designs against it and wished to quiet them. For he was not aware of the drift or of the effect of Hamilton's schemes. Unversed in financial projects and calculations and budgets, his approbation of them was bottomed on his confidence in the man.

But Hamilton was not only a monarchist, but for a monarchy bottomed on corruption. In proof of this, I will relate an anecdote, for the truth of which I attest the God who made me. Before the President set out on his southern tour in April 1791, he addressed a letter of the 4th of that month from Mount Vernon, to the secretaries of state, treasury, and war, desiring that if any serious and important cases should arise during his absence, they would consult and act on them. And he requested that the Vice-President should also be consulted. This was the only occasion on which that officer was ever requested to take part in a cabinet question. Some occasion for consultation arising, I invited those gentlemen (and the attorney general, as well as I remember) to dine with me in order to confer on the subject.

After the cloth was removed, and our question agreed and dismissed, conversation began on other matters and, by some circumstance, was led to the British constitution, on which Mr. Adams observed, "Purge that constitution of its corruption, and give to its popular branch equality of representation, and it would be the most perfect constitution ever devised by the wit of man." Hamilton paused and said, "Purge it of its corruption, and give to its popular branch equality of representation, and it would become an *impracticable* government: as it stands at present, with all its supposed defects, it is the most perfect government which ever existed." And this was assuredly the exact line which separated the political creeds of these two gentlemen. The one was for two hereditary branches and an honest elective one; the other, for a hereditary king, with a House of Lords and Commons corrupted to his will, and standing between him and the people.

Hamilton was, indeed, a singular character. Of acute understanding, disinterested, honest, and honorable in all private transactions, amiable in society, and duly valuing virtue in private life, yet so bewitched and perverted by the British example as to be under thorough conviction that corruption was essential to the government of a nation.

---

84

## Benjamin Franklin: Against the Slave Trade

*On March 25, 1790, an essay against the slave trade written by Benjamin Franklin and signed "Historicus" appeared in the* Federal Gazette. *The article was occasioned by a speech of James Jackson, a U.S. senator from Georgia, who argued in favor of Negro slavery. Franklin parodied Jackson's arguments, satirically claiming that his essay was an old African speech that the Senator "perhaps [had] not seen."*

Source: Sparks, II, pp. 517-521.

Reading last night in your excellent paper the speech of Mr. Jackson in Congress against their meddling with the affair of slavery, or attempting to mend the condition of the slaves, it put me in mind of a similar one made about 100 years since by Sidi Mehemet Ibrahim, a member of the Divan of Algiers, which may be seen in Martin's Account of his Consulship, *anno* 1687. It was against granting the petition of the sect called Erika, or Purists, who prayed for the abolition of piracy and slavery as being unjust. Mr. Jackson does not quote it; perhaps he has not seen it. If, therefore, some of its reasonings are to be found in his eloquent speech, it may only show that men's interests and intellects operate and are operated on with surprising similarity in all countries and climates, whenever they are under similar circumstances. The African's speech, as translated, is as follows.

Allah Bismillah, etc., God is great, and Mahomet is his Prophet.

Have these Erika considered the consequences of granting their petition? If we cease our cruises against the Christians, how shall we be furnished with the commodities their countries produce and which are so necessary for us? If we forbear to make slaves of their people, who in this hot climate are to cultivate our lands? Who are to perform the common labors of our city and in our families? Must we not then be our own slaves? And is there not more compassion and more favor due to us as Mussulmen, than to these Christian dogs? We have now above 50,000 slaves in and near Algiers. This number, if not kept up by fresh supplies, will soon diminish, and be gradually annihilated. If we then cease taking and plundering the infidel ships, and making slaves of the seamen and passengers, our lands will become of no value for want of cultivation; the rents of houses in the city will sink one-half; and the revenue of government arising from its share of prizes be totally destroyed! And for what? To gratify the whims of a whimsical sect, who would have us not only forbear making more slaves, but even manumit those we have.

But who is to indemnify their masters for the loss? Will the state do it? Is our treasury sufficient? Will the Erika do it? Can they do it? Or would they, to do what they think justice to the slaves, do a greater injustice to the owners? And if we set our slaves free, what is to be done with them? Few of them will return to their countries; they know too well the greater hardships they must there be subject to; they will not embrace our holy religion; they will not adopt our manners; our people will not pollute themselves by intermarrying with them. Must we maintain them as beggars in our streets, or suffer our properties to be the prey of their pillage? For men accustomed to slavery will not work for a livelihood when not compelled. And what is there so pitiable in their present condition? Were they not slaves in their own countries?

Are not Spain, Portugal, France, and the Italian states governed by despots, who hold all their subjects in slavery without exception? Even England treats its sailors as slaves; for they are, whenever the government pleases, seized, and confined in ships of war, condemned not only to work, but to fight, for small wages or a mere subsistence, not better than our slaves are allowed by us. Is their condition then made worse by their falling into our hands? No; they have only exchanged one slavery for another, and I may say a better; for here they are brought into a land where the sun of Islamism gives forth its light, and shines in full splendor, and they have an opportunity of making themselves acquainted with the true doctrine, and thereby saving their immortal souls. Those who remain at home have not that happiness. Sending the slaves home then would be sending them out of light into darkness.

I repeat the question: What is to be done with them? I have heard it suggested that they may be planted in the wilderness, where there is plenty of land for them to subsist on and where they may flourish as a free state; but they are, I doubt, too little disposed to labor without compulsion, as well as too ignorant to establish a good government; and the wild Arabs would soon molest and destroy or again enslave them. While serving us, we take care to provide them with everything, and they are treated with humanity. The laborers in their own country are, as I am well informed, worse fed, lodged, and clothed. The condition of most of them is therefore already mended and requires no further improvement. Here their lives are in safety. They are not liable to be impressed for soldiers, and forced to cut one another's Christian throats, as in the wars of their own countries. If some of the religious mad bigots, who now tease us with their silly petitions, have in a fit of blind zeal freed their slaves, it was not generosity, it was not humanity, that moved them to the action; it was from the conscious burden of a load of sins, and a hope, from the supposed merits of so good a work, to be excused from damnation.

How grossly are they mistaken to suppose slavery to be disallowed by the Alcoran! Are not the two precepts (to quote no more): "Masters, treat your slaves with kindness; Slaves, serve your masters with cheerfulness and fidelity," clear proofs to the contrary? Nor can the plundering of infidels be in that sacred book forbidden, since it is well known from it that God has given the world, and all that it contains, to His faithful Mussulmen, who are to enjoy it of right as fast as they conquer it. Let us then hear no more of this detestable proposition, the manumission of Christian slaves, the adoption of which would, by depreciating our lands and houses and thereby depriving so many good citizens of their properties, create universal discontent and provoke insurrections to the endangering of government and producing [of] general confusion. I have therefore no doubt, but this wise council will prefer the comfort and happiness of a whole nation of true believers to the whim of a few Erika and dismiss their petition.

The result was, as Martin tells us, that the Divan came to this resolution: "The doctrine that plundering and enslaving the Christians is unjust is at best problematical; but that it is the interest of this state to continue the practice is clear; therefore let the petition be rejected."

Library of Congress

Engraving of Benjamin Franklin from "Massachusetts Magazine"

And it was rejected accordingly.

And since like motives are apt to produce in the minds of men like opinions and resolutions, may we not, Mr. Brown, venture to predict from this account that the petitions to the Parliament of England for abolishing the slave trade, to say nothing of other legislatures, and the debates upon them, will have a similar conclusion? I am, sir, your constant reader and humble servant,

Historicus

---

*A dying man can do nothing easy.*

Benjamin Franklin, to his daughter who advised him to change his position in bed so he could breathe more easily, April 17, 1790

85.

## NOAH WEBSTER: The Education of Youth in America

*Having spent some time teaching, Noah Webster was concerned with such questions as the proper curriculum of the schools and the role of the Bible in education, particularly in American schools. "On the Education of Youth in America" was first published in Webster's* American Magazine *between 1787 and 1788. In 1790, it was revised and reissued in* A Collection of Essays and Fugitiv Writings, *from which the following selection is taken.*

Source: *A Collection of Essays and Fugitiv Writings,* Boston, 1790, pp. 1-37.

EDUCATION IS A SUBJECT which has been exhausted by the ablest writers, both among the ancients and moderns. I am not vain enough to suppose I can suggest any new ideas upon so trite a theme as education in general; but perhaps the manner of conducting the youth in America may be capable of some improvement. Our constitutions of civil government are not yet firmly established; our national character is not yet formed; and it is an object of vast magnitude that systems of education should be adopted and pursued which may not only diffuse a knowledge of the sciences but may implant in the minds of the American youth the principles of virtue and of liberty and inspire them with just and liberal ideas of government and with an inviolable attachment to their own country. It now becomes every American to examine the modes of education in Europe, to see how far they are applicable in this country, and whether it is not possible to make some valuable alterations adapted to our local and political circumstances. Let us examine the subject in two views. First, as it respects arts and sciences. Second, as it is connected with morals and government. In each of these articles let us see what errors may be found and what improvements suggested in our present practice.

The first error that I would mention is a too general attention to the dead languages, with a neglect of our own. . . .

In deliberating upon any plan of instruction, we should be attentive to its future influence and probable advantages. What advantage does a merchant, a mechanic, a farmer, derive from an acquaintance with the Greek and Roman tongues? It is true, the etymology of words cannot be well understood without a knowledge of the original languages of which ours is composed. . . .

But, when we have an elegant and copious language of our own, with innumerable writers upon ethics, geography, history, commerce, and government — subjects immediately interesting to every man — how can a parent be justified in keeping his son several years over rules of syntax, which he forgets when he shuts his book, or which, if remembered, can be of little or no use in any branch of business?

It is not my wish to discountenance totally the study of the dead languages. On the other hand, I should urge a more close attention to them among young men who are designed for the learned professions. The poets, the orators, the philosophers, and the historians of Greece and Rome furnish the most excellent models of style and the richest treasures of science. The slight attention given to a few of these authors in our usual course of education is rather calculated to make pedants than scholars, and the time employed in gaining superficial knowledge is really wasted.

> A little learning is a dangerous thing,
> Drink deep, or taste not the Pierian
> spring. . . .

Merchants often have occasion for a knowledge of some foreign living language as the French, the Italian, the Spanish, or the German, but men whose business is wholly domestic have little or no use for any language but their own, much less for languages known only in books. . . .

But the high estimation in which the learned languages have been held has discouraged a due attention to our own. People find themselves able without much study to write and speak the English intelligibly and thus have been led to think rules of no utility. This opinion has produced various and arbitrary practices in the use of the language, even among men of the most information and accuracy; and this diversity has produced another opinion, both false and injurious to the language, that there are no rules or principles on which the pronunciation and construction can be settled.

This neglect is so general that there is scarcely an institution to be found in the country where the English tongue is taught regularly, from its elements to its true and elegant construction, in prose and verse. Perhaps in most schools boys are taught the definition of the parts of speech and a few hard names which they do not understand and which the teacher seldom attempts to explain; this is called learning grammar. This practice of learning questions and answers without acquiring any ideas has given rise to a common remark: that grammar is a dry study; and so is every other study which is prosecuted without improving the head or the heart. The study of geography is equally dry when the subject is not understood. But when grammar is taught by the help of visible objects, when children perceive that differences of words arise from differences in things, which they may learn at a very early period of life, the study becomes entertaining as well as improving. In general, when a study of any kind is tiresome to a person, it is a presumptive evidence that he does not make any proficiency in knowledge, and this is almost always the fault of the instructor. . . .

There is one general practice in schools which I censure with diffidence, not because I doubt the propriety of the censure but because it is opposed to deep-rooted prejudices: this practice is the use of the Bible as a schoolbook. There are two reasons why this practice has so generally prevailed: the first is that families in the country are not generally supplied with any other book; the second, an opinion that the reading of the Scriptures will impress upon the minds of youth the important truths of religion and morality. The first may be easily removed, and the purpose of the last is counteracted by the practice itself.

If people design the doctrines of the Bible as a system of religion, ought they to appropriate the book to purposes foreign to this design? Will not a familiarity, contracted by a careless, disrespectful reading of the sacred volume, weaken the influence of its precepts upon the heart? . . .

Objects that affect the mind strongly, whether the sensations they excite are painful or pleasurable, always lose their effect by a frequent repetition of their impressions. Those parts of the Scripture, therefore, which are calculated to strike terror to the mind lose their influence by being too frequently brought into view. The same objection will not apply to the history and morality of the Bible, select passages of which may be read in schools to great advantage. In some countries the common people are not permitted to read the Bible at all. In ours, it is as common as a newspaper and in schools is read with nearly the same degree of respect. Both these practices appear to be extremes. My wish is not to see the Bible excluded from schools but to see it is used as a system of religion and morality.

These remarks suggest another error which is often committed in our inferior schools: I mean that of putting boys into difficult sciences while they are too young to exercise their reason upon abstract subjects. For example, boys are often put to the study of mathematics at the age of eight or ten years and before they can either read or write. In order to show the impropriety of such a practice, it is necessary to repeat what was just now observed, that our senses are the avenues of knowledge. This fact proves that the most natural course of education is that which employs, first, the senses or powers of the body or those faculties of the mind which first acquire strength, and then proceeds to those studies which depend on the power of comparing and combining ideas.

The art of writing is mechanical and imitative; this may therefore employ boys as soon as their fingers have strength sufficient to command a pen. A knowledge of letters requires the exercise of a mental power, memory, but this is coeval almost with the first operations of the human mind, and with respect to objects of sense is almost perfect, even in childhood. Children may therefore be taught reading as soon as their organs of speech have acquired strength sufficient to articulate the sounds of words.

But those sciences, a knowledge of which is acquired principally by the reasoning faculties, should be postponed to a more advanced period of life. In the course of an English education, mathematics should be perhaps the last study of youth in schools. Years of valuable time are sometimes thrown away in a fruitless application to sciences, the principles of which are above the comprehension of the students.

There is no particular age at which every boy is qualified to enter upon mathematics to advantage. The proper time can be best determined by the instructors, who are acquainted with the different capacities of their pupils.

Another error which is frequent in America is that a master undertakes to teach many different branches in the same school. In new settlements, where people are poor and live in scattered situations, the practice is often unavoidable, but in populous towns it must be considered as a defective plan of education. For suppose the teacher to be equally master of all the branches which he attempts to teach, which seldom happens, yet his attention must be distracted with a multiplicity of objects and consequently painful to himself and not useful to the pupils. Add to this the continual interruptions which the students of one branch suffer from those of another, which must retard the progress of the whole school. It is a much more eligible plan to appropriate an apartment to each branch of education, with a teacher who makes that branch his sole employment. The principal academies in Europe and America are on this plan, which both reason and experience prove to be the most useful.

With respect to literary institutions of the first rank, it appears to me that their local situations are an object of importance. It is a subject of controversy whether a large city or a country village is the most eligible situation for a college or university. But the arguments in favor of the latter appear to me decisive. Large cities are always scenes of dissipation and amusement, which have a tendency to corrupt the hearts of youth and divert their minds from their literary pursuits. Reason teaches this doctrine, and experience has uniformly confirmed the truth of it.

Strict discipline is essential to the prosperity of a public seminary of science, and this is established with more facility and supported with more uniformity in a small village where there are no great objects of curiosity to interrupt the studies of youth or to call their attention from the orders of the society. . . .

But if the amusements, dissipation, and vicious examples in populous cities render them improper places for seats of learning, the monkish mode of sequestering boys from other society and confining them to the apartments of a college appears to me another fault. The human mind is like a rich field, which, without constant care, will ever be covered with a luxuriant growth of weeds. It is extremely dangerous to suffer young men to pass the most critical period of life, when the passions are strong, the judgment weak, and the heart susceptible and unsuspecting, in a situation where there is not the least restraint upon their inclinations. My own observations lead me to draw the veil of silence over the ill effects of this practice. But it is to be wished that youth might always be kept under the inspection of age and superior wisdom; that literary institutions might be so situated that the students might live in decent families, be subject in some measure to their discipline, and even under the control of those whom they respect.

Perhaps it may also be numbered among the errors in our systems of education that in all our universities and colleges the students are all restricted to the same course of study and, by being classed, limited to the same progress. Classing is necessary, but whether students should not be removable from the lower to the higher classes as a reward for their superior industry and improvements is submitted to those who know the effect of emulation upon the human mind.

But young gentlemen are not all designed for the same line of business, and why should they pursue the same studies? . . . Life is too short to acquire, and the mind of man too feeble, to contain the whole circle of sciences. . . . In order to qualify persons in any profession, it is necessary that they should attend closely to those branches of learning which lead to it.

There are some arts and sciences which are necessary for every man. Every man should be able to speak and write his native tongue with correctness and have some knowledge of mathematics. The rules of arithmetic are indispensably requisite. But besides the learning which is of common utility, lads should be directed to pursue those branches which are connected more immediately with the business for which they are destined.

It would be very useful for the farming part of the community to furnish country schools with some easy system of practical husbandry. By repeatedly reading some book of this kind, the mind would be stored with ideas which might not indeed be understood in youth but which would be called into practice in some subsequent period of life. This would lead the mind to the subject of agriculture and pave the way for improvements.

Young gentlemen designed for the mercantile line, after having learned to write and speak English correctly, might attend to French, Italian, or such other living language as they will probably want in the course of business. These languages should be learned early in youth, while the organs are yet pliable; otherwise the pronunciation will probably be imperfect. These studies might be succeeded by some attention to chronology, and a regular application to geography, mathematics, history, the general regulations of commercial nations, principles of advance in trade, of insurance, and to the general principles of government.

It appears to me that such a course of education, which might be completed by the age of fifteen or sixteen, would have a tendency to make better merchants than the usual practice which confines boys to Lucian, Ovid, and Tully till they are fourteen and then turns them into a store, without an idea of their business or one article of education necessary for them, except perhaps a knowledge of writing and figures.

Such a system of English education is also much preferable to a university education, even with the usual honors, for it might be finished so early as to leave young persons time to serve a regular apprenticeship, without which no person should enter upon business. But by the time a university education is completed, young men commonly commence gentlemen; their age and their pride will not suffer them to go through the drudgery of a counting house, and they enter upon business without the requisite accomplishments. Indeed it appears to me that what is now called a liberal education disqualifies a man for business. Habits are formed in youth and by practice, and as business is in some measure mechanical, every person should be exercised in his employment in an early period of life, that his habits may be formed by the time his apprenticeship expires. An education in a university interferes with the forming of these habits and perhaps forms opposite habits; the mind may contract a fondness for ease, for pleasure or for books, which no efforts can overcome. An academic education, which should furnish the youth with some ideas of men and things and leave time for an apprenticeship before the age of twenty-one years, would, in my opinion, be the most eligible for young men who are designed for active employments.

The method pursued in our colleges is better calculated to fit youth for the learned professions than for business. But perhaps the period of study required as the condition of receiving the usual degrees is too short. Four years, with the most assiduous application, are a short time to furnish the mind with the necessary knowledge of the languages and of the several sciences. It might perhaps have been a period sufficiently long for an infant settlement, as America was, at the time when most of our colleges were founded. But as the country becomes populous, wealthy, and respectable, it may be worthy of consideration whether the period of academic life should not be extended to six or seven years.

But the principal defect in our plan of education in America is the want of good teachers in the academies and common schools. By good teachers I mean men of unblemished reputation and possessed of abilities competent to their stations. That a man should be master of what he undertakes to teach is a point that will not be disputed, and yet it is certain that abilities are often dispensed with, either thro inattention or fear of expense.

To those who employ ignorant men to instruct their children, permit me to suggest one important idea: that it is better for youth to have no education than to have a bad one, for it is more difficult to eradicate habits than to impress new ideas. The tender shrub is easily bent to any figure, but the tree which has acquired its full growth resists all impressions.

Yet abilities are not the sole requisites. The instructors of youth ought, of all men, to be the most prudent, accomplished, agreeable, and respectable. What avail a man's parts if, while he is the "wisest and brightest," he is the "meanest of mankind?" The pernicious effects of bad example on the minds of youth will probably be acknowledged, but with a view to improvement it is indispensably necessary that the teachers should possess good breeding and agreeable manners. In order to give full effect to instructions, it is requisite that they should proceed from a man who is loved and respected. But a lowbred clown or morose tyrant can command neither love nor respect, and that pupil who has no motive for application to books but the fear of a rod will not make a scholar. . . .

The only practicable method to reform mankind is to begin with children, to banish, if possible, from their company every lowbred, drunken, immoral character. Virtue and vice will not grow together in a great degree, but they will grow where they are planted, and when one has taken root, it is not easily supplanted by the other. The great art of correcting mankind, therefore, consists in prepossessing the mind with good principles. . . .

Another defect in our schools, which, since the Revolution, is become inexcusable, is the want of proper books. The collections which are now used consist of essays that respect foreign and ancient nations. The minds of youth are perpetually led to the history of Greece and Rome or to Great Britain; boys are constantly repeating the declamations of Demosthenes and Cicero or debates upon some political question in the British Parliament. These are excellent specimens of good sense, polished style, and perfect oratory, but they are not interesting to children. They cannot be very useful, except to young gentlemen who want them as models of reasoning and eloquence in the pulpit or at the bar.

But every child in America should be acquainted with his own country. He should read books that furnish him with ideas that will be useful to him in life and practice. As soon as he opens his lips, he should rehearse the history of his own country; he should lisp the praise of liberty and of those illustrious heroes and statesmen who have wrought a revolution in her favor.

A selection of essays respecting the settlement and geography of America, the history of the late Revolution and of the most remarkable characters and events that distinguished it, and a compendium of the principles of the federal and provincial governments should be the principal schoolbook in the United States. These are interesting objects to every man; they call home the minds of youth and fix them upon the interests of their own country, and they assist in forming attachments to it, as well as in enlarging the understanding. . . .

Two regulations are essential to the continuance of republican governments. (1) Such a distribution of lands and such principles of descent and alienation as shall give every citizen a power of acquiring what his industry merits. (2) Such a system of education as gives every citizen an opportunity of acquiring knowledge and fitting himself for places of trust. These are fundamental articles, the *sine qua non* of the existence of the American republics. . . .

In several states we find laws passed establishing provision for colleges and academies where people of property may educate their sons, but no provision is made for instructing the poorer rank of people even in reading and writing. Yet in these same states every citizen who is worth a few shillings annually is entitled to vote for legislators. This appears to me a most glaring solecism in government. The constitutions are *republican* and the laws of education are *monarchical.* The former extend civil rights to every honest industrious man, the latter deprive a large proportion of the citizens of a most valuable privilege. In our American republics, where government is in the hands of the people, knowledge should be universally diffused by means of public schools. . . .

Every small district should be furnished with a school, at least four months in a year, when boys are not otherwise employed. This school should be kept by the most reputable and well-informed man in the district. Here children should be taught the usual branches of learning, submission to superiors and to laws, the moral or social duties, the history and transactions of their own country, the principles of liberty and government. Here the rough manners of the wilderness should be softened and the principles of virtue and good behavior inculcated. The virtues of men are of more consequence to society than their abilities, and for this reason the heart should be cultivated with more assiduity than the head.

Are parents and guardians ignorant that children always imitate those with whom they live or associate? That a boy, bred in the woods, will be a savage? That another, bred in the army, will have the manners of a soldier? That a third, bred in a kitchen, will speak the language and possess the ideas of servants? And that a fourth, bred in genteel company, will have the manners of a gentleman? We cannot believe that many people are ignorant of these truths. Their conduct therefore can be ascribed to nothing but inattention or fear of expense. It is perhaps literally true that a wild life among savages is preferable to an education in a kitchen or under a drunken tutor, for savages would leave the mind uncorrupted with the vices which reign among slaves and the depraved part of civilized nations. It is therefore a point of infinite importance to society that youth should not associate with persons whose manners they ought not to imitate; much less should they be doomed to pass the most susceptible period of life with clowns, profligates, and slaves. . . .

For these reasons children should keep the best of company that they might have before them the best manners, the best breeding, and the best conversation. Their minds should be kept untainted till their reasoning faculties have acquired strength and the good principles which may be planted in their minds have taken deep root. They will then be able to make a firm and probably a successful resistance against the attacks of secret corruption and brazen libertinism.

Our legislators frame laws for the suppression of vice and immorality; our divines thunder from the pulpit the terrors of infinite wrath against the vices that stain the characters of men. And do laws and preaching effect a reformation of manners? Experience would not give a very favorable answer to this inquiry. The reason is obvious: the attempts are directed to the wrong objects. Laws can only check the public effects of vicious principles but can never reach the principles themselves, and preaching is not very intelligible to people till they arrive at an age when their principles are rooted or their habits firmly established. An attempt to eradicate old habits is as absurd as to lop off the branches of a huge oak in order to root it out of a rich soil. The most that such clipping will effect is to prevent a further growth.

Such a general system of education is neither impracticable nor difficult, and, excepting the formation of a federal government that shall be efficient and permanent, it demands the first attention of American patriots. Until such a system shall be adopted and pursued, until the statesman and divine shall unite their efforts in forming the human mind, rather than in lopping its excrescences after it has been neglected, until legislators discover that the only way to make good citizens and subjects is to nourish them from infancy, and until parents shall be convinced that the worst of men are not the proper teachers to make the best, mankind cannot know to what a degree of perfection society and government may be carried. America affords the fairest opportunities for making the experiment and opens the most encouraging prospect of success.

In a system of education that should embrace every part of the community the female sex claim no inconsiderable share of our attention.

The women in America (to their honor it is mentioned) are not generally above the care of educating their own children. Their own education should therefore enable them to implant in the tender mind such sentiments of virtue, propriety, and dignity as are suited to the freedom of our governments. Children should be treated as children, but as children that are in a future time to be men and women. By treating them as if they were always to remain children, we very often see their childishness adhere to them, even in middle life. The silly language called baby talk, in which most persons are initiated in infancy, often breaks out in discourse at the age of forty and makes a man appear very ridiculous. In the same manner, vulgar, obscene, and illiberal ideas imbibed in a nursery or a kitchen often give a tincture to the conduct through life. In order to prevent every evil bias, the ladies, whose province it is to direct the inclinations of children on their first appearance and to choose their nurses, should be possessed, not only of amiable manners but of just sentiments and enlarged understandings.

But the influence of women in forming the dispositions of youth is not the sole reason why their education should be particularly guarded; their influence in controlling the manners of a nation is another powerful reason. Women, once abandoned, may be instrumental in corrupting society, but such is the delicacy of the sex and such the restraints which custom imposes upon them that they are generally the last to be corrupted. There are innumerable instances of men who have been restrained from a vicious life and even of very abandoned men who have been reclaimed by their attachments to ladies of virtue. A fondness for the company and conversation of ladies of character may be considered as a young man's best security against the attractives of a dissipated life. A man who is attached to good company seldom frequents that which is bad. For this reason, society requires that females should be well educated and extend their influence as far as possible over the other sex.

But a distinction is to be made between a good education and a showy one, for an education merely superficial is a proof of corruption of taste and has a mischievous influence on manners. The education of females, like that of males, should be adapted to the principles of the government and correspond with the stage of society. Education in Paris differs from that in Petersburg, and the education of females in London or Paris should not be a model for the Americans to copy.

In all nations a good education is that which renders the ladies correct in their manners, respectable in their families, and agreeable in society. That education is always wrong which raises a woman above the duties of her station.

In America female education should have for its object what is useful. Young ladies should be taught to speak and write their own language with purity and elegance, an article in which they are often deficient. The French language is not necessary for ladies. In some cases it is convenient, but, in general, it may be considered as an article of luxury. As an accomplishment, it may be studied by those whose attention is not employed about more important concerns.

Some knowledge of arithmetic is necessary for every lady. Geography should never be neglected. Belles-lettres learning seems to correspond with the dispositions of most females. A taste for poetry and fine writing should be cultivated, for we expect the most delicate sentiments from the pens of that sex which is possessed of the finest feelings.

A course of reading can hardly be prescribed for all ladies. But it should be remarked that this sex cannot be too well acquainted with the writers upon human life and manners. The *Spectator* should fill the first place in every lady's library. Other volumes of periodical papers, though inferior to the *Spectator*, should be read, and some of the best histories.

With respect to novels, so much admired by the young and so generally condemned by the old, what shall I say? Perhaps it may be said with truth that some of them are useful, many of them pernicious, and most of them trifling. A hundred volumes of modern novels may be read without acquiring a new idea. Some of them contain entertaining stories, and where the descriptions are drawn from nature and from characters and events in themselves innocent, the perusal of them may be harmless.

Were novels written with a view to exhibit only one side of human nature, to paint the social virtues, the world would condemn them as defective, but I should think them more perfect. Young people, especially females, should not see the vicious part of mankind. At best, novels may be considered as the toys of youth, the rattle boxes of sixteen. The mechanic gets his pence for his toys, and the novel writer, for his books, and it would be happy for society if the latter were in all cases as innocent playthings as the former.

In the large towns in America music, drawing, and dancing constitute a part of female education. They, however, hold a subordinate rank, for my fair friends will pardon me when I declare that no man ever marries a woman for her performance on a harpsichord or her figure in a minuet. However ambitious a woman may be to command admiration abroad, her real merit is known only at home. Admiration is useless when it is not supported by domestic worth. But real honor and permanent esteem are always secured by those who preside over their own families with dignity. . . .

A tour through the United States ought now to be considered as a necessary part of a liberal education. Instead of sending young gentlemen to Europe to view curiosities and learn vices and follies, let them spend twelve or eighteen months in examining the local situation of the different states — the rivers, the soil, the population, the improvements and commercial advantages of the whole — with an attention to the spirit and manners of the inhabitants, their laws, local customs, and institutions. Such a tour should at least precede a tour to Europe, for nothing can be more ridiculous than a man traveling in a foreign country for information when he can give no account of his own. When, therefore, young gentlemen have finished an academic education, let them travel through America, and afterward to Europe, if their time and fortunes will permit. But if they cannot make a tour through both, that in America is certainly to be preferred, for the people of America, with all their information, are yet extremely ignorant of the geography, policy, and manners of their neighboring states.

Except a few gentlemen whose public employments in the Army and in Congress have extended their knowledge of America, the people in this country, even of the higher classes, have not so correct information respecting the United States as they have respecting England or France. Such ignorance is not only disgraceful but is materially prejudicial to our political friendship and federal operations.

Americans, unshackle your minds and act like independent beings. You have been children long enough, subject to the control and subservient to the interest of a haughty parent. You have now an interest of your own to augment and defend: you have an empire to raise and support by your exertions and a national character to establish and extend by your wisdom and virtues. To effect these great objects, it is necessary to frame a liberal plan of policy and build it on a broad system of education. Before this system can be formed and embraced, the Americans must believe and act from the belief that it is dishonorable to waste life in mimicking the follies of other nations and basking in the sunshine of foreign glory.

86.

# On the Blessings of Civil and Religious Liberty

*In the summer of 1790, George Washington toured the new republic. When he arrived at the seacoast town of Newport, Rhode Island, he was greeted with enthusiasm. Moses Seixas, the warden of the town's Hebrew congregation and a friend of Washington, warmly welcomed him to Newport in a letter of August 17, which is reprinted here. There had originally been a plan for all of the Jewish congregations in the United States to send a joint memorial of congratulations to the President. But the Newport synagogue had been reluctant to join in an earlier message, owing to Rhode Island's peculiar position with regard to the Constitution. The state had taken no part in the Philadelphia convention and had not ratified until May 1790. Washington's tour of 1790 to consolidate the new government's position seemed the appropriate time for the congregation at Newport to express its appreciation for the tolerance of the new government. The second part of this selection is Washington's reply to the Hebrew congregation.*

Source: Seixas original in the possession of B'nai B'rith Committee on Jewish Americana, Washington, D.C.
Washington original in the "Letter Book" in the *Washington Papers* in the Library of Congress.

I.

## Moses Seixas to George Washington

Permit the children of the stock of Abraham to approach you with the most cordial affection and esteem for your person and merits — and to join with our fellow citizens in welcoming you to Newport.

With pleasure we reflect on those days, those days of difficulty and danger when the God of Israel, who delivered David from the peril of the sword, shielded your head in the day of battle; and we rejoice to think that the same Spirit who rested in the bosom of the greatly beloved Daniel enabling him to preside over the provinces of the Babylonish Empire rests and ever will rest upon you, enabling you to discharge the arduous duties of chief magistrate in these states.

Deprived as we heretofore have been of the invaluable rights of free citizens, we now (with a deep sense of gratitude to the Almighty Disposer of all events) behold a government, erected by the majesty of the people — a government which to bigotry gives no sanction, to persecution no assistance, but generously affording to all liberty of conscience, and immunities of citizenship, deeming every one, of whatever nation, tongue, or language, equal parts of the great government machine. This so ample and extensive federal Union whose basis is philanthropy, mutual confidence, and public virtue, we cannot but acknowledge to be the work of the Great God, who rules in the armies of heaven and among the inhabitants of the earth, doing whatsoever seems to Him good.

For all these blessings of civil and religious liberty which we enjoy under an equal and benign administration, we desire to send up our thanks to the Ancient of Days, the great preserver of men, beseeching him that the angel who conducted our forefathers through the wilderness into the promised land may graciously conduct you through all the difficulties and dangers of this mortal life. And, when like Joshua full of days, and full of honor, you are gathered to your fathers, may you be admitted into the heavenly paradise to partake of the water of life and the tree of immortality.

## II.

## Washington to the Hebrew Congregation at Newport, R.I.

While I receive with much satisfaction your address replete with expressions of affection and esteem, I rejoice in the opportunity of assuring you that I shall always retain a grateful remembrance of the cordial welcome I experienced in my visit to Newport from all classes of citizens.

The reflection on the days of difficulty and danger which are past is rendered the more sweet from a consciousness that they are succeeded by days of uncommon prosperity and security. If we have wisdom to make the best use of the advantages with which we are now favored, we cannot fail, under the just administration of a good government, to become a great and a happy people.

The citizens of the United States of America have a right to applaud themselves for having given to mankind examples of an enlarged and liberal policy, a policy worthy of imitation. All possess alike liberty of conscience and immunities of citizenship. It is now no more that toleration is spoken of as if it was by the indulgence of one class of people that another enjoyed the exercise of their inherent natural rights. For happily the government of the United States, which gives to bigotry no sanction, to persecution no assistance, requires only that they who live under its protection should demean themselves as good citizens, in giving it on all occasions their effectual support.

It would be inconsistent with the frankness of my character not to avow that I am pleased with your favorable opinion of my administration, and fervent wishes for my felicity. May the children of the stock of Abraham, who dwell in this land, continue to merit and enjoy the good will of the other inhabitants, while everyone shall sit in safety under his own vine and fig tree, and there shall be none to make him afraid. May the Father of all mercies scatter light and not darkness in our paths, and make us all in our several vocations useful here, and in His own due time and way everlastingly happy.

---

*Indeed I tremble for my country when I reflect that God is just.*

Thomas Jefferson, Notes on Virginia

87.

## Patrick Henry: Resolution on the Assumption of State Debts

*Though the vocal anti-Federalist Patrick Henry had lost the fight against the ratification of the Constitution, he continued his crusade against a strong central government. When Hamilton proposed to have the federal government assume the debts of the states in his* First Report on the Public Credit, *many feared that Congress would be exercising a power that properly belonged to the states. Henry prepared a protest against this action that the Virginia Assembly passed on December 23, 1790. Hamilton hailed the protest as "the first symptom of a spirit which must either be killed, or will kill the Constitution of the United States."*

Source: Hening, XIII, pp. 237-239.

The General Assembly of the Commonwealth of Virginia to the United States in Congress assembled represent:

That it is with great concern they find themselves compelled from a sense of duty to call the attention of Congress to an act of their last session entitled "An act making provision for the debt of the United States," which the General Assembly conceive neither policy, justice, nor the Constitution warrants. Republican policy, in the opinion of your memorialists, could scarcely have suggested those clauses in the aforesaid act which limit the right of the United States in their redemption of the public debt.

On the contrary, they discern a striking resemblance between this system and that which was introduced into England at the Revolution; a system which has perpetuated upon that nation an enormous debt, and has moreover insinuated into the hands of the executive an unbounded influence which, pervading every branch of the government, bears down all opposition, and daily threatens the destruction of everything that appertains to English liberty. The same causes produce the same effects! In an agricultural country like this, therefore, to erect, and concentrate, and perpetuate a large monied interest is a measure which your memorialists apprehend must, in the course of human events, produce one or other of two evils — the prostration of agriculture at the feet of commerce, or a change in the present form of federal government fatal to the existence of American liberty.

The General Assembly pass by various other parts of the said act which they apprehend will have a dangerous and impolitic tendency, and proceed to show the injustice of it, as it applies to this Commonwealth. It pledges the faith of the United States for the payment of certain debts due by the several states in the Union, contracted by them during the late war. A large proportion of the debt thus contracted by this state has been already redeemed by the collection of heavy taxes levied on its citizens, and measures have been taken for the gradual payment of the balance, so as to afford the most certain prospect of extinguishing the whole at a period not very distant. But, by the operation of the aforesaid act, a heavy debt, and consequently heavy taxes, will be entailed on the citizens of this Commonwealth, from which they never can be relieved by all the efforts of the General Assembly while any part of the debts contracted by any state in the American Union, and so assumed, shall remain unpaid; for it is with great anxiety your memorialists perceive that the said act, without the smallest necessity, is calculated to extort from the General Assembly the power of taxing their own constituents for the payment of their own debts, in such a manner as would be best suited to their own ease and convenience.

Your memorialists cannot suppress their uneasiness at the discriminating preference which is given to the holders of the principal of the Continental debt over the holders of the principal of the state debts, in those instances where states have made ample provision for the annual payment of the interest, and where, of course, there can be no interest to compound with the principal, which happens to be the situation of this Commonwealth. The Continental creditors have preferences in other respects, which the General Assembly forbear to mention, satisfied that Congress must allow that policy, justice, and the principles of public credit abhor discriminations between fair creditors. Your memorialists turn away from the impolicy and injustice of the said act, and view it in another light, in which to them it appears still more odious and deformed.

During the whole discussion of the federal Constitution by the convention of Virginia, your memorialists were taught to believe "that every power not granted was retained." Under this impression and upon this positive condition, declared in the instrument of ratification, the said government was adopted by the people of this Commonwealth. But your memorialists can find no clause in the Constitution authorizing Congress to assume the debts of the states! As the guardians, then, of the rights and interests of their constituents, as sentinels placed by them over the ministers of the federal government to shield it from their encroachments, or at least to sound the alarm when it is threatened with invasion, they can never reconcile it to their consciences silently to acquiesce in a measure which violates that hallowed maxim: a maxim on the truth and sacredness of which the federal government depended for its adoption in this Commonwealth.

New York Historical Society

Patrick Henry, portrait by an unidentified artist.

But this injudicious act not only deserves the censure of the General Assembly because it is not warranted by the Constitution of the United States but because it is repugnant to an express provision of that Constitution; this provision is "that all debts contracted and engagements entered into, before the adoption of this Constitution, shall be as valid against the United States under this Constitution as under the Confederation," which amounts to a constitutional ratification of the contracts respecting the state debts in the situation in which they existed under the Confederation; and, resorting to that standard, there can be no doubt that in the present question the rights of states as contracting parties with the United States must be considered as sacred.

The General Assembly of the Commonwealth of Virginia confide so fully in the justice and wisdom of Congress upon the present occasion as to hope that they will revise and amend the aforesaid act generally, and repeal in particular so much of it as relates to the assumption of the state debts.

# 1791

88.

## Petition by Free Negroes for Equality Under the Law

*Before the emancipation of the slaves after the Civil War, Negroes were severely restricted by laws in both the South and the North. Many states had laws prohibiting them from bringing a suit against another party, or even testifying under oath in a court. One of the earliest protests against these laws is reprinted below. It was presented in January 1791, to the South Carolina legislature by the free Negroes of Charleston.*

Source: Manuscript in Slavery File No. 1, Free Persons of Colour, Historical Commission of South Carolina, Columbia.

To the Honorable David Ramsay, Esquire, president, and to the rest of the honorable new members of the Senate of the state of South Carolina,

The memorial of Thomas Cole, bricklayer, P. B. Mathews and Mathew Webb, butchers, on behalf of themselves and others, free men of color, humbly shows:

That in the enumeration of free citizens by the Constitution of the United States for the purpose of representation of the Southern states in Congress your memorialists have been considered under that description as part of the citizens of this state.

Although by the fourteenth and twenty-ninth clauses in an Act of Assembly made in the year 1740 and entitled an Act for the Better Ordering and Governing Negroes and Other Slaves in this Province, commonly called the Negro Act, now in force, your memorialists are deprived of the rights and privileges of citizens by not having it in their power to give testimony on oath in prosecutions on behalf of the state; from which cause many culprits have escaped the punishment due to their atrocious crimes, nor can they give their testimony in recovering debts due to them, or in establishing agreements made by them within the meaning of the Statutes of Frauds and Perjuries in force in this state except in cases where persons of color are concerned, whereby they are subject to great losses and repeated injuries without any means of redress.

That by the said clauses in the said Act, they are debarred of the rights of free citizens by being subject to a trial without the benefit of a jury and subject to prosecution by testimony of slaves without oath by which they are placed on the same footing.

Your memorialists show that they have at all times since the independence of the United States contributed and do now contribute to the support of the government by cheerfully paying their taxes proportionable to their property with others who have been during such period, and now are, in full enjoyment of the rights and immunities of citizens, inhabitants of a free independent state.

That as your memorialists have been and are considered as free citizens of this state, they hope to be treated as such; they are ready and willing to take and subscribe to such oath of allegiance to the states as shall be prescribed by this honorable House, and are also willing to take upon them any duty for the preservation of the peace in the city or any other occasion if called on.

Your memorialists do not presume to hope that they shall be put on an equal footing with the free white citizens of the state in general. They only humbly solicit such indulgence as the wisdom and humanity of this honorable House shall dictate in their favor by repealing the clauses in the Act beforementioned, and substituting such a clause as will effectually redress the grievances which your memorialists humbly submit in this their memorial, but under such restrictions as to your honorable House shall seem proper.

May it therefore please Your Honors to take your memorialists' case into tender consideration, and make such Acts or insert such clauses for the purpose of relieving your memorialists from the unremitted grievance they now labor under as in your wisdom shall seem meet.

---

89.

## Robert Coram: The Origin and Rights of Property

*Robert Coram, a native of South Carolina who had fought in the Revolution, settled eventually in Wilmington, Delaware, where he became the publisher of the* Delaware Gazette. *Politically he was an anti-Federalist and would probably have found himself in the Jeffersonian party had he lived, but he died at the age of thirty-five, in 1796. His essay,* Political Inquiries, *appeared in 1791. Most of the essay deals with the responsibility of government to provide free compulsory and equal education for all with an emphasis on practical training. The tract concluded with an attack on the "wretched state of country schools throughout the United States, and the absolute necessity of a reformation." The work is in five parts and the portion reprinted here is on the origin of private property.*

Source: *Political Inquiries: To Which Is Added, a Plan for the General Establishment of Schools Throughout the United States,* Wilmington, 1791, Ch. 2.

"In the beginning of the world," says Dr. Blackstone,[1] "we are informed by Holy Writ the All-Bountiful Creator gave to man 'dominion over all the earth, and over the fish of the sea, and over the fowl of the air, and over every living thing that moveth upon the earth.' This is the only true and solid foundation of man's dominion over external things, whatever airy metaphysical

1. Sir William Blackstone (1723-1780), most famous of English jurists and authority on English property law.

notions may have been started by fanciful writers upon that subject."

The Doctor, not the least fanciful of metaphysical writers, quotes the text in Genesis as a demonstration of his creed, to tell us that he believes in the Bible, which is in some measure necessary, as many of his arguments militate against such belief. If, then, the text in Genesis is the only true and solid foundation of man's dominion over external things, every son and daughter of Adam is co-heir to this paternal inheritance, for the gift was made in common to the whole race of Adam. How then have part of mankind forfeited their right to the bounties of Providence? Or from what source does the monopoly of lands originate, since it is plain it cannot be derived from the text in Genesis? The Doctor, indeed, tells us that "the earth, and all things thereon, are the general property of all mankind, exclusive of other beings from the immediate gift of the Creator. And while the earth continued bare of inhabitants, it is reasonable to suppose that all was in common among them and that everyone took from the public stock to his own use such things as his immediate necessities required."

And why not take from the public stock, when men multiplied? The command from the Creator was, increase and multiply. And must men then forfeit their right to the bounties of Providence by acting in obedience to this precept? Or does Dr. Blackstone suppose that the earth can support only a part of mankind, and that the rest live upon air, light, fire, or water, the only inheritance he has left them? It is plain, if the earth supports its inhabitants in the present unequal division of property, it will support them under an equal division. "These general notions of property," continues the Doctor, "were then sufficient to answer all the purposes of human life." That is, the solid foundation of man's dominion over external things is a notion: this notion was, however, sufficient to answer all the purposes of human life; "and might still have answered them," continues the Doctor, "had it been possible for mankind to have remained in a state of primeval simplicity, as may be collected from the manners of many American nations when first discovered by the Europeans." . . .

"*Erant omnia communia et indivisa omnibus, veluti unum cunctis patrimonium esset.* Not," says the Doctor, "that this communion of goods seems ever to have been applicable, even in the earliest ages, to aught but the substance of the thing; nor could it be extended to the use of it." Why not? Let us translate the passage. "All things were common and undivided to all, even as one inheritance might be to all." The sense of this passage is so obvious and plain that a person could hardly think it possible to be misunderstood, but Dr. Blackstone is determined to understand it, not as common sense but as unintelligible jargon. By a peculiar application of the adjective *indivisa*, the Doctor infers that the community of goods could not be extended to the use of such goods, which is making downright nonsense of the sentence: it is making the patrimony left in such manner that not a single heir can enjoy the least use or benefit of it at all. Why should so much stress be laid on the adjective *indivisa*, in the first part of the sentence, when the second part of the sentence is explanatory of the first? The goods were left *communia et indivisa;* but in what manner? *Veluti unum cunctis patrimonium esset:* even as one inheritance might be to all. The Doctor appears designedly obscure in this very paragraph and seems rather desirous to perplex his reader than to throw any light upon the subject.

Continues the Doctor:

> For by the law of nature and reason he who first began to use a thing acquired therein a kind of transient property that lasted so long as he was using it, and no longer; or, to speak with greater precision, the right of possession continued for the same time only that the act

> of possession lasted. Thus the ground was in common, and no part of it was the permanent property of any man in particular; yet, whoever was in the occupation of any determinate spot of it for rest, for shade, or the like, acquired, for the time, a sort of ownership from which it would have been unjust and contrary to the law of nature to have driven him by force, but the instant that he quitted the use or occupation of it another might seize it without injustice.

According to this vague account of natural law, it appears that men had a right to that quantity of ground which happened to be in immediate contact with their feet, when standing up; with their backsides, when sitting; and with their body, when lying down; and no more. No provision is made for agriculture; indeed it would not have suited the Doctor to have allowed the existence of agriculture at that period of the world. . . .

Any person possessed of common sense and some erudition who was not previously bent upon establishing a favorite system at the expense of truth might give us a rational account in what manner property should be regulated under the law of nature. Such a person would probably say, all things subject to the dominion of man may be included in two classes, land and movables; the rational foundation of the tenure of each is labor. Thus fruit growing on a tree was common, but when collected it became the exclusive property of the collector; land uncultivated was common, but when cultivated, it became the exclusive possession of the cultivator. Men, then, according to the laws of nature, had an exclusive property in movables and an exclusive possession in lands, both which were founded on labor and bounded by it. For as labor employed in the collection of fruit could give an exclusive right only to the fruit so collected, so labor in the soil could give exclusive possession only to the spot so labored. But this kind of reasoning would by no means suit Dr. Blackstone.

"But," continues the Doctor, "when mankind increased in number, craft, and ambition, it became necessary to entertain conceptions of more permanent dominion and to appropriate to individuals, not the immediate use only, but the very substance of the thing to be used." Query: Could a man eat an apple without entertaining conceptions of permanent dominion over the substance? Those conceptions existed then anterior to the increase of men in number, craft, and ambition, and were not the consequence of it.

"Otherwise," continues the Doctor, "innumerable tumults must have arisen, and the good order of the world been continually broken and disturbed, while a variety of persons were striving who should get the first occupation of the same thing or disputing which of them had actually gained it." From a system so vague as the Doctor's, and which he would pawn upon us for natural law, nothing but disputes could be expected, for nothing is determinate. His futile distinctions between the use of a thing and the substance of a thing and his notions of possession are truly ridiculous. But those contests for occupancy, this mighty bugbear so fatal to the good order of the world, we can easily prove to be a mere phantom of the Doctor's brain; like the raw head and bloody bones with which ignorant nurses scare their children, it has no existence in nature.

As labor constitutes the right of property in movables and the right of possession in lands, it is evident no disputes could arise merely from the nature of the right, for before labor was employed there could be no right to squabble about, and after labor was employed the right was completely vested. In fact, the whole of Blackstone's chapter on property was artfully contrived to countenance the monopoly of lands as held in Europe. "When men increased in number, craft, and ambition, it became necessary to entertain conceptions of more permanent dominion." If the Doctor means anything, he means that more permanent dominion was established as a check to craft and ambition; or, in other words, that the laws vested a permanent property in lands in some persons to prevent their being dispossessed by unruly individuals.

But this clearly demonstrates the Doctor to be as ignorant of the affections of the human heart as he is of natural law. For a community of lands is the most effectual check which human wisdom could devise against the ambition of individuals. What is the civilized man's ambition? To procure a property in the soil. But there is no such ambition among savages, for no man, civilized or savage, is ambitious of what is common to every man: land is common among savages; therefore they set no value upon it. In most civilized nations, land is held only by a few and also made essential to the qualification of candidates for public offices; hence, to possess property in lands is the ambition of civilized nations.

But, continues the Doctor:

> As human life also grew more and more refined, abundance of conveniences were contrived to render it more easy and agreeable, as habitations for shelter and safety and raiment for warmth and decency. But no man would be at the trouble to provide either, so long as he had only a *usufructuary* property in them, which was to cease the instant that he quitted possession, if, as soon as he walked out of his tent or pulled off his garment, the next stranger who came by would have a right to inhabit the one and wear the other.

If his wise head would have suffered him to reason and not sophisticate, Dr. Blackstone would have found that there never was nor could be a *usufructuary* property in a garment or a house; the property in this case was, from its nature, always absolute. For a house or a garment in *statu quo* is no production of the earth and was certainly never considered as a part of the general stock of society. The materials of which the house or the garment was formed might have been common stock, but when by manual labor or dexterity the materials became converted into a house or a garment, it became the exclusive property of the maker. And this is not merely a scholastic or speculative distinction, but a distinction founded in nature and well known to the American Indians.

"The Indians," says Carver, "are strangers to all distinction of property, except in the articles of domestic use, which everyone considers as his own." . . .

Says the Doctor:

> The art of agriculture by regular connection and consequence introduced the idea of more permanent property in the soil than had been hitherto received and adopted. It was clear that the earth could not produce her fruits in sufficient quantities without the assistance of tillage. But who would be at the pains of tilling it, if another might watch an opportunity to seize upon and enjoy the product of his industry, art, and labor. Had not, therefore, a separate property in lands, as well as movables, been vested in some individual, the world must have continued a forest and men have been mere animals of prey, which according to some philosophers is the genuine state of nature.

But we deny that by any connection or consequence the art of agriculture necessarily introduced more permanent property in the soil than was known in the days of Cain or than is now known by the American Indians. We deny that by the laws of nature any man could seize upon the product of the art, industry, or labor of another, and surely the Doctor forgets not only the Bible but his own words, for he has already established the position that bodily labor bestowed upon any subject which before lay in common gives the fairest and most reasonable title to exclusive property therein.

We deny that by any necessary consequence a community of lands would have detained the world a forest. A right to exclusive possession in lands, founded on the equitable and rational principle of labor, would at all times have been sufficient for all the purposes of men. What does the Doctor mean by *mere animals of prey?* The savage, as we are pleased to call him, takes his bow and repairs to some forest to obtain subsistence by the death of some animal: the polished citizen takes his pence and repairs to some butcher; the brute creation are equally victims, and men equally animals of prey. . . .

The Doctor's premises being therefore false, his conclusions of the necessity of a separate property in lands being vested in some individuals falls to the ground of course. But, continues the Doctor:

> Whereas now (so graciously has Providence interwoven our duty and our happiness together) the result of this very necessity has been the ennobling of the human species, by giving it opportunity of improving its rational faculties, as well as of exerting its natural, necessity begat property and order to insure that property, recourse was had to civil society, which brought with it a train of inseparable concomitants, states, governments, laws, punishments, and the public exercise of religious duties.

That is to say, God created man imperfect and ignoble, a mere animal of prey, but when, with the sword of violence and the pen of sophistry, a few had plundered or cheated the bulk of their rights, the few became ennobled and the many were reduced from mere animals of prey to beasts of burden. But why not mention a few more concomitants of civil society, such as poverty, vices innumerable, and diseases unknown in the state of nature. Look around your cities, ye who boast of having established the civilization and happiness of man, see at every corner of your streets some wretched object with tattered garments, squalid look, and hopeless eye, publishing your lies in folio to the world. Hedged in the narrow strait between your sanguinary laws and the pressing calls of hunger, he has no retreat, but like an abortive being created to no manner of purpose, his only wish is death. For of what use can life be but to augment his sufferings by a comparison of his desperate lot with yours?

But to continue, the Doctor says:

> The only question remaining is how this property became actually vested, or what is it that gave a man an exclusive right to retain in a permanent manner that specific land which before belonged generally to everybody but particularly to nobody. And as we before observed that occupancy gave a right to the temporary use of the soil, so it is agreed upon all hands that occupancy gave also the original right to the permanent property in the substance of the earth itself, which excludes everyone else but the owner from the use of it.
>
> There is indeed some difference among the writers of natural law concerning the reason why occupancy should convey this right and invest one with this absolute property. Grotius and Pufendorf insisting that this right of occupancy is founded upon a tacit and implied assent of all mankind, that the first occupant should become the owner; and Barbeyrac, Titius, Mr. Locke, and others holding that there is no such implied assent, neither is it necessary that there should be, for that the very act of occupancy alone being a degree of bodily labor is from a principle of natural justice without any consent or compact sufficient of itself to gain a title. A dispute that favors too much of nice and scholastic refinement! However, both sides agree in this, that occupancy is the thing by which the title was in fact originally gained, every man seizing to his own continued use such spots of ground as he found most agreeable to his own convenience, provided he found them unoccupied by any man.

But why this snarl at Barbeyrac, Titius, Mr. Locke, and others? It is plain that Dr. Blackstone had predetermined, when he wrote his *Commentaries*, to exclude the great body of mankind from any right to the bounties of Providence — light, air, and water excepted — or else why would he turn up his nose at a distinction absolutely necessary to set bounds to the quantum and prevent a monopoly of all the lands among a few? The position has been before established "that bodily labor bestowed on any subject before common gives the best title to exclusive property."

But the act of occupancy is a degree of bodily labor; that is, the occupancy extends as far as the labor, or, in other words, a man has a right to as much land as he cultivates and no more, which is Mr. Locke's doctrine. This distinction is therefore absolutely necessary to determine the quantum of lands any individual could possess under the laws of nature. For shall we say a man can possess only the ground in immediate contact with his feet, or, if he climbs to the top of a mountain and exclaims, "Behold, I possess as far as I can see!" shall there be any magic in the words or the expression which shall convey the right of all that land, in fee simple, to him and his heirs forever? No: as labor constitutes the right, so it sensibly defines the boundaries of possession.

How then shall we detect the empty sophist who, in order to establish his system of monopoly, would fain persuade us that the Almighty did not know what He was about when He made man; that He made him an animal of prey and intended him for a polished citizen; that He gave His bounties in common to all and yet suffered a necessity to exist by which they could be enjoyed only by a few. Had Dr. Blackstone been disposed to give his readers a true account of the origin of landed property in Europe he might have said exclusive property in lands originated with government; but most of the governments that we have any knowledge of were founded by conquest: property, therefore, in its origin, seems to have been arbitrary. He might then have expatiated upon the difficulty and inconvenience of attempting any innovations upon the established rules of property. This would have sufficiently answered his purpose and saved him much sophistry and absurdity and not a little impiety; for it is surely blasphemy to say there is a necessity of abrogating the divine law contained in the text of Genesis to make room for human laws which starve and degrade one-half of mankind, to pamper and intoxicate the rest.

"But after all," continues the Doctor, "there are some few things which must still unavoidably remain in common: such (among others) are the elements of light, air, and water." Thank you for nothing, Doctor. It is very generous, indeed, to allow us the common right to the elements of light, air, and water, or even the blood which flows in our veins. Blackstone's *Commentaries* have been much celebrated, and this very chapter, so replete with malignant sophistry and absurdity, has been inserted in all the magazines, museums, registers, and other periodical publications in England and cried up as the most ingenious performance ever published. Dr. Priestley and Mr. Furneaux both attacked Mr. Blackstone on the subject of some invectives against the dissenters and a mal-exposition of the Toleration Act, but no champion was to be found to take the part of poor, forlorn Human Nature, and the Doctor was suffered, unmolested, to quibble away all the rights of the great brotherhood of mankind.

Reduced to light, air, and water for an inheritance, one would have thought their situation could not be easily made worse, but it is not difficult to be mistaken. The bulk of mankind were not only cheated out of their right to the soil but were held ineligible to offices in the government because they were not freeholders. First cruelly to wrest from them the paternal inheritance of their universal Father, and then to make this outrageous act an excuse for denying them the rights of citizenship — this is the history of civil society in which our duty and happiness are so admirably interwoven together. We will, however, never believe that men originally entered into a compact by which they excluded themselves from all right to the bounties of Providence; and if they did, the contract could not be binding on their posterity, for although a man may give away his own right, he cannot give away the right of another.

"The only true and natural foundations of society," says Dr. Blackstone, "are the wants and fears of individuals." The word "society" here is a vague term by which we are at liberty to understand any government which has existed from the creation of the world to the present day. But if the European governments were erected to supply the wants and lessen the fears of individuals, we may venture to assert that the first projectors of them were errant blockheads. The wants of man, instead of having been lessened, have been multiplied, and that in proportion to his boasted civilization; and the fear of poverty alone is more than sufficient to counterbalance all the fears to which he was subject in the rudest stage of natural liberty.

From this source arise almost all the disorders in the body politic. The fear of poverty has given a double spring to avarice, the deadliest passion in the human breast; it has erected a golden image to which all mankind, with reverence, bend the knee, regardless of their idolatry. Merit is but an abortive, useless gift to the possessor, unless accompanied with wealth; he might choose which tree whereon to hang himself, did not his virtuous mind tell him to "dig, beg, rot, and perish well content, so he but wrap himself in honest rags at his last gasp and die in peace."

It is a melancholy reflection that in almost all ages and countries men have been cruelly butchered for crimes occasioned by the laws and which they never would have committed had they not been deprived of their natural means of subsistence. But the governors of mankind seem never to have made any allowance for poverty, but, like the stupid physician who prescribed bleeding for every disorder, they seem ever to have been distinguished by an insatiable thirst for human blood. The altars of a merciful God have been washed to their foundation from the veins of miserable men; and the double-edged sword of Justice, with all its formality and parade, seems calculated to cut off equally the innocent and guilty. Between religion and law, man has had literally no rest for the sole of his foot.

In the dark ages of Gothic barbarity, ignorance was some excuse for the framing of absurd systems, but in the age in which Dr. Blackstone lived, he should have known better, he should have known that the unequal distribution of property was the parent of almost all the disorders of government; nay, he did know it, for he had read Beccaria, who treating upon the crime of robbery, says, "But this crime, alas! is commonly the effect of misery and despair, the crime of that unhappy part of mankind to whom the right of exclusive property (a terrible and perhaps unnecessary right) has left but a bare subsistence." There is no necessity for concealing this important truth, but much benefit may be expected from its promulgation. It offers a foundation whereon to erect a system which, like the sun in the universe, will transmit light, life, and harmony to all under its influence. I mean a system of equal education.

90.

# John Leland: The Rights of Conscience

*John Leland, a Baptist clergyman, was a strong spokesman for religious liberty and had been influential in the passage of the Virginia Statute of Religious Freedom of 1786. He advocated the separation of church and state and in 1788 would not support the Constitution until convinced by Madison that it was not a threat to religious freedom. In 1791, Leland moved to Massachusetts and in the same year published a pamphlet, part of which appears below, which expressed his sympathies with the liberal thought of the enlightenment.*

Source: *The Rights of Conscience Inalienable, and Therefore Religious Opinions not Cognizable by Law: or, The High-flying Church-man Stript of his Legal Robe,* New London, Conn., 1791.

The question is, "Are the rights of conscience alienable, or inalienable?"

The word *conscience* signifies *common science,* a court of judicature which the Almighty has erected in every human breast: a *censor morum* over all his conduct. Conscience will ever judge right, when it is rightly informed, and speak the truth when it understands it. But to advert to the question, "Does a man upon entering into social compact surrender his conscience to that society to be controlled by the laws thereof, or can he in justice assist in making laws to bind his children's consciences before they are born?" I judge not, for the following reasons:

1. Every man must give an account of himself to God, and therefore every man ought to be at liberty to serve God in that way that he can best reconcile it to his conscience. If government can answer for individuals at the day of judgment, let men be controlled by it in religious matters; otherwise let men be free.

2. It would be sinful for a man to surrender that to man which is to be kept sacred for God. A man's mind should be always open to conviction, and an honest man will receive that doctrine which appears the best demonstrated; and what is more common than for the best of men to change their minds? Such are the prejudices of the mind, and such the force of tradition, that a man who never alters his mind is either very weak or very stubborn. How painful then must it be to an honest heart to be bound to observe the principles of his former belief, after he is convinced of their imbecility; and this ever has been and ever will be the case while the rights of conscience are considered alienable.

3. But supposing it was right for a man to bind his own conscience, yet surely it is very iniquitous to bind the consciences of his children; to make fetters for them before they are born is very cruel. And yet such has been the conduct of men in almost all ages that their children have been bound to believe and worship as their fathers did, or suffer shame, loss, and sometimes life; and at best to be called dissenters, because they dissent from that which they never joined voluntarily. Such conduct in parents is worse than that of the father of Hannibal who imposed an oath upon his son while a child never to be at peace with the Romans.

4. Finally, religion is a matter between God and individuals, religious opinions of

men not being the objects of civil government nor in any way under its control.

It has often been observed by the friends of religious establishment by human laws that no state can long continue without it; that religion will perish, and nothing but infidelity and atheism prevail.

Are these things facts? Did not the Christian religion prevail during the first three centuries, in a more glorious manner than ever it has since, not only without the aid of law, but in opposition to all the laws of haughty monarchs? And did not religion receive a deadly wound by being fostered in the arms of civil power and regulated by law? These things are so.

From that day to this we have but a few instances of religious liberty to judge by; for in almost all states civil rulers (by the instigation of covetous priests) have undertaken to steady the ark of religion by human laws; but yet we have a few of them without leaving our own land.

The state of Rhode Island has stood above 160 years without any religious establishment. The state of New York never had any. New Jersey claims the same. Pennsylvania has also stood from its first settlement until now upon a liberal foundation; and if agriculture, the mechanical arts, and commerce have not flourished in these states equal to any of the states I judge wrong.

It may further be observed that all the states now in union, saving two or three in New England, have no legal force used about religion, in directing its course or supporting its preachers. And moreover the federal government is forbidden by the Constitution to make any laws establishing any kind of religion. If religion cannot stand, therefore, without the aid of law, it is likely to fall soon in our nation, except in Connecticut and Massachusetts.

To say that "religion cannot stand without a state establishment" is not only contrary to fact . . . but is a contradiction in phrase. Religion must have stood a time before any law could have been made about it; and if it did stand almost 300 years without law it can still stand without it.

The evils of such an establishment are many.

1. Uninspired fallible men make their own opinions tests of orthodoxy, and use their own systems, as Procrustes used his iron bedstead, to stretch and measure the consciences of all others by. Where no toleration is granted to non-conformists, either ignorance and superstition prevail or persecution rages; and if toleration is granted to restricted non-conformists, the minds of men are biased to embrace that religion which is favored and pampered by law (and thereby hypocrisy is nourished), while those who cannot stretch their consciences to believe anything and everything in the established creed are treated with contempt and opprobrious names; and by such means some are pampered to death by largesses and others confined from doing what good they otherwise could by penury. The first lie under a temptation to flatter the ruling party, to continue that form of government which brings the sure bread of idleness; the last to despise that government and those rulers that oppress them. The first have their eyes shut to all further light that would alter the religious machine; the last are always seeking new light, and often fall into enthusiasm. Such are the natural evils of establishment in religion by human laws.

2. Such establishments not only wean and alienate the affections of one from another on account of the different usages they receive in their religious sentiments, but are also very impolitic, especially in new countries; for what encouragement can strangers have to migrate with their arts and wealth into a state, where they cannot enjoy their religious sentiments without exposing themselves to the law, when at the same time their religious opinions do not lead them to be mutinous? And further, how often have kingdoms and states been greatly weakened by religious tests! In the

time of the persecution in France not less than 20,000 people fled for the enjoyment of religious liberty.

3. These establishments metamorphose the church into a creature, and religion into a principle of state, which has a natural tendency to make men conclude that *Bible religion* is nothing but a *trick of state.* Hence it is that the greatest part of the well-informed in literature are overrun with deism and infidelity; nor is it likely that it will ever be any better while preaching is made a trade of emolument. And if there is no difference between *Bible religion* and *state religion* I shall soon fall into infidelity.

4. There are no two kingdoms and states that establish the same creed or formularies of faith. . . . In one kingdom a man is condemned for not believing a doctrine that he would be condemned for believing in another kingdom. Both of these establishments cannot be right — but both of them can be, and surely are, wrong.

5. The nature of such establishments, further, is to keep from civil office the best of men. Good men cannot believe what they cannot believe; and they will not subscribe to what they disbelieve, and take an oath to maintain what they conclude is error: and as the best of men differ in judgment there may be some of them in any state: their talents and virtue entitle them to fill the most important posts, yet because they differ from the established creed of the state, they cannot — will not fill those posts. Whereas villains make no scruple to take any oath.

If these and many more evils attend such establishments, what were and still are the causes that ever there should be a state establishment of religion? The causes are many — some of them follow.

1. The love of importance is a general evil. It is natural to men to dictate for others; they chose to command the bushel and use the whiprow, to have the halter around the necks of others to hang them at pleasure.

2. An over-fondness for a particular system or sect. This gave rise to the first human establishment of religion, by Constantine the Great. Being converted to the Christian system, he established it in the Roman Empire, compelled the pagans to submit, and banished the Christian heretics, built fine chapels at public expense, and forced large stipends for the preachers. All this was done out of love to the Christian religion: but his love operated inadvertently; for he did the Christian church more harm than all the persecuting emperors did. It is said that in his day a voice was heard from Heaven, saying, "Now is poison spewed into the churches." If this voice was not heard, it nevertheless was a truth; for from that day to this, the Christian religion has been made a stirrup to mount the steed of popularity, wealth, and ambition.

3. To produce uniformity in religion is another evil. Rulers often fear that if they leave every man to think, speak and worship as he pleases, the whole cause will be wrecked in diversity; to prevent which they establish some standard of orthodoxy to effect uniformity. But is uniformity attainable? Millions of men, women, and children have been tortured to death to produce uniformity, and yet the world has not advanced one inch towards it. And as long as men live in different parts of the world, have different habits, education, and interests, they will be different in judgment, humanly speaking.

Is conformity of sentiments in matters of religion essential to the happiness of civil government? Not at all. Government has no more to do with the religious opinions of men than it has with the principles of the mathematics. Let every man speak freely without fear — maintain the principles that he believes — worship according to his own faith, either one God, three Gods, no God, or twenty Gods; and let government protect him in so doing, *i.e.,* see that he meets with no personal abuse or loss of property for his religious opinions. Instead of discouraging him with proscriptions, fines, confiscation or death, let him be encouraged, as a free man, to bring forth his arguments and maintain his points with all boldness; then if his doctrine is false it will be confuted, and if it is true (though ever so novel) let others credit it. When every man has this liberty what can he wish for more? A liberal man asks for nothing more of government.

It is not supposable that any established creed contains the whole truth and nothing but the truth; but supposing it did, which established church has got it? All bigots contend for it — each society cries out, "The temple of the Lord are we." Let one society be supposed to be in possession of the whole — let that society be established by law — the creed of faith that they adopt be so consecrated by government that the man that disbelieves it must die — let this creed finally prevail over the whole world. I ask what honor *truth* gets by all this? None at all. It is famed of a Prussian, called John the Cicero, that by one oration he reconciled two contending princes actually in war; but, says the historian, "it was his 6,000 horse of battle that had the most persuasive oratory." So when one creed or church prevails over another, being armed with (a coat of mail) law and sword, truth gets no honor by the victory. Whereas if all stand upon one footing, being equally protected by law as citizens (not as saints) and one prevails over another by cool investigation and fair argument, then truth gains honor, and men more firmly believe it than if it was made an essential article of salvation by law.

Truth disdains the aid of law for its defense — it will stand upon its own merits. The heathens worshiped a goddess called truth, stark naked; and all human decorations of truth serve only to destroy her virgin beauty. It is error, and error alone, that needs human support; and whenever men fly to the law or sword to protect their system of religion and force it upon others, it is evident that they have something in their system that will not bear the light and stand upon the basis of truth.

4. The common objection "that the ignorant part of the community are not capacitated to judge for themselves" supports the popish hierarchy, and all protestants as well as Turkish and pagan establishments, in idea.

But is this idea just? Has God chosen many of the wise and learned? Has He not hid the mystery of gospel truth from them and revealed it unto babes? Does the world by wisdom know God? Did many of the rulers believe in Christ when He was upon earth? Were not the learned clergy (the scribes) His most inveterate enemies? Do not great men differ as much as little men in judgment? Have not almost all lawless errors crept into the world through the means of wise men (so called)? Is not a simple man, who makes nature and reason his study, a competent judge of things? Is the Bible written (like Caligula's laws) so intricate and high that none but the letter-learned (according to common phrase) can read it? Is not the vision written so plain that he that runs may read it? Do not those who understand the original languages which the Bible was written in differ as much in judgment as others? Are the identical copies of Matthew, Mark, Luke and John, together with the epistles, in every university and in the hands of every master of arts? If not, have not the learned to trust to a human transcription, as much as the unlearned have to a translation? If these questions and others of a like nature can be confuted, then I will confess that it is wisdom for a conclave of bishops or a convocation of clergy to frame a system out of the Bible and persuade the legislature to legalize it. No. It would be attended with so much expense, pride, domination, cruelty and bloodshed, that let me rather fall into infidelity; for no religion at all is better than that which is worse than none.

5. The groundwork of these establishments of religion is *clerical influence*. Rulers, being persuaded by the clergy that an establishment of religion by human laws would promote the knowledge of the gospel, quell religious disputes, prevent heresy, produce uniformity, and finally be advantageous to the state, establish such creeds as are framed by the clergy; and this they often do the more readily when they are flattered by the clergy that if they thus defend the truth they will become *nursing fathers* to the church and merit something considerable for themselves.

What stimulates the clergy to recommend this mode of reasoning is,

1. Ignorance — not being able to confute error by fair argument.

2. Indolence — not being willing to spend any time to confute the heretical.

3. But chiefly covetousness, to get money — for it may be observed that in all these establishments settled salaries for the clergy recoverable by law are sure to be interwoven; and was not this the case, I am well convinced that there would not be many if any religious establishments in the Christian world.

---

91.

# Controversy Over the Constitutionality of a United States Bank

*On December 14, 1790, Alexander Hamilton presented a plan to Congress for the adoption of a national bank designed along the lines of the Bank of England. The bank would provide the government with a source for short-term borrowing, increasing the amount of available capital and credit for business, and thereby strengthening the national economy. Congress passed a bill incorporating most of Hamilton's plan in February 1791. Before signing the bill, George Washington, being unsure of its constitutionality, sought the advice of his cabinet. The written opinions of Thomas Jefferson (against the bill) and Alexander Hamilton (for the bill), reprinted here in part, were submitted, respectively, on February 15 and 23, 1791. Washington followed Hamilton's advice and signed the bill into law, thereby chartering the first Bank of the United States.*

Source: Ford, V, pp. 284-289. J. C. Hamilton, IV, pp. 104-138.

I.

## Thomas Jefferson: Against the Bank

The bill for establishing a national bank undertakes, among other things:

1. To form the subscribers into a corporation.

2. To enable them in their corporate capacities to receive grants of land; and so far is against the laws of mortmain.

3. To make alien subscribers capable of holding lands; and so far is against the laws of alienage.

4. To transmit these lands, on the death of a proprietor, to a certain line of successors; and so far changes the course of descents.

5. To put the lands out of the reach of

forfeiture or escheat; and so far is against the laws of forfeiture and escheat.

6. To transmit personal chattels to successors in a certain line; and so far is against the laws of distribution.

7. To give them the sole and exclusive right of banking under the national authority; and so far is against the laws of monopoly.

8. To communicate to them a power to make laws paramount to the laws of the states; for so they must be construed, to protect the institution from the control of the state legislatures; and so, probably, they will be construed.

I consider the foundation of the Constitution as laid on this ground: That "all powers not delegated to the United States, by the Constitution, nor prohibited by it to the states, are reserved to the states or to the people" (Tenth Amendment). To take a single step beyond the boundaries thus specially drawn around the powers of Congress is to take possession of a boundless field of power, no longer susceptible of any definition.

The incorporation of a bank, and the powers assumed by this bill, have not, in my opinion, been delegated to the United States by the Constitution.

1. They are not among the powers specially enumerated; for these are:

First, a power to lay taxes for the purpose of paying the debts of the United States; but no debt is paid by this bill, nor any tax laid. Were it a bill to raise money, its origination in the Senate would condemn it by the Constitution.

Second, "to borrow money." But this bill neither borrows money nor insures the borrowing it. The proprietors of the bank will be just as free as any other moneyholders to lend or not to lend their money to the public. The operation proposed in the bill, first, to lend them $2,000,000, and then to borrow them back again, cannot change the nature of the latter act, which will still be a payment and not a loan, call it by what name you please.

Third, to "regulate commerce with foreign nations, and among the states, and with the Indian tribes." To erect a bank and to regulate commerce are very different acts. He who erects a bank creates a subject of commerce in its bills; so does he who makes a bushel of wheat or digs a dollar out of the mines; yet neither of these persons regulates commerce thereby. To make a thing which may be bought and sold is not to prescribe regulations for buying and selling. Besides, if this was an exercise of the power of regulating commerce, it would be void, as extending as much to the internal commerce of every state as to its external.

For the power given to Congress by the Constitution does not extend to the internal regulation of the commerce of a state (that is to say of the commerce between citizen and citizen), which remain exclusively with its own legislature; but to its external commerce only, that is to say, its commerce with another state, or with foreign nations, or with the Indian tribes. Accordingly the bill does not propose the measure as a regulation of trade, but as "productive of considerable advantages to trade." Still less are these powers covered by any other of the special enumerations.

2. Nor are they within either of the general phrases, which are the two following:

First, to lay taxes to provide for the general welfare of the United States, that is to say, "to lay taxes for *the purpose* of providing for the general welfare." For the laying of taxes is the *power*, and the general welfare the *purpose* for which the power is to be exercised. They are not to lay taxes *ad libitum* [at pleasure] *for any purpose they please but only to pay the debts or provide for the welfare of the Union.* In like manner, they are not *to do anything they please* to provide for the general welfare but only to *lay taxes* for that purpose. To consider the latter phrase, not as describing the purpose of the first but as giving a distinct and independent power to do any act they please which might be for the good of the Union, would render all the preceding and subsequent enumerations of power completely useless.

It would reduce the whole instrument to a single phrase, that of instituting a Congress with power to do whatever would be for the good of the United States; and, as they would be the sole judges of the good or evil, it would be also a power to do whatever evil they please.

It is an established rule of construction where a phrase will bear either of two meanings to give it that which will allow some meaning to the other parts of the instrument and not that which would render all the others useless. Certainly no such universal power was meant to be given them. It was intended to lace them up straitly within the enumerated powers, and those without which, as means, these powers could not be carried into effect. It is known that the very power now proposed *as a means* was rejected *as an end* by the Convention which formed the Constitution. A proposition was made to them to authorize Congress to open canals, and an amendatory one to empower them to incorporate. But the whole was rejected, and one of the reasons for rejection urged in debate was that then they would have a power to erect a bank, which would render the great cities, when there were prejudices and jealousies on the subject, adverse to the reception of the Constitution.

Second. The second general phrase is "to make all laws necessary and proper for carrying into execution the enumerated powers." But they can all be carried into execution without a bank. A bank therefore is not necessary and consequently not authorized by this phrase.

It has been urged that a bank will give great facility or convenience in the collection of taxes. Suppose this were true; yet the Constitution allows only the means which are "necessary," not those which are merely "convenient" for effecting the enumerated powers. If such a latitude of construction be allowed to this phrase as to give any nonenumerated power, it will go to everyone, for there is not one which ingenuity may not torture into a convenience in some instance or other, to some one of so long a list of enumerated powers. It would swallow up all the delegated powers and reduce the whole to one power, as before observed. Therefore it was that the Constitution restrained them to the necessary means, that is to say, to those means without which the grant of power would be nugatory.

But let us examine this convenience and see what it is. The report on this subject . . . states the only *general* convenience to be the preventing the transportation and retransportation of money between the states and the Treasury (for I pass over the increase of circulating medium, ascribed to it as a want, and which, according to my ideas of paper money, is clearly a demerit). Every state will have to pay a sum of tax money into the Treasury; and the Treasury will have to pay, in every state, a part of the interest on the public debt and salaries to the officers of government resident in that state. In most of the states there will still be a surplus of tax money to come up to the seat of government for the officers residing there.

The payments of interest and salary in each state may be made by Treasury orders on the state collector. This will take up the greater part of the money he has collected in his state, and consequently prevent the great mass of it from being drawn out of the state. If there be a balance of commerce in favor of that state against the one in which the government resides, the surplus of taxes will be remitted by the bills of exchange drawn for that commercial balance.

And so it must be if there was a bank. But if there be no balance of commerce, either direct or circuitous, all the banks in the world could not bring up the surplus of taxes but in the form of money. Treasury orders, then, and bills of exchange may prevent the displacement of the main mass of the money collected, without the aid of any bank; and, where these fail, it cannot be prevented even with that aid.

Perhaps, indeed, bank bills may be a more convenient vehicle than Treasury orders. But a little difference in the degree of convenience cannot constitute the necessity which the Constitution makes the ground for assuming any nonenumerated power.

Besides, the existing banks will, without a doubt, enter into arrangements for lending their agency, and the more favorable, as there will be a competition among them for it; whereas the bill delivers us up bound to the national bank, who are free to refuse all arrangement, but on their own terms, and the public not free, on such refusal, to employ any other bank. That of Philadelphia, I believe, now does this business by their post notes, which, by any arrangement with the Treasury, are paid by any state collector to whom they are presented. This expedient alone suffices to prevent the existence of that *necessity* which may justify the assumption of a nonenumerated power as a means for carrying into effect an enumerated one. The thing may be done, and has been done, and well done, without this assumption; therefore, it does not stand on that degree of *necessity* which can honestly justify it.

It may be said that a bank whose bills would have a currency all over the states would be more convenient than one whose currency is limited to a single state. So it would be still more convenient that there should be a bank whose bills should have a currency all over the world. But it does not follow from this superior conveniency that there exists anywhere a power to establish such a bank or that the world may not go on very well without it.

Can it be thought that the Constitution intended that for a shade or two of *convenience,* more or less, Congress should be authorized to break down the most ancient and fundamental laws of the several states; such as those against mortmain, the laws of alienage, the rules of descent, the acts of distribution, the laws of escheat and forfeiture, the laws of monopoly? Nothing but a necessity invincible by any other means can justify such a prostitution of laws, which constitute the pillars of our whole system of jurisprudence. Will Congress be too strait-laced to carry the Constitution into honest effect, unless they may pass over the foundation laws of the state government for the slightest convenience of theirs?

The negative of the President is the shield provided by the Constitution to protect against the invasions of the legislature: (1) the right of the executive; (2) of the judiciary; (3) of the states and state legislatures. The present is the case of a right remaining exclusively with the states, and consequently one of those intended by the Constitution to be placed under its protection.

It must be added, however, that unless the President's mind on a view of everything which is urged for and against this bill is tolerably clear that it is unauthorized by the Constitution; if the pro and con hang so even as to balance his judgment, a just respect for the wisdom of the legislature would naturally decide the balance in favor of their opinion. It is chiefly for cases where they are clearly misled by error, ambition, or interest that the Constitution has placed a check in the negative of the President.

## II.

## ALEXANDER HAMILTON: For the Bank

THE SECRETARY OF THE TREASURY, having perused with attention the papers containing the opinions of the secretary of state and attorney general concerning the constitutionality of the bill for establishing a national bank, proceeds, according to the order of the President, to submit the reasons which have induced him to entertain a different opinion. . . .

In entering upon the argument, it ought to be premised that the objections of the secretary of state and attorney general are founded on a general denial of the authority of the United States to erect corporations. The latter, indeed, expressly admits that if there be anything in the bill which is not warranted by the Constitution, it is the clause of incorporation.

Now it appears to the secretary of the treasury that this general principle is *inherent* in the very *definition* of government and *essential* to every step of the progress to be made by that of the United States, namely: that every power vested in a government is in its nature sovereign and includes, by force of the term, a right to employ all the *means* requisite and fairly applicable to the attainment of the *ends* of such power, and which are not precluded by restrictions and exceptions specified in the Constitution, or not immoral, or contrary to the essential ends of political society. . . .

The circumstance that the powers of sovereignty are in this country divided between the national and state governments does not afford the distinction required. It does not follow from this that each of the portion of powers delegated to the one or to the other is not sovereign with regard to its proper objects. It will only follow from it that each has sovereign power as to certain things and not as to other things. To deny that the government of the United States has sovereign power as to its declared purposes and trusts, because its power does not extend to all cases, would be equally to deny that the state governments have sovereign power in any case, because their power does not extend to every case. The 10th Section of the 1st Article of the Constitution exhibits a long list of very important things which they may not do. And thus the United States would furnish the singular spectacle of a political society without sovereignty, or of a people governed without government.

If it would be necessary to bring proof to a proposition so clear as that which affirms that the powers of the federal government, as to its objects, were sovereign, there is a clause of its Constitution which would be decisive. It is that which declares that the Constitution, and the laws of the United States made in pursuance of it, and all treaties made, or which shall be made, under their authority, shall be the supreme law of the land. The power which can create the supreme law of the land in any case is doubtless sovereign as to such case.

This general and indisputable principle puts at once an end to the abstract question whether the United States have power to erect a corporation; that is to say, to give a legal or artificial capacity to one or more persons, distinct from the natural. For it is unquestionably incident to sovereign power to erect corporations, and consequently to that of the United States, in relation to the objects entrusted to the management of the government. The difference is this: where the authority of the government is general, it can create corporations in all cases; where it is confined to certain branches of legislation, it can create corporations only in those cases.

Here then, as far as concerns the reasonings of the secretary of state and the attorney general, the affirmative of the constitutionality of the bill might be permitted to rest. It will occur to the President that the principle here advanced has been untouched by either of them.

For a more complete elucidation of the point, nevertheless, the arguments which they had used against the power of the government to erect corporations, however foreign they are to the great and fundamental rule which has been stated, shall be particularly examined. . . .

The first of these arguments is that the

foundation of the Constitution is laid on this ground: "That all powers not delegated to the United States by the Constitution, nor prohibited to it by the states, are reserved for the states, or to the people." Whence it is meant to be inferred that Congress can in no case exercise any power not included in those not enumerated in the Constitution. And it is affirmed that the power of erecting a corporation is not included in any of the enumerated powers. . . .

It is not denied that there are implied as well as express powers and that the former are as effectually delegated as the latter. . . . Then it follows that as a power of erecting a corporation may as well be implied as any other thing, it may as well be employed as an instrument or mean of carrying into execution any of the specified powers as any other instrument or mean whatever.

The only question must be, in this, as in every other case, whether the mean to be employed or, in this instance, the corporation to be erected, has a natural relation to any of the acknowledged objects or lawful ends of the government. Thus a corporation may not be erected by Congress for superintending the police of the city of Philadelphia, because they are not authorized to regulate the police of that city. But one may be erected in relation to the collection of taxes, or to the trade with foreign countries, or to the trade between the states, or with the Indian tribes; because it is the province of the federal government to regulate those objects, and because it is incident to a general sovereign or legislative power to regulate a thing, to employ all the means which relate to its regulation to the best and greatest advantage. . . .

Through this mode of reasoning respecting the right of employing all the means requisite to the execution of the specified powers of the government, it is objected that none but necessary and proper means are to be employed; and the secretary of state maintains that no means are to be considered as *necessary* but those without which the grant of the power would be nugatory. Nay, so far does he go in his restrictive interpretation of the *word* as even to make the case of the *necessity* which shall warrant the constitutional exercise of the power to depend on casual and temporary circumstances — an idea which alone refutes the construction. The expediency of exercising a particular power, at a particular time, must, indeed, depend on circumstances; but the constitutional right of exercising it must be uniform and invariable, the same today as tomorrow.

All the arguments, therefore, against the constitutionality of the bill derived from the accidental existence of certain state banks — institutions which happen to exist today and, for aught that concerns the government of the United States, may disappear tomorrow — must not only be rejected as fallacious but must be viewed as demonstrative that there is a radical source of error in the reasoning.

It is essential to the being of the national government that so erroneous a conception of the meaning of the word "necessary" should be exploded.

It is certain that neither the grammatical nor popular sense of the term requires that construction. According to both, "necessary" often means no more than needful, requisite, incidental, useful, or conducive to. It is a common mode of expression to say that it is *necessary* for a government or a person to do this or that thing, when nothing more is intended or understood than that the interests of the government or person require, or will be promoted by, the doing of this or that thing. The imagination can be at no loss for exemplifications of the use of the word in this sense. And it is the true one in which it is to be understood as used in the Constitution.

The whole turn of the clause containing

it indicates that it was the intent of the Convention, by that clause, to give a liberal latitude to the exercise of the specified powers. The expressions have peculiar comprehensiveness. They are, "to make all laws necessary and proper for carrying into execution the foregoing powers, and all other powers vested by the Constitution in the government of the United States, or in any department or officer thereof."

To understand the word as the secretary of state does would be to depart from its obvious and popular sense and to give it a restrictive operation, an idea never before entertained. It would be to give it the same force as if the word "absolutely" or "indispensably" had been prefixed to it. . . . To insist upon it would be to make the criterion of the exercise of any implied power a *case of extreme necessity;* which is rather a rule to justify the overleaping of the bounds of constitutional authority than to govern the ordinary exercise of it.

It may be truly said of every government, as well as that of the United States, that it has only a right to pass such laws as are necessary and proper to accomplish the objects entrusted to it, for no government has a right to do *merely what it pleases.* Hence, by a process of reasoning similar to that of the secretary of state, it might be proved that neither of the state governments has a right to incorporate a bank. It might be shown that all the public business of the state could be performed without a bank, and inferring thence it was unnecessary, it might be argued that it could not be done, because it is against the rule which has been just mentioned. A like mode of reasoning would prove that there was no power to incorporate the inhabitants of a town, with a view to a more perfect police. For it is certain that an incorporation may be dispensed with, though it is better to have one. It is to be remembered that there is no *express* power in any state constitution to erect corporations. . . .

This restrictive interpretation of the word "necessary" is also contrary to this sound maxim of construction; namely, that the powers contained in a constitution of government, especially those which concern the general administration of the affairs of a country, its finances, trade, defense, etc., ought to be construed liberally in advancement of the public good. This rule does not depend on the particular form of a government, or on the particular demarcation of the boundaries of its powers, but on the nature and objects of government itself. The means by which national exigencies are to be provided for, national inconveniences obviated, national prosperity promoted, are of such infinite variety, extent, and complexity that there must of necessity be great latitude of discretion in the selection and application of those means. Hence, consequently, the necessity and propriety of exercising the authorities entrusted to a government on principles of liberal construction. . . .

The truth is that difficulties on this point are inherent in the nature of the federal Constitution; they result inevitably from a division of the legislative power. The consequence of this division is that there will be cases clearly within the power of the national government; others, clearly without its powers; and a third class which will leave room for controversy and difference of opinion, and concerning which a reasonable latitude of judgment must be allowed.

But the doctrine which is contended for is not chargeable with the consequences imputed to it. It does not affirm that the national government is sovereign in all respects but that it is sovereign to a certain extent; that is, to the extent of the objects of its specified powers.

It leaves, therefore, a criterion of what is constitutional and of what is not so. This criterion is the *end* to which the measure relates as a *mean.* If the end be clearly comprehended within any of the specified powers, and if the measure have an obvious relation to that end, and is not forbidden by a particular provision of the Constitution, it may safely be deemed to come within the compass of the national authority.

There is also this further criterion, which may materially assist the decision: Does the proposed measure abridge a preexisting right of any state or of any individual? If it does not, there is a strong presumption in favor of its constitutionality, and slighter relations to any declared object of the Constitution may be permitted to turn the scale. . . .

There are two points in the suggestions of the secretary of state . . . that are peculiarly incorrect. One is that the proposed incorporation is against the laws of monopoly, because it stipulates an exclusive right of banking under the national authority; the other, that it gives power to the institution to make laws paramount to those of the states.

But, with regard to the first point: The bill neither prohibits any state from erecting as many banks as they please, nor any number of individuals from associating to carry on the business, and consequently, is free from the charge of establishing a monopoly; for monopoly implies a *legal impediment* to the carrying on of the trade by others than those to whom it is granted.

And with regard to the second point, there is still less foundation. The bylaws of such an institution as a bank can operate only on its own members — can only concern the disposition of its own property, and must essentially resemble the rules of a private mercantile partnership. They are expressly not to be contrary to law; and law must here mean the law of a state as well as of the United States. There never can be a doubt that a law of a corporation, if contrary to a law of a state, must be overruled as void, unless the law of the state is contrary to that of the United States, and then the question will not be between the law of the state and that of the corporation, but between the law of the state and that of the United States. . . .

It is presumed to have been satisfactorily shown in the course of the preceding observations:

1. That the power of the government, as to the objects entrusted to its management, is, in its nature, sovereign.

2. That the right of erecting corporations is one inherent in, and inseparable from, the idea of sovereign power.

3. That the position that the government of the United States can exercise no power but such as is delegated to it by its Constitution does not militate against this principle.

4. That the word "necessary," in the general clause, can have no restrictive operation derogating from the force of this principle; indeed, that the degree in which a measure is or is not necessary cannot be a test of constitutional right but of expediency only.

5. That the power to erect corporations is not to be considered as an independent or substantive power but as an incidental and auxiliary one and was therefore more properly left to implication than expressly granted.

6. That the principle in question does not extend the power of the government beyond the prescribed limits, because it only affirms a power to incorporate for purposes within the sphere of the specified powers.

And, lastly, that the right to exercise such a power in certain cases is unequivocally granted in the most positive and comprehensive terms. . . .

It shall now be endeavored to be shown that there is a power to erect one of the kind proposed by the bill. This will be done by tracing a natural and obvious relation between the institution of a bank and the objects of several of the enumerated powers of the government; and by showing that, politically speaking, it is necessary to the effectual execution of one or more of those powers. . . .

The proposed bank is to consist of an association of persons, for the purpose of creating a joint capital, to be employed chiefly and essentially in loans. So far the object is not only lawful but it is the mere exercise of a right which the law allows to every individual. The Bank of New York, which is not incorporated, is an example of such an association. The bill proposes, in addition, that the government shall become a joint proprietor in this undertaking, and that it shall permit the bills of the company, payable on demand, to be receivable in its revenues; and stipulates that it shall not grant privileges, similar to those which are to be allowed to this company, to any others. All this is incontrovertibly within the compass of the discretion of the government. The only question is, whether it has a right to incorporate this company in order to enable it the more effectually to accomplish ends which are in themselves lawful.

To establish such a right, it remains to show the relation of such an institution to one or more of the specified powers of the government. Accordingly, it is affirmed that it has a relation, more or less direct, to the power of collecting taxes, to that of borrowing money, to that of regulating trade between the states, and to those of raising and maintaining fleets and armies. To the two former the relation may be said to be immediate; and in the last place it will be argued that it is clearly within the provision which authorizes the making of all needful rules and regulations concerning the property of the United States, as the same has been practised upon by the government.

A bank relates to the collection of taxes in two ways — indirectly, by increasing the quantity of circulating medium and quickening circulation, which facilitates the means of paying directly, by creating a convenient species of medium in which they are to be paid. To designate or appoint the *money* or *thing* in which taxes are to be paid is not only a proper but a *necessary exercise* of the power of collecting them. . . . The appointment, then, of the *money* or *thing* in which the taxes are to be paid is an incident to the power of collection. And among the expedients which may be adopted is that of bills issued under the authority of the United States. . . .

A bank has a direct relation to the power of borrowing money, because it is a usual, and in sudden emergencies an essential, instrument in the obtaining of loans to government. . . . The essentiality of such an institution as an instrument of loans is exemplified at this very moment. An Indian expedition is to be prosecuted. The only fund out of which the money can arise, consistently with the public engagements, is a tax, which only begins to be collected in July next. The preparations, however, are instantly to be made. The money must, therefore, be borrowed — and of whom could it be borrowed if there were no public banks? It happens that there are institutions of this kind, but if there were none, it would be indispensable to create one.

Let it then be supposed that the necessity existed (as but for a casualty would be the case); that proposals were made for obtaining a loan; that a number of individuals came forward and said, "We are willing to accommodate the government with the money; with what we have in hand, and the credit we can raise upon it, we doubt not of being able to furnish the sum required, but in order to do this it is indispensable that we should be incorporated as a bank. This is essential toward putting it in our power to do what is desired, and we are obliged on that account to make it the consideration or condition of the loan."

Can it be believed that a compliance with this proposition would be unconstitutional? Does not this alone evince the contrary? . . .

The institution of a bank has also a natural relation to the regulation of trade between the states, insofar as it is conducive to the creation of a convenient medium of exchange between them, and to the keeping up a full circulation, by preventing the frequent displacement of the metals in reciprocal remittances. Money is the very hinge on which commerce turns. And this does not merely mean gold and silver; many other things have served the purpose, with different degrees of utility. Paper has been extensively employed. It cannot, therefore, be admitted with the attorney general that the regulation of trade between the states, as it concerns the medium of circulation and exchange, ought to be considered as confined to coin. . . .

The secretary of state objects to the relation here insisted upon, by the following mode of reasoning: To erect a bank, says he, and to regulate commerce are very different acts. He who creates a bank, creates a subject of commerce; so does he who makes a bushel of wheat, or digs a dollar out of the mines; yet neither of these persons regulate commerce thereby. To make a thing which may be bought and sold is not to prescribe regulations for *buying* and *selling*. . . .

The secretary of state further argues that if this was a regulation of commerce, it would be void, as extending as much to the internal commerce of every state as to its external. But what regulation of commerce does not extend to the internal commerce of every state? What are all the duties upon imported articles, amounting to prohibitions, but so many bounties upon domestic manufactures, affecting the interests of different classes of citizens in different ways? What are all the provisions in the Coasting Act which relate to the trade between district and district of the same state? In short, what regulation of trade between the states but must affect the internal trade of each state? What can operate upon the whole but must extend to every part?

The relation of a bank to the execution of the powers that concern the common defense has been anticipated. It has been noted that, at this very moment, the aid of such an institution is essential to the measures to be pursued for the protection of our frontiers.

It now remains to show that the incorporation of a bank is within the operation of the provision which authorizes Congress to make all needful rules and regulations concerning the property of the United States. But it is previously necessary to advert to a distinction which has been taken by the attorney general.

He admits that the word "property" may signify personal property, however acquired, and yet asserts that it cannot signify money arising from the sources of revenue pointed out in the Constitution, "because," says he, "the disposal and regulation of money is the final cause for raising it by taxes."

But it would be more accurate to say that the object to which money is intended to be applied is the final cause for raising it than that the disposal and regulation of it is such.

The support of government — the support of troops for the common defense — the payment of the public debt, are the true final causes for raising money. The disposition and regulation of it, when raised, are the steps by which it is applied to the ends for which it was raised, not the ends themselves. Hence, therefore, the money to be raised by taxes, as well as any other personal property, must be supposed to come within the meaning, as they certainly do within the letter, of authority to make all needful rules and regulations concerning the property of the United States. . . .

A hope is entertained that it has, by this time, been made to appear, to the satisfaction of the President, that a bank has a natural relation to the power of collecting taxes — to that of regulating trade — to that of providing for the common defense — and that, as the bill under consideration contemplates the government in the light of a joint proprietor of the stock of the bank, it brings the case within the provision of the clause of the Constitution which immediately respects the property of the United States.

Under a conviction that such a relation subsists, the secretary of the treasury, with all deference, conceives that it will result as a necessary consequence from the position that all the specified powers of government are sovereign, as to the proper objects; that the incorporation of a bank is a constitutional measure; and that the objections taken to the bill, in this respect, are ill-founded. . . .

It has been stated as an auxiliary test of constitutional authority to try whether it abridges any preexisting right of any state, or any individual. The proposed investigation will stand the most severe examination on this point. Each state may still erect as many banks as it pleases. Every individual may still carry on the banking business to any extent he pleases.

92.

## Alexander Hamilton: Report on Manufactures

*Hamilton's fiscal program had fostered an unprecedented prosperity for some segments of American business. The Bank of the United States, which centralized a large part of the nation's capital, had been instituted under the direction of the secretary of the treasury. The next question to be considered was the purpose for which the national wealth should be used. In January 1790, the government asked Hamilton to prepare a plan "for the encouragement and promotion of such manufactures as will tend to render the United States independent of other nations for essentials. . . ." The nation's strong agrarian interests protested the growth of industry; thus a plan for increasing the growth of manufactures had to be a tactful and convincing argument. Economic experts who favored the development of industry, such as Tench Coxe, were asked to help prepare the necessary data for the report. The project resulted in the* Report on Manufactures, *presented by Hamilton to the House of Representatives on December 5, 1791. At the time it was issued, the* Report *aroused little enthusiasm. However, following the War of 1812, it came to be used as a source of arguments in favor of the protection of manufacturing without the interference of any government regulation. A portion of the* Report *is reprinted here.*

Source: *American State Papers, Documents, Legislative and Executive, of the Congress of the United States, etc., etc.,* Walter Lowrie and Matthew Clarke, eds., Vol. V, Washington, 1832, pp. 123-144.

The secretary of the treasury, in obedience to the order of the House of Representatives, of the 15th day of January, 1790, has applied his attention, at as early a period as his other duties would permit, to the subject of manufactures; and particularly to the means of promoting such as will tend to render the United States independent of foreign nations for military and other essential supplies; and he thereupon respectfully submits the following report.

The expediency of encouraging manufactures in the United States, which was not long since deemed very questionable, appears at this time to be pretty generally admitted. The embarrassments which have obstructed the progress of our external trade have led to serious reflections on the necessity of enlarging the sphere of our domestic commerce.

The restrictive regulations which, in foreign markets, abridge the vent of the increasing surplus of our agricultural produce serve to beget an earnest desire that a more extensive demand for that surplus may be created at home; and the complete success which has rewarded manufacturing enterprise, in some valuable branches, conspiring with the promising symptoms which attend some less mature essays in others, justify a hope that the obstacles to the growth of this species of industry are less formidable than they were apprehended to be; and that it is not difficult to find, in its further extension, a full indemnification for any external disadvantages which are or may be experienced, as well as an accession of resources favorable to national independence and safety.

There still are, nevertheless, respectable patrons of opinions unfriendly to the encouragement of manufactures. The following are, substantially, the arguments by which these opinions are defended:

In every country (say those who entertain them), agriculture is the most beneficial and productive object of human industry. This position, generally if not universally true, applies with peculiar emphasis to the United States, on account of their immense tracts of fertile territory uninhabited and unimproved. Nothing can afford so advantageous an employment for capital and labor as the conversion of this extensive wilderness into cultivated farms. Nothing, equally with this, can contribute to the population, strength, and real riches of the country.

To endeavor, by the extraordinary patronage of government, to accelerate the growth of manufactures is, in fact, to endeavor by force and art to transfer the natural current of industry from a more to a less beneficial channel. Whatever has such a tendency must necessarily be unwise; indeed, it can hardly ever be wise in a government to attempt to give a direction to the industry of its citizens. This, under the quick-sighted guidance of private interest, will, if left to itself, infallibly find its own way to the most profitable employment; and it is by such employment that the public prosperity will be most effectually promoted. To leave industry to itself, therefore, is in almost every case the soundest as well as the simplest policy.

This policy is not only recommended to the United States by considerations which affect all nations; it is in a manner dictated to them by the imperious force of a very peculiar situation. The smallness of their population compared with their territory; the constant allurements to emigration from the settled to the unsettled parts of the country; the facility with which the less independent condition of an artisan can be exchanged for the more independent condition of a farmer — these, and similar causes, conspire to produce, and for a length of time must continue to occasion, a scarcity of hands for manufacturing occupation and dearness of labor generally. To these disadvantages for the prosecution of manufactures, a deficiency of pecuniary capital being added, the prospect of a successful competition with the manufactures of Europe must be regarded as little less than desperate. Extensive manufactures can only be the offspring of a redundant, at least of a full, population. Till the latter shall characterize the situation of this country, it is vain to hope for the former.

If, contrary to the natural course of things, an unseasonable and premature spring can be given to certain fabrics by heavy duties, prohibitions, bounties, or by other forced expedients, this will only be to sacrifice the interests of the community to those of particular classes. Besides the misdirection of labor, a virtual monopoly will be given to the persons employed on such fabrics; and an enhancement of price, the inevitable consequence of every monopoly, must be defrayed at the expense of the other parts of the society. It is far preferable that those persons should be engaged in the cultivation of the earth; and that we should procure, in exchange for its productions, the commodities with which foreigners are able to supply us in greater perfection and upon better terms. . . .

In order to form an accurate judgment how far that which has been just stated ought to be deemed liable to a similar imputation, it is necessary to advert carefully to the considerations which plead in favor of manufactures, and which appear to recommend the special and positive encouragement of them in certain cases, and under certain reasonable limitations.

It ought readily to be conceded that the cultivation of the earth, as the primary and most certain source of national supply, as the immediate and chief source of subsistence to man, as the principal source of those materials which constitute the nutriment of other kinds of labor, as including a state most favorable to the freedom and independence of the human mind — one, perhaps, most conducive to the multiplication of the human species — has intrinsically a strong claim to preeminence over every other kind of industry. But that it has a title to anything like an exclusive predilection, in any country, ought to be admitted with great caution; that it is even more productive than every other branch of industry requires more evidence than has yet been given in support of the position. That its real interests, precious and important as (without the help of exaggeration) they truly are, will be advanced rather than injured by the due encouragement of manufactures may, it is believed, be satisfactorily demonstrated. And it is also believed that the expediency of such encouragement, in a general view, may be shown to be recommended by the most cogent and persuasive motives of national policy.

It has been maintained that agriculture is not only the most productive but the only productive species of industry. The reality of this suggestion, in either respect, has, however, not been verified by any accurate detail of facts and calculations; and the general arguments which are adduced to prove it are rather subtle and paradoxical than solid or convincing.

Those which maintain its exclusive productiveness are to this effect:

Labor bestowed upon the cultivation of land produces enough not only to replace all the necessary expenses incurred in the business and to maintain the persons who are employed in it but to afford, together with the ordinary profit on the stock or capital of the farmer, a net surplus or rent for the landlord or proprietor of the soil. But the labor of artificers does nothing more than replace the stock which employs them (or which furnished materials, tools, and wages), and yield the ordinary profit upon that stock. It yields nothing equivalent to the rent of the land; neither does it add anything to the total value of the whole annual produce of the land and labor of the country. The additional value given to those parts of the produce of land which are wrought into manufactures is counterbalanced by the value of those other parts of that produce which are consumed by the manufacturers. It can, therefore, only be by saving or parsimony, not by the positive productiveness of their labor, that the classes of artificers can, in any degree, augment the revenue of the society.

To this it has been answered:

1. That inasmuch as it is acknowledged that manufacturing labor reproduces a value equal to that which is expended or consumed in carrying it on, and continues in existence the original stock or capital employed, it ought, on that account alone, to escape being considered as wholly unproductive. That though it should be admitted,

as alleged, that the consumption of the produce of the soil, by the classes of artificers or manufacturers, is exactly equal to the value added by their labor to the materials upon which it is exerted, yet it would not thence follow that it added nothing to the revenue of the society or to the aggregate value of the annual produce of its land and labor. If the consumption for any given period amounted to a given sum, and the increased value of the produce manufactured, in the same period, to a like sum, the total amount of the consumption and production, during that period, would be equal to the two sums, and consequently double the value of the agricultural produce consumed; and though the increment of value produced by the classes of artificers should at no time exceed the value of the produce of the land consumed by them, yet there would be, at every moment, in consequence of their labor, a greater value of goods in the market than would exist independent of it.

2. That the position that artificers can augment the revenue of a society only by parsimony is true in no other sense than in one which is equally applicable to husbandmen or cultivators. It may be alike affirmed of all these classes that the fund acquired by their labor, and destined for their support, is not, in an ordinary way, more than equal to it. And hence it will follow that augmentation of the wealth or capital of the community (except in the instances of some extraordinary dexterity or skill) can only proceed, with respect to any of them, from the savings of the more thrifty and parsimonious.

3. That the annual produce of the land and labor of a country can only be increased in two ways — by some improvement in the productive powers of the useful labor which actually exists within it, or by some increase in the quantity of such labor. That, with regard to the first, the labor of artificers being capable of greater subdivision and simplicity of operation than that of cultivators, it is susceptible, in a proportionably greater degree, of improvement in its productive powers, whether to be derived from an accession of skill or from the application of ingenious machinery; in which particular, therefore, the labor employed in the culture of land can pretend to no advantage over that engaged in manufactures. That, with regard to an augmentation of the quantity of useful labor, this, excluding adventitious circumstances, must depend essentially upon an increase of capital, which again must depend upon the savings made out of the revenues of those who furnish or manage that which is at any time employed, whether in agriculture or in manufactures, or in any other way.

But while the exclusive productiveness of agricultural labor has been thus denied and refuted, the superiority of its productiveness has been conceded without hesitation. As this concession involves a point of considerable magnitude in relation to maxims of public administration, the grounds on which it rests are worthy of a distinct and particular examination.

One of the arguments made use of in support of the idea may be pronounced both quaint and superficial. It amounts to this — that in the productions of the soil, nature cooperates with man; and that the effect of their joint labor must be greater than that of the labor of man alone.

This, however, is far from being a necessary inference. It is very conceivable that the labor of man alone, laid out upon a work requiring great skill and art to bring it to perfection, may be more productive in value than the labor of nature and man combined, when directed toward more simple operations and objects; and when it is recollected to what an extent the agency of nature, in the application of the mechanical powers, is made auxiliary to the prosecution of manufactures, the suggestion which has been noticed loses even the appearance of plausibility.

It might also be observed, with a contrary view, that the labor employed in agriculture is, in a great measure, periodical and occasional, depending on seasons, and liable to various and long intermissions; while that occupied in many manufactures is constant and regular, extending through the year, embracing, in some instances, night as well as day. It is also probable that there are among the cultivators of land more examples of remissness than among artificers.

The farmer, from the peculiar fertility of his land, or some other favorable circumstance, may frequently obtain a livelihood even with a considerable degree of carelessness in the mode of cultivation; but the artisan can with difficulty effect the same object, without exerting himself pretty equally with all those who are engaged in the same pursuit. And if it may likewise be assumed as a fact that manufactures open a wider field to exertions of ingenuity than agriculture, it would not be a strained conjecture that the labor employed in the former, being at once more constant, more uniform, and more ingenious than that which is employed in the latter, will be found, at the same time, more productive. . . .

Another, and that which seems to be the principal argument offered for the superior productiveness of agricultural labor, turns upon the allegation that labor employed on manufactures yields nothing equivalent to the rent of land; or to that net surplus, as it is called, which accrues to the proprietor of the soil.

But this distinction, important as it has been deemed, appears rather verbal than substantial.

It is easily discernible, that what, in the first instance, is divided into two parts, under the denominations of the ordinary profit of the stock of the farmer and rent to the landlord, is, in the second instance, united under the general appellation of the ordinary profit on the stock of the undertaker; and that this formal or verbal distribution constitutes the whole difference in the two cases. It seems to have been overlooked that the land is itself a stock or capital, advanced or lent by its owner to the occupier or tenant, and that the rent he receives is only the ordinary profit of a certain stock in land, not managed by the proprietor himself but by another, to whom he lends or lets it, and who, on his part, advances a second capital, to stock and improve the land, upon which he also receives the usual profit. The rent of the landlord and the profit of the farmer are, therefore, nothing more than the ordinary profits of two capitals belonging to two different persons, and united in the cultivation of a farm; as, in the other case, the surplus which arises upon any manufactory, after replacing the expenses of carrying it on, answers to the ordinary profits of one or more capitals engaged in the prosecution of such manufactory. It is said one or more capitals, because, in fact, the same thing which is contemplated in the case of the farm sometimes happens in that of a manufactory.

There is one, who furnishes a part of the capital or lends a part of the money by which it is carried on, and another, who carries it on with the addition of his own capital. Out of the surplus which remains after defraying expenses, an interest is paid to the moneylender, for the portion of the capital furnished by him, which exactly agrees with the rent paid to the landlord; and the residue of that surplus constitutes the profit of the undertaker or manufacturer, and agrees with what is denominated the ordinary profits on the stock of the farmer. Both together make the ordinary profits of two capitals employed in a manufactory; as, in the other case, the rent of the landlord and the revenue of the farmer compose the ordinary profits of two capitals employed in the cultivation of a farm.

The rent, therefore, accruing to the proprietor of the land, far from being a criterion of exclusive productiveness as has been argued, is no criterion even of superior productiveness. The question must still be, whether the surplus, after defraying expenses of a given capital employed in the purchase and improvement of a piece of land, is greater or less than that of a like capital, employed in the prosecution of a manufactory; or whether the whole value produced from a given capital and a given quantity of labor, employed in one way, be greater or less than the whole value produced from an equal capital and an equal quantity of labor, employed in the other way; or rather, perhaps, whether the business of agriculture, or that of manufactures, will yield the greatest product, according to a compound ratio of the quantity of the capital and the quantity of labor, which are employed in the one or in the other. . . .

It is extremely probable that on a full and accurate development of the matter, on the ground of fact and calculation, it would be discovered that there is no material difference between the aggregate productiveness of the one and of the other kind of industry; and that the propriety of the encouragements which may, in any case, be proposed to be given to either ought to be determined upon considerations irrelative to any comparison of that nature. . . .

It is now proper to proceed a step further and to enumerate the principal circumstances from which it may be inferred that manufacturing establishments not only occasion a positive augmentation of the produce and revenue of the society but that they contribute essentially to rendering them greater than they could possibly be without such establishments. These circumstances are:

1. The division of labor.
2. An extension of the use of machinery.
3. Additional employment to classes of the community not ordinarily engaged in the business.
4. The promoting of emigration from foreign countries.
5. The furnishing greater scope for the diversity of talents and dispositions, which discriminate men from each other.
6. The affording a more ample and various field for enterprise.
7. The creating, in some instances, a new, and securing, in all, a more certain and steady demand for the surplus produce of the soil.

Each of these circumstances has a considerable influence upon the total mass of industrious effort in a community; together, they add to it a degree of energy and effect which is not easily conceived. Some comments upon each of them, in the order in which they have been stated, may serve to explain their importance.

1. *As To The Division Of Labor*

It has justly been observed that there is scarcely anything of greater moment in the economy of a nation than the proper division of labor. The separation of occupations causes each to be carried to a much greater perfection than it could possibly acquire if they were blended. This arises principally from three circumstances.

First, the greater skill and dexterity naturally resulting from a constant and undivided application to a single object. It is evident that these properties must increase in proportion to the separation and simplification of objects, and the steadiness of the attention devoted to each; and must be less in proportion to the complication of objects, and the number among which the attention is distracted.

Second, the economy of time, by avoiding the loss of it, incident to a frequent transition from one operation to another of a different nature. This depends on various circumstances: the transition itself; the orderly disposition of the implements, machines, and materials employed in the operation to be relinquished; the preparatory steps to the commencement of a new one; the interruption of the impulse which the mind of the workman acquires from being engaged in a particular operation; the distractions, hesitations, and reluctances which attend the passage from one kind of business to another.

Third, an extension of the use of machinery. A man occupied on a single object will have it more in his power, and will be more naturally led to exert his imagination in devising methods to facilitate and abridge labor, than if he were perplexed by a variety of independent and dissimilar operations. Besides this, the fabrication of machines, in numerous instances, becoming itself a distinct trade, the artist who follows it has all the advantages which have been enumerated for improvement in his particular art; and, in both ways, the invention and application of machinery are extended.

And, from these causes united, the mere separation of the occupation of the cultivator from that of the artificer has the effect of augmenting the productive powers of labor and, with them, the total mass of the produce or revenue of a country. In this single view of the subject, therefore, the utility of artificers or manufacturers toward promoting an increase of productive industry is apparent.

### 2. *As To An Extension Of The Use Of Machinery; A Point Which, Though Partly Anticipated, Requires To Be Placed In One Or Two Additional Lights*

THE EMPLOYMENT OF MACHINERY forms an item of great importance in the general mass of national industry. It is an artificial force brought in aid of the natural force of man; and, to all the purposes of labor, is an increase of hands — an accession of strength, unencumbered, too, by the expense of maintaining the laborer. May it not, therefore, be fairly inferred that those occupations which give greatest scope to the use of this auxiliary contribute most to the general stock of industrious effort and, in consequence, to the general product of industry?

It shall be taken for granted, and the truth of the position referred to observation, that manufacturing pursuits are susceptible in a greater degree of the application of machinery than those of agriculture. If so, all the difference is lost to a community which, instead of manufacturing for itself, procures the fabrics requisite to its supply from other countries. The substitution of foreign for domestic manufactures is a transfer to foreign nations of the advantages accruing from the employment of machinery in the modes in which it is capable of being employed with most utility and to the greatest extent.

The cotton mill, invented in England within the last twenty years, is a signal illustration of the general proposition which has just been advanced. In consequence of it, all the different processes for spinning cotton are performed by means of machines which are put in motion by water, and attended chiefly by women and children; and by a smaller number of persons, in the whole, than are requisite in the ordinary mode of spinning. And it is an advantage of great moment that the operations of this mill continue, with convenience, during the night as well as through the day. The prodigious effect of such a machine is easily conceived. To this invention is to be attributed, essentially, the immense progress which has been so suddenly made in Great Britain in the various fabrics of cotton.

### 3. *As To The Additional Employment Of Classes Of The Community Not Originally Engaged In The Particular Business*

THIS IS NOT AMONG the least valuable of the means by which manufacturing institutions contribute to augment the general stock of industry and production. In places where those institutions prevail, besides the persons regularly engaged in them, they afford occasional and extra employment to industrious individuals and families who are willing to devote the leisure resulting from the intermissions of their ordinary pursuits to collateral labors, as a resource for multiplying their acquisitions or their enjoyments. The husbandman himself experiences a new source of profit and support from the increased industry of his wife and daughters, invited and stimulated by the demands of the neighboring manufactories.

Besides this advantage of occasional employment to classes having different occupations, there is another, of a nature allied to it, and of a similar tendency. This is the employment of persons who would otherwise be idle and, in many cases, a burden on the community, either from the bias of temper, habit, infirmity of body, or some other cause indisposing or disqualifying them for the toils of the country. It is worthy of particular remark that, in general, women and children are rendered more useful, and the latter more early useful, by manufacturing establishments, than they would otherwise be. Of the number of persons employed in the cotton manufactories of Great Britain, it is computed that four-sevenths, nearly, are women and children; of whom the greatest proportion are children, and many of them of a tender age.

And thus it appears to be one of the attributes of manufactures, and one of no small consequence, to give occasion to the exertion of a greater quantity of industry, even by the same number of persons, where they happen to prevail, than would exist if there were no such establishments.

### 4. *As To The Promoting Of Emigration From Foreign Countries*

Men reluctantly quit one course of occupation and livelihood for another unless invited to it by very apparent and proximate advantages. Many who would go from one country to another, if they had a prospect of continuing with more benefit the callings to which they have been educated, will often not be tempted to change their situation by the hope of doing better in some other way.

Manufacturers who, listening to the powerful invitations of a better price for their fabrics or their labor; of greater cheapness of provisions and raw materials; of an exemption from the chief part of the taxes, burdens, and restraints which they endure in the Old World; of greater personal independence and consequence under the operation of a more equal government; and of what is far more precious than mere religious toleration — a perfect equality of religious privileges — would probably flock from Europe to the United States to pursue their own trades or professions if they were once made sensible of the advantages they would enjoy, and were inspired with an assurance of encouragement and employment, will, with difficulty, be induced to transplant themselves with a view to becoming cultivators of land.

If it be true, then, that it is the interest of the United States to open every possible avenue to emigration from abroad, it affords a weighty argument for the encouragement of manufactures; which, for the reasons just assigned, will have the strongest tendency to multiply the inducements to it.

Here is perceived an important resource, not only for extending the population and, with it, the useful and productive labor of the country but likewise for the prosecution of manufactures, without deducting from the number of hands which might otherwise be drawn to tillage; and even for the indemnification of agriculture, for such as might happen to be diverted from it. Many, whom manufacturing views would induce to emigrate, would afterward yield to the temptations which the particular situation of this country holds out to agricultural pursuits; and while agriculture would, in other respects, derive many signal and unmingled advantages from the growth of manufactures, it is a problem whether it would gain or lose, as to the article of the number of persons employed in carrying it on.

### 5. *As To The Furnishing Greater Scope For The Diversity Of Talents And Dispositions Which Discriminate Men From Each Other*

This is a much more powerful means of augmenting the fund of national industry than may at first sight appear. It is a just observation that minds of the strongest and most active powers for their proper objects fall below mediocrity and labor without effect if confined to uncongenial pursuits; and it is thence to be inferred that the results of human exertion may be immensely increased by diversifying its objects. When all the different kinds of industry obtain in a community, each individual can find his proper element and can call into activity the whole vigor of his nature; and the community is benefited by the services of its respective members in the manner in which each can serve it with most effect.

If there be anything in a remark often to be met with, namely, that there is in the genius of the people of this country a peculiar aptitude for mechanic improvements, it would operate as a forcible reason for giving opportunities to the exercise of that species of talent by the propagation of manufactures.

### 6. *As To The Affording A More Ample And Various Field For Enterprise*

This also is of greater consequence in the general scale of national exertion than might perhaps on a superficial view be supposed, and has effects not altogether dissimilar from those of the circumstance last noticed. To cherish and stimulate the activity of the human mind by multiplying the objects of enterprise is not among the least considerable of the expedients by which the wealth of a nation may be promoted. Even things in themselves not positively advantageous sometimes become so by their tendency to provoke exertion. Every new scene which is opened to the busy nature of man to rouse and exert itself is the addition of a new energy to the general stock of effort.

The spirit of enterprise, useful and prolific as it is, must necessarily be contracted or expanded in proportion to the simplicity or variety of the occupations and productions which are to be found in a society. It must be less in a nation of mere cultivators than in a nation of cultivators and merchants; less in a nation of cultivators and merchants than in a nation of cultivators, artificers, and merchants.

### 7. *As To The Creating, In Some Instances, A New, And Securing, In All, A More Certain And Steady Demand For The Surplus Produce Of The Soil*

This is among the most important of the circumstances which have been indicated. It is a principal means by which the establishment of manufactures contributes to an augmentation of the produce or revenue of a country and has an immediate and direct relation to the prosperity of agriculture.

It is evident that the exertions of the husbandman will be steady or fluctuating, vigorous or feeble, in proportion to the steadiness or fluctuation, adequateness or inadequateness, of the markets on which he must depend for the vent of the surplus which may be produced by his labor; and that such surplus, in the ordinary course of things, will be greater or less in the same proportion.

For the purpose of this vent, a domestic market is greatly to be preferred to a foreign one; because it is, in the nature of things, far more to be relied upon.

It is a primary object of the policy of nations to be able to supply themselves with subsistence from their own soils; and manufacturing nations, as far as circumstances permit, endeavor to procure from the same source the raw materials necessary for their own fabrics. This disposition, urged by the spirit of monopoly, is sometimes even carried to an injudicious extreme.

It seems not always to be recollected that nations who have neither mines nor manufactures can only obtain the manufactured articles of which they stand in need by an exchange of the products of their soils; and that if those who can best furnish them with such articles are unwilling to give a due course to this exchange, they must, of necessity, make every possible effort to manufacture for themselves; the effect of which is that the manufacturing nations abridge the natural advantages of their situation through an unwillingness to permit the agricultural countries to enjoy the advantages of theirs, and sacrifice the interests of a mutually beneficial intercourse to the vain project of selling everything and buying nothing.

But it is also a consequence of the policy which has been noted that the foreign demand for the products of agricultural countries is, in a great degree, rather casual and occasional than certain or constant. To what extent injurious interruptions of the demand for some of the staple commodities of the United States may have been experienced from that cause must be referred to the judgment of those who are engaged in carrying on the commerce of the country; but it may be safely affirmed that such interruptions are at times very inconveniently felt, and that cases not unfrequently occur in which markets are so confined and restricted as to render the demand very unequal to the supply.

Independently, likewise, of the artificial impediments which are created by the policy in question, there are natural causes tending to render the external demand for the surplus of agricultural nations a precarious reliance. The differences of seasons in the countries which are the consumers make immense differences in the produce of their own soils in different years and, consequently, in the degrees of their necessity for foreign supply. Plentiful harvests with them, especially if similar ones occur at the same time in the countries which are the furnishers, occasion, of course, a glut in the markets of the latter.

Considering how fast and how much the progress of new settlements in the United States must increase the surplus produce of the soil, and weighing seriously the tendency of the system which prevails among most of the commercial nations of Europe; whatever dependence may be placed on the force of natural circumstances to counteract the effects of an artificial policy, there appear strong reasons to regard the foreign demand for that surplus as too uncertain a reliance and to desire a substitute for it in an extensive domestic market.

To secure such a market there is no other expedient than to promote manufacturing establishments. Manufacturers, who constitute the most numerous class after the cultivators of land, are for that reason the principal consumers of the surplus of their labor.

This idea of an extensive domestic market for the surplus produce of the soil is of the first consequence. It is, of all things, that which most effectually conduces to a flourishing state of agriculture. If the effect of manufactories should be to detach a portion of the hands which would otherwise be engaged in tillage, it might possibly cause a smaller quantity of lands to be under cultivation; but by their tendency to procure a more certain demand for the surplus produce of the soil, they would, at the same time, cause the lands which were in cultivation to be better improved and more productive. And while, by their influence, the condition of each individual farmer would be meliorated, the total mass of agricultural production would probably be increased; for this must evidently depend as much upon the degree of improvement (if not more) as upon the number of acres under culture.

It merits particular observation that the multiplication of manufactories not only furnishes a market for those articles which have been accustomed to be produced in abundance in a country but it likewise creates a demand for such as were either unknown or produced in inconsiderable quantities. The bowels as well as the surface of the earth are ransacked for articles which were before neglected. Animals, plants, and minerals acquire a utility and value which were before unexplored.

The foregoing considerations seem sufficient to establish, as general propositions, that it is the interest of nations to diversify the industrious pursuits of the individuals who compose them; that the establishment of manufactures is calculated not only to increase the general stock of useful and productive labor but even to improve the state of agriculture in particular; certainly to advance the interests of those who are engaged in it. . . .

It may be observed (and the idea is of no inconsiderable weight) that, however true it might be, a state which, possessing large tracts of vacant and fertile territory, was at the same time secluded from foreign commerce, would find its interest and the interest of agriculture in diverting a part of its population from tillage to manufactures; yet it will not follow that the same is true of a state which, having such vacant and fertile territory, has at the same time ample opportunity of procuring from abroad, on good terms, all the fabrics of which it stands in need for the supply of its inhabitants. The power of doing this at least secures the great advantage of a division of labor, leaving the farmer free to pursue, exclusively, the culture of his land, and enabling him to procure with its products the manufactured supplies requisite either to his wants or to his enjoyments.

And though it should be true that in settled countries the diversification of industry is conducive to an increase in the productive powers of labor and to an augmentation of revenue and capital, yet it is scarcely conceivable that there can be anything of so solid and permanent advantage to an uncultivated and unpeopled country as to convert its wastes into cultivated and inhabited districts. If the revenue, in the meantime, should be less, the capital, in the event, must be greater. . . .

If Europe will not take from us the products of our soil upon terms consistent with our interest, the natural remedy is to contract, as fast as possible, our wants of her.

Second, the conversion of their waste into cultivated lands is certainly a point of great moment in the political calculations of the United States. But the degree in which this may possibly be retarded, by the encouragement of manufactories, does not appear to countervail the powerful inducements to afford that encouragement.

An observation, made in another place, is of a nature to have great influence upon this question. If it cannot be denied that the interests, even of agriculture, may be advanced more by having such of the lands of a state as are occupied, under good cultivation, than by having a greater quantity occupied under a much inferior cultivation; and if manufactories, for the reasons assigned, must be admitted to have a tendency to promote a more steady and vigorous cultivation of the lands occupied than would happen without them, it will follow that they are capable of indemnifying a country for a diminution of the progress of new settlements; and may serve to increase both the capital value and the income of its lands, even though they should abridge the number of acres under tillage.

But it does by no means follow that the progress of new settlements would be retarded by the extension of manufactures. The desire of being an independent proprietor of land is founded on such strong principles in the human breast that, where the opportunity of becoming so is as great as it is in the United States, the proportion will be small of those (whose situations would otherwise lead to it) who would be diverted from it toward manufactures. And it is highly probable, as already intimated, that the accessions of foreigners who, originally drawn over by manufacturing views, would afterward abandon them for agricultural, would be more than an equivalent for those of our own citizens who might happen to be detached from them.

The remaining objections to a particular encouragement of manufactures in the United States now require to be examined.

One of these turns on the proposition that industry, if left to itself, will naturally find its way to the most useful and profitable employment. Whence it is inferred that manufactures, without the aid of government, will grow up as soon and as fast as the natural state of things and the interest of the community may require.

Against the solidity of this hypothesis, in the full latitude of the terms, very cogent reasons may be offered. These have relation to the strong influence of habit and the spirit of imitation; the fear of want of success in untried enterprises; the intrinsic difficulties incident to first essays toward a competition with those who have previously attained to perfection in the business to be attempted; the bounties, premiums, and other artificial encouragements with which foreign nations second the exertions of their own citizens in the branches in which they are to be rivaled. . . .

There remains to be noticed an objection to the encouragement of manufactures, of a nature different from those which question the probability of success. This is derived from its supposed tendency to give a monopoly of advantages to particular classes, at the expense of the rest of the community, who, it is affirmed, would be able to procure the requisite supplies of manufactured articles on better terms from foreigners than from our own citizens; and who, it is alleged, are reduced to necessity of paying an enhanced price for whatever they want, by every measure which obstructs the free competition of foreign commodities.

It is not an unreasonable supposition that measures which serve to abridge the free competition of foreign articles have a tendency to occasion an enhancement of prices; and it is not to be denied that such is the effect, in a number of cases; but the fact does not uniformly correspond with the theory. A reduction of prices has, in several instances, immediately succeeded the establishment of a domestic manufacture. Whether it be that foreign manufacturers endeavor to supplant, by underselling our own, or whatever else be the cause, the effect has been such as is stated, and the reverse of what might have been expected.

But, though it were true that the immediate and certain effect of regulations controlling the competition of foreign with domestic fabrics was an increase of price, it is universally true that the contrary is the ultimate effect with every successful manufacture. When a domestic manufacture has attained to perfection, and has engaged in the prosecution of it a competent number of persons, it invariably becomes cheaper. Being free from the heavy charges which attend the importation of foreign commodities, it can be afforded, and accordingly seldom never fails to be sold cheaper, in process of time, than was the foreign article for which it is a substitute. The internal competition which takes place soon does away everything like monopoly, and by degrees reduces the price of the article to the minimum of a reasonable profit on the capital employed. This accords with the reason of the thing, and with experience.

Whence it follows, that it is the interest of a community, with a view to eventual and permanent economy, to encourage the growth of manufactures. In a national view, a temporary enhancement of price must always be well compensated by a permanent reduction of it. . . .

There seems to be a moral certainty that the trade of a country which is both manufacturing and agricultural will be more lucrative and prosperous than that of a country which is merely agricultural.

One reason for this is found in that general effort of nations . . . to procure from their own soils the articles of prime necessity requisite to their own consumption and use, and which serves to render their demand for a foreign supply of such articles, in a great degree, occasional and contingent. . . . Another circumstance, which gives a superiority of commercial advantages to states that manufacture as well as cultivate, consists in the more numerous attractions which a more diversified market offers to foreign customers, and in the greater scope which it affords to mercantile enterprise. . . .

A third circumstance, perhaps not inferior to either of the other two . . . has relation to the stagnations of demand for certain commodities, which, at some time or other, interfere more or less with the sale of all. The nation which can bring to market but few articles is likely to be more quickly and sensibly affected by such stagnations than one which is always possessed of a great variety of commodities; the former frequently finds too great a proportion of its stock of materials for sale or exchange lying on hand, or is obliged to make injurious sacrifices to supply its wants of foreign articles, which are numerous and urgent, in proportion to the smallness of the number of its own. The latter commonly finds itself indemnified by the high prices of some articles for the low prices of others; and the prompt and advantageous sale of those articles which are in demand enables its merchants the better to wait for a favorable change in respect to those which are not. There is ground to believe that a difference of situation, in this particular, has immensely different effects upon the wealth and prosperity of nations.

From these circumstances, collectively, two important inferences are to be drawn: one, that there is always a higher probability of a favorable balance of trade in regard to countries in which manufactures founded on the basis of a thriving agriculture flourish than in regard to those which are confined wholly, or almost wholly, to agriculture; the other (which is also a consequence of the first), that countries of the former description are likely to possess more pecuniary wealth, or money, than those of the latter. . . .

It is not uncommon to meet with an opinion that, though the promoting of manufactures may be the interest of a part of the Union, it is contrary to that of another part. The Northern and Southern regions are sometimes represented as having adverse interests in this respect. Those are called manufacturing, these agricultural states; and a species of opposition is imagined to subsist between the manufacturing and agricultural interests. . . .

Ideas of a contrariety of interests between the Northern and Southern regions of the Union, are, in the main, as unfounded as they are mischievous. The diversity of circumstances on which such contrariety is usually predicated authorizes a directly contrary conclusion. Mutual wants constitute one of the strongest links of political connection; and the extent of these bears a natural proportion to the diversity in the means of mutual supply.

Suggestions of an opposite complexion are ever to be deplored as unfriendly to the steady pursuit of one great common cause and to the perfect harmony of all the parts.

In proportion as the mind is accustomed to trace the intimate connection of interest which subsists between all the parts of a society, united under the same government, the infinite variety of channels will serve to circulate the prosperity of each, to and through the rest — in that proportion will it be little apt to be disturbed by solicitudes and apprehensions, which originate in local discriminations.

It is a truth, as important as it is agreeable, and one to which it is not easy to imagine exceptions, that everything tending to establish substantial and permanent order in the affairs of a country, to increase the total mass of industry and opulence, is ultimately beneficial to every part of it. On the credit of this great truth, an acquiescence may safely be accorded, from every quarter, to all institutions and arrangements which promise a confirmation of public order and an augmentation of national resource.

But there are more particular considerations which serve to fortify the idea that the encouragement of manufactures is the interest of all parts of the Union. If the Northern and Middle states should be the principal scenes of such establishments, they would immediately benefit the more southern, by creating a demand for productions, some of which they have in common with the other states, and others, which are either peculiar to them, or more abundant, or of better quality, than elsewhere. . . .

If, then, it satisfactorily appears that it is the interest of the United States, generally, to encourage manufactures, it merits particular attention that there are circumstances which render the present a critical moment for entering, with zeal, upon the important business. The effort cannot fail to be materially seconded by a considerable and increasing influx of money, in consequence of foreign speculations in the funds, and by the disorders which exist in different parts of Europe.

---

93.

## James Madison: Concerning Public Opinion

*James Madison wrote a number of short political essays reflecting his concern for the new government he had helped to create and for the direction it would take in the future. The sovereign power of the United States resided in its people, he felt, and only through an enlightened public could the government seek guidance for its tasks. Madison's awareness of the unpredictability of the public mind is reflected in the following essay, which first appeared in the* National Gazette *on December 19, 1791, long before the public opinion polls of today had come into existence.*

Source: *Madison Letters,* IV: "Public Opinion."

Public opinion sets bounds to every government, and is the real sovereign in every free one.

As there are cases where the public opinion must be obeyed by the government, so there are cases where, not being fixed, it may be influenced by the government. This distinction, if kept in view, would prevent or decide many debates on the respect due from the government to the sentiments of the people.

In proportion as government is influenced by opinion, it must be so by whatever influences opinion. This decides the question concerning a constitutional Declaration of Rights, which requires an influence on government by becoming a part of public opinion.

The larger a country, the less easy for its real opinion to be ascertained, and the less difficult to be counterfeited; when ascertained or presumed, the more respectable it is in the eyes of individuals. This is favorable to the authority of government. For the same reason, the more extensive a country, the more insignificant is each individual in his own eyes. This may be unfavorable to liberty.

Whatever facilitates a general intercourse of sentiments, as good roads, domestic commerce, a free press, and particularly a circulation of newspapers through the entire body of the people, and representatives going from and returning among every part of them, is equivalent to a contraction of territorial limits, and is favorable to liberty, where these may be too extensive.

---

94.

## Sea Chanteys

*In the years after independence, when the restrictive British Navigation Acts could be safely ignored, America's merchant marine grew both in size and efficiency until by the 1790s it was probably the leading ocean carrier of the world. The increase in the number of vessels meant an increase in the number of sailing men, and this in turn led to an efflorescence of sea songs that is one of the high points in America's folk song tradition. For America's sailors, as for those of other countries, there was likely to be a "fair maid" in every port. Nevertheless, the first song reprinted below records one sailor's choice of a hometown girl, who will be his "little wife," over the fair maid of Amsterdam, who is "mistress of her trade." The second song is a "short drag" chantey, sung when the foresail was being sheeted home. On each repetition of the word "Joe," the sailors hauled on the ropes.*

### A-ROVING

In Amsterdam there lived a maid,
Mark well what I do say;
In Amsterdam there lived a maid,
And she was mistress of her trade;
I'll go no more a-roving with you, fair maid.
*Chorus:*
A-roving, a-roving, since roving's been my ru-i-in
I'll go no more a-roving with you, fair maid.

Her eyes are like two stars so bright,
Mark well what I do say;
Her eyes are like two stars so bright,
Her face is fair, her step is light;
I'll go no more a-roving with you, fair maid.

Her cheeks are like the rosebuds red,
Mark well what I do say;
Her cheeks are like the rosebuds red,
There's wealth of hair upon her head;
I'll go no more a-roving with you, fair maid.

I love this fair maid as my life,
Mark well what I do say;
I love this fair maid as my life,
And soon she'll be my little wife;
I'll go no more a-roving with you, fair maid.

And if you'd know this maiden's name,
Mark well what I do say;
And if you'd know this maiden's name,
Why soon like mine, 'twill be the same;
I'll go no more a-roving with you, fair maid.

## HAUL AWAY, JOE

When I was a little boy
And so my mother told me,
Way haul away, we'll haul away, Joe!
That if I did not kiss the girls
My lips would grow all moldy.
Way haul away, we'll haul away, Joe!

Once I had a Southern gal
But she was fat and lazy,
Way haul away, we'll haul away, Joe!
But now I've got a Yankee gal
And she is just a daisy.
Way haul away, we'll haul away, Joe!

Oh, Louis was the king of France
Before the Revolution,
Way haul away, we'll haul away, Joe!
But then he got his head cut off
Which spoiled his constitution.
Way haul away, we'll haul away, Joe!

The cook is in the galley now
Making duff so handy,
Way haul away, we'll haul away, Joe!
And the captain's in his cabin
Drinkin' wine and brandy.
Way haul away, we'll haul away, Joe!

*Chorus:*
Way haul away,
We'll haul away together,
Way haul away,
We'll haul away, Joe!

The Library Company of Philadelphia

# THE NATION TAKES SHAPE

The Revolutionary War completely disrupted the American economy, but the new nation had both natural and human resources for a strong recovery. Britain, unconsciously, contributed greatly to the growth of American economic self-reliance by restricting trade with England and its possessions: though its short-range commerce was hurt, America was forced to find new export markets. Also, Americans had to learn to use their own manufactured goods, rather than the more familiar imported goods. Demands on the relatively small number of skilled craftsmen in America grew accordingly. The artisans, shipwrights, and metal founders, whose function it had been to fill the gap between imports and consumption, found themselves faced by the need to build the basis of a total native economy. Men of means, landed gentry and merchants, quickly saw the bountiful, capital-producing potential of the natural resources of the continent. Economically, the United States had more advantages than most new nations have had since.

The awareness of this latent material and industrial potential was expressed in several ways: in Hamilton's "Report on Manufactures," in the establishment of the Patent Office. It was also expressed in Noah Webster's advocacy of practical education, and in John Adams' interest in the study of natural science as the basis for sound resource development. Independence also brought forth an indigenous publishing trade and the burgeoning of national literature.

Library of Congress

**Boston viewed from the harbor**

Yale University Library

**New Haven, Connecticut, in 1786**

**New York City from Hobuck Ferry House, New Jersey**

Library of Congress

In the first years of independence the new nation remained as closely tied to the Atlantic coast as it had been during the colonial period. Distances were great and roads primitive. As a result, most travelers and goods moved by water, and the cities along the coast came to dominate their inland neighbors. Duties that the port cities charged on goods moving through them to other states greatly hindered internal trade and impaired relations between states until interstate duties were eliminated by the Constitution. The primary commodities in interstate, as well as international, trade were fish, rice, tobacco, and cotton.

**View of the town of Baltimore, 1796**

Maryland Historical Society

Pennsylvania Historical Society

**Blue Anchor Inn, Philadelphia**

The towns not dependent on trade continued to develop as self-contained communities. The church was the focal point of the town, serving as a gathering place for town meetings and celebrations, as well as worship.

The general spirit of independence following the Revolution pervaded all institutions. It extended as well to the churches: many broke away from old affiliations, and new sects proliferated.

Valentine Museum, Richmond

Library of Congress

**St. John's Church in Richmond (above) was the setting for Patrick Henry's "give me liberty or give me death" speech. The Baptist Meeting House in Providence, R.I. (left) and Trinity Church in New York (right) are examples of the styles of church architecture still prevailing in America**

New York Public Library

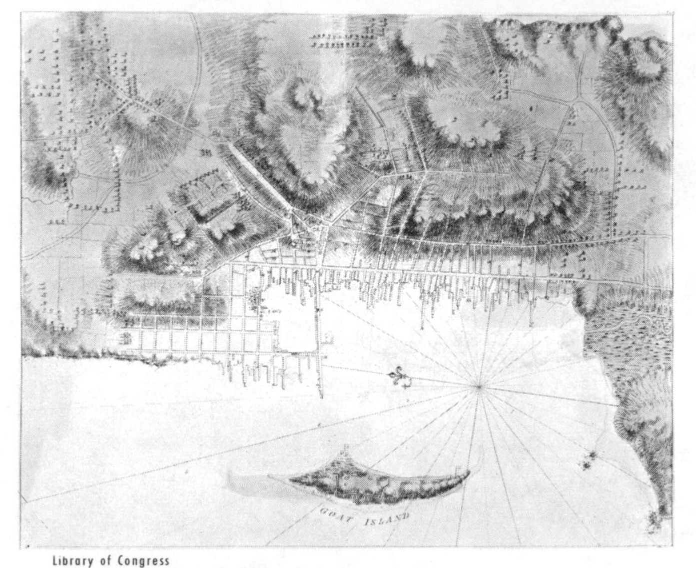


Library of Congress

**Town and harbor of Newport, R.I.; from "Atlantic Neptune"**

Library of Congress

**Lighthouse, Cape Henlopen**

Old Dartmouth Whaling Museum

**Thomas Nye, New Bedford ship captain**

# American Shipping

Following the Revolution, American merchants no longer enjoyed a favored trade position in the British Empire. They were compelled to seek new markets in the Orient, the Mediterranean, and the Baltic. These markets proved so profitable that shipping was the first of all the American trades to recover from the war. Only in the Mediterranean were American vessels threatened, and it was partly in response to the Barbary pirates who roamed there that the American Navy launched its first vessel, the "United States," in 1797.

**Frigate "United States"**

Library of Congress

Library of Congress

Library of Congress

**(Above) View of the Narrows above New York harbor, 1798; (below) plan of Charlestown, S.C., and the harbor, from "Atlantic Neptune"**

Library of Congress

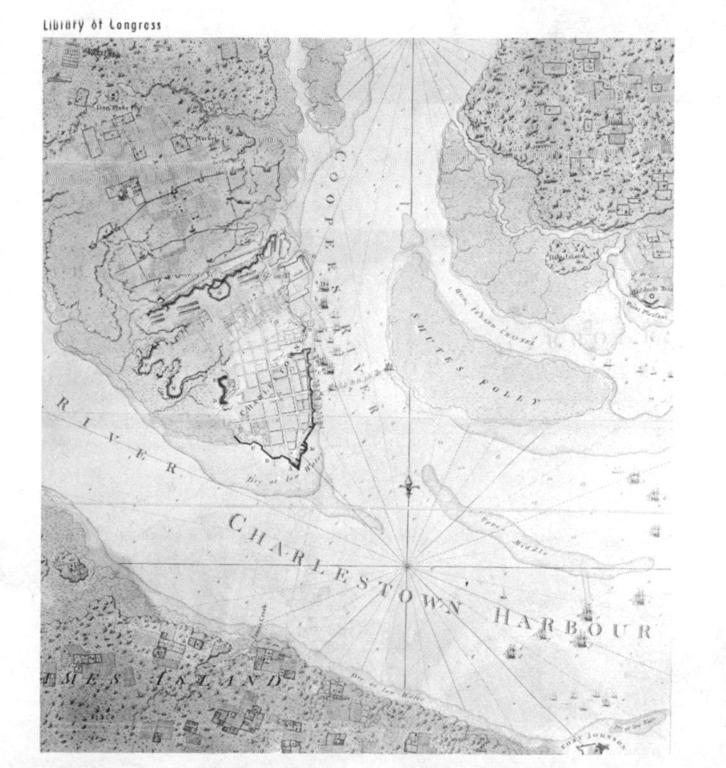

U.S. Naval Academy Museum

**Abraham Whipple, American privateer and naval officer during the Revolution**

# Town . . .

Library of Congress

Although gains in American commerce and industry after the Revolution spurred the growth of the cities, the great bulk of the people still lived on farms. For the most part these farms were primitive and poor, but in the northern states men who had achieved professional or commercial success often invested in farming estates. These estates, together with smaller farms clustered around the towns, set a pattern of northern community life that contrasted sharply with the scattered plantations of the South.

**(Above) The green at Lexington, Mass.; (left) etching depicting a carpenter in his shop; (below) view of the farm of John Hancock, 1789; (bottom) Leeds overmantle, 18th century, portraying a farm in New York State**

Library of Congress

Library of Congress

New York State Historical Association

# and Farm

By the end of the war, the soil on the small, backwoods farms, and on many plantations as well, had been either wholly or partially depleted by a century and a half of continuous cultivation. The gentlemen farmers, who had the time and the capital to invest, set about studying ways of restoring American agriculture, and several societies, such as the New York Agricultural Society and the Philadelphia Society, appeared in northern cities to further experiments with new methods.

Rockefeller Collection, Colonial Williamsburg

**(Above) "Residence of David Twining as it was in 1797," by Edward Hicks; (right) Green Hill, an estate in Pennsylvania in 1792; (below) St. George's Manor on Long Island, 1792**

Library of Congress

Library of Congress

# The South

The plantation system that had developed during the colonial period continued to dominate Southern life. Slavery was general in the plantation system. Commercial ties with the mother country were quickly reestablished, since England valued the rice, tobacco, and indigo produced in the South.

**(Above) Stages in the handling of tobacco: preparation for drying, inspection in a public warehouse, and bringing it to market; (below) "Start of the Hunt" by an unknown artist, about 1780**

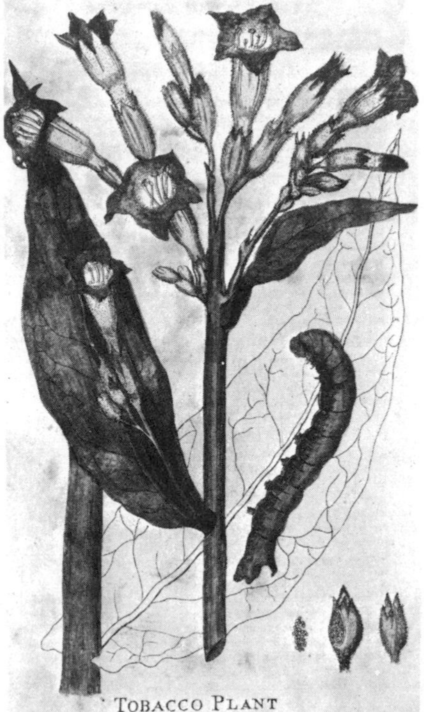


(All) Library of Congress

Garbisch Collection, National Gallery of Art

Library of Congress

Scene on a plantation near the Indian River in Delaware, painted about 1788

(Left) Painting of Colonial Dame (South Carolina) attributed to James Earl; (right) oil painting, "Alexander Spotswood Payne and His Brother, John Robert Danbridge Payne, with their Nurse," 1790

Virginia Museum of Fine Arts

Princeton Art Museum

"The End of the Hunt"; painted about 1780 by an unknown artist

National Gallery of Art

# Science

Library Company of Philadelphia

**"Chemistry Experiment," by an anonymous artist**

Following the Revolution most of those devoted to science were men of wealth and leisure. John Adams, feeling that the promotion of science protected the popular form of government, helped form the American Academy of Arts and Sciences in Boston in 1780. A strong influence on experimental science was exerted by Joseph Priestley, friend of Ben Franklin and political refugee from England.

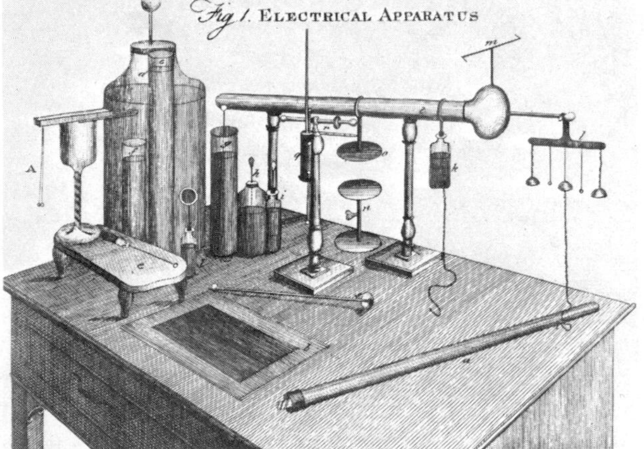


(All) Encyclopaedia Britannica

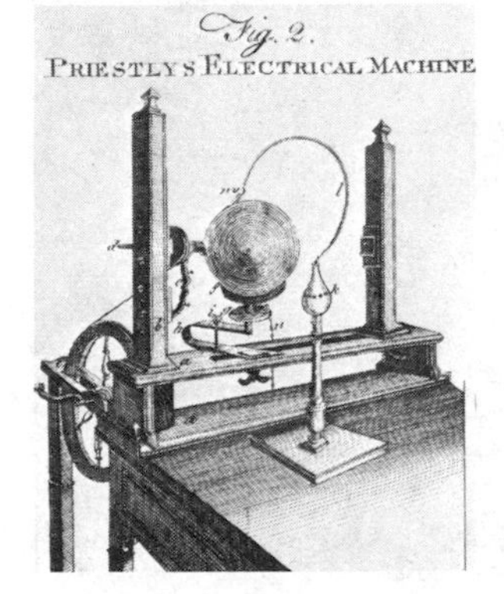


Library of Congress

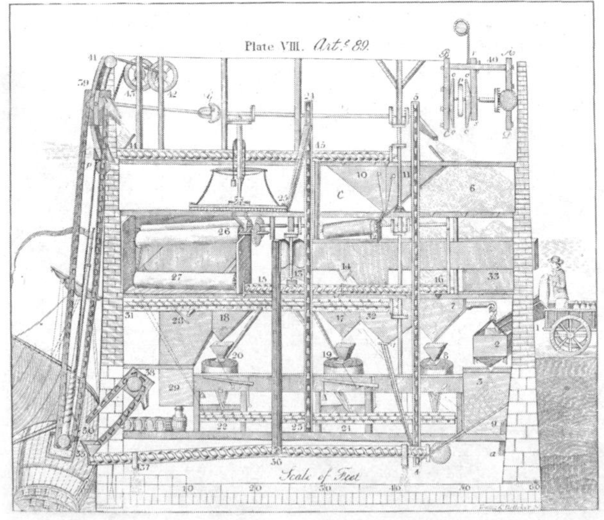


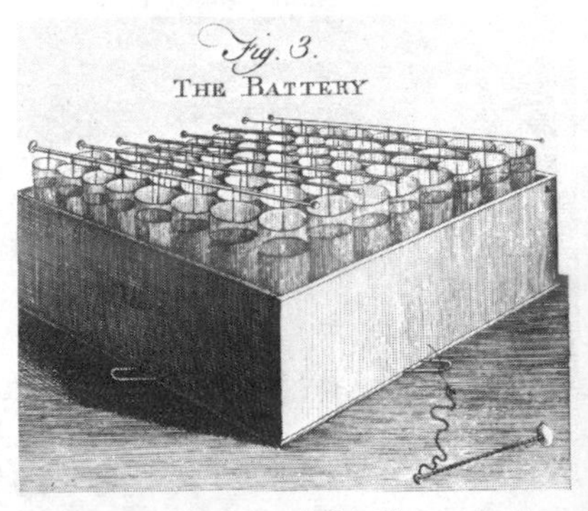


**(Above and above left) Three devices used in Priestley's experiments with electricity**

**(Left) Evans' grist mill produced flour from grain in a continuous process requiring only one laborer**

Library of Congress

**A machine dredge in operation, 1775**

# Technology

A general attitude of innovation and self-confidence was brought about by independence and precipitated a tremendous surge in American technology. To encourage this trend Congress passed a Federal Patent Law in 1790 to protect inventors. One of the first patents granted under this law was to Oliver Evans for his automatic grist mill. Evans, a prodigious inventor, had previously improved the design of the steam engine. The American inventor of the steamboat, John Fitch, used a small steam engine to propel a system of oars in his early models.

Library of Congress

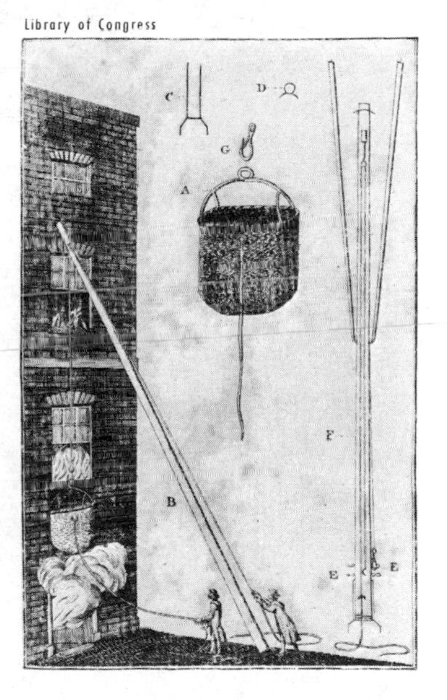

**(Right) A fire-fighting rescue device, 1775; (below) Fitch's steamboat in which he took some Constitutional Congress delegates up the Delaware River**

Library of Congress

New York Public Library

Harvard Theater Collection

(Above) The Chestnut Street Theater; (left) scene from the 1790 production of "The Contrast"

# Expressions of Independence

In an attempt to be free of British influence in any form, the presentation of theatrical performances was prohibited in the early postwar years. However, the demand for dramatic entertainment increased, and a few short-lived companies were founded in New York and Philadelphia. In 1787 the first American play, "The Contrast," by Royall Tyler, was staged in New York. William Dunlap was inspired to give up his painting career and organize a theater in New York to produce his own plays. Thomas Wignell established the Old American Company at the Chestnut Street Theater in 1794, presenting primarily foreign dramatic road companies.

The White House Collection

Detail from the 1778 drawing, "The Apotheosis of Franklin," by Fragonard, which demonstrates the esteem with which Franklin was regarded. At the time of his death in 1790, he was honored as the most enlightened man of his time and his influence had been felt in almost all aspects of the developing American culture

The New-York Journal, and Daily Patriotic Register.

NUMB. 21, of VOL. XLII ] SATURDAY, January 26, 1788. [Total NUMB. 2189.

HERE TRUTH UNLICENS'D REIGNS; AND DARES ACCOST—E'EN KINGS THEMSELVES, OR RULERS OF THE FREE. Thompson's Liberty

NEW-YORK: Printed and Published by THOMAS GREENLEAF, at the PRINTING-OFFICE, NO. 25, WATER-STREET.

Library of Congress

The number of newspapers, gazettes, and magazines increased during this period. New York and Philadelphia each had a daily paper serving the mercantile industry in 1785, and by the end of the century, political papers in the cities were also issued daily. During Washington's second term, the press became highly partisan and remained so thereafter

Library of Congress

Pennsylvania Historical Society

The postwar period saw a creative outpouring that had more enthusiasm than quality. But it indicated a desire for a new culture to complement the new political union. Francis Hopkinson (right) was not only a politician, but he also wrote patriotic poems and composed music. The "American Experiment" was a subject of great curiosity to Europeans. William Winterbotham (above) wrote about America without ever leaving England, and visitors from many countries soon were publishing their "True accounts based on a recent visit . . ."

Library of Congress

FRIDAY, 13th FEBRUARY, 1789. THE NUMB. CXVII.

FEDERAL GAZETTE,

And PHILADELPHIA EVENING POST.

*Whatever measures have a tendency to dissolve the union, or contribute to violate or lessen the sovereign authority, ought to be considered as hostile to the liberties and independence of America.* Gen. *Washington's* Circ. Let

TO BE HAD,
Ready made, for the very moderate price of ONE DOLLAR each, at
JOSEPH COOKE'S,
GOLD-SMITH, JEWELER & HAIR-WORKER,
In Second-street, between Market and Chesnut streets,
COMPLEAT
Counting House or Watch

The Eastern Shore line of
POST-COACHES

*To the Honourable the Representatives of Pennsylvania, in General Assembly.*
*(Continued from last evening's Gazette.)*

" 2WHEN any trustee shall remove far from the city of Philadelphia, reside beyond sea, "or die, the remaining trustees, with all convenient "speed, shall elect another residing in or near the city." This part was afterwards explained and inserted in their charter, so as to limit the residence of every trustee to the (then) province, and a distance not more than five miles from the city; which shews that the semi-

Dartmouth College

**Dartmouth College in 1793**

Hampden-Sydney College

**Samuel S. Smith, head of Hampden-Sydney College when it was begun by the Presbyterians in 1776; he was later president of Princeton**

Old Print Shop, New York

**Transylvania, the first college in Kentucky, 1780**

# Colleges in the New Nation

During the immediate postwar period, it was believed that to strengthen national unity Americans should be educated in their own country. This stimulated the creation of many new colleges, particularly in the South. Religious groups were still the primary sponsors. In New England, Dartmouth College grew most rapidly and by the 1790s was second only to Harvard in the number of degrees awarded. In 1795 George Washington called for a national academy to train military officers. West Point, a military fortress during the war, was the site chosen.

New York Public Library

**(Above) Harvard College, which elected the first layman to the Board of Overseers in 1792; (below) West Point in the 1780s, proposed site for the national military academy**

Library of Congress

# 1792

95.

## James Madison: Freedom, Power, and the Stability of Governments

*Madison once said that "every step in writing the Constitution was a contest between power and liberty." As the proponent of a strong Constitution in 1787, he had helped to establish the government that he felt would best protect the rights of the people. As a defender of the new government, he wrote the following essay, printed on January 19, 1792, in the* National Gazette, *on the nature of charter government.*

Source: *National Gazette,* January 19, 1792: "Charters."

In Europe, charters of liberty have been granted by power. America has set the example and France has followed it, of charters of power granted by liberty. This revolution in the practice of the world may, with an honest praise, be pronounced the most triumphant epoch of its history, and the most consoling presage of its happiness. We look back already with astonishment at the daring outrages committed by despotism on the reason and rights of man; we look forward with joy to the period when it shall be despoiled of all its usurpations, and bound forever in the chains with which it had loaded its miserable victims.

In proportion to the value of this revolution; in proportion to the importance of instruments, every word of which decides a question between power and liberty; in proportion to the solemnity of acts proclaiming the will and authenticated by the seal of the people, the only earthly source of authority ought to be the vigilance with which they are guarded by every citizen in private life, and the circumspection with which they are executed by every citizen in public trust.

As compacts, charters of government are superior in obligation to all others because they give effect to all others. As trusts, none can be more sacred because they are bound on the conscience by the religious sanctions of an oath. As metes and bounds of government, they transcend all other landmarks because every public usurpation is an encroachment on the private right, not of one but of all.

The citizens of the United States have peculiar motives to support the energy of their constitutional charters.

Having originated the experiment, their merit will be estimated by its success.

The complicated form of their political system arising from the partition of government between the states and the Union, and from the separations and subdivisions of the several departments in each, requires a more than common reverence for authority which is to preserve order through the whole.

Being republicans, they must be anxious to establish the efficacy of popular charters in defending liberty against power and power against licentiousness, and in keeping every portion of power within its proper limits, by this means discomfiting the partisans of antirepublican contrivances for the purpose.

All power has been traced up to opinion. The stability of all governments and security of all rights may be traced to the same source. The most arbitrary government is controlled where the public opinion is fixed. The despot of Constantinople dares not lay a new tax because every slave thinks he ought not. The most systematic governments are turned by the slightest impulse from their regular path when the public opinion no longer holds them in it. We see at this moment the *executive* magistrate of Great Britain exercising, under the authority of the representatives of the *people*, a *legislative* power over the West India commerce.

How devoutly is it to be wished, then, that the public opinion of the United States should be enlightened; that it should attach itself to their governments as delineated in the great charters, derived not from the usurped power of kings but from the legitimate authority of the people; and that it should guarantee, with a holy zeal, these political scriptures from every attempt to add to or diminish from them. Liberty and order will never be perfectly safe until a trespass on the constitutional provisions for either shall be felt with the same keenness that resents an invasion of the dearest rights, until every citizen shall be an Argus to espy, and an Aegeon to avenge, the unhallowed deed.

96.

## James Madison: Political Parties

*James Madison had expressed his concern for the danger of factions in* Federalist, *Number 10. By the 1790s, irreconcilable differences had developed between the Jeffersonians and the Hamiltonians, convincing Madison that parties would be an inevitable part of American political life. Actual political parties were not in existence until the end of the eighteenth century, when Madison himself became a staunch defender of Jefferson's ideas and helped organize the Republican Party. On January 23, 1792, Madison published the following short essay in the* National Gazette.

Source: *National Gazette*, January 23, 1792: "Parties."

In every political society, parties are unavoidable. A difference of interests, real or supposed, is the most natural and fruitful source of them. The great object should be to combat the evil: (1) by establishing a political equality among all; (2) by withholding *unnecessary* opportunities from a few to increase the inequality of property by an immoderate, and especially an unmerited, accumulation of riches; (3) by the silent operation of laws, which, without violating the rights of property, reduce extreme wealth toward a state of mediocrity and raise extreme indigence toward a state of comfort; (4) by abstaining from measures which operate differently on different interests, and particularly such as favor one interest at the expense of another; (5) by making one party a check on the other, so far as the existence of parties cannot be prevented nor their views accommodated. If this is not the language of reason, it is that of republicanism.

In all political societies, different interests and parties arise out of the nature of things, and the great art of politicians lies in making them checks and balances to each other. Let us then increase these natural distinctions by favoring an inequality of property; and let us add to them artificial distinctions, by establishing kings and nobles and plebeians. We shall then have the more checks to oppose to each other; we shall then have the more scales and the more weights to perfect and maintain the equilibrium. This is as little the voice of reason as it is that of republicanism.

From the expediency, in politics, of making natural parties mutual checks on each other, to infer the propriety of creating artificial parties in order to form them into mutual checks is not less absurd than it would be in ethics to say that new vices ought to be promoted where they would counteract each other, because this use may be made of existing vices.

97.

# John Laurance and James Madison: General Welfare and the Limits of Government Authority

*New England and Canadian fishermen shared fishing grounds along the Atlantic coast, and thus were in direct competition. A tariff on imported salt, a necessary commodity, particularly for the cod fisheries, had been levied by the American government, thereby giving an economic advantage to Canadian fishermen. In order to rectify this economic disadvantage, Congress proposed a "bounty" that actually was a rebate for the duty paid on salt by the fisheries. Reprinted in part below is the text of a debate in the House of Representatives in February 1792, between John Laurance of New York and James Madison of Virginia. The debate, which centered around the "general welfare" clause of the Constitution, is one of the earliest attempts to clarify the constitutional powers of Congress.*

Source: *Abridgement of the Debates of Congress from 1789 to 1856,* Thomas Hart Benton, ed., Vol. 1, New York, 1857, pp. 360-364.

Mr. Laurance said, from examining the section, he conceived it contemplated no more than what the merchant is entitled to by existing laws. The merchant is now entitled to the drawback; but it is found by experience that the effect has not been to produce that encouragement to the fishermen which was expected; and he presumed the way was perfectly clear to give a new direction to the drawback, and this is all that is aimed at in the bill. He supposed that the clause had no necessary connection with the question which had been started respecting the right of the government to grant bounties; but, since the question has been brought forward, it may be proper to consider it. In discussing the question he inquired, What has Congress already done? Have we not laid extra duties on various articles expressly for the purpose of encouraging various branches of our own manufactures? These duties are bounties to all intents and purposes, and are founded on the idea only of their conducing to the general interest. Similar objections to those now advanced were not made to these duties. They were advocated, some of them, by gentlemen from the southward. He traced the effects of these duties, and showed that they operated fully as indirect bounties.

Mr. L. then adverted particularly to the Constitution, and observed that it contains *general* principles and powers only. These powers depend on *particular* laws for their operation; and on this idea, he contended that the powers of the government must in various circumstances extend to the granting bounties. He instanced, in case of a war with a foreign power, will any gentleman say that the general government has not a power to grant a bounty on arms, ammunition, etc., should the general welfare require it? The general welfare is inseparably connected with any object or pursuit which in its effects adds to the riches of the country. He conceived that the argument was given up by gentlemen in opposition to the bill, when they admit of encouragement to the fishermen in any possible modification of it. He then adverted particularly to the fisheries, stated the number of men employed, the tons of shipping necessary to export the fish taken, and inferred the sound policy of encouraging so important a branch of business.

Gentlemen say that we do not want a navy. Grant it; but can they say that we shall never have a war with any European power? May not the time arrive when the protection to the commerce of this country, derived from this source, may be of the utmost necessity to its existence? Adverting to Mr. Williamson's objection from the unequal operation of bounties, and who had referred to the article of the Constitution which says that taxes shall be equal in all the states, Mr. L. observed that this article in the Constitution could only respect the rates of the duties, and that the *same* duties should be paid in Virginia that are paid in New York — at the northward as at the southward. It surely could not mean that every individual should pay exactly the same sum in every part of the Union. This was a provision that no law could possibly contemplate.

He concluded by a summary recapitulation of his arguments, and saying he hoped the section would be retained.

*Mr. Madison:* In the conflict I feel between my disposition on one hand to afford every constitutional encouragement to the fisheries, and my dislike, on the other, of the consequences apprehended from some clauses of the bill, I should have forborne to enter into this discussion, if I had not found that over and above such arguments as appear to be natural and pertinent to the subject, others have been introduced which are, in my judgment, contrary to the true meaning, and even strike at the characteristic principles of the existing Constitution.

Let me premise, however, to the remarks which I shall briefly offer on the doctrine maintained by these gentlemen, that I make a material distinction, in the present case, between an allowance as a mere commutation and modification of a drawback, and an allowance in the nature of a real and positive bounty. I make a distinction, also, as a subject of fair consideration at least, between a bounty granted under the particular terms in the Constitution, "a power to regulate trade," and one granted under the in-

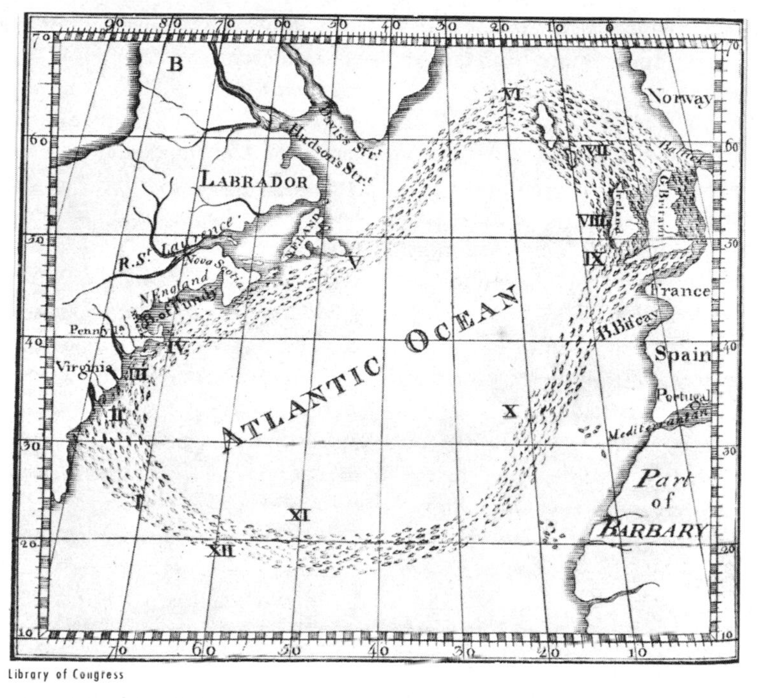


Library of Congress

Map of the Atlantic Ocean, showing the route of the annual passage of herring and the location of major fisheries

definite terms which have been cited as authority on this occasion. I think, however, that the term "bounty" is in every point of view improper as it is here applied, not only because it may be offensive to some, and in the opinion of others carries a dangerous implication, but also because it does not express the true intention of the bill, as avowed and advocated by its patrons themselves. For if, in the allowance, nothing more is proposed than a mere reimbursement of the sum advanced, it is only paying a debt; and when we pay a debt, we ought not to claim the merit of granting a bounty.

It is supposed by some gentlemen that Congress have authority not only to grant bounties in the sense here used, merely as a commutation for drawbacks, but even to grant them under a power by virtue of which they may do anything which they may think conducive to the "general welfare." This, sir, in my mind, raises the important and fundamental question whether the general terms which had been cited are to be considered as a sort of caption or general description of the specified powers, and as having no further meaning, and giving no further power than what is found in that specification; or as an abstract and indefinite delegation of power extending to all cases whatever, to all such, at least, as will admit the application of money, which is giving as much latitude as any government could well desire.

I, sir, have always conceived — I believe those who proposed the Constitution conceived, and it is still more fully known, and more material to observe that those who ratified the Constitution conceived — that this is not an indefinite government, deriving its powers from the general terms prefixed to the specified powers, but a limited government, tied down to the specified powers which explain and define the general terms. The gentlemen who contend for a contrary doctrine are surely not aware of the consequences which flow from it, and which they must either admit or give up their doctrine.

It will follow, in the first place, that if the terms be taken in the broad sense they maintain, the particular powers afterwards so carefully and distinctly enumerated would be without any meaning, and must go for nothing. It would be absurd to say, first, that Congress may do what they please, and then that they may do this or that particular thing. After giving Congress power to raise money and apply it to all purposes which they may pronounce necessary to the general welfare, it would be absurd, to say the least, to superadd a power to raise armies, to provide fleets, etc. In fact, the meaning of the general terms in question must either be sought in the subsequent enumeration which limits and details them, or they convert the government from one limited, as hitherto supposed, to the enumerated powers, into a government without any limits at all.

It is to be recollected that the terms "common defense and general welfare," as here used, are not novel terms first introduced into this Constitution. They are terms familiar in their construction and well known to the people of America. They are repeatedly found in the old Articles of Confederation, where, although they are susceptible of as great latitude as can be given them by the context here, it was never supposed or pretended that they conveyed any such power as is now assigned to them. On the contrary, it was always considered as clear and certain that the old Congress was limited to the enumerated powers, and that the enumeration limited and explained the general terms. I ask the gentlemen themselves whether it ever was supposed or suspected that the old Congress could give away the moneys of the states in bounties, to encourage agriculture, or for any other purpose they pleased? If such a power had been possessed by that body, it would have been much less impotent, or have borne a very different character from that universally ascribed to it.

The novel idea now annexed to these terms, and never before entertained by the friends or enemies of the government, will have a further consequence, which cannot have been taken into the view of the gentlemen. Their construction would not only give Congress the complete legislative power I have stated, it would do more — it would supersede all the restrictions understood at present to lie on their power with respect to the judiciary. It would put it in the power of Congress to establish courts throughout the United States, with cognizance of suits between citizen and citizen, and in all cases whatsoever.

This, sir, seems to be demonstrable; for if the clause in question really authorizes Congress to do whatever they think fit, provided it be for the general welfare, of which they are to judge, and money can be applied to it, Congress must have power to create and support a judiciary establishment, with a jurisdiction extending to all cases favorable, in their opinion, to the general welfare, in the same manner as they have power to pass laws and apply money, providing in any other way for the general welfare.

I shall be reminded, perhaps, that according to the terms of the Constitution, the judicial power is to extend to certain cases only, not to all cases. But this circumstance can have no effect in the argument, it being presupposed by the gentlemen that the specification of certain objects does not limit the import of general terms. Taking these terms as an abstract and indefinite grant of power, they comprise all the objects of legislative regulation, as well such as fall under the judiciary article in the Constitution as those falling immediately under the legislative article; and if the partial enumeration of objects in the legislative article does not, as these gentlemen contend, limit the general power, neither will it be limited by the partial enumeration of objects in the judiciary article.

There are consequences, sir, still more extensive, which, as they follow clearly from the doctrine combated, must either be admitted, or the doctrine must be given up. If Congress can apply money indefinitely to the general welfare, and are the sole and supreme judges of the general welfare, they may take the care of religion into their own hands; they may establish teachers in every state, county, and parish, and pay them out of the public treasury; they may take into their own hands the education of children, establishing in like manner schools throughout the Union; they may undertake the regulation of all roads other than post roads. In short, everything, from the highest object of state legislation down to the most minute object of police, would be thrown under the power of Congress; for every object I have mentioned would admit the application of money, and might be called, if Congress pleased, provisions for the general welfare.

The language held in various discussions of this House is a proof that the doctrine in question was never entertained by this body. Arguments, wherever the subject would permit, have constantly been drawn from the peculiar nature of this government, as limited to certain enumerated powers, instead of extending, like other governments, to all cases not particularly excepted. In a very late instance — I mean the debate on the Representation Bill — it must be remembered that an argument much urged, particularly by a gentleman from Massachusetts, against the ratio of one for 30,000, was that this government was unlike the state governments, which had an indefinite variety of objects within their power; that it had a small number of objects only to attend to, and therefore that a smaller number of representatives would be sufficient to administer it.

Several arguments have been advanced to show that because, in the regulation of trade, indirect and eventual encouragement is given to manufactures, therefore Congress have power to give money in direct bounties, or to grant it in any other way that would answer the same purpose. But surely, sir, there is a great and obvious difference, which it cannot be necessary to enlarge upon. A duty laid on imported implements of husbandry would, in its operation, be an indirect tax on exported produce; but will anyone say that by virtue of a mere power to lay duties on imports, Congress might go directly to the produce or implements of agriculture, or to the articles exported? It is true, duties on exports are expressly prohibited; but if there were no article forbidding them, a power directly to tax exports could never be deduced from a power to tax imports, although such a power might directly and incidentally affect exports.

In short, sir, without going further into the subject, which I should not have here touched on at all but for the reasons already mentioned, I venture to declare it as my opinion that were the power of Congress to be established in the latitude contended for, it would subvert the very foundation and transmute the very nature of the limited government established by the people of America; and what inferences might be drawn, or what consequences ensue from such a step, it is incumbent on us all well to consider.

With respect to the question before the House, for striking out the clause, it is immaterial whether it be struck out, or so amended as to rest on the avowed principle of a commutation for the drawback; but as a clause has been drawn up by my colleague, in order to be substituted, I shall concur in a vote for striking out, reserving to myself a freedom to be governed in my final vote by the modification which may prevail.

98.

## James Madison: The Mutability of Fashion

*In a short essay that appeared in the* National Gazette *on March 20, 1792, James Madison commented on the contrast between the British and American economies. In England, fashion was dictated by the aristocracy. At the whim of a prince or nobleman, an entire industry that was producing an item then in vogue could suddenly become obsolete. The plea of a Birmingham buckle manufacturer to the Prince of Wales came to the attention of Madison. He seized the opportunity to point out the superiority of American self-reliance and the danger to individuals and nations of an economic system that depended, at least in part, on the caprice of one man.*

Source: *Madison Letters,* IV: "Fashion."

A humble address has been lately presented to the Prince of Wales by the buckle manufacturers of Birmingham, Wassal, Wolverhampton, and their environs, stating that the buckle trade gives employment to more than 20,000 persons, numbers of whom, in consequence of the prevailing fashion of shoestrings and slippers, are at present without employ, almost destitute of bread, and exposed to the horrors of want at the most inclement season; that to the manufacturers of buckles and buttons, Birmingham owes its important figure on the map of England; that it is to no purpose to address Fashion herself, she being void of feeling and deaf to argument, but fortunately accustomed to listen to his voice, and to obey his commands. Finally, imploring His Royal Highness to consider the deplorable condition of their trade, which is in danger of being ruined by the mutability of fashion, and to give that direction to the public taste which will insure the lasting gratitude of the petitioners.

Several important reflections are suggested by this address.

1. The most precarious of all occupations which give bread to the industrious are those depending on mere fashion, which generally changes so suddenly, and often so considerably, as to throw whole bodies of people out of employment.

2. Of all occupations those are the least desirable in a free state which produce the most servile dependence of one class of citizens on another class. This dependence must increase as the mutuality of wants is diminished. Where the wants on one side are the absolute necessaries, and on the other are neither absolute necessaries, nor result from the habitual economy of life, but are the mere caprices of fancy, the evil is in its extreme; or if not —

3. The extremity of the evil must be in the case before us, where the absolute necessaries depend on the caprices of fancy, and the caprice of a single fancy directs the fashion of the community. Here the dependence sinks to the lowest point of servility. We see a proof of it in the spirit of the address. Twenty thousand persons are to get or go without their bread as a wanton youth may fancy to wear his shoes with or without straps, or to fasten his straps with strings or with buckles. Can any despotism be more cruel than a situation in which the

existence of thousands depends on one will, and that will on the most slight and fickle of all motives, a mere whim of the imagination?

4. What a contrast is here to the independent situation and manly sentiments of American citizens, who live on their own soil, or whose labor is necessary to its cultivation, or who are occupied in supplying wants which, being founded in solid utility, in comfortable accommodation, or in settled habits, produce a reciprocity of dependence, at once insuring subsistence and inspiring a dignified sense of social rights!

5. The condition of those who receive employment and bread from the precarious source of fashion and superfluity is a lesson to nations as well as to individuals. In proportion as a nation consists of that description of citizens, and depends on external commerce, it is dependent on the consumption and caprice of other nations. If the laws of propriety did not forbid, the manufacturers of Birmingham, Wassal, and Wolverhampton had as real an interest in supplicating the arbiters of fashion in America as the patron they have addressed. The dependence in the case of nations is even greater than among individuals of the same nation; for, besides the mutability of fashion, which is the same in both, the mutability of policy is another source of danger in the former.

---

99.

## James Madison: The Right to Property and Property in Rights

*Madison felt that Hamilton's program was geared to the wealthy in society and did not reflect the intent of the Constitution. Fearing that the farmers and workers would lose faith in a government based on oligarchic principles, and believing that Hamilton's conception of property was too narrow, Madison wrote a short essay on the subject that has been termed "a dramatic piece of political journalism." In it Madison drew on the Lockeian thesis that government is "for the mutual preservation of [men's] lives, liberties, and estates, which I call by the general name, property." He distinguished, as Locke had done, between "rights to property" and "property in rights"; the latter pertained to freedom of thought, religious practice, and other intangible freedoms. According to Madison, governments should preserve and protect both kinds of property, not just one of them. The essay appeared in the* National Gazette *on March 27, 1792.*

Source: *Madison Letters,* IV: "Property."

This term [Property], in its particular application, means "that dominion which one man claims and exercises over the external things of the world, in exclusion of every other individual."

In its larger and juster meaning, it embraces everything to which a man may attach a value and have a right; and which leaves to everyone else the like advantage.

In the former sense, a man's land, or merchandise, or money is called his property.

In the latter sense, a man has property in his opinions and the free communication of them.

He has a property of peculiar value in his religious opinions, and in the profession and practice dictated by them.

He has property very dear to him in the safety and liberty of his person.

He has an equal property in the free use of his faculties and free choice of the objects on which to employ them.

In a word, as a man is said to have a right to his property, he may be equally said to have a property in his rights.

Where an excess of power prevails, property of no sort is duly respected. No man is safe in his opinions, his person, his faculties, or his possessions.

Where there is an excess of liberty, the effect is the same, though from an opposite cause.

Government is instituted to protect property of every sort, as well that which lies in the various rights of individuals, as that which the term particularly expresses. This being the end of government, that alone is a *just* government which *impartially* secures to every man whatever is his *own.*

According to this standard of merit, the praise of affording a just security to property should be sparingly bestowed on a government which, however scrupulously guarding the possessions of individuals, does not protect them in the enjoyment and communication of their opinions, in which they have an equal, and, in the estimation of some, a more valuable property.

More sparingly should this praise be allowed to a government where a man's religious rights are violated by penalties, or fettered by tests, or taxed by a hierarchy.

Conscience is the most sacred of all property; other property depending in part on positive law, the exercise of that being a natural and unalienable right. To guard a man's house as his castle, to pay public and enforce private debts with the most exact faith can give no title to invade a man's conscience, which is more sacred than his castle, or to withhold from it that debt of protection for which the public faith is pledged by the very nature and original conditions of the social pact.

That is not a just government, nor is property secure under it, where the property which a man has in his personal safety and personal liberty is violated by arbitrary seizures of one class of citizens for the service of the rest. A magistrate issuing warrants to a press gang would be in his proper functions in Turkey or Hindustan, under appellations proverbial of the most complete despotism.

That is not a just government, nor is property secure under it, where arbitrary restrictions, exemptions, and monopolies deny to part of its citizens that free use of their faculties and free choice of their occupations which not only constitute their property in the general sense of the word but are the means of acquiring property strictly so called. What must be the spirit of legislation where a manufacturer of linen cloth is forbidden to bury his own child in a linen shroud in order to favor his neighbor who manufactures woolen cloth; where the manufacturer and wearer of woolen cloth are again forbidden the economical use of buttons of that material in favor of the manufacturer of buttons of other materials!

A just security to property is not afforded by that government under which unequal taxes oppress one species of property and reward another species; where arbitrary taxes invade the domestic sanctuaries of the rich and excessive taxes grind the faces of the poor; where the keenness and competitions of want are deemed an insufficient spur to labor, and taxes are again applied by an unfeeling policy as another spur; in violation of that sacred property which heaven, in decreeing man to earn his bread by the sweat of his brow, kindly reserved to him in the small repose that could be spared from the supply of his necessities.

If there be a government, then, which

prides itself in maintaining the inviolability of property; which provides that none shall be taken *directly*, even for public use, without indemnification to the owner, and yet *directly* violates the property which individuals have in their opinions, their religion, their passions, and their faculties; nay, more, which *indirectly* violates their property in their actual possessions, in the labor that acquires their daily subsistence, and in the hallowed remnant of time which ought to relieve their fatigues and soothe their cares — the inference will have been anticipated that such a government is not a pattern for the United States.

If the United States mean to obtain or deserve the full praise due to wise and just governments, they will equally respect the rights of property and the property in rights; they will rival the government that most sacredly guards the former; and by repelling its example in violating the latter, will make themselves a pattern to that and all other governments.

100.

## Philip Freneau: Rules for Changing a Republic into a Monarchy

*Those who had opposed the Constitution thought their fears justified by the conduct of the government that began to function in 1789. Under the aggressive leadership of Alexander Hamilton, the secretary of the treasury, economic measures were taken that favored the few, while an effective party machine was organized and the army strengthened in such a way as to suggest an intent to control rather than to represent the many. The whole tone of Washington's administration was aristocratic, favoring as it did the educated, the wealthy, the clergy, and the press, who were fearful of "mob-rule" and preferred to see what Hamilton called "gentlemen of principle and property" in command. As Hamilton had at his service a newspaper — John Fenno's* Gazette of the United States *— to support his policies, his opponents, led by Jefferson and Madison, decided to establish a rival newspaper, the* National Gazette. *Philip Freneau, an experienced journalist of known democratic leanings, was chosen to edit the paper. The editorial, reprinted here, is typical of those in which Freneau criticized the Hamiltonian program from 1791 to 1793.*

Source: *American Museum*, July 1792: "Rules for Changing a Limited Republican Government into an Unlimited Hereditary One."

*Rules for changing a limited republican government into an unlimited hereditary one.*

1. It being necessary, in order to effect the change, to get rid of constitutional shackles and popular prejudices, all possible means and occasions are to be used for both these purposes.

2. Nothing being more likely to prepare the vulgar mind for aristocratical ranks and hereditary powers than *titles*, endeavor in the offset of the government to confer these

on its most dignified officers. If the principal magistrate should happen to be particularly venerable in the eyes of the people, take advantage of that fortunate circumstance in setting the example.

3. Should the attempt fail through his republican aversion to it, or from the danger of alarming the people, do not abandon the enterprise altogether, but lay up the proposition in record. Time may gain it respect, and it will be there always ready, cut and dried, for any favorable conjuncture that may offer.

4. In drawing all bills, resolutions, and reports, keep constantly in view that the limitations in the Constitution are ultimately to be explained away. Precedents and phrases may thus be shuffled in, without being adverted to by candid or weak people, of which good use may afterward be made.

5. As the novelty and bustle of inaugurating the government will for some time keep the public mind in a heedless and unsettled state, let the press during this period be busy in propagating the doctrines of monarchy and aristocracy. For this purpose it will be particularly useful to confound a mobbish democracy with a representative republic, that by exhibiting all the turbulent examples and enormities of the former, an odium may be thrown on the character of the latter. Review all the civil contests, convulsions, factions, broils, squabbles, bickerings, black eyes, and bloody noses of ancient, middle, and modern ages; caricature them into the most frightful forms and colors that can be imagined; and unfold one scene of the horrible tragedy after another till the people be made, if possible, to tremble at their own shadows. Let the discourses on Davila then contrast with these pictures of terror the quiet of hereditary succession, the reverence claimed by birth and nobility, and the fascinating influence of stars, and ribands, and garters, cautiously suppressing all the bloody tragedies and unceasing oppressions which form the history of this species of government. No pains should be spared in this part of the undertaking, for the greatest will be wanted, it being extremely difficult, especially when a people have been taught to reason and feel their rights, to convince them that a king, who is always an enemy to the people, and a nobility, who are perhaps still more so, will take better care of the people than the people will take of themselves.

6. But the grand nostrum will be a public debt, provided enough of it can be got and it be medicated with the proper ingredients. If by good fortune a debt be ready at hand, the most is to be made of it. Stretch it and swell it to the utmost the items will bear. Allow as many extra claims as decency will permit. Assume all the debts of your neighbors — in a word, get as much debt as can be raked and scraped together, and when you have got all you can, "advertise" for more, and have the debt made *as big as possible.* This object being accomplished, the next will be to make it *as perpetual as possible;* and the next to that, to get it into *as few hands as possible.* The more effectually to bring this about, modify the debt, complicate it, divide it, subdivide it, subtract it, postpone it, let there be one-third of two-thirds, and two-thirds of one-third, and two-thirds of two-thirds; let there be 3 percents, and 4 percents, and 6 percents, and present 6 percents, and future 6 percents. To be brief, let the whole be such a mystery that a *few only* can understand it; and let all possible opportunities and informations fall in the way of *these few,* to clinch their advantages over the many.

7. It must not be forgotten that the members of the legislative body are to have a deep stake in the game. This is an essential point, and happily is attended with no difficulty. A sufficient number, properly disposed, can alternately legislate and speculate, and speculate and legislate, and buy

and sell, and sell and buy, until a due portion of the property of their constituents has passed into their hands to give them an interest against their constituents, and to ensure the part they are to act. All this, however, must be carried on under cover of the closest secrecy; and it is particularly lucky that dealings in paper admit of more secrecy than any other. Should a discovery take place, the whole plan may be blown up.

8. The ways in which a great debt, so constituted and applied, will contribute to the ultimate end in view are both numerous and obvious. (1) The favorite few, thus possessed of it, whether within or without the government, will feel the staunchest fealty to it, and will go through thick and thin to support it in all its oppressions and usurpations. (2) Their money will give them consequence and influence, even among those who have been tricked out of it. (3) They will be the readiest materials that can be found for a hereditary aristocratic order, whenever matters are ripe for one. (4) A great debt will require great taxes; great taxes, many taxgatherers and other officers; and all officers are auxiliaries of power. (5) Heavy taxes may produce discontents; these may threaten resistance; and in proportion to this danger will be the pretense for a standing army to repel it. (6) A standing army, in its turn, will increase the moral force of the government by means of its appointments, and give it physical force by means of the sword, thus doubly forwarding the main object.

9. The management of a great funded debt and an extensive system of taxes will afford a plea, not to be neglected, for establishing a great incorporated bank. The use of such a machine is well understood. If the Constitution, according to its fair meaning, should not authorize it, so much the better. Push it through by a forced meaning and you will get in the bargain an admirable precedent for future misconstructions.

In fashioning the bank, remember that it is to be made particularly instrumental in enriching and aggrandizing the elect few, who are to be called in due season to the honors and felicities of the kingdom preparing for them, and who are the pillars that must support it. It will be easy to throw the benefit entirely into their hands, and to make it a solid addition of 50, or 60, or 70 percent to their former capitals of 800 percent, or 900 percent, without costing them a shilling; while it will be so difficult to explain to the people that this gain of the few is at the cost of the many, that the contrary may be boldly and safely pretended. The bank will be pregnant with other important advantages. It will admit the same men to be, at the same time, members of the bank and members of the government. The two institutions will thus be soldered together, and each made the stronger. Money will be put under the direction of the government, and government under the direction of money. To crown the whole, the bank will have a proper interest in swelling and perpetuating the public debt and public taxes, with all the blessings of both, because its agency and its profits will be extended in exact proportion.

10. "Divide and govern" is a maxim consecrated by the experience of ages, and should be as familiar in its use to every politician as the knife he carries in his pocket. In the work here to be executed, the best effects may be produced by this maxim, and with peculiar facility. An extensive republic made up of lesser republics necessarily contains various sorts of people, distinguished by local and other interests and prejudices. Let the whole group be well examined in all its parts and relations, geographical and political, metaphysical and metaphorical; let there be first a northern and a southern section, by a line running east and west, and then an eastern and western section, by a line running north and south. By a suitable nomenclature, the landholders cultivating different articles can be discriminated from

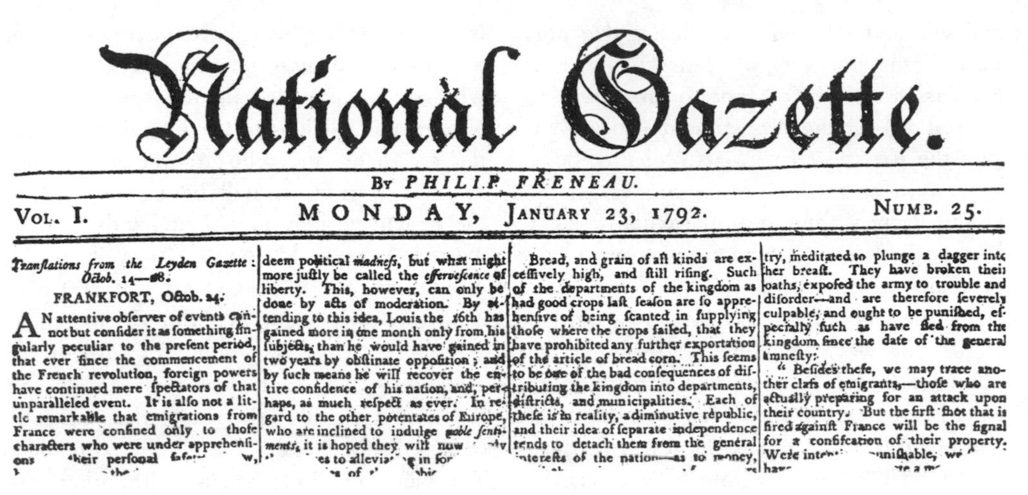

National Gazette.

By PHILIP FRENEAU.

VOL. I. MONDAY, JANUARY 23, 1792. NUMB. 25.

*Translations from the Leyden Gazette: Octob. 14—18.*

FRANKFORT, Octob. 24.

AN attentive obſerver of events cannot but conſider it as ſomething ſingularly peculiar to the preſent period, that ever ſince the commencement of the French revolution, foreign powers have continued mere ſpectators of that unparalleled event. It is alſo not a little remarkable that emigrations from France were confined only to thoſe characters who were under apprehenſions [of] their perſonal ſafe[ty] ... w,

deem political *madneſs*, but what might more juſtly be called the *efferveſcence* of liberty. This, however, can only be done by acts of moderation. By attending to this idea, Louis the 16th has gained more in one month only from his ſubjects, than he would have gained in two years by obſtinate oppoſition; and by ſuch means he will recover the entire confidence of his nation, and, perhaps, as much reſpect as ever. In regard to the other potentates of Europe, who are inclined to indulge *noble ſentiments*, it is hoped they will now ... es to allevia[t]e in for...

Bread, and grain of all kinds are exceſſively high, and ſtill riſing. Such of the departments of the kingdom as had good crops laſt ſeaſon are ſo apprehenſive of being ſcanted in ſupplying thoſe where the crops failed, that they have prohibited any further exportation of the article of bread corn. This ſeems to be one of the bad conſequences of diſtributing the kingdom into departments, diſtricts, and municipalities. Each of theſe is in reality, a diminutive republic, and their idea of ſeparate independence tends to detach them from the general intereſts of the nation—as to money,

try, meditated to plunge a dagger into her breaſt. They have broken their oaths, expoſed the army to trouble and diſorder—and are therefore ſeverely culpable, and ought to be puniſhed, eſpecially ſuch as have fled from the kingdom ſince the date of the general amneſty:

" Beſides theſe, we may trace another claſs of emigrants,—thoſe who are actually preparing for an attack upon their country. But the firſt ſhot that is fired againſt France will be the ſignal for a confiſcation of their property. Were inte[ntions] ... puniſhable, we ...

Banner of "National Gazette," the newspaper edited by Philip Freneau

one another, all from the class of merchants, and both from that of manufacturers.

One of the subordinate republics may be represented as a commercial state, another as a navigation state, another as a manufacturing state, others as agricultural states; and although the great body of the people in each be really agricultural, and the other characters be more or less common to all, still it will be politic to take advantage of such an arrangement. Should the members of the great republic be of different sizes, and subject to little jealousies on that account, another important division will be ready formed to your hand. Add again the divisions that may be carved out of personal interests, political opinions, and local parties. With so convenient an assortment of votes, especially with the help of the *marked ones,* a majority may be packed for any question with as much ease as the odd trick by an adroit gamester, and any measure whatever be carried or defeated, as the great revolution to be brought about may require.

It is only necessary, therefore, to recommend that full use be made of the resource; and to remark that, besides the direct benefit to be drawn from these artificial divisions, they will tend to smother the true and natural one, existing in all societies, between the few who are always impatient of political equality and the many who can never rise above it; between those who are to mount to the prerogatives and those who are to be saddled with the burdens of the hereditary government to be introduced — in one word, between the general mass of the people, attached to their republican government and republican interests, and the chosen band devoted to monarchy and Mammon. It is of infinite importance that this distinction should be kept out of sight. The success of the project absolutely requires it.

11. As soon as sufficient progress in the intended change shall have been made, and the public mind duly prepared according to the rules already laid down, it will be proper to venture on another and a bolder step toward a removal of the constitutional landmarks. Here the aid of the former encroachments and all the other precedents and way-paving maneuvers will be called in of course. But, in order to render success the more certain, it will be of special moment to give the most plausible and popular name that can be found to the power that is to be usurped. It may be called, for example, a power for the common safety or the public good, or, "the general welfare." If the people should not be too much enlightened, the name will have a most im-

posing effect. It will escape attention that it means, in fact, the same thing with a power to do anything the government pleases "in all cases whatsoever." To oppose the power may consequently seem to the ignorant, and be called by the artful, opposing the "general welfare," and may be cried down under that deception.

As the people, however, may not run so readily into the snare as might be wished, it will be prudent to bait it well with some specious popular interest, such as the encouragement of manufactures, or even of agriculture, taking due care not even to mention any unpopular object to which the power is equally applicable, such as religion, etc. By this contrivance, particular classes of people may possibly be taken in who will be a valuable reinforcement.

With respect to the patronage of agriculture there is not indeed much to be expected from it. It will be too quickly seen through by the owners and tillers of the soil, that to tax them with one hand and pay back a part only with the other is a losing game on their side. From the power over manufactures more is to be hoped. It will not be so easily perceived that the premium bestowed may not be equal to the circuitous tax on consumption which pays it. There are particular reasons, too, for pushing the experiment on this class of citizens.

(1) As they live in towns and can act together, it is of vast consequence to gain them over to the interest of monarchy. (2) If the power over them be once established, the government can grant favors or monopolies, as it pleases; can raise or depress this or that place, as it pleases; can gratify this or that individual, as it pleases; in a word, by creating a dependence in so numerous and important a class of citizens, it will increase its own independence of every class and be more free to pursue the grand object in contemplation. (3) The expense of this operation will not in the end cost the government a shilling, for the moment any branch of manufacture has been brought to a state of tolerable maturity the exciseman will be ready with his constable and his search warrant to demand a reimbursement, and as much more as can be squeezed out of the article. All this, it is to be remembered, supposes that the manufacturers will be weak enough to be cheated, in some respects, out of their own interests, and wicked enough, in others, to betray those of their fellow citizens; a supposition that, if known, would totally mar the experiment. Great care, therefore, must be taken to prevent it from leaking out.

12. The expediency of seizing every occasion of external danger for augmenting and perpetuating the standing military force is too obvious to escape. So important is this matter that for any loss or disaster whatever attending the national arms, there will be ample consolation and compensation in the opportunity for enlarging the establishment. A military defeat will become a political victory, and the loss of a little vulgar blood contribute to ennoble that which flows in the veins of our future dukes and marquesses.

13. The same prudence will improve the opportunity afforded by an increase of military expenditures for perpetuating the taxes required for them. If the inconsistency and absurdity of establishing a *perpetual* tax for a temporary service should produce any difficulty in the business, Rule 10 must be resorted to. Throw in as many extraneous motives as will make up a majority, and the thing is effected in an instant. What was before evil will become good as easily as black could be made white by the same magical operation.

14. Throughout this great undertaking it will be wise to have some particular model constantly in view. The work can then be carried on more systematically, and every measure be fortified, in the progress, by apt illustrations and authorities. Should there exist a particular monarchy against which there are fewer prejudices than against any

other; should it contain a mixture of the representative principle so as to present on one side the semblance of a republican aspect; should it, moreover, have a great, funded, complicated, irredeemable debt, with all the apparatus and appurtenances of excises, banks, etc., upon that a steady eye is to be kept. In all cases it will assist, and in most its statute book will furnish a precise pattern by which there may be cut out any moneyed or monarchical project that may be wanted.

15. As it is not to be expected that the change of a republic into a monarchy, with the rapidity desired, can be carried through without occasional suspicions and alarms, it will be necessary to be prepared for such events. The best general rule on the subject is to be taken from the example of crying "Stop thief" first — neither lungs nor pens must be spared in charging every man who whispers, or even thinks, that the revolution on foot is meditated, with being himself an enemy to the established government and meaning to overturn it. Let the charge be reiterated and reverberated till at last such confusion and uncertainty be produced that the people, being not able to find out where the truth lies, withdraw their attention from the contest.

Many other rules of great wisdom and efficacy might be added; but it is conceived that the above will be abundantly enough for the purpose. This will certainly be the case if the people can be either kept asleep so as not to discover, or be thrown into artificial divisions so as not to resist, what is silently going forward. Should it be found impossible, however, to prevent the people from awaking and uniting; should all artificial distinctions give way to the natural division between the lordly minded few and the well-disposed many; should all who have common interest make a common cause and show an inflexible attachment to republicanism in opposition to a government of monarchy and of money, why then. . . . .

---

101.

## Joel Barlow: Equality in America

*Joel Barlow spent a number of years in Europe, where he became enamored with the democratic and religious thought of many European contemporaries. In 1792, he departed from his usual poetic form to write a forceful political essay, in which he presented the doctrine of governmental responsibility. Considered to be heretical by more conservative standards,* Advice to the Privileged Orders *was proscribed by the British government.*

Source: *Advice to the Privileged Orders in the Several States of Europe,* London, 1792-1795 [Ithaca, N. Y., 1956].

In the United States of America, the science of liberty is universally understood, felt and practised as much by the simple as the wise, the weak as the strong. Their deep-rooted and inveterate habit of thinking is that all men are equal in their rights, that it is impossible to make them otherwise; and this being their undisturbed belief, they have no conception how any man in his senses can entertain any other. This point once settled, everything is settled. Many operations, which in Europe have been considered as incredible tales or dangerous experiments, are but the infallible consequences of this great principle.

The first of these operations is the business of election, which with that people is carried on with as much gravity as their daily labor. There is no jealousy on the occasion, nothing lucrative in office; any man in society may attain to any place in the government and may exercise its functions. They believe that there is nothing more difficult in the management of the affairs of a nation than the affairs of a family; that it only requires more hands. They believe that it is the juggle of keeping up impositions to blind the eyes of the vulgar that constitutes the intricacy of state. Banish the mysticism of inequality and you banish almost all the evils attendant on human nature.

The people being habituated to the election of all kinds of officers, the magnitude of the office makes no difficulty in the case. The President of the United States, who has more power while in office than some of the kings of Europe, is chosen with as little commotion as a churchwarden. There is a public service to be performed, and the people say who shall do it. The servant feels honored with the confidence reposed in him, and generally expresses his gratitude by a faithful performance.

Another of these operations is making every citizen a soldier, and every soldier a citizen; not only permitting every man to arm but obliging him to arm. This fact, told in Europe previous to the French Revolution, would have gained little credit; or at least it would have been regarded as a mark of an uncivilized people, extremely dangerous to a well-ordered society. Men who build systems on an inversion of nature are obliged to invert everything that is to make part of that system. It is because the people are civilized that they are with safety armed. It is an effect of their conscious dignity, as citizens enjoying equal rights, that they wish not to invade the rights of others. The danger (where there is any) from armed citizens, is only to the government, not to the society; and as long as they have nothing to revenge in the government (which they cannot have while it is in their own hands) there are many advantages in their being accustomed to the use of arms, and no possible disadvantage.

Power, habitually in the hands of a whole community, loses all the ordinary associated ideas of power. The exercise of power is a relative term; it supposes an opposition — something to operate upon. We perceive no exertion of power in the motion of the planetary system, but a very strong one in the movement of a whirlwind; it is because we see obstructions to the latter, but none to the former. Where the government is *not* in the hands of the people, there you find opposition, you perceive two contending interests, and get an idea of the exercise of power, and whether this power be in the hands of the government or of the people, or whether it change from side to side, it is always to be dreaded. But the word "people" in America has a different meaning from what it has in Europe. It there means the whole community, and comprehends every human creature; here it means something else, more difficult to define.

Another consequence of the habitual idea of equality is the facility of changing the structure of their government whenever and as often as the society shall think there is anything in it to amend. As Mr. Burke has written no "reflections on the revolution" in America, the people there have never yet been told that they had no right "to frame a government for themselves"; they have, therefore, done much of this business without ever affixing to it the idea of "sacrilege" or "usurpation," or any other term of rant to be found in that gentleman's vocabulary.

Within a few years the fifteen states have not only framed each its own state constitution, and two successive federal constitutions, but since the settlement of the present general government in the year 1789, three of the states — Pennsylvania, South Carolina, and Georgia — have totally new modeled their own. And all this is done without the least confusion, the operation being scarcely known beyond the limits of the state where it is performed. Thus they are in the habit of "choosing their own governors," of "cashiering them for misconduct," of "framing a government for themselves," and all those abominable things, the mere naming of which, in Mr. Burke's opinion, has polluted the pulpit. . . .

Another consequence of a settled belief in the equality of rights is that under this belief there is no danger from anarchy. This word has likewise acquired a different meaning in America from what we read of it in books. In Europe it means confusion, attended with mobs and carnage, where the innocent perish with the guilty. But it is very different where a country is used to a representative government, though it should have an interval of no government at all. Where the people at large feel and know that they can do everything by themselves personally, they really do nothing by themselves personally. In the heat of the American Revolution, when the people in some states were for a long time without the least shadow of law or government, they always acted by committees and representation. This they must call anarchy, for they know no other.

These are materials for the formation of governments, which need not be dreaded, though disjointed and laid asunder to make some repairs. They are deep-rooted habits of thinking, which almost change the moral nature of man; they are principles as much unknown to the ancient republics as to the modern monarchies of Europe. . . .

Only admit the original, unalterable truth: that all men are equal in their rights, and the foundation of everything is laid — to build the superstructure requires no effort but that of natural deduction. The first necessary deduction will be that the people will form an equal representative government in which it will be impossible for orders or privileges to exist for a moment; and consequently the first materials for standing armies will be converted into peaceable members of the state. Another deduction follows — that the people will be universally armed. They will assume those weapons for security which the art of war has invented for destruction. You will then have removed the necessity of a standing army by the organization of the legislature, and the possibility of it by the arrangement of the militia; for it is as impossible for an armed soldiery to exist in an armed nation as for a nobility to exist under an equal government.

It is curious to remark how ill we reason on human nature, from being accustomed to view it under the disguise which the unequal governments of the world have always imposed upon it. During the American war, and especially toward its close, General Washington might be said to possess the hearts of all the Americans. His recommendation was law, and he was able to command the whole power of that people for any purpose of defense. The philosophers of Europe considered this as a dangerous crisis to the cause of freedom. They knew, from the example of Caesar and Sulla and Marius and Alcibiades and Pericles and Cromwell, that Washington would never lay down his arms till he had given his country a master. But after he did lay them down, then came the miracle — his virtue was cried up to be more than human; and it is by this miracle of virtue in him that the Americans are supposed to enjoy their liberty at this day.

I believe the virtue of that great man to be equal to the highest human virtue that has ever yet been known; but to an American eye no extraordinary portion of it could appear in that transaction. It would have been impossible for the general or the army to have continued in the field after the enemy left it; for the soldiers were all citizens; and if it had been otherwise, their numbers were not the hundredth part of the citizens at large, who were all soldiers. To say that he was wise in discerning the impossibility of success in an attempt to imitate the great heroes above mentioned is to give him only the same merit for sagacity which is common to every other person who knows that country, or who has well considered the effects of equal liberty. . . .

A people that legislate for themselves ought to be in the habit of protecting themselves, or they will lose the spirit of both. A knowledge of their own strength preserves a temperance in their own wisdom, and the performance of their duties gives a value to their rights.

That is likewise the way to increase the solid domestic force of a nation, to a degree far beyond any ideas we form of a standing army; and at the same time to annihilate its capacity as well as inclination for foreign aggressive hostilities. The true guarantee of perpetual tranquillity at home and abroad, in such a case, would arise from this truth, which would pass into an incontrovertible maxim, that offensive operations would be impossible and defensive ones infallible.

This is undoubtedly the true and only secret of exterminating wars from the face of the earth; and it must afford no small degree of consolation to every friend of humanity to find this unspeakable blessing resulting from that equal mode of government, which alone secures every other enjoyment for which mankind unite their interests in society. Politicians, and even sometimes honest men, are accustomed to speak of war as an uncontrollable event, falling on the human race like a concussion of the elements — a scourge which admits no remedy, but for which we must wait with trembling preparation, as for an epidemical disease, whose force we may hope to lighten but can never avoid. They say that mankind are wicked and rapacious, and "it must be that offenses will come."

This reasoning applies to individuals and to countries when governed by individuals, but not to nations deliberately speaking a national voice. I hope I shall not be understood to mean that the nature of man is totally changed by living in a free republic. I allow that it is still interested men and passionate men that direct the affairs of the world. But in national assemblies, passion is lost in deliberation and interest balances interest, till the good of the whole community combines the general will. Here, then, is a great moral entity, acting still from interested motives, but whose interest it never can be, in any possible combination of circumstances, to commence an offensive war. . . .

The boundaries of nations have been fixed for the accommodation of the government, without the least regard to the convenience of the people. Kings and ministers, who make a profitable trade of governing, are interested in extending the limits of their dominion as far as possible. They have a property in the people and in the territory that they cover. The country and its inhabitants are to them a farm stocked with sheep. . . .

In America it is not so. Among the several states, the governments are all equal in their force, and the people are all equal in their rights. Were it possible for one state to conquer another state, without any expense of money, or of time, or of blood, neither of the states, nor a single individual in either of them, would be richer or poorer for the event. The people would all be upon their own lands and engaged in their own occupations, as before; and whether the territory on which they live were called New York or Massachusetts is a matter of total indifference, about which they have no superstition. For the people belong not to the government, but the government belongs to the people.

Since the independence of those states, many territorial disputes have been settled, which had risen from the interference of their ancient charters. The interference of charters is a kind of policy which, I suppose, every mother country observes toward her colonies in order to give them a subject of contention; that she may have the opportunity of keeping all parties quiet by the parental blessing of a standing army. But on the banishment of foreign control and all ideas of European policy, the enjoyment of equal liberty has taught the Americans the secret of settling these disputes with as much calmness as they have formed their constitutions. It is found that questions about the boundaries between free states are not matters of interest but merely of form and convenience. And though these questions may involve a tract of country equal to a European kingdom, it alters not the case; they are settled as merchants settle the course of exchange between two commercial cities. Several instances have occurred, since the Revolution, of deciding in a few days, by amicable arbitration, territorial disputes which determine the jurisdiction of larger and richer tracts of country than have formed the objects of all the wars of the two last centuries between France and Germany.

It is needless to spend any time in applying this idea to the circumstances of all countries, where the government should be freely and habitually in the hands of the people. It would apply to all Europe, and will apply to it as soon as a revolution shall take place in the principle of government. For such a revolution cannot stop short of fixing the power of the state on the basis allotted by nature, the unalienable rights of man, which are the same in all countries. It will eradicate the superstitions about territorial jurisdiction; and this consideration must promise an additional security against the possibility of war. . . .

It is a truth, I believe, not to be called in question, that every man is born with an imprescriptible claim to a portion of the elements, which portion is termed his birthright. Society may vary this right as to its form, but never can destroy it in substance. She has no control over the man till he is born; and the right being born with him and being necessary to his existence, she can no more annihilate the one than the other, though she has the power of new-modeling both. But on coming into the world, he finds that the ground which nature had promised him is taken up and in the occupancy of others. Society has changed the form of his birthright; the general stock of elements from which the lives of men are to be supported has undergone a new modification; and his portion among the rest. He is told that he cannot claim it in its present form as an independent inheritance; that he must draw on the stock of society, instead of the stock of nature; that he is banished from the mother, and must cleave to the nurse. In this unexpected occurrence he is unprepared to act; but knowledge is a part of the stock of society; and an indispensable part to be allotted in the portion of the claimant is instruction relative to the new arrangement of natural right. To withhold this instruction, therefore, would be not merely the omission of a duty but the commission of a crime; and society, in this case, would sin against the man before the man could sin against society.

I should hope to meet the assent of all unprejudiced readers in carrying this idea still farther. In cases where a person is born of poor parents, or finds himself brought into the community of men without the means of subsistence, society is bound in duty to furnish him the means. She ought not only to instruct him in the artificial laws by which property is secured but in the artificial industry by which it is obtained. She is bound, in justice as well as policy, to give him some art or trade. For the reason of his incapacity is that she has usurped his birthright; and this is restoring it to him in another form, more convenient for both parties. The failure of society in this branch of her duty is the occasion of much the greater part of the evils that call for criminal jurisprudence. The individual feels that he is robbed of his natural right; he cannot bring his process to reclaim it from the great community, by which he is overpowered; he, therefore, feels authorized in reprisal, in taking another's goods to replace his own. And it must be confessed that in numberless instances the conduct of society justifies him in this proceeding; she has seized upon his property and commenced the war against him. . . .

Society, then, is bound, in the first place, to distribute knowledge to every person according to his wants to enable him to be useful and happy, so far as to dispose him to take an active interest in the welfare of the state. Second, where the faculties of the individual are naturally defective, so that he remains unable to provide for himself, she is bound still to support and render him happy. It is her duty in all cases to induce every human creature, by rational motives, to place his happiness in the tranquillity of the public and in the security of individual peace and property. But third, in cases where these precautions shall fail of their effect, she is driven indeed to the last extremity — she is to use the rod of correction. These instances would doubtless be rare; and, if we could suppose a long continuance of wise administration, such as a well-organized government would ensure to every nation in the world, we may almost persuade ourselves to believe that the necessity for punishment would be reduced to nothing.

Proceeding however on the supposition of the existence of crimes, it must still remain an object of legislative wisdom to discriminate between their different classes, and apply to each its proper remedy, in the quantity and mode of punishment. It is no part of my subject to enter into this inquiry any farther than simply to observe that it is the characteristic of arbitrary governments to be jealous of their power. And, as jealousy is, of all human passions, the most vindictive and the least rational, these governments seek the revenge of injuries in the most absurd and tremendous punishments that their fury can invent. As far as any rule can be discovered in their gradation of punishments, it appears to be this — that the severity of the penalty is in proportion to the injustice of the law. The reason of this is simple — the laws which counteract nature the most are the most likely to be violated. . . .

A method of communicating instruction to every member of society is not difficult to discover, and would not be expensive in practice. The government generally establishes ministers of justice in every part of the dominion. The first object of these ministers ought to be to see that every person is well instructed in his duties and in his rights; that he is rendered perfectly acquainted with every law, in its true spirit and tendency, in order that he may know the reason of his obedience and the manner of obtaining redress, in case he should deem it unjust; that he is taught to feel the cares and interests of an active citizen, to consider himself as a real member of the state, know that the government is his own, that the society is his friend, and that the officers of the state are the servants of the people. A person possessing these ideas will never violate the law, unless it be from necessity; and such necessity is to be prevented by means which are equally obvious.

For the purposes of compulsive justice, it is not enough that the laws be rendered familiar to the people; but the tribunals ought to be near at hand, easy of access, and equally open to the poor as to the rich. The means of coming at justice should be cheap, expeditious, and certain; the mode of process should be simple and perfectly intelligible to the meanest capacity, unclouded with mysteries and unperplexed with forms.

In short, justice should familiarize itself as the well-known friend of every man; and the consequence seems natural, that every man would be a friend to justice.

After considering what is the duty of society and what would be the practice of a well-organized government, relative to the subject of this chapter, it is almost useless to inquire what *is* the practice of all the old governments of Europe. We may be sure beforehand that it is directly the contrary; that, like all other parts of the system, it is the inversion of everything that is right and reasonable. The pyramid is everywhere set on the little end, and all sorts of extraneous rubbish are constantly brought to prop it up.

Unequal governments are necessarily founded in ignorance, and they must be supported by ignorance; to deviate from their principle would be voluntary suicide. The first great object of their policy is to perpetuate that undisturbed ignorance of the people, which is the companion of poverty, the parent of crimes, and the pillar of the state. . . .

There is a strange idea prevalent in England (it has had its day in America) that it is good policy to raise the expenses of legal proceedings above the reach of the lower classes of people, as it lessens the number of suits. This kind of reasoning appears too absurd to support its own weight for a moment; and it would be beneath our serious notice, were it not for the reflection that men of superficial research are perpetually caught by it. The human mind is fitted, from its own indolence, to be dazzled by the glare of a proposition; and to receive and utter for truth what it never gives itself the trouble to examine. There is no paradox among all the enormities of despotism but what finds its advocates from this very circumstance. We must not, therefore, scorn to encounter an argument because it is foolish. The business of sober philosophy is often a task of drudgery; it must sometimes listen to the most incoherent clamors, which would be unworthy of its attention did they not form a part of the general din, by which mankind are deafened and misled.

For a man to bring into court a suit that is manifestly unjust is a crime against the state; to hinder him from bringing one that is just is a crime of the state against him. It is a poor compliment to the wisdom of a nation to suppose that no method can be devised for preventing the first of these evils without running into the last; and the last is ten times the greatest of the two. The French, who appear to have been destined to give lessons to the world by the wisdom of their new institutions as well as by the folly of their old have found the secret of imposing a small fine on a vexatious plaintiff; and of establishing many other regulations on this subject, which effectually shut the door of the tribunal against the oppressor, while it easily opens to the feeblest cry of the oppressed.

They have likewise established a method of communicating the knowledge of the laws to every human creature in the kingdom, however ignorant he may be in other respects. They are printed and pasted up on public buildings in every town and village, and read and explained by the curate from the pulpit in every parish. It is in contemplation likewise to institute a general system of public instruction, on a more useful and extensive plan than has ever yet been devised. Several enlightened philosophers are busied in these researches; and several societies are formed, whose object is to discover and bring forward the best concerted plan for this important purpose. In their whole system of distributing knowledge and justice, they seem to be aiming at a degree of perfection which promises great success. With all my partiality for the institutions of the United States, I should quote them (in comparison to those of France) with less confidence on the subject of this chapter than of any other.

In the administration of justice, the Americans are too much attached to the English forms; which serve to increase the expense and to mysticize the business to a degree that is manifestly inconsistent with the dignity of a true republic. But in respect to public instruction, there are some circumstances which deserve to be mentioned to their praise. I am going to speak only of the particular state with which I am best acquainted. How many of the others are better regulated in this respect, and how many are worse, I am not accurately informed. This state (which contains less than 240,000 inhabitants) is divided into about 100 towns. These are subdivided into small portions, called school districts, suitable for the support of small schools. Each of these districts has a drawback on the state treasury for a sum which bears a proportion to the public taxes paid by the inhabitants of the district, and which is about half equal to the support of a schoolmaster. But this sum can be drawn only on condition that a school is maintained in the district.

The following remarkable consequences seem to have resulted from this provision: There is not perhaps in that state a person of six years old and of common intellects who cannot read, and very few who cannot write and cast accounts; besides the useful books that are found in every family, it is computed that there are in the state about 300 public libraries, which have been formed by voluntary subscription among the people of the districts and the parishes; till about the year 1768, which was more than 130 years after the settlement of the state, no capital punishment, as I am informed, had been inflicted within its jurisdiction, nor any person convicted of a capital offense — since that period, very few have been convicted, and those few are generally Europeans by birth and education; there is no extreme poverty in the state, and no extraordinary wealth accumulated by individuals.

It would be absurd to suppose that public instruction is by any means carried to the perfection that it ought to be in this or any other state in the universe. But this experiment proves that good morals and equal liberty are reciprocal causes and effects; and that they are both the parents of national happiness and of great prosperity.

All governments that lay any claim to respectability or justice have proscribed the idea of ex post facto laws, or laws made after the performance of an action, constituting that action a crime, and punishing the party for a thing that was innocent at the time of its being done. Such laws would be so flagrant a violation of natural right that in the French and several of the American state constitutions they are solemnly interdicted in their declarations of rights. This proscription is likewise considered as a fundamental article of English liberty, and almost the only one that has not been habitually violated within the present century. But let us resort to reason and justice and ask what is the difference between a violation of this article and the observance of that tremendous maxim of jurisprudence, common to all the nations abovementioned, *ignorantia legis neminem excusat* [ignorance of the law is no excuse].

Most of the laws of society are positive regulations, not taught by nature. Indeed, such only are applicable to the subject now in question. For *ignorantia legis* can have reference only to laws arising out of society, in which our natural feelings have no concern; and where a man is ignorant of such a law, he is in the same situation as if the law did not exist. To read it to him from the tribunal, where he stands arraigned for the breach of it, is to him precisely the same thing as it would be to originate it at the time by the same tribunal for the express purpose of his condemnation. The law till then, as relative to him, is not in being. He is, therefore, in the same predicament that the society in general would be, under the operation of an ex post facto law. Hence we ought to conclude that, as it seems difficult for a government to dispense with the maxim abovementioned, a free people ought, in their declaration of rights, to provide for universal public instruction. If they neglect to do this, and mean to avoid the absurdity of a self-destroying policy by adhering to a system of justice which would preserve a dignity and inspire a confidence worthy the name of liberty, they ought to reject the maxim altogether, and insert in their declaration of rights that instruction alone can constitute a duty; and that laws can enforce no obedience but where they are explained.

It is truly hard and sufficiently to be regretted that any part of society should be obliged to yield obedience to laws to which they have not literally and personally consented. Such is the state of things; it is necessary that a majority should govern. If it be an evil to obey a law to which we have not consented, it is at least a necessary evil; but to compel a compliance with orders which are unknown is carrying injustice beyond the bounds of necessity; it is absurd and even impossible. Laws in this case may be avenged but cannot be obeyed; they may inspire terror but can never command respect. . . .

The Americans cannot be said as yet to have formed a national character. The political part of their revolution, aside from the military, was not of that violent and convulsive nature which shakes the whole fabric of human opinions, and enables men to decide which are to be retained as proper to their situation and which are to be rejected as the offspring of unnatural connections. Happily the weight of oppression there had never been so great nor of so long duration as to have distorted in any extravagant degree the moral features of man. He recognized himself as the same being under the new system as the old; for the change of form had not been so perceptible as to require a great change of principle. Under these circumstances, the people continued most of their ancient maxims, though they were a mixture of foreign and domestic, and, as habit is a coin current in all countries, it is not surprising that whatever had received the stamp of authority in the polished nations of Europe should be adopted without scruple by the offspring of those nations in America.

The circumstance of their not being invested with what is called national character, though hitherto a subject of regret, will in future be much in their favor. The public mind being open to receive impressions from abroad, they will be able to profit by the practical lessons which will now be afforded them from the change of system in this quarter of the world. It will be found there, as it is now found in France, that the display of wealth will cease to be challenged as an emblem or a substitute for personal talents; and it will be coveted everywhere in a less degree than at present, as it will fail to gratify the passion for respect. It may be farther remarked that this is not the only circumstance in which the state of society in America will be essentially benefited by a change of manners in Europe.

# 1792 - 1793

102.

## Hugh H. Brackenridge: A Satirical View of Senators and Philosophers

*Hugh Brackenridge, a political leader in western Pennsylvania, sympathized with the republican sentiments of James Madison and Philip Freneau, who had been his classmates at what is now Princeton. He is best remembered for his novel,* Modern Chivalry, *on which he spent the leisure of his lifetime, and which appeared in parts between 1792 and 1815. The novel, part of which appears here, owes a good deal to* Don Quixote, *as well as to* Tristram Shandy *and* Gulliver's Travels. *It deals with the adventures of Captain John Farrago and his servant, Teague O'Regan, who ride through western Pennsylvania observing the life and manners of the people. Farrago is more or less a Jeffersonian democrat, Teague a self-assured but ignorant braggart, part fool and part knave. The story was in part an attack on the Society of the Cincinnati, a fraternal organization founded by officers of the disbanding Continental Army in 1783. Brackenridge disapproved of it, and it was frequently criticized at the time as an aristocratic military order.*

Source: *Modern Chivalry, 2nd edition,* Philadelphia, 1846, Vol. I, Chs. 3, 6.

At an early hour, our knight-errant and his squire set out on their way, and soon arrived at a place of crossroads, at a public house and store, where a number of people were convened for the purpose of electing persons to represent them in the legislature of the state. This was not the annual election, but to fill an occasional vacancy. There was a weaver who was a candidate, and seemed to have a good deal of interest among the people. But another, who was a man of education, was his competitor. Relying on some talent of speaking which he thought he possessed, and getting on the stump of a large oak tree for the convenience of a more elevated position, he thus addressed the people:

> Fellow citizens, I pretend not to any great abilities; but am conscious to myself that I have the best goodwill to serve you. But it is very astonishing to me that this man should conceive himself qualified for the trust; for though my acquirements are not great, yet his are still less. The business which he pursues must necessarily take up so much of his time that he cannot apply himself to political studies. I should, therefore, think it would be more answerable to your dig-

nity, and conducive to your interest, to be represented by a man at least of some letters than by an illiterate man like this. It will be more honorable for himself to remain at his loom and knot threads than to come forward in a legislative capacity, because, in the one case, he is in the sphere suited to his education; in the other, he is like a fish out of water, and must struggle for breath in a new element. It is not because he is a weaver that I object to him, but because he is nothing but a weaver, and entirely destitute of the qualifications necessary to fill the office to which he aspires. The occupation a man pursues for a livelihood is but a secondary consideration, if any consideration at all. Warriors and statesmen and sages may be found at the plough, and the work bench, but this man has not the slightest pretensions beyond the mysteries of his trade.

Is it possible that he can understand the affairs of government, whose mind has been entirely concentered to the small object of weaving webs; to the price by the yard, the grist of the thread; and suchlike matters as concern the manufacturer of cloths? The feet of him who weaves are more occupied than the head, or at least as much; and, therefore, he must be, at least, but in half accustomed to exercise his mental powers. For these reasons, all other things set aside, the chance is in my favor, with respect to information. However, you will decide, and give your suffrages to him or to me, as you shall judge expedient.

The captain, hearing these observations, and looking at the weaver, made free to subjoin something in support of what had been just said. Said he,

I have no prejudice against a weaver more than another man. Nor do I know any harm in the trade, save that from the sedentary life in a damp place, there is usually a paleness of the countenance; but this is a physical not a moral evil. Such usually occupy subterranean apartments, not for the purpose, like Demosthenes, of shaving their heads and writing over eight times the history of Thucydides, and perfecting a style of oratory but rather to keep the thread moist; or because this is considered but as an inglorious sort of trade, and is frequently thrust away into cellars and damp outhouses, which are not occupied for a better use.

But to rise from the cellar to the Senate House would be an unnatural hoist for one whose mind had not been prepared for it by a previous course of study or training, either self-instructed and gifted with superior intellect, or having the good fortune to have received an education, with also the advantage of actual experience in public affairs. To come from counting threads and adjusting them to the splits of a reed to regulate the finances of a government would be preposterous, there being no congruity in the case. There is no analogy between knotting threads and framing laws. It would be a reversion of the order of things. Not that a manufacturer of linen or woolen, or other stuffs, is an inferior character but a different one from that which ought to be employed in affairs of state.

It is unnecessary to enlarge on this subject; for you must all be convinced of the truth and propriety of what I say. But if you will give me leave to take the manufacturer aside a little, I think I can explain to him my ideas on the subject; and very probably prevail with him to withdraw his pretensions.

The people, seeming to acquiesce, and beckoning to the weaver, they withdrew aside, and the captain addressed him in the following words:

Mr. Traddle, I have not the smallest idea of wounding your feelings, but it would seem to me it would be more your interest to pursue your occupation than to launch out into that of which you have no knowledge. When you go to the Senate House, the application to you will not be to warp a web but to make laws for the commonwealth. Now, suppose that the making these laws requires a knowledge of commerce, of finance, and of the infinite variety of subjects embraced by the laws, civil, or criminal, what service could you render? It is possible you might think justly, but could you speak? You are not in the habit of public speaking. You are not furnished with those commonplace ideas with which even very ignorant men can pass for knowing something. There is nothing makes a man so ridiculous as to attempt what is beyond his capacity. You are no tumbler, for instance; yet should you give out that you could vault upon a man's back, or turn heels over head like the wheels of a cart, the stiffness of your joints would encumber you and you would fall to the ground. Such a squash as that would do you damage. The getting up to ride on the state is an unsafe thing to those who are not accustomed to such horsemanship. It is a disagreeable thing for a man to be laughed at, and there is no way of keeping one's self from it but by avoiding all affectation.

These observations did not seem to make much impression on the weaver, who argued that common sense was often better than learning.

While they were thus discoursing, a bustle had taken place among the crowd. Teague, hearing so much about elections and serving the government, took it into his head that he could be a legislator himself. The thing was not displeasing to the people, who seemed to favor his pretensions, owing, in some degree, to there being several of his countrymen among the crowd, but more especially to the fluctuation of the popular mind, and a disposition to what is new and ignoble; for though the weaver was not the most elevated object of choice, yet he was still preferable to this tatterdemalion.

The captain coming up and finding what was on the carpet, was chagrined at not having been able to give the voters a better idea of the importance of a legislative trust; alarmed, also, from an apprehension of the loss of his servant. Under these impressions he resumed his address to the people. Said he,

This is making the matter still worse, gentlemen; this servant of mine is but a bogtrotter who can scarcely speak the dialect in which your laws ought to be written, but certainly has never read a single treatise on any political subject; for the truth is, he cannot read at all.

The young people of the lower class in Ireland have seldom the advantage of a good education; especially the descendants of the ancient Irish, who have most of them a great assurance of countenance but little information or literature. This young man, whose family name is O'Regan, has been my servant for several years; and, except a too great fondness for whiskey, which now and then brings him into scrapes, he has demeaned himself in a manner tolerable enough. But he is totally ignorant of the great principles of legislation, and more especially the particular interests of the government. A free government is a noble acquisition to a people; and this freedom consists in an equal right to make laws, and to have the benefit of the laws when made. Though doubtless, in such a government, the lowest citizen may become chief magistrate; yet it is sufficient to possess the right, not absolutely necessary to exercise it.

Or even if you should think proper, now and then, to show your privilege and exert, in a signal manner, the democratic prerogative, yet is it not descending too low to filch away from me a servant whom I cannot well spare, and for whom I have paid my money? You are surely carrying the matter too far in thinking to make a senator of this hostler; to take him away from an employment to which he has been bred, and put him to another, to which he has served no apprenticeship; to set those hands, which have lately been employed in currying my horse, to the drafting bills, and preparing business for the House.

The people were tenacious of their choice, and insisted on giving Teague their suffrages; and by the frown upon their brows, seemed to indicate resentment at what had been said, as indirectly charging them with want of judgment or calling in question their privilege to do what they thought proper. "It is a very strange thing," said one of them, who was a speaker for the rest, that after having conquered Burgoyne and Cornwallis, and got a government of our own, we cannot put in whom we please. This young man may be your servant, or another man's servant; but if we choose to make him a delegate, what is that to you? He may not be yet skilled in the matter, but there is a good day coming. We will empower him; and it is better to trust a plain man like him than one of your highflyers that will make laws to suit their own purposes.

Said the captain:

I had much rather you would send the weaver, though I thought that improper, than to invade my household, and thus take from me the person who is employed to curry my horse and black my boots.

The prolocutor of the people gave him to understand that his objections were useless, for the people had determined on the choice, and Teague they would have for a representative.

Finding it answered no end to expostulate, he requested to speak a word with Teague by himself. Stepping aside, he said to him, composing his voice, and addressing him in a soft manner:

Teague, you are quite wrong in this matter they have put into your head. Do you know what it is to be a member of a deliberative body? What qualifications are necessary? Do you understand anything of geography? If a question should be put to make a law to dig a canal in some part of the state, can you describe the bearing of the mountains and the course of the rivers? Or, if commerce is to be pushed to some new quarter, by the force of regulations, are you competent to decide in such a case? There will be questions of law and astronomy on the carpet. How you must gape and stare like a fool when you come to be asked your opinion on these subjects! Are you acquainted with the principles of finance; with the funding public securities; the ways and means of raising the revenue; providing for the discharge of the public debts, and all other things which respect the economy of the government? Even if you had knowledge, have you a facility of speaking? I would suppose you would have too much pride to go to the House just to say ay or no. This is not the fault of your nature but of your education, having been accustomed to dig turf in your early years rather than instructing yourself in the classics or common-school books.

When a man becomes a member of a public body, he is like a raccoon, or other beast that climbs up the fork of a tree; the boys pushing at him with pitchforks, or throwing stones, or shooting at him with arrows; the dogs barking in the meantime. One will find fault with your not speaking; another with your speaking, if you speak at all. They will put you in the newspapers, and ridicule you as a perfect beast. There is what they call the *caricatura;* that is, representing you with a dog's head, or a cat's claw. It is the devil to be exposed to the squibs and crackers of the gazette wits and publications. You know no more about these matters than a goose; and yet you would undertake rashly, without advice, to enter on the office; nay, contrary to advice. For I would not for a hundred guineas, though I have not the half to spare, that the breed of the O'Regans should come to this; bringing on them a worse stain than stealing sheep. You have nothing but your character, Teague, in a new country to depend upon. Let it never be said, that you quitted an honest livelihood, the taking care of my horse, to follow the new-fangled whims of the times, and be a statesman. And, besides, have I not promised to do something clever toward settling you in life hereafter, provided you will serve me faithfully in my travels? Something better than you have thought of may turn up in the course of our rambles.

Teague was moved chiefly with the last part of the address, and consented to relinquish his pretensions.

The captain, glad of this, took him back to the people, and announced his disposition to decline the honor which they had intended him.

Teague acknowledged that he had changed his mind, and was willing to remain in a private station.

Library of Congress

"Captain Farrago and Teague O'Regan," a cartoon from the 1846 edition of "Modern Chivalry" by Hugh H. Brackenridge

The people did not seem well pleased; but as nothing more could be said about the matter, they turned their attention to the weaver and gave him their suffrages. . . .

There was, in a certain great city, a society who called themselves philosophers. They had published books, under the title of *Transactions*. These contained dissertations on the nature and causes of things, from the stars of heaven to the fireflies of the earth; and from the sea crab to the woodland buffalo. Such disquisitions are doubtless useful and entertaining to an inquisitive mind.

There is no question but there were in this body some very great men whose investigations of the arcana of nature deserve attention. But so it was, there had been introduced by some means many individuals who were no philosophers at all. This is no unusual thing with institutions of this nature; though, by the bye, it is a very great fault. For it lessens the incentives of honor to have the access made so easy that every-one may obtain admission. It has been a reproach to some colleges that a diploma could be purchased for half a crown. This society were still more moderate for the bare scratching the back of a member has been known to procure a membership. At least, there have been those admitted who appeared capable of nothing else.

Nevertheless, it was necessary, even in these cases, for the candidates to procure some token of a philosophic turn of mind; such as the skin of a dead cat, or some odd kind of a mousetrap; or have praises in their mouths about minerals and petrifactions, so as just to support some idea of natural knowledge, and pass muster. There was one who got in by finding, accidentally, the tail of a rabbit, which had been taken off in a boy's trap. The beard of an old fox, taken off and dried in the sun, was the means of introducing another; or, rather, as I have already hinted, it was beforehand intended he should be introduced; and these spoils of the animal kingdom were but the tokens and apologies for admission.

It happened as the captain was riding this day, and Teague trotting after him, he saw a large owl that had been shot by somebody, and was placed in the crotch of a tree, about the height of a man's head from the ground, for those that passed by to look at. Being struck with it as somewhat larger than such birds usually are, he desired Teague to reach it to him, and tying it to the hinder part of his saddle, rode along.

He had not rode more than two or three miles before he was met and accosted by a respectable looking traveler, well-mounted, and attended by a servant following him on another horse with the portmanteau. This traveler, who proved to be a member of the Philosophical Society, seeing the bird at the saddle skirts, stopped to make inquiry with regard to the genus and nature of the fowl.

"Sir," said the captain, "I know nothing more about it than that it is nearly as large as a turkey buzzard."

"It is doubtless," said the other, "the

great Canada owl, that comes from the lakes; and if you will give me leave, squire, I will take it and submit it to the Society, and have yourself made a member."

Consent was readily given to the first; but as to the second, the being a member, he chose rather to decline it, conceiving himself unqualified for a place in such a body. The other assured him that he was under a very great mistake; for there were members who scarcely knew a *B* from a bull's foot. "That may be," said the captain, "but if others choose to degrade themselves by suffering their names to be used in so preposterous a way as that, it was no reason he [I] should."

The other gave him to understand that the society would certainly wish to express their sense of his merit, and show themselves not inattentive to a virtuoso; that as he declined the honor himself, he probably might not be averse to let his attendant take a seat among them.

"He is but a simple Irishman," said the captain,

> and of a low education; his language being that spoken by the aborigines of his country. And if he speaks a little English, it is with the brogue on his tongue, which would be unbecoming in a member of your body. It would seem to me that a philosopher ought to know how to write, or at least to read; but Teague can neither write nor read. He can sing a song or whistle an Irish tune, but is totally illiterate in all things else. I question much if he could tell you how many new moons there are in the year; or any the most common things you could ask him. He is a long-legged fellow, it is true, and might be of service in clambering over rocks, or going to the shores of rivers to gather curiosities. But could you not get persons to do this without making them members? I have more respect for science than to suffer this bogtrotter to be so advanced at its expense. In these American states there is a wide field for philosophical research; and these researches may be of great use in agriculture, manufactures, and architecture. There is but little immediate profit attending these pursuits; but if there can be inducements of honor, these may supply the place. What more alluring to a young man than the prospect of being one day received into the society of men truly learned, the admission being a test and a proof of distinguished knowledge. But the fountain of honor, thus contaminated by a sediment foreign from its nature, who would wish to drink of it?

"As to that," said the philosopher,

> at the first institution of the Society by Dr. Franklin and others, it was put upon a narrow basis, and only men of science were considered proper to compose it; and this might be a necessary policy at that time, when the institution was in its infancy and could not bear much drawback of ignorance. But it has not been judged so necessary of late years. The matter stands now on a broad and catholic bottom; and, like the gospel itself, it is our orders "to go out into the highways and hedges, and compel them to come in." There are hundreds whose names you may see on our list who are not more instructed than your man Teague.

"They must be a sad set indeed then," said the captain.

"Sad or no sad," said the other, "it is the case; and if you will let Teague go, I will engage him a membership."

"I take it very ill of you, Mr. Philosopher," said the captain, "to put this nonsense in his head.

> If you knew what trouble I have lately had with a parcel of people that were for sending him to Congress, you would be unwilling to draw him from me for the purpose of making him a philosopher. It is not an easy matter to get servants nowadays; and when you do get one, it is a mere chance whether he will suit your purpose. It would be a very great loss to me to have him taken off at this time, when I have equipped myself for a journey.

Teague, who had been attentive to what had been passing but without comprehending it, supposed that he was about to be prevented from the possession of something to his advantage, declared that he would accept of his honor's offer, and be a philosopher in spite of his master.

"You are an ignoramus," said the captain. "It is not the being among philosophers will make you one."

He insisted that he had a right to make the best of his fortune; and, as there was a door open to his advancement, he did not see why he might not make use of it.

The captain, finding that it answered no end to dispute the matter with him by words of sense and reason, took a contrary way to manage him.

"Teague," said he,

> I have a regard for you, and would wish to see you do well. I have not forgotten my promise; but if you will be a philosopher, which you erroneously suppose will lead to fortune, let me speak a word or two in private on the subject. If you will go, I may perhaps suggest some things that may be of service to you for your future conduct in this new line of life.

Teague consenting, they stepped aside, and his master addressed him in the following manner:

> Teague, do you know what you are about? It is a fine thing, at first sight, to be a philosopher and get into this society, as they call it. And, indeed, if you were a real philosopher, it might be some honor, and also safe, to take that leap. But do you think it is to make a philosopher of you that they want you? Far from it. It is their great study to find curiosities; and they will have you away through the bogs and marshes, catching fireflies, or oblige you to descend into draw-wells for fogs and phlogistic air. You must go into wolves' dens, run over mountains like a catamount, and dig the earth like a groundhog. You will have to climb over trees and be bit by flying squirrels. There will be no end to the mosquitoes you will have to dissect. What is all this, to diving into milldams and rivers to catch crawfish? Or if you go to the ocean, there are sharks to devour you. Will they give wages, think you? No, certainly — you must work for the honor of the thing, and find your own food and clothing. Who knows but it may come your turn, in a windy night, to go aloft to the heavens, to rub down the stars, and give fodder to the goats and rams? The keeping the stars clean and bright is a laborious work. There is a bull there would think no more of tossing you on his horns than he would a puppy dog. If the crab should get you into his claws, he would squeeze you like a lobster. But what is all that to your having no place to stand on? How would you like to be up at the moon, and to fall down when you had missed your hold, like a boy from the topmast of a ship, and have your brains beat out upon the top of some great mountain, where your skeleton would be picked by the turkey buzzards?
>
> Or if they should, in the meantime, excuse you from such out-of-door services, they will rack and torture you with hard questions. You must tell them how long the rays of light are coming from the sun; how many drops of rain fall in a thundergust; what makes the grasshopper chirp when the sun is hot; how mussel shells get up to the top of the mountains; how the Indians got over to America. You will have to prove that the Negroes were once white, and that their flat noses came by someone giving a slap in the face when the clay was soft.
>
> Take my advice and stay where you are. Many men have ruined themselves by their ambition, and made bad worse. There is another kind of philosophy which lies more within your sphere; that is, moral philosophy. Every hostler or hireling can study this, and you have the most excellent opportunity of acquiring this knowledge in our traverses through the country, or communications at the different taverns or villages, where we may happen to sojourn.

Teague had long ago, in his own mind, given up all thoughts of the Society, and would not for the world have any more to do with it; especially as there was nothing to be got; therefore, without bidding the philosopher adieu, they pursued their route as usual.

# 1793

103.

## George Washington: Proclamation of Neutrality

*When France, America's ally during the Revolution, declared war on England on February 1, 1793, the United States was faced with a complex question of foreign policy in a strictly European war. Members of the Cabinet agreed with George Washington that a policy of neutrality was in the best interest of the United States. On April 22, 1793, the President issued the following statement to this effect. It should be noted that within the proclamation the actual word "neutrality" is not used. The word was omitted in order not to offend Great Britain, whose capital was important to American shipowners.*

Source: Richardson, I, pp. 156-157.

BY THE PRESIDENT
OF THE UNITED STATES
OF AMERICA
*A Proclamation*

*Whereas* it appears that a state of war exists between Austria, Prussia, Sardinia, Great Britain, and the United Netherlands on the one part and France on the other, and the duty and interest of the United States require that they should with sincerity and good faith adopt and pursue a conduct friendly and impartial toward the belligerent powers:

I have therefore thought fit by these presents to declare the disposition of the United States to observe the conduct aforesaid toward those powers respectively, and to exhort and warn the citizens of the United States carefully to avoid all acts and proceedings whatsoever which may in any manner tend to contravene such disposition.

And I do hereby also make known that whosoever of the citizens of the United States shall render himself liable to punishment or forfeiture under the law of nations by committing, aiding, or abetting hostilities against any of the said powers, or by carrying to any of them those articles which are deemed contraband by the modern usage of nations, will not receive the protection of the United States against such punishment or forfeiture; and further, that I have given instructions to those officers to whom it belongs to cause prosecutions to be instituted against all persons who shall, within the cognizance of the courts of the United States, violate the law of nations with respect to the powers at war, or any of them.

Library of Congress

Wayne Andrews

# Federal Architecture

(Top) The Capitol, Washington, D.C., begun in 1793 under architect William Thornton, as it appeared in 1850; (left) state capitol, Richmond, Va., by Thomas Jefferson, 1785-88; (bottom left) first U.S. Bank, Philadelphia, built 1795; (below) Baltimore cathedral, Md., by Benjamin Latrobe, 1809-21

American Museum of Photography

Wayne Andrews

Wayne Andrews

In the years following the Revolution, American architects turned away from the influence of England and sought inspiration for the public buildings needed by the new Republic in the ancient republican states of Greece and Rome. Roman ideals influenced Thomas Jefferson's designs for his home, Monticello, and for public

Library of Congress

**(Top) Monticello, Charlottesville, Va., home of Thomas Jefferson, who supervised its design and construction, 1773-79; (center) the White House, Washington, D. C., by James Hoban, 1792-1817, photographed by Mathew Brady before the Civil War; (right) Pingree House, Salem, Mass., by Samuel McIntire, 1804**

Essex Institute

buildings shown here and on the preceding page. His lead was later followed by professional architects such as Benjamin Latrobe, who initiated the Greek revival. Plans for the new capital city were drawn up by a French engineer, Pierre Charles L'Enfant, and work was begun on the presidential home, later to become known as the White House, and on the halls for Congress on Capitol Hill.

Boston Chamber of Commerce

(Top) State capitol, Boston, Mass., by Charles Bulfinch, 1795-98; the two wings of white marble were constructed later; (right) Harvard's University Hall, Cambridge, Mass., by Charles Bulfinch, 1813-15; (below) the Peirce-Nichols House, Salem, Mass., by Samuel McIntire, 1782

Harvard University

Library of Congress

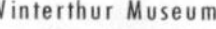

Winterthur Museum

(Above and right) Albany Institute of History and Art

Winterthur Museum

Winterthur Museum

**(Above left) Girondole looking glass, 1805-1810; (center) mahogany knife box, c. 1795, and detail from a bed by Charles Lannuier, c. 1817; (right) room setting before 1800 and drawing room of the Federal period; (below) gilded pier table, c. 1825; console table by Lannuier**

Albany Institute of History and Art

Museum of the City of New York

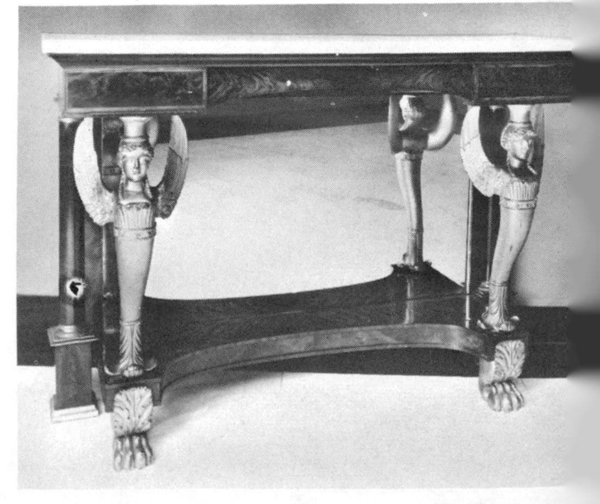

Albany Institute of History and Art

Winterthur Museum

The Revolution led to a rejection of English influence and popular American taste turned to France, an ally in the war, for inspiration. French neoclassical designs replaced rococo styles in American furniture making.

**(Top) Detail from bed by Lannuier, c. 1817; (left) dining room in French style, late 18th century; (below left) pre-Revolutionary parlor; (below) free-hanging stairway, Montmorenci, N.C.**

Winterthur Museum

Winterthur Museum

Old Sturbridge Village Photos

Philadelphia Museum of Art

# Woodworking

The new settlers, who arrived in a land rich in forests, used the wide variety of woods for utensils as well as for building homes. The earliest objects, made by village craftsmen, were of a purely utilitarian nature. Craftsmen of the post-Revolutionary years produced more elaborate carvings for decorative purposes and also to identify inns and other buildings. The eagle soon became a popular symbol.

**(Top) Pail; bed wrench used for tightening rope springs; butter paddle; (center) piggin, used as dipper for water; wooden reel used in textile production, mortar and pestle; (right) butter mold with figure of swan**

Pennsylvania Farm Museum of Landis Valley

Winterthur Museum

Bostonian Society

(Above and below) Rockefeller Folk Art Collection

**(Above) "Hope," carved in white pine by Simeon and John Skillin, c. 1800; (right, top to bottom) "Bell in Hand," from a Boston tavern, 1795; eagle by Wilhelm Schimmel; rooster, polychromed pine, 19th century; eagle, carved and gilded by Samuel McIntire for gate of Salem Common, c. 1805; (below) cartouche with arms of Massachusetts, also by McIntire for Salem Common**

(Both) Essex Institute

# Pennsylvania Dutch Folk Art

Winterthur Museum

Winterthur Museum

Pennsylvania Farm Museum

**(Top) Fraktur baptismal certificate, 1826; pottery jar with slip decoration by Christian Klinker, 1787; (center) fraktur decoration by Heinrich Otto, 1792; pottery bulb kettle with slip decoration, 1830; (bottom) painted tulipwood marriage chest, 1788; tin tray with brightly painted patterns; (right) pottery lion ornament by John Nase**

(Others) Philadelphia Museum of Art

Winterthur Museum

**(Top) Pottery pie plates by David Spinner, 1800-10; (second row) pottery plates and a covered jar, made between 1800-30; (third row) stoneware teapot with tulip design, 1770-1800; pie dish with figure of George Washington on horseback, probably by Johannes Neeze, 1805; (fourth row) pottery mugs, 1801 and 1816; dish by George Hubener, 1786; (right) pie plate depicting couples dancing, 1786**

(Others) Philadelphia Museum of Art

Winterthur Museum Corning Museum of Glass Winterthur Museum

**Three pieces of glass manufactured by John Frederick Amelung: (left to right) green sugar bowl, 1785; goblet, one of a pair, 1793; covered flip glass, 1788**

# Textiles and Glass

The most important glass producer at the end of the 18th century was John Frederick Amelung, an immigrant from Germany who landed at Baltimore in 1784. Despite the excellence of his design and execution, his business went bankrupt in 1795. Many fine pieces survive to indicate the wide range of his production. Needlework and textiles were largely made by the women for use in their own homes. They ranged from simple cross-stitched samplers worked by young girls to the elaborate set of bed hangings embroidered by a 30-year-old widow.

Winterthur Museum

**Woven wool bedspread, Pennsylvania, 1778**

**(Below) Linen sampler embroidered in cross-stitch, early 19th century; (right) crewel bed hangings made by Mary Bulman, 1745**

Philadelphia Museum of Art

Old Gaol Museum

104.

# Thomas Jefferson: For Our Alliance with France

*Washington's decision to remain neutral in the war between Britain and France precipitated a series of debates over the Treaty of 1778, which had allied France and the United States. Many pro-French Americans, including Thomas Jefferson, felt that the alliance was a binding agreement to come to France's aid. Hamilton reasoned that the treaty had not been made with the French revolutionary government, but with the monarchy, and that the United States therefore had no legal obligation to France. On April 28, 1793, Jefferson wrote a reply to Hamilton, part of which is reprinted here, stating that* moral, *not legal, considerations should guide the country's foreign policy.*

Source: Ford, VI, pp. 219-231.

I PROCEED, IN COMPLIANCE with the requisition of the President, to give an opinion in writing on the general question — Whether the U.S. have a right to renounce their treaties with France, or to hold them suspended till the government of that country shall be established?

In the consultation at the President's on the 19th inst., the secretary of the treasury took the following positions and consequences.

> France was a monarchy when we entered into treaties with it; but it has now declared itself a republic, and is preparing a republican form of government. As it may issue in a republic, or a military despotism, or in something else which may possibly render our alliance with it dangerous to ourselves, we have a right of election to renounce the treaty altogether, or to declare it suspended till their government shall be settled in the form it is ultimately to take; and then we may judge whether we will call the treaties into operation again, or declare them forever null. Having that right of election now, if we receive their minister without any qualifications, it will amount to an act of election to continue the treaties; and if the change they are undergoing should issue in a form which should bring danger on us, we shall not be then free to renounce them. To elect to continue them is equivalent to the making a new treaty at this time, in the same form, that is to say, with a clause of guarantee; but to make a treaty with a clause of guarantee, during a war, is a departure from neutrality and would make us associates in the war. To renounce or suspend the treaties therefore is a necessary act of neutrality.

If I do not subscribe to the soundness of this reasoning, I do most fully to its ingenuity. I shall now lay down the principles which according to my understanding govern the case.

I consider the people who constitute a society or nation as the source of all authority in that nation, as free to transact their common concerns by any agents they think proper to change these agents individually, or the organization of them in form or function whenever they please; that all the acts done by those agents under the authority of the nation are the acts of the nation, are obligatory on them, and enure to their use, and can in no wise be annulled or affected by any change in the form of the government, or of the persons administering it. Consequently, the treaties between the U.S. and France were not treaties between the U.S. and Louis Capet but between the two nations of America and France, and the nations remaining in existence, though both of them have since changed their forms of government, the treaties are not annulled by these changes.

The law of nations by which this question is to be determined is composed of three branches: (1) the moral law of our nature; (2) the usages of nations; (3) their special conventions.

The first of these only concerns this question, that is to say the moral law to which man has been subjected by his Creator, and of which his feelings, or conscience as it is sometimes called, are the evidence with which his Creator has furnished him. The moral duties which exist between individual and individual in a state of nature accompany them into a state of society, and the aggregate of the duties of all the individuals composing the society constitutes the duties of that society toward any other; so that between society and society, the same moral duties exist as did between the individuals composing them while in an unassociated state, their Maker not having released them from those duties on their forming themselves into a nation. Compacts then between nation and nation are obligatory on them by the same moral law which obliges individuals to observe their compacts. There are circumstances, however, which sometimes excuse the nonperformance of contracts between man and man; so are there also between nation and nation.

When performance, for instance, becomes *impossible,* nonperformance is not immoral. So, if performance becomes *self-destructive* to the party, the law of self-preservation overrules the laws of obligation to others. For the reality of these principles, I appeal to the true fountains of evidence, the head and heart of every rational and honest man. It is there nature has written her moral laws, and where every man may read them for himself. He will never read there the permission to annul his obligations for a time, or forever, whenever they become "dangerous, useless, or disagreeable." Certainly not when merely *useless* or *disagreeable,* as seems to be said in an authority which has been quoted . . . and though he may under certain degrees of *danger,* yet the danger must be imminent and the degree great.

Of these, it is true, that nations are to be judges for themselves, since no one nation has a right to sit in judgment over another. But the tribunal of our consciences remains, and that, also, of the opinion of the world. These will revise the sentence we pass in our own case, and as we respect these, we must see that in judging ourselves we have honestly done the part of impartial and vigorous judges.

But reason, which gives this right of self-liberation from a contract in certain cases, has subjected it to certain just limitations.

The danger which absolves us must be great, inevitable, and imminent. Is such the character of that now apprehended from our treaties with France? What is that danger?

1. Is it that if their government issues in a military despotism, an alliance with them may taint us with despotic principles? But their government, when we allied ourselves to it, was a perfect despotism, civil and military, yet the treaties were made in that very state of things and, therefore, that danger can furnish no just cause.

2. Is it that their government may issue in a republic, and too much strengthen our republican principles? But this is the hope of the great mass of our constituents and

not their dread. They do not look with longing to the happy mean of a limited monarchy.

3. But, says the doctrine I am combating, the change the French are undergoing may possibly end in something we know not what, and bring on us danger we know not whence. In short, it may end in raw head and bloody bones in the dark. Very well. Let raw head and bloody bones come, and then we shall be justified in making our peace with him, by renouncing our ancient friends and his enemies. For observe, it is not the *possibility of danger* which absolves a party from his contract; for that possibility always exists, and in every case. It existed in the present one at the moment of making the contract. If *possibilities* would avoid contracts, there never could be a valid contract; for possibilities hang over everything. Obligation is not suspended till the danger is become real, and the moment of it so imminent that we can no longer avoid decision without forever losing the opportunity to do it. But can a danger which has not yet taken its shape, which does not yet exist, and never may exist, which cannot, therefore, be defined, can such a danger, I ask, be so imminent that if we fail to pronounce on it in this moment we can never have another opportunity of doing it?

4. The danger apprehended, is it that the treaties remaining valid, the clause guaranteeing their West India islands will engage us in the war? But does the guarantee engage us to enter into the war in any event? Are we to enter into it before we are called on by our allies? Have we been called on by them — shall we ever be called on? Is it their interest to call on us? Can they call on us before their islands are invaded, or imminently threatened? If they can save them themselves, have they a right to call on us? Are we obliged to go to war at once, without trying peaceable negotiations with their enemy?

If all these questions be against us, there are still others behind. Are we in a condition to go to war? Can we be expected to begin before we are in condition? Will the islands be lost if we do not save them? Have we the means of saving them? If we cannot save them, are we bound to go to war for a desperate object? Will not a ten-year forbearance in us to call them into the guarantee of our posts entitle us to some indulgence?

Many if not most of these questions offer grounds of doubt whether the clause of guarantee will draw us into the war. Consequently, if this be the danger apprehended, it is not yet certain enough to authorize us in sound morality to declare, at the moment, the treaties null.

5. Is the danger apprehended from the 17th Article of the Treaty of Commerce, which admits French ships of war and privateers to come and go freely, with prizes made on their enemies, while their enemies are not to have the same privilege with prizes made on the French? But Holland and Prussia have approved of this article in our treaty with France by subscribing to an express salvo of it in our treaties with them. And England in her last treaty with France has entered into the same stipulation verbatim, and placed us in her ports on the same footing on which she is in ours, in case of a war of either of us with France. If we are engaged in such a war, England must receive prizes made on us by the French and exclude those made on the French by us. Nay, further, in this very article of her treaty with France is a salvo of any similar article in any anterior treaty of either party, and ours with France being anterior, this salvo confirms it expressly. Neither of these three powers, then, have a right to complain of this article in our treaty.

6. Is the danger apprehended from the 22nd Article of our Treaty of Commerce which prohibits the enemies of France from fitting out privateers in our ports, or selling their prizes here? But we are free to refuse

the same thing to France, there being no stipulation to the contrary, and we ought to refuse it on principles of fair neutrality.

7. But the reception of a minister from the Republic of France without qualifications, it is thought, will bring us into danger; because this, it is said, will determine the continuance of the treaty, and take from us the right of self-liberation, when at anytime hereafter our safety would require us to use it. The reception of the minister at all (in favor of which Colonel Hamilton has given his opinion, though reluctantly, as he confessed) is an acknowledgement of the legitimacy of their government; and if the qualifications meditated are to deny that legitimacy, it will be a curious compound which is to admit and deny the same thing. But I deny that the reception of a minister has anything to do with the treaties. There is not a word, in either of them, about sending ministers. This has been done between us under the common usage of nations and can have no effect either to continue or annul the treaties.

But how can any act of election have the effect to continue a treaty which is acknowledged to be going on still? For it was not pretended the treaty was void, but only voidable if we choose to declare it so. To make it void would require an act of election, but to let it go on requires only that we should do nothing, and doing nothing can hardly be an infraction of peace or neutrality.

But I go further and deny that the most explicit declaration made at this moment, that we acknowledge the obligation of the treaties, could take from us the right of noncompliance at any future time when compliance would involve us in great and inevitable danger.

I conclude, then, that few of these sources threaten any danger at all; and from none of them is it inevitable; and consequently, none of them give us the right at this moment of releasing ourselves from our treaties.

A second limitation on our right of releasing ourselves is that we are to do it from so much of the treaties only as is bringing great and inevitable danger on us, and not from the residue, allowing to the other party a right at the same time to determine whether on our noncompliance with that part they will declare the whole void. This right they would have, but we should not. . . . The only part of the treaties which can really lead us into danger is the clause of guarantee. That clause is all then we could suspend in any case, and the residue will remain or not at the will of the other party.

A third limitation is that where a party from necessity or danger withholds compliance with part of a treaty, it is bound to make compensation where the nature of the case admits and does not dispense with it. . . . If actual circumstances excuse us from entering into the war under the clause of guarantee, it will be a question whether they excuse us from compensation. Our weight in the war admits of an estimate; and that estimate would form the measure of compensation.

If, in withholding a compliance with any part of the treaties, we do it without just cause or compensation, we give to France a cause of war, and so become associated in it on the other side. An injured friend is the bitterest of foes, and France had not discovered either timidity or overmuch forbearance on the late occasions. Is this the position we wish to take for our constituents? It is certainly not the one they would take for themselves. . . .

Upon the whole I conclude:

That the treaties are still binding, notwithstanding the change of government in France; that no part of them, but the clause of guarantee, holds up *danger*, even at a distance.

And, consequently, that a liberation from no other part could be proposed in any case; that if that clause may ever bring *danger,* it is neither extreme, nor imminent, nor even probable; that the authority for renouncing a treaty, when *useless* or *disagreeable,* is either misunderstood or in opposition to itself, to all their writers, and to every moral feeling; that were it not so, these treaties are in fact neither useless nor disagreeable.

That the receiving a minister from France at this time is an act of no significance with respect to the treaties, amounting neither to an admission nor a denial of them, forasmuch as he comes not under any stipulation in them.

That were it an explicit admission, or were an express declaration of this obligation now to be made, it would not take from us that right which exists at all times of liberating ourselves when an adherence to the treaties would be *ruinous* or *destructive* to the society; and that the not renouncing the treaties now is so far from being a breach of neutrality that the doing it would be the breach, by giving just cause of war to France.

---

105.

## James Monroe: On the Role of the Executive in Foreign Affairs

*From the time he entered the Senate in 1790, James Monroe of Virginia was critical of the Washington administration. As a close friend of Jefferson, he opposed the Federalist domination of the government. It was in this role as critic that he wrote the following letters to Jefferson on the problems Monroe felt were created by Washington's Neutrality Proclamation. In 1794, Monroe was appointed minister to France, a position in which his efforts were anything but an unqualified success. The letters to Jefferson are dated May 28 and June 27, 1793.*

Source: *The Writings of James Monroe,* Stanislaus M. Hamilton, ed., Vol. I, New York, 1898.

*May 28, 1793*

The European war becomes daily as it progresses more interesting to us. I was happy to find M. Genet, whom I passed on the road between Fredericksburg and Richmond, had made a most favorable impression on the inhabitants of the latter city. It furnishes a favorable presage of his impression on a more important, though if possible, not a more prejudiced theater.

There can be no doubt that the general sentiment of America is favorable to the French Revolution. The minority compared with the strength of those in that interest, if the division could be properly drawn, would, in my opinion, be as the aggregate of Richmond and Alexandria to Virginia — but general as this sentiment is I believe it is equally so in favor of our neutrality. And this seems to be dictated by the soundest policy even as it may respect the object in view, the success of the French Revolution. For if we were to join France we should from that moment put it out of her power to derive any advantage from these states. We could neither aid her with men nor money. Of the former we have none; and of the latter our weak and improvident war with the Indians together with the debts we have assumed will completely exhaust us.

Our declaration would not be felt on the Continent. It would produce no effect on the general combination of European powers — would not retard the movements of Brunswick's or any other invading army. It would in fact be simply a declaration against Great Britain, which would prove beneficial to her, and highly injurious to France and ourselves. From the view I have of the subject it would relieve her from restraints growing out of the present state of things, which would be both gratifying and advantageous to her. For while the rights of neutrality belong to us some respect will be shown to those rights, nor is it probable that an invasion of them by her will be countenanced by her other associates in the war. Under the protection of these rights the ports and the bottoms of America will be free to France; in addition to which every act of gratuity and favor which a generous and grateful people can bestow, without an infringement of them on the other side, will be shown.

France may greatly profit from this situation, for under a wise management immense resources may be gathered hence to aid her operations and support her cause. And America must flourish under it, if indeed it were generous to count her profits arising from the general misfortunes of mankind. Let it be noticed as a posterior consideration, after estimating the effect our declaration of neutrality might produce upon the affairs of France.

On the other hand, I am persuaded our declaration in favor of France would not only, in a correspondent degree, injure that nation and ourselves but benefit the party we meant to injure. Freed from any embarrassing questions respecting the rights of neutrality, our commerce would be her lawful plunder, and commanding, as I presume she will, the seas, but little would escape her. Neither the vessels of France nor even our own would be safe in our ports, unless we raised fortifications in each for their protection. I shall not, therefore, be surprised to find Great Britain endeavoring to draw us into the war, even against her, by every species of insult and outrage which a proud, selfish, and vindictive nation can impose, or that this disposition should show itself in the impressment of our ships, sailors, and other violations of our neutrality.

Whether an appeal from such conduct should be made to the general sense even of the combined powers, with whom I see no reason why we should not stand on good terms, with a view of degrading her among all civilized nations as the Algiers of Europe, or to any other means for the purpose of teaching her better principles and manners, I will not pretend to determine. Certain however I am, at least this is my present impression, that it is our duty to avoid by every possible dexterity a war which must inevitably injure ourselves and our friends and benefit our enemies.

One circumstance seems to press us at present, and which I fear will lessen, before any possible remedy can be applied, the benefits of our neutrality and to those for whom they are wished — I mean the scarcity of American bottoms. I am told such cannot be procured, and in consequence that our productions cannot be exported. The injury that must arise from such a course will be universally felt. Can this be otherwise remedied than by allowing the American merchants to buy in the bottoms of other nations, for a limited time: twelve months for instance?

I can perceive no other cause at present

which can make the meeting of Congress necessary before, or much before the time appointed; and the fact I hope does not exist, or so partially as will admit of a remedy under the regular operation of the existing law by the great encouragement offered to American ships. If such an event should take place (a more early meeting of Congress), which is much spoken of here by letters from Philadelphia, I shall thank you to mention the time you think it will sit, as it will regulate me in my family and law concerns, and particularly whether I shall bring Mrs. M. with me or leave her behind. If such a call should be made, however injurious it may be to me, I shall obey it, for while I hold the present station, I shall always endeavor to perform its duties.

*June 27, 1793*

In my last I made some observations evincing the propriety and policy of our neutrality in the present European war, but as that sentiment appears to be general, I refer to it now only as a proof that it is likewise mine. It leaves me more at liberty to comment on the conduct of the executive since, which I do the more freely as I do not know what part you have borne in it. The measure I particularly refer to is the proclamation declaring this neutrality, with the reply to the address of some merchants of Philadelphia and the order for the prosecution of two Marines who had embarked in a privateer licensed by the French minister.

I must confess I had considered the proclamation at first as only an admonition to the people to mind their own business and not interfere in the controversy; and in this view, although I could not perceive the necessity of the measure, yet I was inclined to deem it harmless. As the executive magistrate, the competent authority having not otherwise declared, the President might, if he was distrustful of his constituents, endeavor to restrain them within the limits such authority had prescribed, or rather allowed; if indeed there exists in the government a right to inhibit the citizens of the states from taking commissions from either of the powers at war and fighting in their service. I did not suppose it was intended as a matter of right to declare what should be the conduct of these states in relation to that controversy, but the reply to the merchants and the prosecution above mentioned seem to denote the contrary, and to show that the President meant it as such. Upon this construction I deem it both unconstitutional and impolitic.

I cannot conceive upon what principle the right is claimed. I think the position incontrovertible that if he possesses the right to say we shall be neutral, he might say we should not be. The power in both instances must be in the same hands, for if the executive could say we should be neutral, how could the legislature say that we should war? In truth, a right to declare our neutrality, as a distinct authority, cannot exist, for that is only the natural state of things, when the positive power of declaring war is not exerted, and this belongs to the legislature only; any interference therefore with it, by the executive, must be unconstitutional and improper.

As little can in my opinion be said in favor of its policy. 'Tis possible Great Britain might wish to keep us neutral. If such were her disposition, it became her interest to cultivate our friendship by surrendering the posts, etc., while our conduct was in suspense that anxiety would be increased; but by this precipitate declaration the point has been given up, and for what object? What do we gain by it? We committed no offense, until we should violate the laws of neutrality. And no power could compel us to say what part we would take in the controversy, by holding aloof on that head nor could be dissatisfied except France in case she should claim the guarantee — declarations of neutrality I believe generally succeed applications for them, or the contrary course. Had France applied for our aid, or had Britain that we would not aid her, then in either case, such notification would have been regular. But a declaration like ours is, I suspect, without precedent. It loses the merit of having not refused France, or of accommodating Britain. It gives us no claim upon either court. France indeed it outrages, for it denies her claim of guarantee, or yielding it up, the merit of the concession. And Britain it assures of an accommodation where she may wish it, without even the trouble of asking for it.

Again, why prosecute our citizens for taking commissions in the French service; against what law have they offended, or upon what principle are they charged? The mere acceptance of the commission cannot be deemed criminal, and the act of hostility upon the British vessel was without the jurisdiction of these states, as I presume upon the high seas — and the doctrine is well established that no offense can be committed against the laws of any society beyond the limits within which they operate; for instance, that an offense such as murder or the like, committed in France, cannot be punished here; and if upon the sea, the principle is the same unless the party be a pirate, and in that case amenable to the Admiralty tribunals of every country. The subsequent act of bringing the vessel into port here does not, I suppose, constitute the ground for prosecution, more than if these men had carried, or aided in carrying her, to the Island of St. Croix or elsewhere and returned her, for if it does, the purchasers or mariners afterwards hired to take care of her are equally criminal.

This I take to be the doctrine of the common law — 'tis certainly the base upon which separate and independent societies are erected. Nor has it been enlarged by any act of the legislature that I know of; though indeed I have not the acts with me. So far upon the idea that the French commission gives no separate rights or immunities to one of our citizens, otherwise than if he had none. But does it give none, and of which he may avail himself against the opposite power, and even against his own country? If taken, can he be treated as a pirate? The laws and usages of nations are otherwise. Can we be made answerable for his conduct? If we had hired him to France or Britain, as the Swiss in particular do, we could not be. As a volunteer, then, we certainly are not.

I do not absolutely deny the right of a society to restrain its members from the commission of certain enormities, beyond the limits of its own jurisdiction, under such penalties as it may impose, though according to my present view of the subject, but few if any benefits can be derived from it, and some objections occur. The local tribunal will always be sufficient for his punishment if apprehended and if he escapes, yet the power disposed may surrender him to justice. This I should think enough either for the suppression of vice, or national security. But to give our laws cognizance of offenses committed in other countries must be deemed not only sanguinary as it respects our citizens but a derogation of the sovereignties in which they may be. The offense, for instance, by a fiction of the law must be considered as committed here. May we demand them and rescue him from their courts to be punished here, or shall he be twice punished for the same offense? Nor am I an advocate for privateering; on the contrary could wish the practice suppressed — but presume such reformation should be brought about by conventions throughout the world, and not the desultory operations of any one nation.

But by taking the laws as they are, I cannot perceive wherein they have offended, or upon what principle the prosecution can be supported — in this position I think myself founded in relation to foreign authorities, for there, where the doctrine of allegiance binds the subject in perpetual obedience to his sovereign, it has never been otherwise construed or applied than to prohibit the right of expatriation and, of course, the taking up arms against his native country. To fight in the service of one prince against another was never denied, I believe, to anyone. I suspect it was never asked unless the party were already in the service of his own — but with us will not the rights of citizenship be construed more freely? Will that of expatriation be denied? And may not the mere act of accepting a commission in a foreign service be deemed such if the party pleases? In this state there is a law to authorize it, but the law is drawn in such cautious terms as to leave the point as it stood before, upon foreign authorities, improved by the principles of our Revolution, and was intended not to abrogate any rights but to make sure what had been doubted.

But admitting it to be an offense and punishable by our laws, why prosecute these people until formally demanded by that court, in case she had a right to demand it? Is it that we affect an extraordinary degree of refinement and political purity? The parties at war will not, I apprehend, ascribe it to that motive. Nations more generally shelter their citizens from punishment when due and demanded than otherwise. But to commence it ourselves unauthorized, as I believe, and pursue it with such vigor will be ascribed to some other. If we so seriously abhorred vice, and were disposed to banish it from our country, has no other instance of enormity presented itself worthy of reprehension?

I have but little hope of a fortunate issue from the negotiation in Spain, for I observe that it is conducted on the part of that court by Gardoqui, a subtle and malignant little wretch, highly incensed against us for defeating him on that point here, and he well knows the support he received upon that occasion from a party still high in office and all-powerful in the present administration. The association of Carmel too will, I fear, prove a clog on it, for 'tis possible he might deem a rapid success as a feather to his colleague taken from himself. And with Britain my expectation is on the same level, for our conduct to her since the adoption of the present government, as more fully shown by this declaration of neutrality, and the acceptance of her patronage (for such I presume to be the case by our commission taking the route of Niagara) to obtain our peace with the Indians, must convince them of our subservience to their views, or how extremely impotent and contemptible we are.

We forced that nation to abandon those very Indians in her treaty with us, and now, when opposed to them alone, divided too on their part, and strengthened on ours by alliances with several tribes, we accept, if not solicit, her aid to make our peace with those whom they had sacrificed. Either this nation must be among the most unprincipled, or she will endeavor to compensate her allies at our expense. To expect the contrary, unless we have the fullest assurance of her perfidy, must show the weakness of our councils. I trust that our humiliation has attained its lowest point, when we are capable of placing ourselves in a situation so degrading and shameful. But the solidity of our credit with the brokers at Amsterdam is a medicine of sufficient virtue to heal every wound that can be given to the national honor and reputation.

106.

## Alexander Hamilton: Neutrality and the National Interest

*Many Americans were convinced that Washington had exceeded his constitutional authority in the Neutrality Proclamation. Alexander Hamilton, using the pseudonym, "Pacificus," responded to these accusations in a series of newspaper articles in which he broadly interpreted the powers of the executive as stated in the Constitution. In these essays, printed in July 1793, Hamilton denied that international politics should be treated as relations between individuals, claiming that the self-interest of a nation took precedence over any acts of benevolence or generosity to another nation. He pointed out that France's participation in the American Revolution had been prompted not by her love for liberty, but by her commercial objectives and particularly her hope to crush Great Britain's interests in America. The selections that follow first appeared on July 6 and July 13, respectively, in the* Gazette of the United States.

Source: *The Works of Alexander Hamilton,* Henry Cabot Lodge, ed., Vol. IV, New York, 1885, pp. 157-162, 167-175.

I.

### Pacificus, No. III

France, at the time of issuing the proclamation, was engaged in war with a considerable part of Europe, and likely to be embroiled with almost all the rest, without a single ally in that quarter of the globe. In such a situation, it is evident that however she may be able to defend herself at home, of which her factions and internal agitations furnish the only serious doubt, she cannot make external efforts in any degree proportioned to those which can be made against her.

This state of things alone discharges the United States from an obligation to embark in her quarrel.

It is known that we are wholly destitute of naval force. France, with all the great maritime powers united against her, is unable to supply this deficiency. She cannot afford us that species of cooperation which is necessary to render our efforts useful to her, and to prevent our experiencing the destruction of our trade and the most calamitous inconveniences in other respects.

Our guaranty does not look to France herself. It does not relate to her immediate defense but to the defense and preservation of her American colonies; objects of which she might be deprived, and yet remain a great, a powerful, and a happy nation. In the actual situation of this country, and in relation to a matter of only secondary importance to France, it may fairly be maintained that an ability in her to supply, in a competent degree, our deficiency of naval force is a condition of our obligation to perform the guaranty on our part. Had the United States a powerful marine, or could they command one in time, this reasoning would not be solid; but circumstanced as they are, it is presumed to be well-founded.

There would be no proportion between the mischiefs and perils to which the United States would expose themselves, by embarking in the war, and the benefit which the nature of their stipulation aims at securing to France, or that which it would be in their power actually to render her by becoming a party.

This disproportion would be a valid reason for not executing the guaranty. All contracts are to receive a reasonable construction. Self-preservation is the first duty of a nation; and though in the performance of stipulations relating to war, good faith requires that its ordinary hazards should be fairly met because they are directly contemplated by such stipulations, yet it does not require that extraordinary and extreme hazards should be run, especially where the object to be gained or secured is only a partial or particular interest of the ally, for whom they are to be encountered.

As in the present instance, good faith does not require that the United States should put in jeopardy their essential interests, perhaps their very existence, in one of the most unequal contests in which a nation could be engaged to secure to France — what? Her West India islands and other less important possessions in America. For it is always to be remembered that the stipulations of the United States do, in no event, reach beyond this point. If they were, upon the strength of their guaranty, to engage in the war, and could make any arrangement with the belligerent powers for securing to France those islands and those possessions, they would be at perfect liberty instantly to withdraw. They would not be bound to prosecute the war one moment longer. They are under no obligation in any event, as far as the faith of treaties is concerned, to assist France in defense of her liberty; a topic on which so much has been said, so very little to the purpose, as it regards the present question.

The contest in which the United States would plunge themselves, were they to take part with France, would possibly be still more unequal than that in which France herself is engaged. With the possessions of Great Britain and Spain on both flanks, the numerous Indian tribes under the influence and direction of those powers along our whole interior frontier, with a long extended seacoast, with no maritime force of our own, and with the maritime force of all Europe against us, with no fortifications whatever, and with a population not exceeding 4,000,000, it is impossible to imagine a more unequal contest than that in which we should be involved in the case supposed. From such a contest we are dissuaded by the most cogent motives of self-preservation, no less than of interest.

We may learn from [Emmerich de] Vattel, one of the best writers on the laws of nations, that

> if a state which has promised succors finds itself unable to furnish them, its very inability is its exemption; and if the furnishing the succors would expose it to an evident danger, this also is a lawful dispensation. The case would render the treaty pernicious to the state, and therefore not obligatory. But this applies to an imminent danger threatening the safety of the state; the case of such a danger is tacitly and necessarily reserved in every treaty.

If, too, as no sensible and candid man will deny, the extent of the present combination against France is in a degree to be ascribed to imprudences on her part, the exemption to the United States is still more manifest and complete. No country is bound to partake in hazards of the most critical kind, which may have been produced or promoted by the indiscretion and intemperance of another. This is an obvious dictate of reason, with which the common sense and common practice of mankind coincide.

To the foregoing considerations, it may perhaps be added with no small degree of force that military stipulations in national treaties contemplate only the ordinary case of foreign war, and are irrelative to the contests which grow out of revolutions of government, unless where they have express reference to a revolution begun, or where there is a guaranty of the existing constitution of a nation, or where there is a personal alliance for the defense of a prince and his family.

The revolution in France is the primitive source of the war in which she is engaged. The restoration of the monarchy is the avowed object of some of her enemies, and the implied one of all. That question, then, is essentially involved in the principle of the war, a question certainly never in the contemplation of the government with which our treaty was made, and, it may thence be fairly inferred, never intended to be embraced by it.

The inference is that the United States fulfilled the utmost that could be claimed by the nation of France when they so far respected its decision as to recognize the newly constituted authorities, giving operation to the treaty of alliance for future occasions, but considering the present war as a tacit exception. Perhaps, too, this exception is in other respects due to the circumstances under which the engagements between the two countries were contracted. It is impossible, prejudice apart, not to perceive a delicate embarrassment between the theory and fact of our political relations to France.

On these grounds, also, as well as that of the present war being offensive on the side of France, the United States have valid and honorable pleas to offer against the execution of the guaranty if it should be claimed by France; and the President was in every view fully justified in pronouncing that the duty and interest of the United States dictated a neutrality in the war.

## II.

## Pacificus, No. V

France, the rival, time immemorial, of Great Britain, had, in the course of the war which ended in 1763, suffered, from the successful arms of the latter, the severest losses and the most mortifying defeats. Britain, from that moment, had acquired an ascendant in the affairs of Europe and in the commerce of the world, too decided and too humiliating to be endured without extreme impatience, and an eager desire of finding a favorable opportunity to destroy it and to repair the breach which had been made in the national glory. The animosity of wounded pride conspired with calculations of interest to give a keen edge to that impatience and to that desire.

The American Revolution offered the occasion. It early attracted the notice of France, though with extreme circumspection. As far as countenance and aid may be presumed to have been given prior to the epoch of the acknowledgement of our independence, it will be no unkind derogation to assert that they were marked neither with liberality nor with vigor; that they wore the appearance rather of a desire to keep alive disturbances which might embarrass a rival than of a serious design to assist a revolution, or a serious expectation that it could be effected.

The victories of Saratoga, the capture of an army, which went a great way toward deciding the issue of the contest, decided also the hesitations of France. They established in the government of that country a confidence of our ability to accomplish our purpose, and, as a consequence of it, produced the treaties of alliance and commerce.

It is impossible to see in all this anything more than the conduct of a jealous competitor, embracing a most promising opportunity to repress the pride and diminish the power of a dangerous rival by seconding a successful resistance to its authority, with the object of lopping off a valuable portion of its dominions. The dismemberment of this country from Great Britain was an obvious and a very important interest of France. It cannot be doubted that it was both the determining motive and an adequate compensation for the assistance afforded to us.

Men of sense, in this country, derived encouragement to the part which their zeal for liberty prompted them to take in our revolution, from the probability of the cooperation of France and Spain. It will be remembered that this argument was used in the publications of the day; but upon what was it bottomed? Upon the known competition between those nations and Great Britain, upon their evident interest to reduce her power and circumscribe her empire; not certainly from motives of regard to our interest, or of attachment to our cause. Whoever should have alleged the latter as the grounds of the expectation held out would have been then justly considered as a visionary or a deceiver. And whoever shall now ascribe to such motives the aid which we did receive would not deserve to be viewed in a better light.

The inference from these facts is not obscure. Aid and cooperation, founded upon a great interest, pursued and obtained by the party rendering them, is not a proper stock upon which to engraft that enthusiastic gratitude which is claimed from us by those who love France more than the United States.

This view of the subject, extorted by the extravagancy of such a claim, is not meant to disparage the just pretensions of France to our goodwill. Though neither in the motives to the success which she furnished, nor in their extent (considering how powerfully the point of honor, in such war, reinforced the considerations of interest when she was once engaged), can be found a sufficient basis for that gratitude which is the theme of so much declamation, yet we shall find, in the manner of affording them, just cause for our esteem and friendship.

France did not attempt, in the first instance, to take advantage of our situation to extort from us any humiliating or injurious concessions as the price of her assistance; nor afterwards, in the progress of the war, to impose hard terms as the condition of particular aids. Though this course was certainly dictated by policy, yet it was a magnanimous policy, such as always constitutes a title to the approbation and esteem of mankind, and a claim to the friendship and acknowledgement of the party in whose favor it is practised.

But these sentiments are satisfied on the part of the nation when they produce sincere wishes for the happiness of the party from whom it has experienced such conduct, and a cordial disposition to render all good and friendly offices which can be rendered without prejudice to its own solid and permanent interests.

To ask of a nation so situated, to make a sacrifice of substantial interest; to expose itself to the jealousy, ill will, or resentment of the rest of the world; to hazard, in an eminent degree, its own safety for the benefit of the party who may have observed toward it the conduct which has been described would be to ask more than the nature of the case demands, more than the fundamental maxims of society authorize, more than the dictates of sound reason justify.

A question has arisen with regard to the proper object of that gratitude which is so much insisted upon: whether it be the unfortunate prince by whom the assistance received was given, or the nation of whom he was the chief or the organ? It is extremely interesting to the national justice, to form right conceptions on this point. The arguments which support the latter idea are as follows:

> Louis XVI was but the constitutional agent of the French people. He acted for and on behalf of the nation; it was with their money and their blood he supported our cause. It is to them, therefore, not to him, that our obligations are due. Louis XVI, in taking our part, was no doubt actuated by state policy. An absolute prince could not love liberty. But the people of France patronized our cause with zeal, from sympathy in its object. The people, therefore, not its monarch, are entitled to our sympathy.

This reasoning may be ingenious, but it is not founded in nature or fact.

Louis XVI, though no more than the constitutional agent of the nation, had, at the time, the sole power of managing its affairs, the legal right of directing its will and its force. It belonged to him to assist us, or not, without consulting the nation; and he did assist without such consultation. His will alone was active; that of the nation passive. If there was kindness in the decision, demanding a return of goodwill, it was the kindness of Louis XVI — his heart was the depository of the sentiment. Let the genuine voice of nature, then, unperverted by political subtleties, pronounce whether the acknowledgement, which may be due for that kindness, can be equitably transferred from him to others who had no share in the decision; whether the principle of gratitude ought to determine us to behold with indifference his misfortunes, and with satisfaction the triumphs of his foes.

The doctrine that the prince is the organ of his nation is conclusive to enforce the obligations of good faith between two states — in other words, the observance of duties stipulated in treaties for national purposes; and it will even suffice to continue to a nation a claim to the friendship and goodwill of another, resulting from friendly offices done by its prince; but it would be to carry the principle much too far, and to render it infinitely too artificial, to attribute to it the effect of transferring such a claim from the prince to the nation by way of opposition and contrast. Friendship, goodwill, gratitude for favors received have so inseparable a reference to the motives with which, and to the persons by whom, they were rendered as to be incapable of being transferred to another at his expense.

But Louis XVI, it is said, acted from reasons of state, without regard to our cause, while the people of France patronized it with zeal and attachment.

As far as the assertion with regard to the monarch may be well-founded, and is an objection to our gratitude to him, it destroys the whole fabric of gratitude to France. For our gratitude is, and must be, relative to the services performed. The nation can only claim it on the score of their having been rendered by their agent with their means. If the views with which he performs them divested them of the merit which ought to inspire gratitude, none is due. The nation no more than their agent can claim it.

With regard to the individual good wishes of the citizens of France, as they did not produce the services rendered to us as a nation, they can be no foundation for national gratitude. They can only call for a reciprocation of individual good wishes. They cannot form the basis of public obligation.

But the assertion takes more for granted than there is reason to believe true.

Louis XVI no doubt took part in our contest from reasons of state; but Louis XVI was a man, humane and kindhearted. The acts of his early youth had entitled him to this character. It is natural for a man of this disposition to become interested in the cause of those whom he protects or aids;

and if the concurrent testimony of the period may be credited, there was no man in France more personally friendly to the cause of this country than Louis XVI. I am much misinformed if repeated declarations of the venerable Franklin did not attest this fact.

It is a just tribute to the people of France to admit that they manifested a lively interest in the cause of America; but while motives are scanned, who can say how much of it is to be ascribed to the antipathy which they bore to their rival neighbor — how much to their sympathy in the object of our pursuit? It is certain that the love of liberty was not a national sentiment in France when a zeal for our cause first appeared among that people.

There is reason to believe, too, that the attachment to our cause, which ultimately became very extensive, if not general, did not originate with the mass of the French people. It began with the circles more immediately connected with the court, and was thence diffused through the nation.

This observation, besides its tendency to rectify ideas which are calculated to give a false current to the public feeling, may serve to check the spirit of illiberal invective which has been wantonly indulged against those distinguished friends of America, who, though the authors of the French Revolution, have fallen victims to it; because their principles would not permit them to go the whole length of an entire subversion of the monarchy.

The preachers of gratitude are not ashamed to brand Louis XVI as a tyrant, Lafayette as a traitor. But how can we wonder at this, when they insinuate a distrust even of a ——— !!!

In urging the friendly disposition to our cause, manifested by the people of France, as a motive to our gratitude toward that people, it ought not to be forgotten that those dispositions were not confined to the inhabitants of that country. They were eminently shared by the people of the United Provinces, produced to us valuable pecuniary aids from their citizens, and eventually involved them in the war on the same side with us. It may be added, too, that here the patronage of our cause emphatically began with the mass of the community, not originating, as in France, with the government, but finally implicating the government in the consequences.

Our cause had also numerous friends in other countries — even in that with which we were at war. Conducted with prudence, moderation, justice, and humanity, it may be said to have been a popular cause among mankind, conciliating the countenance of princes and the affection of nations.

The dispositions of the individual citizens of France can, therefore, in no sense be urged as constituting a peculiar claim to our gratitude. As far as there is foundation for it, it must be referred to the services rendered to us, and, in the first instance, to the unfortunate monarch that rendered them. This is the conclusion of nature and reason.

---

*The English know very well that the Americans would give their lives in defense of their national soil, but that they dislike fighting a war away from their homes. They have not yet reached the point where they can seriously worry the English. Some day, perhaps, they will be the avengers of the seas, but that day is still far off. The Americans will become great slowly, or not at all.*

NAPOLEON BONAPARTE

107.

# James Madison: For Congressional Leadership in Foreign Affairs

*Thomas Jefferson was astounded by Hamilton's interpretation of foreign policy, particularly his explanation of the President's Neutrality Proclamation. Jefferson continued to believe that loyalty, gratitude, and generosity should play their part in foreign policy decisions. The secretary of state begged his friend, James Madison, to write a rebuttal to the "Pacificus" articles. "For God's sake, my dear sir," Jefferson wrote, "take up your pen, select the most striking heresies and cut him to pieces in the face of the public." Under the pen name, "Helvidius," Madison followed Jefferson's advice, holding that the Congress, not the executive, should direct foreign policy. The Neutrality Proclamation, he claimed, had the force of law, and the President had thus usurped a strictly congressional power. The "Helvidius" letters first appeared in the* Gazette of the United States *from August 24 to September 18, 1793. The selection that follows is Letter V.*

Source: *Madison Letters,* I, pp. 646-654.

Having seen that the executive has no constitutional right to interfere in any question, whether there be or be not a cause of war, and the extensive consequences flowing from the doctrines on which such a claim has been asserted, it remains to be inquired whether the writer is better warranted in the fact which he assumes, namely, that the proclamation of the executive has undertaken to decide the question whether there be a cause of war or not, in the article of guaranty between the United States and France, and in so doing has exercised the right which is claimed for that department.

Before I proceed to the examination of this point, it may not be amiss to advert to the novelty of the phraseology, as well as of the doctrines espoused by this writer. The source from which the former is evidently borrowed may enlighten our conjectures with regard to the source of the latter. It is a just observation also, that words have often a gradual influence on ideas, and when used in an improper sense may cover fallacies which would not otherwise escape detection.

I allude particularly to his application of the term "government" to the *executive authority alone.* The proclamation is a "manifestation of the sense of the *government.*" "Why did not the *government* wait, etc." "The policy on the part of the *government* of removing all doubt as to *its own disposition.*" "It was of great importance that our citizens should understand as early as possible the opinion entertained by the *government,* etc." "If, in addition to the rest, the early manifestation of *the views* of the *government* had any effect *in fixing the public opinion,* etc."

The reader will probably be struck with the reflection that if the proclamation really possessed the character and was to have the effects here ascribed to it, something more than the authority of *the government,* in the writer's sense of government, would have been a necessary sanction to the act; and if the term "government" be removed and that of "president" substituted, in the sentences quoted, the justice of the reflection will be felt with peculiar force. But I remark only on the singularity of the style adopted by the writer as showing either that the phraseology of a foreign government is more familiar to him than the phraseology proper to our own, or that he wishes to propagate a familiarity of the former in preference to the latter. I do not know what degree of disapprobation others may think due to this innovation of language; but I consider it as far above a trivial criticism to observe that it is by no means unworthy of attention, whether viewed with an eye to its probable cause or its apparent tendency.

"The government" unquestionably means, in the United States, the whole government, not the executive part, either exclusively or *preeminently,* as it may do in a monarchy, where the splendor of prerogative eclipses, and the machinery of influence directs, every other part of the government. In the former and proper sense, the term has hitherto been used in official proceedings, in public discussions, and in private discourse. It is as short and as easy, and less liable to misapprehension, to say the executive or the president as to say the government. In a word, the new dialect could not proceed either from necessity, conveniency, propriety, or perspicuity; and being in opposition to common usage, so marked a fondness for it justifies the notice here taken of it. It shall no longer detain me, however, from the more important subject of the present paper.

I proceed therefore to observe, that as a "proclamation," in its *ordinary* use, is an address to citizens or subjects only; as it is always understood to relate to the law *actually in operation,* and to be an act *purely* and *exclusively* executive, there can be no implication in the *name* or the *form* of such an instrument, that it was meant principally for the information of foreign nations; far less that it related to an *eventual stipulation* on the subject *acknowledged* to be within the *legislative province.*

When the writer, therefore, undertook to engraft his new prerogative on the proclamation by ascribing to it so unusual and unimplied a meaning, it was evidently incumbent on him to show that the *text* of the instrument could not be satisfied by any other construction than his own. Has he done this? No. What has he done? He has called the proclamation a proclamation of neutrality; he has put his own arbitrary meaning on that phrase, and has then proceeded in his arguments and his inferences with as much confidence as if no question was ever to be asked, whether the term "neutrality" be in the proclamation, or whether if there, it could justify the use he makes of it.

It has appeared from observations already made that if the term "neutrality" was in the proclamation, it could not avail the writer in the present discussion; but the fact is, no such term is to be found in it, nor any other term of a meaning equivalent to that in which the term "neutrality" is used by him.

There is the less pretext in the present case for hunting after any latent or extraordinary object, because an obvious and legal one is at hand to satisfy the occasion on which the proclamation [was] issued. The existence of war among several nations with which the United States have an extensive intercourse; the duty of the executive to preserve peace by enforcing its laws while those laws continued in force; the danger that indiscreet citizens might be tempted or surprised by the crisis into unlawful proceedings, tending to involve the United States in a war which the competent authority might decide them to be at liberty to avoid, and which, if they should be judged not at liberty to avoid, the other party to the *eventual contract* might be willing not to impose on them; these surely might have been sufficient grounds for the measure pursued by the executive; and being legal and rational grounds, it would be wrong, if there be no necessity to look beyond them.

If there be anything in the proclamation of which the writer could have made a handle, it is the part which declares the *disposition,* the *duty,* and the *interest* of the United States in relation to the war existing in Europe. As the legislature is the only competent and constitutional organ of the will of the nation, that is of its disposition, its duty, and its interest in relation to a commencement of war, in like manner as the President and Senate *jointly,* not the President *alone,* are in relation to peace after war has been commenced, I will not dissemble my wish that a language less exposed to criticism had been preferred. But taking the expressions, in the sense of the writer himself, as analogous to the language which might be proper on the reception of a public minister or any similar occasion, it is evident that his construction can derive no succor even from this source.

If the proclamation, then, does not *require* the construction which this writer has taken the liberty of putting on it, I leave it to be decided whether the following considerations do not forbid us to suppose that the President could have intended, by that act, to embrace and prejudge the legislative question, whether there was or was not, under the circumstances of the case, a cause of war in the article of guaranty.

It has been shown that such an intention would have usurped a prerogative not vested in the executive, and even *confessedly* vested in another department.

In exercising the constitutional power of deciding a question of war, the legislature ought to be as free to decide, according to its own sense of the public good, on one side as on the other side. Had the proclamation prejudged the question on either side and *proclaimed its decision to the world,* the legislature, instead of being as free as it ought, might be thrown under the dilemma of either sacrificing its judgment to that of the executive, or, by opposing the executive judgment, of producing a relation between the two departments extremely delicate among ourselves, and of the worst influence on the national character and interests abroad. A variance of this nature, it will readily be perceived, would be very different from a want of conformity to the *mere recommendations* of the executive in the measures adopted by the legislature.

It does not appear that such a proclamation could have even pleaded any call, from either of the parties at war with France, for an explanation of the light in which the guaranty was viewed. While, indeed, no positive indication whatever was given of hostile purposes, it is not conceived that any power could have decently made such an application, or if it had, that a proclamation would have been either a satisfactory or an honorable answer. It could not have been satisfactory if serious apprehensions were entertained, because it would not have proceeded from that authority which alone could definitely pronounce the will of the United States on the subject. It would not have been honorable, because a private diplomatic answer only is due to a private diplomatic application; and to have done so much more would have marked a pusillanimity and want of dignity in the executive.

But whether the executive was or was not applied to, or whatever weight be allowed to that circumstance, it ought never to be presumed that the executive would so abruptly, so publicly, and so solemnly proceed to disclaim a sense of the contract, which the other party might consider and wish to support by discussion, as its true and reasonable import. It is asked, indeed, in a tone that sufficiently displays the spirit in which the writer construes both the proclamation and the treaty, "Did the executive stand in need of the logic of a foreign agent to enlighten it as to the duties or the interests of the nation; or was it bound to ask his consent to a step which appeared to itself consistent with the former and conducive to the latter? The sense of treaties was to be learned from the treaties themselves."

Had he consulted his Vattel instead of his animosity to France, he would have discovered that however humiliating it might be to wait for a foreign logic, to assist the interpretation of an act depending on the national authority alone, yet in the case of a treaty, which is as much the treaty of a foreign nation as it is ours, and in which foreign duties and rights are as much involved as ours, the sense of the treaty, though to be learned from the treaty itself, is to be equally learned by both parties to it. Neither of them can have a right more than the other to say what a particular article means; and where there is equality without a judge, consultation is as consistent with dignity as it is conducive to harmony and friendship; let Vattel, however, be heard on the subject.

> The third general maxim, or principle, on the subject of interpretation [of treaties] is: *that neither the one nor the other of the interested or contracting powers has a right to interpret the act or treaty at its pleasure.* For if you are at liberty to give my promise what sense you please, you will have the power of obliging me to do whatever you have a mind, contrary to my intention, and beyond my real engagement; and reciprocally, if I am allowed to explain my promises as I please, I may render them vain and illusive, by giving them a sense quite different from that in which they were presented to you, and in which you must have taken them in accepting them.

The writer ought to have been particularly sensible of the improbability that a precipitate and *ex parte* decision of the question arising under the guaranty could have been intended by the proclamation. He had but just gone through his undertaking to prove that the article of guaranty like the rest of the treaty is defensive, not offensive. He had examined his books and retailed his quotations to show that the criterion between the two kinds of war is the circumstance of priority in the attack. He could not, therefore, but know that according to his own principles the question whether the United States were under an obligation or not to take part in the war was a *question of fact* whether the first attack was made by France or her enemies.

And to decide a question of fact, as well as of principle, without waiting for such representations and proofs as the absent and interested party might have to produce would have been a proceeding contrary to the ordinary maxims of justice, and requiring circumstances of a very peculiar nature to warrant it toward any nation. Toward a nation which could verify her claim to more than bare justice by our own reiterated and formal acknowledgements, and which must in her present singular and interesting situation have a peculiar sensibility to marks of our friendship or alienation, the impropriety of such a proceeding would be infinitely increased, and in the same proportion the improbability of its having taken place.

There are reasons of another sort which would have been a bar to such a proceeding. It would have been as impolitic as it would have been unfair and unkind.

If France meant not to insist on the guaranty, the measure, without giving any present advantage, would have deprived the United States of a future claim which may be of importance to their safety. It would have inspired France with jealousies of a secret bias in this country toward some of her enemies, which might have left in her breast a spirit of contempt and revenge of which the effects might be felt in various ways. It must, in particular, have tended to inspire her with a disinclination to feed our commerce with those important advantages which it already enjoys, and those more important ones, which it anxiously contemplates. The nation that consumes more of the fruits of our soil than any other nation in the world, and supplies the only foreign raw material of extensive use in the United States, would not be unnecessarily provoked by those who understand the public interest, and make it their study, as it is their interest to advance it.

I am aware that the commonplace remark will be interposed that "commercial privileges are not worth having when not secured by mutual interest; and never worth purchasing because they will grow of themselves out of a mutual interest." Prudent men, who do not suffer their reason to be misled by their prejudices, will view the subject in a juster light. They will reflect that if commercial privileges are not worth purchasing, they are worth having without purchase; that in the commerce of a great nation, there are valuable privileges which may be granted or not granted, or granted either to this or that country, without any sensible influence on the interest of the nation itself; that the friendly or unfriendly disposition of a country is always an article of moment in the calculations of a comprehensive interest; that some sacrifices of interest will be made to other motives, by nations as well as by individuals, though not with the same frequency, or in the same proportions; that more of a disinterested conduct or of a conduct founded on liberal views of interest prevails in some nations than in others; that as far as can be seen of the influence of the Revolution on the genius and the policy of France, particularly with regard to the United States, everything is to be hoped by the latter on this subject, which one country can reasonably hope from another. In this point of view a greater error could not have been committed than in a step that might have turned the present disposition of France to open her commerce to us as far as a liberal calculation of her interest would permit, and her friendship toward us, and confidence in our friendship toward her, could prompt into a disposition to shut it as closely against us as the united motives of interest, of distrust, and of ill will could urge her.

On the supposition that France might intend to claim the guaranty a hasty and harsh refusal before we were asked, on a ground that accused her of being the aggressor in the war against every power in the catalogue of her enemies, and in a crisis when all her sensibility must be alive toward the United States, would have given every possible irritation to a disappointment which every motive that one nation could feel toward another and toward itself, required to be alleviated by all the circumspection and delicacy that could be applied to the occasion.

The silence of the executive since the accession of Spain and Portugal to the war against France throws great light on the present discussion. Had the proclamation been issued in the sense and for the purposes ascribed to it, that is to say, as a declaration of neutrality, another would have followed, on that event. If it was the right and duty of the *government,* that is, the *President,* to manifest to Great Britain and Holland, and to the American merchants and citizens, his *sense,* his *disposition,* and his *views* on the question, whether *the United States were under the circumstances of the case, bound or not, to execute the clause of guaranty, and not to leave it uncertain whether the executive did or did not believe a state of neutrality,* to be consistent with our treaties, the *duty* as well as the right prescribed a similar manifestation to all the parties concerned after Spain and Portugal had joined the other maritime enemies of France. The opinion of the executive with respect to a consistency or inconsistency of neutrality with treaties in the *latter case* could not be *inferred* from the proclamation in the former, because the *circumstances might be different.*

Taking the proclamation in its proper sense, as reminding all concerned that as the United States were at peace (that state not being affected by foreign wars, and only to be changed by the legislative authority of the country) the laws of peace were still obligatory and would be enforced, and the inference is so obvious and so applicable to all other cases *whatever circumstances* may distinguish them, that another proclamation would be unnecessary. Here is a new aspect of the whole subject, admonishing us in the most striking manner at once of the danger of the prerogative contended for, and the absurdity of the distinctions and arguments employed in its favor. It would be as impossible in practice as it is in theory to separate the power of judging and concluding that the obligations of a treaty do not impose war from that of judging and concluding that the obligations *do impose war*. In certain cases, silence would proclaim the latter conclusion as intelligibly as words could do the former. The writer, indeed, has himself abandoned the distinction . . . by declaring expressly that the object of the proclamation would have been defeated "by leaving it uncertain whether the executive did or *did not* believe a state of neutrality to be consistent with our treaties."

108.

## Eli Whitney: The Invention of the Cotton Gin

*Following his graduation from Yale University in 1792, Eli Whitney traveled to Savannah, Georgia, where he became fascinated with the slow and tedious process of cleaning cotton by hand. He began to sketch on paper some ideas for a machine that would speed up the operation, and within a few weeks he had developed the cotton engine, which quickly became elided to "cotton gin." This amazing invention produced fifty pounds of cleaned cotton per day, whereas only one pound could be processed in the same time by hand. Upon returning to New Haven, Whitney sent the following letter, written on September 11, 1793, to his father discussing his ventures of the preceding summer.*

Source: *American Historical Review*, October 1897.

I went from New York with the family of the late Major General Greene to Georgia. I went immediately with the family to their plantation, about twelve miles from Savannah, with an expectation of spending four or five days and then proceed into Carolina to take the school. . . .

During this time I heard much said of the extreme difficulty of ginning cotton, that is, separating it from its seeds. There were a number of very respectable gentlemen at Mrs. Greene's who all agreed that if a machine could be invented which would clean the cotton with expedition, it would be a great thing both to the country and to the inventor. I involuntarily happened to be thinking on the subject and struck out a plan of a machine in my mind, which I communicated to Miller (who is agent to the executors of General Greene and resides in the family, a man of respectability and property); he was pleased with the plan and said if I would pursue it and try an experiment to see if it would answer, he would be at the whole expense; I should lose nothing but my time, and if I succeeded we would share the profits.

Previous to this I found I was like to be disappointed in my school, that is, instead of 100, I found I could get only 50 guineas a year. I, however, held the refusal of the school until I tried some experiments. In about ten days I made a little model, for which I was offered, if I would give up all right and title to it, 100 guineas. I concluded to relinquish my school and turn my attention to perfecting the machine. I made one before I came away which required the labor of one man to turn it and with which one man will clean ten times as much cotton as he can in any other way before known, and also cleanse it much better than in the usual mode. This machine may be turned by water or with a horse with the greatest ease, and one man and a horse will do more than fifty men with the old machines. It makes the labor fifty times less, without throwing any class of people out of business.

I returned to the northward for the purpose of having a machine made on a large scale and obtaining a patent for the invention. I went to Philadelphia soon after I arrived, made myself acquainted with the steps necessary to obtain a patent, took several of the steps and the Secretary of State, Mr. Jefferson, agreed to send the patent to me as soon as it could be made out — so that I apprehended no difficulty in obtaining the patent. Since I have been here I have employed several workmen in making machines, and as soon as my business is such that I can leave it a few days, I shall come to Westboro. . . .

I am certain I can obtain a patent in England. As soon as I have got a patent in America I shall go with the machine which I am now making to Georgia, where I shall stay a few weeks to see it at work. From thence I expect to go to England, where I shall probably continue two or three years. How advantageous this business will eventually prove to me, I cannot say. It is generally said by those who know anything about it that I shall make a fortune by it. I have no expectation that I shall make an independent fortune by it, but think I had better pursue it than any other business into which I can enter. Something which cannot be foreseen may frustrate my expectations and defeat my plan; but I am now so sure of success that $10,000, if I saw the money counted out to me, would not tempt me to give up my right and relinquish the object. I wish you, sir, not to show this letter nor communicate anything of its contents to anybody except my brothers and sister, *enjoining* it on them to keep the whole a *profound secret.*

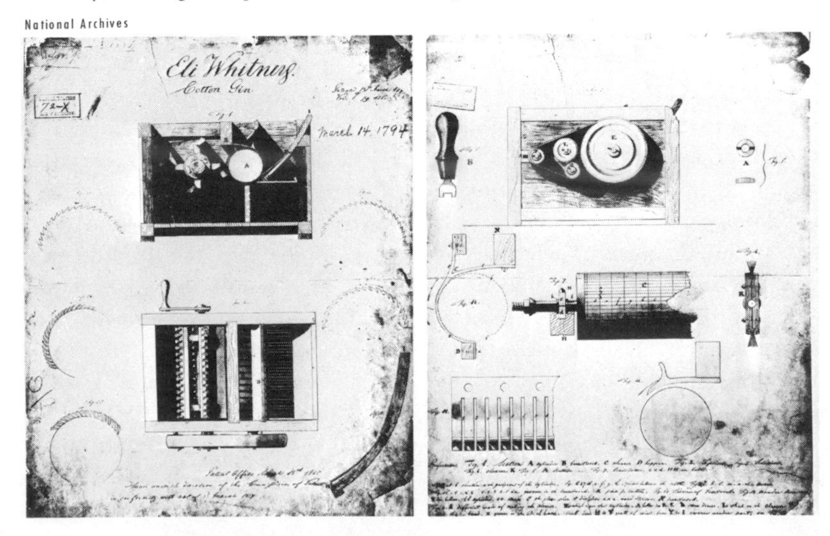


Sketches submitted to the Patent Office by Eli Whitney, showing the operation of the cotton gin

National Archives

# 1794

109.

## Alexander Hamilton: Against an Alliance with France

*Early in 1794, Hamilton published the "Americanus" papers, a continuation of his "Pacificus" papers against United States involvement in European wars. The selection, reprinted below, was written on February 8, 1794.*

Source: *The Works of Alexander Hamilton,* Henry Cabot Lodge, ed., Vol. IV, New York, 1885, pp. 272-282.

Let us now turn to the other side of the medal; to be struck with it, it is not necessary to exaggerate.

All who are not willfully blind must see and acknowledge that this country at present enjoys an unexampled state of prosperity. That war would interrupt it need not be affirmed. We should then, by war, lose the advantage of that astonishing progress in strength, wealth, and improvement which we are now making, and which, if continued for a few years, will place our national rights and interests upon immovable foundations. This loss alone would be of infinite moment; it is such a one as no prudent or good man would encounter but for some clear necessity or some positive duty. If, while Europe is exhausting herself in a destructive war, this country can maintain its peace, the issue will open to us a wide field of advantages, which even imagination can with difficulty compass.

But a check to the progress of our prosperity is not the greatest evil to be anticipated. Considering the naval superiority of the enemies of France, we cannot doubt that our commerce would in a very great degree be annihilated by a war. Our agriculture would of course with our commerce, receive a deep wound. The exportations which now continue to animate it could not fail to be essentially diminished. Our mechanics would experience their full share of the common calamity. That lively and profitable industry, which now spreads a smile over all of our cities and towns, would feel an instantaneous and rapid decay.

Nine-tenths of our present revenues are derived from commercial duties. Their declension must of course keep pace with that of the trade. A substitute cannot be found in other sources of taxation without imposing heavy burdens on the people. To support public credit and carry on the war would suppose exactions really grievous. To abandon public credit would be to renounce an important means of carrying on the war, besides the sacrifice of the public creditors and the disgrace of a national bankruptcy.

We will not call in the aid of savage butcheries and depredations to heighten the picture. It is enough to say that a general Indian war, excited by the united influence of Britain and Spain, would not fail to spread desolation throughout our frontier. To a people who have so recently and so severely felt the evils of war, little more is necessary than to appeal to their own recollection for their magnitude and extent.

The war which now rages is, and for obvious reasons is likely to continue to be, carried on with unusual animosity and rancor. It is highly probable that the resentment of the combined powers against us, if we should take part in it, would be, if possible, still more violent than it is against France. Our interference would be regarded as altogether officious and wanton. How far this idea might lead to the aggravation of the ordinary calamities of war would deserve serious reflection.

The certain evils of our joining France in the war are sufficient dissuasives from so intemperate a measure. The possible ones are of a nature to call for all our caution, all our prudence.

To defend its own rights, to vindicate its own honor, there are occasions when a nation ought to hazard even its existence. Should such an occasion occur, I trust those who are most averse to commit the peace of the country will not be the last to face the danger, nor the first to turn their backs upon it.

But let us at least have the consolation of not having rashly courted misfortune. Let us have to act under the animating reflection of being engaged in repelling wrongs, which we neither sought nor merited; in vindicating our rights, invaded without provocation; in defending our honor, violated without cause. Let us not have to reproach ourselves with having voluntarily bartered blessings for calamities.

But we are told that our own liberty is at stake upon the event of the war against France — that if she falls, we shall be the next victim. The combined powers, it is said, will never forgive in us the origination of those principles which were the germs of the French Revolution. They will endeavor to eradicate them from the world. If this suggestion were ever so well-founded, it would perhaps be a sufficient answer to it to say that our interference is not likely to alter the case; that it would only serve prematurely to exhaust our strength.

But other answers more conclusive present themselves. The war against France requires, on the part of her enemies, efforts unusually violent. They are obliged to strain every nerve, to exert every resource. However it may terminate, they must find themselves spent in an extreme degree; a situation not very favorable to the undertaking anew, and even to Europe combined, an immense enterprise.

To subvert, by force, republican liberty in this country, nothing short of entire conquest would suffice. This conquest, with our present increased population, greatly distant as we are from Europe, would either be impracticable, or would demand such exertions as, following immediately upon those which will have been requisite to the subversion of the French Revolution, would be absolutely ruinous to the undertakers. It is against all probability that an undertaking, pernicious as this would be, even in the event of success, would be attempted against an unoffending nation, by its geographical position little connected with the political concerns of Europe.

But impediments would arise from more special causes. Suppose France subdued, and a restoration of the monarchy in its ancient form, or a partition, effected — to uphold either state of things, after the general impulse in favor of liberty which has been given to the minds of 24,000,000 people, would in one way or another find occupation for a considerable part of the forces which had brought it about.

In the event of an unqualified restoration of the monarchy, if the future monarch did not stand in need of foreign legions for the support of his authority, still the powers which had been concerned in the restoration could not sufficiently rely upon the solidity of the order of things reestablished by them, not to keep themselves in a posture to be prepared against the disturbance of it, till there had been time to compose the discordant interests and passions produced by the Revolution, and bring back the nation to ancient habits of subordination. In the event of a partition of France, it would of course give occupation to the forces of the conquerors to secure the submission of the dismembered parts.

The new dismemberment of Poland will be another obstacle to the detaching of troops from Europe for a crusade against this country — the fruits of that transaction can only be secured to Russia and Prussia by the agency of large bodies of forces, kept on foot for the purpose, within the dismembered territories.

Of the powers combined against France, there are only three whose interests have any material reference to this country — England, Spain, Holland. As to Holland, it will be readily conceded that she can have no interest or feeling to induce her to embark in so mad and wicked a project. Let us see how the matter will stand with regard to Spain and England.

The object of the enterprise against us must be either the establishment in this country of a royal in place of our present republican government, the subjugation of the country to the dominion of one of the parties, or its division among them.

The establishment of an independent monarchy in this country would be so manifestly against the interests of both those nations, in the ordinary acceptation of this term in politics, that neither of them is at all likely to desire it.

It may be adopted as an axiom in our political calculations that no foreign power which has valuable colonies in America will be propitious to our remaining one people under a vigorous government.

No man, I believe, but will think it probable, however disadvantageous the change in other respects, that a monarchical government, from its superior force, would ensure more effectually than our present form our permanent unity as a nation. This at least would be the indubitable conclusion of European calculators; from which may be confidently inferred a disinclination in England and Spain to our undergoing a change of that kind. The only thing that can be imagined capable of reconciling either of those powers to it would be the giving us for monarch a member of its own royal family, and forming something like a family compact.

But here would arise a direct collision of interests between them. Which of them would agree that a prince of the family of the other should, by reigning over this country, give to that other a decided preponderancy in the scale of American affairs? The subjugation of the United States to the dominion of those powers would fall more strongly under a like consideration. It is impossible that either of them should consent that the other should become master of this country, and neither of them without madness could desire a mastery which would cost more than it was worth to maintain it, and which, from an irresistible course of things, could be but of very short duration.

The third, namely, the division of it between them, is the most colorable of the three suppositions. But even this would be the excess of folly in both. The dominion of neither of them could be of any permanency, and while it lasted, would cost more than it was worth. Spain on her part could scarcely fail to be sensible that, from obvious causes, her dominion over the part which was allotted to her would be altogether transient.

The first collision between Britain and Spain would indubitably have one of two effects — either a temporary reunion of the whole country under Great Britain, or a dismission of the yoke of both. The latter, by far the most probable and eventually certain, would discover to both the extreme absurdity of the project. If the first step was a reunion under Great Britain; the second, and one not long deferred, would be a rejection of her authority.

The United States, rooted as are now the ideas of independence, are happily too remote from Europe to be governed by her; dominion over any part of them would be a real misfortune to any nation of that quarter of the globe.

To Great Britain, the enterprise supposed would threaten serious consequences in more ways than one. It may safely be affirmed that she would run by it greater risks of bankruptcy and revolution than we of subjugation. A chief proportion of the burden would unavoidably fall upon her as the monied and principal maritime power, and it may emphatically be said that she would make war upon her own commerce and credit. There is the strongest ground to believe that the nation would disrelish and oppose the project. The certainty of great evils attending it, the dread of much greater experience of the disasters of the last war would operate upon all; many, not improbably a majority, would see in the enterprise a malignant and wanton hostility against liberty, of which they might themselves expect to be the next victim. Their judgments and their feelings would easily distinguish this case from either that of their former contest with us or their present contest with France. In the former they had pretensions to support which were plausible enough to mislead their pride and their interest. In the latter there were strong circumstances to rouse their passions, alarm their fears, and induce an acquiescence in the course which was pursued.

But a future attack upon us, as is apprehended, would be so absolutely pretextless as not to be understood. Our conduct will have been such as to entitle us to the reverse of unfriendly or hostile dispositions, while powerful motives of self-interest would advocate with them our cause.

But Britain, Spain, Austria, Prussia, and perhaps even Russia will have more need and a stronger desire of peace and repose, to restore and recruit their wasted strength and exhausted treasures, to reinvigorate the interior order and industry of their respective kingdoms, relaxed and depressed by war, than either means or inclination to undertake so extravagant an enterprise against the liberty of this country.

If there can be any danger to us, it must arise from our voluntarily thrusting ourselves into the war. Once embarked, nations sometimes prosecute enterprises of which they would not otherwise have dreamed. The most violent resentment, as before intimated, would no doubt in such a case, be kindled against us for what would be called a wanton and presumptuous intermeddling on our part; what this might produce, it is not easy to calculate.

There are two great errors in our reasoning upon this subject: one, that the combined powers will certainly attribute to us the same principles which they deem so exceptionable in France; the other, that our principles are in fact the same.

If left to themselves they will all, except one, naturally see in us a people who originally resorted to a revolution in government as a refuge from encroachments on rights and privileges *antecedently* enjoyed, not as a people who from choice sought a radical and entire change in the established government, in pursuit of new privileges and rights carried to an extreme, irreconcilable perhaps with any form of regular government. They will see in us a people who have a due respect for property and personal security; who, in the midst of our revolution, abstained with exemplary moderation from everything violent or sanguinary, instituting governments adequate to the protection of persons and property; who, since the completion of our revolution, have in a very short period, from mere reasoning and reflection, without tumult or bloodshed, adopted a form of general government calculated, as well as the nature of things would permit, to remedy antecedent defects, to give strength and security to the nation, to rest the foundations of liberty on the basis of justice, order, and law, who have at all times been content to govern themselves without intermeddling with the affairs or governments of other nations. In fine, they will see in us sincere republicans, but decided enemies to licentiousness and anarchy; sincere republicans, but decided friends to the freedom of opinion, to the order and tranquillity of all mankind.

They will not see in us a people whose best passions have been misled, and whose best qualities have been perverted from their true direction by headlong, fanatical, or designing leaders, to the perpetration of acts from which humanity shrinks, to the commission of outrages over which the eye of reason weeps, to the profession and practice of principles which tend to shake the foundations of morality, to dissolve the social bands, to disturb the peace of mankind, to substitute confusion to order, anarchy to government.

Such at least is the light in which the reason or the passions of the powers confederated against France lead them to view her principles and conduct. And it is to be lamented that so much cause has been given for their opinions. If, on our part, we give no incitement to their passions, facts too prominent and too decisive to be combated will forbid their reason to bestow the same character upon us.

It is, therefore, matter of real regret that there should be an effort on our part to level the distinctions which discriminate our case from that of France, to confound the two cases in the view of foreign powers, and to pervert or hazard our own principles by persuading ourselves of a similitude which does not exist.

Let us content ourselves with lamenting the errors into which a great, a gallant, an amiable, a respectable nation has been betrayed, with uniting our wishes and our prayers that the Supreme Ruler of the world will bring them back from those errors to a more sober and more just way of thinking and acting; and will overrule the complicated calamities which surround them, to the establishment of a government under which they may be free, secure, and happy. But let us not corrupt ourselves by false comparisons or glosses, nor shut our eyes to the true nature of transactions which ought to grieve and warn us, nor rashly mingle our destiny in the consequences of the errors and extravagances of another nation.

---

*Every man has two countries, France and his own* (Chaque homme a deux patries, la sienne et la France).

Benjamin Franklin

110.

## George Washington: Proclamation on the Whiskey Rebellion

*Alexander Hamilton's financial scheme to raise money for the federal government included an excise tax on domestic liquor. The farmers of western Pennsylvania protested because they gained much of their income from whiskey, which could be transported more economically than grain. In the summer of 1794, the farmers, under the leadership of local demagogues, resorted to armed rebellion. In an unprecedented show of national over local governmental authority, George Washington issued the following proclamation on August 7, 1794, calling for the militia of several states to suppress the rebellion.*

Source: WGW, XII, pp. 445-448.

*Whereas,* combinations to defeat the execution of the laws laying duties upon spirits distilled within the United States and upon stills have from the time of the commencement of those laws existed in some of the western parts of Pennsylvania;

*And whereas,* the said combinations, proceeding in a manner subversive equally of the just authority of government and of the rights of individuals, have hitherto effected their dangerous and criminal purpose by the influence of certain irregular meetings whose proceedings have tended to encourage and uphold the spirit of opposition by misrepresentations of the laws calculated to render them odious; by endeavors to deter those who might be so disposed from accepting offices under them through fear of public resentment and of injury to person and property, and to compel those who had accepted such offices by actual violence to surrender or forbear the execution of them; by circulating vindictive menaces against all those who should otherwise, directly or indirectly, aid in the execution of the said laws, or who, yielding to the dictates of conscience and to a sense of obligation, should themselves comply therewith; by actually injuring and destroying the property of persons who were understood to have so complied; by inflicting cruel and humiliating punishments upon private citizens for no other cause than that of appearing to be the friends of the laws; by intercepting the public officers on the highways, abusing, assaulting, and otherwise ill treating them; by going to their houses in the night, gaining admittance by force, taking away their papers, and committing other outrages, employing for these unwarrantable purposes the agency of armed banditti disguised in such manner as for the most part to escape discovery;

*And whereas,* the endeavors of the legislature to obviate objections to the said laws by lowering the duties and by other alterations conducive to the convenience of those whom they immediately affect (though they have given satisfaction in other quarters), and the endeavors of the executive officers to conciliate a compliance with the laws by explanations, by forbearance, and even by

Winterthur Museum

George Washington reviewing the federal troops sent to suppress the Whiskey Rebellion; painting by Kremmelmeyer

particular accommodations founded on the suggestion of local considerations, have been disappointed of their effect by the machinations of persons whose industry to excite resistance has increased with every appearance of a disposition among the people to relax in their opposition and to acquiesce in the laws, insomuch that many persons in the said western parts of Pennsylvania have at length been hardy enough to perpetrate acts, which I am advised amount to treason, being overt acts of levying war against the United States, the said persons having on the 16th and 17th of July last past proceeded in arms (on the second day amounting to several hundreds) to the house of John Neville, inspector of the revenue for the fourth survey of the district of Pennsylvania; having repeatedly attacked the said house with the persons therein, wounding some of them; having seized David Lenox, marshal of the district of Pennsylvania, who previous thereto had been fired upon while in the execution of his duty by a party of armed men, detaining him for some time prisoner, till, for the preservation of his life and the obtaining of his liberty, he found it necessary to enter into stipulations to forbear the execution of certain official duties touching processes issuing out of a court of the United States; and having finally obliged the said inspector of the revenue and the said marshal from considerations of personal safety to fly from that part of the country, in order, by a circuitous route, to proceed to the seat of government, avowing as the motives of these outrageous proceedings an intention to prevent by force of arms the execution of the said laws, to oblige the said inspector of the revenue to renounce his said office, to withstand by open violence the lawful authority of the government of the United States, and to compel thereby an alteration in the measures of the legislature and a repeal of the laws aforesaid;

*And whereas,* by a law of the United States entitled "An act to provide for calling forth the militia to execute the laws of the Union, suppress insurrections, and repel invasions," it is enacted

> that whenever the laws of the United States shall be opposed or the execution thereof obstructed in any state by combinations too powerful to be suppressed by the ordinary course of judicial proceedings or by the powers vested in the marshals by that act, the same being notified by an associate justice or the district judge, it shall be lawful for the President of the United States to call forth the militia of such state to suppress such combinations and to cause the laws to be duly executed. And if the militia of a state, when such combinations may happen, shall refuse or be insufficient to suppress the same, it shall be lawful for the President, if the legislature of the United States shall not be in session, to call forth and employ such numbers of the militia of any other state or states most convenient thereto as may be necessary; and the use of the militia so to be called forth may be continued, if necessary, until the expiration of thirty days after the commencement of the ensuing session: *Provided always,* that, whenever it may be necessary in the judgment of the President to use the military force hereby directed to be called forth, the President shall forthwith, and previous thereto, by proclamation, command such insurgents to disperse and retire peaceably to their respective abodes within a limited time;

*And whereas,* James Wilson, an associate justice, on the 4th instant, by writing under his hand, did from evidence which had been laid before him notify to me that "in the counties of Washington and Allegany, in Pennsylvania, laws of the United States are opposed and the execution thereof obstructed by combinations too powerful to be suppressed by the ordinary course of judicial proceedings or by the powers vested in the marshal of that district";

*And whereas,* it is in my judgment necessary under the circumstances of the case to take measures for calling forth the militia in order to suppress the combinations aforesaid, and to cause the laws to be duly executed; and I have accordingly determined so to do, feeling the deepest regret for the occasion, but withal the most solemn conviction that the essential interests of the Union demand it, that the very existence of government and the fundamental principles of social order are materially involved in the issue, and that the patriotism and firmness of all good citizens are seriously called upon, as occasions may require, to aid in the effectual suppression of so fatal a spirit:

*Therefore,* and in pursuance of the proviso above recited, I, George Washington, President of the United States, do hereby command all persons, being insurgents, as aforesaid, and all others whom it may concern, on or before the 1st day of September next to disperse and retire peaceably to their respective abodes. And I do moreover warn all persons whomsoever against aiding, abetting, or comforting the perpetrators of the aforesaid treasonable acts; and do require all officers and other citizens, according to their respective duties and the laws of the land, to exert their utmost endeavors to prevent and suppress such dangerous proceedings.

Pittsburgh Allegheny County

I DO solemnly promise, henceforth to submit to the Laws of the United States; that I will not directly nor indirectly oppose the execution of the Acts for raising a Revenue on Distilled Spirits and Stills, and that I will support as far as the Laws require the civil authority in affording the protection due to all officers and other Citizens.

September 11, 1794.



Extract from the document of submission signed by the leaders of the Whiskey Rebellion, 1794

111.

## Alexander Hamilton: Liberty and Anarchy

*Washington's order to ready the militias for fighting the "whiskey rebels" in the West was opposed by many Americans. Hamilton, fearful that the militias would not respond to the President's proclamation, attempted to win public support for the government's action. In another of his efforts to influence public opinion, he wrote under the pseudonym, "Tully," a series of letters that were so convincing that enlistment had to be curtailed in order to keep the army to a manageable size. On August 28, 1794, he presented the following defense of the government's policies.*

Source: *The Works of Alexander Hamilton,* Henry Cabot Lodge, ed., Vol. VI, New York, 1886, pp. 26-32.

If it were to be asked — "What is the most sacred duty, and the greatest source of security in a republic?" — the answer would be — "An inviolable respect for the Constitution and laws, the first growing out of the last." It is by this, in a great degree, that the rich and the powerful are to be restrained from enterprises against the common liberty — operated upon by the influence of a general sentiment, by their interest in the principle, and by the obstacles which the habit it produces erects against innovation and encroachment. It is by this in a still greater degree that caballers, intriguers, and demagogues are prevented from climbing on the shoulders of faction to the tempting seats of usurpation and tyranny.

Were it not that it might require too long a discussion, it would not be difficult to demonstrate that a large and well-organized republic can scarcely lose its liberty from any other cause than that of anarchy, to which a contempt of the laws is the high road.

But without entering into so wide a field, it is sufficient to present to your view a more simple and a more obvious truth, which is this: that a sacred respect for the constitutional law is the vital principle, the sustaining energy, of a free government.

Government is frequently and aptly classed under two descriptions — a government of *force,* and a government of *laws.* The first is the definition of despotism; the last, of liberty. But how can a government of laws exist when the laws are disrespected and disobeyed? Government supposes control. It is that *power* by which individuals in society are kept from doing injury to each other, and are brought to cooperate to a common end. The instruments by which it must act are either the *authority* of the laws or *force.* If the first be destroyed, the last must be substituted, and where this becomes the ordinary instrument of government, there is an end to liberty!

Those, therefore, who preach doctrines, or set examples which undermine or subvert the authority of the laws, lead us from freedom to slavery; they incapacitate us for a *government of laws,* and, consequently, prepare the way for one of *force,* for mankind must have *government of one sort or another.* There are, indeed, great and urgent cases where the bounds of the Constitution are manifestly transgressed, or its constitutional authorities so exercised as to produce unequivocal oppression on the community and to render resistance justifiable. But such cases can give no color to the resistance by a comparatively inconsiderable part of a community, of constitutional laws distinguished by no extraordinary features of rigor or oppression, and acquiesced in by the body of the community.

Such a resistance is treason against society, against liberty, against everything that ought to be dear to a free, enlightened, and prudent people. To tolerate it were to abandon your most precious interests. Not to subdue it were to tolerate it. Those who openly or covertly dissuade you from exertions adequate to the occasion are your worst enemies. They treat you either as fools or cowards, too weak to perceive your interest or your duty, or too dastardly to pursue them. They, therefore, merit and will, no doubt, meet your contempt. To the plausible but hollow harangue of such conspirators you cannot fail to reply — "How long, ye Catilines, will ye abuse our patience?"

To urge the execution of that system would manifest, it is said, an intemperate spirit; and to excite your disapprobation of that course, you are threatened with the danger of a civil war which is called the consummation of human evil.

To crown the outrage upon your understandings, the insurgents are represented as men who understand the principles of freedom, and know the horrors and distresses of anarchy, and who, therefore, must have been tempted to hostility against the laws by a *radical defect either* in the government *or* in those entrusted with its administration. How *thin* the partition which divides the insinuation from the assertion, that the government is in fault and the insurgents in the right!

Fellow citizens: a name, a sound has too often had influence on the affairs of nations; an *excise* has too long been the successful watchword of party. It has even sometimes led astray well-meaning men. The experiment is now to be tried whether there be any spell in it of sufficient force to unnerve the arm which may be found necessary to be raised in defense of law and order.

The jugglers who endeavor to cheat us with the sound have never dared to venture into the fair fields of argument. They are conscious that it is easier to declaim than to reason on the subject. They know it to be better to play a game with the passions and prejudices than to engage seriously with the understanding of the auditory. You have already seen that the merits of excise laws are immaterial to the question to be decided; that you have prejudged the point by a solemn constitutional act; and that until you shall have revoked or modified that act, resistance to its operation is a criminal infraction of the social compact, an inversion of the fundamental principles of republican government, and a daring attack upon *your* sovereignty, which you are bound by every motive of duty and self-preservation to withstand and defeat. The matter might safely be suffered to rest here; but I shall take a future opportunity to examine the reasonableness of the prejudice which is inculcated against excise laws, and which has become the pretext for excesses tending to dissolve the bands of society.

Fellow citizens: you are told that it will be intemperate to urge the execution of the laws which are resisted. What? Will it be indeed intemperate in your chief magistrate, sworn to maintain the Constitution, charged faithfully to execute the laws, and authorized to employ for that purpose force when the ordinary means fail — will it be intemperate in him to exert that force when the Constitution and the laws are opposed by force? Can he answer it to his conscience, to you, not to exert it? Yes, it is said; because the execution of it will produce civil war — the consummation of human evil.

Fellow citizens: civil war is, undoubtedly, a great evil. It is one that every good man would wish to avoid, and will deplore if inevitable. But it is incomparably a less evil than the destruction of government. The first brings with it serious but temporary and partial ills; the last undermines the foundations of our security and happiness. And where should we be if it were once to grow into a maxim that force is not to be used against the seditious combinations of parts of the community to resist the laws? This would be to give a *carte blanche* to ambition, to licentiousness, to foreign intrigue, to make you the prey of the gold of other nations — the sport of the passions and vices of individuals among yourselves. The hydra anarchy would rear its head in every quarter. The goodly fabric you have established would be rent asunder, and precipitated into the dust.

You knew how to encounter civil war rather than surrender your liberty to foreign domination; you will not hesitate now to brave it rather than to surrender your sovereignty to the tyranny of a faction; you will be as deaf to the apostles of anarchy now as you were to the emissaries of despotism then. Your love of liberty will guide you now as it did then; you know that the *power* of the majority and *liberty* are inseparable. Destroy that, and this perishes. But, in truth, that which properly can be called civil war is not to be apprehended — unless from the act of those who endeavor to fan the flame by rendering the government odious. A civil war is a contest between two great parts of the same empire. The exertion of the strength of the nation to suppress resistance to its laws by a sixtieth part of itself, is not of that description.

After endeavoring to alarm you with the horrors of civil war, an attempt is made to excite your sympathy in favor of the armed faction by telling you that those who compose it are men who understand the principles of freedom, and know the horrors and distresses of anarchy, and must, therefore, have been prompted to hostility against the laws by a radical defect *either* in the government *or* in its administration. Fellow citizens, for an answer to this you have only to consult your senses. The natural consequences of radical defect in a government, or in its administration, are national distress and suffering. Look around you — where is it? Do you feel it? Do you see it?

Go in quest of it beyond the Allegheny, and instead of it you will find that there also a scene of unparalleled prosperity upbraids the ingratitude and madness of those who are endeavoring to cloud the bright face of our political horizon, and to mar the happiest lot that beneficent Heaven ever indulged to undeserving mortals.

When you have turned your eyes toward that scene, examine well the men whose knowledge of the principles of freedom is so emphatically vaunted — where did they get their better knowledge of those principles than that which you possess? How is it that you have been so blind or tame as to remain quiet while they have been goaded into hostility against the laws by a *radical defect* in the government or its administration? Are you willing to yield them the palm of discernment, or patriotism, or of courage?

112.

# The Jay Treaty

*The decision to remain neutral in European affairs proved to be fraught with grave difficulties. United States navigation laws had been passed that were potentially discriminatory against Great Britain. Duties on British imports were a major source of United States revenue, and, consequently, a commercial war would be most detrimental to the health of the American economy. In addition, despite the Treaty of 1783 which had guaranteed British evacuation of posts on the western frontier, no action to this effect had taken place. In 1794, John Jay was sent to Britain as minister plenipotentiary and envoy extraordinary for the purpose of negotiating these and several other differences between the two governments. Jay's Treaty was signed on November 19, 1794; portions of it are reprinted here.*

Source: Malloy, I, pp. 590-606.

Article I. There shall be a firm, inviolable, and universal peace, and a true and sincere friendship between His Britannic Majesty, His Heirs, and Successors, and the United States of America; and between their respective countries, territories, cities, towns, and people of every degree, without exception of persons or places.

Article II. His Majesty will withdraw all his troops and garrisons from all posts and places within the boundary lines assigned by the treaty of peace to the United States. This evacuation shall take place on or before June 1, 1796, and all the proper measures shall in the interval be taken by concert between the government of the United States and His Majesty's governor-general in America for settling the previous arrangements which may be necessary respecting the delivery of the said posts. The United States, in the meantime, at their discretion, extending their settlements to any part within the said boundary line, except within the precincts or jurisdiction of any of the said posts. All settlers and traders within the precincts or jurisdiction of the said posts shall continue to enjoy, unmolested, all their property of every kind, and shall be protected therein. They shall be at full liberty to remain there, or to remove with all or any part of their effects; and it shall also be free to them to sell their lands, houses, or effects, or to retain the property thereof, at their discretion.

Such of them as shall continue to reside within the said boundary lines shall not be compelled to become citizens of the United States, or to take any oath of allegiance to the government thereof; but they shall be at full liberty so to do if they think proper, and they shall make and declare their election within one year after the evacuation aforesaid. And all persons who shall continue there after the expiration of the said year, without having declared their intention of remaining subjects of His Britannic Majesty, shall be considered as having elected to become citizens of the United States.

Article III. It is agreed that it shall at all times be free to His Majesty's subjects, and to the citizens of the United States, and also to the Indians dwelling on either side of the said boundary line, freely to pass and repass by land or inland navigation into the respective territories and countries of the two parties, on the continent of America (the country within the limits of the Hudson's Bay Company only excepted) and to navigate all the lakes, rivers, and waters thereof, and freely to carry on trade and commerce with each other.

But it is understood that this article does not extend to the admission of vessels of the United States into the seaports, harbors, bays, or creeks of His Majesty's said territories; nor into such parts of the rivers in His Majesty's said territories as are between the mouth thereof and the highest port of entry from the sea, except in small vessels trading bona fide between Montreal and Quebec, under such regulations as shall be established to prevent the possibility of any frauds in this respect. Nor to the admission of British vessels from the sea into the rivers of the United States beyond the highest ports of entry for foreign vessels from the sea.

The River Mississippi shall, however, according to the treaty of peace, be entirely open to both parties; and it is further agreed that all the ports and places on its eastern side, to whichsoever of the parties belonging, may freely be resorted to and used by both parties in as ample a manner as any of the Atlantic ports or places of the United States, or any of the ports or places of His Majesty in Great Britain.

All goods and merchandise whose importation into His Majesty's said territories in America shall not be entirely prohibited may freely, for the purposes of commerce, be carried into the same, in the manner aforesaid, by the citizens of the United States; and such goods and merchandise shall be subject to no higher or other duties than would be payable by His Majesty's subjects on the importation of the same from Europe into the said territories. And, in like manner, all goods and merchandise whose importation into the United States shall not be wholly prohibited may freely, for the purposes of commerce, be carried into the same, in the manner aforesaid, by His Majesty's subjects, and such goods and merchandise shall be subject to no higher or other duties than would be payable by the citizens of the United States on the importation of the same in American vessels into the Atlantic ports of the said states. And all goods not prohibited to be exported from the said territories respectively may, in like manner, be carried out of the same by the two parties respectively, paying duty as aforesaid. . . .

Article IV. Whereas it is uncertain whether the River Mississippi extends so far to the northward as to be intersected by a line to be drawn due west from the Lake of the Woods, in the manner mentioned in the treaty of peace . . . it is agreed that measures shall be taken . . . for making a joint survey of the said river from one degree of latitude below the Falls of St. Anthony to the principal source or sources of the said river, and also of the parts adjacent thereto; and that if, on the result of such survey, it should appear that the said river would not be intersected by such a line as is above mentioned, the two parties will thereupon proceed by amicable negotiation to regulate the boundary line in that quarter, as well as all other points to be adjusted between the said parties. . . .

Article V. Whereas doubts have arisen what river was truly intended under the name of the River St. Croix, mentioned in the said treaty of peace, and forming a part of the boundary therein described; that question shall be referred to the final decision of commissioners to be appointed. . . .

Article VI. Whereas it is alleged by diverse British merchants and others, His Majesty's subjects, that debts, to a considerable amount, which were bona fide contracted before the peace, still remain owing to them by citizens or inhabitants of the United States, and that by the operation of various lawful impediments since the peace, not only the full recovery of the said debts has been delayed but also the value and security thereof have been, in several instances, impaired and lessened, so that by the ordinary course of judicial proceedings the British creditors cannot now obtain, and actually have and receive full and adequate compensation for the losses and damages which they have thereby sustained: It is agreed that in all such cases where full compensation for such losses and damages cannot, for whatever reason, be actually obtained, had, and received by the said creditors in the ordinary course of justice, the United States will make full and complete compensation for the same to the said creditors. But it is distinctly understood that this provision is to extend to such losses only as have been occasioned by the lawful impediments aforesaid, and is not to extend to losses occasioned by such insolvency of the debtors or other causes as would equally have operated to produce such loss, if the said impediments had not existed; nor to such losses or damages as have been occasioned by the manifest delay or negligence or willful omission of the claimant. . . .

Article VII. Whereas complaints have been made by diverse merchants and others, citizens of the United States, that during the course of the war in which His Majesty is now engaged they have sustained considerable losses and damage, by reason of irregular or illegal captures or condemnations of their vessels and other property, under color of authority or commissions from His Majesty, and that from various circumstances belonging to the said cases adequate compensation for the losses and damages so sustained cannot now be actually obtained, had, and received by the ordinary course of judicial proceedings; it is agreed that in all such cases where adequate compensation cannot, for whatever reason, be now actually obtained, had, and received by the said merchants and others, in the ordinary course of justice, full and complete compensation for the same will be made by the British government to the said complainants. But it is distinctly understood that this provision is not to extend to such losses or damages as have been occasioned by the manifest delay or negligence or willful omission of the claimant. . . .

And whereas certain merchants and others, His Majesty's subjects, complain that in the course of the war they have sustained loss and damage by reason of the capture of their vessels and merchandise, taken within the limits and jurisdiction of the States and brought into the ports of the same, or taken by vessels originally armed in ports of the said States: It is agreed that in all such cases where restitution shall not have been made . . . the complaints of the parties shall be and hereby are referred to the commissioners . . . who are hereby authorized and required to proceed in the like manner relative to these as to the other cases committed to them; and the United States undertake to pay to the complainants or claimants in specie, without deduction, the amount of such sums as shall be awarded to them respectively by the said commissioners, and at the times and places which in such awards shall be specified; and on condition of such releases or assignments to be given by the claimants as in the said awards may be directed. And it is further agreed that not only the now-existing cases of both descriptions but also all such as shall exist at the time of exchanging the ratifications of this treaty shall be considered as being within the provisions, intent, and meaning of this article. . . .

Article IX. It is agreed that British subjects who now hold lands in the territories of the United States, and American citizens who now hold lands in the dominions of His Majesty, shall continue to hold them according to the nature and tenure of their respective estates and titles therein; and may grant, sell, or devise the same to whom they please, in like manner as if they were natives; and that neither they nor their heirs or assigns shall, so far as may respect the said lands and the legal remedies incident thereto, be regarded as aliens.

Article X. Neither the debts due from individuals of the one nation to individuals of the other, nor shares nor monies which they may have in the public funds, or in the public or private banks, shall ever in any event of war or national differences be sequestered or confiscated, it being unjust and impolitic that debts and engagements contracted and made by individuals, having confidence in each other and in their respective governments, should ever be destroyed or impaired by national authority on account of national differences and discontents.

Article XI. It is agreed between His Majesty and the United States of America that there shall be a reciprocal and entirely perfect liberty of navigation and commerce between their respective people, in the manner, under the limitations, and on the conditions specified in the following articles:

Article XII. His Majesty consents that it shall and may be lawful, during the time hereinafter limited, for the citizens of the United States to carry to any of His Majesty's islands and ports in the West Indies from the United States, in their own vessels, not being above the burden of seventy tons, any goods or merchandises, being of the growth, manufacture, or produce of the said States, which it is or may be lawful to carry to the said islands or ports from the said States in British vessels; and that the said American vessels shall be subject there to no other or higher tonnage duties or charges than shall be payable by British vessels in the ports of the United States; and that the cargoes of the said American vessels shall be subject there to no other or higher duties or charges than shall be payable on the like articles if imported there from the said States in British vessels.

And His Majesty also consents that it shall be lawful for the said American citizens to purchase, load, and carry away in their said vessels to the United States, from the said islands and ports, all such articles, being of the growth, manufacture, or produce of the said islands, as may now by law be carried from thence to the said States in British vessels, and subject only to the same duties and charges on exportation to which British vessels and their cargoes are or shall be subject in similar circumstances. . . .

Article XIII. His Majesty consents that the vessels belonging to the citizens of the United States of America shall be admitted and hospitably received in all the seaports and harbors of the British territories in the East Indies. And that the citizens of the said United States may freely carry on a trade between the said territories and the said United States in all articles of which the importation or exportation respectively to or from the said territories shall not be entirely prohibited; provided only that it shall not be lawful for them, in any time of war between the British government and any other power or state whatever, to export from the said territories, without the special permission of the British government there, any military stores, or naval stores, or rice.

The citizens of the United States shall pay for their vessels, when admitted into the said ports, no other or higher tonnage duty than shall be payable on British vessels when admitted into the ports of the United States. And they shall pay no other or higher duties or charges on the importation or exportation of the cargoes of the said vessels than shall be payable on the same articles when imported or exported in British vessels. But it is expressly agreed that the vessels of the United States shall not carry any of the articles exported by them from the said British territories to any port or place except to some port or place in America, where the same shall be unladen, and such regulations shall be adopted by both parties as shall from time to time be found necessary to enforce the due and faithful observance of this stipulation.

It is also understood that the permission granted by this article is not to extend to allow the vessels of the United States to carry on any part of the coasting trade of the said British territories; but vessels going with their original cargoes, or part thereof, from one port of discharge to another are not to be considered as carrying on the coasting trade. Neither is this article to be construed to allow the citizens of the said States to settle or reside within the said territories, or to go into the interior parts thereof, without the permission of the British government established there.

And if any transgression should be attempted against the regulations of the British government in this respect, the observance of the same shall and may be enforced against the citizens of America in the same manner as against British subjects or others transgressing the same rule. And the citizens of the United States, whenever they arrive in any port or harbor in the said territories, or if they should be permitted, in manner aforesaid, to go to any other place therein, shall always be subject to the laws, government, and jurisdiction of what nature established in such harbor, port, or place, according as the same may be. The citizens of the United States may also touch for refreshment at the island of St. Helena, but subject in all respects to such regulations as the British government may from time to time establish there.

Article XIV. There shall be between all the dominions of His Majesty in Europe and the territories of the United States a reciprocal and perfect liberty of commerce and navigation. . . .

Article XV. It is agreed that no other or higher duties shall be paid by the ships or merchandise of the one party in the ports of the other than such as are paid by the like vessels or merchandise of all other nations. . . .

Article XVI. It shall be free for the two contracting parties, respectively, to appoint consuls for the protection of trade, to reside in the dominions and territories aforesaid; and the said consuls shall enjoy those liberties and rights which belong to them by reason of their function. . . .

Article XVII. It is agreed that in all cases where vessels shall be captured or detained on just suspicion of having on board enemy's property, or of carrying to the enemy any of the articles which are contraband of war, the said vessel shall be brought to the nearest or most convenient port; and if any property of an enemy should be found on board such vessel, that part only which belongs to the enemy shall be made prize, and the vessel shall be at liberty to proceed with the remainder without any impediment. . . .

Article XVIII. And whereas the difficulty of agreeing on the precise cases in which alone provisions and other articles not generally contraband may be regarded as such, renders it expedient to provide against the inconveniences and misunderstandings which might thence arise; it is further agreed that whenever any such articles so becoming contraband, according to the existing laws of nations, shall for that reason be seized, the same shall not be confiscated, but the owners thereof shall be speedily and completely indemnified. . . .

And whereas it frequently happens that vessels sail for a port or place belonging to an enemy without knowing that the same is either besieged, blockaded, or invested, it is agreed that every vessel so circumstanced may be turned away from such port or place; but she shall not be detained, nor her cargo, if not contraband, be confiscated, unless after notice she shall again attempt to enter, but she shall be permitted to go to any other port or place she may think proper; nor shall any vessel or goods of either party that may have entered into such port or place before the same was besieged, blockaded, or invested by the other, and be found therein after the reduction or surrender of such place, be liable to confiscation, but shall be restored to the owners or proprietors there.

Article XIX. And that more abundant

care may be taken for the security of the respective subjects and citizens of the contracting parties, and to prevent their suffering injuries by the men of war or privateers of either party, all commanders of ships of war and privateers, and all others the said subjects and citizens, shall forbear doing any damage to those of the other party, or committing any outrage against them, and if they act to the contrary, they shall be punished, and shall also be bound in their persons and estates to make satisfaction and reparation for all damages. . . .

Article XX. It is further agreed that both the said contracting parties shall not only refuse to receive any pirates into any of their ports, havens, or towns, or permit any of their inhabitants to receive, protect, harbor, conceal, or assist them in any manner, but will bring to condign punishment all such inhabitants as shall be guilty of such acts or offenses.

And all their ships, with the goods or merchandises taken by them and brought into the port of either of the said parties, shall be seized as far as they can be discovered, and shall be restored to the owners, or their factors or agents, duly deputed and authorized in writing by them (proper evidence being first given in the Court of Admiralty for proving the property), even in case such effects should have passed into other hands by sale, if it be proved that the buyers knew or had good reason to believe or suspect that they had been piratically taken.

Article XXI. It is likewise agreed that the subjects and citizens of the two nations shall not do any acts of hostility or violence against each other, nor accept commissions or instructions so to act from any foreign prince or state, enemies to the other party; nor shall the enemies of one of the parties be permitted to invite, or endeavor to enlist in their military service, any of the subjects or citizens of the other party; and the laws against all such offenses and aggressions shall be punctually executed. And if any subject or citizen of the said parties respectively shall accept any foreign commission or letters of marque for arming any vessel to act as a privateer against the other party, and be taken by the other party, it is hereby declared to be lawful for the said party to treat and punish the said subject or citizen having such commission or letters of marque as a pirate.

Article XXII. It is expressly stipulated, that neither of the said contracting parties will order or authorize any acts of reprisal against the other, on complaints of injuries or damages, until the said party shall first have presented to the other a statement thereof, verified by competent proof and evidence, and demanded justice and satisfaction, and the same shall either have been refused or unreasonably delayed. . . .

Article XXVI. If at any time a rupture should take place (which God forbid) between His Majesty and the United States, the merchants and others of each of the two nations, residing in the dominions of the other, shall have the privilege of remaining and continuing their trade, so long as they behave peaceably and commit no offense against the laws; and in case their conduct should render them suspected, and the respective governments should think proper to order them to remove, the term of twelve months from the publication of the order shall be allowed them for that purpose, to remove with their families, effects, and property; but this favor shall not be extended to those who shall act contrary to the established laws. . . .

Article XXVII. It is further agreed that His Majesty and the United States, on mutual requisitions, by them respectively, or by their respective ministers or officers authorized to make the same, will deliver up to justice all persons who, being charged with murder or forgery, committed within the jurisdiction of either, shall seek an asylum within any of the countries of the other, provided that this shall only be done on such evidence of criminality as, according to the laws of the place where the fugitive or person so charged shall be found, would justify his apprehension and commitment for trial, if the offense had there been committed. The expense of such apprehension and delivery shall be borne and defrayed by those who make the requisition and receive the fugitive.

Article XXVIII. It is agreed that the first ten articles of this treaty shall be permanent, and that the subsequent articles, except the 12th, shall be limited in their duration to twelve years.

113.

## Ann Julia Hatton: "Alknomook"

*James Hewitt, an Englishman who immigrated to America, composed one of the first ballad operas to be written in the United States,* Tammany; or the Indian Chief. *The opera was first performed in 1794 under the auspices of the Tammany Society, whose poetess, Ann Julia Hatton, wrote the libretto for the work. "Alknomook," subtitled "The Death Song of the Cherokee Indians," is the only piece that has survived from the opera. It reflects the widespread feeling among Easterners at the time that the Indian, though primitive and a savage, was somehow noble. Westerners felt differently, of course.*

Source: *The Little American Songster, Containing a Choice Collection of Modern and Popular Songs,* New York, n.d. [184-].

### ALKNOMOOK

The sun sets at night, and the stars shun the day,
But glory remains when the light fades away.
Begin, ye tormentors, your threats are in vain,
For the son of Alknomook shall never complain.

Remember the arrows he shot from his bow,
Remember your chiefs by his hatchet laid low.
Why so slow, do you wait till I shrink from my pain?
No, the son of Alknomook shall never complain.

Remember the wood where in ambush we lay,
And the scalps which we bore from your nation away.
Now the flame rises fast, you exult in my pain,
But the son of Alknomook shall never complain.

I'll go to the land where my father is gone,
His ghost shall rejoice at the fame of his son.
Death comes like a friend, to relieve me from pain,
And thy son, O! Alknomook, has scorned to complain.

114.

## Gustavus Vassa: The Slave Ship

*Olaudah Equiano was taken as a child from his African village, Benin, located near the present-day country of Nigeria, and shipped to the West Indies as a slave. His fate was not to be that of an ordinary slave, as he traveled extensively, eventually exploring the Arctic. On one of his many sea voyages, a captain named him Gustavus Vassa, for the sixteenth-century Swedish king, Gustavus I (Gustavus Vasa), and he was eventually baptized with that name. He was one of the few slaves who became educated and thus was equipped to write his journal,* The Interesting Narrative of the Life of Gustavus Vassa, The African; *it is a rare autobiographical account of the life of an eighteenth-century slave. The work depicts not only Gustavus' trials and sorrows, but also the miseries of other Africans who were abducted into slavery. Excerpts are reprinted here.*

Source: *The Life of Olaudah Equiano or Gustavus Vassa, The African,* Boston, 1837, pp. 30-52.

I hope the reader will not think I have trespassed on his patience in introducing myself to him with some account of the manners and customs of my country. They had been implanted in me with great care, and made an impression on my mind, which time could not erase, and which all the adversity and variety of fortune I have since experienced served only to rivet and record; for, whether the love of one's country be real or imaginary, or a lesson of reason, or an instinct of nature, I still look back with pleasure on the first scenes of my life, though that pleasure has been for the most part mingled with sorrow. . . .

My father, besides many slaves, had a numerous family, of which seven lived to grow up, including myself and a sister, who was the only daughter. As I was the youngest of the sons, I became, of course, the greatest favorite with my mother, and was always with her; and she used to take particular pains to form my mind. I was trained up from my earliest years in the art of war; my daily exercise was shooting and throwing javelins; and my mother adorned me with emblems, after the manner of our greatest warriors.

In this way I grew up till I was turned the age of eleven, when an end was put to my happiness in the following manner. Generally, when the grown people in the neighborhood were gone far in the fields to labor, the children assembled together in some of the neighboring premises to play; and, commonly, some of us used to get up a tree to look out for any assailant, or kidnapper, that might come upon us — for they sometimes took those opportunities of our parents' absence to attack and carry off as many as they could seize. One day, as I was watching at the top of a tree in our yard, I saw one of those people come into the yard of our next neighbor but one to kidnap, there being many stout young people in it. Immediately on this I gave the alarm of the rogue, and he was surrounded by the stoutest of them, who entangled him with cords, so that he could not escape till some of the grown people came and secured him.

But, alas! ere long it was my fate to be thus attacked, and to be carried off, when none of the grown people were nigh. One day, when all our people were gone out to their works as usual, and only I and my dear sister were left to mind the house, two men and a woman got over our walls, and in a moment seized us both, and, without giving us time to cry out or make resistance, they stopped our mouths and ran off with us into the nearest wood. Here they tied our hands, and continued to carry us as far as they could, till night came on, when we reached a small house where the robbers halted for refreshment and spent the night. We were then unbound, but were unable to take any food; and, being quite overpowered by fatigue and grief, our only relief was some sleep, which allayed our misfortune for a short time. The next morning we left the house, and continued traveling all the day.

For a long time we had kept the woods, but at last we came into a road which I believed I knew. I had now some hopes of being delivered; for we had advanced but a little way before I discovered some people at a distance, on which I began to cry out for their assistance; but my cries had no other effect than to make them tie me faster and stop my mouth, and then they put me into a large sack. They also stopped my sister's mouth and tied her hands; and in this manner we proceeded till we were out of sight of these people. When we went to rest the following night, they offered us some victuals, but we refused it; and the only comfort we had was in being in one another's arms all that night, and bathing each other with our tears. But, alas! we were soon deprived of even the small comfort of weeping together. The next day proved a day of greater sorrow than I had yet experienced; for my sister and I were then separated, while we lay clasped in each other's arms. It was in vain that we besought them not to part us; she was torn from me and immediately carried away, while I was left in a state of distraction not to be described. I cried and grieved continually; and for several days did not eat anything but what they forced into my mouth.

At length, after many days traveling, during which I had often changed masters, I got into the hands of a chieftain in a very pleasant country. This man had two wives and some children, and they all used me extremely well, and did all they could to comfort me; particularly the first wife, who was something like my mother. Although I was a great many days' journey from my father's house, yet these people spoke exactly the same language with us. This first master of mine, as I may call him, was a smith, and my principal employment was working his bellows, which were the same kind as I had seen in my vicinity. They were in some respects not unlike the stoves here in gentlemen's kitchens, and were covered over with leather; and in the middle of that leather a stick was fixed, and a person stood up and worked it in the same manner as is done to pump water out of a cask with a hand pump. I believe it was gold he worked, for it was of a lovely bright yellow color, and was worn by the women on their wrists and ankles.

I was there, I suppose, about a month, and they at last used to trust me some little distance from the house. This liberty I used in embracing every opportunity to inquire the way to my own home; and I also sometimes, for the same purpose, went with the maidens, in the cool of the evenings, to bring pitchers of water from the springs for the use of the house. I had also remarked where the sun rose in the morning and set in the evening as I had traveled along; and I had observed that my father's house was toward the rising of the sun. I therefore determined to seize the first opportunity of making my escape, and to shape my course for that quarter; for I was quite oppressed and weighed down by grief after my mother and friends; and my love of liberty, ever great, was strengthened by the mortifying circumstance of not daring to eat with the freeborn children, although I was mostly their companion.

While I was projecting my escape one day, an unlucky event happened, which quite disconcerted my plan and put an end to my hopes. I used to be sometimes employed in assisting an elderly slave to cook and take care of the poultry; and one morning, while I was feeding some chickens, I happened to toss a small pebble at one of them, which hit it on the middle and directly killed it. The old slave, having soon after missed the chicken, inquired after it; and on my relating the accident (for I told her the truth, for my mother would never suffer me to tell a lie), she flew into a violent passion and threatened that I should suffer for it; and, my master being out, she immediately went and told her mistress what I had done. This alarmed me very much, and I expected an instant flogging, which to me was uncommonly dreadful, for I had seldom been beaten at home. I therefore resolved to fly; and accordingly I ran into a thicket that was hard by, and hid myself in the bushes. Soon afterward my mistress and the slave returned, and, not seeing me, they searched all the house, but not finding me, and I not making answer when they called to me, they thought I had run away, and the whole neighborhood was raised in the pursuit of me.

In that part of the country, as in ours, the houses and villages were skirted with woods, or shrubberies, and the bushes were so thick that a man could readily conceal himself in them so as to elude the strictest search. The neighbors continued the whole day looking for me, and several times many of them came within a few yards of the place where I lay hid. I expected every moment when I heard a rustling among the trees to be found out and punished by my master; but they never discovered me, though they were often so near that I even heard their conjectures as they were looking about for me; and I now learned from them that any attempts to return home would be hopeless. Most of them supposed I had fled toward home; but the distance was so great, and the way so intricate, that they thought I could never reach it, and that I should be lost in the woods. When I heard this, I was seized with a violent panic and abandoned myself to despair. Night, too, began to approach, and aggravated all my fears. I had before entertained hopes of getting home, and had determined when it should be dark to make the attempt; but I was now convinced it was fruitless, and began to consider that, if possibly I could escape all other animals, I could not those of the human kind; and that, not knowing the way, I must perish in the woods. Thus was I like the hunted deer

Every leaf and every whisp'ring breath,
Conveyed a foe, and every foe a death.

I heard frequent rustlings among the leaves, and being pretty sure they were snakes, I expected every instant to be stung by them. This increased my anguish, and the horror of my situation became now quite insupportable. I at length quitted the thicket, very faint and hungry, for I had not eaten or drank anything all the day, and crept to my master's kitchen, from whence I set out at first, which was an open shed, and laid myself down in the ashes with an anxious wish for death, to relieve me from all my pains. I was scarcely awake in the morning when the old woman slave, who was the first up, came to light the fire, and saw me in the fireplace. She was very much surprised to see me, and could scarcely believe her own eyes. She now promised to intercede for me, and went for her master, who soon after came, and, having slightly reprimanded me, ordered me to be taken care of and not ill-treated.

Soon after this, my master's only daughter, and child by his first wife, sickened and died, which affected him so much that for some time he was almost frantic, and really would have killed himself had he not been watched and prevented. However, in a short time afterward he recovered, and I was again sold.

I was now carried to the left of the sun's rising, through many dreary wastes and dismal woods, amidst the hideous roarings of wild beasts. The people I was sold to used to carry me very often, when I was tired, either on their shoulders or on their backs. I saw many convenient well-built sheds along the road at proper distances to accommodate the merchants and travelers who lay in those buildings along with their wives, who often accompany them; and they always go well armed.

From the time I left my own nation, I always found somebody that understood me till I came to the seacoast. The languages of different nations did not totally differ, nor were they so copious as those of the Europeans, particularly the English. They were therefore easily learned; and, while I was journeying thus through Africa, I acquired two or three different tongues.

In this manner I had been traveling for a considerable time, when, one evening, to my great surprise, whom should I see brought to the house where I was but my dear sister! As soon as she saw me, she gave a loud shriek and ran into my arms — I was quite overpowered; neither of us could speak, but, for a considerable time, clung to each other in mutual embraces, unable to do anything but weep. Our meeting affected all who saw us; and, indeed, I must acknowledge, in honor of those sable destroyers of human rights, that I never met with any ill-treatment, or saw any offered to their slaves, except tying them, when necessary, to keep them from running away. When these people knew we were brother and sister, they indulged us to be together; and the man to whom I supposed we belonged lay with us, he in the middle, while she and I held one another by the hands across his breast all night; and thus, for a while, we forgot our misfortunes in the joy of being together. But even this small comfort was soon to have an end; for scarcely had the fatal morning appeared when she was again torn from me forever!

I was now more miserable, if possible, than before. The small relief which her presence gave me from pain was gone, and the wretchedness of my situation was redoubled by my anxiety after her fate, and my apprehensions lest her sufferings should be greater than mine, when I could not be with her to alleviate them. Yes, thou dear partner of all my childish sports! thou sharer of my joys and sorrows! happy should I have ever esteemed myself to encounter every misery for you and to procure your freedom by the sacrifice of my own. Though you were early forced from my arms, your image has been always riveted in my heart, from which neither time nor fortune have been able to remove it; so that, while the thoughts of your sufferings have damped my prosperity, they have mingled with adversity and increased its bitterness. To that Heaven which protects the weak from the strong, I commit the care of your innocence and virtues, if they have not already received their full reward, and if your youth and delicacy have not long since fallen victims to the violence of the African trader, the pestilential stench of a Guinea ship, the seasoning in the European colonies, or the lash and lust of a brutal and unrelenting overseer.

I did not long remain after my sister. I was again sold and carried through a number of places, till after traveling a considerable time I came to a town called Tinmah, in the most beautiful country I had yet seen in Africa. It was extremely rich, and there were many rivulets which flowed through it, and supplied a large pond in the center of the town, where the people washed. Here I first saw and tasted coconuts, which I thought superior to any nuts I had ever tasted before; and the trees which were loaded were also interspersed among the houses, which had commodious shades adjoining, and were in the same manner as ours, the insides being neatly plastered and whitewashed. Here I also saw and tasted, for the first time, sugarcane.

Their money consisted of little white shells, the size of the fingernail. I was sold here for 172 of them by a merchant who lived and brought me there. I had been about two or three days at his house when a wealthy widow, a neighbor of his, came there one evening and brought with her an only son, a young gentleman about my own age and size. Here they saw me; and, having taken a fancy to me, I was bought of the merchant and went home with them. Her house and premises were situated close to one of those rivulets I have mentioned, and were the finest I ever saw in Africa; they were very extensive, and she had a number of slaves to attend her. The next day I was washed and perfumed; and when mealtime came, I was led into the presence of my mistress, and ate and drank before her with her son. This filled me with astonishment; and I could scarce help expressing my surprise that the young gentleman should suffer me, who was bound, to eat with him who was free; and not only so, but that he would not at any time either eat or drink till I had taken first, because I was the eldest, which was agreeable to our custom.

Indeed, everything here, and all their treatment of me, made me forget that I was a slave. The language of these people resembled ours so nearly that we understood each other perfectly. They had also the very same customs as we. There were likewise slaves daily to attend us, while my young master and I, with other boys, sported with our darts and bows and arrows, as I had been used to do at home. In this resemblance to my former happy state, I passed about two months; and I now began to think I was to be adopted into the family, and was beginning to be reconciled to my situation and to forget by degrees my misfortunes, when all at once the delusion vanished; for, without the least previous knowledge, one morning early, while my dear master and companion was still asleep, I was awakened out of my reverie to fresh sorrow, and hurried away even among the uncircumcised.

Thus, at the very moment I dreamed of the greatest happiness, I found myself most miserable; and it seemed as if fortune wished to give me this taste of joy only to render the reverse more poignant. The change I now experienced was as painful as it was sudden and unexpected. It was a change, indeed, from a state of bliss to a scene which is inexpressible by me, as it discovered to me an element I had never before beheld, and till then had no idea of, and wherein such instances of hardship and cruelty continually occurred as I can never reflect on but with horror.

All the nations and people I had hitherto passed through resembled our own in their manners, customs, and language; but I came at length to a country, the inhabitants of which differed from us in all those particulars. I was very much struck with this difference, especially when I came among a people who did not circumcise, and ate without washing their hands. They cooked also in iron pots, and had European cutlasses and crossbows, which were unknown to us, and fought with their fists among themselves. Their women were not so modest as ours, for they ate and drank and slept with their men. But above all, I was amazed to see no sacrifices or offerings among them.

In some of those places the people ornamented themselves with scars, and likewise filed their teeth very sharp. They wanted sometimes to ornament me in the same manner, but I would not suffer them; hoping that I might some time be among a people who did not thus disfigure themselves, as I thought they did.

At last I came to the banks of a large river which was covered with canoes, in which the people appeared to live with their household utensils and provisions of all kinds. I was beyond measure astonished at this, as I had never before seen any water larger than a pond or a rivulet; and my surprise was mingled with no small fear when I was put into one of these canoes, and we began to paddle and move along the river. We continued going on thus till night, and when we came to land and made fires on the banks, each family by themselves, some dragged their canoes on shore, others stayed and cooked in theirs, and laid in them all night. Those on the land had mats, of which they made tents, some in the shape of little houses; in these we slept; and after the morning meal, we embarked again and proceeded as before. I was often very much astonished to see some of the women, as well as the men, jump into the water, dive to the bottom, come up again, and swim about.

Thus I continued to travel, sometimes by land, sometimes by water, through different countries and various nations, till, at the end of six or seven months after I had been kidnapped, I arrived at the seacoast. It would be tedious and uninteresting to relate all the incidents which befell me during this journey, and which I have not yet forgotten; of the various hands I passed through, and the manners and customs of all the different people among whom I lived. I shall, therefore, only observe that in all the places where I was, the soil was exceedingly rich; the pumpkins, eadas, plantains, yams, etc., were in great abundance and of incredible size. There were also vast quantities of different gums, though not used for any purpose, and everywhere a great deal of tobacco. The cotton even grew quite wild, and there was plenty of redwood. I saw no mechanics whatever in all the way, except such as I have mentioned. The chief employment in all these countries was agriculture, and both the males and females, as with us, were brought up to it, and trained in the arts of war.

The first object which saluted my eyes when I arrived on the coast was the sea, and a slave ship, which was then riding at anchor and waiting for its cargo. These filled me with astonishment, which was soon converted into terror when I was carried on board. I was immediately handled and tossed up to see if I were sound by some of the crew; and I was now persuaded that I had gotten into a world of bad spirits, and that they were going to kill me. Their complexions, too, differing so much from ours, their long hair, and the language they spoke (which was very different from any I had ever heard) united to confirm me in this belief. Indeed, such were the horrors of my views and fears at the moment that, if 10,000 worlds had been my own, I would have freely parted with them all to have exchanged my condition with that of the meanest slave in my own country. When I looked round the ship, too, and saw a large furnace of copper boiling, and a multitude of black people of every description chained together, every one of their countenances expressing dejection and sorrow, I no longer doubted of my fate; and, quite overpowered with horror and anguish, I fell motionless on the deck and fainted.

When I recovered a little, I found some black people about me, who I believed were some of those who had brought me on board and had been receiving their pay; they talked to me in order to cheer me, but all in vain. I asked them if we were not to be eaten by those white men with horrible looks, red faces, and long hair. They told me I was not; and one of the crew brought me a small portion of spirituous liquor in a wine glass, but, being afraid of him, I would not take it out of his hand. One of the blacks, therefore, took it from him and gave it to me, and I took a little down my palate, which, instead of reviving me, as they thought it would, threw me into the greatest consternation at the strange feeling it produced, having never tasted any such liquor before. Soon after this, the blacks who brought me on board went off and left me abandoned to despair.

I now saw myself deprived of all chance of returning to my native country, or even the least glimpse of hope of gaining the shore, which I now considered as friendly; and I even wished for my former slavery in preference to my present situation, which was filled with horrors of every kind, still heightened by my ignorance of what I was to undergo. I was not long suffered to indulge my grief. I was soon put down under the decks, and there I received such a salutation in my nostrils as I had never experienced in my life; so that, with the loathsomeness of the stench and crying together, I became so sick and low that I was not able to eat, nor had I the least desire to taste anything. I now wished for the last friend, death, to relieve me; but soon, to my grief, two of the white men offered me eatables; and, on my refusing to eat, one of them held me fast by the hands and laid me across, I think, the windlass, and tied my feet, while the other flogged me severely.

I had never experienced anything of this kind before, and although not being used to the water, I naturally feared that element the first time I saw it, yet, nevertheless, could I have got over the nettings, I would have jumped over the side, but I could not; and, besides, the crew used to watch us very closely who were not chained down to the decks lest we should leap into the water. And I have seen some of these poor African prisoners most severely cut for attempting to do so, and hourly whipped for not eating. This, indeed, was often the case with myself. In a little time after, among the poor chained men, I found some of my own nation, which in a small degree gave ease to my mind. I inquired of these what was to be done with us? They gave me to understand we were to be carried to these white people's country to work for them. I then was a little revived, and thought, if it were no worse than working, my situation was not so desperate; but still I feared I should be put to death, the white people looked and acted, as I thought, in so savage a manner; for I had never seen among any people such instances of brutal cruelty; and this not only shown toward us blacks but also to some of the whites themselves. One white man in particular I saw, when we were permitted to be on deck, flogged so unmercifully with a large rope near the foremast that he died in consequence of it; and they tossed him over the side as they would have done a brute. This made me fear these people the more; and I expected nothing less than to be treated in the same manner.

I could not help expressing my fears and apprehensions to some of my countrymen; I asked them if these people had no country, but lived in this hollow place (the ship). They told me they did not, but came from a distant one. "Then," said I, "how comes it in all our country we never heard of them?" They told me because they lived so very far off. I then asked where were their women? had they any like themselves? I was told they had. "And why," said I, "do we not see them?" They answered, because they were left behind. I asked how the vessel could go? They told me they could not tell; but that there was cloth put upon the masts by the help of the ropes I saw, and then the vessel went on; and the white men had some spell or magic they put in the water when they liked in order to stop the vessel. I was exceedingly amazed at this account, and really thought they were spirits. I therefore wished much to be from among them, for I expected they would sacrifice me; but my wishes were vain, for we were so quartered that it was impossible for any of us to make our escape.

While we stayed on the coast, I was mostly on deck; and one day, to my great astonishment, I saw one of these vessels coming in with the sails up. As soon as the whites saw it, they gave a great shout, at which we were amazed; and the more so as the vessel appeared larger by approaching nearer. At last, she came to an anchor in my sight, and when the anchor was let go, I and my countrymen who saw it were lost in astonishment to observe the vessel stop — and were now convinced it was done by magic. Soon after this the other ship got her boats out, and they came on board of us, and the people of both ships seemed very glad to see each other. Several of the strangers also shook hands with us black people, and made motions with their hands, signifying, I suppose, we were to go to their country, but we did not understand them.

At last, when the ship we were in had got in all her cargo, they made ready with many fearful noises, and we were all put under deck, so that we could not see how they managed the vessel. But this disappointment was the least of my sorrow. The stench of the hold while we were on the coast was so intolerably loathsome that it was dangerous to remain there for any time, and some of us had been permitted to stay on the deck for the fresh air; but now that the whole ship's cargo were confined together, it became absolutely pestilential. The closeness of the place and the heat of the climate, added to the number in the ship, which was so crowded that each had scarcely room to turn himself, almost suffocated us. This produced copious perspirations, so that the air soon became unfit for respiration, from a variety of loathsome smells, and brought on a sickness among the slaves, of which many died — thus falling victims to the improvident avarice, as I may call it, of their purchasers. This wretched situation was again aggravated by the galling of the chains, now became insupportable; and the filth of the necessary tubs, into which the children often fell and were almost suffocated. The shrieks of the women and the groans of the dying rendered the whole a scene of horror almost inconceivable.

Happily, perhaps, for myself, I was soon reduced so low here that it was thought necessary to keep me almost always on deck; and from my extreme youth I was not put in fetters. In this situation I expected every hour to share the fate of my companions, some of whom were almost daily brought upon deck at the point of death, which I began to hope would soon put an end to my miseries. Often did I think many of the inhabitants of the deep much more happy than myself. I envied them the freedom they enjoyed, and as often wished I could change my condition for theirs. Every circumstance I met with served only to render my state more painful, and heightened my apprehensions and my opinion of the cruelty of the whites.

One day they had taken a number of fishes; and when they had killed and satisfied themselves with as many as they thought fit, to our astonishment who were on deck, rather than give any of them to us to eat, as we expected, they tossed the remaining fish into the sea again, although we begged and prayed for some as well as we could, but in vain; and some of my countrymen, being pressed by hunger, took an opportunity, when they thought no one saw them, of trying to get a little privately. But they were discovered, and the attempt procured them some very severe floggings. One day, when we had a smooth sea and moderate wind, two of my wearied countrymen who were chained together (I was near them at the time), preferring death to such a life of misery, somehow made through the nettings and jumped into the sea. Immediately, another quite dejected fellow, who, on account of his illness, was suffered to be out of irons, also followed their example; and I believe many more would very soon have done the same if they had not been prevented by the ship's crew, who were instantly alarmed. Those of us that were the most active were in a moment put down under the deck, and there was such a noise and confusion among the people of the ship, as I never heard before, to stop her and get the boat out to go after the slaves. However, two of the wretches were drowned, but they got the other, and afterward flogged him unmercifully for thus attempting to prefer death to slavery.

In this manner we continued to undergo more hardships than I can now relate, hardships which are inseparable from this accursed trade. Many a time we were near suffocation from the want of fresh air, which we were often without for whole days together. This, and the stench of the necessary tubs, carried off many.

During our passage, I first saw flying fishes, which surprised me very much; they used frequently to fly across the ship, and many of them fell on the deck. I also now first saw the use of the quadrant; I had often with astonishment seen the mariners make observations with it, and I could not think what it meant. They at last took notice of my surprise; and one of them, willing to increase it as well as to gratify my curiosity, made me one day look through it. The clouds appeared to me to be land, which disappeared as they passed along. This heightened my wonder; and I was now more persuaded than ever that I was in another world, and that everything about me was magic.

At last, we came in sight of the island of Barbados, at which the whites on board gave a great shout and made many signs of joy to us. We did not know what to think of this; but as the vessel drew nearer, we plainly saw the harbor, and other ships of different kinds and sizes, and we soon anchored among them, off Bridgetown.

Many merchants and planters now came on board, though it was in the evening. They put us in separate parcels and examined us attentively. They also made us jump, and pointed to the land, signifying we were to go there. We thought by this we should be eaten by these ugly men, as they appeared to us; and, when soon after we were all put down under the deck again, there was much dread and trembling among us, and nothing but bitter cries to be heard all the night from these apprehensions, insomuch that at last the white people got some old slaves from the land to pacify us. They told us we were not to be eaten but to work, and were soon to go on land, where we should see many of our country people. This report eased us much. And sure enough, soon after we were landed, there came to us Africans of all languages.

We were conducted immediately to the merchant's yard, where we were all pent up together, like so many sheep in a fold, without regard to sex or age. As every object was new to me, everything I saw filled me with surprise. What struck me first was that the houses were built with bricks and stories, and in every other respect different from those I had seen in Africa; but I was still more astonished on seeing people on horseback. I did not know what this could mean; and, indeed, I thought these people were full of nothing but magical arts. While I was in this astonishment, one of my fellow prisoners spoke to a countryman of his about the horses, who said they were the same kind they had in their country. I understood them, though they were from a distant part of Africa; and I thought it odd I had not seen any horses there; but afterward, when I came to converse with different Africans, I found they had many horses among them, and much larger than those I then saw.

We were not many days in the merchant's custody before we were sold after their usual manner, which is this. On a signal given (as the beat of a drum), the buyers rush at once into the yard where the slaves are confined and make choice of that parcel they like best. The noise and clamor with which this is attended, and the eagerness visible in the countenances of the buyers, serve not a little to increase the apprehension of terrified Africans, who may well be supposed to consider them as the ministers of that destruction to which they think themselves devoted. In this manner, without scruple, are relations and friends separated, most of them never to see each other again. I remember, in the vessel in which I was brought over, in the men's apartment, there were several brothers, who, in the sale, were sold in different lots; and it was very moving, on this occasion, to see and hear their cries at parting.

O, ye nominal Christians! might not an African ask you — Learned you this from your God, who says unto you, "Do unto all men as you would men should do unto you"? Is it not enough that we are torn from our country and friends to toil for your luxury and lust of gain? Must every tender feeling be likewise sacrificed to your avarice? Are the dearest friends and relations, now rendered more dear by their separation from their kindred, still to be parted from each other, and thus prevented from cheering the gloom of slavery, with the small comfort of being together and mingling their sufferings and sorrows? Why are parents to lose their children, brothers their sisters, or husbands their wives? Surely, this is a new refinement in cruelty which, while it has no advantage to atone for it, thus aggravates distress and adds fresh horrors even to the wretchedness of slavery.

**Negroes for Sale.**

*A Cargo of very fine ſtout Men and Women, in good order and fit for immediate ſervice, juſt imported from the Windward Coaſt of Africa, in the Ship* Two Brothers.— *Conditions are one half Caſh or Produce, the other half payable the firſt of January next, giving Bond and Security if required.*

*The Sale to be opened at* 10 *o'Clock each Day, in* Mr. Bourdeaux's *Yard, at No,* 48, *on the Bay.*

*May* 19, 1784. JOHN MITCHELL.

# 1795

115.

## The Naturalization of Immigrants

*The Constitution empowered Congress "to establish a uniform rule of naturalization." In 1790, a liberal act was passed providing for the admission of immigrants to citizenship. However, because of the increasing turbulence in Europe, many feared that a growth in the number of political refugees, particularly those aristocratic elements driven out by the revolution in France, would be harmful to American liberty. On January 29, 1795, Congress modified the Act of 1790 to require five years of residence before a person could be naturalized. The main provisions of the Act are revealed in the selection that is reprinted below.*

Source: John P. Sanderson, *The Views and Opinions of American Statesmen on Foreign Immigration,* Philadelphia, 1856, pp. 128-129.

Any alien, being a free white person, may be admitted to become a citizen of the United States, or any of them, on the following conditions, and not otherwise. First, he shall have declared, on oath or affirmation, before the Supreme, Superior, District, or Circuit Court of some one of the states, or of the territories northwest or south of the Ohio River, or a Circuit or District Court of the United States, three years at least before his admission, that it was, bona fide, his intention to become a citizen of the United States, and to renounce forever all allegiance and fidelity to any foreign prince, potentate, state, or sovereignty whereof such alien may at that time be a citizen or subject.

Second, he shall, at the time of his application to be admitted, declare on oath or affirmation before some one of the courts aforesaid that he has resided within the United States five years at least, and within the state or territory where such court is at the time held, one year at least; that he will support the Constitution of the United States; and that he does absolutely and entirely renounce and abjure all allegiance and fidelity to any foreign prince, potentate, state, or sovereignty whatever, and particularly by name the prince, potentate, state, or sovereignty whereof he was before a citizen or subject; which proceedings shall be recorded by the clerk of the court.

Third, the court admitting such alien shall

be satisfied that he has resided within the limits and under the jurisdiction of the United States five years. It shall further appear to their satisfaction that during that time he has behaved as a man of a good moral character, attached to the principles of the Constitution of the United States, and well-disposed to the good order and happiness of the same.

Fourth, in case the alien applying to be admitted to citizenship shall have borne any hereditary title, or been of any of the orders of nobility, in the kingdom or state from which he came, he shall, in addition to the above requisites, make an express renunciation of his title or order of nobility in the court to which his application shall be made; which renunciation shall be recorded in said court. . . .

*Provided always, and be it further enacted,* that any alien now residing within the limits and under the jurisdiction of the United States may be admitted to become a citizen on his declaring, on oath or affirmation, in some one of the courts aforesaid, that he has resided two years, at least, within and under the jurisdiction of the same, and one year, at least, within the state or territory where such court is at the time held; that he will support the Constitution of the United States; and that he does absolutely and entirely renounce and abjure all allegiance and fidelity to any foreign prince, potentate, state, or sovereignty whatever, and particularly by name the prince, potentate, state, or sovereignty whereof he was before a citizen or subject. Moreover, on its appearing to the satisfaction of the court that, during the said term of two years, he has behaved as a man of good moral character, attached to the Constitution of the United States, and well-disposed to the good order and happiness of the same; and when the alien applying for admission to citizenship shall have borne any hereditary title, or been of any of the orders of nobility in the kingdom or state from which he came, on his, moreover, making in the court an express renunciation of his title or order of nobility, before he shall be entitled to such admission; all of which proceedings, required in this proviso to be performed in the court, shall be recorded by the clerk thereof. . . . .

*And be it further enacted,* that the children of persons duly naturalized, dwelling within the United States, and being under the age of twenty-one years at the time of such naturalization, and the children of citizens of the United States born out of the limits and jurisdiction of the United States, shall be considered as citizens of the United States. The right of citizenship shall not descend on persons whose fathers have never been resident of the United States. No person heretofore proscribed by any state, or who has been legally convicted of having joined the army of Great Britain during the late war, shall be admitted as aforesaid, without the consent of the legislature of the state in which such person was proscribed.

---

*It is immensely difficult to create a country out of states without any community of religion and interests, states which have been peopled by different stocks, and are living on varied soils and under diverse climates. What link is there between a Frenchman of Louisiana, a Spaniard of Florida, a German of New York, an Englishman of New England, Carolina, Georgia — all considered Americans? . . . How many centuries will be needed to make these elements homogeneous?*

CHATEAUBRIAND

116.

## Timothy Pickering: On Peace with the Indians

*In the eighteenth century, the threat of Indian wars had hindered the development and settling of western lands. However, on August 20, 1794, General Anthony Wayne won an important victory over the Indians at Fallen Timbers, in northwest Ohio. The Indians of the area made peace overtures, which eventually led to the Greenville Treaty. Signed on August 3, 1795, this agreement was not completely satisfactory to the Indians, who lost many tribal holdings because of it. Until the Department of the Interior was organized in 1849, Indian affairs were handled by the War Department. Thus, when Timothy Pickering became the secretary of war early in 1795, he was charged with the conduct of this area. On April 8, 1795, he wrote the following letter to General Wayne, outlining his proposals to end the Indian conflicts.*

Source: *Anthony Wayne, A Name in Arms ... The Wayne-Knox-Pickering-McHenry Correspondence*, Richard C. Knopf, ed., Pittsburgh, 1959, pp. 393-403.

The overtures for peace which have been made by the Indians northwest of the Ohio bear the appearance of sincerity, and viewed in connection with the events of the last year, it is hardly to be doubted that their overtures have been made in good faith. Taking this for granted, it becomes necessary to communicate to you the ideas of the President of the United States relative to the terms on which peace is now to be negotiated. To gratify the usual expectation of Indians assembling for the purposes of treaty and thereby facilitate the negotiation, it is thought best to provide and forward a quantity of goods. These will amount to at least $25,000, but are to be delivered only in case of a successful treaty: except such small portions of them as humanity may call for pending the negotiation. The residue are to be delivered to them as one of the conditions for their final relinquishment of the lands which the treaty shall comprehend.

Besides the goods, you will stipulate to pay them a sum not exceeding $10,000 annually, as a further and full consideration for all the lands they relinquish.

You will consider how the goods for the treaty should be distributed. Perhaps Indians of several nations will attend, who have no sort of claim to any of the lands we shall retain: yet being present they will expect to participate, and they must participate. In what degree can be adjusted with the chiefs of the tribes who were the true owners of the land. These alone (the true owners), if they can be ascertained or agreed on, are to enjoy the annuity, the share of each nation to be fixed if possible; and it is presumed they will agree on the principles by which your calculation will be governed. They will doubtless, as formerly, manifest their wishes to recover a large part of their best hunting ground as necessary to their subsistence; but the annuity is intended to compensate them for the loss of the game, while its amount granted under the present circumstances will evince the liberality of the United States.

With respect to the general boundary

line, that described in the treaty made at Fort Harmar January 9, 1789, will still be satisfactory to the United States; and you will urge it accordingly.

The reservations of diverse pieces of land for trading posts, as in the tenth article of the Treaty of Fort Harmar, and the strip six miles wide from the River Rosine to Lake St. Clair in the eleventh article, as a convenient appendage to Detroit, to give room for settlements, it is desirable to have retained for those uses. Some of the military posts which are already established, or which you may judge necessary to have established to preserve or complete a chain of communication from the Ohio to the Miami of the Lake; and from the Miami villages to the head of the Wabash, and down the same to the Ohio and from the Miami villages down to the mouth of the Miami River at Lake Erie, it will also be desirable to secure: but all these cessions are not to be insisted on; for peace and not increase of territory has been the object of this expensive war. Yet, the success of the last campaign authorizes a demand of some indemnification for the blood and treasure expended. Such a boundary line, therefore, as would formerly have been acquiesced in, for the sake of peace, will not now be proposed.

The Treaty of Fort Harmar, as you have announced to the chiefs, is to be the basis of the new treaty. The old boundary line from the mouth of Cuyahoga to the forks of Muskingum, at the crossing place above Fort Lawrance [Laurens], and thence westerly straight to the portage between a branch of the Miami of the Ohio and the river St. Marys (which is a branch of the Miami of the Lake) is still to be adhered to; but from this portage the line may run down the aforementioned branch of the Miami of the Ohio to the main river and thence down the same to the Ohio, making the line now described from the mouth of Cuyahoga to the mouth of the Miami of the Ohio the general boundary of the lands of the United States over the Ohio.

All the lands north and west of this general boundary line to which, by virtue of former treaties with the western Indians, the United States have claims, may be relinquished excepting:

1. The lands which being occupied by the British troops and subjects, and the Indian title to the same being extinguished, were ceded by Great Britain in full right to the United States by the treaty of 1783.

2. Those detached pieces of land on which you have established or shall think proper to establish military posts to form or complete a chain of communication between the Miami of the Ohio and the Miami of Lake Erie, and by the latter from the Lake to Fort Wayne and thence to the Wabash and down the same to the Ohio.

3. The 150,000 acres granted to General Clarke for himself and his warriors near the rapids of the Ohio.

4. The lands in possession of the French people and other white settlers among them, who hold their lands by the consent of the United States.

5. The military posts now occupied by the troops of the United States on the Wabash and the Ohio.

The object of these reservations may be explained to the Indians. They are not destined for their annoyance, or to impose the smallest restraint on their enjoyment of their lands, but to connect the settlements of the people of the United States by rendering a passage from one to the other more practicable and convenient. These posts will also prove convenient to the Indians themselves, as traders may reside at some or all of them to supply them with goods. For these reasons some land about each of these posts, not less than two square miles, should also be reserved, together with a right of passage from one to another.

If the Indians are sincere, and desire to have our friendship, they cannot object to these means of useful intercourse, which will cement that friendship while they will afford a very necessary and important accommodation to the people of the United States, and in the way of trade to the Indians themselves.

The reservations to the United States of the lands occupied by the British troops will of course comprehend the post of Michilimackinac, but without any definite boundary. The present post there is on an island, but a very barren one. If the former post on the main is situated in a better soil, and it can be ascertained that the Indian title to any quantity of land there was extinguished, it will be ours of course. But if the Indian title was not extinguished, an attempt may be made to obtain it. If objected to there need be no difficulty in renouncing it.

The treaties heretofore made with the western Indians have comprised a number of nations; and if there be any truth in their pretensions of late years, their interests are blended together. Hence may result the necessity of continuing their former mode of treating. And their uniting in one instrument will save much time and trouble, and prevent tedious and perhaps inconvenient altercations among themselves about their boundaries which are often extremely vague. For instance, the chiefs of the Six Nations last autumn declared that their title to the lands between the Allegany and French Creek on the east and the Muskingum and Cuyahoga on the west was acknowledged by all the western Indians. But when I pressed them on this point to cede that tract to the United States, they confessed that the four most hostile tribes denied their right to it. I am well satisfied that whatever claim the Six Nations might formerly have to the lands westward of the Allegany, they long ago relinquished the same to the Delawares, and others of the present western Indians. The relinquishment of the country, therefore, to the United States by the Six Nations I consider as affording us but the shadow of a title to it.

The principal reasons given by the western Indians for not adhering to the treaties of Fort McIntosh, Miami, and Fort Harmar have been these:

1. That the chiefs who treated were not an adequate representation of the nations to whom the lands belonged.

2. That they were compelled by threats to subscribe some of the treaties.

3. That the claim of the United States to the full property of the Indians' lands, under color of the treaty of 1783 with Great Britain, was unfounded and unjust.

To prevent a repetition of such complaints you will use every practicable means to obtain a full representation of all the nations claiming property in the lands in question. And to obviate future doubts it may be expedient to get lists of all the principal and other chiefs of each nation to ascertain who are absent, and whether those present may be fairly considered as an adequate representation of their nation. The explanations and declarations of the chiefs on this point may be noted, and subscribed by them upon each list.

As they will be collected within your power at Greenville, it will highly concern the honor and justice of the United States that strong and decided proofs be given them that they are not under even the shadow of duress. Let them feel that they are at perfect liberty to speak their sentiments, and to sign or refuse to sign such a treaty as you are now authorized to negotiate.

The unfortunate construction put by the first commissioners on our treaty of peace with Great Britain and thence continued by General St. Clair in 1789 has since been repeatedly renounced. The commissioners who went to Canada in 1793 were explicit on this head in their messages to the western Indians — copies whereof you will receive. As this construction grasped the whole Indian country southward of the Great Lakes and eastward of the Mississippi as the full and absolute property of the United States, a construction as unfounded in itself as it was unintelligible and mysterious to the Indians — a construction which, with the use made of it by the British advisers of those Indians, has probably been the mainspring of the distressing war on our frontiers — it cannot be too explicitly renounced. At the same time you will carefully explain and maintain the preemption right of the United States. Some delicacy, however, will be required to state even this claim without exciting their displeasure. If the land is theirs (and this we acknowledge) they will say "Why shall we not sell it to whom we please?" Perhaps in some such way as the following it may be rendered inoffensive.

The white nations, in their treaties with one another, agree on certain boundaries, beyond which neither is to advance a step. In America, where these boundaries agreed on by the white people pass along the countries of the Indians, the meaning of the treaties is this: that one white nation shall not purchase or take possession of any Indian land beyond their own boundary so agreed on, even although the Indians should offer to sell or give it to them. The individuals indeed have often attempted to purchase and possess such lands, but being bound by the treaty of their nation, their purchases and possessions have no strength, and the other nation has a right to dispossess and drive them off.

So likewise the individuals of a white nation have no right to purchase and possess Indian lands within the boundaries of their own nations, unless the nation consents. For each white nation makes certain rules about Indian lands, which everyone of the people is obliged to follow. The most important of these rules is that which forbids individuals taking hold of Indian lands without the consent of the nation. When individuals do such things, it is because they wish to cheat not only the Indians but their own nation, which, therefore, has a right to punish them and to take away the lands so unlawfully obtained. The United States has made such a rule, the design of which is to protect the Indian lands against such bad men.

With respect to our citizens who are prisoners among the Indians, the most diligent and strenuous endeavors are to be used to recover them. Their restoration must be made an essential condition of the peace. The withholding any of them will be deemed a breech of the treaty. Perhaps the most effectual method will be what has been often practised, the taking of hostages. It has been by former instructions, and still is left to your judgment to stipulate or not a ransom for our prisoners. On one hand it would introduce a precedent that would not seem the most honorable; on the other hand, the expectation of reward might save the lives of prisoners in future wars, and perhaps of some of those now in captivity, whom their possessors may sacrifice rather than surrender without a compensation.

It has been thought necessary to appoint agents to reside among the Creeks and Cherokees to gain their good will to counteract the influence of agents from another quarter, to protect them from abuse by our own people, and to receive and represent their complaints. But the northwestern hostile tribes are separately so small, it will probably be unnecessary to adopt the like measure with them, especially if trading posts, on public account, should be established. This, by the way of experiment, will be attempted this year with the southern Indians, and there is a disposition to extend the provision, if it can be guarded from abuses. The plan proposed has been to sell the goods to the Indians and receive their skins and furs in exchange, at such rates as would merely balance the expenses of the establishment. Whatever shall be said to the western Indians on this subject must be to represent the measure as probable only and not certain, for it depends on the future decision of the legislature. But if public traffic should not be carried on, private trade will be regulated with a view to prevent abuses, and the regulations it is hoped will be effectual, as soon as the United States are in the possession of the posts which can control the traders.

The instructions on the subject of a treaty with the western Indians, given at the War Office on the 4th day of April, 1794, are still to be attended to, and to aid and influence your negotiations in all matters not varied by the present instructions, the chief of which have resulted from a change in our relative situation to the hostile Indians and to the European powers, especially the British.

One great principle ought to govern all public negotiations — *a rigid adherence to truth* — a principle that is essential in negotiations with Indians if we would gain their permanent confidence and a useful influence over them. Jealousy is strongest in minds uninformed, so that the utmost purity and candor will hardly escape suspicion. Suspicions occasion delays, and issue in discontents, and these in depredations and war.

---

117.

# Debate on the Jay Treaty

*Furious opposition greeted Jay's Treaty when it was publicized in March 1795. Many Republicans accused Jay of selling out his country and betraying the nation's ally, France. A leader of this opposition was Robert Livingston, a well-known jurist of New York, who published an essay,* Examination of the Treaty of Amity, Commerce, and Navigation, Between the United States and Great Britain, *under the pen name, "Cato." Alexander Hamilton, though then retired, felt it was his obligation to defend the work of Jay and thus took up his pen, this time under the name, "Camillus." Excerpts from Camillus, No. I, and from Livingston's attack, are reprinted here.*

Source: *The Works of Alexander Hamilton*, Henry Cabot Lodge, ed., Vol. IV, New York, 1885, pp. 371-380.
*Examination of the Treaty of Amity, Commerce, and Navigation, Between the United States and Great Britain, in Several Numbers: by Cato*, n.p., 1795, pp. 3-9.

## I.

### Alexander Hamilton: In Defense of the Treaty

It was to have been foreseen that the treaty which Mr. Jay was charged to negotiate with Great Britain, whenever it should appear, would have to contend with many perverse dispositions and some honest prejudices; that there was no measure in which the government could engage so little likely to be viewed according to its intrinsic merits — so very likely to encounter misconception, jealousy, and unreasonable dislike. For this, many reasons may be assigned.

It is only to know the vanity and vindictiveness of human nature to be convinced that while this generation lasts there will always exist among us men irreconcilable to our present national Constitution; embittered in their animosity in proportion to the

New York Historical Society

Robert Livingston, portrait by John Vanderlyn

success of its operations, and the disappointment of their inauspicious predictions. It is a material inference from this that such men will watch, with lynx's eyes, for opportunities of discrediting the proceedings of the government, and will display a hostile and malignant zeal upon every occasion where they think there are any prepossessions of the community to favor their enterprises. A treaty with Great Britain was too fruitful an occasion not to call forth all their activity. . . . It was natural that the contrary spirit should produce efforts of foreign counteraction to the treaty; and it was certain that the partisans of the counteracting power would second its efforts by all the means which they thought calculated to answer the end.

It was known that the resentment produced by our revolution war with Great Britain had never been entirely extinguished, and that recent injuries had rekindled the flame with additional violence. It was a natural consequence of this that many should be disinclined to any amicable arrangement with Great Britain, and that many others should be prepared to acquiesce only in a treaty which should present advantages of so striking and preponderant a kind as it was not reasonable to expect could be obtained, unless the United States were in a condition to give the law to Great Britain, and as, if obtained under the coercion of such a situation, could only have been the short-lived prelude of a speedy rupture to get rid of them.

Unfortunately, too, the supposition of that situation has served to foster exaggerated expectations; and the absurd delusion to this moment prevails, notwithstanding the plain evidence to the contrary, which is deducible from the high and haughty ground still maintained by Great Britain against victorious France.

It was not to be mistaken that an enthusiasm for France and her revolution, throughout all its wonderful vicissitudes, has continued to possess the minds of the great body of the people of this country; and it was to be inferred that this sentiment would predispose to a jealousy of any agreement or treaty with her most persevering competitor — a jealousy so excessive as would give the fullest scope to insidious arts to perplex and mislead the public opinion. It was well understood that a numerous party among us, though disavowing the design because the avowal would defeat it, have been steadily endeavoring to make the United States a party in the present European war by advocating all those measures which would widen the breach between us and Great Britain, and by resisting all those which would tend to close it; and it was morally certain that this party would eagerly improve every circumstance which would serve to render the treaty odious, and to frustrate it, as the most effectual road of their favorite goal. . . .

Before the treaty was known, attempts were made to prepossess the public mind against it. It was absurdly asserted that it was not expected by the people that Mr. Jay was to make any treaty; as if he had been sent not to accommodate differences by negotiation and agreement but to dictate to Great Britain the terms of an unconditional submission.

Before it was published at large, a sketch, calculated to produce false impressions, was handed out to the public, through a medium noted for hostility to the administration of the government. Emissaries flew through the country, spreading alarm and discontent; the leaders of clubs were everywhere active to seize the passions of the people and preoccupy their judgments against the treaty.

At Boston it was published one day, and the next a town meeting was convened to condemn it; without ever being read, without any serious discussion, sentence was pronounced against it. . . .

To every man who is not an enemy to the national government, who is not a prejudiced partisan, who is capable of comprehending the argument, and dispassionate enough to attend to it with impartiality, I flatter myself I shall be able to demonstrate satisfactorily in the course of some succeeding papers:

1. That the treaty adjusts, in a reasonable manner, the points in controversy between the United States and Great Britain, as well those depending on the inexecution of the treaty of peace, as those growing out of the present European war.

2. That it makes no improper concessions to Great Britain, no sacrifices on the part of the United States.

3. That it secures to the United States equivalents for what they grant.

4. That it lays upon them no restrictions which are incompatible with their honor or their interest.

5. That in the articles which respect war, it conforms to the laws of nations.

6. That it violates no treaty with, nor duty toward, any foreign power.

7. That, compared with our other commercial treaties, it is, upon the whole, entitled to a preference.

8. That it contains concessions of advantages by Great Britain to the United States, which no other nation has obtained from the same power.

9. That it gives to her no superiority of advantages over other nations with whom we have treaties.

10. That the interests of primary importance to our general welfare are promoted by it.

11. That the too probable result of a refusal to ratify is war, or, what would be still worse, a disgraceful passiveness under violations of our rights, unredressed, and unadjusted; and consequently that it is the true interest of the United States that the treaty should go into effect.

It will be understood that I speak of the treaty as advised to be ratified by the Senate — for this is the true question before the public.

## II.

## Robert Livingston: An Attack on the Treaty

As the embassy extraordinary to Great Britain, from the appointment of the envoy to the conclusion of the treaty, is unequaled in the annals of negotiation, it becomes *us, the people,* who are, as yet, the *constitutional sovereigns* of the country, to consider it with attention, that it may in future either serve as a friendly beacon to point out a secure harbor in political storms, or avoided as a light perfidiously hung out to lure our unsuspecting barks on rocks and quicksands.

It is essential to the due consideration of the advantages and disadvantages of a treaty to examine the situation of the contracting parties, because the same treaty may be good under some and bad under other circumstances. . . .

Britain, on the day of the signature of the treaty, was involved in a war with the bravest people in Europe. In the whole course of this war, she had experienced continued defeats and disgraces; her treasures were wasted upon allies that either deserted or were too feeble to afford her effectual aid; her debt had grown to the enormous sum of three hundred millions; her Navy could only be manned by the most destructive burdens upon her commerce; her manufactures were languishing; her fleets were unable to protect her trade, which had suffered unexampled losses. And while she was sinking under her burdens, her antagonist was consolidating her government, and growing so rapidly in strength, reputation, and vigor, as to threaten her existence as a nation.

The United States were, on the other hand, in the highest prosperity; their numbers had doubled since they had successfully measured swords with Britain; they possessed men, arms, military stores, and an ally, who was alone too powerful for her enemies. Sweden and Denmark, who had received insults from Britain, were ready to make a common cause with her. As the marine of England and France were nearly balanced, the weight of America, had she been forced into the war, would have turned the scale and completed the ruin of the British commerce, without any other effort than that of granting letters of marque. Independent of which, without a violation of their neutrality by those acts of sovereignty which no one would dispute their right to exercise, they could involve the British trade in the utmost distress, by an additional duty on British tonnage, by granting advantages to rival manufactures, by retaining debts due to her merchants until the injuries ours had sustained were compensated.

By following her example, both in the present and in the late American war, and suffering no part of the public debt to be paid to her citizens until justice was done us, we could have forced her into any measure that it was just or proper for us to ask. And, indeed, so fully satisfied were the Americans, of every party, of the superiority of our situation, that no doubt was entertained of a favorable issue to Mr. Jay's negotiation, and all that his friends lamented and his enemies rejoiced in was that the principal credit of them would be ascribed rather to the victories of France than to the address of our minister. Under these happy auspices the negotiation began. We shall proceed to see how it concluded.

The next point of inquiry is into the objects of the negotiation, for as every treaty is an abridgment of the natural freedom of nations, no wise state ever enters into one but with a view to remove some evil or acquire some advantage. It is upon this ground that many of our most distinguished patriots have been of opinion that all commercial treaties were injurious trammels, and bargains in which we might probably be overreached at the moment, or which circumstances might thereafter render inconvenient; that America, having nothing to sell but articles necessary to the nations with which she deals, and affording a market to their manufactures, her own trade laws are her best treaties, since she may alter and modify them at pleasure; and, indeed, experience has justified their opinion. Independent of the depredations we have suffered from the war, our trade enjoyed every advantage we could reasonably wish.

A commercial treaty was not the object of Mr. Jay's mission; the British nation, in direct violation of the Treaty of Paris, refused to surrender the western posts; extended the limits of their jurisdiction; availed themselves of their situation to possess the Indian trade, and stimulated the savages to ravage our frontiers. British officers even accompanying them in their incursions, it became the dignity of the nation to demand a delivery of the posts — reparation for the loss of trade — a compensation for the expense of the war the British had excited with the Indians — a public punishment of the British subjects who had personally appeared in arms against us, with the removal from office of Lord Dorchester, who had, in his address to the Indians, encouraged them to violate the treaty of peace. Mr. Jay was thought the properest person to make this demand. Let us see how far he has justified that sentiment, in fulfilling his duty with respect to this single point.

By the 2nd Article of the treaty, the British promise to evacuate the western posts by the 1st of June, 1796. By the Treaty of Paris, in 1782, they promised to evacuate with all convenient speed; which, if we may judge by the speed with which they have found it convenient to evacuate all their posts in France, Flanders, Germany, Holland, and Brabant, one would have supposed must have meant a much shorter time than eighteen months, so that all that the treaty acquires with respect to the posts is less than we were entitled to by the Treaty of Paris. Surely we might expect better security than a mere promise from a nation which has already shown, in their violation of the past, the little reliance that can be placed on their future engagements.

By June 1796, it is not improbable that our situation, or that of Britain, may be changed. What security shall we then have for the performance of the treaty? It is said (by those shameless apologists who are determined to find every ministerial measure right) that every treaty is a promise, and that if we are not to rely upon a promise, there can be no treaties. I answer that it is the practice of negotiators, where the character of the nation, or other circumstances, give reason to suspect a violation of their engagements, *not to rely* upon a naked promise, but to expect some guarantee or surety for the performance; that in the present case, as the promise was evidently extorted by the pressure of existing circumstances, we should see to the performance while those circumstances continue to exist.

It is evident, before Mr. Jay left this country, that the British were so far from intending to evacuate the posts, that they had determined to extend their limits; this may not only be inferred from the encouragement they gave to the depredations of the Indians, but undeniably proved by Lord Dorchester's speech, which, though disavowed by Dundas, is now admitted to have been made in consequence of express instructions. The promise, then, to evacuate has been extorted by French victories, by the humiliation of the British nation, and by their apprehension that we might at last be provoked to do ourselves justice while they were embarrassed with France. Surely then the evacuation should have been insisted upon while these circumstances operated with full force.

What was there to impede an immediate evacuation of Oswego, which is only occupied by a lieutenant's command? What was to prevent our troops being put in immediate possession of Niagara and the upper posts, under an engagement to protect, for a limited time, the British property that remained there? In one week this might have been effected, considering the situation of the posts, upon navigable waters, as well as in one year. May we not reasonably suppose that the British still entertain a hope that peace between them and France, dissensions between the United States and that republic, the seeds of which are so plentifully sown by the treaty itself, may enable them to violate their second with the same impunity that they have their first engagement. If the supposed nonperformance of the Treaty of Paris (which, however, has been so ably refuted by Mr. Jefferson in his correspondence with Mr. Hammond on that subject) has hitherto served us as a pretext for retaining the posts, how many such pretenses must the complexity and obscurity of the present treaty afford?

But suppose the war with France to continue; suppose they have the magnanimity to forgive our predilection for the enemy; suppose the spirit of our own nation to get the better of that disgraceful stupor into which a venal system has lulled it; suppose the increasing imbecility of Britain shall forbid her to hope for impunity in a further breach of faith — will it still be a matter of little moment whether or not she retains garrisons in the midst of our territory for twelve months longer?

Are we not at this moment at war with the savages? Is not this war attended with much expense to the nation, and much private distress? Is not the blood of our citizens daily shed? These evils must continue as long as the posts are in the hands of the British, or a peace, if practicable, must be purchased by the United States at very considerable expense. Were we to estimate the difference in this point of view, between an immediate evacuation and one that is to take place in June 1796, it would certainly not fall short of $1,000,000, independent of the destruction of our fellow citizens, whose lives are beyond all price. If to this we add the annual profits of the Indian trade, amounting to $800,000, it will appear that the United States lose above $1,000,000 by the retention of the posts, supposing (which is at least problematical) that they will be surrendered at the period proposed. Those who think with me that decision on the part of our government and firmness in our minister could not have failed to effect an immediate restitution of our territory, will know to what account to charge this heavy loss of blood and treasure.

But was the evacuation of the posts all we had a right to ask on that subject, if the retention of them occasioned those expensive Indian wars which have so often drained our Treasury and thinned our ranks? If, for twelve years, we have left thereby a lucrative branch of commerce, are we entitled to no compensation for these losses? If the honor of the nation has been insulted, both by Lord Dorchester and the subjects of Great Britain under his command, are we to expect no reparation for these insults? Have we reason, from what we have seen of Mr. Jay's correspondence with Lord Grenville, to presume that any has been asked? Are we not assured that none has been obtained? What, then, is the boasted article about which so much has already been said, which was the only one communicated to the public as the only one that it was imagined would bear the light? What is it but a declaration, on the part of Britain, that though she has already stripped us of millions, though she has occasioned the death of thousands of our fellow citizens, yet she now *promises* that if we will let her pocket another million, and pay as much more out of our own Treasury for a peace with her Indian allies, she will consent, in case the war with France should continue and she should be too weak to contend with us, to let us possess our own territory.

And what is our submission to these terms, and the unrequited insults we have received, but the lowest political degradation? If it is said that these were the best that could be obtained, I boldly deny the assertion; the state of Europe, the state of England itself, their submission to Denmark and Sweden, even to the little state of Genoa, warrant the denial. But should it even have been otherwise, it would have been infinitely better, both in point of honor and interest, to have waited, after having spoken with dignity of our rights, until circumstances should have enabled us to enforce them than to have relinquished our well-founded claim to a compensation of millions; to have relinquished that satisfaction which our national honor demanded. Can we doubt, if we were ourselves too weak, which I am far from supposing, that the magnanimity of France would have permitted her to conclude a peace with England without procuring us the satisfaction which her guarantee of our territories entitled us to ask? I am warranted in asserting, from the best authority, that she would not.

National Gallery of Art

**"The Washington Family" by Edward Savage, 1796; the children are George Washington Parke Custis and Eleanor Parke Custis, grandchildren of Martha Washington by her first marriage**

# WASHINGTON RETIRES TO MOUNT VERNON

Washington had inherited Mount Vernon from his half-brother Lawrence in 1752. When he married Martha Dandridge Custis, on Jan. 6, 1759, he devoted much time to his estate. Later that year, he entered the Virginia House of Burgesses. He became involved in the revolutionary movement and in 1775 was selected as the commander of the Continental Army. After bringing the Revolutionary War to a victorious conclusion, he retired in disappointment to Mount Vernon in 1783, when he was accused of desiring to be king of the new nation. Recalled to public life, he presided over the drafting of the Constitution in 1787. Two years later he was unanimously elected the first president of the United States and served effectively for two terms. He could not be prevailed upon to serve a third term, and he retired again to the congenial rural life of Mount Vernon. He was called away from his estate on one more occasion when, in 1798, war with France was impending. But the danger passed, and Washington returned for the last time to his beloved haven. He remained there, as the elder statesman of the Revolution, until his death on Dec. 14, 1799. George and Martha were laid to final rest in a tomb adjoining the estate, overlooking the Potomac.

Library of Congress

Washington was the active manager of his estate and took particular interest in experiments with seed and livestock. He began tests of crop rotation in 1766 when the soil became depleted from continuous cultivation of tobacco, and he is said to have been the first to import mules. Like other landowners, he owned slaves. Over the years Washington increased his holdings to over 8,000 acres and devoted considerable attention to enlarging the mansion, and landscaping the surrounding grounds.

Huntington Library

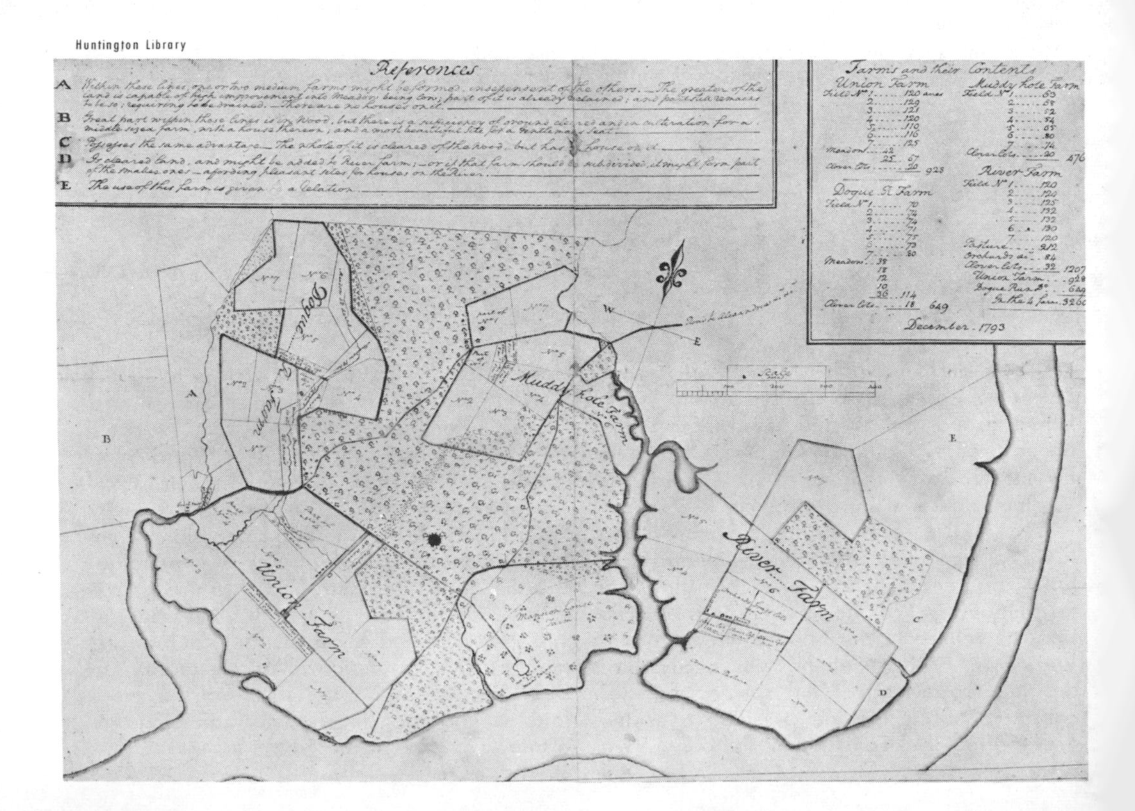

Library of Congress

**OPPOSITE PAGE: View of Mount Vernon from the landing on the Potomac, and Washington's survey of his property in 1793, with suggestions for subdividing some of the fallow land**

**(Above) Engraving by William Birch of the mansion house at Mount Vernon; (right) aquatint showing mansion and grounds by Francis Jukes, both early 19th century; (below and below right) two sketches by Benjamin Latrobe done while he was a guest in 1796**

Library of Congress

Maryland Historical Society

Sketch of General Washington, stolen at Mount Vernon while he was looking to discover a distant Vessel on the Potowmac, in which he expected some of his friends from Alexandria.

Maryland Historical Society

# Washington Portraits

In 1795, Washington was painted by C. W. Peale, Gilbert Stuart, and Adolph Wertmuller. Of the three portraits, Stuart's has come to be regarded as the definitive Washington. The original life study remained unfinished in Stuart's studio and served as the basis for numerous copies, which Stuart referred to as his "one hundred dollar bills."

**(Right) Portrait by Charles Willson Peale; (below left) Adolph Wertmuller's portrait; (below right) the "Athenaeum" Washington by Stuart**

New York Historical Society

Metropolitan Museum of Art; bequest of Charles Allen Munn

Boston Athenaeum; on deposit, Museum of Fine Arts

# 1796

118.

## Samuel Harrison Smith: The Objects Proper to Liberal Education

*Samuel Harrison Smith was a Philadelphia banker and newspaper publisher. In 1797, the American Philosophical Society offered a prize for the best essay on education and the public schools. For this contest, Smith submitted* Remarks on Education . . . To Which Is Annexed a System of Liberal Education, *an essay he had written in the summer of 1796. The essay won him part of the prize and brought him to the attention of Thomas Jefferson. Subsequently, Smith affiliated himself with the Jeffersonian faction in American politics and his newspaper, the* National Intelligencer, *became the organ of the Jefferson administration. Excerpts from Smith's essay are reprinted below.*

Source: *Remarks on Education: Illustrating the Close Connection Between Virtue and Wisdom. To Which Is Annexed a System of Liberal Education,* Philadelphia, 1798, pp. 40-70.

It is necessary that the principle of a universal diffusion of knowledge should be in the highest degree energetic. This is a principle which cannot be too extensively embraced, for it is too true that all the efforts of an enlightened zeal will never make a whole nation as well informed as its interests would prescribe. . . . We are correct, therefore, in declaring a diffusion of knowledge the best, perhaps the only, pledge of virtue, of equality, and of independence. . . .

In forming a system of liberal education, it is necessary to avoid ideas of too general a character as well as those which involve too minute a specification. Considerable latitude must be allowed for the different degrees of natural capacity and the varying shades of temper and bias. It seems, therefore, fit to lay down principles which possess properties common to every mind and which will, of course, in their application, admit of few, if any, exceptions.

The first great object of a liberal system of education should be the admission into the young mind of such ideas only as are either absolutely true or in the highest degree probable; and the cautious exclusion of all error. . . .

If this view be correct, should it not be thought treason against truth and virtue to instill prejudice and error into the young mind? If this be treason against truth and virtue, what shall we say of those who inculcate principles which they know to be false and attempt in this way to establish systems that only exist in the midst of human carnage and destruction?

Whether we consider man's existence as terminated by the grave or view him, as he doubtless is, the heir of a future life, we must consider his happiness as altogether dependent on the observance of certain moral principles. The universality with which these have been received may be considered as the test of their truth. These principles are few and simple. As the mind expands they should be explained. They require no other aid than clear illustration. The unperverted understanding acknowledges their truth as it were by intuition.

Let then those truths in which all men agree be firmly impressed, let those which are probable be inculcated with caution, and let doubt always hang over those respecting which the good and the wise disagree. Above all things let the infant mind be protected from conviction without proof.

But it will be said that in almost all the departments of a general plan of education the perusal of approved books must be chiefly relied on. The indispensable economy of arrangements which are to pervade a whole society will prohibit the employment of preceptors of either great or original talents. It will therefore be fit that the preceptor, instead of inculcating his own immature ideas, should be guided by prescribed works. It is asked where performances explaining and enforcing plain and undeniable truths and avoiding prejudices or falsehoods are to be found. Such productions are acknowledged to be rare. It is also granted that this difficulty presents one of the most serious obstacles to successful education. But it is not insurmountable. It is attempted to be removed . . . by offering large rewards for books of this nature and by inciting the learned by other inducements to embark in so noble a service. At present we must be satisfied in giving the preference to those works which abound most with truth and are the most exempt from error.

The elements of education, viz., reading and writing, are so obviously necessary that it is useless to do more than enumerate them.

Of nearly equal importance are the first principles of mathematics, as at present almost universally taught.

A tolerably correct idea of geography would seem, in a republic especially, to involve great advantages. The interest of the mercantile part of the community is closely connected with correct geographical knowledge. Many important departments of science include an accurate knowledge of it. But the most important consideration is that which contemplates the United States as either allied in friendship or arrayed in hostility with the other nations of the earth. In both which cases it becomes the duty of the citizen to have just ideas of the position, size, and strength of nations, that he may as much as possible confide in his own judgment in forming an opinion of our foreign relations instead of yielding his mind to a dangerous credulity. A most interesting part of geography relates to a knowledge of our own country. Correct information on this subject will always conduce to strengthen the bands of friendship and to dissipate the misrepresentations of party prejudice.

The cultivation of natural philosophy, particularly so far as it relates to agriculture and manufactures, has been heretofore almost entirely neglected. The benefits, however, which it would produce are great, both as they regard the happiness of the individual and as they regard national wealth. Many of the labors of the farmer and the mechanic, so far from forbidding reflection, invite it. Thus the constant development of new beauties in nature and the almost as constant production of new wonders in art extort admiration from the most ignorant and even impress their minds with considerable delight. And yet how little do they know of the energies of nature or art? Lost in the contemplation of effects, the tribute of a grateful mind finds vent in simple wonder.

If we reverse the scene and behold the farmer enlightened by the knowledge of chemistry, how wide a field of reflection and pleasure, as well as profit, would acknowledge his empire?

The ingenuity of the mechanic would not long remain passive. Repeated efforts at improvement would often prove successful and be the source of new and rapid wealth. At any rate, in all these cases, whether prospered with the expected success or not, an adequate compensation would be conferred on the mind thus employed whose thoughts generally bring with them their own reward.

The circumscribed advantages attending geographical knowledge will be greatly enlarged by a liberal acquaintance with history. In proportion as this branch of education shall be cultivated, men will see the mighty influence of moral principle, as well on the private individuals of a community as on those who are called to preside over its public concerns. It will be distinctly seen that ambition has generally risen on a destruction of every sentiment of virtue and that it much oftener merits execration than applause. Power, long enjoyed, will appear to be hostile to the happiness and subversive of the integrity of the individual in whom it centers. Fanaticism and superstition will appear surrounded with blood and torture. War will stand forth with the boldest prominence of vice and folly, and make it, for a while, doubtful whether man is most a villain or a fool. In short, the mirror which history presents will manifest to man what it is probable he will become should he surrender himself up to those selfish pursuits which, centering in his own fame alone, have enabled him without horror to wade through the blood and tears of millions. . . .

The second leading object of education should be to inspire the mind with a strong disposition to improvement.

It is acknowledged that science is still in its infancy. The combination of ideas is infinite. As this combination advances, the circle of knowledge is enlarged and, of course, the sphere of happiness extended. At present, science is only cultivated by a few recluse students, too apt to mingle the illusions of imagination with the results of indistinct observation. Hence the reproach that theory and practice oppose each other. But no sooner shall a whole nation be tributary to science than it will dawn with new luster. To adopt a physical illustration, its rays may be expected to meet with little absorption from ignorance, but to be reflected with additional luster from every object they strike.

The most splendid discoveries have not been made by philosophers of profound erudition and abstracted reflection but by men of moderate attainments and correct observation. They have proceeded from steady and patient observation.

Were the progress of a mind to improvement attended with no other effects than internal delight, it would still deserve the highest rank among those objects which produce happiness. Banishing from the mind all those sensations of indifference, ennui, and vacancy which produce effects the more cruel from their being almost wholly without remedy, it would give to existence a thousand new charms, not fleeting, but constant and always at command. The periods of youth and of active life would be invigorated, the close of existence would become a blessing instead of a burden. Is there anything in existence more interesting than an old man whose mind is stored with wisdom and whose heart is full of sensibility? . . .

This progressive improvement would be

promoted, in the third place, by inspiring youth with a taste for, and an attachment to, science, so firm that it should be almost impossible to eradicate it in the subsequent periods of life.

For this purpose, studies which address themselves to the heart, as well as those which require strong mental attention, should invite the exercise of their thoughts. Rewards should be liberally bestowed, as well those which furnish the means of moderate pleasure, as those which confer distinction. Coercion should be seldom, if ever, applied.

But this great object would be assisted more than by any other consideration by rendering, in the fourth place, knowledge as highly practical as possible. . . . Next to the first object it claims the greatest notice.

All science ought to derive its rank from its utility. The real good which it actually does, or is capable of doing, is the only genuine criterion of its value. Man may indulge himself in sublime reveries, but the world will forever remain uninterested in them. It is only when he applies the powers of his mind to objects of general use that he becomes their benefactor; until he does this he is neither entitled to their gratitude or applause.

He is the best friend of man who makes discoveries involving effects which benefit mankind the most extensively. Moral truths are therefore of importance but little short of infinite. For they apply to numbers which almost evade enumeration and to time which loses itself in eternity. These truths, all agree, are not to be sought in the cloister. They are only acquired by uniting the calm and patient reflection of retirement with the bold and penetrating observation of active life. . . .

As the period of education will, it is probable, in most instances be protracted till the child shall be engaged in preparing himself for some employment in life, it would be important to confine his attention, in a considerable degree, to the acquisition of that kind of knowledge which would be of the greatest practical use in the profession for which he is destined. Give the mind an object worthy of its efforts and you may rely upon their being made. In this case the child would realize the connection between its present pursuits and its future prosperity, and this impression could not fail to kindle new ardor in its youthful breast.

The fifth object should be the inspiring youth with an ardent love for mankind. To accomplish this end, the preceptor should cautiously avoid instilling into the mind of his pupil a mean idea of human nature. . . .

Should education be public or private? The most distinguished talents have been engaged in the discussion of this subject, and here, as in most controversies of a speculative cast, we find a great diversity of sentiment. Quintilian and Milton are warm in their eulogium on a public, while Locke is equally animated in his praise of a private system of education. The great argument, which may be called the center of all others urged, is the production of emulation by a public education, while the great objection made to public education is the sacrifice, alleged to be produced, of morality and honesty.

As there is, undoubtedly, truth on both sides, it becomes necessary to consider what weight the alleged advantages and disadvantages ought to possess in determining the preference of the judgment to one over the other system. It will, perhaps, be possible to reconcile the apparently conflicting ideas in such a way as to make the result of benefit produced infinitely larger than the risk of injury sustained.

The early period of life is under parental, and especially maternal, control. The solicitude of a mother is now the best, the only protection, which the child can receive. Some years elapse before the mind seems capable of being impressed with true or false knowledge in a degree sufficient to influence its future expansion, and during this period it is fortunate that we have not occasion to regret the unenlightened state of the female mind. But though these years do not mark much strength of mind, yet they rapidly unfold and form the disposition which seldom fails to receive a virtuous bias from a mother who, however vicious herself, feels deeply interested in the virtue of her offspring. Hence those amiable affections are excited which are the ornament of human nature. Before the age of five the child seldom feels a disposition to do an immoral thing, and even if it should exhibit such a symptom, the temper is so flexible that it easily yields to a more virtuous direction.

The young mind, having passed five years of its existence free from much corruption, and a plan of education being now commenced, it becomes an object of consideration whether the child should remain with its parents or be separated from them.

As a large portion of parental solicitude still exists which alone seems capable of securing a vigilant attention to those little indications of temper and mind which now so profusely appear, it seems highly important that the child should still remain under the immediate control of parental authority. That affection which on the part of the child is but half formed will have time and opportunity to gain strength, a love of domestic tranquillity will be produced, and both these principles will form a firm shield to virtue.

On the other hand, the daily attendance at school will withdraw the mind of the child from an *entire* dependence on its parents, will place it in situations demanding the exercise of its faculties, and will strengthen, instead of weakening, its attachment to domestic scenes. To be deprived of that which we love is in some degree painful to us all; to children it is painful in the highest degree. Yet a habit of voluntary or compulsory abstinence from pleasure is absolutely necessary to human happiness.

The child, in this situation, having its time divided between school, the hours of diversion, and those spent in the house of its parents, will, perhaps, remain as free from a prostration of morals as can be expected in infancy. This, indeed, is the plan which universally prevails in the civilized world, and its universality is certainly some argument in its favor.

Let this plan, partly domestic and partly public, be pursued till the mind begins boldly to expand itself and to indicate an ability and an inclination to think for itself. The commencement of this capacity of combining ideas takes place about the age of ten. We have now reached the period which claims the closest attention. The mind now feels its vigor and delights in displaying it. Ambition is kindled, emulation burns, a desire of superiority and distinction are roused.

This, then, appears to be the era, if ever, of public education. The indulgence of parental tenderness should now be exchanged for the patient and unobstructed exercise of the mental powers. Let us attend to the advantages of the two rival systems at this period.

With regard to the plan of public education:

1. Emulation is excited. Without numbers there can be no emulation. It is founded on the love of distinction. In a private family this distinction cannot be acquired.

2. An attention to study when the child is removed from the house of its parent may be uninterrupted, whereas, while it resides with him, a thousand trifling, menial avocations will always take precedence. From this results the conviction in the mind of the child that study is altogether subordinate to the objects to which it is compelled to attend.

3. But, above every other consideration, the system of public education inspires a

spirit of independent reflection and conduct. Removed from a scene where it has little occasion to think and less to act, the child now finds itself placed in a situation free from rigid parental authority. Placed in the midst of objects of pursuit, its preference of one object to another is often determined by its own volition. Hence reflection is excited; and with children there is certainly no danger of too much thought, the only apprehension is that [of] there being too little.

Let a spirit of independent reflection animate a large number of even youthful minds and the acquisition of useful truths will soon be rapid. This spirit, aided by the instruction of enlightened precepts, must give an undeniable ascendancy to the public over the private plan.

Error is never more dangerous than in the mouth of a parent. The child, from the dawn of its existence, accustomed to receive as undoubted every idea from this quarter, seldom if ever questions the truth of what it is told. Hence prejudices are as hereditary as titles, and you may almost universally know the sentiments of the son by those of the father. Now, by education remote from parental influence, the errors of the father cease to be entailed upon the child. Still further, the child, having acquired true ideas, very often, from the superior force of truth, dissipates the errors of his parent by the remonstrances of reason.

As education professes to improve the state and character of men and not barely to oppose their declension, it must follow that domestic education is improper, as it does no more, even if successful, than secure the last at the expense of the first.

When we consider the argument urged against public education (for only one is urged with any tenacity), we shall find that the evil it deprecates arises from the imperfection of human nature more than from any appropriate and exclusive property of public education. . . .

The discussion of this subject appears in some measure superseded and the preference unequivocally established of the public over the private plan by the small expense of the first compared with the impracticable expense of the last. If parents educated their children, the hours withdrawn from business would alone impoverish them. . . .

Guided by these principles it is proposed:

1. That the period of education be from five to eighteen.

2. That every male child, without exception, be educated.

3. That the instructor in every district be directed to attend to the faithful execution of this injunction. That it be made punishable by law in a parent to neglect offering his child to the preceptor for instruction.

4. That every parent who wishes to deviate in the education of his children from the established system be made responsible for devoting to the education of his children as much time as the established system prescribes.

5. That a fund be raised from the citizens in the ratio of their property.

6. That the system be composed of primary schools, of colleges, and of a *university*.

7. That the primary schools be divided into two classes, the first consisting of boys from five to ten years old, the second consisting of boys from ten to eighteen, and that these classes be subdivided, if necessary, into smaller ones.

8. That the instruction given to the first class be the rudiments of the English language, writing, arithmetic, the commission to memory and delivery of select pieces, inculcating moral duties, describing natural phenomena, or displaying correct fancy.

9. Though this class is formed of boys between the age of five and ten years, yet should rapid acquisitions be made in the above branches of knowledge at an earlier age than that of ten, the boy is to be promoted into the second class.

10. The most solemn attention must be

paid to avoid instilling into the young mind any ideas or sentiments whose truth is not unequivocally established by the undissenting suffrage of the enlightened and virtuous part of mankind.

11. That the instruction given to the second class be an extended and more correct knowledge of arithmetic; of the English language, comprising plain rules of criticism and composition; the concise study of general history and a more detailed acquaintance with the history of our own country; of geography; of the laws of nature, practically illustrated. That this practical illustration consist in an actual devotion of a portion of time to agriculture and mechanics, under the superintendence of the preceptor. That it be the duty of this class to commit to memory and frequently to repeat the Constitution and the fundamental laws of the United States.

12. That each primary school consist of fifty boys.

13. That such boys be admitted into the college as shall be deemed by the preceptor to be worthy, from a manifestation of industry and talents, of a more extended education. That one boy be annually chosen out of the second class of each primary school for this preferment.

14. That the students at college so promoted be supported at the public expense, but that such other students may be received as shall be maintained by their parents.

15. That the studies of the college consist in a still more extended acquaintance with the above stated branches of knowledge, together with the cultivation of polite literature.

16. That each college admit 200 students.

17. That an opportunity be furnished to those who have the ability, without interfering with the established studies, of acquiring a knowledge of the modern languages, music, drawing, dancing, and fencing, and that the permission to cultivate these accomplishments be held forth as the reward of diligence and talents.

18. That a national university be established in which the highest branches of science and literature shall be taught. That it consist of students promoted from the colleges. That one student out of ten be annually chosen for this promotion by a majority of the suffrages of the professors of the college to which he may belong.

19. That the student so promoted be supported at the public expense and be lodged within the walls of the university, remaining so long as he please on a salary, in consideration of his devoting his time to the cultivation of science or literature, in which last case he shall become a fellow of the university.

20. The number of professors in the college and the university is not fixed, but it is proposed that the last contain a professor of every branch of useful knowledge.

21. It is proposed that the professors be in the first instance designated by law; that afterward, in all cases of vacancy, the professors of the college choose the preceptors of the primary schools and that the professors of the university choose the professors of the colleges.

22. For the promotion of literature and science, it is proposed that a board of literature and science be established.

119.

# George Washington: A National University

*Though a plan for a federal university had been proposed by a number of men, among them Benjamin Rush and Joel Barlow, no official action had been taken to establish one. On December 7, 1796, George Washington spoke to Congress of a project he had long cherished: a national university in the future capital. Such an institution would diminish regional loyalties, he believed, and symbolize the unity of the nation. To help finance the venture, the President had personally offered the Commissioners of the Federal District an endowment in 1795, and eventually left a bequest to Congress for the same purpose. However, the idea for a federal university never materialized. Sectional loyalty was too strong, as was the desire to enhance regional customs, ideas, and interests. A portion of the President's message to Congress is reprinted below.*

Source: WGW, XIII, pp. 344-351.

I have heretofore proposed to the consideration of Congress the expediency of establishing a national university, and also a military academy. The desirableness of both these institutions has so constantly increased with every new view I have taken of the subject that I cannot omit the opportunity of once for all recalling your attention to them.

The assembly to which I address myself is too enlightened not to be fully sensible how much a flourishing state of the arts and sciences contributes to national prosperity and reputation. True it is that our country, much to its honor, contains many seminaries of learning, highly respectable and useful; but the funds upon which they rest are too narrow to command the ablest professors in the different departments of liberal knowledge for the institution contemplated, though they would be excellent auxiliaries.

Among the motives to such an institution, the assimilation of the principles, opinions, and manners of our countrymen, by the common education of a portion of our youth from every quarter, well deserves attention. The more homogeneous our citizens can be made in these particulars, the greater will be our prospect of permanent union; and a primary object of such a national institution should be the education of our youth in the science of government. In a republic, what species of knowledge can be equally important, and what duty more pressing on its legislature, than to patronize a plan for communicating it to those who are to be the future guardians of the liberties of the country?

The institution of a military academy is also recommended by cogent reasons. However pacific the general policy of a nation may be, it ought never to be without an adequate stock of military knowledge for emergencies. The first would impair the energy of its character, and both would hazard its safety or expose it to greater evils when war could not be avoided. Besides, that war might often not depend upon its own choice. In proportion as the observance of pacific maxims might exempt a nation from the necessity of practising the rules of the military art ought to be its care in preserving and transmitting, by proper establishments, the knowledge of that art.

Whatever argument may be drawn from particular examples, superficially viewed, a thorough examination of the subject will evince that the art of war is at once comprehensive and complicated; that it demands much previous study; and that the possession of it, in its most improved and perfect state, is always of great moment to the security of a nation. This, therefore, ought to be a serious care of every government; and for this purpose, an academy, where a regular course of instruction is given, is an obvious expedient which different nations have successfully employed.

---

120.

## "The Right of Free Elections"

*The year 1796 saw the first contested presidential election in our country's history, for Washington had had little opposition in 1792, and none in 1789. The pride with which American voters participated in the choice of their chief executive (indirectly during this period, of course) and of other government officials is reflected in the following song, which probably dates from the election of 1796 and was widely sung in the succeeding years. The tune was that of "Yankee Doodle," a fact that emphasizes the closeness, in the minds of the early citizens of the Republic, of patriotism and the suffrage.*

Source: *Songs, Odes, and Other Poems, on National Subjects,* compiled by Wm. McCarty, Philadelphia, 1842, pp. 176-177.

### THE RIGHT OF FREE ELECTIONS

While some on rights, and some on wrongs,
Prefer their own reflections,
The people's right demands our songs —
The right of free elections.

For government and order's sake,
And law's important sections,
We should support, and pleasure take
In frequent free elections.

Our agricultural interest, marts,
And mercantile connections,
With manufactures, science, arts,
Must thrive by free elections.

To thwart the schemes of factious bands,
Who for us plan subjections,
The cause of liberty demands
Our votes at all elections.

Should enemies beset us round,
Of foreign, fierce complexions;
Undaunted we will stand our ground,
Upheld by free elections.

We'll never from our duty swerve,
Let who will make objections;
But while we live, unchanged preserve
The freedom of elections.

121.

## George Washington: Farewell Address

*Washington's* Farewell Address *was never delivered by him. It appeared first by his own arrangement in a newspaper at Philadelphia, then the seat of the national government. Designed in part to remove him from consideration for a third term as President of the United States, the address as published was similar to one he had prepared at the end of his first term, in 1792, when he had contemplated retiring from office. In July 1796, he sent a copy of this earlier address to Alexander Hamilton, requesting him to write a new one. Hamilton, who until the year before had been secretary of the treasury and the chief architect of Washington's administration, did as he was asked, but the result, again reworked by Washington, still reflects the ideas of the retiring President. It was printed in the* American Daily Advertiser, *September 19, 1796.*

Source: WGW, XIII, pp. 277-325.

Friends and Fellow Citizens:

The period for a new election of a citizen to administer the executive government of the United States being not far distant, and the time actually arrived when your thoughts must be employed in designating the person who is to be clothed with that important trust, it appears to me proper, especially as it may conduce to a more distinct expression of the public voice, that I should now apprise you of the resolution I have formed to decline being considered among the number of those out of whom a choice is to be made.

I beg you, at the same time, to do me the justice to be assured that this resolution has not been taken without a strict regard to all the considerations appertaining to the relation which binds a dutiful citizen to his country; and that, in withdrawing the tender of service which silence in my situation might imply, I am influenced by no diminution of zeal for your future interest, no deficiency of grateful respect for your past kindness, but act under . . . a full conviction that the step is compatible with both.

The acceptance of and continuance hitherto in the office to which your suffrages have twice called me have been a uniform sacrifice of inclination to the opinion of duty and to a deference for what appeared to be your desire. I constantly hoped that it would have been much earlier in my power, consistently with motives which I was not at liberty to disregard, to return to that retirement from which I had been reluctantly drawn. The strength of my inclination to do this, previous to the last election, had even led to the preparation of an address to declare it to you; but mature reflection on the then perplexed and critical posture of our affairs with foreign nations, and the unanimous advice of persons entitled to my confidence, impelled me to abandon the idea.

I rejoice that the state of your concerns, external as well as internal, no longer renders the pursuit of inclination incompatible with the sentiment of duty or propriety; and am persuaded, whatever partiality may be retained for my services, that, in the present circumstances of our country, you will not disapprove my determination to retire.

The impressions with which I first undertook the arduous trust were explained on the proper occasion. In the discharge of this trust, I will only say that I have, with good intentions, contributed toward the organization and administration of the government the best exertions of which a very fallible judgment was capable. Not unconscious, in the outset, of the inferiority of my qualifications, experience in my own eyes, perhaps still more in the eyes of others, has strengthened the motives to diffidence of myself; and every day the increasing weight of years admonishes me more and more that the shade of retirement is as necessary to me as it will be welcome. Satisfied that, if any circumstances have given peculiar value to my services, they were temporary, I have the consolation to believe that, while choice and prudence invite me to quit the political scene, patriotism does not forbid it. . . .

If benefits have resulted to our country from these services, let it always be remembered to your praise, and as an instructive example in our annals, that, under circumstances in which the passions agitated in every direction were liable to mislead, amidst appearances sometimes dubious, vicissitudes of fortune often discouraging, in situations in which not unfrequently want of success has countenanced the spirit of criticism, the constancy of your support was the essential prop of the efforts and a guarantee of the plans by which they were effected.

Profoundly penetrated with this idea, I shall carry it with me to the grave as a strong incitement to unceasing vows that Heaven may continue to you the choicest tokens of its beneficence; that your Union and brotherly affection may be perpetual; that the free Constitution, which is the work of your hands, may be sacredly maintained; that its administration in every department may be stamped with wisdom and virtue; that, in fine, the happiness of the people of these States, under the auspices of liberty, may be made complete by so careful a preservation and so prudent a use of this blessing as will acquire to them the glory of recommending it to the applause, the affection, and adoption of every nation which is yet a stranger to it.

Here, perhaps, I ought to stop. But a solicitude for your welfare, which cannot end but with my life, and the apprehension of danger natural to that solicitude, urge me, on an occasion like the present, to offer to your solemn contemplation, and to recommend to your frequent review, some sentiments which are the result of much reflection, of no inconsiderable observation, and which appear to me all-important to the permanency of your felicity as a people. These will be offered to you with the more freedom as you can only see in them the disinterested warnings of a parting friend who can possibly have no personal motive to bias his counsels. Nor can I forget, as an encouragement to it, your indulgent reception of my sentiments on a former and not dissimilar occasion.

Interwoven as is the love of liberty with every ligament of your hearts, no recommendation of mine is necessary to fortify or confirm the attachment.

The unity of government which constitutes you one people is also now dear to you. It is justly so, for it is a main pillar in the edifice of your real independence; the support of your tranquillity at home, your peace abroad; of your safety; of your prosperity in every shape; of that very liberty which you so highly prize. But as it is easy to foresee that, from different causes and from different quarters, much pains will be taken, many artifices employed to weaken in your minds the conviction of this truth;

as this is the point in your political fortress against which the batteries of internal and external enemies will be most constantly and actively (though often covertly and insidiously) directed, it is of infinite moment that you should properly estimate the immense value of your national Union to your collective and individual happiness; that you should cherish a cordial, habitual, and immovable attachment to it, accustoming yourselves to think and speak of it as of the palladium of your political safety and prosperity, watching for its preservation with jealous anxiety, discountenancing whatever may suggest even a suspicion that it can in any event be abandoned, and indignantly frowning upon the first dawning of every attempt to alienate any portion of our country from the rest or to enfeeble the sacred ties which now link together the various parts.

For this you have every inducement of sympathy and interest. Citizens by birth or choice of a common country, that country has a right to concentrate your affections. The name of *American,* which belongs to you, in your national capacity, must always exalt the just pride of patriotism more than any appellation derived from local discriminations. With slight shades of difference, you have the same religion, manners, habits, and political principles. You have in a common cause fought and triumphed together. The independence and liberty you possess are the work of joint councils and joint efforts, of common dangers, sufferings, and successes.

But these considerations, however powerfully they address themselves to your sensibility, are greatly outweighed by those which apply more immediately to your interest. Here every portion of our country finds the most commanding motives for carefully guarding and preserving the Union of the whole.

The North, in an unrestrained intercourse with the South, protected by the equal laws of a common government, finds in the productions of the latter great additional resources of maritime and commercial enterprise and precious materials of manufacturing industry. The South, in the same intercourse, benefiting by the agency of the North, sees its agriculture grow and its commerce expand. Turning partly into its own channels the seamen of the North, it finds its particular navigation invigorated; and while it contributes, in different ways, to nourish and increase the general mass of the national navigation, it looks forward to the protection of a maritime strength, to which itself is unequally adapted.

The East, in a like intercourse with the West, already finds, and in the progressive improvement of interior communications by land and water will more and more find, a valuable vent for the commodities which it brings from abroad or manufactures at home. The West derives from the East supplies requisite to its growth and comfort, and, what is perhaps of still greater consequence, it must of necessity owe the secure enjoyment of indispensable outlets for its own productions to the weight, influence, and the future maritime strength of the Atlantic side of the Union, directed by an indissoluble community of interest, as *one nation.* Any other tenure by which the West can hold this essential advantage, whether derived from its own separate strength or from an apostate and unnatural connection with any foreign power, must be intrinsically precarious.

While then every part of our country thus feels an immediate and particular interest in Union, all the parts combined in the united mass of means and efforts cannot fail to find greater strength, greater resource, proportionably greater security from external danger, a less frequent interruption of their peace by foreign nations; and — what is of inestimable value! — they must derive from Union an exemption from those broils and wars between themselves which so frequently afflict neighboring countries not tied together by the same government, which their own rivalships alone would be sufficient to produce but which opposite foreign alliances, attachments, and intrigues would stimulate and embitter. Hence, likewise, they will avoid the necessity of those overgrown military establishments which under any form of government are inauspicious to liberty and which are to be regarded as particularly hostile to republican liberty. In this sense it is that your Union ought to be considered as a main prop of your liberty and that the love of the one ought to endear to you the preservation of the other.

These considerations speak a persuasive language to every reflecting and virtuous mind and exhibit the continuance of the *Union* as a primary object of patriotic desire. Is there a doubt whether a common government can embrace so large a sphere? Let experience solve it. To listen to mere speculation in such a case were criminal. We are authorized to hope that a proper organization of the whole, with the auxiliary agency of governments for the respective subdivisions, will afford a happy issue to the experiment. It is well worth a fair and full experiment. With such powerful and obvious motives to Union affecting all parts of our country, while experience shall not have demonstrated its impracticability, there will always be reason to distrust the patriotism of those who in any quarter may endeavor to weaken its bands.

In contemplating the causes which may disturb our Union, it occurs as matter of serious concern that any ground should have been furnished for characterizing parties by geographical discriminations: Northern and Southern; Atlantic and Western; whence designing men may endeavor to excite a belief that there is a real difference of local interests and views. One of the expedients of party to acquire influence, within particular districts, is to misrepresent the opinions and aims of other districts. You cannot shield yourselves too much against the jealousies and heartburnings which spring from these misrepresentations. They tend to render alien to each other those who ought to be bound together by fraternal affection.

The inhabitants of our Western country have lately had a useful lesson on this head. They have seen, in the negotiation by the executive, and in the unanimous ratification by the Senate of the treaty with Spain, and in the universal satisfaction at that event throughout the United States, a decisive proof how unfounded were the suspicions propagated among them of a policy in the general government and in the Atlantic states unfriendly to their interests in regard to the Mississippi. They have been witnesses to the formation of two treaties, that with Great Britain and that with Spain, which secure to them everything they could desire, in respect to our foreign relations, toward confirming their prosperity. Will it not be their wisdom to rely for the preservation of these advantages on the Union by which they were procured? Will they not henceforth be deaf to those advisers, if such there are, who would sever them from their brethren and connect them with aliens?

To the efficacy and permanency of your Union, a government for the whole is indispensable. No alliances, however strict between the parts, can be an adequate substitute. They must inevitably experience the infractions and interruptions which all alliances in all times have experienced. Sensible of this momentous truth, you have improved upon your first essay by the adoption of a Constitution of government better calculated than your former for an intimate Union and for the efficacious management of your common concerns. This government, the offspring of our own choice uninfluenced and unawed, adopted upon full investigation and mature deliberation, completely free in its principles, in the distribution of its powers, uniting security with energy, and containing within itself a provision for its own amendment, has a just claim to your confidence and your support.

Respect for its authority, compliance with its laws, acquiescence in its measures are duties enjoined by the fundamental maxims of true liberty. The basis of our political systems is the right of the people to make and to alter their constitutions of government. But the constitution which at any time exists, till changed by an explicit and authentic act of the whole people, is sacredly obligatory upon all. The very idea of the power and the right of the people to establish government presupposes the duty of every individual to obey the established government.

All obstructions to the execution of the laws, all combinations and associations, under whatever plausible character, with the real design to direct, control, counteract, or awe the regular deliberation and action of the constituted authorities, are destructive of this fundamental principle, and of fatal tendency. They serve to organize faction, to give it an artificial and extraordinary force, to put in the place of the delegated will of the nation the will of a party, often a small but artful and enterprising minority of the community; and, according to the alternate triumphs of different parties, to make the public administration the mirror of the ill-concerted and incongruous projects of faction rather than the organ of consistent and wholesome plans digested by common councils and modified by mutual interests.

However combinations or associations of the above description may now and then answer popular ends, they are likely, in the course of time and things, to become potent engines by which cunning, ambitious, and unprincipled men will be enabled to subvert the power of the people and to usurp for themselves the reins of government, destroying afterward the very engines which have lifted them to unjust dominion.

Toward the preservation of your government and the permanency of your present happy state, it is requisite not only that you steadily discountenance irregular oppositions to its acknowledged authority but also that you resist with care the spirit of innovation upon its principles, however specious the pretexts. One method of assault may be to effect, in the forms of the Constitution, alterations which will impair the energy of the system and thus to undermine what cannot be directly overthrown. In all the changes to which you may be invited, remember that time and habit are at least as necessary to fix the true character of governments as of other human institutions; that experience is the surest standard by which to test the real tendency of the existing constitution of a country; that facility in changes upon the credit of mere hypothesis and opinion exposes to perpetual change, from the endless variety of hypothesis and opinion; and remember, especially, that for the efficient management of your common interests, in a country so extensive as ours, a government of as much vigor as is consistent with the perfect security of liberty is indispensable.

Liberty itself will find in such a government, with powers properly distributed and adjusted, its surest guardian. It is, indeed, little else than a name where the government is too feeble to withstand the enterprises of faction, to confine each member of the society within the limits prescribed by the laws and to maintain all in the secure and tranquil enjoyment of the rights of person and property.

I have already intimated to you the danger of parties in the state, with particular reference to the founding of them on geographical discriminations. Let me now take a more comprehensive view and warn you in the most solemn manner against the baneful effects of the spirit of party generally.

This spirit, unfortunately, is inseparable

from our nature, having its root in the strongest passions of the human mind. It exists under different shapes in all governments, more or less stifled, controlled, or repressed; but, in those of the popular form, it is seen in its greatest rankness and is truly their worst enemy.

The alternate domination of one faction over another, sharpened by the spirit of revenge natural to party dissension, which in different ages and countries has perpetrated the most horrid enormities, is itself a frightful despotism. But this leads at length to a more formal and permanent despotism. The disorders and miseries which result gradually incline the minds of men to seek security and repose in the absolute power of an individual; and sooner or later the chief of some prevailing faction, more able or more fortunate than his competitors, turns this disposition to the purposes of his own elevation on the ruins of public liberty.

Without looking forward to an extremity of this kind (which nevertheless ought not to be entirely out of sight), the common and continual mischiefs of the spirit of party are sufficient to make it the interest and duty of a wise people to discourage and restrain it.

It serves always to distract the public councils and enfeeble the public administration. It agitates the community with ill-founded jealousies and false alarms, kindles the animosity of one part against another, foments occasionally riot and insurrection. It opens the door to foreign influence and corruption, which find a facilitated access to the government itself through the channels of party passions. Thus the policy and the will of one country are subjected to the policy and will of another.

There is an opinion that parties in free countries are useful checks upon the administration of the government and serve to keep alive the spirit of liberty. This within certain limits is probably true, and, in governments of a monarchical cast, patriotism may look with indulgence, if not with favor, upon the spirit of party. But in those of the popular character, in governments purely elective, it is a spirit not to be encouraged. From their natural tendency, it is certain there will always be enough of that spirit for every salutary purpose. And there being constant danger of excess, the effort ought to be, by force of public opinion, to mitigate and assuage it. A fire not to be quenched, it demands a uniform vigilance to prevent its bursting into a flame, lest instead of warming it should consume.

It is important, likewise, that the habits of thinking in a free country should inspire caution in those entrusted with its administration to confine themselves within their respective constitutional spheres, avoiding in the exercise of the powers of one department to encroach upon another. The spirit of encroachment tends to consolidate the powers of all the departments in one and thus to create, whatever the form of government, a real despotism. A just estimate of that love of power and proneness to abuse it which predominates in the human heart is sufficient to satisfy us of the truth of this position.

The necessity of reciprocal checks in the exercise of political power, by dividing and distributing it into different depositories, and constituting each the guardian of the public weal against invasions by the others, has been evinced by experiments ancient and modern, some of them in our country and under our own eyes. To preserve them must be as necessary as to institute them. If, in the opinion of the people, the distribution or modification of the constitutional powers be in any particular wrong, let it be corrected by an amendment in the way which the Constitution designates. But let there be no change by usurpation; for, though this, in one instance, may be the instrument of good, it is the customary weapon by which free governments are destroyed. The precedent must always greatly overbalance in permanent evil any partial or transient benefit which the use can at any time yield.

Of all the dispositions and habits which lead to political prosperity, religion and morality are indispensable supports. In vain would that man claim the tribute of patriotism who should labor to subvert these great pillars of human happiness, these firmest props of the duties of men and citizens. The mere politician, equally with the pious man, ought to respect and to cherish them. A volume could not trace all their connections with private and public felicity.

Let it simply be asked — Where is the security for property, for reputation, for life, if the sense of religious obligation desert the oaths, which are the instruments of investigation in courts of justice? And let us with caution indulge the supposition that morality can be maintained without religion. Whatever may be conceded to the influence of refined education on minds of peculiar structure, reason and experience both forbid us to expect that national morality can prevail in exclusion of religious principle.

It is substantially true that virtue or morality is a necessary spring of popular government. The rule indeed extends with more or less force to every species of free government. Who that is a sincere friend to it can look with indifference upon attempts to shake the foundation of the fabric?

Promote, then, as an object of primary importance, institutions for the general diffusion of knowledge. In proportion as the structure of a government gives force to public opinion, it is essential that public opinion should be enlightened.

As a very important source of strength and security, cherish public credit. One method of preserving it is to use it as sparingly as possible, avoiding occasions of expense by cultivating peace, but remembering also that timely disbursements to prepare for danger frequently prevent much greater disbursements to repel it; avoiding likewise the accumulation of debt, not only by shunning occasions of expense but by vigorous exertions in time of peace to discharge the debts which unavoidable wars may have occasioned, not ungenerously throwing upon posterity the burden which we ourselves ought to bear. The execution of these maxims belongs to your representatives, but it is necessary that public opinion should cooperate.

To facilitate to them the performance of their duty, it is essential that you should practically bear in mind that toward the payment of debts there must be revenue; that to have revenue there must be taxes; that no taxes can be devised which are not more or less inconvenient and unpleasant; that the intrinsic embarrassment inseparable from the selection of the proper objects (which is always a choice of difficulties) ought to be a decisive motive for a candid construction of the conduct of the government in making it, and for a spirit of acquiescence in the measures for obtaining revenue which the public exigencies may at any time dictate.

Observe good faith and justice toward all nations. Cultivate peace and harmony with all. Religion and morality enjoin this conduct; and can it be that good policy does not equally enjoin it? It will be worthy of a free, enlightened, and, at no distant period, a great nation to give to mankind the magnanimous and too novel example of a people always guided by an exalted justice and benevolence. Who can doubt that in the course of time and things the fruits of such a plan would richly repay any temporary advantages which might be lost by a steady adherence to it? Can it be that Providence has not connected the permanent felicity of a nation with its virtue? The experiment, at least, is recommended by every sentiment which ennobles human nature. Alas! is it rendered impossible by its vices?

In the execution of such a plan nothing is more essential than that permanent, inveterate antipathies against particular nations and passionate attachments for others should be excluded and that in place of them just and amicable feelings toward all should be cultivated. The nation which indulges toward another an habitual hatred or an habitual fondness is in some degree a slave. It is a slave to its animosity or to its affection, either of which is sufficient to lead it astray from its duty and its interest. Antipathy in one nation against another disposes each more readily to offer insult and injury, to lay hold of slight causes of umbrage, and to be haughty and intractable when accidental or trifling occasions of dispute occur.

Hence, frequent collisions, obstinate, envenomed, and bloody contests. The nation prompted by ill will and resentment sometimes impels to war the government, contrary to the best calculations of policy. The government sometimes participates in the national propensity, and adopts, through passion, what reason would reject; at other times, it makes the animosity of the nation subservient to projects of hostility instigated by pride, ambition, and other sinister and pernicious motives. The peace often, sometimes perhaps the liberty, of nations has been the victim.

So, likewise, a passionate attachment of one nation for another produces a variety of evils. Sympathy for the favorite nation, facilitating the illusion of an imaginary common interest in cases where no real common interest exists, and infusing into one the enmities of the other, betrays the former into a participation in the quarrels and wars of the latter without adequate inducement or justification. It leads also to concessions to the favorite nation of privileges denied to others, which is apt doubly to injure the nation making the concessions, by unnecessarily parting with what ought to have been retained, and by exciting jealousy, ill will, and disposition to retaliate in the parties from whom equal privileges are withheld.

And it gives to ambitious, corrupted, or deluded citizens (who devote themselves to the favorite nation) facility to betray or sacrifice the interests of their own country, without odium, sometimes even with popularity, gilding with the appearances of a virtuous sense of obligation, a commendable deference for public opinion, or a laudable zeal for public good, the base or foolish compliances of ambition, corruption, or infatuation. As avenues to foreign influence in innumerable ways, such attachments are particularly alarming to the truly enlightened and independent patriot. How many opportunities do they afford to tamper with domestic factions, to practise the arts of seduction, to mislead public opinion, to influence or awe the public councils! Such an attachment of a small or weak toward a great and powerful nation dooms the former to be the satellite of the latter.

Against the insidious wiles of foreign influence, I conjure you to believe me, fellow citizens, the jealousy of a free people ought to be *constantly* awake, since history and experience prove that foreign influence is one of the most baneful foes of republican government. But that jealousy, to be useful, must be impartial, else it becomes the instrument of the very influence to be avoided instead of a defense against it. Excessive partiality for one foreign nation and excessive dislike of another cause those whom they actuate to see danger only on one side and serve to veil and even second the arts of influence on the other. Real patriots, who may resist the intrigues of the favorite, are liable to become suspected and odious, while its tools and dupes usurp the applause and confidence of the people to surrender their interests.

The great rule of conduct for us, in regard to foreign nations, is in extending our commercial relations to have with them as little political connection as possible. So far as we have already formed engagements, let them be fulfilled with perfect good faith. Here let us stop.

Europe has a set of primary interests which to us have none, or a very remote relation. Hence she must be engaged in frequent controversies, the causes of which are essentially foreign to our concerns. Hence, therefore, it must be unwise in us to implicate ourselves, by artificial ties, in the ordinary vicissitudes of her politics or the ordinary combinations and collisions of her friendships or enmities.

Our detached and distant situation invites and enables us to pursue a different course. If we remain one people, under an efficient government, the period is not far off when we may defy material injury from external annoyance; when we may take such an attitude as will cause the neutrality we may at any time resolve upon to be scrupulously respected; when belligerent nations, under the impossibility of making acquisitions upon us, will not lightly hazard the giving us provocation; when we may choose peace or war, as our interest guided by our justice shall counsel.

Why forgo the advantages of so peculiar a situation? Why quit our own to stand upon foreign ground? Why, by interweaving our destiny with that of any part of Europe, entangle our peace and prosperity in the toils of European ambition, rivalship, interest, humor, or caprice?

It is our true policy to steer clear of permanent alliances with any portion of the foreign world. So far, I mean, as we are now at liberty to do it, for let me not be understood as capable of patronizing infidelity to existing engagements (I hold the maxim no less applicable to public than to private affairs that honesty is always the best policy). I repeat it, therefore: let those engagements be observed in their genuine sense. But, in my opinion, it is unnecessary and would be unwise to extend them.

Taking care always to keep ourselves, by suitable establishments, on a respectably defensive posture, we may safely trust to temporary alliances for extraordinary emergencies.

Harmony, liberal intercourse with all nations are recommended by policy, humanity, and interest. But even our commercial policy should hold an equal and impartial hand, neither seeking nor granting exclusive favors or preferences; consulting the natural course of things; diffusing and diversifying by gentle means the streams of commerce but forcing nothing; establishing with powers so disposed, in order to give to trade a stable course, to define the rights of our merchants, and to enable the government to support them, conventional rules of intercourse, the best that present circumstances and mutual opinion will permit, but temporary and liable to be from time to time abandoned or varied, as experience and circumstances shall dictate; constantly keeping in view that it is folly in one nation to look for disinterested favors from another; that it must pay with a portion of its independence for whatever it may accept under that character; that, by such acceptance, it may place itself in the condition of having given equivalents for nominal favors and yet of being reproached with ingratitude for not giving more. There can be no greater error than to expect, or calculate, upon real favors from nation to nation. It is an illusion which experience must cure, which a just pride ought to discard.

In offering to you, my countrymen, these counsels of an old and affectionate friend, I dare not hope they will make the strong and lasting impression I could wish; that they will control the usual current of the passions or prevent our nation from running the course which has hitherto marked the destiny of nations. But if I may even flatter myself that they may be productive of some partial benefit, some occasional good; that they may now and then recur to moderate the fury of party-spirit, to warn against the mischiefs of foreign intrigue, to guard against the impostures of pretended patriotism, this hope will be a full recompense for the solicitude for your welfare by which they have been dictated.

In relation to the still subsisting war in Europe, my proclamation of the 22nd of April, 1793, is the index to my plan. Sanctioned by your approving voice and by that of your representatives in both houses of Congress, the spirit of that measure has continually governed me — uninfluenced by any attempts to deter or divert me from it.

After deliberate examination with the aid of the best lights I could obtain, I was well satisfied that our country, under all the circumstances of the case, had a right to take, and was bound in duty and interest to take, a neutral position. Having taken it, I determined, as far as should depend upon me, to maintain it, with moderation, perseverance, and firmness. . . .

The inducements of interest for observing that conduct will best be referred to your own reflections and experience. With me, a predominant motive has been to endeavor to gain time to our country to settle and mature its yet recent institutions, and to progress without interruption to that degree of strength and consistency which is necessary to give it, humanly speaking, the command of its own fortune.

Though, in reviewing the incidents of my administration, I am unconscious of intentional error, I am nevertheless too sensible of my defects not to think it probable that I may have committed many errors. Whatever they may be, I fervently beseech the Almighty to avert or mitigate the evils to which they may tend. I shall also carry with me the hope that my country will never cease to view them with indulgence, and that, after forty-five years of my life dedicated to its service, with an upright zeal, the faults of incompetent abilities will be consigned to oblivion as myself must soon be to the mansions of rest.

Relying on its kindness in this as in other things, and actuated by that fervent love toward it which is so natural to a man who views in it the native soil of himself and his progenitors for several generations, I anticipate with pleasing expectations that retreat in which I promise myself to realize, without alloy, the sweet enjoyment of partaking, in the midst of my fellow citizens, the benign influence of good laws under a free government, the ever favorite object of my heart, and the happy reward, as I trust, of our mutual cares, labors, and dangers.

*Washington, the brave, the wise, the good,*
*Supreme in war, in council, and in peace.*
*Valiant without ambition, discreet without fear, confident without presumption.*
*In disaster, calm; in success, moderate; in all, himself.*
*The hero, the patriot, the Christian.*
*The father of nations, the friend of mankind,*
*Who, when he had won all, renounced all, and sought in the bosom of*
*his family and of nature, retirement, and in the hope of religion, immortality.*

Inscription at Mount Vernon

# Index of Authors

*The numbers in brackets indicate selection numbers in this volume*

Filson, John (1747-1788), explorer and historian. His *Discovery, Settlement, and Present State of Kentucke* (1784) was the first descriptive history of that region and fostered the legend of Daniel Boone. **[2]**

Franklin, Benjamin (Jan. 17, 1706-April 17, 1790), printer, author, philanthropist, inventor, scientist, diplomat, and statesman. Born Boston; published *Poor Richard's Almanack* (1732-57); signed the Declaration of Independence; in France, 1776-85; member of the Constitutional Convention (1787); author of *Autobiography*. **[74, 76, 84]** See also Author Index, Vols. 1, 2.

Freneau, Philip (Jan. 2, 1752-Dec. 18, 1832), poet and essayist. Editor (1791-93) of the *National Gazette;* author of satiric essays on the British and Tories, patriotic works, and nature poems. **[45, 64, 66, 100]**

Grover, Thomas (fl. 1786), spokesman for the Hampshire County, Mass., participants in Shays's Rebellion. **[17]**

Hamilton, Alexander (?Jan. 11, 1755-July 12, 1804), soldier, lawyer, and statesman. Member (1782-83) of the Congress of the Confederation; New York delegate to the Constitutional Convention (1787); author with James Madison and John Jay of *The Federalist* (1787-88); secretary of the treasury (1789-95) under Washington and creator of the first Bank of the United States. Mortally wounded in a duel with Aaron Burr. **[4, 31, 47, 82, 91, 92, 106, 109, 111, 117]** See also Author Index, Vols. 2, 4.

Hatton, Ann Julia (fl. 1794), poetess. Wrote the libretto for James Hewitt's opera *Tammany* (1794), one of the first ballad operas composed in U.S. **[113]**

Henry, Patrick (May 29, 1736-June 6, 1799), lawyer, orator, and statesman. Member (1765-73) of the Virginia House of Burgesses and (1774-75) of the Continental Congress; governor (1776-79, 1784-86); a principal advocate of the Bill of Rights. **[56, 87]** See also Author Index, Vol. 2.

Iredell, James (1751-1799), jurist and public official. Attorney general of North Carolina (1779-81); delegate to the Constitutional Convention (1787); associate justice (1790-99) of the U.S. Supreme Court. **[48]**

Jay, John (Dec. 12, 1745-May 17, 1829), jurist, diplomat, and statesman. Member (1774) and president (1778) of the Continental Congress; commissioner to Great Britain (1782); author with James Madison and Alexander Hamilton of *The Federalist* (1787-88); first chief justice (1789-95) of the U.S. Supreme Court. **[18, 54]** See also Author Index, Vol. 2.

Jefferson, Thomas (April 13, 1743-July 4, 1826), lawyer, architect, agriculturalist, educator, political philosopher, diplomat, and statesman. Third President of the United States (1801-09); member (1775-76) of the Continental Congress; author of the Declaration of Independence; governor of Virginia (1779-81); minister to France (1785-89); secretary of state (1790-93) under Washington; Vice-President of the United States under John Adams; founder of the University of Virginia. **[11, 12, 15, 22, 23, 27, 39, 60, 69, 79, 83, 91, 104]** See also Author Index, Vols. 2, 4, 5.

Lansing, John (fl. 1787), lawyer and mayor of Albany, N.Y. Ardent anti-Federalist; resigned from the Constitutional Convention of 1787. **[41]**

Laurance, John (1750-Nov. 11, 1810), Revolutionary War soldier, jurist, and public official. New York delegate (1785-87) to the Congress of the Confederation; U.S. representative (1789-93); U.S. senator (1796-1800). **[97]**

Lee, Richard Henry (Jan. 20, 1732-June 19, 1794), statesman. Member (1758-75) of the Virginia House of Burgesses; delegate (1774-76) to the Continental Congress; signed the Declaration of Independence; president (1784-85) of the Congress of the Confederation; U.S. senator (1789-92). **[30]**

Leland, John (May 14, 1754-Jan. 14, 1841), Baptist clergyman. Member of the Virginia Ratifying Convention of 1788; author of *Virginia Chronicle* (1790); leading advocate of religious freedom. **[90]**

Lenoir, William (fl. 1788), public official. Leading anti-Federalist in the North Carolina Ratifying Convention of 1788. **[59]**

Published several Jeffersonian newspapers, notably the *National Intelligencer* (1800-10); president (from 1828) of the Washington branch, Bank of the United States; director of the Washington, D.C., library; treasurer of the Washington National Monument Society. **[118]**

Trumbull, John (June 6, 1756-Nov. 10, 1843), artist, architect, and author. Aide and cartographer to George Washington in the Revolutionary War; president (1817-36) of the American Academy of Fine Arts; painter of four of the eight large pictures in the rotunda of the Capitol at Washington, D.C. **[68]** See also Author Index, Vol. 2.

Tyler, Royall (1757-1826), author and jurist. Chief justice (1807-13) of the Vermont Supreme Court; his play *The Contrast,* the first comedy written by an American, was professionally staged in New York, April 16, 1787. **[81]**

Vassa, Gustavus (fl. 1758-94), slave and explorer. Born Olaudah Equiano in Benin (Nigeria), Africa; captured and sent to West Indies as a slave; later freed and renamed for King Gustavus I of Sweden; traveled widely, even to the Arctic, and described his adventures in a journal. **[114]**

Washington, George (Feb. 22, 1732-Dec. 14, 1799), surveyor, planter, soldier, and statesman. First President of the United States (1789-97); member (1759-74) of the Virginia House of Burgesses; delegate (1774-75) to the Continental Congress; commander (1775-83) of all Continental armies; president of the Constitutional Convention (1787); commander in chief (1798-99) of U.S. Army. **[18, 70, 86, 103, 110, 119, 121]** See also Author Index, Vols. 2, 4.

Webster, Noah (Oct. 16, 1758-May 28, 1843), lexicographer, journalist, educator, lawyer, and statesman. Massachusetts legislator (1815, 1819); founder of Connecticut Academy of Arts and Sciences, president (1820-21) of Amherst Academy and founder (1819-21) of Amherst College; his *American Spelling Book* has never been out of print; published the *American Dictionary of the English Language* (1828). **[8, 19, 77, 85]**

Whitney, Eli (Dec. 8, 1765-Jan. 8, 1825), inventor. Devised the cotton gin (1793) for cleaning seed from cotton fibers; introduced the system of manufacturing interchangeable parts for firearms (*c.* 1798). **[108]**

Wilson, James (Sept. 14, 1742-Aug. 21, 1798), lawyer and political philosopher. Member (1775-77) of the Continental Congress; signed the Declaration of Independence; advocate general for France (1779); Pennsylvania delegate to the Constitutional Convention (1787); associate justice (1789-98) of the U.S. Supreme Court. **[34, 78]** See also Author Index, Vol. 2.

Yates, Robert (1738-1801), jurist. Chief justice (1790-98) of the New York Supreme Court; leading anti-Federalist in the Constitutional Convention (1787). **[41]**